Lecture Notes in Computer Science   **11579**

Commenced Publication in 1973
Founding and Former Series Editors:
Gerhard Goos, Juris Hartmanis, and Jan van Leeuwen

More information about this series at http://www.springer.com/series/7409

Gabriele Meiselwitz (Ed.)

Social Computing and Social Media

Communication and Social Communities

11th International Conference, SCSM 2019
Held as Part of the 21st HCI International Conference, HCII 2019
Orlando, FL, USA, July 26–31, 2019
Proceedings, Part II

 Springer

Editor
Gabriele Meiselwitz
Computer Science
Towson University
Towson, MD, USA

ISSN 0302-9743   ISSN 1611-3349 (electronic)
Lecture Notes in Computer Science
ISBN 978-3-030-21904-8   ISBN 978-3-030-21905-5   (eBook)
https://doi.org/10.1007/978-3-030-21905-5

LNCS Sublibrary: SL3 – Information Systems and Applications, incl. Internet/Web, and HCI

This Springer imprint is published by the registered company Springer Nature Switzerland AG
The registered company address is: Gewerbestrasse 11, 6330 Cham, Switzerland

Foreword

The 21st International Conference on Human-Computer Interaction, HCI International 2019, was held in Orlando, FL, USA, during July 26–31, 2019. The event incorporated the 18 thematic areas and affiliated conferences listed on the following page.

A total of 5,029 individuals from academia, research institutes, industry, and governmental agencies from 73 countries submitted contributions, and 1,274 papers and 209 posters were included in the pre-conference proceedings. These contributions address the latest research and development efforts and highlight the human aspects of design and use of computing systems. The contributions thoroughly cover the entire field of human-computer interaction, addressing major advances in knowledge and effective use of computers in a variety of application areas. The volumes constituting the full set of the pre-conference proceedings are listed in the following pages.

This year the HCI International (HCII) conference introduced the new option of "late-breaking work." This applies both for papers and posters and the corresponding volume(s) of the proceedings will be published just after the conference. Full papers will be included in the *HCII 2019 Late-Breaking Work Papers Proceedings* volume of the proceedings to be published in the Springer LNCS series, while poster extended abstracts will be included as short papers in the HCII 2019 *Late-Breaking Work Poster Extended Abstracts* volume to be published in the Springer CCIS series.

I would like to thank the program board chairs and the members of the program boards of all thematic areas and affiliated conferences for their contribution to the highest scientific quality and the overall success of the HCI International 2019 conference.

This conference would not have been possible without the continuous and unwavering support and advice of the founder, Conference General Chair Emeritus and Conference Scientific Advisor Prof. Gavriel Salvendy. For his outstanding efforts, I would like to express my appreciation to the communications chair and editor of *HCI International News,* Dr. Abbas Moallem.

July 2019   Constantine Stephanidis

HCI International 2019 Thematic Areas and Affiliated Conferences

Thematic areas:

- HCI 2019: Human-Computer Interaction
- HIMI 2019: Human Interface and the Management of Information

Affiliated conferences:

- EPCE 2019: 16th International Conference on Engineering Psychology and Cognitive Ergonomics
- UAHCI 2019: 13th International Conference on Universal Access in Human-Computer Interaction
- VAMR 2019: 11th International Conference on Virtual, Augmented and Mixed Reality
- CCD 2019: 11th International Conference on Cross-Cultural Design
- SCSM 2019: 11th International Conference on Social Computing and Social Media
- AC 2019: 13th International Conference on Augmented Cognition
- DHM 2019: 10th International Conference on Digital Human Modeling and Applications in Health, Safety, Ergonomics and Risk Management
- DUXU 2019: 8th International Conference on Design, User Experience, and Usability
- DAPI 2019: 7th International Conference on Distributed, Ambient and Pervasive Interactions
- HCIBGO 2019: 6th International Conference on HCI in Business, Government and Organizations
- LCT 2019: 6th International Conference on Learning and Collaboration Technologies
- ITAP 2019: 5th International Conference on Human Aspects of IT for the Aged Population
- HCI-CPT 2019: First International Conference on HCI for Cybersecurity, Privacy and Trust
- HCI-Games 2019: First International Conference on HCI in Games
- MobiTAS 2019: First International Conference on HCI in Mobility, Transport, and Automotive Systems
- AIS 2019: First International Conference on Adaptive Instructional Systems

Pre-conference Proceedings Volumes Full List

1. LNCS 11566, Human-Computer Interaction: Perspectives on Design (Part I), edited by Masaaki Kurosu
2. LNCS 11567, Human-Computer Interaction: Recognition and Interaction Technologies (Part II), edited by Masaaki Kurosu
3. LNCS 11568, Human-Computer Interaction: Design Practice in Contemporary Societies (Part III), edited by Masaaki Kurosu
4. LNCS 11569, Human Interface and the Management of Information: Visual Information and Knowledge Management (Part I), edited by Sakae Yamamoto and Hirohiko Mori
5. LNCS 11570, Human Interface and the Management of Information: Information in Intelligent Systems (Part II), edited by Sakae Yamamoto and Hirohiko Mori
6. LNAI 11571, Engineering Psychology and Cognitive Ergonomics, edited by Don Harris
7. LNCS 11572, Universal Access in Human-Computer Interaction: Theory, Methods and Tools (Part I), edited by Margherita Antona and Constantine Stephanidis
8. LNCS 11573, Universal Access in Human-Computer Interaction: Multimodality and Assistive Environments (Part II), edited by Margherita Antona and Constantine Stephanidis
9. LNCS 11574, Virtual, Augmented and Mixed Reality: Multimodal Interaction (Part I), edited by Jessie Y. C. Chen and Gino Fragomeni
10. LNCS 11575, Virtual, Augmented and Mixed Reality: Applications and Case Studies (Part II), edited by Jessie Y. C. Chen and Gino Fragomeni
11. LNCS 11576, Cross-Cultural Design: Methods, Tools and User Experience (Part I), edited by P. L. Patrick Rau
12. LNCS 11577, Cross-Cultural Design: Culture and Society (Part II), edited by P. L. Patrick Rau
13. LNCS 11578, Social Computing and Social Media: Design, Human Behavior and Analytics (Part I), edited by Gabriele Meiselwitz
14. LNCS 11579, Social Computing and Social Media: Communication and Social Communities (Part II), edited by Gabriele Meiselwitz
15. LNAI 11580, Augmented Cognition, edited by Dylan D. Schmorrow and Cali M. Fidopiastis
16. LNCS 11581, Digital Human Modeling and Applications in Health, Safety, Ergonomics and Risk Management: Human Body and Motion (Part I), edited by Vincent G. Duffy

34. CCIS 1033, HCI International 2019 - Posters (Part II), edited by Constantine Stephanidis
35. CCIS 1034, HCI International 2019 - Posters (Part III), edited by Constantine Stephanidis

http://2019.hci.international/proceedings

11th International Conference on Social Computing and Social Media (SCSM 2019)

Program Board Chair(s): **Gabriele Meiselwitz**, *USA*

- Rocío Abascal-Mena, Mexico
- Francisco Alvarez, Mexico
- James Braman, USA
- Adheesh Budree, South Africa
- Adela Coman, Romania
- Panagiotis Germanakos, Germany
- Tamara Heck, Germany
- Sara Hook, USA
- Hung-Hsuan Huang, Japan
- Carsten Kleiner, Germany
- Erick López-Ornelas, Mexico
- Joon Suk Lee, USA
- Marilia S. Mendes, Brazil
- Takashi Namatame, Japan
- Hoang D. Nguyen, Singapore
- Kohei Otake, Japan
- Daniela Quinones, Chile
- Cristian Rusu, Chile
- Christian W. Scheiner, Germany
- Simona Vasilache, Japan
- Giovanni Vincenti, USA
- Kathy Wang, USA
- June Wei, USA
- Brian Wentz, USA

The full list with the Program Board Chairs and the members of the Program Boards of all thematic areas and affiliated conferences is available online at:

http://www.hci.international/board-members-2019.php

HCI International 2020

The 22nd International Conference on Human-Computer Interaction, HCI International 2020, will be held jointly with the affiliated conferences in Copenhagen, Denmark, at the Bella Center Copenhagen, July 19–24, 2020. It will cover a broad spectrum of themes related to HCI, including theoretical issues, methods, tools, processes, and case studies in HCI design, as well as novel interaction techniques, interfaces, and applications. The proceedings will be published by Springer. More information will be available on the conference website: http://2020.hci.international/.

General Chair
Prof. Constantine Stephanidis
University of Crete and ICS-FORTH
Heraklion, Crete, Greece
E-mail: general_chair@hcii2020.org

http://2020.hci.international/

Contents – Part II

Social Media in Education

Digital Marketing and Consumer Experience

Contents – Part I

Human Behaviour in Social Media

Social Network Analysis

Community Engagement and Social Participation

Computer Mediated Communication

Examining Parent Versus Child Reviews of Parental Control Apps on Google Play

Turki Alelyani[1(✉)], Arup Kumar Ghosh[2], Larry Moralez[2],
Shion Guha[3], and Pamela Wisniewski[2]

[1] Stevens Institute of Technology, Hoboken, NJ 07030, USA
`talelyan@stevens.edu`
[2] University of Central Florida, Orlando, FL 32816, USA
`{arupkumar.ghosh,pamela.wisniewski}@ucf.edu,`
`larrymoralez@knights.ucf.edu`
[3] Marquette University Milwaukee, Milwaukee, WI 53233, USA
`shion.guha@marquette.edu`

Abstract. Mobile devices have become a ubiquitous means for teens and younger children to access the internet and social media. Such pervasive access affords many benefits but also exposes children to potential online risks, including cyberbullying, exposure to explicit content, and sexual solicitations. Parents who are concerned about their children's online safety may use parental control apps to monitor, manage, and curate their children's online access and mobile activities. This creates tension between the privacy rights and interests of children versus the legal, emotional, and moral imperatives of parents seeking to protect their children from online risks. To better understand the unique perspectives of parents and children, we conducted an analysis of 29,272 reviews of 52 different parental control apps from the Google Play store. We found that reviews written by parents differed statistically from those written by children such that it is possible to computationally automate the process of differentiating between them. Furthermore, latent themes emerged from the reviews that revealed the complexities and tensions in parent-child relationships as mediated by parental control app use. Natural Language Processing (NLP) revealed that the underlying themes within the reviews went beyond a description of the app, its features or performance and more towards an expression of the relationship between parents and teens as mediated through parental control apps. These insights can be used to improve parental control app design, and therefore the user experience of both parents and children.

Keywords: Privacy · Parental control apps · User reviews ·
Computational analysis · Classification · Parent-child relationships ·
Google Play

1 Introduction

With the proliferation of smartphones among youth, online safety has become a considerable concern within families [1, 2]. This is especially true because mobile smart devices have become the norm for teenagers [3], providing constant access to the

© Springer Nature Switzerland AG 2019
G. Meiselwitz (Ed.): HCII 2019, LNCS 11579, pp. 3–21, 2019.
https://doi.org/10.1007/978-3-030-21905-5_1

internet that is often not monitored by their parents. However, parents have a legal and emotional duty to ensure safety for their children in online contexts [4]. To do this, parents use a wide array of strategies to monitor their teens' technology use, including 16% of parents, according to a Pew Research, who install parental control applications apps on their teens' mobile devices to filter and block inappropriate online activities [3]. An analysis of 75 Google Play parental control apps found that the features of these apps may be too clumsy and privacy invasive for families that value open communication, trust, and a teen's desire to gain independence from his or her parents [5]. Ghosh et al. confirmed this claim from the perspective of teens and younger children by qualitatively analyzing online reviews posted from the vantage point of child users [6]. However, a key limitation of these studies is that researchers used qualitative methods on a relatively small sample of child reviews and were unable to conduct a comparative study of parent versus child reviews.

We build upon this work by conducting the first large-scale analysis of 29,272 reviews for 52 parental control apps to understand the unique perspectives of parents and children. We conducted a quantitative examination of the online reviews for parental control apps to understand whether parents and teens rate and write about parental control apps differently in their online reviews. We also examine the interpersonal relationships between parents and children through the lens of online privacy and surveillance. Specifically, we pose the following research questions:

RQ1: *Can we use computational methods to accurately distinguish between online reviews written by parents versus those written by children?*

RQ2: *Does the content of online reviews differ depending on whether the user is a parent or child? If so, how?*

To answer these questions, we scraped and analyzed publicly posted online reviews for 52 parental control apps available for download on the Google Play store. We first analyzed the reviews by applying Topic Modeling and N-Grams techniques to extract our linguistic prediction drivers. We then evaluated six predictive models including Naïve Bayes, Support Vector Machines, Neural Network, Logistic Regression, K-Nearest Neighbors, and Classification and Regression Trees. We compared the results of N-grams and Topic Modeling as different techniques for features extraction. We then generated topics based on parent versus child and high versus low rated reviews (Low: 1–3 ratings; High: 4–5 ratings to understand the key differences in these reviews.

Our paper makes two unique contributions. First, we show that it is possible to build computational models that accurately predict the origin of online reviews (parents or children) using linguistic indicators. We compared and contrasted six common machine learning algorithms to highlight their performance in such classification tasks. Second, we reveal that latent themes expressed within online app reviews reveal more insights than just the strengths and weakness of the app. They express a multitude of emotions and a manifestation of the complex tensions that exist in parent-teen relationships, specifically those around privacy rights and parental control through surveillance tactics. These findings have important implications for the analysis of online reviews that extend beyond the context of adolescent online safety and serve as an important lens for future social computational research.

2 Background

2.1 Teen Technology Use and Parental Relationships

Technology use among teens and parental mediation have become an important research topic [7–12]. Yet, the majority of research in this space derives from the social sciences with little contribution from a social computational perspective. For instance, several researchers have conducted interview-based studies to highlight the tensions between parents and children when it comes to rule-setting and ensuring the online safety of youth [1, 13]. Others found that teens desire privacy as they are in the process of individuating and establishing their identities online [14, 15].

2.2 "Practical Obscurity" Versus "Parental Stalking"

Teens are often forced to disclose personal information to their parents, as parents want more transparency into their teens' online activities for the purpose of ensuring their online safety [11]. Yet, according to privacy theories, everyone should have some level of authority to decide how their personal information is disclosed to others [16, 17]. Blackwell et al. studied how "practical obscurity" (i.e., the limited visibility) of mobile devices makes it harder for parents to know their children's online activities and, as a consequence, parents often misjudge the frequency and nature of their teens' technology use [1]. For instance, they under-estimate how often their teens use social media apps or even which apps their children use.

To increase access to their teens online mobile activities, parents can install parental control apps on the teens' smartphone that allow them to monitor and restrict various functions, including calls, text messaging, web browsing, and installations [18]. In general, parental control apps are a way for parents to control their children's behavior as a means to protect them, as opposed to helping teens self-regulate and protect themselves [5]. Recent research has shown that teens equate such parental control apps to a form of "parental stalking" [6]. Others have argued that these apps engender an incongruency with the core values (e.g., privacy, autonomy) important to different families and may negatively impact parent-teen relationships [19] and shown that the use of currently available apps was associated with children experiencing more (not fewer) online risks [20]. Human-Computer Interaction (HCI) researchers have recommended and conceptualized that more collaborative approaches be used to manage these tensions [6, 8, 21, 22].

2.3 Online Reviews and Parental Control Apps

Ghosh et al.'s qualitative analysis of online reviews for 37 parental control apps examined what children think about parental control apps' effectiveness and invasiveness [6]. They found that most children felt that the apps were excessively restrictive and privacy invasive. This previous work focused only on Google Play reviews posted by children. To our knowledge, online reviews have not been used yet to understand parents' perspectives on these apps, nor how they differ from the perspectives of the children. To fill this gap, we scraped 29,272 reviews for 52 parental control apps to conduct a social computational analysis that differentiates between parent and child reviews, as well as models the different themes expressed within these reviews.

Analyzing online reviews is valuable as they have been shown to effectively help make better products [30–32] and boost profits [33]. For example, Epstein et al. used online app reviews, a survey, and interviews to improve the design of menstrual apps for women [34]. Wang et al. created a framework for product recommendation by leveraging the power of online reviews [26]. In addition, user feedback was also used to understand reasons for disliking apps [35]. Analyzing online reviews is also a common approach among computational social science researchers [23–26] and is a newer approach used within intersectional fields, such as Human-Computer Interaction (HCI) and Natural Language Processing (NLP) [27–29].

3 Study Design

App stores such as Google Play let users review their downloaded apps and assign a numerical rating (i.e. 1–5 stars). Users may highlight specific strengths and weaknesses of the app. Ratings for each app are then aggregated and displayed for the user to view. This data source captures different perspectives regarding aspects such as the app's functionality, benefits, and cost. These reviews can help developers overcome some of their flaws in the development process [30–32], as well as helping consumers make important decisions as to what apps will meet their needs as end users.

Below, we describe our approach to data collection, data cleaning, and analysis. Our methodology consisted of two phases: First, we applied machine learning techniques to identify different features and perspectives mentioned in the user reviews for both teens and parents, as well as the sentiments and opinions associated to these features. Second, we classified these reviews based on the extracted features. Table 1 shows all of the app used in the analysis. For each app reviewed contained more than one review, and the total number of reviews is included in the table as well.

3.1 Data Collection

We scraped publicly available user reviews on Google Play using the app review downloading tool Heedzy[1]. Each review had the following attributes: (1) app name, (2) date, (3) user name, (4) review, and (5) rating. Ratings were numerical values (represented as a star) given by the user, ranging from 1 = worst to 5 = best. As shown in Table 1, a total of 29,272 user reviews for 52 apps were collected for this analysis. No users were involved in this study and IRB approval was not obtained. We excluded user names from the exemplar quotations shared in this paper to maintain anonymity.

---

[1] www.heedzy.com/feedback.

Table 1. Summary of app names and number of reviews used in the analysis

App name	Reviews	App name	Reviews
Bitdefender	95	Dashboard	117
Cerberus	3000	Board	109
Cybersafe	9	iNetClean	16
ESET	84	Parental Control	145
SecureKids	13	Familoop	38
Funamo	555	Launcher	17
Kakatu	114	PhoneWatcher - Mobile Tracker	314
KIDOZ	2113	Qustodio	996
Kids Place	3000	Ranger Pro Safe Browser	42
Kidslox	50	Remote Control	50
Kids Zone	490	ReThink - Stops Cyberbullying	121
MamaBear	465	Safe Browser	634
McAfee	312	Safe Browsing	222
MMGuardian	1060	Screen Time Companion App	2935
Mobicip	413	Screen Time	3002
Mobile Fence	2103	SecureTeen	2605
Net Nanny	646	Securkin	9
Norton Family	922	ShieldMyTeen	609
NQ Family Guardian	198	TeenSafe Child	132
Land of Kids	23	Trackidz	52
Xooloo	47	SafeKiddo	57
Web Blocker	98	TangTracker	32
Mobile Security	33	SURFIE	11
shieldMyTeen	609	Safe Kids	3
Parental Control and Locator	3	Privacy Camp	3
Block	6	Family Safety	8

3.2   Data Preprocessing

NLTK[2], a third-party library for Python for natural language processing, was used to remove stop-words and frequently used words from each review. A MALLET list was used to identify stop words [36]. We followed an iterative process to remove frequently used words that would mislead our models by giving additional weight to specific keywords. Many of these words are common in the English language (e.g., "and", "this", "is", "are"). We also removed words that appeared too frequently (e.g., "app," "please," and "fix"). We note that these words suggest that users often post reviews for developers to fix problems within the app, but otherwise, were irrelevant to this research.

---

[2] www.nltk.org.

3.3 RQ1: Classifying App Review Authors

We employed a rule-based classification technique to extract rules for both parents and teens reviews based on research conducted by Ghosh et al. [6]. This helped in mapping the attributes of a review with a parents/teen label. A rule set consists of multiple rules $R_s = \{R_1, R_2, .., R_{1n}\}$. For example, in teen reviews, attributes such as "my parents", "my mom", and "my dad" were identified. For parents, "my teen", "my son", and "my child" were key attributes. We used these rules to establish ground truth for classifying the authors of these reviews. After classification, we extracted different linguistic features for each group. These features can be represented as collections of words or a set of variables categorizing a specific context [37]. We then added Term Frequency-Inverse Document Frequency (TF-IDF) vectorization to identify other important features that represent the parent and teen classes. These features served as predictors for the model to classify authors of app reviews.

3.4 RQ2: Understanding Themes in App Reviews

We represented each review as a bag-of-words, using n-grams as features [38]. N-grams can capture groups of words in each review that may represent some patterns or important features. Relevant examples of useful 2-grams include "keep track", "sucks worst", and "parents allow." This enabled us to build a text corpus to test against the full dataset for extracting latent themes. We tested this corpus against six common machine learning algorithms. Tables 2 and 3 show the performance accuracy for both N-grams and Topic Modeling, the mean absolute error, as well as a comparison of the confusion matrices for each of the 5 classifiers.

Table 2. Performance accuracy of N-grams and topic modeling

Algorithm	Accuracy		Mean absolute error	
	NG	TM	NG	TM
Logistic Regression	0.73	0.59	0.48	1.08
K-Nearest Neighbors	0.67	0.57	0.74	1.08
Classification and Regression Trees	0.64	0.52	0.70	1.51
Naive Bayes	0.73	0.53	0.51	1.33
Support Vector Machines	0.53	0.53	1.35	1.32
Neural Network	0.68	0.63	0.58	0.93

Next, we used topic modeling, specifically the latent Dirichlet allocation algorithm (LDA) via MALLET, to extract the hidden semantic structure for both parent and teen reviews [39]. Topics are collections of word tokens which represent the context of the analyzed text. MALLET identifies the most relevant topic for each review by converting collection of text to features.

Table 3. Comparison of confusion matrix results

Algorithm	Precision		Recall		F1 - Score	
	NG	TM	NG	TM	NG	TM
Logistic Regression	0.69	**0.45**	0.73	**0.59**	0.70	**0.48**
K-Nearest Neighbors	0.59	**0.51**	0.67	**0.57**	0.61	**0.53**
Classification and Regression Trees	0.61	**0.50**	0.64	**0.52**	0.63	**0.50**
Naive Bayes	0.66	**0.28**	0.73	**0.53**	0.68	**0.37**
Support Vector Machines	0.53	**0.51**	0.53	**0.53**	0.37	**0.37**
Neural Network	0.67	**0.49**	0.68	**0.63**	0.67	**0.54**

The LDA algorithm is a generative statistical model often applied to discrete data such as text corpora and is used to categorize texts from a document to a specific category. Textual features are then transformed into numerical representations that can be processed efficiently. HCI research has increasingly begun use of topic models [40–42] to explore and make sense of large-scale text data in conjunction with qualitative inferences from topic models, particularly from online communities. This allows us to understand what influences how parents and teens administer a given rating. We used a common convention of selecting the number of topics that represent 80% of the overall variance to set the number of topics for each group [5, 42]. Tables 4, 5, 6 and 7 show the extracted topics with respect to the followings:

(1) An exploratory analysis for both parent and child as well as apps rating, Tables 4, 5 and 6.
(2) Parent versus child and high versus low rated reviews (Low: 1–3 ratings; High: 4–5) to understand the key differences in these reviews, Table 7.

4   Results

4.1   Examining Apps Reviews by Ratings

Initially, we did an exploratory analysis across three groups of reviews irrespective of if the review was posted by a parent or child. To do so, we classified the extracted reviews into three groups according to their rating. Our team interpreted the results qualitatively based on table topic models. The first group of ratings consists of reviews with rating 1 and 2. The second group consists of reviews with rating 3 and 4. The third group consists of reviews with rating 5.

The groups provided insights into the relationship between apps rating ranges and the extracted topics. Tables 4, 5 and 6 outline relevant topics for each category. For instance, Tables 4 and 5, which represent reviews with high and medium ratings, reflect some satisfactions with the apps by both teens and parent, along with suggestions for improvements. These include payment issues, user interface, installations and blocking issues. Table 6 shows the first group, which represents the majority of reviews - 8742 - and has the range of occurrences between 436 and 1453.

These topics were mainly reflecting users' dissatisfactions with several apps' features including license, upgrading, installations as well as some compatibility issues. For example, some of the extracted topics may reflect functionality issues as in Topic 2, Topic 3, and Topic 4. Other topics may reflect dissatisfaction with the apps due to other reasons mentioned earlier as in Topics 4–10. Additionally, the reported topics show that there is a relationship between apps with low rating scores and the review themes. For instance, Topic 3 may explain some concerns regarding apps setting or security.

Table 4. Topics on high rating apps reviews

ID	Topic	Occurrence
1	Play kid google found pretty turn block	263
2	Browser monitor internet mode safe text content sites	338
3	Device settings password stars working uninstall issue blocking	395
4	Kids add option make feature works nice pay problem	457
5	Screen love son year day home button times	489
6	Time control set tablet parents limit children parental	490
7	Good daughter update games location days show awesome	559
8	Free works web phones find stars website trial	650
9	Great work features easy android version track install service	745
10	Phone child access kids lock back blocked things usage installed	808

Table 5. Topics on medium rating apps reviews

ID	Topic	Occurrence
1	Year free worth make download pay blocked trial	589
2	Access device android installed lock block put feature monitoring	815
3	Kids play games phones things bad hate worry tool	1071
4	Love parent son kids great usage limits tablet helps	1063
5	Parents children easy control monitor safe parental internet online web	1589
6	Time screen set limit tablets tablet day chores tasks school	1794
7	Control devices recommend highly found amazing reviews lot	1559
8	Phone child daughter track mind content thing peace location block	2042
9	Great good works features work job happy nice needed	2479
10	Kid settings back perfect awesome home life mobile	2315

Table 6. Topics on low rating apps reviews

ID	Topic	Occurrence
1	Tablet great update son working support year internet	436
2	Child block access sites lock parent blocks porn	534
3	Work uninstall stupid works deactivate chrome useless	654
4	Settings screen browser mode android open home website	811

(continued)

Table 6. (*continued*)

ID	Topic	Occurrence
5	Kids hate parents bad install version control games	771
6	Good back times uninstalled buy change delete star location	721
7	Play google download give features people stars sucks	974
8	Time device password account set waste devices reset found problem	1010
9	Phone won kid thing daughter locked longer call	1408
10	Lifetime free license pay money email make trust trial years	1453

4.2 Distinguishing Between Parent Versus Child Reviews

To address RQ1, we ran three different classifiers on the data set to determine which worked best to classify parent and teen reviews. Table 2 shows the results of Naïve Bayes (NB), Support Vector Machines (SVM), and Neural Network (NN) to predict whether a review was entered by a teen or parent. Based on the extracted N-Grams features, the output depended upon whether or not the model estimated the right class (parent or teen). There were 10 reviews and each review were associated with the top three topics. The scores represent the weight these topics have within each review, so they can be used later on to build our models. To train our proposed models, we used 80% of the dataset for training and 20% for testing on 29,272 reviews, and we reported the results on 10-fold cross validation. We analyzed the results from the accuracy measure for each classifier. Naïve Bayes (NB) produced the highest score having correctly classified 75% of the reviews. The Support Vector Machines (SVM), which has been described as an outstanding classifier in the context of text classification, achieved a 72% accuracy measure [43–45]. Neural Network (NN) produced the worst results with an accuracy measure score of 69%.

The reported findings illustrate that the extracted features by N-Grams technique contributed in identifying parents' reviews from child reviews. From our analyses, parents' reviews were associated with concerns including functionality issues, suggestions for improvement and cost issues. Some of these features include "monitors usage including", "google play doesn't", "support unable", and "app reason rooted."

Child reviews were mostly expressing frustration toward their parents. For instance, some of the extracted features for teens include negative sentiments regarding the parental control apps installed on their devices explicitly mentioned their parent or parents. Examples include "even stupid parents", "people creating disgusting", "hate parents", and "dislike dad put."

The coherence of our analysis shows how well the extracted features by N-Grams can be contributed to improving the performance of the proposed models. In other words, parents and teens features may have shared a common theme within each group which led to the increasing of the models' performance accuracy. Additionally, reviews written by either group may reveal that concerns are centered around specific type of issues. A more thorough research of parental control apps can provide an array of clues to providing future strategies for apps designers.

Our findings show that the both models, (NB) and (LR), substantially outperformed the other models. This finding confirmed previous studies' conclusions that NB is an outstanding classifier in text classifications [45]. K-Nearest Neighbors (KNN) and Neural Network (NN) scored 63% and 68%, respectively. Support Vector Machines (SVM) and Classification and Regression Trees (CART) produced the lowest performance in accuracy scoring 53% and 64%, respectively.

On the contrary, we observe low accuracy measure on topic modeling results co pared to N-Grams results. For instance, LR and NN scored 59% and 63%, the highest performance with higher MAE 1.08 and 0.93, respectively. A discrepancy between the calculated performance for N-Grams (NG) and Topic modeling (TB) can be explained by the text length where classifiers tend to perform better on shorter text. KNN scored 57% on accuracy for both techniques. NN and LR scored the highest a curacy for Topic modeling. KNN produced 57% in accuracy compared to lower accuracy when it is applied on N-Grams. Finally, CART, SVM, and NB produced the worst accuracy with low variance among each other, 52% and 53%. This finding confirms previous research findings that Naïve Bayes is very sensitive to the dataset [43].

Table 3 shows Precision, recall, and F-measure of each proposed classifier. We compared the results when using N-grams and Topic Modeling as different techniques for features extraction. As explained earlier, N-Grams produce short text containing 2–3 words. In contrast, topic modeling produces different topics where each topic consists of several words. We experienced a high discrepancy between the two results produced by N-gram and topic modeling. In N-Grams, we achieved the highest precision of 69% and highest recall for LR. NN achieved the second highest precision 67% and 68% in recall. NB performed 66% and 73% in precision and recall. Finally, KNN, CART, and SVM range between 53% and 61% for Precision and between 53% and 57% for recall.

Our N-Grams classifiers performance seems promising given the experienced limitation in the extracted reviews. For instance, teens' reviews tend to be very short compare to parents' reviews which can be hard for classifiers to identify the correct pattern. Additionally, some apps had a larger number of reviews compared to others. Consequently, high variance can be achieved within the dataset which can diminish the classification accuracy. The other category was performed on topic modeling achieved the range between 45% and 59% for precision and recall in the following classifiers: LR, KNN, CART, and SVM. NB reported the lowest precision 28%. Finally, we investigated the misclassification issues in the topic modeling analysis and found that the variability of the used vocabulary by different users can be a significant factor in achieving lower scores in precision and recall. This finding of the low precision and recall in topic modeling is consistent with previous study [46].

4.3 Contrasting Parent Versus Child Reviews

To understand the different themes expressed in the reviews by parents and teens (RQ2), we compared the results of N-grams and Topic Modeling as different techniques for features extraction. As shown in Table 7, we then generated topics based on parent versus child and high versus low rated reviews (Low: 1–3 ratings; High: 4–5) to understand the key differences in these reviews.

Latent themes emerged from the data to reveal differences between parent and child reviews. The topics demonstrated a relationship between apps rating scores and the review themes for both parents and children.

Table 7. Parent and child topics under high and low app rating.

Parents: High Ratings	Child: High Ratings
1. Phone, app, games, chores, **times, earn, daughters,** knowing, downloaded, **amount**	1. Works, hate, **screen,** games, day, year, bad, isn, website, sad
2. **Time, limit, usage,** tasks, limits, helps, **track,** extra, helped, **helpful**	2. **Dad,** installed, things, doesn, happy, im, date, **helps,** lol, block,
3. Apps, access, devices, give, year, **lock, tablets,** web, **content, ability**	3. App, recommend, lot, homework, likes, mind, step, **helped,** likes, heck, **understand**
4. **Daughter,** good, works, found, free, home, find, check, perfect	4. Tablet, play, **limit,** make, playing, **life** brother, glad, delete, quot
5. Son, tablet, app, **love, mind,** online, settings, manage, **peace,** keeping	5. **Love,** kids, years, kid, device, find, teen nice, downloaded, control,
6. Phone, child, **safe,** play, don, things, children, **block,** phones, **worry**	6. Phone, kid, stop, thing, found, **hope,** won, **addicted,** cousin, face
7. App, children, internet, **recommend,** highly, activity, **problem,** happy, add, service	7. **Good, mom,** great, loves, apps, spend dang, fix, world, back
8. App, child, **great,** parents, parent, device, **features,** feel, android **protect**	8. **Parents,** don, put, pretty, settings, usage, didn, airplane, setting, review
9. **Control, monitor, easy,** great, work, make, installed, parental, feature, **love**	9. **Time, safe,** made, hour, track, mobile, control, change, manage, tab
10. Kids, **screen,** set, ve, day, school, long, hours, back, put	10. App, **child,** work, password, deleted, give, blocked, mad, hey, feature
Parents: Low Ratings	**Child: Low Ratings**
1. Time, son, good, day, **useless,** hours, **password,** application, change, show	1. **Parents,** don, **sucks,** people, school, friends, makes, anymore, youtube, talk
2. App, doesn, games, parent, mode, buy, **allowed, blocking,** sites, kid	2. Life, child, **privacy,** thing, children, feel, hour, parent, app, text
3. Child, great, **blocked,** home, place, open, site, videos, button, received	3. **Hate,** download, stuff, **horrible,** person, net, wont, great, forever, times
4. Device, **uninstall,** times, back, google, **trial,** don, message, log, find	4. Kids, apps, **blocked,** good, control, screen, **freedom,** block, things, stop
5. App, update, working, **free,** data, year, features, school, monitoring, **stopped**	5. Time, **dad, stupid,** doesn, made, uninstall, work, worst, easy, game
6. Son, work, location, give, settings, days, norton, **pay,** android 11	6. Phone, put, **parents,** day, hours, making, gonna, **dumb,** unlock, set
7. Apps, tablet, **works, won,** screen, control, play, account, phones, fix	7. App, quot, trust, play, install, dont, delete, lot, teen, ve
8. Children, access, installed, kids, **block,** worked, monitor, stars, make, **problem**	8. Kid, tablet, im, games, won, make, **bad,** downloaded fix, internet
9. Phone, put, don, locked, service, call, thing, email, long, issue	9. **Mom,** device, settings, **blocks,** google, mode, safe, watch, teens, volume
10. Daughter, quot, set, lock, support, ve, version, **paid,** didn, samsung	10. App, password, installed, kid, give, **minutes,** didn, star, **stalking,** back

High parental ratings accounted for 54% of reviews. Parent reviews tended to range from one complete sentence to more than 5 sentences. Positive reviews focused on the app's ability to protect the online safety of their child. For instance, one positive review explained, *"I can monitor everything my son does."* Low parental ratings accounted for 17% of reviews. Negative reviews were associated with concerns such as functionality, installation, licensing, and cost. In one example, the parent wrote, "Keeps crashing after update making my phone unusable because it takes forever to get the program to close and you are locked out of everything."

In contrast, child reviews tended to be short sentence fragments emoting anger and frustration towards their parent. High child ratings represented only 5% of reviews. The few positive reviews from children showed that they appreciate some of the app's features. For instance, one child explained, *"I'm 9...with kid search it has kid friendly things that work for my age! Keep up!."* These reviews also suggested that some children understood their parents' concerns regarding their safety and the negative effects of technology overuse. Keywords such as *"safe, help, addicted"* appeared in several topics. Low child ratings comprised 24% of the reviews and included emotional charged words, such as *"Hate it,"* *"F you,"* *"sucks,"* *"stupid,"* *"dumb,"* and *"bad."* Topics in this group often reflected a child's frustration regarding privacy violations by their parents and limits on their freedom.

These quotes highlight how teens are not satisfied with the apps being installed on their devices. On the other hand, parents expressed satisfaction or positive feedback. For instance, *"safe online remote"* and *"Good app children"* may explain a positive experience with an app's features. Table 4 contains examples of the extracted topics using LDA for common parent and teen topics from high and low rating reviews.

5   Discussion

5.1   Parents and Children Write Reviews in Different Ways

Our analysis addresses the parent and teen communities' perspectives on parental control app reviews which range from enjoyment and satisfaction to sadness and displeasure. Parents reviews are largely found to be long and complete, varying in the range of one complete sentence to more than five sentences. For instance, one complete sentence may explain an app's feature, "I can monitor everything my son does." Complete reviews of an app with a 5-star may highlight elements that the developer has designed well, for instance:

> *"I can now let my son uses my phone without worrying if he is going to get into something he shouldn't! I also love how easy the app was to set up! I cannot recommend this highly enough for anyone that has children or works around children."* – Parent, Parental Control by Familoop, 2016.

This parent praised the apps ability to alleviate their worries about what their son was looking at on his phone. Furthermore, it indicates that the app was easy to set up. The parent is happy with the effectiveness of the app and its initial usability. Thus, effectiveness and ease of use are elements that will engender a positive experience in parents and should be noted by developers.

Parental reviews with a 1-star rating often remark on their dissatisfaction with the app. These types of reviews tend to be longer given that the parent may want to justify their rating, for example:

> "I have had sooooooo many issues with this application! It has week days/ends mixed up, the timer doesn't work properly with games, it's a day behind in its reporting, etc. Those issues I have come to live with because at least it blocks inappropriate apps. NOPE! The last straw was when I found out today that my son has FULL access to the Internet even though I have it all blocked with this app. I'm talking FULL ACCESS! PORN GALORE! Do NOT trust this application!" – Parent, ESET Parental Control, 2016.

This example demonstrates the types of frustrations a parent may have using parental control apps. Simple UI elements like the calendar and timers are misfunctioning. This may be indicative of two scenarios. In one, the app developer lacked adequate quality controls and shipped a product that is malfunctioning. In the other, the apps usability may not be intuitive or learnable enough for parents of various technological backgrounds. Distinguishing between parent and teen reviews may help inform developers on how to design effective UI elements for both parent and teen users. New designs can then be user tested by parents and teens separately to ensure that the needs of both user groups are being met.

While these reviews suggest that parents are eager to share their positive and negative experiences, they tend to not share their teens frustration or displeasure. Positive reviews by teens accounted for only 5% of the total reviews, compared to 54% by parents. This suggests that teens are having fewer positive experiences with the parental control apps. Indeed, teen reviews often feature expressions of anger related to restrictive features. Some examples include short descriptions such as "Hate it", "F you", and "Cuz I am child". However, teens also admit that control apps can be helpful, but some features should be improved:

> "I am a kid. I used to be on my phone all the time but this app got me up and out. Now though, it glitches and says I've been on my phone for 11 h when I only play on it on the bus, which is an hour max. It also doesn't let me respond to texts when time is used up. I also cannot get on contacts without having my parents unblock it. Still is a great app though. Hope this glitch will be fixed soon". – Teen, Screen Time Companion App, 2015.

In addition to expressing their frustrations with the control app's restrictions, reviews by teens were found to be shorter than those of their parents. Despite their shortened length, however, these shortened reviews may reveal additional security concerns not initially considered by the developers. For instance, in the quote below, the teen highlights the possibility of their parent's phones being stolen. Criminals with access to the parent's phone may also have access to critical information regarding their teen.

> "Freaking hate this. It's bullshit. My parents are hacking me. No one get this all. It's more safe without it. Imagine if some one got hold of their phones. It's bullshit." –Teen, Secure Teen Parental Control, 2015.

One review revealed that parental control apps can contribute to the increased toxic relationship between teens and their parents, while also exacerbating other social issues:

"Im 15. my dad got this app just to limit time on my phone. I have no problem with that and i agree that i use my phone too often. but how you can restrict apps is the worst. i could have a really nice conversation with a new person i met at school. not anymore. i have a social problem and texting helps me talk to people. well now im screwed. my friends dont want to text me anymore because they know my dad can see my messages. I am not even gonna start on not having a wifi signal because its such bullshit..." –Teen, Screen Time Companion App, 2015

This review suggests that teens may be understanding of the parent's desire to control their mobile phone usage but disagree to the extent to which their behaviors are restricted. This not only creates tension between the teen and the parent, but also limits the teen's ability to socialize according to current conventions of their age group. The latter may lead to a sense of alienation. Understanding the needs and desires of teen mobile users could potentially avoid this conflict by way of curating restrictions based on the varying interpersonal dynamics of parents and teens.

In general, our results show that teens were open to communicate and share their frustrations where it seems like there is a lack of communication with their parents when it comes to privacy issues. Teens demand privacy and more autonomy as they feel more restricted and disclosed by installing these apps.

5.2   Reviews Reveal Relational Tensions Between Parents and Children

Topic modeling revealed additional insights into the relationship between the extracted features and app rating. The three groups in topic modeling, Tables 5, 6 and 7, show different patterns for low, medium, and high rating apps. For instance, low rating apps tend to be mostly negative and include keywords such as mom, dad, block, hate, privacy, horrible, stupid, and ruin. Many of these keywords represent teens expressing their anger and irritation regarding the apps. Some of these keywords such as 'block' or 'blocked' occur in low rating reviews by both parents and teens.

However, in light of the explicit quotes examined in Sect. 5.1, it is likely that these words are being used by each group differently. That is, parents are going to use the word blocked in a negative review if the app failed at blocking the teen's mobile usage. Whereas a teen is likely to use it in a negative review when it successfully blocks their access. Topics in high rating apps are similar between both user groups with keywords such as 'help' or 'helped' and 'safe.' While tensions are likely to occur between parents and teens, in many cases the app was able to help the family solve problems regarding their safety and that these safety concerns were understood by both parties. It is important, then, for developers to search for common needs that overlap between the two user groups to design effective solutions.

These findings have implications beyond classifying parent and teen reviews based on their linguistic factors. In many cases, topic modeling revealed that the underlying themes within the reviews went beyond a description of the app, its features, or its performance. Instead, reviews were often an expression of the relationship between parents and teens as mediated through parental control apps. Thus, the written component of a review appears far more important than a quantitative rating of app usability, and more, a valuable signal of the underlying parent-teen relationship. Future studies should focus on review content as an important indicator of understanding these relationships.

Our work is consistent with previous studies where N-Grams outperformed other techniques due to the length of the extracted text [46]. Topic modeling and N-Grams helped to generate some labels related to different domains including design, privacy, license, and app costs. These types of analyses can be used to inspire designers to embrace new communication strategies so users can be pro-active in sharing their experience. Finally, our study found that both teens and parents are willing to explain the reasoning behind their rating. This can be demonstrated in the three groups as each one may represent different categories. One implication of this finding is that both teens and parents are encouraged to communicate and share their thoughts.

These analyses are an important source of information for apps developers to improve the quality of the developed apps. The applied techniques and generated features assessed the model to improve the performance accuracy for the six machine learning classifiers.

5.3   Implications for the Future Design of Parental Control Apps

Key insights that arose from our results may help us shape the future design of parental control apps. Our results showed that parents and children liked and disliked the currently available apps for different reasons. Although most parents were generally positive about the apps, they were mainly concerned about apps cost, license, bugs, and functionality issues. So, app designers need to make sure that: (1) their apps offer free and low-cost versions, (2) apps are bug-free, and (3) they provide tech support for parents who may not be tech savvy or intuitive help documentation.

Teens, on the other hand, posted positive reviews when they felt that the apps helped them break addictive patterns and better manage their screen-time. However, they more often left low ratings because of how the parental control app negatively changed the relationship dynamic between themselves and their parents. Stalking, restriction, and privacy were common themes among the low-rated child reviews. This finding raises the question of how parental control apps might be designed in a way that is more supportive of nurturing positive parent-teen relationships while still ensuring a teen's online safety? To do this, developers and researchers should pro-actively embrace direct interactions with teen users for more feedback. Doing so will provide additional clarification regarding the teen's concerns. Teens need to have their voice heard being a major stakeholder in the design process. What's more, giving teens a voice in the design process will allow for the development of parental control apps that respect a teen's need for autonomy and privacy, while providing security that parents seek. This can benefit the teens' mobile experience while also facilitating more positive relationships between teens and their parents.

5.4   Limitations and Future Research

Several limitations should be considered while interpreting the reported results. First, our topic modeling Parameter K were set to be 10, based on common convention derived from our observation of each group's size. This result can change in the case of different parameters. Second, our analysis was based on 52 parental control apps found on Google Play with large variance of the number of reviews for each app. Finally, the extracted reviews for teens were small compare to the parents' reviews, so results could differ in future studies with more teen reviews. Therefore, we suggest that future research consider validating the generalizability of our findings across different platforms (i.e., iOS) and a wider range of adolescent online safety apps to see if the patterns we uncovered hold in these new contexts. We also encourage social computational researchers to work with qualitative researchers to find synergistic ways to meaningfully analyze large data sets from the strengths of both perspectives.

6 Conclusion

Our N-Grams and Topic Modeling analyses revealed new insights into the relationship and tensions. These analyses are an important source of information for analysts and apps developers to improve the quality of the developed apps between parents and children by applying computational methods to parental control app reviews. A key contribution of this work is that we integrated domain knowledge into computational models for empirical validation at a reasonable scale. Yet, these findings have implications beyond classifying parent and child reviews based on their linguistic factors. In many cases, topic modeling revealed that the underlying themes within the reviews went beyond a description of the app and its features or performance, and more towards an expression of the relationship between parents and teens as mediated through parental control apps. Thus, reviews seem to be far more important than a quantitative rating of app usability and more, a valuable signal of the underlying parent-teen relationship. These insights can be used to improve parental control app design, and therefore the user experience of both parents and children.

References

1. Blackwell, L., Gardiner, E., Schoenebeck, S.: Managing expectations: technology tensions among parents and teens. In: Proceedings of the 19th ACM Conference on Computer-Supported Cooperative Work & Social Computing, pp. 1390–1401. ACM, New York (2016a)
2. Boyd, D.: It's Complicated: The Social Lives of Networked Teens. Yale University Press, New Haven (2014)
3. Anderson, M.: Parents, Teens and Digital Monitoring (2016). http://www.pewinternet.org/2016/01/07/parents-teens-and-digital-monitoring/
4. Baumrind, D.: A developmental perspective on adolescent risk taking in contemporary America. In: New Directions for Child and Adolescent Development, pp. 93–125 (1987). https://doi.org/10.1002/cd.23219873706
5. Wisniewski, P., Ghosh, A.K., Rosson, M.B., Xu, H., Carroll, J.M.: Parental control vs. teen self-regulation: is there a middle ground for mobile online safety? In: Proceedings of the 20th ACM Conference on Computer Supported Cooperative Work & Social Computing. ACM, Portland (2017)

6. Ghosh, A.K., Badillo-Urquiola, K., Guha, S., LaViola Jr., J., Wisniewski, P.: Safety vs. surveillance: what children have to say about mobile apps for parental control. In: Proceedings of the 2018 CHI Conference on Human Factors in Computing Systems. ACM, New York (2018)

7. Ashktorab, Z., Vitak, J.: Designing cyberbullying mitigation and prevention solutions through participatory design with teenagers. In: Proceedings of the 2016 CHI Conference on Human Factors in Computing Systems, pp. 3895–3905. ACM, New York (2016)

8. Hashish, Y., Bunt, A., Young, J.E.: Involving children in content control: a collaborative and education-oriented content filtering approach. In: Proceedings of the 32nd Annual ACM Conference on Human Factors in Computing Systems, pp. 1797–1806. ACM, New York (2014)

9. Wisniewski, P., et al.: Resilience mitigates the negative effects of adolescent internet addiction and online risk exposure. In: Proceedings of the 33rd Annual ACM Conference on Human Factors in Computing Systems, pp. 4029–4038. ACM, New York (2015)

10. Wisniewski, P., Xu, H., Rosson, M.B., Perkins, D.F., Carroll, J.M.: Dear diary: teens reflect on their weekly online risk experiences. In: Proceedings of the 2016 CHI Conference on Human Factors in Computing Systems, pp. 3919–3930. ACM, New York (2016)

11. Yardi, S., Bruckman, A.: Social and technical challenges in parenting teens' social media use. In: Proceedings of the SIGCHI Conference on Human Factors in Computing Systems, pp. 3237–3246. ACM, New York (2011)

12. Yardi, S., Bruckman, A.: Income, race, and class: exploring socioeconomic differences in family technology use. In: Proceedings of the SIGCHI Conference on Human Factors in Computing Systems, pp. 3041–3050. ACM, New York (2012)

13. Hiniker, A., Schoenebeck, S.Y., Kientz, J.A.: Not at the dinner table: parents' and children's perspectives on family technology rules. In: Proceedings of the 19th ACM Conference on Computer-Supported Cooperative Work & Social Computing, pp. 1376–1389. ACM, New York (2016)

14. Cranor, L.F., Durity, A.L., Marsh, A., Ur, B.: Parents' and teens' perspectives on privacy in a technology-filled world. In: Proceedings of the Tenth Symposium on Usable Privacy and Security. USENIX, Menlo Park (2014)

15. Livingstone, S.: Taking risky opportunities in youthful content creation: teenagers' use of social networking sites for intimacy, privacy, and self-expression. New Media Soc. **10**, 393–411 (2008)

16. Nissenbaum, H.: Privacy as Contextual Integrity. Washington Law Rev. **79** (2004)

17. Petronio, S.S.: Boundaries of Privacy: Dialects of Disclosure. SUNY Press (2002)

18. Zaman, B., Nouwen, M.: Parental controls: advice for parents, researchers and industry. http://www.lse.ac.uk/media@lse/research/EUKidsOnline/Home.aspx

19. Czeskis, A., et al.: Parenting from the pocket: value tensions and technical directions for secure and private parent-teen mobile safety. In: Proceedings of the Sixth Symposium on Usable Privacy and Security, pp. 15:1–15:15. ACM, New York (2010)

20. Ghosh, A.K., Badillo-Urquiola, K., Rosson, M.B., Xu, H., Carroll, J., Wisniewski, P.: A matter of control or safety? Examining parental use of technical monitoring apps on teens' mobile devices. In: Proceedings of the 2018 CHI Conference on Human Factors in Computing Systems. ACM, New York (2018)

21. Amato, G., Bolettieri, P., Costa, G., Torre, F., Martinelli, F.: Detection of images with adult content for parental control on mobile devices? In: Proceedings of the 6th International Conference on Mobile Technology, Application & Systems, pp. 35:1–35:5. ACM, New York (2009)

22. Ko, M., Choi, S., Yang, S., Lee, J., Lee, U.: FamiLync: facilitating participatory parental mediation of adolescents' smartphone use. In: Proceedings of the 2015 ACM International Joint Conference on Pervasive and Ubiquitous Computing, pp. 867–878. ACM, New York (2015)

23. Kim, S., Zhang, J., Chen, Z., Oh, A., Liu, S.: A hierarchical aspect-sentiment model for online reviews. In: Proceedings of the Twenty-Seventh AAAI Conference on Artificial Intelligence, pp. 526–533. AAAI Press, Bellevue (2013)

24. Mason, R., et al.: Microsummarization of online reviews: an experimental study. In: Proceedings of the Thirtieth AAAI Conference on Artificial Intelligence, pp. 3015–3021. AAAI Press, Phoenix (2016)

25. Michael, L., Otterbacher, J.: Write like I write: herding in the language of online reviews. In: Proceedings of the 8th International Conference on Weblogs and Social Media, ICWSM 2014, pp. 356–365 (2014)

26. Wang, J., Zhao, W.X., He, Y., Li, X.: Leveraging product adopter information from online reviews for product recommendation. In: Ninth International AAAI Conference on Web and Social Media. AAAI Publications (2015)

27. Ida, Y., Nakamura, T., Matsumoto, T.: Domain-dependent/independent topic switching model for online reviews with numerical ratings. In: Proceedings of the 22nd ACM International Conference on Information & Knowledge Management, pp. 229–238. ACM, New York (2013)

28. Zhao, W.X., Wang, J., He, Y., Wen, J.-R., Chang, E.Y., Li, X.: Mining product adopter information from online reviews for improving product recommendation. ACM Trans. Knowl. Discov. Data. **10**, 29:1–29:23 (2016). https://doi.org/10.1145/2842629

29. Moghaddam, S., Jamali, M., Ester, M.: Review recommendation: personalized prediction of the quality of online reviews. In: Proceedings of the 20th ACM International Conference on Information and Knowledge Management, pp. 2249–2252. ACM, New York (2011)

30. Jawecki, G., Fuller, J.: How to use the innovative potential of online communities? Netnography – an unobtrusive research method to absorb the knowledge and creativity of online communities. Int. J. Bus. Process Integr. Manage. **3**, 248–255 (2008). https://doi.org/10.1504/IJBPIM.2008.024982

31. Korfiatis, N., García-Bariocanal, E., Sánchez-Alonso, S.: Evaluating content quality and helpfulness of online product reviews: the interplay of review helpfulness vs review content. Electron. Commer. Res. Appl. **11**, 205–217 (2012). https://doi.org/10.1016/j.elerap.2011.10.003

32. Vasa, R., Hoon, L., Mouzakis, K., Noguchi, A.: A preliminary analysis of mobile app user reviews. In: Proceedings of the 24th Australian Computer-Human Interaction Conference, pp. 241–244. ACM, New York (2012)

33. Duan, W., Gu, B., Whinston, A.B.: Do online reviews matter?—an empirical investigation of panel data. Decis. Support Syst. **45**, 1007–1016 (2008). https://doi.org/10.1016/j.dss.2008.04.001

34. Epstein, D.A., et al.: Examining menstrual tracking to inform the design of personal informatics tools. In: Proceedings of the 2017 CHI Conference on Human Factors in Computing Systems, pp. 6876–6888. ACM, New York (2017)

35. Fu, B., Lin, J., Li, L., Faloutsos, C., Hong, J., Sadeh, N.: Why people hate your app: making sense of user feedback in a mobile app store. In: Proceedings of the 19th ACM SIGKDD International Conference on Knowledge Discovery and Data Mining, pp. 1276–1284. ACM, New York (2013)

36. McCallum, A.K.: MALLET: A Machine Learning for Language Toolkit (2002)

37. Guyon, I., Elisseeff, A.: An introduction to feature extraction. In: Guyon, I., Nikravesh, M., Gunn, S., Zadeh, L.A. (eds.) Feature Extraction, pp. 1–25. Springer, Heidelberg (2006). https://doi.org/10.1007/978-3-540-35488-8_1

38. Brown, P.F., deSouza, P.V., Mercer, R.L., Pietra, V.J.D., Lai, J.C.: Class-Based n-gram Models of Natural Language. Comput. Linguist. (1992)

39. Blei, D.M.: Latent Dirichlet Allocation **30**

40. Guha, S., Baumer, E.P.S., Gay, G.K.: Regrets, I've had a few: when regretful experiences do (and don't) compel users to leave Facebook. In: Proceedings of the 2018 ACM Conference on Supporting Groupwork, pp. 166–177. ACM, New York (2018)

41. Muller, M., Guha, S., Baumer, E.P.S., Mimno, D., Shami, N.S.: Machine learning and grounded theory method: convergence, divergence, and combination. In: Proceedings of the 19th International Conference on Supporting Group Work, pp. 3–8. ACM, New York (2016)

42. Baumer, E.P.S., Mimno, D., Guha, S., Quan, E., Gay, G.K.: Comparing grounded theory and topic modeling: extreme divergence or unlikely convergence? J. Assoc. Inf. Sci. Technol. **68**, 1397–1410 (2017). https://doi.org/10.1002/asi.23786

43. Alelyani, T., Mao, K., Yang, Y.: Context-centric pricing: early pricing models for software crowdsourcing tasks. In: Proceedings of the 13th International Conference on Predictive Models and Data Analytics in Software Engineering, pp. 63–72. ACM, New York (2017)

44. Friedman, J.H.: On bias, variance, 0/1—loss, and the curse-of-dimensionality. Data Min. Knowl. Discov. **1**, 55–77 (1997). https://doi.org/10.1023/A:1009778005914

45. Friedman, N., Geiger, D., Goldszmidt, M.: Bayesian network classifiers. Mach. Learn. **29**, 131–163 (1997). https://doi.org/10.1023/A:1007465528199

46. Ciurumelea, A., Schaufelbühl, A., Panichella, S., Gall, H.C.: Analyzing reviews and code of mobile apps for better release planning. In: 2017 IEEE 24th International Conference on Software Analysis, Evolution and Reengineering (SANER), pp. 91–102 (2017)

Every Picture Tells a Story - Exploring Personal Branding Communication Activities on Social Media

Christian V. Baccarella[✉], Lukas Maier, Sabine Eibl,
and Kai-Ingo Voigt

School of Business and Economics, Friedrich-Alexander-Universität
Erlangen-Nürnberg, Lange Gasse 20, 90403 Nürnberg, Germany
{christian.baccarella,lukas.maier,sabine.eibl,
kai-ingo.voigt}@fau.de

Abstract. Social media has significantly transformed the way we communicate with each other. It is now possible to let the whole world participate in one's own life, thus having the opportunity to easily create one's own personal brand. In this study, we aim to explore the factors of successful personal branding activities on social media. The present paper aims to find out which aspects of personal brand identities are communicated on social media and how they affect user interaction. More particular, we look at the communication activities of five popular female musicians on the social networking site Instagram. Due to its emphasis on visuals (images and short films), Instagram is particularly suitable to analyze personal branding activities to find out why some individuals excel in creating their personal brand. From a theoretical perspective, this study contributes to the fields of personal branding and social media. From a practical perspective, this study provides important insights for social media managers, artists, and everybody who is interested in building a strong personal brand on social media.

Keywords: Social media · Personal branding · Brand communication · Personal brand identity

1 Introduction

Social media has significantly transformed the way we communicate with each other [1]. It is now possible to let the whole world participate in one's own life, thus having the opportunity to become one's own brand more easily. Although the concept of personal branding is not entirely new [2], it has become increasingly relevant in the digital age. Once considered a marketing tactic especially for celebrities [3] or personalities from business and politics, social media applications have allowed personal branding to become a significant opportunity for anyone willing to fascinate the online community [4]. Moreover, for a long time the creation of an appealing personal brand as well as the communication of it was associated with great effort and with high financial expenses. Today, social media offer a fast and more cost efficient opportunity to create and maintain a personal brand [5].

© Springer Nature Switzerland AG 2019
G. Meiselwitz (Ed.): HCII 2019, LNCS 11579, pp. 22–33, 2019.
https://doi.org/10.1007/978-3-030-21905-5_2

Similar to the more widespread idea of product branding, self-branding begins by defining a distinct brand identity before actively communicating it to the targeted market in order to achieve a specific goal, such as gaining employment, establishing new friendships, or as a way for self-expression [4, 6]. Despite the growing importance of the self-branding phenomenon –especially on social media– there is surprisingly a lack of studies that deal with the *how* of personal branding and that consider the special circumstances of the fast-changing online environment [5].

Thus, in this study we aim to explore the factors leading to successful personal branding activities on social media. The present paper aims to find out which aspects of personal brand identities are communicated on social media and how they affect user interaction. More particular, we look at the communication activities of five popular female musicians on the social networking site (SNS) Instagram. Due to its emphasis on visuals (images and short films), Instagram is particularly suitable to analyze personal branding activities to find out why some individuals excel in creating their personal brand.

2 Theoretical Background

2.1 Social Media

Kaplan and Haenlein [7] define social media as Internet-based applications that provide users the opportunity to create, exchange, and share content using the technological foundations of Web 2.0. Social media includes a variety of different formats, such as blogs, corporate discussion forums, and chat rooms, product or service reviews from users and various social networks [8]. Individuals do not only interact with each other, but can also directly reach out to companies or other organizations [9]. The inherent interactivity of social media applications thus offers individuals and newly formed interest groups the opportunity to share, develop, discuss and modify content they have created themselves [10].

Of course, companies have already recognized the enormous potential of social media for their marketing purposes, [1] such as brand communication [11], customer relationship management [12], or product marketing [13–15]. Felix, Rauschnabel and Hinsch [16] define social media marketing as an interdisciplinary and cross-functional concept, which mainly (often in combination with other communication channels) uses the platforms of the social web to achieve corporate goals by creating value for various interest groups. SNS like Facebook, Instagram or Twitter have become particularly important for companies since they accumulate a huge amount of potential customers [17]. SNS allow companies to create an online presence to reach out to their target audience at relatively low cost to provide them with information about their products and to develop a strong relationship with their customers [7]. However, the possibilities social media offer to create a strong brand are not only limited to companies or organizations. On the contrary, it is now more than ever also possible for "regular" individuals to seize all the opportunities social media offer in the same way.

2.2   Personal Branding

The traditional notion of branding mainly focused on organizations and/or products [18]. Contrary to this traditional view, Peters [2] introduced the idea of personal branding. He describes a person's personality as a 'human brand' that can be formed and communicated to others [2]. Montoya and Vandehey [19] see personal values, skills, and actions as the core of the personal brand. Similarly, Schwabel [6] understands the goal of personal branding as the expansion of one's own existing personality into a brand rather than the change of one's own personality to correspond to a desired brand image. Rampersad [20] describes personal branding as the sum of personal marketing activities to create a consistent external image with the ultimate goal of creating publicity. Accordingly, Hood, Robles and Hopkins [21] define personal branding as the dissemination and promotion of one's own abilities and individual strengths in the sense of a classic product using integrated marketing communication.

Even though the idea of product and personal branding may sound similar at first, they differ in various respects. The biggest difference between corporate brands and personal brands lies in their development process. Whereas product brands are developed based on an existing demand and identified target group preferences, the creation of a personal brand is predetermined by innate personal traits that lie within an individual. Personal brands are therefore more likely to change over time than if they were created from scratch [22]. Consequently, Leland [23] describes personal branding as a continuous stream of small developments instead of a series of drastic modifications.

And yet, the process of personal branding has a lot in common with traditional product branding. A comprehensive self-reflection and self-evaluation of one's own strengths and particularities are regarded as the starting point for the creation of a strong brand [24]. Subsequently, unique and valuable characteristics must be emphasized to allow differentiation from the competition. At the same time, however, these characteristics must also be relevant and important for a certain target group [25]. In summary, all successful branding activities include the core activities of analyzing and communicating individual strengths as well as highlighting their uniqueness for a specific target group [26].

A special category of personal brands are the so-called "celebrity brands". The idea of using the popularity of celebrities and tuning them into (human) trademarks is not new and has a long tradition in theory and practice. Due to their special role as individuals in the public eye, celebrities are admired by their fans and serve as "landmarks" for their own way of living [27].

Although celebrities have already been the subject of various scientific studies [e.g. 28–30], the concept of having a celebrity status, i.e. conceptualizing what exactly the characteristics of a celebrity are, have surprisingly attracted less attention. In an early study, McCracken [31] describes a celebrity as part of a social elite, which is gaining popularity primarily through public relations in the form of press articles or TV appearances. In the marketing literature, research mainly focused on the idea of using celebrities as brand ambassadors for product brands [32, 33]. Thomson [34], however, argues that public figures or celebrities represent brands themselves, since they (1) can be professionally managed and (2) also have characteristics of traditional product brands. Similarly, Close et al. [18] as well as Rindova, Pollock and Hayward [35] do not see any differences between celebrities and traditional brands as they also can be at the center of planned marketing activities with the aim of attracting public attention.

More recently, studies have emphasized the importance of simultaneous self-presentation on a variety of media channels as a central element in creating celebrity brands [36]. Since the emergence of the Internet, communication possibilities for self-portrayal have changed dramatically, certainly making it easier to be omnipresent on a variety of different media formats. Thus, the number of people who are considered "famous" is steadily growing [37], because social media and better access to a wider range of communication channels in general have made it much easier to achieve "celebrity status" these days [38].

2.3 Brand Identity

The creation of a unique and recognizable identity as well as its authentic communication are considered central success factors for a brand [39]. Through direct interaction on social media, brands can build a strong identity and can therefore establish an emotional bond that makes consumers feel strongly connected to them [40]. Thus, it is worthwhile to investigate how individuals can leverage social media to create a strong brand identity.

Aaker [41] defines the personality of a brand as the set of human characteristics primarily associated with a brand. It was also Aaker, who, based on the Big Five personality traits [see e.g. 42], developed the Brand Personality Scale (BPS) with five core brand personality traits: *sophistication, excitement, competence, sincerity*, and *ruggedness* (later also *rudeness*) [41]. The first dimension of the brand personality, *sophistication*, refers strongly to the representation of outer beauty. A further expression of the brand identity is the category *excitement*, which generally describes the presence of energy and activity. *Competence* is described, among other things, by the characteristics successful, intelligent and trustworthy and, similar to sophistication and excitement, is regarded as a personality trait with positive associations [43]. *Sincerity* is characterized by the attributes down-to-earth and honest. Honesty has already been identified in various studies as a central factor in building trust between a brand and the consumer [44]. The last category, *ruggedness*, is described by the attributes outdoorsy and tough and is considered as less important compared to the other attributes of the brand identity [41].

As already mentioned, individuals can also have a distinct brand identity that can be professionally marketed [34, 45]. Moreover, a strong brand identity is generally regarded as an important factor in distinguishing oneself from the competition [46]. Based on the growing importance of social media for personal branding activities, two questions arise: (1) How can individuals use SNS to communicate their own personal brand identity, i.e. which characteristics of their brand identity are particularly highlighted; and (2) which of the shared content generates the greatest user interactivity?

3   Methodology

We chose the popular photo-sharing SNS site Instagram (www.instagram.com) for our study due to its increasing significance for modern marketing and its particular suitability for personal branding activities [47, 48]. In order to answer the research questions, we first analyzed the most popular Instagram profiles. The profiles were selected based on the number of followers indicating the status and impact of an artist on social media [49]. Our initial analysis revealed that ten out of the 25 most successful Instagram profiles were female musicians. After excluding profiles that were not active during our period of analysis or that showed unconventional communication patterns (e.g. posting identical pictures multiple times) and in order to ensure a manageable and homogenous sample, we based our analysis on five Instagram profiles of popular female musicians: Demi Lovato, Jennifer Lopez, Katy Perry, Miley Cyrus, and Tylor Swift.

All profile contents were collected, categorized, and coded over a period of three months from January to March 2018. Overall, data collection resulted in 470 posts across all analyzed profiles. From the 470 posts, 114 posts (24%) were contributed by Demi Lovato, 148 posts (31%) by Jennifer Lopez, 73 posts (16%) by Katy Perry, 122 posts (26%) by Miley Cyrus, and 13 posts (3%) by Taylor Swift. For each post, we first examined whether the post was an advertisement post (e.g. for a certain product or an upcoming tour) or a regular Instagram post (e.g. picture without any reference to a commercial product). We excluded that advertisements from our analysis and continued to explore the regular posts to further find out about the brand personality characteristics of the artists. In a first step, we conducted free analysis based on a short description of the shown picture. In a second step, we categorized the posts into the deductively derived brand traits based on Aaker's [41] brand personality scale: sophistication, sincerity, competence, excitement, and rudeness.

4   Results

From our analyzed 470 posts, 132 posts (28%) clearly communicated an invitation to buy or at least to use a commercial offering (for example the invitation to watch a TV program that features the artist or the invitation for the upcoming world tour of the artist). The remaining 338 posts (72%) contained cues related to the artists' personal brand identities and served as our final sample.

We found each of the five personality traits in communication activities of the artists. However, the occurrence of them differs considerably. For an overview of the different personality traits across the artists, please see Fig. 1.

In particular, our findings show that the most frequently communicated personality trait is sophistication (50%). Accordingly, the category sophistication highlights the physical appearance of the person. Figure 2 shows an example of a post that displays the personality trait sophistication. Moreover, our findings show that within the brand trait sophistication, the sub attributes *beautiful* and *attractive* are the most communicated

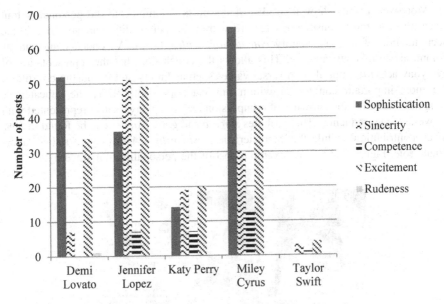

Fig. 1. Distribution of personality traits across the artists

ones (each 93%). Additionally, the artists also communicate the sub attributes *sexy* (71%), *stylish* (63%), and *glamorous* (52%). However, the attribute *cute* is hardly communicated by the artists (8%).

Fig. 2. Example for sophistication personality trait [50]

The second most communicated personality trait is excitement (45%). Findings show that the most communicated sub categories of the excitement personality trait, are *dynamic* (72%), *exciting* (83%), and *good energy* (93%).

Moreover, results show that 33% of the posts communicate the personality trait sincerity. The most conspicuous feature within the personality trait sincerity is the accumulation of the subcategory *can identify with* (100%). All coded contributions communicate this subcategory. This allows the conclusion that the representation of everyday activities, but also universal values such as family and friendship constitutes the most important component within this category. With 97%, the subcategory *compassionate*, i.e. the showing of compassion and sympathy, is also represented with above-average frequency. The attributes *sincere* and *good listener* can be found in 50% of all contributions, while the characteristic *trustworthy* (34%) plays a rather subordinate role. Figure 3 shows an example post of the personality trait sincerity.

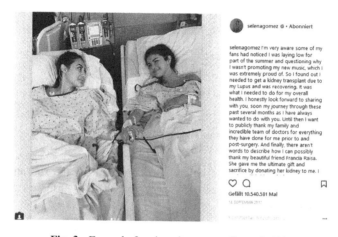

Fig. 3. Example for sincerity personality trait [51]

The personality trait competence is communicated by 8% of the posts. Within this personality trait, artists most often communicate the subcategories *experienced* (96%) and *successful* (61%). The subcategory *intelligent* (43%) is also still presented very frequently, while the subcategory *interesting* is only communicated in 32% of the posts that communicate competence. Even though competence generally receives less attention, the presentation of professional competence or experience in one's own field as well as achieved successes are important for personal brands. Only one post contained the personality trait rudeness (0.3%).

To gain further insights which posts generated the greatest user interaction, we first analyzed the three most successful posts (measured by the number of "likes") for each of the five artists. Findings show that a clear majority of the most successful posts (ten of the 15) focus on "self-portrayal" (i.e. showing portraits or full-body photographs of the artists). Other communicated key themes, such as "family and friends", "backstage insights" or information about the artist's personal "interests and hobbies" have attracted considerably less interest and therefore achieved far fewer likes. Regarding containing brand personality traits, we find that 80% of the most successful posts contain the personality trait sophistication and 33% reflect the category excitement.

In addition, we analyzed the three most successful posts regarding their number of comments of four of the five artists (one of the artists disabled to comment function). Similar to our other findings, results show that 67% of the most commented posts fall into the category "self-portrayal". Moreover, 92% of the posts contained the personality trait sophistication and 25% the personality trait excitement.

5 Discussion

5.1 General Discussion

The aim of this study was to identify how personality traits are communicated on social media by successful personal brands. There exist only a few studies examining brand identities of celebrities such as writers [52], athletes [53], or politicians [54]. Despite the growing importance of digital communication activities, there is still a lack of studies that deal with personal branding activities on social media. From a theoretical perspective, we therefore contribute to the fields of personal branding and social media by shedding light on how successful personal branding on social media takes place.

Our findings show that the analyzed artists mostly communicate the brand personality traits sophistication and excitement and that both characteristics lead to high user interaction. In that context, visual appearance and a positive attitude seem to be central factors in order to create a strong personal brand. These findings are consistent with existing research in the field of personal branding. For example, Lunardo et al. [55] see sophistication as the main characteristic of an attractive personal brand. Moreover, Choi and Rifon [56] state that external attractiveness (sophistication) is the primary determining factor for successful personal brands. Besides that, previous studies identified the personality trait excitement as one of the most valued personality traits of both product brands and personal brands (e.g. [57]). This study contributes to the ongoing discussion by showing that the personality trait excitement is also an important characteristic of successful personal brands on social media.

Moreover, we show that the personality trait sincerity can help to build a successful personal brand on social media. The analyzed artists often present themselves as compassionate, lovable, and approachable persons with whom the fans can identify.

Moreover, we find that the personality trait competence can be used to build strong personal brands. Compared to the already mentioned brand identity traits we however find that competence seems not so important for the social media personal brand identity. One reason for the low representation of one's own competence could be the artists' aim to be close to the target group instead of clearly distinguishing themselves from them. Fans may find it more difficult to identify themselves with attributes such as experience and intelligence, which is why they could play a minor role in the representation of the analyzed brand personalities.

Finally and not surprisingly, our study shows that the personality trait rudeness is not at all relevant for presenting artists' brand personalities on social media.

5.2   Practical Implications

Our study provides important insights for social media managers, artists, and everybody who is interested in building a strong personal brand on social media.

First, to build a successful personal brand on social media, users should primarily communicate the personality traits sophistication and excitement. Sophistication and excitement proved to be major aspects of successful personal brand on social media, which was also clearly shown in the high user interaction. Thus, in order to increase their popularity and user interaction, social media managers and artists should primarily focus on communicating sophistication and excitement. Through a high level of interaction, followers can become even closer and more emotionally attached to an individual (or his profile), thus contributing to the establishment of a long-term relationship with the personal brand.

Second, users on social media should avoid communicating the personality trait rudeness when aiming to build a strong personal brand. Our study shows that rudeness does not play a role in the representation of the artists' brand personality. It can therefore be assumed that this personality trait is largely connected with negative associations and is therefore avoided. Social media managers should also regularly review their clients' posts for potentially negative content such as rudeness, and amend them if necessary. Therefore, it can make sense to make a "brand personality map" for their clients in order to plan the content that should be communicated in their social media posts. Due to the fast pace of SNS' like Instagram, consistency and a clear brand identity strategy help to shape a personal brand in the long run.

Third, when developing a successful brand strategy and its communication within social media, users must be aware of possible damage to the image due to lack of authenticity. Authenticity is crucial for positive consumer and follower reaction and can lead to significant and irreparable damage to brand identity if insufficient attention is paid to it [58]. Thus, it is also important to constantly monitor the reaction of social media followers. Qualitative approaches could help to find out how communication activities are perceived by the audience. Solely focusing on likes and comments may not be sufficient to find out more subtle aspects.

6   Limitations and Future Research

Our study has some limitations that, however, provide possibilities for future research. First, we used a relatively small sample from a specific industry for our study. Thus, our findings from the music industry cannot necessarily be generalized for other industries or other settings. Future research should examine whether our findings can also be confirmed for other industries or whether they are also relevant for private, non-celebrity personal brands. Furthermore, as we analyzed only profiles of female artists, further research should investigate whether and to what extent the brand identity on social media differs between male and female individuals.

Second, we only considered the social media platform Instagram for our study. To gain a more comprehensive understanding on how to build strong personal brands on social media, research should also consider other social media platforms (e.g. Facebook or LinkedIn) for their analysis.

Third, we focused on visual content in our study and neglected images' captions or texts. Here, future research should clarify how different types of information may influence the perception of brand identities.

References

1. Wagner, T.F., Baccarella, C.V., Voigt, K.I.: Framing social media communication: investigating the effects of brand post appeals on user interaction. Eur. Manag. J. **35**(5), 606–616 (2017)
2. Peters, T.: The brand called you. Fast Company **10**(10), 83–90 (1997)
3. Rein, I., Kotler, P., Shields, B.: The Elusive Fan: Reinventing Sports in a Crowded Marketplace. McGraw-Hill, London (2006)
4. Shepherd, I.D.: From cattle and coke to charlie: meeting the challenge of self marketing and personal branding. J. Mark. Manag. **21**(5–6), 589–606 (2005)
5. Karaduman, I.: The effect of social media on personal branding efforts of top level executives. In: Özşahin, M. (ed.) Proceedings of 9th International Strategic Management Conference, Riga (2013)
6. Schwabel, D.: Me 2.0: A Powerful Way to Achieve Brand Success. Kaplan Publishers, New York (2009)
7. Kaplan, A.M., Haenlein, M.: Users of the world, unite! The challenges and opportunities of social media. Bus. Horiz. **53**(1), 59–68 (2010)
8. Mangold, W.G., Faulds, D.J.: Social media: the new hybrid element of the promotion mix. Bus. Horiz. **52**(4), 357–365 (2009)
9. Saboo, A.R., Kumar, V., Ramani, G.: Evaluating the impact of social media activities on human brand sales. Int. J. Res. Mark. **33**(3), 524–541 (2016)
10. Kietzmann, J.H., Hermkens, K., McCarthy, I.P., Silvestre, B.S.: Social media? Get serious! Understanding the functional building blocks of social media. Bus. Horiz. **54**(3), 241–251 (2011)
11. Asmussen, B., Harridge-March, S., Occhiocupo, N., Farquhar, J.: The multi-layered nature of the internet-based democratization of brand management. J. Bus. Res. **66**(9), 1473–1483 (2013)
12. Trainor, K.J., Andzulis, J.M., Rapp, A., Agnihotri, R.: Social media technology usage and customer relationship performance: a capabilities-based examination of social CRM. J. Bus. Res. **67**(6), 1201–1208 (2014)
13. Chang, Y.T., Yu, H., Lu, H.P.: Persuasive messages, popularity cohesion, and message diffusion in social media marketing. J. Bus. Res. **68**(4), 777–782 (2015)
14. Kumar, A., Bezawada, R., Rishika, R., Janakiraman, R., Kannan, P.K.: From social to sale: the effects of firm-generated content in social media on customer behavior. J. Mark. **80**(1), 7–25 (2016)
15. Relling, M., Schnittka, O., Sattler, H., Johnen, M.: Each can help or hurt: negative and positive word of mouth in social network brand communities. Int. J. Res. Mark. **33**(1), 42–58 (2016)
16. Felix, R., Rauschnabel, P.A., Hinsch, C.: Elements of strategic social media marketing: a holistic framework. J. Bus. Res. **70**, 118–126 (2017)

17. Tuten, T., Mintu-Wimsatt, A.: Advancing our understanding of the theory and practice of social media marketing: introduction to the special issue. J. Mark. Theor. Pract. **26**(1–2), 1–3 (2018)
18. Close, A.G., Moulard, J.G., Monroe, K.B.: Establishing human brands: determinants of placement success for first faculty positions in marketing. J. Acad. Mark. Sci. **39**(6), 922–941 (2011)
19. Montoya, P., Vandehey, T.: The Brand Called You: The Ultimate Brand-Building and Business Development Handbook to Transform Anyone into an Indispensable Personal Brand. Personal Branding Press, Santa Ana (2003)
20. Rampersad, H.K.: Authentic Personal Branding: A New Blueprint for Building and Aligning a Powerful Leadership Brand. Information Age Publishing, Charlotte (2009)
21. Hood, K.M., Robles, M., Hopkins, C.D.: Personal branding and social media for students in today's competitive job market. J. Res. Bus. Educ. **56**(2), 33–47 (2014)
22. Rangarajan, D., Gelb, B.D., Vandaveer, A.: Strategic personal branding—and how it pays off. Bus. Horiz. **60**(5), 657–666 (2017)
23. Leland, K.T.: The Brand Mapping Strategy. Entrepreneur Press, Irvine (2006)
24. Johnson, K.: The importance of personal branding in social media: educating students to create and manage their personal brand. Int. J. Educ. Soc. Sci. **4**(1), 21–27 (2017)
25. Lair, D.J., Sullivan, K., Cheney, G.: Marketization and the recasting of the professional self: the rhetoric and ethics of personal branding. Manag. Commun. **Q18**(3), 307–343 (2005)
26. Khedher, M.: Personal branding phenomenon. Int. J. Inf. Bus. Manag. **6**(2), 29–40 (2014)
27. Boon, S.D., Lomore, C.D.: Admirer-celebrity relationships among young adults: explaining perceptions of celebrity influence on identity. Hum. Commun. Res. **27**(3), 432–465 (2001)
28. Goldsmith, R.E., Lafferty, B.A., Newell, S.J.: The impact of corporate credibility and celebrity credibility on consumer reaction to advertisements and brands. J. Advert. **29**(3), 43–54 (2000)
29. Newman, G.E., Diesendruck, G., Bloom, P.: Celebrity contagion and the value of objects. J. Consum. Res. **38**(2), 215–228 (2011)
30. Tanner, R.J., Maeng, A.: A tiger and a president: imperceptible celebrity facial cues influence trust and preference. J. Consum. Res. **39**(4), 769–783 (2012)
31. McCracken, G.: Who is the celebrity endorser? Cultural foundations of the endorsement process. J. Consum. Res. **16**, 310–321 (1989)
32. Ford, J.B.: What do we know about celebrity endorsement in advertising. J. Adver. Res. **58**(1), 1–2 (2018)
33. Winterich, K.P., Gangwar, M., Grewal, R.: When celebrities count: power distance and celebrity endorsements. J. Mark. **82**(5), 70–86 (2018)
34. Thomson, M.: Human brands: investigating antecedents to consumers' strong attachments to celebrities. J. Mark. **70**(3), 104–119 (2006)
35. Rindova, V.P., Pollock, T.G., Hayward, M.L.: Celebrity firms: the social construction of market popularity. Acad. Manag. Rev. **31**(1), 50–71 (2006)
36. Fournier, S.: Taking stock in martha stewart: a cultural critique of the marketing practice of building person-brands. Adv. Consum. Res. **37**(1), 37–40 (2010)
37. McCutcheon, L.E., Lange, R., Houran, J.: Conceptualization and measurement of celebrity worship. Br. J. Psychol. **93**(1), 67–87 (2002)
38. McQuarrie, E.F., Miller, J., Phillips, B.J.: The megaphone effect: taste and audience in fashion blogging. J. Consum. Res. **40**, 136–158 (2013)
39. Parmentier, M.A., Fischer, E., Reuber, A.R.: Positioning person brands in established organizational fields. J. Acad. Mark. Sci. **41**(3), 373–387 (2013)

40. Stever, G.S., Lawson, K.: Twitter as a way for celebrities to communicate with fans: implications for the study of parasocial interaction. Noth Am. J. Psychol. **15**(2), 339–354 (2013)
41. Aaker, J.L.: Dimensions of brand personality. J. Mark. Res. **34**(3), 347–356 (1997)
42. Barrick, M.R., Mount, M.K.: The big five personality dimensions and job performance: a meta-analysis. Pers. Psychol. **44**(1), 1–26 (1991)
43. Maehle, N., Shneor, R.: On congruence between brand and human personalities. J. Prod. Brand Manag. **19**(1), 44–53 (2009)
44. Campbell, M.C., Kirmani, A.: Consumers' use of persuasion knowledge: the effects of accessibility and cognitive capacity on perceptions of an influence agent. J. Consum. Res. **27**(1), 69–83 (2000)
45. Park, W.C., MacInnis, D.J., Priester, J., Eisingerich, A.B., Iacobucci, D.: Brand attachment and brand attitude strength: conceptual and empirical differentiation of two critical brand equity drivers. J. Mark. **74**(6), 1–17 (2010)
46. Aaker, D.A.: Innovation: brand it or lose it. Calif. Manag. Rev. **50**(1), 8–24 (2007)
47. Khamis, S., Ang, L., Welling, R.: Self-branding, 'micro-celebrity' and the rise of social media influencers. Celebrity Stud. **8**(2), 191–208 (2017)
48. Stelzner, M.: Social media marketing industry report. Soc. Media Exam., 1–52 (2018)
49. Barnes, N.G., Jacobsen, S.L.: Missed eWOM opportunities: a cross-sector analysis of online monitoring behavior. J. Mark. Commun. **20**(1–2), 147–158 (2014)
50. Instagram (2017) selenagomez. https://www.instagram.com/p/BZBHr4Pg5Wd/?taken-by= selenagomez. Accessed 29 June 2018
51. Instagram (2018) selenagomez. https://www.instagram.com/p/BU-msH8ggkA/?taken-by= selenagomez. Accessed 27 July 2018
52. Johns, R., English, R.: Transition of self: repositioning the celebrity brand through social media – the case of Elizabeth Gilbert. J. Bus. Res. **69**(1), 65–72 (2016)
53. Carlson, B.D., Donavan, D.T.: Human brands in sport: athlete brand personality and identification. J. Sport Manage. **27**(3), 193–206 (2013)
54. Smith, G.: Conceptualizing and Testing Brand personality in British Politics. J. Polit. Mark. **8**(3), 209–232 (2009)
55. Lunardo, R., Gergaud, O., Livat, F.: Celebrities as human brands: an investigation of the effects of personality and time on celebrities' appeal. J. Market Manage. **31**(5–6), 685–712 (2015)
56. Choi, S.M., Rifon, N.J.: It is a match: the impact of congruence between celebrity image and consumer ideal self on endorsement effectiveness. Psychol. Market **29**(9), 639–650 (2012)
57. Buss, D.M., Barnes, M.: Preferences in human mate selection. J. Pers. Soc. Psychol. **50**(3), 559–570 (1986)
58. Beverland, M.B., Farrelly, F.J.: The quest for authenticity in consumption: consumers' purposive choice of authentic cues to shape experienced outcomes. J. Consum. Res. **36**(5), 838–856 (2010)

Using Social Media to Express Grief While Considering Security Vulnerabilities of Inactive Accounts of the Deceased

James Braman[1]([⊠]), Alexander Wood[2]([⊠]), Alfreda Dudley[2]([⊠]), and Giovanni Vincenti[3]([⊠])

[1] Computer Science/Information Technology,
Community College of Baltimore County, Rosedale, MD 21237, USA
jbraman@ccbcmd.edu
[2] Department of Computer and Information Sciences, Towson University,
Towson, MD 21252, USA
awood13@students.towson.edu, adudley@towson.edu
[3] Division of Science, Information Arts and Technologies,
University of Baltimore, Baltimore, MD 21201, USA
gvincenti@ubalt.edu

Abstract. It is through social media profiles that we can express loss, find support, and create online memorials of those who have died. Online profiles can be a powerful medium to both create a digital memorial and to also "communicate" with the dead. It is the communication with the deceased that is important to consider as we strive to understand how these tools can be used in the context of bereavement. At the same time, there are many security issues related to data and personal information of the deceased. The various profiles and user data we leave behind after our death can be a cause for concern from a security perspective. Complicating this issue is not knowing where data is located or account details and not having accounts secured. It is also problematic when it is not known when an account belongs to a deceased user, opening the door for exploitation. This project follows previous research on our efforts to automatically identify accounts through SADD - A Social Media Agent for the Detection of the Deceased. This project focuses on digital legacy issues from a security perspective and implications to consider for various digital platforms. In addition, we examine how social media can be used to express grief and continue bonds with the deceased.

Keywords: Digital legacy security · Thanatechnology · SADD · Profiles · Social networks · Grief

1 Introduction

Most online activities leave "digital footprints" behind or require creating and maintaining some form of user profile where various types of information is stored. As an increasing number of users interact with and use social media platforms, cloud services, streaming media, online financial accounts and more, the number of separate accounts

© Springer Nature Switzerland AG 2019
G. Meiselwitz (Ed.): HCII 2019, LNCS 11579, pp. 34–44, 2019.
https://doi.org/10.1007/978-3-030-21905-5_3

each person has continues to grow. Many people have several password-protected accounts. Some of these accounts may not be known to friends or family members. Social media data, including postings and profile interactions, contribute to our profile and timeline which chronicles the many activities of our daily lives. We leave a trail of data and information in our everyday interactions with technology. Sometimes this "trail" becomes part of our digital legacy, often unintentionally.

Social media has also influenced how we grieve as individuals are increasingly expressing themselves online. As a Web 2.0 technology, social media allows for dynamic interaction with other people where users can post many types of information, such as text, video, images, and more [1]. These pieces of information can also be thought of as "narrative bits" that describe and represent a person and their interactions over time, essentially building a digital narrative [2]. A great deal of personal information is posted in online profiles each day describing our lives representing who we are while serving as a communication tool. However, what happens to this online narrative when we die? How does this affect those we are connected with online? An increasing amount of people are living out parts of their lives through online social media, and as an extension, these platforms are becoming vehicles for expressing grief and for memorialization of the dead [3].

It is through these profiles that we can express loss, find support, and create online memorials of those who have died. Online memorial sites and profiles can take many forms and include an array of features and content. Some of this content may be originally posted by the now deceased when they were using the account, while other content may have been posted by the bereaved after the person had died. Online profiles can be powerful a medium to both create a digital memorial and to also "communicate" with the dead. It is the communication with the deceased that is important to consider as we strive to understand how these tools can be used in the context of bereavement. This paper, therefore, examines how social media can be used to express grief and continue bonds with the deceased. Following, a discussion of how social media accounts of deceased users can create security concerns.

2 Using Social Media to Express Grief

As social networking sites have become more integrated into our lives, it has become an important technology that we use to communicate and express ourselves. Many forms of social media allow users to create profiles and interact with others such as Facebook, Twitter, Instagram, Snapchat, and many more. Each platform has different features, and some are more popular within specific age groups. These profiles and connections to others represent aspects of our lives, and at the same time, end up representing us in death allowing other users to stay connected. This connection to others (those alive and dead) afford new ways to express our grief. "In the coming years, the opportunities available to integrate technology into the grieving process will become more pronounced and nuanced" [4, p. 23]. How then do current models of bereavement fit in with varying emerging technologies and different grieving styles? When examining grief and loss through online social media, research suggests that the dual process model (DPM) of coping with bereavement be considered [5, 6].

With DPM, the management of coping with the loss oscillates between stressors (loss-oriented and restoration-oriented) as the person attempts to reorient his or her self and his or her life without the deceased [7]. In other words, people have both good and bad moments as they adjust with such a life change. DPM combines several aspects of bereavement in its description of coping which fit the polymorphic nature of Web content. Social media offers the ability for the bereaved to interact with digital artifacts in a way that allows for expressions (confronting the loss) and to seek support from others while participating in everyday online activities (attending to life changes). At the same time developing a new but continued bond with the deceased can occur through their online presence. However, [5] notes that sometimes sites like Facebook may present bereaved users interaction with the deceased person's profile unexpectedly when they are in a restoration "phase" which could lead to maladaptation. This occurs when a social media platform is unaware that an account is of a deceased user and may suggest the account as a connection to add as a "friend," promote the account in one's timeline or list "remembrance" photos automatically. Receiving a "friendship request" from someone that you know is deceased can be unsettling [8]. A brief discussion on detecting these accounts to preserve the content will be presented later.

Preserving important content in a digital format has also become a changing practice related to expressing grief through the digitization of pictures and other content [9]. Popular digital content often includes photographs, video, and text. Reminiscing through photographs is a way to interact with memories about the deceased that evokes emotions and can be seen as a ritual activity to help cope with the loss [10]. With digital information, storage of the content will not degrade over time or take up physical space, which is a problem with traditional photographs. These digital "memories" can be shared with others along with comments expressing emotion through social media. The technology not only allows for the sharing of content but affords the bereaved a unique opportunity to express themselves in a variety of ways. Social media allows text-based posting that can be commented on, reposted and shared in a multitude of ways and puts grieving into public view, which is most often expressed privately.

In expressing grief publicly online, categorization of how social media was being used by the bereaved was examined through feedback from 454 survey responses, yielding categories for news dissemination, preservations (memorialization) and community (connections, support, witness to grief) [5]. In terms of news dissemination, it is becoming more commonplace to post information about someone's death online. This sometimes is to serve as a notification to those connected to the person's profile online or to serve as an online obituary containing contact information. In terms of preservation, the deceased's profile becomes a memorial of their life based on content that they have previously posted in life, their friended connections and interactions. Often these profiles were never intended to be turned into a memorial but were inadvertently made so through the interaction of bereaved friends and family members. Facebook, for instance, will memorialize an account if notified (with proof) so that a profile can be preserved. Lastly, a community of grief can be observed within the set of connected "friends." In addition to expressing grief, there are several bereavement support groups available within some social networking sites. Sites like Facebook, "provide users with a return to communal mourning through its affordances of interactive, user-generated, and co-constructed expression of emotions" [11, p. 25]. Using technology, our expressions of grief can be viewed by others, used to request support, or sent even sent to the deceased in the form of a message.

3 Continuing Bonds with the Deceased

There is a growing set of literature supporting a continuing bonds theory for the bereaved to engage with memories of the deceased [12]. Social media is full of memories in the form of interactive digital artifacts available any time of the day, as long as the profile is still active or has been memorialized. The asynchronous nature of social media, combined with the distorted sense of time, connection over long distances (including death) and social barriers presents unique ways to stay connected with the deceased [13]. Most often when we post content on another person's profile, the user on the other side is not active on their page at that moment, but we assume they will see the post eventually. Extending this idea to the deceased, we may get a sense that they are still listening. Kasket's [16] research supports the theory that users in this context have the perception that "the dead are listening." Social media may give us a false sense that nothing has changed, mainly if the loss is a friend or family member with whom we seldom had interactions.

Brubaker et al. [13] argue that relationships with the deceased continue through the creation of virtual bonds through online profiles. The technology itself allows a stable connection with the deceased's profile, allowing for continued and unchanged interaction (except for the interaction we would otherwise get back from the person). We are still able to share the mundane interactions of everyday life, accomplishments, news, and gossip. Posting this content on the profile itself would be publicly available to other users in the network. Private messages to the deceased could also be sent as a private instant message. However, if the account was designated with a caretaker, then private messages could potentially be accessed by a living person to whom the message was not intended. Memorialized accounts allow those connected to the deceased to still stay connected, but new connections cannot be created. Within Facebook, this process ensures that the content is preserved and prevents the profiles of deceased users from showing up in search results and friend suggestions within the platform. Posthumous interaction with the deceased through social media is an interesting phenomenon that allows continued bonds long after a loss. Rossetto et al. [5] discuss that social media enables users to continue connections or to reconnect with the dead, possibly leading to more adaptive grief outcomes.

On a more extreme side of continuing bonds, there have been projects such as Eter9, a program driven by artificial intelligence that algorithmically examines a person's posts and interaction to learn the behaviors of a person to serve as a replacement in the event of death or absence. Their website states, "The Counterpart is your Virtual Self that will stay in the system and interact with the world just like you would if you were present" [14, p. 1]. Programs like Eter9 are applications that can control someone's profile and post content, comments and other items as it was the original person. However, interacting with a technology-based doppelganger of the deceased has not been well studied as these technologies are still under development. These applications will still take many more years to become more realistic and natural but may warrant much more research from the thanatology community.

Related to more traditional social media interaction, there have been studies examining how users interact with profiles of deceased users. Facebook can be used to honor the deceased, allowing one to visit postmortem profiles to share memories and maintain connections [15]. In maintaining these connections, research suggests that users found viewing pictures on a deceased person's profile as being beneficial in the coping process [13, 17]. Pictures can be viewed and commented on over time. In observations from [18], while examining Myspace profiles of deceased individuals, other users often posted comments on the deceased user's page most frequently on the day of their death until about day ten. They also noticed an increase in activity on these pages on anniversaries and holidays. As social media has only been around for the past several years, the long-term interaction with this content and its effect on bereavement are yet unknown. A study of teenage Facebook users noted that it was atypical to de-friend a deceased profile [17]. Doing so would be disconnecting the virtual bond between themselves and the deceased. Instead of de-friending, users adjust their relationship with the deceased redefining their bonds [6]. Keeping the friendship allows the deceased to remain part of a circle of friends and family online, just as they were in life.

Another way to continue bonds with the deceased using social media is through the creation of official memorial pages. These pages are typically built with the purpose of memorializing the deceased instead of using a page that was their actual profile. This has the added benefit of filtering out specific perceived negative photos, comments or other content. A family member or personal friend could be designated to create the memorial after the death or could be created spontaneously as a group page from the user's network of friends. "Memorial websites and web cemeteries are designed to commemorate and remember the deceased, and they provide site users an outlet for emotional expression, reminiscing, disclosure, paying tribute continuing bods, sharing grief, and establishing community following a loss" [5, p. 975]. These are more permanent sites that would be open to the public, but more in-depth than an online obituary. Just like in a traditional cemetery where someone may leave a note or flowers, in a similar fashion comments can be posted along with images to not only communicate to the deceased, but to other users that may be grieving.

4 Security Concerns

The data contained in profiles, databases, and accounts of the deceased can be of great value. This value can be measured monetarily by a variety of factors or by its sentimental worth to family, friends and loved ones. Protecting this content can become a source of concern for those engaged in protecting the memory and legacy of the deceased. Therefore, protecting this data and the integrity of the contents is a crucial area of concern. The increase in accounts owned by deceased users will inevitably become a growing security concern. There is value in these accounts in terms of possibilities of what can be done and in terms of the confidential information they contain from a hacker's perspective. If compromised, the inactive accounts of the deceased can be used for malicious purposes. All this data is useful; however, the question emerges about what happens to it after one's death? There is a growing need for digital asset management in the context of death. Complicating the transference of digital assets is the many legal issues tied to the terms of service agreements and other contracts between users and the company that provides services or storage [19]. In many cases, accounts and content cannot be transferred to other users.

4.1 Identity

Social media platforms that allow for the memorialization of accounts can be useful for families and friends of the deceased in preserving content and memories. These online memorials provide a way to express grief and to preserve content for remembrance. We need to be mindful of these memorials as they open the door to a possible venue for identity theft. A deceased user's profile contains a narrative of the person's life including images and other content that could be used for malicious purposes. How easy would it be to copy the content and create a new profile under a new name? Most likely family and friends of the deceased would be unaware.

Hacked profiles of the deceased are problematic for several reasons. Most obvious is the potential harm caused by upsetting those connected to the deceased that know they are dead. Having the profile suddenly active again, posting content could be very unsettling and harmful to the bereaved. These re-activated accounts could then be used to "connect" with other users (previously not connected) in order to cause harm. Unsuspecting users may visit these compromised pages, and viewing the activity of the page, friended accounts and pictures, may believe the account is of a valid user. Compromised pages could also allow a hacker access to other information, messages and important information that can be used for additional harm. These accounts could easily be used for phishing scams as they were once held by their legitimate owners but are now being used illegally. We also need to be mindful and always on guard for malicious web crawlers that scour online sources for information. These programs may devour large amounts of content while the person is alive without their knowledge. This information can be saved for long periods of time to be used later after the person is deceased and their accounts are not being closely monitored. Therefore, it is important to monitor traffic to protect web content from malicious web crawlers using a variety of techniques [20–22]. The data of the deceased that was thought to be "safe," and protected could be deleted and misappropriated by hackers. Therefore, it is vital to protect these accounts through some form of memorialization or deletion.

As data breaches are becoming common for many types of accounts and involve a wealth of information, the deceased are still susceptible. As companies often notify current users of compromised accounts, the deceased cannot act on these notifications. Family and friends of the deceased most likely will not receive these notifications on their behalf or even realize what accounts the deceased had active before their death. What data then was compromised and what steps could be made to protect this information? It is also possible that the data contained in the breach could impact the living in unknown ways. These accounts are still technically active and compromised, and the deceased user cannot monitor or take corrective security actions to repair the issue. There may be other information that would be useful to hackers such as data stored in the cloud, particularly in accounts that remain active and unmonitored.

Similar to information that can be reconstructed from obtaining data printed on documents through "dumpster diving," discarded electronic devices of the deceased should also be presumed to contain sensitive data. What data could be gained from discarded wearable devices, cell phones, tablets, cameras and more? Family members or those dealing with the person's estate that are managing the items may not realize its importance and discard potentially sensitive items that contain information of concern. Were there passwords for sensitive accounts saved on a spreadsheet that was discarded?

There is a growing importance of considering some type of death management as part of computer services. Particularly useful would be a systematic "dead man's switch" that automatically flags and deactivates all accounts and profiles associated with the deceased. This is a similar approach that some companies are taking to protect user data in the event of a death, such as through Google's Inactive Account Manager [23]. A user can set a period of inactivity before the account is considered inactive and steps are taken to send a message to individual email accounts or phone numbers. A user has a choice to send out messages to up to ten people that the account is no longer in use (based on the time frame selected) as well as the option to delete the account. It is essential to consider if someone should be notified or have access to an essential account in the case of a death. Increasingly as part of a will, this information is being recorded in case of an emergency. Although this too raises many questions, as sharing passwords are generally not allowed as part of most terms of service agreements, can change many times since the account was created, or seen by those in which it was not intended. Additionally, the security of the saved account information must be maintained.

4.2   Transitional Weakness

Our previous work described four states of being related to death as viewed in Fig. 1 [24]. Type A represents users who are physically alive and maintain an active presence in an online platform or environment. Type B represents users who are alive, but who do not have a presence in an online platform. Type C users are those who have physically died but have an "active" virtual memorial or social networking site. This includes the set of users who have died, and someone else created a memorial on their behalf, hence still having an active online presence. Type D users represent those that have died and have no online presence or memorial. The online persona of a type D user could have been erased after their death.

There is a time period where the deceased's data is more vulnerable. This temporal transition period in the states of being can be problematic. Essentially this attack window comprises the time period in which it is not known that the user is deceased, opening several vulnerabilities. For instance, the accounts of the deceased are still active with an expectation that there will still be activity. Therefore, unauthorized access and use of the account might not be detected for some time. This attack window also includes the time when family and friends know that the person is deceased, but due to their grief may not be actively monitoring certain account information. Although for some, these accounts may be visited much more often during this time. It may take a significant amount of time to identify what accounts and information the now deceased stored online or kept in some digital format.

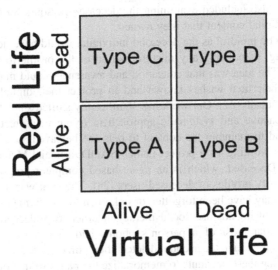

Fig. 1. Four states of Being [24]

Consider the scenario where a distant friend might not know that their friend has died. Perhaps their death was only a day or so ago (or even longer in some cases), and news of the death is not well known. Perhaps the friend lives far away and has limited contact with others that are close to the deceased. If the deceased's profile becomes compromised by an attacker, they could then send messages to everyone connected to the user asking for information or financial "assistance" relying on the relationship between the friend and the deceased. The friend may have no reason to question the request. Until the death is known and the deceased's profile transitions from Type A to Type C for instance, there are vulnerabilities. More research is needed regarding these transitions, timing and ways to protect content in these situations.

5 Conclusion and Future Work

The term thanatechnology, coined by [25] was a way to describe the multidisciplinary intersection of computing technology and thanatology. In the field of human-computer interaction, limited consideration is given to the content of deceased users when designing applications or the protection of the content long-term. Our view is that as more people use social media throughout their lives, we will inadvertently construct a lifelong timeline through our profile which will most likely become our digital legacy (and thus our memorial). However, most social media users do not think about this or the long-term consequences of their actions in creating their legacy through social media. This then led us to research college student's perceptions of death and social media to create a set of guidelines in posting content online, merely to make people more aware. This also included examining the deceased person's final wishes in preserving (or not) digital content that they owned.

It is crucial to be mindful as the deceased individual would have no means of self-cleansing, auditing, or policing any misinformation of the profile to remove content themselves [26]. The idea was that education and awareness could make people more alert at making their final wishes known and to protect their digital content in the likelihood of their death [27]. Our work has significantly shifted since then as we have taken a more proactive and systematic approach in trying to protect the content of deceased users and to maintain the content to help the bereaved.

We have been working on a project named SADD, a Social Media Agent for the Detection of the Deceased, which is an agent-based computer program designed to automatically identify profiles of deceased users [28]. The goal was to find profiles of the deceased that may have been forgotten or unknown to family members (mainly for family members that do not use social media) in order to protect and preserve the content. Imagine that most of a person's photos and videos were only saved in Facebook or Twitter, to have the account deleted after a time of inactivity. Another goal of SADD was to flag these accounts to memorialize the pages so that other users could continue their online relationship with the deceased.

Currently, SADD can search Twitter for users tweeting a designated hashtag, for example, #RIP, then isolate the tweets for each user. Those tweets are then analyzed for trends or emotional cues from word choice, otherwise known as sentiment analysis. Individuals who have experienced a loss are identified and tracked for long term data gathering. Selected user's tweets are categorized as confronting or avoiding the tasks of grieving, based on the dual process model of coping. The publicly available Twitter data plus automated collection and analysis provide the ability for large scale collection for large sample sizes to identify markers for negative emotional stress. Potential issues with the methodology include verification and protection of user identity, sample population selection, and screening user's experiencing loss. Technical issues with the data collection include rate limitations on queries by Twitter, storage of tweets as large numbers of users are identified, and resource commitment for analysis.

Areas of further research would include networks of users and application of the model for groups of users providing insight into the effects of social interaction on the grief process. Identification of networks requires a rigorous definition of social networks within Twitter. The propagation of emotion through twitter networks can also be explored. We intend to expand the technical application of SADD and continue to explore social media in the context of death.

References

1. Cormode, G., Krishnamurthy, B.: Key differences between Web 1.0 and Web 2.0. First Monday **13**(6) (2008)
2. Mitra, A.: Creating a presence on social networks via narbs. Glob. Media J. **9**(16), 1–18 (2010)
3. Gibbs, M., Mori, J., Arnold, M., Kohn, T.: Tombstones, uncanny monuments and epic quests: memorials in World of Warcraft. Game Stud. **12**(1), 13–22 (2012)
4. Gilbert, K.R., Massimi, M.: From digital divide to digital immortality: Thanatechnology at the turn of the 21st century. In: Dying, Death, and Grief in an Online Universe: For Counselors and Educators, pp. 16–27 (2012)
5. Rossetto, K.R., Lannutti, P.J., Strauman, E.C.: Death on Facebook: examining the roles of social media communication for the bereaved. J. Soc. Pers. Relat. **32**(7), 974–994 (2015)
6. Bassett, D.J.: Who wants to live forever? Living, dying and grieving in our digital society. Soc. Sci. **4**(4), 1127–1139 (2015)
7. Stroebe, M., Schut, H.: The dual process model of coping with bereavement: a decade on. OMEGA-J. Death Dying **61**(4), 273–289 (2010)
8. Goldberg, L.: Posthumous profiles on virtual social networks: death and language (2017). [Blog post] https://www.leonardogoldberg.com/single-post/2017/06/07/Posthumous-profiles-on-virtual-social-networks-death-and-language
9. Gray, S.E., Coulton, P.: Living with the dead: emergent post-mortem digital curation and creation practices. In: Maciel, C., Pereira, V. (eds.) Digital Legacy and Interaction. HCI, pp. 31–47. Springer, Cham (2013). https://doi.org/10.1007/978-3-319-01631-3_2
10. Winokuer, H., Harris, D.: Principles and Practice of Grief Counseling, 2nd edn. Springer, New York (2016)
11. Sabra, J.B.: "I hate when they do that!" Netiquette in mourning and memorialization among Danish Facebook users. J. Broadcast. Electron. Media **61**(1), 24–40 (2017)
12. Klass, D., Silverman, P.R., Nickman, S. (eds.): Continuing Bonds: New Understandings of Grief. Taylor & Francis, Washington, DC (2014)
13. Brubaker, J.R., Hayes, G.R., Dourish, P.: Beyond the grave: Facebook as a site for the expansion of death and mourning. Inf. Soc. **29**(3), 152–163 (2013)
14. Eter9: Eter9 main page (2018). https://www.eter9.com/auth/login
15. Brubaker, J.R., Callison-Burch, V.: Legacy contact: designing and implementing post-mortem stewardship at Facebook. In: Proceedings of the 2016 CHI Conference on Human Factors in Computing Systems, pp. 2908–2919. ACM (2016)
16. Kasket, E.: Continuing bonds in the age of social networking: Facebook as a modern-day medium. Bereavement Care **31**(2), 62–69 (2012)
17. Pennington, N.: You don't de-friend the dead: an analysis of grief communication by college students through Facebook profiles. Death Stud. **37**(7), 617–635 (2013)
18. Brubaker, J.R., Hayes, G.R.: We will never forget you [online]: an empirical investigation of post-mortem MySpace comments. In: Proceedings of the ACM 2011 Conference on Computer Supported Cooperative Work, pp. 123–132. ACM (2011)
19. Banta, N.M.: Inherit the cloud: the role of private contracts in distributing or deleting digital assets at death. Fordham L. Rev. **83**, 799 (2014)
20. Stevanovic, D., Vlajic, N., An, A.: Unsupervised clustering of Web sessions to detect malicious and non-malicious website users. Procedia Comput. Sci. **5**, 123–131 (2011)
21. Suchacka, G., Sobkow, M.: Detection of Internet robots using a Bayesian approach. In: IEEE 2nd International Conference on Cybernetics (CYBCONF), pp. 365–370. IEEE (2015)
22. Wan, S.: Protecting Web Contents Against Persistent Crawlers (2016)

23. Elliott, M.: How to set up Google's inactive account manager (2013). https://www.cnet.com/how-to/how-to-set-up-googles-inactive-account-manager/
24. Braman, J., Dudley, A., Vincenti, G.: Death, social networks and virtual worlds: a look into the digital afterlife. In: Proceedings of the 9th International Conference on Software Engineering Research, Management and Applications (SERA). Baltimore, MD USA (2011)
25. Sofka, C.J.: Social support internetworks, caskets for sale, and more: thanatology and the information superhighway. Death Stud. **21**(6), 553–574 (1997)
26. Wang, Y., Norcie, G., Komanduri, S., Acquisti, A., Leon, P.G., Cranor, L.F.: I regretted the minute I pressed share: a qualitative study of regrets on Facebook. In: Proceedings of the 7th Symposium on Usable Privacy and Security, p. 10. ACM (2011)
27. Braman, J., Dudley, A., Vincenti, G.: Thana-technology education: the importance of considering social networks and virtual worlds. In: The Quarterly Publication of the Association for Death Education and Counseling. The Thanatology Association, vol. 41, no. 1, January–February 2015
28. Braman, J., Dudley, A., Vincenti, G.: Designing SADD: a social media agent for the detection of the deceased. In: Meiselwitz, G. (ed.) SCSM 2018. LNCS, vol. 10914, pp. 345–356. Springer, Cham (2018). https://doi.org/10.1007/978-3-319-91485-5_26

Estimating Interpersonal Reactivity Scores Using Gaze Behavior and Dialogue Act During Turn-Changing

Ryo Ishii[1]($\boxtimes$), Kazuhiro Otsuka[2], Shiro Kumano[2], Ryuichiro Higashinaka[1], and Junji Tomita[1]

[1] NTT Media Intelligence Laboratories, NTT Corporation, 1-1 Hikarinooka, Yokosuka-shi, Kanagawa, Japan
{ishii.ryo,higashinaka.ryuichiro,tomita.junji}@lab.ntt.co.jp
[2] NTT Communication Science Laboratories, NTT Corporation, 3-1 Morinosato Wakamiya, Atsugi-shi, Kanagawa, Japan
{otsuka.kazuhiro,kumano.shiro}@lab.ntt.co.jp

Abstract. We explored the effectiveness of external observable behaviors in multi-party discussions to estimate an individual's empathy skill level. In our previous research, we estimated personal empathy skills from the external observable behavior in multi-person dialogues. We demonstrated that the gaze behavior towards the end of utterances and dialogue act (DA), i.e., verbal-behavior information indicating the intension of an utterance during turn-keeping/changing, are important for estimating empathy level. We focused on Davis' Interpersonal Reactivity Index (IRI), which measures empathy skill level and consists of four dimensions of empathy, i.e., empathic concern (EC), perspective taking (PT), personal distress (PD), and fantasy (FS), as the estimation target. We particularly focused on estimating an individual's EC score. In this research, we explored whether gaze behavior and DA during turn-keeping/changing are useful regarding the other three dimensions, i.e., PT, PD, and FS by constructing and evaluating estimation models based on these dimensions. We found that gaze behavior and DA are useful for estimating the scores of these three dimensions. Therefore, gaze behavior and DA during turn-changing/keeping are useful for estimating the scores of all four Davis' IRI dimensions.

Keywords: Interpersonal reactivity scores · Gaze behavior · Dialogue act · Empathy skill · Multiparty meeting

1 Introduction

Social communication skills are fundamental for successful communication in globalized and multi-cultural societies as they are central to education, work, and daily life. Although there is great interest in the notion of communication skills in scientific and real-life applications, the concept is difficult to generally define due

© Springer Nature Switzerland AG 2019
G. Meiselwitz (Ed.): HCII 2019, LNCS 11579, pp. 45–53, 2019.
https://doi.org/10.1007/978-3-030-21905-5_4

to the complexity of communication, wide variety of related cognitive and social abilities, and huge situational variability [7]. Techniques that involve nonverbal behaviors to estimate communication skills have been receiving much attention. For example, researchers have developed models for estimating public speaking skills [29,32], persuasiveness [28], communication skills during job interviews [25] and group work [26], and leadership [31].

We are working on constructing models for estimating "the empathy skill level" in multi-party discussions. Empathy, which is the ability to understand and share the feelings of others, is one of the most important social skills and has long been studied in psychology [4,5]. Davis' Interpersonal Reactivity Index (IRI) [3] includes four dimensions of empathy: perspective taking (PT), i.e., the tendency to adopt another's psychological perspective; fantasy (FS), i.e., the tendency to strongly identify with fictitious characters; empathic concern (EC), i.e., the tendency to experience feelings of warmth, sympathy, and concern toward others; and personal distress (PD), i.e., the tendency to have feelings of discomfort and concern when witnessing others' negative experiences. Davis' IRI has been translated into many languages [6] and used in a wide variety of fields such as neuroscience [1] and genetics [30].

In our previous study, we developed an estimation model of an individual's EC score that uses the gaze behavior and dialogue act (DA) near the end of utterances during turn-keeping/changing as feature values [17]. The model has a higher estimation accuracy than one using the overall values of verbal/nonverbal behaviors in an entire discussion such as the amount of utterances and physical motion used in many previous studies on skill estimation [7,25,26,28,29,31,32]. This suggests that behavior during turn-keeping/turn-changing in a very short time interval is useful for estimating individual empathy skill level. We demonstrated that the gaze behavior towards the end of utterances and DA, i.e., verbal-behavior information indicating the intension of an utterance, during turn-keeping/changing are important for estimating an individual's EC score.

Since we focused on estimating only an individual's EC score, it is necessary to verify whether gaze behavior and DA are useful for estimating the scores of the other three dimensions, i.e., PT, PD, and FS.

In this research, we explored whether gaze behavior and DA during turn-keeping/changing are useful in estimating the scores of the remaining three Davis' IRI dimensions by constructing and evaluating estimation models based on these dimensions. We found that gaze behavior and DA are useful for estimating the scores of PT, PD, and FS. Therefore, gaze behavior and DA during turn-changing/keeping are useful for estimating the scores of all four Davis' IRI dimensions.

2   Corpus Data

We previously created a face-to-face conversation corpus for developing our estimation model of an individual's empathy skill level using gaze behavior and DA in multi-party discussions [13,17]. In this section, we give details of our corpus. The corpus includes eight face-to-face four-person discussions held by four

Fig. 1. Photograph of multi-party discussion.

groups of four different people (16 participants in total). In each group, the four participants were Japanese women in their 20's and 30's who had never met before. They sat facing each other (Fig. 1). We labeled the participants, from left to right, P1, P2, P3, and P4. They argued and gave opinions in response to highly divisive questions, such as "Is marriage the same as love?", and needed to reach a conclusion within ten minutes. All four four-person groups took part in two discussions.

The participants' voices were recorded with a pin microphone attached to their chests, and the entire discussions were videoed. Upper body shots of each participant (recorded at 30 Hz) were also taken. From the collected data for all eight discussions (80 min in total) and from the recorded data, we constructed a multimodal corpus consisting of the following verbal/nonverbal behaviors and the participants' empathy skill levels.

- Utterances and DAs: We built the utterance unit using the inter-pausal unit (IPU) [23]. The utterance interval was extracted manually from the speech wave. The portion of an utterance followed by 200 ms of silence was used as the unit of one utterance. From the created IPU, backchannels were excluded, and an utterance unit continued from the same person was considered as one utterance turn. IPU pairs adjoined in time, and IPU groups during turn-keeping/changing were created. The data for speech overlaps, i.e., when a listener interrupted during a speaker's utterance or two or more participants spoke simultaneously at turn-changing, were excluded from the IPU pairs for analysis. Eventually, there were 1227 IPUs during turn-keeping and 129 during turn-changing.
- Gaze objects: A skilled annotator manually annotated the gaze objects by using bust/head and overhead views in each video frame. The gaze objects were the four participants (labeled P1, P2, P3, and P4, as mentioned above) and non-persons, i.e., the walls or floor. Three annotators annotated the gaze behavior in our conversation dataset to verify the annotation quality. Conger's Kappa coefficient was 0.887. Based on the benchmarks of [8], the gaze annotations were of excellent quality.

– Empathy skill level: All participants were asked to answer a questionnaire that was based on Davis' IRI [3]. We collected the scores of the four Davis' IRI dimensions to estimate the participants' empathy skill levels.

All verbal and nonverbal behavior data were integrated at 30 Hz for visual display using the NTT Multimodal Meeting Viewer [27]. This viewer enables us to annotate the multimodal data frame-by-frame and observe the data intuitively.

3 Feature Values

We used the gaze behavior and DA during turn-changing/turn-keeping as feature values for developing our estimation model of empathy skill level [13,17]. In this section, we give details of these feature values.

We first introduce the feature values of gaze behavior. We focused on Gaze Transition pattern (GTP) for analyzing gaze behavior, which are temporal transitions of participant's gaze behavior near the end of utterances [10,15,18,19,21]. A GTP is expressed as an n-gram, which is defined as a sequence of gaze-direction shifts. We demonstrated that the occurrence frequencies of GTPs differ significantly for a speaker and listener during turn-keeping and a speaker, listener who becomes the next speaker (hereafter called "next-speaker"), and listeners who do not become the next speaker (hereafter called "listeners") during turn-changing. We also demonstrated that GTP is effective for estimating the next speaker in multi-party discussions. Thus, we used GTPs as analysis gaze parameters. To generate a GTP, we focused on the gazed object for 1200 ms: 1000 ms before and 200 ms after the utterance since the GTP during 1200 ms is important for turn-taking [10,15,18,19,21]. A GTP is composed of a person or object classified as "speaker", "listener", or "non-person" and labeled. We considered whether there was mutual gaze and classified gaze behavior using the following seven gaze labels.

– S: Person looks at a speaker without mutual gaze (speaker does not look at the listener.).
– SM: Person looks at the speaker with mutual gaze (speaker looks at a listener.).
– $L1 \sim L3$: Person looks at another listener without mutual gaze. Labels $L1$, $L2$, and $L3$ indicate different people. The sitting position does not matter. For example, if P1 who is speaking looks at P2 followed by P3 then P2 again, the gaze transition pattern of P1 is $L1\text{-}L2\text{-}L1$.
– $LM1 \sim LM3$: Person looks at another listener with mutual gaze. Labels $LM1$, $LM2$, and $LM3$ indicate different people.
– N: Person looks at the next speaker without mutual gaze only during turn-changing.
– NM: Person looks at the next speaker with mutual gaze only during turn-changing.
– X: Person looks at non-persons, such as the floor or ceiling, i.e., gaze aversion.

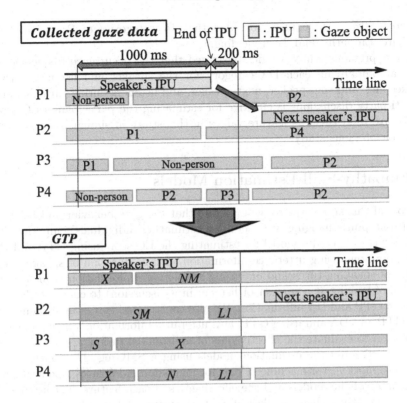

Fig. 2. Example of generating GTPs in turn-changing situation

Figure 2 shows how GTPs are constructed: P1 finishes speaking, then P2 starts to speak. Person P1 gazes at P2 after she gazes at a non-person during the analysis interval. When P1 looks at P2, P2 looks at P1; that is, there is mutual gaze. Therefore, P1's GTP is X-NM. Person P2 looks at P4 after making eye contact with P1; thus, P2's GTP is SM-$L1$. Person P3 looks at a non-person after looking at P1; thus, P3's GTP is S-X. Person P4 looks at P2 and P3 after looking at a non-person; thus, P4's GTP is X-N-$L1$.

A DA for each IPU was extracted using an estimation technique for Japanese [9,24] for DA analysis. This technique can estimate a DA of a sentence from among 33 DA categories using word n-grams, semantic categories (obtained from a Japanese thesaurus Goi-Taikei), and character n-grams. The technique outputs 33 DA categories. We grouped them into the following five major categories.

- Provision: Utterance for providing information
- Self-discourse: Utterance for disclosing oneself
- Empathy: Utterance intending empathy
- Turn-yielding: Utterance intending a listener to speak next (ex. utterance of question, suggestion, or confirmation)
- Others: Utterance not included in the above four categories

About 90% of utterances included the DA categories of Provision, Self-disclosure, Empathy, and Turn-yielding.

In our previous study, we demonstrated that the occurrence frequencies of GTPs accompanying each DA category for the speaker and listeners during turn-keeping; and the speaker, next-speaker, and listeners during turn-changing in multi-party discussions is effective for estimating the participant's EC score [13,17]. We used them as feature values in this study in similar manner as we did in our previous study.

4   Empathy-Skill-Estimation Models

The goal of this study was to demonstrate that the gaze behavior and DA during turn-keeping/changing are useful for estimating individuals' empathy skill levels. We constructed a model for estimating the EC score using GTP and DA information, one using utterance information such as duration of speaking and number of speaking-turns and one using simple gaze information (which is the duration of looking at a speaker or listener in a discussion) to compare the usefulness of GTP and DA information. We also constructed two estimation models using GTP and DA and using GTP, DA, utterance information, and simple gaze information to evaluate the effectiveness of multimodal fusion.

We constructed the estimation models using a SMOreg [22], which implements a support vector machine (SVM) for regression in Weka [2], and evaluated the accuracy of the models and the effectiveness of each feature. The settings of the SVM, i.e., the polynomial kernel, cost parameter (C), and hyper parameter of the kernel (γ), were determined using a grid-search technique. The objective variable is the EC score of each person.

The details of the five estimation models are as follows.

- Chance level: This model outputs the mean value of all participants.
- Utterance amount model: This model uses the ratio of utterances and turns in the discussion.
- Gaze amount model: This model uses the duration a person was looking at the speaker and listeners in the discussion.
- GTP+DA model: This model uses the occurrence frequencies of GTPs for each DA category when the person is either the speaker or a listener during turn-keeping and the speaker, next-speaker, or a listener during turn-changing.
- All model: This model uses the ratio of utterances and turns, duration of looking, and occurrence frequencies of GTPs for each DA category. In other words, the features are integrated with an early-fusion method.

We used ten-fold cross validation with the data of the 16 participants. The mean absolute error of each estimation model is shown in Fig. 3. The GTP+DA model (0.081 for PT; 0.052 for EC, 0.076 for FS: 0.055 for PD) performed significantly better than the Utterance amount model (0.0840 for PT; 0.742 for EC, 0.530 for FS: 0.454 for PD) and Gaze amount model (0.529 for PT; 0.477 for

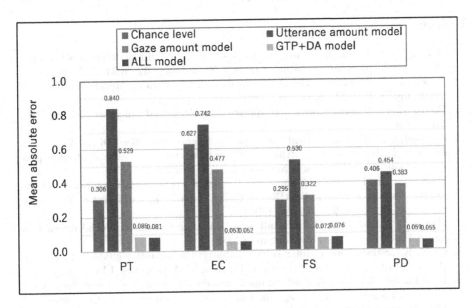

Fig. 3. Mean absolute errors of estimation models based on Davis' IRI dimensions during turn-keeping/changing

EC, 0.322 for FS: 0.383 for PD) for all scores. Moreover, there was no difference in mean absolute error between the GTP+DA model and All model (0.081 for PT; 0.052 for EC, 0.076 for FS: 0.055 for PD). These results indicate that the combination of GTP and DA information during turn-keeping/changing is a good estimator of an individual's empathy skill level even without using utterance information or simple gaze information. Therefore, we demonstrated that the gaze behavior and DA during turn-keeping/changing are useful in estimating the scores of PT, FS, PD as well as EC. In other words, they are useful for estimating the scores of all four Davis' IRI dimensions.

5 Conclusion

We explored whether gaze behavior and DA during turn-keeping/changing are useful for estimating the scores of the three Davis' IRI dimensions of PT, PD, and FS. We constructed and evaluated five estimation models based on these dimensions. We found that gaze behavior and DA are useful for estimating the scores of PT, PD, and FS. Therefore, the gaze behavior and DA during turn-changing/keeping are useful for estimating the scores of all four Davis' IRI dimensions.

In the future, we plan to verify how effective gaze behavior and DA are for scores of other social-skill indices and personal traits. We will also explore how the other behaviors such as head nods [11,14], respiration [16,20] and mouth movement [12] during turn-taking is effective for estimating individual's social skill.

References

1. Banissy, M.J., Kanai, R., Walsh, V., Rees, G.: Inter-individual differences in empathy are reflected in human brain structure. NeuroImage **62**, 2034–2039 (2012)
2. Bouckaert, R.R., et al.: WEKA-experiences with a Java open-source project. J. Mach. Learn. Res. **11**, 2533–2541 (2010)
3. Davis, M.H.: A multidimensional approach to individual differences in empathy. **10** (1980)
4. de Waal, F.B.M.: The antiquity of empathy. Science **336**, 874–876 (2012)
5. Decetya, J., Svetlova, M.: Putting together phylogenetic and ontogenetic perspectives on empathy. Dev. Cogn. Neurosci. **2**(1), 1–24 (2012)
6. Fernandez, A., Dufey, M., Kramp, U.: Testing the psychometric properties of the interpersonal reactivity index (IRI) in Chile: empathy in a different cultural context. Eur. J. Assess. **27**, 179–185 (2011)
7. Greene, J.O., Burleson, B.R.: Handbook of Communication and Social Interaction Skills. Psychology Press, Philadelphia (2003)
8. Gwet, K.L.: Handbook of inter-rater reliability: the definitive guide to measuring the extent of agreement among raters. In: Advanced Analytics, LLC (2014)
9. Higashinaka, R., et al.: Towards an open-domain conversational system fully based on natural language processing. In: International Conference on Computational Linguistics, pp. 928–939 (2014)
10. Ishii, R., Kumano, S., Otsuka, K.: Multimodal fusion using respiration and gaze behavior for predicting next speaker in multi-party meetings. In: ICMI, pp. 99–106 (2015)
11. Ishii, R., Kumano, S., Otsuka, K.: Predicting next speaker using head movement in multi-party meetings. In: ICASSP, pp. 2319–2323 (2015)
12. Ishii, R., Kumano, S., Otsuka, K.: Analyzing mouth-opening transition pattern for predicting next speaker in multi-party meetings. In: Proceedings of the International Conference on Acoustics, Speech and Signal Processing, pp. 209–216 (2016)
13. Ishii, R., Kumano, S., Otsuka, K.: Analyzing gaze behavior during turn-taking for estimating empathy skill level. In: Proceedings of the 19th ACM International Conference on Multimodal Interaction, ICMI 2017, pp. 365–373. ACM, New York (2017)
14. Ishii, R., Kumano, S., Otsuka, K.: Prediction of next-utterance timing using head movement in multi-party meetings. In: Proceedings of the 5th International Conference on Human Agent Interaction, HAI 2017, pp. 181–187. ACM, New York (2017)
15. Ishii, R., Otsuka, K., Kumano, S., Yamamoto, J.: Predicting of who will be the next speaker and when using gaze behavior in multiparty meetings. ACM Trans. Interact. Intell. Syst. **6**(1), 4 (2016)
16. Ishii, R., Otsuka, K., Kumano, S., Yamamoto, J.: Using respiration to predict who will speak next and when in multiparty meetings. ACM Trans. Interact. Intell. Syst. **6**(2), 20 (2016)
17. Ishii, R., Otsuka, K., Kumano, S., Higashinaka, R., Tomita, J.: Analyzing gaze behavior and dialogue act during turn-taking for estimating empathy skill level. In: Proceedings of the 20th ACM International Conference on Multimodal Interaction, ICMI 2018, pp. 31–39. ACM, New York (2018)
18. Ishii, R., Otsuka, K., Kumano, S., Matsuda, M., Yamato, J.: Predicting next speaker and timing from gaze transition patterns in multi-party meetings. In: Proceedings of the International Conference on Multimodal Interaction, pp. 79–86 (2013)

19. Ishii, R., Otsuka, K., Kumano, S., Yamato, J.: Analysis and modeling of next speaking start timing based on gaze behavior in multi-party meetings. In: Proceedings of the International Conference on Acoustics, Speech, and Signal Processing, pp. 694–698 (2014)
20. Ishii, R., Otsuka, K., Kumano, S., Yamato, J.: Analysis of respiration for prediction of who will be next speaker and when? In multi-party meetings. In: Proceedings of the International Conference on Multimodal Interaction, pp. 18–25 (2014)
21. Ishii, R., Otsuka, K., Kumano, S., Yamato, J.: Analysis of timing structure of eye contact in turn-changing. In: Proceedings of the 7th Workshop on Eye Gaze in Intelligent Human Machine Interaction, GazeIn 2014, pp. 15–20. ACM, New York (2014)
22. Keerthi, S.S., Shevade, S.K., Bhattacharyya, C., Murthy, K.R.K.: Improvements to platt's SMO algorithm for SVM classifier design. Neural Comput. **13**(3), 637–649 (2001)
23. Koiso, H., Horiuchi, Y., Tutiya, S., Ichikawa, A., Den, Y.: An analysis of turn-taking and backchannels based on prosodic and syntactic features in Japanese map task dialogs. Lang. Speech **41**, 295–321 (1998)
24. Meguro, T., Higashinaka, R., Minami, Y., Dohsaka, K.: Controlling listening-oriented dialogue using partially observable Markov decision processes. In: International Conference on Computational Linguistics, pp. 761–769 (2010)
25. Nguyen, L., Frauendorfer, D., Mast, M., Gatica-Perez, D.: Hire me: computational inference of hirability in employment interviews based on nonverbal behavior. IEEE Trans. Multimed. **16**(4), 1018–1031 (2014)
26. Okada, S., et al.: Estimating communication skills using dialogue acts and nonverbal features in multiple discussion datasets. In: Proceedings of the International Conference on Multimodal Interaction, pp. 169–176 (2016)
27. Otsuka, K., Araki, S., Mikami, D., Ishizuka, K., Fujimoto, M., Yamato, J.: Realtime meeting analysis and 3D meeting viewer based on omnidirectional multimodal sensors. In: ACM International Conference on Multimodal Interfaces and Workshop on Machine Learning for Multimodal Interaction, pp. 219–220 (2009)
28. Park, S., Shim, H.S., Chatterjee, M., Sagae, K., Morency, L.-P.: Computational analysis of persuasiveness in social multimedia: a novel dataset and multimodal prediction approach. In: Proceedings of the ACM ICMI, pp. 50–57 (2014)
29. Ramanarayanan, V., Leong, C.W., Feng, G., Chen, L., Suendermann-Oeft, D.: Evaluating speech, face, emotion and body movement time-series features for automated multimodal presentation scoring. In: Proceedings of the ACM ICMI, pp. 23–30 (2015)
30. Rodrigues, S.M., Saslow, L.R., Garcia, N., John, O.P., Keltner, D.: Oxytocin receptor genetic variation relates to empathy and stress reactivity in humans. Proc. Nat. Acad. Sci. U.S.A. **106**, 21437–21441 (2009)
31. Sanchez-Cortes, D., Aran, O., Mast, M.S., Gatica-Perez, D.: A nonverbal behavior approach to identify emergent leaders in small groups. IEEE Trans. Multimed. **14**(3), 816–832 (2012)
32. Wortwein, T., Chollet, M., Schauerte, B., Morency, L.-P., Stiefelhagen, R., Scherer, S.: Multimodal public speaking performance assessment. In: Proceedings of the ACM ICMI, pp. 43–50 (2015)

Human-Computer Interaction (HCI) Between "Virtual Family" Members: A Bulgarian Case

Mariyan Tomov[(⊠)]

Sofia University "St. Kliment Ohridski", Sofia, Bulgaria
mariyan.d.tomov@gmail.com

Abstract. The proposed text discusses some major social changes taking place in the modern society and transforming the nuclear family model. Along with the various forms of family life including cohabitation relationships, living apart together families, reconstituted families, rainbow families, migrant families, this study defines "the virtual family" as a new family form. The aim is to outline the nature of communication and relationships between its members.

Using a number of in-depth interviews (N = 50), the analysis of the responses displays that the communication from a distance is essential for the preservation and maintenance of the family relationships, structure and intimacy. The results also show that the interviewees use more mobile phone than Viber, Skype or Facebook, do not communicate with the same frequency, duration and quality with all their relatives, the quantity and the quality of communication correspond to the period of absence.

Keywords: Virtual family · Social changes · Family relationships · Communication · HCI

1 Introduction

The family patterns in Europe have changed noticeably in the 1960s and 1970s [1] and marked the end of the "Golden Age of the Family" [2, 3] which is characterized by high birth and marriage rates at relatively young ages, low divorce levels and of non-traditional family patterns. The idea of a traditional family household with a married heterosexual couple and their biological children is replaced by variety of alternative family patterns and lifestyles [4]. Although the extent of these transformations is not the same throughout Europe, the variety of lone-parent families, stepfamilies, homosexual "families of choice" defined by Weston [5] continued to increase rapidly. Furthermore, new forms such as living apart together families, reconstituted families, rainbow families, migrant families emerged.

These family transformations due to an influence of complex demographic factors are theorized in early 1929 by Warren Thompson [6]. In the "First Demographic Transition" theory, Thompson describes that the transition takes place in four stages. High birth and mortality levels characterize the first stage. The second one begins with a sharp drop in mortality, but with the same birth levels. As a result there is a rapid increase of the population. In the third stage, the birth rate also decreases, thus, a low

© Springer Nature Switzerland AG 2019
G. Meiselwitz (Ed.): HCII 2019, LNCS 11579, pp. 54–67, 2019.
https://doi.org/10.1007/978-3-030-21905-5_5

level balance is achieved. The latter stage occurs with low birth and mortality rates as the population does not provide its simple reproduction.

Decades later, the "Second Demographic Transition" theory [7] is developed, according to which European populations are undergoing into a new phase of demographic transition, mainly affecting the family. The most important elements are related to: marriage reduction, increasing of non-native born children, distribution of cohabitation relationship (arrangement where non married couple live together), higher divorce rates and reconstructed families (where children live with their mother's or father's spouse), a decrease in birth rate below the simple reproduction level of the population, appearance and spread of conscious childlessness (conscious abandonment of parenthood), as well as an increasing share of migrants. The latter phenomenon is analyzed in the theory of the "Third Demographic Transition" [8].

Many sociologists use the Second Demographic Transition concept in an attempt to summarize the exciting and complex demographic changes of the mid-1960s, as well as a valuable framework in designing their study. Contrary, different authors [9–13] claim that this is a continuous process arguing the Second Demographic Transition universality and value. Nowadays, for many modern families the communication from a distance characterize their daily relationships and lifestyle.

The development of Human-computer interaction (HCI) and free movement across the National borders facilitate some virtual relationships to develop into long-distance relationships [14]. In this sense, at macro level, the Oxford Dictionary uses the definition "virtual community" described as a "community of people sharing common interests, ideas and feelings on the Internet". Therefore, at micro level (family), the term "virtual family" may be used. In an attempt to describe more precisely what the virtual family is, the definition must be close to the virtual community, but also "tailored" to the specificities of the new form of family life. It is also necessary to frame the structure of the family as well as the blood or bloodless kinship relationships. On this basis, the study proposes the following working definition:

The virtual family is an alternative family form composed of a married or unmarried couple, a family with children (narrowly) and their ancestors (broadly) where single, several or all members of the family unit do not live in the same household. Usually they use HCI to share everyday challenges, to exchange ideas and feelings from a distance.

The older population in Israel, for example, is extensively attending courses devoted on computer literacy. The main goal, mostly for the elderly women, is to learn to use social networks to communicate almost daily with their grandchildren, who live in different countries around the world. The communication process includes not only sharing of feelings or telling intergenerational stories. These grandmothers teach their young heirs of Jewish culture, history, religion, which helps to maintain and preserve the Jewish identity, roots and belonging.

Nowadays, more and more Bulgarians, like Jews, live separately from their close relatives. A research, conducted by the non-governmental organization "Here and there" [15] shows that almost every third person in Bulgaria has relatives or friends who are living abroad.

The increasing number of people moving from global "peripheries" to "core" countries in the North/West [16] is well-reflected in the large-scale post-communist (after 1989) Bulgarian migration to Western Europe and North America. The end of 2012 marked a period of gradually increasing migration, the direction of which, however, has shifted from the previously preferred Southern European migration destinations (such as Spain, Italy and Greece) towards the UK and Germany. The waving of the transitional labour market restrictions for Bulgarian and Romanian citizens at the beginning of 2014 led to another relative upsurge in the number of newcomers to the UK [17].

These mobility and migrant processes brought several changes and challenges to the Bulgarian families. HCI ease to maintain family relations and therefore create mediatised or virtual ways of communication and living. The emergence of the Internet has changed the balance between communication and spatial distance, promising to put into action what Marshall McLuhan [18] predicted, and Manuel Castells [19] called the "space of streams" (Castells 2000) where communication is a function regardless of the place. The distance between persons could vary - within one village, city or different countries. The space often corresponds to the frequency and quality of communication between individuals, which the current study analyzes. In the family context, the distance relationship could exist between both intimate partners in a marriage or non-marital union (narrowly) as well as between other family members, as their children or grandparents.

Along with the spatial distance, we should consider the time concept. In this regard, the relatives have the possibility to meet (face to face) at different frequency and have relatively free time devoted on communication. Thus, this correlates with the frequency, the duration and in many cases reflects the quality of their communication. Personal motivation and feelings of absence, loneliness, self-isolation are among the major factors motivating the personal contact with the closest people. Although the communication is not a universal substitute of the physical contact or "remedy", it could "mild" the negative feelings, but in some cases to intensify them, which corresponds with Fortunati's [20] statement that the ideal form of communication is the personal interaction. Her statement is strengthened by the fact that the physical intimacy and care (including healthcare) could not be replaced. In order to be able to grasp the complexity of the issue, the paper focuses on the virtual families in the Bulgarian context, analyzing the communication between the family members.

2   Methodology

In-depth face-to-face and Skype interviews with 50 (N = 50) respondents are conducted. The interviewees are between 18 and 55 years as all of them were separated from their Bulgarian families when the interviews were conducted (in 2018). The selection of the interviewees includes mediated and snowball sampling. The methodology follows the theory of Duncombe and Marsden [21], according to which remote communication is distinguished by the presence of many emotional aspects that are often obscure and confused. This, according to the authors, requires qualitative research.

3 Results and Discussion

3.1 Reasons for the Family Dispersion

The possibility to work or/and study in another place are among the main reasons for the interviewees (82%) to move to another city in the country or abroad. Many of the young people in Bulgaria, identified as "risk group", are seeking for better life abroad because: (1) the education does not correspond to the needs of the labor market; (2) experience difficulties in finding proper first job; (3) lower payment, (4) desire to migrate after graduation in search of a better realization [22]. These trends correspond to the Bulgarian Statistical Institute data for 2018[1].

The complicated financial, social and political situation in Bulgaria sometimes disperses the whole family. One of the interviewees shared:

My father works in The United States, my mother in Greece. I am making career in Cyprus, while my brother studies in Bulgaria.

This revelation is not an isolated case within the current study. Exactly 50% of the interviewees said that they are divided with two or more family members, including their intimate partner.

For four of the interviewees who live in different households but within one city, the hectic everyday life and the lack of personal time urge them to communicate mostly from a distance. Divorce or parents' separation also determines the structural change of the family. As a result, the intimate partners often choose to live in separate households. Inevitably, children become a kind of "hostages" to the separation of their parents and remain in the household of one of them. It is not a precedent for children to live separately in mother and father's households. In such complicated situation, the traumatic consequences affect every member of the family. In some cases, the disagreements and dissensions of parents during their marriage or intimate relationship continue after their actual separation. The sincerity of a father and his daughter, interviewed independently from one another, is indicative:

Daughter: *After the divorce of my parents, it's difficult to keep in touch with my father.*

Father: *My ex-wife's attitude towards me is extremely negative, which influences my children as well. She imposes restrictions on my communication with them. That's why we don't talk often, and even if we succeed to do so, it's very short conversation.*

The structural change of the family may be due to both separation between intimate partners and reconstruction. It is necessary to specify that it can occur after the separation of intimate partners, but also in the cases of death of one of the parents. Two interviewees mentioned this reason:

---

[1] National Statistical Institute (2018) http://www.nsi.bg/bg/content/3435/%D1%83%D1%87%D0%B0%D1%89%D0%B8-%D0%BD%D0%B0%D0%BF%D1%83%D1%81%D0%BD%D0%B0%D0%BB%D0%B8-%D0%BF%D0%BE-%D0%BF%D1%80%D0%B8%D1%87%D0%B8%D0%BD%D0%B8-%D1%81%D1%82%D0%B5%D0%BF%D0%B5%D0%BD-%D0%BD%D0%B0-%D0%BE%D0%B1%D1%80%D0%B0%D0%B7%D0%BE%D0%B2%D0%B0%D0%BD%D0%B8%D0%B5.

After my mother's death, my father hurried up to marry again. As a result, I stayed at my deceased mom's home. I don't see regularly my father and my little sister from my father's second marriage. They live in another household, although in the same city (Sofia), and live their lives. After my mother's death, my brother went to live with my grandmother in Stara Zagora (city in Bulgaria). The distance is crucial and I'm not able to meet them often.

Family reconstruction, the grief, the transformed pattern of life are capable of radically altering past family relationships by replacing them with new relationships. Separation turns out to be a tough but preferable choice, especially when grown-up children have to get used to living with a stepparent. It looks like that the quest for happiness and the quest to "mitigate" the negative effect of such a tragedy becomes a value which every family member is likely to strive.

3.2 Dependencies Between Separation Period and Frequency of Communication

In order to determine whether the duration of family separation affects the frequency of the communication, we differentiated the following periods:

(1) Half a year and one year (40% of the interviewees).
(2) One and three years (18% of the interviewees).
(3) More than three years (50% of the interviewees).

The difference of 8% in the values, which exceed 100%, is due to the fact that 4 out of 50 interviewees have two family members living in other countries that had left their family household at different periods.

The aim of the next question was to measure the frequency of communication. Thus, we differentiated the following variations:

(1) Communicate daily (40% of the interviewees).
(2) Communicate two, three times a week (30% of the interviewees).
(3) Communicate two, three times a month (24% of the interviewees).
(4) Communicate several times a year (10% of the interviewees).

The values above 100% are due to differences in the frequency of communication between more than one of the separated members of the family unit.

Thus, on Fig. 1 we compared the period of separation between the family members with the frequency of their communication.

The results showed that "Between half a year and a year" communicate mostly "Daily" and less "2–3 times a week". None of the interviewees indicated the other two options on the scale. Five out of nine of the interviewees separated from their relatives for "One to three years", communicate with them "two, three times a week". Three of nine communicate "Daily" while one indicated "Two, three times a month" connection. There are extreme variations in the frequency of communication in the last group ("Over three years"). An equal number of the interviewees communicate with their relatives "Daily" and "Two, three times a week" (7 of them). Six out of 25 were communicating "Two, three times a month" while five out of 25 communicate "Several times a year".

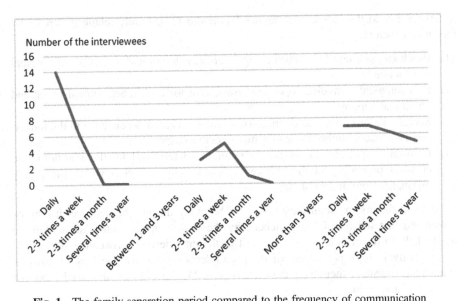

Fig. 1. The family separation period compared to the frequency of communication

The first prolonged separation from the familiar family environment or the separation between the intimate partners generates greater concerns. Undoubted is the concern of the mothers who want to know what is happening to their children at any time, even if they have reached the age of adulthood. The uncertainty about the future of the beloved ones sometimes turns into mutual attacks and jealousy. Over time, separation could be conceived as necessity or inevitability. It is part of the individual choice or predetermined by a number of circumstances and consequences. Gradually, relatives become accustomed to the separation as this has an impact on both the communication frequency and quality.

3.3 The Time and Space Effect on Family Relationships

Separation sometimes rejuvenates feelings, but more often alienates. The distant relationship could be inspiring at the beginning, but when the light is not visible in your eyes and you have no physical contact the intimate communication with the closest people become cool and essentially torn [23]. This is the emotional and the psychological problem of the separated lonely elderly parents or children, of the separated partners, of the distant friends and relatives.

Regarding this, the interviewees were questioned whether they have the feeling that had distanced them from their closest people. The response included dichotomous answer options: "Yes, they have distanced us" and "They have strengthened the relationship". With the "No, I am not distanced" option the interviewees indicated their feeling that the relationship is unchanged. Sometimes, the distance is able to confuse the feelings and objectivity of the assessment. Thus, "I cannot judge" answer was included.

According to the Russian researcher Sidorenko [24], family relations depend by four major factors:

(1) Psychophysiological – relationships between biological relatives and sexual satisfaction
(2) Psychological – involves openness, trust, care for each other, mutual moral and emotional support
(3) Social relations – include distribution of roles, material dependence in the family, and also status: authority, leadership, obedience, etc.
(4) Cultural – special type of family relations, determined by the traditions and customs prevailing in the culture (national, religious, etc.) which the family originates from and exists in.

If these factors maintain their unity and harmony despite the distance, it may be considered that the feelings experienced by the closest people before separation are more likely to remain unchanged, as most of the interviewees answered – 42%.

A relatively high percentage of the respondents (36%) said the lack of physical contact had distanced them from their relatives. A 24-year-old woman shared about her intimate relationship:

I feel we have gone apart because I don't want to go to live with him in Germany. I don't like the way of life there and it will be hard to find a job. The real problem is that he doesn't want to return in Bulgaria regularly.

Another woman, who emigrated in England 10 years ago, lists the main reasons she thought alienated her from her parents:

Generational differences, life in different countries, socio-economic crisis, lack of time because I work hard and I have a number of commitments. When I think about it, there is also a dose of apathy, mostly on my part.

The answer "I cannot judge" is indicated by 14% of the interviewees. The other 8% said that separation had strengthened the relationship between the closest people. The latter values could be attributed to the desire of the separated people to witness and preserve their love. As a result, for example, intimate partners might begin to exchange expensive gifts or gentle revelations, as they have never done when they were together. Parental instinct (especially maternal) could be strengthened by expressing the urgent desire to take more care at a distance – sending money, more frequent and long-lasting communication, giving life guidance without being asked by the children.

3.4 Communication Quality

For 42% of the interviewees the communication has become "clumsy" and "mechanical". A daughter shared one of the reasons for that:

My mother is sometimes annoying, especially when asking me questions that aren't very relevant and concern my personal life.

The various manifestations of dependence on children, the attempts to enter someone's private space interferes the communication smoothness, despite the prior desire of both sides. At the same time, for 24% of the interviewees, "mechanics" and "clumsiness" of their communication are constant and are due to generational differences, unequal socio-economic environment and dynamics of life, multifaceted perception and interpretation of reality, feelings of apathy. A 44-year-old father revealed his own observations of communication with his children:

Communication with my children is extremely difficult. We jump very fast from one topic to another without depleting each of them. Sometimes we have nothing to say. In that case, I mechanically ask any questions.

The communication can be influenced by divorce of the intimate partners or family reorganization. For the remaining 34% of the interviewees the quality of communication has not suffered despite the distance. For some of them the desire to share moments with the closest people favors in finding new themes for conversation, while this is an expression of trust. The sharing is a powerful psychological tool for relaxing from everyday care and problems. It also represents expression of love and concern. A 27-year-old man shared moments of his intimate relationship:

I talk everyday with my girlfriend, even several times a day. Our conversations sometimes last more than an hour. She tells me about her university lectures, about her experiences. I share my impressions of the day, about the people I met. Often we are planning what we will do and where we'll go next time when we see each other.

3.5 Daily Topics

Usually the conversations begin with a discussion of a daily life and everything related directly or indirectly with the family members. Distance generates questions about health, material and financial condition, work or education, career development. In some cases, topics related to close relatives or family friends are also discussed. Some of the interviewees pay attention on political and social events in the country where the family members are located. The majority pointed out the importance of the weather as a topic. As one of the interviewees admitted the weather is a *"rescue shore"* especially when there are no topics left to be discussed.

Additionally the interviewees were questioned if there is a theme taboo for them. A student, first grade, admitted:

I avoid mentioning details of my personal life, my health and financial condition, in order not to disturb my parents if something is wrong. I worry that they, as well as me, are silent about many things concerning their health and everyday problems.

The other topics that the closest people avoid to discuss with each other concern family relations and family issues, mainly because these topics carry negative emotions. In this sense, permanent divisions of property, misunderstandings between relatives to divide the will of their ancestors, muddles and disputes for minor welfare are part of the Bulgarian people-psychology. Probably, this stems from the public policy of state restitution during the socialist period and the return of the property in private hands after the fall of the regime in 1989. One of the interviewees shared:

I endeavor to talk about my job and the working process itself because these conversations are stressful for me!

Policies can also act as a "dividing line" between some relatives:

I do not want to discuss political issues with my father because his beliefs are solid and can't be changed. Such a dispute makes no sense at all.

Some parents and children had built up taboo topics, for example, such as smoking, alcohol or drugs. For 36% of the interviewees there are no topics such a taboo themes because they respect the freedom of thought in their family. A 55-year-old mother admitted she does not avoid discussing any subject with her son. She believes this approach could solve any problems well in advance.

3.6 Emotionality

It is noteworthy that the majority of the interviewees "become emotional" when talking to their family members. The current study assumes that emotionality is supporting the stability of the relationship between relatives and intimate partners. Because on one hand, emotions are a pushing motivation to call someone who is missing, and on the other hand, communicating and experiencing the emotional states show empathy. Otherwise, the closest people can feel lonely and desolate. Furthermore, positive emotions are involving a strong sense of self-esteem and people have the feeling that they are loved. Communicating with the loved ones brings joy and is an immanent characteristic of emotional acceptance [25].

In total 58% of the interviewees express their emotions. A 33-year-old married woman who has two children said:

We always appreciate the expression of emotions in our family. They are important condition for the emotional stability of the whole family.

Emotionality also depends on the current state of the persons. Initiating a long emotional interaction can bring extra fatigue, especially after a long working day, it can be psychologically burdening and disturbing the peace of mind. In some cases, a person can cover up disturbing information in an attempt to rationalize the surrounding circumstances and in attempt not to worry his/her family. About 30% of the interviewees express their emotions openly, which identify them with the first group of respondents, who always share their emotions. One of the respondents shared:

Whether I will express my emotions depends mostly on what happened to me during the day, on the specific situation and my mood, and on my desire to share with my family.

The remaining 12% of the interviewees said they usually did not share their emotions openly. Among the reasons for their answer were the apathetic relations between family members before separation or they were trying not to worry their family. A 28-year-old woman told about communicating with her intimate partner:

Distance drives us apart. There aren't emotions when we talk. I feel we are becoming no family as we were before.

3.7 Communication Between Several Separated Family Members

Half of the interviewees have two or more family members who are living apart. The results show that 68% of them do not communicate equally with their relatives, while the others (32%) have relatively equal frequency and duration of communication. In a similar quantitative study, Lawton et al. [26] also notice that mothers communicate more frequently with their children than fathers do. According to them women in the family perceive their role as advocates of kinship. At the same time, in most cases, the father is unlikely to have such an approach. Father-child based communication is primarily on the benefits of the contact and when the children have financial difficulties.

Further, the current study suggests that communication between intimate partners differs from blood-kinship relations. Homans [27] assume that people have the opportunity to end a relationship that does not bring them satisfaction, referring to friendly relationships [28, 29]. This can refer to intimate partners with no live born children as well. Unlike these two groups, the parents and their children have long-term regulatory obligations. Consequently, blood relatives are more likely to communicate with each other, although the relationship could bring them only stress and discomfort.

The communication between blood relatives correlates with a number of other variables in the model. Established relationship between family members, possibility of reconstruction or divorce of parents, different psychological or personal motives have an influence to the quality and the quantity of their interaction from a distance. One of the interviewees shared:

The relationship with my father broke up in early childhood. He lived with us, but I never felt that he needed me. Obviously, I did not need him. I was afraid to talk to him and we had communication barriers of a different nature. I always felt safe only when I share things from my personal life with my mother. Now, when I'm abroad, I prefer to talk more to her. I avoid doing that with my father.

3.8   Prerequisites for Choosing a Social Network for Communication

The key to choose means of communication, according to Miller and Madianou [30], is the perception of each media as a structure of possibilities, such as the choice between the letter and the recorded voice on the audio cassettes sent by mail in the past. According to the authors, most people use a constellation of different media as an integrated environment in which each medium finds its niche in relation to the others. The polymedia use is inherent for the interviewees in the current study. One of the interviewees shared:

I use Viber when I want to hear with my sister or other friend abroad at the moment. I usually use Facebook when the message I want to leave is not so urgent and does not require an instant response.

In addition, the results indicate that the most common communication media among the interviewees is: (1) mobile phone followed by (2) Viber or Skype and (3) Facebook. However, the use of the latter two media does not fully replace the use of mobile phone because the social media applications are usually installed on it. We must consider also the access and affordability to media technologies, as well as media literacy, which are among the basic prerequisites for communication. Additionally, some subjective preferences for choosing a proper media should be considered. One of the interviewees shared his experiences:

My parents have Viber, but not Facebook – they refuse to participate in, as they call it, "this place for gossip". I respect their choice.

The use of social networks also depends on the individual attitudes, moods and emotional states, as well as the different premises and circumstances. Another interviewee said:

I always want to hear and see my parents on Skype. Sometimes, however, after a long working day, I feel very tired and I feel sad that they are so far away. At these moments, I prefer just to hear with my family members. If I don't have energy to talk at all I'm typing SMS to my mother to know that I'm OK.

3.9   Interpretations and Perceptions of the Virtual Family

About 44% of the interviewees perceived that they represent the virtual family. Part of them is a 32-year-old man for whom the prospect of lucrative work abroad and the inability to realize professionally in his own country are among the main reasons to emigrate in London, UK. He emigrated together with his girlfriend. In Bulgaria he left his mother, father and sister along with his closest friends. According to him:

The virtual family is a phenomenon that has arisen from the lack of perspective in our own country. It is sad but the term is a fact… in the virtual family other processes are running, different in comparison with the live contact… This family is a puzzle with missing pieces.

High levels of emigration in Bulgaria, economic, social and political crisis in the years of transition urged many young people and highly qualified specialists to leave the country. A 44-year-old woman, a cruise ship musician with three children, thought that the virtual family is *the present and the future, because more and more people travel for work and they are far from their relatives.*

Another interviewee, who also has to travel abroad frequently said:

Every family is going through a certain period of separation, which makes it virtual.

Human-computer communication, claimed some of the interviewees, is precondition for the virtual family formation:

If one family spends more time online than being together it could be said its virtual.

The other respondents (56%) do not perceive themselves as part of the virtual family. One of the participants in the study, separated for more than 17 years with his mother and father, argued:

The family structure is largely preserved, which determines that the family is not virtual, although relations between family members have changed and have become more sterile.

A nineteen-year-old student said that *many young people go to study in another city and the communication with their families inevitably becomes virtual.* According to this interviewee, *18-19 years of personal communication and living at her parents' home were enough to build up strong relationship with all family members.*

A 38-year-old woman, mother of two children believes that distant communication is a prerequisite for maintaining family relationship, family existence and even its survival. The interviewee is sure that a virtual family could appear only if the communication stops and would exist as a term.

Brother and sister who live for more than seven years separated expressed an interesting interpretation. The young woman, who shares a household in Bulgaria with her mother and father, does not define her family as a virtual. Her brother however, who studies and works in Denmark, is convinced that his family has been transformed into this alternative virtual form. The different perceptions for the same family could stem from the fact that the sister lives with her parents who are able to fill (but not completely) or partially replace the missing family member. At the same time, her brother is detached from the whole family.

Some of the respondents completely rejected the proposed term "virtual family". Most of them argued briefly: *"This term is incomprehensible to me. These are mutually exclusive words"; "The virtual family does not exist. The family is only real"; "This cannot be a family!"*

4 Discussion and Conclusion

Based on the current research, the following conclusions can be drawn:

(1) Seeking for highly paid work, personal development and education in prestigious universities are among the main reasons for the Bulgarian family separation. The young people are among the risk groups.

(2) The Human-computer interaction between the virtual family members preserve the family relations, structure and intimate proximity.

(3) The different daily routine and lifestyle that family members have could alienate them. The distance further intensifies this feeling. Everyday experiences, emotions, problems and worries often exclude the involvement of the family. Sharing and revelation (if any) are mediated and are often insufficient for a person to sympathize, to be fully involved in the emotional states and affairs of his or her closest people, especially when he is not a direct participant or is not directly involved.

(4) Despite the relatively more stable, intimate relationship between mother and children, their relationships are also dynamic. Mothers desire to patronize and control often does not correlate with the wish of the growing up children for more independence.

(5) Children avoid discussing with their parents topics often related to their personal live, thus trying to prevent interference and to gain personal freedom.

(6) The communication between virtual family members is different in frequency, duration and quality.

(7) Long absence of family members seriously reflects on the quantity and the quality of communication. Conversations between relatives become increasingly rare, the topics are limited to a few basic ones, and the communication process is often "clumsy" and "mechanical".

(8) The common channel of communication among the interviewees is the mobile phone, followed by Viber/Skype, and Facebook.

(9) The use of social networks depends on the individual attitudes, moods and emotional states, as well as the different premises and circumstances. Access and affordability to media technologies, and media literacy also have influence on the interviewees.

(10) Most of the separated relatives and intimate partners do not perceive themselves as a virtual family. This phenomenon can be explained by the emerging "nonexistent family" association and with the negative connotations of the term which the family members do not want to be associated with.

Although virtual relationships and virtual family are extremely complex phenomena, availability of relatively frequent and qualified communication often turns out to be vital for the survival of the family structure and for preservation of the relationship between intimate partners. The communication between family members from a distance is in dynamic dependence on the constant internal and external changes of the environment – cultural, technological, corporate, which determines the need for further in-depth research in this scientific field.

Acknowledgements. The paper has been developed within the framework of the research projects of the National Scientific Fund of Bulgaria: DCOST 01/25-20.02.2017 supporting COST Action CA 16211 "Reappraising Intellectual Debates on Civic Rights and Democracy in Europe" and Program Young Scientists and Post Docs of the Bulgarian Ministry of Education and Science.

References

1. Uhlendorf, U., Rupp, M., Euteneuer, M.: Wellbeing of Families in Future Europe. In: Challenges for Research and Policy. Family Platform – Families in Europe, vol. 1, p. 14 (2011)
2. Sobotka, T.: Fertility in Central and Eastern Europe after 1989: collapse and gradual recovery. Hist. Soc. Res. **36**(2), 246–296 (2011)
3. Skolnick, A.: The Intimate Environment: Exploring Marriage and the Family. Little, Brown and Company, Boston (1978). Cover Worn, Some Underlining edition
4. Kapella, O., Rille-Pfeiffer, C., Rupp, M., Schneider, N.F.: Die Vielfalt der Familie: Tagungsband zum 3. Europäischen Fachkongress Familienforhchung. Barbara Budrich, Opladen (2009)
5. Weston, K.: Families We Choose: Lesbians, Gay Men and Kinship. Columbia University Press, New York (1991)
6. Thompson, W.: Population. Am. J. Sociol. **34**, 959–975 (1929)
7. Lesthaeghe, R., Van de Kaa, D.: Two demographic transitions? Population Growth and Decline, pp. 9–24. Deventer (1986)
8. Coleman, D.: Immigration and ethnic change in low-fertility countries: a third demographic transition. Popul. Dev. Rev. **32**, 401–446 (2006)
9. Vishnevsky, A.: Demographic Revolution and the Future of Fertility; A Systems Approach, pp. 257–280. Academic Press, London (1991)
10. Cliquet, L.: The second demographic transition: Fact or fiction? Population studies No. 23, Council of Europe, Strasbourg (1991)
11. Pavlik, Z.: The concept of demographic development. In: Kuijsten, A., de Gans, H., de Feijter, H. (eds.) The Joy of Demography... and Other Disciplines, Essays in Honour of Dirk van de Kaa, NethurD-publications, Thela Thesis, Amsterdam, pp. 335–348 (1998)
12. Livi Bacci, M.: Comment: desired family size and the future course of fertility. In: Bulatao, R., Casterline, B. (eds.) Global Fertility Transition, Supplement to PDR, vol. 27, Population Council, New York, pp. 282–290 (2001)
13. Coleman, D.: Why we don't have to believe without doubting in the "Second demographic transition" - some agnostic comments. Vienna Yearbook of Population Research, pp. 11–24 (2004)
14. Sánchez, L., Goldani, A.: The changing shape of ties in European families: profiles and intentions of LAT couples. Presented at Population and Association of America 2012, in session 56: Non-marital and diverse family forms (2012)

15. Here and there (2015). https://tuk-tam.bg/tuk-tam-research-2015/. Accessed 3 Oct 2018
16. Castles, S., de Haas, H., Miller, M.: The Age of Migration. International Population Movements in the Modern World, 5th edn. Palgrave Macmillian, Basingstoke (2014)
17. Manolova, P.: "Going to the West Is My Last Chance to Get a Normal Life": Bulgarian would-be migrants' imaginings of life in the UK. Central and Eastern European Migration Review, pp. 1–23 (2018)
18. McLuhan, M.: The Gutenberg Galaxy. University of Toronto Press, Toronto (1962)
19. Castells, M.: The Rise of the Network Society, 2nd edn. Blackwell Publishers, Oxford (2000)
20. Fortunati, L.: Is body to body communication still the prototype? Inf. Soc. **21**(1), 53–61 (2005)
21. Duncombe, J., Marsden, D.: Love and intimacy: the gender division of emotion and emotion work, a neglected aspect of sociological discussion of heterosexual relationships. Sociology **27**(2), 221–241 (1993)
22. Tsoneva, E.: Youth unemployment in Bulgaria - economic and social problems. E-Journal Dialogue, 4458 (2010). issue 01/2010
23. Mirchev, M.: Texts 2. Invitation for sociology. Second edited and revised edition. Ed. M-8-M (2011). Мирчев, М.: Текстове 2. Покана за социология. Второ издание. Изд. М-8-М (2011)
24. Sidorenko, V.: Imagelogy. How to please people. Public education, Moscow, pp. 282–294 (2002). Сидоренко, В.: Имиджелоги. Как нравиться людям. Народное образование, Москва, с 282–294 (2002)
25. Stoyanova, D.: Conceptual and technological approaches to pedagogy of parents in the context of positive-oriented family education. Scientific works of the University of Rousse, vol. 51, ser. 6.2, pp. 129–133 (2012)
26. Lawton, L., Merril, S., Vern, B.: Affection, social contact, and geographic distance between adult children and their parents. J. Marriage Fam. **56**, 57–68 (1994)
27. Homans, G.: The Human Group. Harcourt, Brace & World, New York (1950)
28. Laumann, O.: Bonds of Pluralism. Wiley, New York (1973)
29. Fischer, C.: To Dwell Among Friends: Personal Networks in Town and City. Chicago University Press, Chicago (1982)
30. Miller, D., Madianou, M.: Migration and New Media: Transnational Families and Polymedia. Routledge, New York (2011)

Gaze from and Toward the Silent Third Participant in a Triadic Conversation

Ichiro Umata[1]([⊠]), Koki Ijuin[2], Tsuneo Kato[2], and Seiichi Yamamoto[2]

[1] KDDI Research, Inc., Garden Air Tower, 3-10-10, Iidabashi, Chiyoda-ku,
Tokyo 102-8460, Japan
ic-umata@kddi-research.jp
[2] Department of Information Systems Design, Doshisha University,
Kyotanabe-shi, Kyoto 610-0321, Japan
euqll01@mail4.doshisha.ac.jp,
{tsukato, seyamamo}@mail.doshisha.ac.jp

Abstract. This study reports an analysis of the relationship between gaze and floor apportionment in a triadic conversation, focusing on the gazes from and toward the silent third participant, in other words, the participant who was not involved in the speaker change. Based on the previous observations that mutual gazes between the current and the next speaker do play an important role in coordinating floor apportionment, we analyzed the relationship between gaze and floor apportionment focusing on the silent third participant. The result suggests that the mutual gazes between the next speaker and the silent third participants had little relation to speech turn organization.

Keywords: Multimodal interaction · Multiparty conversation · Gaze · Turn organization

1 Introduction

Multimodal interactions such as meetings, negotiations, and discussions are important social activities in workplaces, classrooms, and community management, and supporting such interactions has been an important research topic in the field of human-computer interaction (HCI) studies [1, 2]. In multimodal interactions, not only verbal but also nonverbal information play an important role. The non-verbal elements have been considered particularly important not only in the affectional and attitudinal aspect of communication [3, 4], but also in coordination of communication [5, 6]. Among nonverbal cues, gaze has attracted the strong interest of researchers. They have reported on the important functions of gaze in communication, such as expressing emotional states, exercising social control, highlighting the informational structure of speech, and organizing speech turn [7–10], and it is expected to be an important cue in evaluating communication characteristics and establishing the roles of the participants in human-computer interactions.

One of the main topics communication study researchers have focused on is the relation between gaze and speech-turn organization. Several earlier psychological studies reported that gaze has a speech-turn organization function in dyadic conversations

© Springer Nature Switzerland AG 2019
G. Meiselwitz (Ed.): HCII 2019, LNCS 11579, pp. 68–76, 2019.
https://doi.org/10.1007/978-3-030-21905-5_6

involving participants who speak the same language [7, 8, 10], although some were skeptical about such findings [11, 12]. Some recent multiparty conversation studies in psychology, cognitive science, and information science fields have confirmed the speech-turn organization function of gaze [9, 13–20], and it is likely that the conditions under which a conversation occurs affect the relative importance of the various functions of gaze in communication [21].

The analyses of gaze and speech-turn organization mentioned above have mainly focused on the interaction between the current speaker and the next speaker. The participants constitute a ratified structure in a multi-party conversation [22], and behaviors of the side participants, in other words, the silent participants who were not involved in the speaker change, are also important cues for capturing the characteristics of such conversations. Holler and Kendrick conducted temporal analyses of the unaddressed participants' gaze shift from the current to the next speaker, and showed they can anticipate next speech turns [9]. However, the general tendency of the gazing activities among the current speaker, the next speaker, and the silent third participants has not been analyzed quantitatively. Analyzing the behavior of silent participants is also important for capturing the characteristics of multimodal multiparty interactions, and for developing systems that support smooth and active communication and designing HCI interfaces.

This study reports a preliminary analysis of the gazing activities involving the silent third participants in triadic conversations, focusing on mutual gaze and shared gaze phenomena. As for mutual gaze, the results of the correlation analysis between the current speaker and the silent third participant suggest that their mutual gaze plays a negligible role as a speech-turn organization signal. As for shared gaze toward the silent third participant, the results of the correlation analysis suggest that the silent third participants might have been attracting less shared attention in utterances without a speaker change when the conversational flow was more predictable. These results are expected to contribute to the development of a future conversation support system and interactive interface design.

2   Corpus

We analyzed a multimodal multi-party interaction corpus with eye-gaze data collected during previous studies [15, 19]. The corpus consists of conversations in the mother tongue of the participants and conversations in a second language involving the same interlocutors (for details, refer to [15, 19]). The mother tongue conversations were the focus of analysis in this study. A total of 60 subjects (23 females and 37 males: 20 groups) between the ages of 18 and 24 participated in the data collection, and each conversational group consisted of three participants. All participants were native speaker of Japanese.

Three participants were seated 1.5 m apart from each other in a triangular formation around a table (see Figs. 1 and 2). The corpus covers two conversation types to examine the effect of the conversation topics on their interaction behaviors. One is free-flowing, natural chatting that ranges over various topics such as hobbies, weekend plans, studies, and travels. The second type is goal-oriented, in which participants collaboratively decided what to take with them on trips to uninhabited islands or mountains. All the participants in the goal-oriented conversations would be under pressure to contribute to the conversation in order to reach an agreement, whereas there would be far less pressure in free-flowing conversations. Conversational flow would be more predictable in the goal-oriented conversations where the vocabulary was more limited and the domain of the discourse was defined more narrowly by the task than in the free-flowing conversations.

The order of the conversation types was arranged randomly to counterbalance any order effect. The order of the languages used in the conversations was also arranged randomly. Each group had six-minute conversations of the two types in both Japanese and English. We collected multimodal data from 80 triadic conversations in L1 (Japanese) and in L2 (English) languages (20 free-flowing in Japanese, 20 free-flowing in English, 20 goal-oriented in Japanese, and 20 goal-oriented in English). Twenty groups engaged in all four conversation types. The average duration of individual conversations was 6 min. All the participants except those in the first three groups answered a questionnaire evaluating their conversation after each conversation condition to be analyzed in other studies (see [20]).

Their eye gazes and voices were recorded via three sets of NAC EMR-9 head-mounted eye trackers and headsets with microphones. The viewing angle of the EMR-9 was 62° and the sampling rate was 60 fps. We used the EUDICO Linguistic Annotator (ELAN) developed by the Max Planck Institute as a tool for gaze and utterance annotation [24] (see Fig. 3). Each utterance is segmented from speech at inserted pauses of more than 500 ms, and the corpus was manually annotated in terms of the time spans for utterances, backchannel, laughing, and eye movements.

Fig. 1. Experimental setup

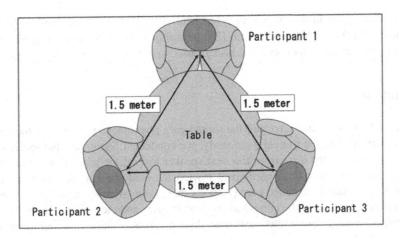

Fig. 2. Seating positions of the three participants.

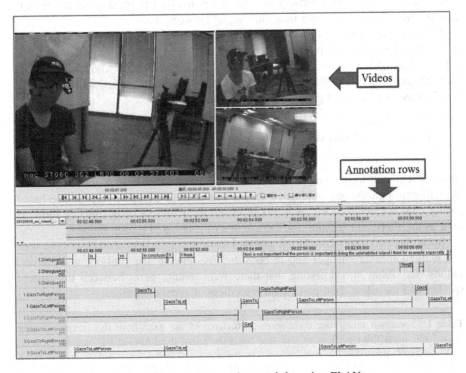

Fig. 3. Example of annotation result by using ELAN.

Studies have been conducted that observed cultural differences in gazing activities, as introduced in [13]. Rosano et al. showed that gazing activities may vary across cultures and may also be strongly related to the social actions the participants are initiating [25]. The participants gaze 1.6-fold more while listening than while speaking in L1 conversations in the corpus analyzed here [19]. This statistical result is highly consistent with that of Vertegaal et al. [26] in multiparty conversations, regardless of the differences in languages, cultural background, and conversation topics.

3   Analyses

We focused on the mutual gaze and the shared gaze phenomena that involve the silent third participant. For the mutual gaze study, we conducted Spearman rank-order correlation analyses of the gaze from the next speaker toward the silent third participant and that from the silent third participant toward the next speaker. A previous study showed that in native language conversations there were significant positive correlations between gazes from the current to the next speaker and those from the next to the current speaker only during utterances preceding the speaker change but not utterances without a speaker change, suggesting that mutual gaze acted as a turn transition signal [20]. We assumed that the same tendency would be observed between the current speaker and the silent third participant, who is not involved in speaking at that time if mutual gaze also acts as a turn transition signal between them.

We used the average of gazing ratios for the correlation analyses based on Ijuin et al. [19]. The participant roles were classified into three types: current speaker (CS), as the speaker of the utterance; next speaker (NS), as the participant who takes the floor after the current speaker releases the floor; and the silent third participant (Silent 3rd). The average of role-based gazing ratios is defined as

$$\text{average role-based gazing ratio (gazing ratio)} = \frac{1}{n} \sum_{i=1}^{n} \frac{DG_{jk(i)}}{DSU_{(i)}} \times 100 (\%)$$

where $DSU(i)$ and $DGjk(i)$ represent the duration of the i-th utterance and the duration of participant j gazing at participant k during that utterance, respectively. A role-based gazing ratio is calculated for each group. In the following sections, "gazing ratio" is used as the shorthand notation for the average of role-based gazing ratios.

Spearman rank-order correlation analyses showed significant correlations both with and without speaker changes and in both the free-flowing and goal-oriented conversations (see Table 1), suggesting that there were mutual gazes between the current speaker and the silent third participant regardless of speaker changes.

Table 1. Spearman rank-order correlation coefficients of the gaze from the current speaker toward the silent third participant and that from the silent third toward the current speaker. (*: p < .05; **: p < .01)

	From CS to Silent-3rd ⇔ From Silent 3rd to CS
Free-flowing: utterances before speaker change	.522* (p = .018)
Free-flowing: utterances without speaker change	.534* (p = .015)
Goal-oriented: utterances before speaker change	.848** (p = .000)
Goal-oriented: utterances without speaker change	.696** (p = .001)

For the shared gaze study, we conducted correlation analyses of the gaze from the current speaker toward the silent third participant and that from the next speaker toward the silent third participant. We expected that the current speaker's gazing activity toward the silent third participant would invite the next speaker's gazing activity resulting in their shared gaze toward the silent third participant. The silent third participants were expected to be less prominent in conversation, and another expectation was that they might do something noteworthy that attracted the current and the next speakers' attention when they were gazed at. We assumed that a correlation would be observed both with and without speaker changes and in both the free-flowing and goal-oriented conversations.

The analyses showed a significant correlation both with and without speaker change in free-flowing conversations, whereas they showed a significant correlation only with a speaker change in goal-oriented conversations (see Table 2), suggesting that there were shared gazes toward the silent third participants other than utterances without speaker change in goal-oriented conversations.

Table 2. Spearman rank-order correlation coefficients of the gaze from the current speaker toward the silent third participant and that from the next speaker toward the silent third.

	From CS to Silent-3rd ⇔ From NS to Silent 3rd
Free-flowing: utterances before speaker change	.752** ($p = .000$)
Free-flowing: utterances without speaker change	.445* ($p = .049$)
Goal-oriented: utterances before speaker change	.866** ($p = .000$)
Goal-oriented: utterances without speaker change	.141 ($p = .552$)

4 Discussion

For the mutual gaze between the next speaker and the silent third participant, our analysis revealed an interesting result: the correlation analysis of the gaze from the next speaker toward the silent third participant and that from the silent third participant toward the next speaker showed that their mutual gaze was not related to speech-turn transition to the same extent as the mutual gaze between the current speaker and the next speaker was. Together with the results of previous studies that showed the duration of the current speaker's gaze toward the next speaker was significantly longer than that toward the silent participants in multiparty conversation [9, 13–17, 19], the results of this study also suggest that their mutual gaze had little relation to speech-turn organization and did not act as a speech-turn organization signal. There might have been other reasons for their mutual gaze, and it would be an interesting future research direction to examine the context of the interaction where their mutual gaze was observed.

In terms of the shared gaze toward the silent third participant, correlation analysis of gaze from the current speaker toward the silent third participant and that from the next speaker toward the silent third participant also revealed an interesting result.

Contrary to our expectation, there was an exception: their shared gaze toward the silent third participant was not observed for utterances without speaker change in goal-oriented conversations.

The cause of this phenomenon is not clear, although the predictability of the goal-oriented conversation might have been an important factor. It may be the case that the silent third participants might have been attracting less shared attention during utterances without a speaker change in goal-oriented conversation where the conversational flow was less dynamic and the current and the next speaker might have felt less need to observe the behavior of the silent third participant who was not actively involved in their speech interaction. Detailed analyses of the differences among these interaction conditions would also be an interesting future extension of this study.

5   Conclusion

We analyzed gazing activities of the current speaker, the next speaker, and the silent third participant during utterances with/without speaker change, from the viewpoints of mutual gaze and shared gaze phenomena that involve the silent third participant.

For mutual gaze between the current speaker and the silent third participant, the analysis of gaze from the current speaker toward the silent third participant and that from the silent third participant toward the current speaker showed significant correlations under all utterance conditions, suggesting that their mutual gaze had little relation to speech-turn organization, contrary to our initial expectation.

For shared gaze toward the silent third participant, the analysis of gaze from the current speaker toward the silent third participant and that from the next speaker toward the silent third participant showed a significant correlation both with and without speaker change in free-flowing conversations, whereas they showed a significant correlation only with a speaker change in goal-oriented conversations. These results suggest that the silent third participants might have been attracting less shared attention for utterances without a speaker change when the conversational flow was more predictable.

Although the causes of these phenomena are still not clear and require more detailed studies in the future, these results show that the functions of gaze are affected by the role of the participants in multimodal multiparty interaction, and are expected to contribute to forming the basis of the development of a conversation support system and interactive interface design.

References

1. Chiu, P., Kapuskar, A., Wilcox, L., Reitmeier, S.: Meeting capture in a media enriched conference room. In: Streitz, N.A., Siegel, J., Hartkopf, V., Konomi, S. (eds.) CoBuild 1999. LNCS, vol. 1670, pp. 79–88. Springer, Heidelberg (1999). https://doi.org/10.1007/10705432_8
2. Cutler, R., et al.: Distributed meetings: a meeting capture and broadcasting system. In: Proceedings of the Tenth ACM International Conference on Multimedia (MULTIMEDIA 2002), pp. 503–512. ACM Press (2002)

3. Mehrabian, A., Ferris, S.R.: Inference of attitudes from nonverbal communication in two channels. J. Consult. Psychol. **31**(3), 248–252 (1967)
4. Mehrabian, A., Wiener, M.: Decoding of inconsistent communications. J. Pers. Soc. Psychol. **6**(1), 109–114 (1967)
5. Clark, H.H.: Using Language. Cambridge University Press, Cambridge (1996)
6. Clark, H.H., Brennan, S.E.: Grounding in communication. In: Resnik, L.B., Levine, J.M., Teasley, S.D. (eds.) Perspectives on Socially Shared Cognition, pp. 503–512. APA Books (1991)
7. Argyle, M., Lallijee, M., Cook, M.: The effects of visibility on interaction in a dyad. Hum. Relat. **21**(1968), 3–17 (1968)
8. Duncan, S.: Some signals and rules for taking speaking turns in conversations. J. Pers. Soc. Psychol. **23**, 283–292 (1972)
9. Holler, J., Kendrick, K.H.: Unaddressed participants' gaze in multi- person interaction: optimizing recipiency. Front. Psychol. **6**, 14 (2015). https://doi.org/10.3389/fpsyg.2015.00098. Article 98
10. Kendon, A.: Some functions of gaze-direction in social interaction. Acta Psychol. **26**, 22–63 (1967)
11. Beattie, G.W.: Floor apportionment and gaze in conversational dyads. Br. J. Soc. Clin. Psychol. **17**(1), 7–15 (1978)
12. Rutter, D.R., Stevenson, G.M., Ayling, K., White, P.A.: The timing of looks in dyadic conversation. Br. J. Soc. Clin. Psychol. **17**, 17–21 (1978)
13. Rossano, F.: Gaze in conversation. In: Stivers, T., Sidnell, J. (ed.) The Handbook of Conversation Analysis, pp. 308–329. Wiley-Blackwell, Malden (2013). https://doi.org/10.1002/9781118325001.ch15
14. Jokinen, K., Furukawa, H., Nishida, M., Yamamoto, S.: Gaze and turn-taking behavior in casual conversational interactions. ACM Trans. Interact. Intell. Syst. **3**(2), 12 (2013)
15. Yamamoto, S., Taguchi, K., Ijuin, K., Umata, I., Nishida, M.: Multimodal corpus of multiparty conversations in L1 and L2 languages and findings obtained from it. Lang. Res. Eval. **49**, 857–882 (2015)
16. Ishii, R., Otsuka, K., Kumano, S., Matsuda, M., Yamato, J.: Predicting next speaker and timing from gaze transition patterns in multi-party meetings. In: Proceedings of the 15th ACM on International Conference on Multimodal Interaction (ICMI 2013), pp. 79–86 (2013). ACM, New York. https://doi.org/10.1145/2522848.2522856
17. Ishii, R., Otsuka, K., Kumano, S., Yamato, J.: Prediction of who will be the next speaker and when using gaze behavior in multiparty meetings. ACM Trans. Interact. Intell. Syst. **6**(1), 31 (2016). https://doi.org/10.1145/2757284. Article 4
18. Auer, P.: Gaze, addressee selection and turn-taking in triadic interaction. In: InLiSt - Interaction and Linguistic Structures, no. 60, August 2017 (2018). http://www.inlist.uni-bayreuth.de/issues/60/index.htm
19. Ijuin, K., Umata, I., Kato, T., Yamamoto, S.: Difference in eye gaze for floor apportionment in native- and second-language conversations. J. Nonverbal Behav. **42**, 113–128 (2018)
20. Umata, I., Ijuin, K., Kato, T., Yamamoto, S.: Floor apportionment and mutual gazes in native and second-language conversation. In: Proceedings of the 20th ACM International Conference on Multimodal Interaction (ICMI 2018), pp. 334–341. ACM, New York (2018). https://doi.org/10.1145/3242969.3242991
21. Kleinke, C.L.: Gaze and eye contact: a research review. Psychol. Bull. **100**, 78–100 (1986)
22. Goffman, E.: Replies and Responses. Lang. Soc. **5**, 257–313 (1976)

23. Umata, I., Yamamoto, S., Ijuin, K., Nishida, M.: Effects of language proficiency on eye-gaze in second language conversations: toward supporting second language collaboration. In: Proceedings of the International Conference on Multimodal Interaction (ICMI 2013), pp. 413–419 (2013)
24. ELAN. http://www.lat-mpi.eu/tools/elan
25. Rossano, F., Brown, P., Levinson., S.C.: Gaze, Questioning, and Culture, pp. 187–249. Cambridge University Press, Cambridge (2009). https://doi.org/10.1017/CBO978051163 5670.008
26. Vertegaal, R., Slagter, R., Verr, G., Nijholt, A.: Eye gaze patterns in conversations: there is more to conversational agents than meets the eyes. In: CHI 2001 Proceedings of the SIGCHI Conference on Human Factors in Computing Systems, pp. 301–308 (2001)

Healthcare Communities

What Health Information Are Consumers Seeking? A Comparison Between Two Types of Online Q&A Sites

Ashwag Alasmari[1,3]([✉]) and Lina Zhou[2]

[1] University of Maryland Baltimore County, Baltimore, MD 21250, USA
ashwag1@umbc.edu
[2] University of North Carolina at Charlotte, Charlotte, NC 920, USA
[3] King Khalid University, Abha, Kingdom of Saudi Arabia

Abstract. Online questioning and answering (Q&A) sites have emerged as an alternative source for serving individuals' health information needs. Despite studies on analyzing user-generated content in online Q&A sites, there is an insufficient understanding of health consumers from the perspective of health-consumer types, information needs and number of questions. Additionally, empirical comparisons of different Q&A platforms are scarce. This research investigates types of health consumers, information seeking needs, and number of questions for asking questions across two types of online Q&A platforms. Empirical analyses of 624 heath questions collected from Yahoo! Answers and WebMD reveal several important differences. In comparison, there were more questions about adverse drug reactions on WebMD, and more questions about seeking similar experiences on Yahoo! Answers. The findings have design implications for online Q&A sites to better support health information seeking.

Keywords: Information needs · Online health seeking · Online Q&A

1 Introduction

Health consumers are increasingly going online to access health information. According to the 2014 Pew Internet and American Life Project survey, 72% of Internet users reported using online resources to obtain health information in the past 12 months [5]. Specifically, over 35% of respondents searched online for medical information to determine what medical condition they or someone else might have. These online resources ranged from general search engines to specific websites devoted to health information. One of the many online resources that meet these information needs is online Question and Answer (or Q&A) sites.

Online Q&A sites [21] allow health consumers to post questions with expectation of getting answers from others. Accordingly, such sites represent the most direct way for a person to seek information. Q&A sites also serve as an alternative source to search engine after consumers fail to find information via the latter [9]. In Q&A research, health has been identified as a major domain for observing user interactions [12]. There are different types of online Q&A sites. Some sites such as Yahoo! Answers are

© Springer Nature Switzerland AG 2019
G. Meiselwitz (Ed.): HCII 2019, LNCS 11579, pp. 79–89, 2019.
https://doi.org/10.1007/978-3-030-21905-5_7

organized as a directory with different sections focusing on different topics, whereas some others like Quora do not provide pre-defined categories for questions. Online Q&A sites also differ based on whether the posted answers are curated or not. In a curated site such as WebMD Answers, experts are considered as an essential part of the community. In contrast, health consumers are able to seek support from peers with similar conditions in some other online Q&A platforms. However, none of the previous studies have compared health consumers' needs across different types of Q&A sites.

To fill the above literature gaps, this research compares curated and community Q&A sites. Specially, it answers the following research questions: (1) How do the health information needs differ between the two online Q&A sites, if any? (2) Are there differences between different types of Q&A sites in terms of health-consumer types and number of questions?

The study answers the above questions by analyzing heath questions collected from two distinct online Q&A platforms: Yahoo! Answers and WebMD Answers. According to the statistic of National Institute of Diabetes and Digestive and Kidney Diseases, kidney disease can lead many complications, and the overall prevalence of chronic kidney disease in general population estimated to be 14%. Thus, data are collected pertaining to questions about the kidney disease from the two platforms in this study.

2 Background and Literature Review

Online Q&A sites provide a venue generally for asking a question and posting answers. While online Q&A usually refers to user-generated answers, there are examples of systems that do automatic extractions of answers, such as Google or Bing, which are also known as machine-driven Q&A. On the other hand, online Q&A has evolved owing to the significant development of Web 2.0. It is an outlet for information seeking where the health consumers' needs are articulated by natural language questions and posted to a community. Therefore, answers to the questions are answered by anyone who share a topic of interest from the community. The answers can include, but are not limited to, information, social, suggestions, advice, or opinions.

With the growing popularity of online Q&A services in recent years, many classification schemes have been proposed for such Q&A sites. Q&A platforms can be focused on a specific topic or general topics. Examples of specific or specialized Q&A include WebMD and Stack Overflow. There is an abundance of examples which fall under the general-purpose Q&A category. These sites typically cover a broad range of topics instead of being organized around just one single (broad) topic. Examples of general focused Q&A include Yahoo! Answers and Quora. To make this classification more precise, Q&A sites further differ based on whether the posted answers are curated or not. In a curated site, experts are considered as an essential part of the community such as WebMD Answers and Quora. Take WebMD as an example, answers posted by experts are featured and ranked top on WebMD Answers, followed by answers posted by other types of contributors. In contrast, health consumers are able to seek support from peers as well in some other Q&A sites such as Yahoo! Answers and Quora and the answers are featured based on the total number of community votes. Choi et al. [3]

proposed a typology of online Q&A platforms consisting of four categories: community-based (such as Yahoo! Answers) Q&A, collaborative Q&A (such as WikiAnswer), expert-based Q&A or curated-based Q&A (such as WebMD Answers) and social Q&A (such as Q&A hashtags on Twitter).

Online Q&A sites provide an alternative paradigm for seeking and sharing information to search engines [21]. These type of sites not only avoid dealing with a large number of search results before getting at the desired information, but also help directly find related information in a short period of time based on the information given in questions. Additionally, the answers are given by other users with knowledge or similar experiences, which are likely to be useful and easy to understand to the information consumers [10]. One promising application of online Q&A is in health, such as health-related information seeking.

The extant studies on online Q&A in health-related topics have centered on two issues: (1) content [15, 23] (e.g., questions and answers) and (2) community dynamics [4] (e.g., information questioners, answerers, and the community in general). Information needs and consumers' behavior in online Q&A have been analyzed for various medical conditions such as HIV/AIDS [14], cancer [16], STD [13], diabetes [22] and H1N1 [7]. One major stream of research in the area of information seeking behavior is comparing and contrasting different Q&A sites. A recent study explored how the health information seeking behavior of lay persons differs from that of professionals across 5 different sites [18]. Based on an analysis of linguistic characteristics of consumers' needs (such as lexical, syntactic, and semantic information), they found that patients ask longer questions, provide background information, and ask for different types of information compared to professionals. Another study aimed to understand health consumers' usage of medical concepts by evaluating the coverage of concepts and semantic types of the Unified Medical Language System (UMLS) in two types of social media: blogs and Q&A [17]. The findings reveal that UMLS concepts appeared more frequently in social Q&A postings when compared to blog postings.

The review of related literature suggests that there is a lack of understanding of possible differences concerning health questions between community and curated online Q&A sites. In addition, they fail to understand the health consumers from the perspective of health-consumer types, information needs and the number of questions. This research aims to address the above limitations by comparing health questions across two main online questioning and answering (Q&A) platforms: community and curated Q&A sites. The comparison is performed along three main dimensions: health-consumer types, health information seeking needs, and the number of questions.

3 Methods

3.1 Q&A Sites Selection

We selected Yahoo! Answers as a community-driven Q&A site for data collection because health is one of the top-level categories in this platform. The platform was released in December 2005, becoming the third most popular internet reference site in the world and the most visited community Q&A site in the United States; 16.64% of

Yahoo! users used Yahoo! Answers [24]. There is a diversity of topics in which health consumers can participate in. For the purpose of our research, we collected 9 years' worth of data (2006 – 2015) from the site.

We chose WebMD Answers as a Curated Q&A site. As one of the most influential online health Q&A websites [2, 11], WebMD is served by professional health organizations, and American certified health experts in a broad range of specialty areas and registered site users. The site covers over 900 health topics ranging from acne to weight loss, and it also serves as a platform for people with similar health concerns and wellness interests to meet and share experiences as well as interact with certified health experts and specialists. We collected all posts starting at August 2008 from the site.

As explained in Introduction, we selected questions related to a specific disease condition of the kidney in this study. The screening of related questions was based on related search keywords or key-phrases such as *kidney, kidney infection, kidney stone, kidney cancer, kidney disease, chronic kidney disease, dialysis, kidney failure, renal artery stenosis,* and *renal cell carcinoma.* For the purpose of this study, we randomly sampled 316 questions from Yahoo! Answers across various kidney related topics by using the stratified sampling method. In addition, we randomly selected 308 questions from WebMD.

We cleaned the datasets by removing noise such as advertisements, non-human subjects (e.g., questions about the kidney problems of pets instead of humans), questions that were non-kidney related, questions related to a student's projects, and posts that did not actually state any questions. The final dataset consisted of 624 questions from the two platforms.

3.2   Dataset Description

For each question post, we collected related information such as questions titles, and descriptions, post-date, and answers. In addition, we collected some other information about the questions such as the categories where the questions posted, total number of answers and the number of votes for each answer. In this study, we only used question titles and descriptions. The descriptive statistics of datasets are reported in Table 1.

Table 1. Descriptive statistics of the Yahoo! Answers and WebMD answers datasets

Yahoo! Answers			WebMD		
Category	# Q	%Q	Category	# Q	%Q
Other diseases	218	69	Kidney	162	52.6
Diabetes	21	6.6	Kidney infection	28	9.1
Heart diseases	8	2.5	Kidney stone	72	23.8
Infectious diseases	10	3.2	Kidney cancer	10	3.24
Cancer	6	1.9	Kidney disease	24	7.8
Other health related topics	36	11.4	Renal cell carcinoma	2	0.60
General topics	17	5.8	Renal artery stenosis	10	3.24

3.3 Analysis Method

Content analysis is one of the most widely used research methods for analyzing the questions and answers in online Q&A platforms [12]. During the content analysis, questions are coded into a set of categories and these categories and frequencies are used to understand the dataset. More specifically, we used directed content analysis in which we followed predefined categories from a previous study [23].

We developed an annotation system to facilitate the analysis of questions. Two coders analyzed the questions independently. The questions are randomly assigned to two coders at a ratio of 6:4. To check the validity of the coding results, we randomly drew a sample of 20% of questions, which were then reanalyzed by a third coder independently. The inter-coder agreement of the sample set was 87.9%. We then discussed discrepancies with the coders to eliminate potential biases.

3.4 Analysis Categories

To answer the research questions, we focused on the following types of information in content analysis.

Health-Consumer Types. A health consumer may post questions about him/herself or on behalf of someone else. Accordingly, the questions were labeled as self and other, respectively. In the latter case, the health information described in the question was typically about the health consumers' family member or friend. In addition, we used non-identified as a third value to cover questions that did not have a clear indication of the role of the health consumers.

Information Seeking Needs. Health consumers ask health-related questions online to address their specific needs. The following is a list of common health information needs in asking questions in online Q&A sites, introduced in a previous study [23].

- Symptom: to gain an understanding of symptoms of a kidney or any other related disease.
- Diagnosis: to confirm the nature of certain disease.
- Causes: to figure out the causes of the disease.
- Prognoses: to inquire about the hypothetical effect of a disease.
- Treatment: to explore treatment alternatives of a kidney disease.
- Supplements and lifestyle: to explore lifestyle and diet in people with a kidney disease as well as using different supplements.
- Information sources, medical profession, and related types of information: to look for medical experts in the field and any kind of resources to fulfill health consumers' needs.
- Drug interaction: to ask for more details about unfavorable and unexpected signs, symptoms, or diseases associated with the use of a drug without any judgment about the causality or relationship to the drug use.
- Similar experiences: to connect to patients with similar conditions.

Number of Questions. The number of sub-questions per question, including the title is calculated in this study. Some questions are asked in different formats; we can only consider one question that shows the same information needs.

4   Results

To fully answer the research questions, we conducted independent sample t-test in addition to reporting descriptive statistics.

4.1   Health-Consumer Types

Table 2 shows the distributions of health-consumer types of the two selected Q&A sites. Overall, more than 60% of health consumers asked questions about themselves or others across the websites. Nevertheless, more questions were posted by family members or friends on behalf of patients on Yahoo! Answers (19.9%) than on WebMD (9.7%). On the other hand, there is a significant percentage of health consumers whose types were not identified, which accounted for 37.7% questions from Yahoo! Answer and 41.2% from WebMD, respectively.

Table 2. Distribution of health-consumer types

Types	Yahoo! Answers	WebMD
	Distribution	Distribution
Self	42.4%	49%
Other	19.9%	9.7%
Non-identified	37.7%	41.2%

4.2   Information Seeking Needs

We identified 10 types of information needs of health consumers, including diagnose, cause, treatments, supplements and lifestyle, prognoses, symptoms, information sources, drug interaction, similar experiences, and others. The descriptive statistics of the different types of information needs (in terms of percentage) is summarized in Table 3. In addition, we report the statistical test results of independent sample t-test in the last column.

Table 3. Descriptive statistics and t-test results of information seeking goals

Information needs	Yahoo! Answers		WebMD		p-value
	Mean	SD	Mean	SD	
Diagnose	0.24	0.43	0.18	0.39	0.0725'
Cause	0.19	0.39	0.19	0.39	0.958
Treatment	0.21	0.4	0.15	0.36	0.0837'
Supplements and lifestyle	0.15	0.35	0.13	0.34	0.6539
Prognoses	0.18	0.38	0.09	0.29	0.0011**
Symptom	0.15	0.36	0.08	0.27	0.0036**
Information source	0.08	0.27	0.07	0.26	0.952
Drug interaction	0.02	0.14	0.07	0.25	0.0027**
Similar experiences	0.07	0.26	0	0	1.09E-06'
Other	0.18	0.38	0.09	0.29	0.0023**

*Note: *: significant at .01, ': significant at .1*

The most common information need of using both Q&A sites was about diagnosis of a health condition (21.2%) (e.g., *"I have been researching Chronic Kidney Disease on WedMd and I've had some of the [symptoms]. Such as lots of headaches, not feel hungry, nauseated.....I've been to the doctors twice. Only one of them a urine sample was taken. ...Anyone know anything useful."*)

The next two common information needs are inquiring about causes (18.6%) and treatment (17.9%). For example, *"How does chronic kidney disease affect homeostatic mechanisms? What is the cause and what is the effect on homeostatic mechanisms?"* *"What is pentoxifylline? [Can] this can help for chronic kidney disease?"*. Questions in the supplements and lifestyle (diet and exercise) category often asked for recommendations on diets or food should be taken to help stay healthy, or recover from a disease. For example, *"is there treatment to cure it? and also what foods to avoid."*

Prognoses is another common information need for questioning. For example, someone asked a question about his father who was recently diagnosed with CKD and had only 30% of his kidney functioning: *"how much longer will he live? how much longer till he needs dialysis//transplant?"*

For questions focusing on symptoms (11.5%) are relatively general. For example, *"Does anyone know the signs of chronic kidney disease?"* and *"How can you tell if you have chronic kidney disease[?]"*

Some health consumers visited the Q&A sites for recommendations on information sources (7.5%). Among the questions, 4.3% were motivated by understanding medication effects, such as learning about side effects (e.g., *"is there a blood pressure medicine that [I] can take that will not harm kidneys"*), comparing and contrasting medications (e.g., *"Does Renal interact with any other medications?"*), or seeking information on available medications, such as whether non-prescription options are available or learning more about medications and interaction between different medications.

Beyond these broad categories, health consumers also asked for advice and experiences from those who were experiencing similar conditions (3.7%). One example is that a health consumer shared her story about some symptoms and was not sure if the hair loss was related to kidney disease. At the end of the question, she asked, *"Does anyone know of anyone that has [experienced] hair loss [due] to a failed kidney or has experienced it themselves?"* In addition, another health consumer shared her husband's case who had recently been diagnosed with CKD stage III and she was wondering about the progression to dialysis. She emphasized at the end of her post that *"Just looking for someone with personal experience."* Another patient who was in early 30s was diagnosed with CKD. He stated, *"The doctor is saying that I am developing chronic kidney disease. Has anyone else been diagnosed with this so young? If so, what lifestyle changes have you had to do to help combat it?"*

The results of T-tests revealed some significant differences in the health information needs between the two platforms. For those needs that showed differences, most of them are more common in Yahoo! than WebMD Answers, such as symptoms, prognoses, similar experience ($p < .01$), and diagnoses and treatment ($p < .1$). The only exception was adverse drug reaction, which were more frequently asked in WebMD (M = 0.07, SD = 0.25) than Yahoo!! Answer (M = 0.02, SD = 0.14) ($p < .001$).

4.3 Number of Questions

The distributions of number questions are reported in Table 4. The data shows that the majority of questions (92.5%) posted on WebMD Answers contains only one question. In contrast, more than 40% of questions on Yahoo! Answers include multiple questions.

Table 4. Distribution of health-consumer types

# of questions	Yahoo! Answers	WebMD
1	57.9%	92.5%
2	31.1%	21.1%
3	7.2%	1.9%
>= 4	3.8%	0

5 Discussion

Q&A platforms generally provide a venue for asking a question and posting answers [12]. Accordingly, such sites represent the most natural way for a person to seek information by supporting the writing of questions fully and explicitly. This research investigates and compares health-consumer types, health information needs and number of questions across two types of online Q&A platforms. Empirical analyses of 624 heath questions collected from Yahoo! Answers and WebMD Answers reveal several important differences.

First, more questions in general were posted by family members on Yahoo! Answers than WebMD. The process of posting a question on the former platform is relatively simpler than the latter. Yahoo! Answer only requires the email address of a health consumer, whereas WebMD not only requires more information, but also encourages the health consumer to create a profile and provide more details about his/her health status.

One main difference between the community-driven and curated online Q&A platforms lies in the type of health information needs. There were more questions concerning adverse drug reactions posted on WebMD than on Yahoo! Answers. A curated site carries authoritative expertise with it, and topics like adverse drug reactions and drug-to-drug interactions are complicated, and responding to such questions requires extensive domain expertise. Although WebMD allows other health consumers to provide answers in addition to medical professionals, the responses from the latter group were given more weights and top listed. This finding has implications for discovering new adverse drug reactions from user-generated content online [1, 8, 20]. To this end, WebMD can serve as a more appropriate source than Yahoo! Answers.

In contrast, a significant percentage of questions posted on Yahoo! Answers were aimed to seek answers from peers with similar conditions, which were absent in WebMD. Community Q&A is a social interaction platforms and built based on user-generated content and the interaction among users. Yahoo! Answers is a large and diverse Q&A platform, acting not only as a medium for sharing technical knowledge, but as a place where one can seek advice, gather opinions, and satisfy health consumers' curiosity about a variety of topics [12]. They include sharing personal stories and experiences, among others, which is confirmed in our study. By the same token, the findings of this study reveal that health consumers were more likely to ask multiple questions at Yahoo! Answers more than WebMD.

Design Implications
The themes emerging from our findings have implications for improving online Q&A sites.

It is important for Q&A sites to support social interaction for effective communication of medical conditions. Our results reveal that family members were active in seeking health information on behalf of patients on Yahoo! Answers. The literature has shown that many people with chronic and unstable conditions co-manage or delegate health management activities to others [19]. However, family members and close friends are often not aware of patients' specific health conditions, treatment recommendations, or care goals, and consequently may not know how to best support lifestyle and medication treatment regimen adherence or decision-making preferences [6]. Therefore, providing support for social interaction would help improve the accuracy and completeness of information described in question posts on these Q&A sites. In addition, extending online Q&A platforms to include family members and friends can facilitate more proactive and impactful involvement of family members in patients' healthcare self-management.

It is worth noting that many health consumers value peers' personal experience and specifically sought for people whom they can talk to. Online Q&A has emerged as a popular and effective paradigm for meeting a wide range of information needs [12]. There is an enormous amount of knowledge and expertise shared in online Q&A sites. As the number of questions posted about looking for similar patients in online Q&A sites increases, routing these questions to anyone who share similar experiences is another way of direction. This is expected to contribute to improved efficiency, engagement, and survivability of online Q&A community. In addition, identifying "authoritative" users and promoting their posts would help better meet the health information needs of other users. Further, online recommendation techniques can be adapted to suggest other related questions and responses to a user's question post in online Q&A sites.

Future Directions
Like all other studies on online information seeking behavior, this study has some limitations. First, we collected data from two online Q&A sites only, and thus the findings may not be generalizable to other online health Q&A platforms. This study can be extended by examining questions about different type of diseases and from other types of platforms. Second, despite that the analysis of question content helped gain insights into contextual characteristics of questions, other types of data from the online Q&A sites such as user activities, profiles, comments, and ratings are also valuable. An integration of data from the various dimensions will help gain a fuller understanding of user behavior in online Q&A communities.

6   Conclusion

Through analyzing questions collected from community Q&A and curated Q&A sites, this study identified both of their similarities and differences in term of health-consumer type, information seeking needs and the number of questions. The findings have implications for the design of online Q&A websites and for effective use of such platforms to meet patients' health information needs.

References

1. Benton, A., Ungar, L., Hill, S., et al.: Identifying potential adverse effects using the web: a new approach to medical hypothesis generation. J. Biomed. Inf. **44**(6), 989–996 (2011)
2. Bramall, A.N., Bernstein, M.: Improving information provision for neurosurgical patients: a qualitative study. Can. J. Neurol. Sci./Journal Canadien des Sciences Neurologiques **41**(01), 66–73 (2014)
3. Choi, E., Kitzie, V., Shah, C.: Developing a typology of online Q&A models and recommending the right model for each question type. Proc. ASIST Ann. Meeting **49**, 1 (2012)
4. Choi, E., Scott, C.R.: Effects of user identity information on key answer outcomes in social Q&A. In: iConference, pp. 302–315 (2013)
5. Susannah Fox. The social life of health information (2014). http://www.pewresearch.org/fact-tank/2014/01/15/the-social-life-of-health-information/
6. Kernisan, L.P., Sudore, R.L., Knight, S.J.: Information-seeking at a caregiving website: a qualitative analysis. J. Med. Internet Res. **12**, 3 (2010)
7. Kim, S., Pinkerton, T., Ganesh, N.: Assessment of H1N1 questions and answers posted on the web. Am. J. Infect. Control **40**(3), 211–217 (2012)
8. Lardon, J., Abdellaoui, R., Bellet, F., et al.: Adverse drug reaction identification and extraction in social media: a scoping review. J. Med. Internet Res. **17**(7), e171–e171 (2015)
9. Liu, Q., Agichtein, E., Dror, G., Maarek, Y., Szpektor, I.: When web search fails, searchers become askers. In: Proceedings of the 35th International ACM SIGIR Conference on Research and Development in Information Retrieval - SIGIR 2012, p. 801 (2012)

10. Molino, P., Aiello, L.M., Lops, P.: Social question answering: textual, user, and network features for best answer prediction. ACM Trans. Inf. Syst. **35**(1), 4–40 (2016)
11. Nowrouzi, B., Gohar, B., Nowrouzi-Kia, B., Garbaczewska, M., Brewster, K.: An examination of scope, completeness, credibility, and readability of health, medical, and nutritional information on the internet: a comparative study of wikipedia, WebMD, and the mayo clinic websites. Can. J. Diabetes **39**(2015), S71 (2015)
12. Oh, S.: Social Q&A. In: Social Information Access, pp. 75–107 (2018)
13. Oh, S., Park, M.S.: Text Mining as a Method of Analyzing Health Questions in Social Q & A, pp. 1–4 (2013)
14. Oh, S., Park, M.S.: HIV/AIDS Question Analysis with Text Mining : Using Concept Maps for Data Analysis and Interpretation Results & Discussion (2014)
15. Sanghee, O., Worrall, A.: Health answer quality evaluation by librarians, nurses, and users in social Q&A. Libr. Inf. Sci. Res. **35**(4), 288–298 (2013)
16. Sanghee, O., Zhang, Y., Park, M.S.: Cancer information seeking in social question and answer services: identifying health-related topics in cancer questions on Yahoo!! answers. Inf. Res. Int. Electron. J. **21**, 3 (2016)
17. Park, M.S., He, Z., Chen, Z., Sanghee, O., Bian, J.: Consumers' use of UMLS concepts on social media: diabetes-related textual data analysis in blog and social Q&A sites. JMIR Med. Inf. **4**(4), e41 (2016)
18. Roberts, K., Demner-Fushman, D.: Interactive use of online health resources: a comparison of consumer and professional questions. J. Am. Med. Inf. Assoc. **23**(4), 802–811 (2016)
19. Ann-Marie Rosland, M.P.A., Michele Heisler, M.D., Janevic, M.R., et al.: NIH public access. Fam. Syst. Health **31**(2), 119–131 (2013)
20. Sarker, A., Ginn, R., Nikfarjam, A., et al.: Utilizing social media data for pharmacovigilance: a review. J. Biomed. Inf. **54**, 202–212 (2015)
21. Shah, C., Oh, S., Oh, J.S.: Research agenda for social Q&A. Libr. Inf. Sci. Res. **31**(4), 205–209 (2009)
22. Zhang, J., Zhao, Y., Dimitroff, A.: A study on health care consumers' diabetes term usage across identified categories. Aslib J. Inf. Manage. **66**(4), 443–463 (2014)
23. Zhang, Y.: Contextualizing consumer health information searching: an analysis of questions in a social Q&A community. In: Proceedings of the 1st ACM International Health, pp. 210–219 (2010)
24. The top 500 sites on the web. https://www.alexa.com/topsites/category/Top/Reference. Accessed 20 Sept 2018

Dr. Google, Please Help Me Understand!

The Quality of Health Information Found Through Web Searches

Lisa Beutelspacher[(✉)]

Department of Information Science, Heinrich Heine University Düsseldorf,
Düsseldorf, Germany
Lisa.Beutelspacher@hhu.de

Abstract. Many patients have a very high need for information about their health conditions even after doctor consultation. As a result, more and more patients are looking for reliable information on the Internet. But how qualitative are health information found online?

This study examines the quality of 49 German websites on health conditions in the field of otolaryngology. The results showed that there is certainly a need for improvement in medical quality, especially with regard to the completeness of the information. The correctness of the information, in general, can be judged as good. However, many sites do not contain references and further information. Consumer health portals scored particularly well while advertising sites performed worst in almost all categories. The readability of the pages is at an average level.

Keywords: Online health information · Quality indicators ·
Information quality · Assessing health information

1 Introduction

The Internet is the largest source of health information for patients. Due to the simple and fast handling more and more users turn to search engines to inform themselves about diseases, their symptoms, treatment possibilities or risks. 77% of online health seekers begin their search at a search engine such as Google [1] and in 2015 5% of all Google searches were health-related [2].

There are different reasons why consumers would choose web search engines as a source for health information: to prepare for a doctor's appointment, to clarify open questions afterward, to make a self-diagnosis or to learn about a health condition in general [3].

This movement is expected to lead to better-informed patients, who have the ability to make wiser treatment decisions. Nevertheless, there are concerns about the quality of health information online [4]. This is mainly due to the huge amount of information available and the fact that anyone can publish and edit information on the web. It is feared that information from the web may be overwhelming and that users who are not

© Springer Nature Switzerland AG 2019
G. Meiselwitz (Ed.): HCII 2019, LNCS 11579, pp. 90–107, 2019.
https://doi.org/10.1007/978-3-030-21905-5_8

medically trained will not be able to distinguish between correct and incorrect information.

The aim of the present study is to give an overview of the quality of the websites that users find through Google after a diagnosis has been made by a medical professional.

1.1 Assessing Online Health Information

Since publishing information on the web is easy for anyone to do, it is essential to take a close look at the quality of online health information. Many studies have been dealing with this topic for years and some gave an overview of evaluation methods for health information on- and offline (e.g., [4–6]). A strong focus here is on the identification and investigation of appropriate quality criteria and indicators.

2002 Eysenbach et al. [4] divided the indicators from 79 different studies into five categories: Accuracy, Completeness, Technical Criteria (e.g., authorship, currency, or disclosure), Readability, and Design. Accuracy and completeness aim at the actual content of the websites whereas technical criteria, readability and design are formal criteria referring to the presentation or the metadata of the websites. Zhang, Sum and Xie [5] also recognized various criteria and divided them into content and design. Frequently, both the design and the content are evaluated using pre-defined lists of criteria taken from medical guidelines or other scientific literature.

Various organizations are also concerned with how the quality of health information can be tested. For this purpose, various quality seals have been developed in recent years to enable users to find high-quality health information. They either rely on the voluntary observance of a code of conduct (e.g., Health on the Net Foundation [7]) or have the websites tested by experts (e.g., MedCertain [8]). For some initiatives, a fee must be paid in order to achieve the seal after successful testing (e.g., Afgis [9], Medisuch [10]).

Zhang et al. [5] identified a variety of tools that were used to assess the quality of health information both on- and offline. In scientific practice, the JAMA benchmarks, the HONcode, and the DISCERN Instrument are most frequently used [5].

The JAMA Benchmarks were created in 1997 by Silberg, Lundberg, and Musacchio [11]. They developed four core standards to make the quality of health information on the Internet assessable: Authorship, Attribution, Disclosure, and Currency. The HONcode is a code of ethics that guides publishers and authors on how to provide high-quality medical information [12]. These two instruments focus only on formal criteria like currency or credibility. The DISCERN Instrument can additionally be used to evaluate the content [13]. However, only the treatment choices are considered here.

It can be summarized that the literature search has shown that different authors examine the quality with very different criteria, indicators and instruments. Zhang et al. [5] also conclude that there is no common definition of quality in the field of health information on the web.

1.2 Aims and Research Questions

Although many patients are satisfied with the general health care, they are not always satisfied with the quality of the communication with their doctor and due to the short time available, questions remain unanswered [14]. Many patients want to know more about their disease. An average doctoral consultation in Germany takes 7.6 min [15]. So it is not surprising that after such a conversation questions about the disease itself, its symptoms, treatment options, etc. may remain open. For many patients, the quickest and easiest way to meet this need for information is an Internet search. But do patients really find qualitative information about a disease by performing a web search?

This study aims to answer five research questions (RQs):

- RQ1: What Google search results are users confronted with if they have already been diagnosed with a disease?
- RQ2: How qualitative are these websites in terms of formal and medical criteria?
- RQ3: How readable are these websites?
- RQ4: Do formal criteria indicate the medical quality of the information?
- RQ5: What are the differences between the results of the various diseases and search terms?

2 Method

A Google search was carried out to collect relevant websites. These results were evaluated according to various criteria by an information scientist and an otolaryn-gologist. The details of the website collection and the rating process and evaluation are presented below. Since web pages and their content are published information, the terms (web)page, (web)site and publication are used synonymously in the following.

2.1 Website Collection

Within the scope of the research questions, we were interested in whether different diseases lead us to expect different outcomes. Therefore, we decided to randomly select three health conditions from the field of otolaryngology, namely tonsillitis (inflam-mation of the tonsils), tinnitus (ringing in the ears), and rhonchopathy (snoring).

We know that many patients still have unanswered questions after diagnosis [14], so it is reasonable for many to turn to the Internet to find answers. These patients have already come into contact with the medical terms, so we chose the official medical name of the respective health condition as a search term. We also decided to use the appropriate German translation as a search term.

Therefore, the search terms were the medical terms and the appropriate German terms (see Table 1).

Table 1. Search terms and corresponding ICD-10 classification

Medical term	German term	ICD-10 classification
Tonsillitis	Mandelentzündung	J03.0, J03.8, J03.9, J35.0
Tinnitus	Ohrgeräusche	H93.1
Rhonchopathy	Schnarchen	R06.5

We conducted the search with Google, as this is the most used search engine in Germany [16]. It is very common among users of search engines to include only the first page of the result list in their search before the search is aborted or the search is restarted with other terms [17]. Therefore, we decided to consider only the first page of the search results list for each search term. All search results except Google Ads were taken into account when searching for web pages. After collecting the websites, all duplicates were removed for the rating process. These pages will be taken into account later during the interpretation concerning the different search terms.

The collection was conducted using the incognito mode of Google Chrome on December 18, 2018.

2.2 Rating Process

Once the pages had been collected and identified, the evaluation was conducted according to the rating catalog below. All links were made accessible in an Excel spreadsheet along with the formal and medical criteria. The evaluation using the formal indicators (e.g., disclosure of authorship, publication aims or additional support) was taken over by the author. Dr. Marbod Kohns, an ENT resident, was responsible for evaluation using the medical indicators with regard to completeness and accuracy.

The rating was performed between 27 December, 2018 and 10 January, 2019.

2.3 Evaluation Catalog

To enable the rating of the pages, an evaluation catalog was developed. This consists of a non-medical and a medical part. The indicators of the non-medical part are used to evaluate the form of the publication and its metadata. The indicators of the medical part serve to evaluate the completeness and correctness of the medical information within the publication. In the following, the non-medical and the medical criteria contained in the evaluation catalog will be described.

Non-medical Criteria. The first part of the evaluation catalog consists of six indicators which are intended to make the formal quality of the publication assessable. The focus here is not on the (medical) content, but rather on the metadata and the external form to assess the credibility and reliability of a publication. This division corresponds to the "Technical Criteria" in Eysenbach et al. [4]. The indicators have been created using various publications and quality assessment tools already mentioned in the Introduction section, but mainly the three most used assessment instruments DISCERN, HONCode and JAMA. The individual indicators are evaluated on a scale from one (lowest rating) to five (highest rating).

Disclosure of Authorship. Numerous sources mention the naming of the author as an essential quality criterion for the evaluation of information (e.g., [11, 12, 18]). It is used to evaluate the reliability of the site or the information. In the ideal case, the profession and expertise of the author are also mentioned.

Disclosure of Currency. Evidence-based patient information should include the latest developments in science and practice [18]. Therefore, this indicator should evaluate whether the creation date and the date of the last revision are identifiable. It is also found in the DISCERN instrument, in the HONcode as well as in the JAMA benchmarks. It should be noted that this is only concerned with the existence of the date, the freshness of the page itself is not evaluated here.

Publication Aims. A qualitative publication should clearly set out its objectives. It should communicate what the publication is about, what areas it covers and to whom it is addressed [13]. This information should be included both in the title and in an introduction.

References and Sources. The medical information in a publication should correspond to the current state of scientific knowledge. The sources on which the information is based must be presented on the website. All DISCERN Instrument, HONCode and JAMA benchmarks contain this indicator.

Balanced Content. To provide balanced and unbiased content is an essential indicator for a qualitative publication. The DISCERN tool advises evaluators to consider whether different treatment options are presented, different sources are used, or whether there is evidence that the publication has been independently reviewed [19]. However, the evaluator is also advised to rely on his feelings. Of course, this fact makes an objective evaluation very difficult.

Additional Support. The provision of further sources of information on a topic enables the reader to obtain more information depending on his or her information needs. These additional sources include other websites, scientific literature as well as organizations or support groups. The DISCERN instrument emphasizes that the information provided must include details such as author, publisher, address or telephone number [19].

Medical Criteria. The second part of the catalog refers to the medical content. Here different categories have been developed, which should be included in patient information (definition of the disease, causes and infection, symptoms, diagnosis, treatments, treatment-risks, and lack of evidence). These categories were taken from various guidelines for patient information [18, 20, 21]. Each of these categories was evaluated according to accuracy and completeness, also mentioned in Eysenbach et al. [4]. The evaluation was carried out on a scale from one (lowest rating) to five (highest rating).

In order to make the individual categories more assessable, the evaluation criteria for each disease were extracted from the respective medical guidelines (Tonsillitis: [22], Rhonchopathy: [23], Tinnitus: [24]). This then resulted in a checklist for each category within the diseases, which the evaluator could adhere to. This made consistent evaluation possible.

Completeness. The completeness of a website or publication is also evaluated on the basis of accepted medical guidelines. According to the study by Chen et al. [6] the completeness is the most-used indicator to assess health information quality.

Accuracy. The accuracy represents the conformance with the current state of research as contained in medical guidelines. The accuracy is only evaluated for the information actually provided. Therefore, the accuracy can be evaluated with 5 (highest score), even if the completeness is only 1 (lowest rating).

2.4 Readability

For each publication, the readability was determined using the Flesch Reading Ease Score [25]. This metric assumes that short words and short sentences are easier for readers to understand. Since the English and German languages differ in length and number of words, we used the formula adapted by Amstad in 1978 [26]. The formula calculates a value between 0 and 100, where a higher number means easier readability. Texts with values between 0 and 40 are difficult or very difficult to read, whereas texts with values between 60 and 100 are easy or very easy to read. Since whole sentences are required for the calculation, titles, list items, and link texts were not taken into account. The readability was tested using the website Schreiblabor [27].

Other characteristics such as the type of page, the intended target group or the existence of quality seals were also noted during the evaluation.

The data resulting from the evaluation were analyzed with Microsoft Excel. The author is aware that the arithmetic analysis of ordinal scales is controversial. However, since the scale is regarded here as an interval scale with equal distances between the points, it was decided to analyze the results with arithmetic methods [28]. This includes the calculation of the mean, the standard deviation and in some cases the pearson correlation.

3 Results

A total of 60 pages were found through the six search queries. After deleting all duplicates, 49 pages remained (16 each for tonsillitis and tinnitus, 17 for rhonchopathy).

3.1 Page Types and Target Groups

The largest part of the web pages has as target group patients without medical knowledge (43 of 49 pages). 17 of the examined pages are websites published by health service providers (doctors, pharmacies or clinics) as shown in Fig. 1. Ten pages are so-called consumer health portals (e.g., *Onmeda.de, Netdoktor.de,* or *Gesundheitsinformation.de*). These websites aim to make medical content understandable to users without medical knowledge. Nine websites advertise medical products or services. Six pages were written for medical professionals, e.g., encyclopedias for doctors or learning platforms for medical students. During the investigation also five non-medical pages were found. These are pages whose purpose is not the mediation of medical contents like online encyclopedias or non-medical journals. Two pages could be assigned to the category "disease-specific sites." This includes one page especially about snoring and sleep apnoea and one page published by a tinnitus self-help organization. It should be noted that among the 49 pages found, there are only two portals that offer user-generated content (Wikipedia.org and Flexikon.com)

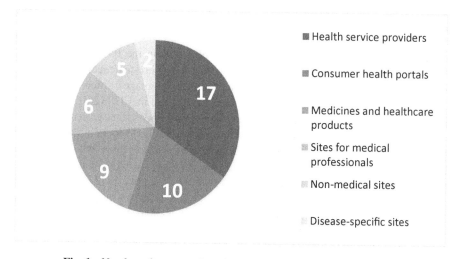

Fig. 1. Number of pages assigned to the different page types (n = 49)

Medical quality seals could be identified on 13 of the 49 pages. 7 pages even had two seals. Three different seals could be found: HONcode (eleven times), AFGIS (six times) and Medisuch (three times).

29 of the 49 pages found contained an indication that the content was not intended for self-diagnosis or self-treatment, but only to provide information. In the case of tonsillitis websites, such information was contained on 12 pages (75%), in the case of tinnitus websites on 10 pages (approx. 63%), and in the case of rhonchopathy websites on 8 pages (approx. 41%).

3.2 Non-medical Criteria

On the scale from one to five, 16 pages in the rating of all non-medical indicators received a mean score of 4 or higher. 13 pages had a rating between 3 and 3.9. 16 pages received a rating between 2 and 2.9, and 4 pages received a rating of less than 2.

The average rating of all pages examined with regard to non-medical criteria was 3.24 (Standard Deviation SD = 1.52) as shown in Table 2.

With a mean value of 4.43 (SD = 0.88), the indicator "balanced content" was given the highest rating. Here 32 of 49 pages reached a value of five. The indicator "references and sources" was rated worst with a value of 2.55 (SD = 1.64). 21 out of 49 pages had no references at all (rating of 1).

The ratings for indicator "disclosure of currency" is very mixed in the evaluation. 16 pages had no information about the timeliness of the publication or its information. On the other hand, 20 pages had complete information, i.e. the date of creation and of the last update.

For the majority of the pages (32), the rating in terms of "publication aims" is three or less. However, no page was rated with a 1. This means that for all pages at least the title indicates the content of the publication.

Table 2. Mean ratings for non-medical indicators (scale: 1-lowest rating to 5-highest rating)

	All sites	Consumer health portals	Sites for medical professionals	Non-medical sites	Health service providers	Medicines and healthcare products	Disease-specific sites
Number of pages (n)	49	10	6	5	17	9	2
Disclosure of authorship	2.96	3.70	3.17	3.20	3.06	1.89	2.00
Publication aims	3.12	3.40	3.50	3.40	2.94	3.00	2.00
References and sources	2.55	4.20	3.00	3.00	2.00	1.56	1.00
Disclosure of currency	3.33	4.20	4.67	4.80	3.06	1.67	1.00
Balanced content	4.43	5.00	4.67	4.40	4.65	3.56	3.00
Additional support	3.06	4.60	3.17	3.20	2.53	2.33	2.50
All non-medical criteria	3.24	4.18	3.69	3.67	3.04	2.33	1.92

If looking at the ratings of the individual page types, consumer health portals have the highest rating with a mean of 4.18 (SD = 1.16). The indicators "balanced content" (5.0) and "additional support" (4.6) were particularly highly rated here. The lowest rating with 1.92 (SD = 0.86) of five points for the non-medical indicators was the group of disease-specific sites. However, it should be noted that only two pages are assigned to this category.

The mean value of pages with a seal was 4.12 (SD = 1.12) and of pages without a seal 2.93 (SD = 1.52).

3.3   Medical Criteria

Completeness. On the scale of 1 to 5, 10 pages in the rating of completeness received a mean score of 4 or higher. 22 pages had a rating of between 3 and 3.9. 14 pages received a rating of between 2 and 2.9, and 3 pages received a rating of less than 2. Table 3 shows the average scores in terms of the completeness of medical information. The overall score is 3.19 (SD = 1.53). The highest rating is found in consumer health portals (3.54), the lowest in medicines and healthcare products (2.68). The most frequently available information is on the definition of disease and symptoms (4.22). 32 out of 40 pages did not contain any information on the treatment risks. Also the indication of areas for which no empirical information was available was completely missing in 31 of 41 pages. In contrast, definition and symptoms were often stated completely. In the criterion "definition" 28 pages, in the criterion "symptoms" 24 pages were rated with a 5.

Table 3. Mean ratings for completeness (scale: 1-lowest rating to 5-highest rating)

Completeness	All sites	Consumer health portals	Health service providers	Non-medical sites	Disease-specific sites	Sites for medical professionals	Medicines and healthcare products
Number of pages (n)	49	10	17	5	2	6	9
Definition	4.22	4.60	4.35	4.20	5.00	4.00	3.56
Causes and infection	3.73	4.10	3.88	3.80	4.50	3.50	3.00
Symptoms	4.22	4.50	4.53	4.00	4.50	3.67	3.78
Diagnosis	2.98	3.70	3.47	2.20	1.50	3.33	1.78
Treatments	3.65	4.00	3.76	4.00	3.50	3.17	3.22
Treatment risks	1.78	1.90	1.53	2.60	1.50	1.50	1.89
Lack of evidence	1.73	2.00	1.71	2.20	1.00	1.50	1.56
Completeness according to all medical criteria	3.19	3.54	3.32	3.29	3.07	2.95	2.68

The overall rating of completeness for pages with a quality seal is 3.49 (SD = 1.36). For pages without seal, the rating is 3.08 (SD = 1.58). For the diseases examined, the rating of completeness is as follows: Tonsillitis: 3.14; Rhonchopathy: 3.24; Tinnitus: 3.19.

Accuracy. On the scale of 1 to 5, 37 out of 49 pages in the accuracy rating received a mean score of 4 or higher. 12 pages had a rating between 3 and 3.9. No page received a rating less than 3.

Table 4 shows the average scores of all pages in terms of accuracy. If a rating of 1 was assigned in terms of completeness, i.e. no information about the specified area was contained, the correctness could not be evaluated and was not included in the calculation. The number of these pages for the respective indicator can be found in the last column of the table. The most correct information can be found on medical professionals' pages (4.55) and on disease-specific sites (4.50). Pages for medicines and healthcare products had the lowest ratings (3.95).

Table 4. Mean ratings for accuracy (scale: 1-lowest rating to 5-highest rating)

Accuracy	All sites	Sites for medical professionals	Disease-specific sites	Consumer health portals	Health service providers	Non-medical sites	Medicines and healthcare products	# Pages that do not contain these information
Number of pages (n)	49	6	2	10	15	5	9	/
Definition	4.39	4.50	5.00	4.50	4.41	4.00	4.22	0
Causes and infection	4.50	4.83	4.50	4.70	4.38	4.80	4.11	1
Symptoms	4.90	4.80	5.00	4.90	4.94	4.80	4.89	1
Diagnosis	4.19	4.60	5.00	4.44	4.21	4.00	3.00	12
Treatments	3.58	4.00	3.00	3.70	3.75	3.80	2.88	4
Treatment risks	4.71	5.00	5.00	5.00	4.80	4.67	4.00	32
Lack of evidence	4.11	4.00	N/A	4.40	3.83	4.33	4.00	31
Accuracy according to all medical criteria	4.34	4.55	4.50	4.48	4.34	4.33	3.95	/

The mean accuracy score for quality seal pages is 4.47 (SD = 0.82). For pages without the seal, the rating is 4.28 (SD = 0.93). The overall accuracy score for the various diseases examined is as follows: Tonsillitis: 4.25; Rhonchopathy: 4.40; Tinnitus: 4.37.

3.4 Readability

On the basis of the German version of the Flesch Reading Score [23] the pages were examined for their readability. Overall, the average readability of all pages was 41.88 (SD = 8.41), which is just about "Average." Two pages were rated as "easy" (see Fig. 2). The majority of the pages (32) had average readability. 12 pages had a readability value of "Demanding." Three pages were classified as "Difficult" and "Very Difficult." The most difficult pages to read are those for medical professionals (33.67). The most readable pages are those of medicines and healthcare products (45.56).

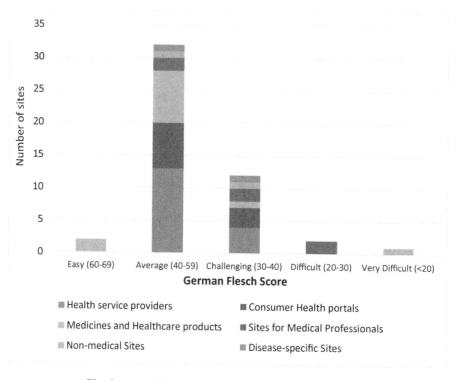

Fig. 2. Readability levels for different page types (n = 49)

On average, the most readable pages were those on Rhonchopathy (46.88) followed by those on Tinnitus (40.38) and Tonsillitis (38.06).

In addition, the readability of the pages found with German and medical search terms was compared. In the case of medical terms, more pages were rated as "Challenging" (nine pages) than in the case of German terms (six pages). The mean value of the readability of all medical pages is 39.93 and is therefore slightly more difficult to read than the pages found with German search terms (43.90).

The average readability of pages with a medical quality seal (41.54) was approximately the same as that of pages without such a seal (42.00).

3.5   Interdependencies

Table 5 shows that pages that have received a high rating within the non-medical indicators (equal to or above the mean) have higher completeness. Accuracy is also higher for these pages than for pages that are below the average. Formally highly rated pages have a higher readability score than low-rated pages.

Table 5. Medical quality and readability in relation to the ratings of non-medical indicators (scale: 1-lowest rating to 5-highest rating)

Non-medical criteria	Completeness	Accuracy	Readability
Sites above mean (>=3.19; n = 26)	3.39	4.43	43.85
Sites below mean (<3.19; n = 23)	2.96	4.19	39.65

Figure 3 shows the average completeness rating for pages with high and low ratings in the various non-medical indicators.

The largest differences can be seen in "references and sources", "disclosure of currency" and "additional support." The Pearson correlation between the non-medical indicators and completeness show values from -0.07 (disclosure of authorship) to 0.5 (additional support). In total, the Pearson correlation between all formal indicators and completeness is about 0.41.

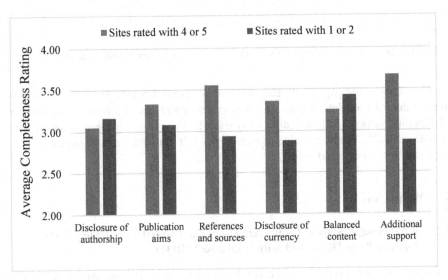

Fig. 3. Mean completeness rating of sites with high and low scores in non-medical indicators

Figure 4 shows the average rating of accuracy for pages with high and low ratings in the various non-medical indicators. Again, the biggest differences between low and high scored sites are in the areas "references and sources", and "additional support."

The Pearson correlation between the non-medical indicators and the accuracy shows values from −0.14 (Disclosure of Authorship) to 0.41 (References and sources). Overall, the correlation coefficient between all formal indicators and accuracy is about 0.32.

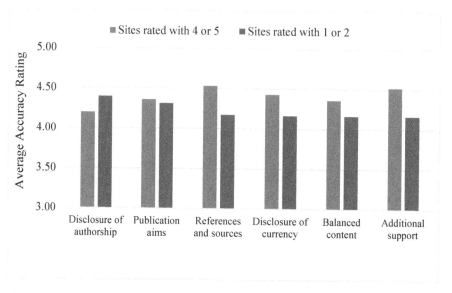

Fig. 4. Mean accuracy rating of sites with high and low scores in non-medical indicators

If looking at the pages with easy to average readability (Flesch Score >=40), the mean value of completeness is 3.15. For pages where readability was evaluated as challenging, difficult and very difficult (Flesch Score < 40), the mean value of completeness is 3.28. The mean value of accuracy is 4.26 for well readable pages and 4.45 for pages with lower readability.

4   Discussion

4.1   What Google Search Results Are Users Confronted with if They Have Already Been Diagnosed with a Disease? (RQ1)

If users search for a specific health condition on Google, they are confronted with a variety of different pages from different providers. The aim for the patient is now to filter out correct, reliable and relevant information.

Most of the websites found have patients as their target group. But also pages for medical professionals are displayed to the user if she/he wants to inform her- or himself about a disease. On some of the pages, it is not immediately apparent that the information is not intended for patients or medically uneducated individuals. This can easily lead to confusion among users.

While some pages are specialized in the communication of health information (e.g., consumer health portals), the user is also confronted with a large number of advertising pages. Approximately one-fifth of all pages have the purpose to advertise a certain medical product. But advertising can also be identified on pages that do not directly focus on a product. For example, pages from medical practices or pharmacies have been grouped under the category "health service providers." Here it may be that these providers want to advertise their medical services.

More than 30% of the pages found contained no indication that the content was suitable only for information purposes but not for self-diagnosis. In particular, pages on the subject of snoring often lacked this information. This can be due to the fact that also many physicians with Rhonchopathie (if it does not accompany a sleep apnea) there is no medical indication for treatment [23].

4.2 RQ 2: How Qualitative Are These Websites in Terms of Formal and Medical Criteria? (RQ2)

The non-medical quality of the pages, based on indicators such as disclosure of authorship or references and sources, can be described as mixed. While after calculating the average score of all formal indicators approx. 60% of the pages had a rating of 3 or higher (scale 1 to 5), many deficits in formal quality can also be identified.

Overall, the high proportion of pages that do not mention any sources of their information is particularly worrying. The user cannot obtain any further information and can therefore not evaluate whether the information provided is correct and complete. The objectivity of the publications was commonly rated as very high. However, the results of this indicator should only be interpreted with caution, as objectivity could only be assessed subjectively.

The completeness of the medical content also provides a mixed picture. Only about one-fifth of the pages was (almost) complete (rating of 4 or higher). It is particularly noticeable that especially the "treatment risks" are very rarely found on websites. 32 of 49 pages had no information about the risks of a treatment. Especially with treatments that a patient could theoretically perform himself, such as taking medication or the like, this may have serious health consequences.

Completeness as a quality criterion must, however, be relativized here. A single website is only part of the information pool from which users can make use and they usually browse different websites to meet their information needs [4].

The accuracy of the medical contents turns out to be quite positive. Approximately 75% of the pages were rated as very accurate (rating of 4 or higher). It should be noted, however, that no evaluation on the accuracy was carried out for non-existing information. Pages that contain little information could still have a very high accuracy value. One area in which the accuracy rating was lowest were information on treatments. Here also quite a lot of wrong information could be identified.

Consumer health portals have the highest formal quality. The ratings were very high, especially with regard to objectivity and the disclosure of sources and further information about a disease. The portals set themselves high quality standards and cooperate with a large number of experts. This could explain the high formal quality. The medical quality of these portals is also very high. Especially in the area of completeness, the ratings are higher than in other categories. While the formal quality of disease-specific sites is very low, the evaluation of accuracy is relatively high. Only pages for medical professionals were rated better here.

It can be clearly seen that sites advertising medical products have low formal as well as low medical quality. This observation was also made by some other studies (e.g., [29, 30]).

4.3   How Readable Are These Websites? (RQ3)

According to Eysenbach [4], many studies come to the conclusion that the readability of medical pages is much too high. This was only partially confirmed in the present study. The majority of the pages showed intermediate readability. On average, pages found using a medical search term were slightly more difficult to read than pages found using German search terms. This could be due to the higher proportion of pages for medical professionals, which has the most difficult readability. The evaluation of these results is based on the premise that the competence level of the German Flesch Scores is adapted to the actual readability of the population. But to the best of my knowledge, there is currently no empirical study on this.

4.4   Do Formal Criteria Indicate the Medical Quality of the Information? (RQ4)

Overall, it can be seen that sites that received a higher rating for non-medical indicators perform better in both completeness and accuracy than sites that received a lower formal rating. These observations lead to the conclusion that pages that are formally better presented also have better medical content so that the non-medical quality can be used as an indicator of content quality. In particular, those who provide sources for their information and offer additional assistance and support perform better both in terms of completeness and accuracy. However, this does not apply to all areas of non-medical indicators. Thus, texts whose authorship was not fully disclosed were still more complete and correct than texts in which the authors are named. As a consequence, formal quality should not be the only indicator for determining the quality of medical information.

In the present study, more readable pages received a somewhat lower rating in the completeness and accuracy of medical information. On the basis of these results, it can be concluded that texts that are more difficult to read contain more complete and correct information.

The existence of a quality seal, based on the pages examined here, only allows us to draw conclusions about the quality of a page to a limited extent. It should be noted that pages with a quality seal have a higher formal quality. Medical quality is also higher for pages with a seal, but only to a small degree. When evaluating these results, it should also be noted that these seals often require a fee for testing and evaluating the pages and awarding a seal and are therefore not easily accessible, especially for non-profit associations or private individuals.

4.5   What Are the Differences Between the Results of the Various Diseases and Search Terms? (RQ5)

No major differences could be identified between the various diseases in the assessment of the non-medical and medical indicators. If looking at the readability, it becomes clear that pages on the subject of rhonchopathy are on average easier to read than for the other two diseases. Also, pages found by medical search terms are on average more difficult to read than the pages found by German search terms.

4.6   Limitations

Some limitations of the study can be identified. The first limitation is the fact that the websites were only evaluated by one person. This is due to the high effort involved in the assessment. More evaluators would be desirable for further studies.

Although indicators for design and navigation were deliberately omitted from the evaluation catalog, these would also be interesting criteria for the quality of online health information in further studies.

Unfortunately, due to the limited number of search results, no user-generated content (like in discussion boards or social networks) could be examined.

The search terms in this paper were created by the researcher. In further studies, actual search queries from users should be included. It would also be interesting to evaluate the perception of the users in comparison to the presented results.

5   Conclusion

When users search Google for a health condition, they are confronted with a wide variety of pages. These include sites that specialize in the mediation of medical content to patients, as well as medical practice sites, pharmacy sites, medical professional sites, and sites whose primary objective is the marketing of medical products.

As the study has shown, the question of whether these results are of high quality cannot be answered with a simple yes or no. While the accuracy is quite high on all pages, many pages lack important information.

On the basis of the results, users could be recommended to inform themselves on a multitude of pages. Consumer health portals are particularly suitable here since both the formal and the medical quality is very high. Users should be cautious with sites that sell a medical product, as the medical information is much more incomplete and sometimes even incorrect.

The formal quality of pages may provide information about their medical quality. For example, users should ensure that the publication offers evidence for given information or other resources. Seals of quality can also provide information about the quality of a page. The readability of the pages can generally be described as average, even if there are major differences between the pages.

In summary, it can be said that the Google search, even it does not substitute a visit to the doctor, is quite useful for further information on a disease. However, the user has to take a critical look at the medical content.

Acknowledgments. The author is sincerely grateful to Dr. Marbod Kohns. On the one hand, for the medical expertise required for this paper, but above all for the time-consuming and labor-intensive evaluation of the pages.

References

1. Fox, S., Duggan, M.: Health Online 2013. Pew Research Center, Washington (2013)
2. Ramaswami, P.: A remedy for your health-related questions: health info in the knowledge graph. In: Google Off. Blog (2015). https://googleblog.blogspot.com/2015/02/health-info-knowledge-graph.html. Accessed 16 Dec 2019
3. Rozmovits, L., Ziebland, S.: What do patients with prostate or breast cancer want from an Internet site? a qualitative study of information needs. Patient Educ. Couns. **53**, 57–64 (2004). https://doi.org/10.1016/S0738-3991(03)00116-2
4. Eysenbach, G., Powell, J., Kuss, O., Sa, E.R.: Empirical studies assessing the quality of health information for consumers on the World Wide Web: a systematic review. J. Am. Med. Assoc. **287**, 2691–2700 (2002). https://doi.org/10.1001/jama.287.20.2691
5. Zhang, Y., Sun, Y., Xie, B.: Quality of health information for consumers on the web: a systematic review of indicators, criteria, tools, and evaluation results. J. Assoc. Inf. Sci. Technol. **66**, 2071–2084 (2015). https://doi.org/10.1002/asi.23311
6. Chen, H., Hailey, D., Wang, N., Yu, P.: A review of data quality assessment methods for public health information systems. Int. J. Environ. Res. Public Health **11**, 5170–5207 (2014). https://doi.org/10.3390/ijerph110505170
7. Health on the Net Foundation. https://www.hon.ch/
8. Eysenbach, G., Yihune, G., Lampe, K., et al.: MedCERTAIN: quality management, certification and rating of health information on the net. In: Proceedings of AMIA Symposium, pp. 230–234 (2000)
9. Aktionsforum Gesundheitsinformation. https://www.afgis.de/
10. MEDISuch. https://www.medisuch.de/
11. Silberg, W.M., Lundberg, G.D., Musacchio, R.A.: Assessing, controlling, and assuring the quality of medical information on the Internet: Caveant lector et viewor—Let the reader and viewer beware. J. Am. Med. Assoc. **277**, 1244–1245 (1997). https://doi.org/10.1001/jama.1997.03540390074039
12. Health on the Net Foundation. Operational definition of the HONcode principles (2010). https://www.hon.ch/HONcode/Guidelines/guidelines.html
13. Charnock, D., Shepperd, S., Needham, G., Gann, R.: DISCERN: an instrument for judging the quality of written consumer health information on treatment choices. J. Epidemiol. Community Health **53**, 105–111 (1999). https://doi.org/10.1136/jech.53.2.105
14. Heydebreck, K.: Das Arzt-Patienten-Gespräch im Kontext von Patientenkompetenz, Patientensouveränität und Patientenzufriedenheit. Universität Bayreuth (2010)
15. van den Brink-Muinen, A., Verhaak, P.F.M., Bensing, J.M., et al.: Communication in general practice: differences between European countries. Fam. Pract. **20**, 478–485 (2003). https://doi.org/10.1093/fampra/cmg426
16. Kuhn, J.: German search engines and what to consider when optimising for them (2018). http://blog.webcertain.com/german-search-engines-and-what-to-consider-when-optimising-for-them/05/03/2018/
17. Eysenbach, G., Köhler, C.: How do consumers search for and appraise health information on the world wide web? qualitative study using focus groups, usability tests, and in-depth interviews. BMJ **324**, 573–577 (2002). https://doi.org/10.1136/bmj.324.7337.573

18. Sänger, S., Lang, B., Klemperer, D., et al.: Manual Patienteninformation. ÄZQ Schriftenreihe, Berlin (2006)
19. Discern Online. The DISCERN Instrument (1997). http://www.discern.org.uk/discern_instrument.php
20. Gesellschaft für Versicherungswissenschaften und -gestaltung e.v. (Hrsg.) Gesundheitsinformationen in Deutschland: Eine Übersicht zu Anforderungen, Angeboten und Herausforderungen. GVG, Köln (2011)
21. Lühnen, J., Albrecht, M., Mühlhauser, I., Steckelberg, A.: Leitlinie evidenzbasierte Gesundheitsinformation. Deutsches Netzwerk Evidenzbasierte Medizin e.V., Hamburg (2017)
22. Berner, R., Steffen, G., Toepfner, N., et al.: Leitlinien: Therapie entzündlicher Erkrankungen der Gaumenmandeln–Tonsillitis. S2k-Leitlinie 017/024 (2015)
23. Stuck, B.A., Dreher, A., Heiser, C., et al.: S2 k-Leitlinie Diagnostik und Therapie des Schnarchens des Erwachsenen. AWMF Leitlinie 017/068 (2013)
24. Deutsche Gesellschaft für Hals-, Nasen-, Ohrenheilkunde KH. Chronischer Tinnitus, S3 Leitlinien. AWMF Leitlinie 017/064 (2015)
25. Flesch, R.: A new readability yardstick. J. Appl. Psychol. 32, 221–233 (1948). https://doi.org/10.1037/h0057532
26. Amstad, T.: Wie verständlich sind unsere Zeitungen? (Dissertation). Universität Zürich (1978)
27. Schreiblabor - Textanalyse. http://www.schreiblabor.com/textanalyse/
28. Sullican, G.M., Artino, A.R.: Analyzing and interpreting data from likert-type scales. J. Grad. Med. Educ. 5, 541–542 (2013). https://doi.org/10.4300/JGME-5-4-18
29. Lissman, T.L., Boehnlein, J.K.: A critical review of internet information about depression. Psychiatr. Serv. 52, 1046–1050 (2001). https://doi.org/10.1176/appi.ps.52.8.1046
30. Sacchetti, P., Zvara, P., Plante, M.K.: The internet and patient education-resources and their reliability: focus on a select urologic topic. Urology 53, 1117–1120 (1999). https://doi.org/10.1016/S0090-4295(98)00662-1

Examining Reply Bias and Effectiveness of Online Community for Suicide Prevention: A Case Study of /r/SuicideWatch

Hsiao-Ying Huang[(⊠)]

University of Illinois at Urbana-Champaign, Urbana, IL 61801, USA
hhuang65@illinois.edu

Abstract. Online community has become a new approach for suicide prevention with the rise of the Internet technology for the past decade. However,
due to the various and dynamic ecosystem of online community, its effects on
suicide prevention remain unknown. We selected SuicideWatch, a forum on
reddit as our research context and investigated users' response bias and the
effects of online response to suicide posters by linguistic analysis. Our findings
indicate two important phenomena: (1) users' responses could be biased by
linguistic cues in title and (2) online response has positive effects on suicide
posters. We believe the findings and approach proposed in this study can offer
insights for suicide prevention.

Keywords: Mental health · Social media · Computational linguistics

1 Introduction

Suicide has been a severe public health issue in the worldwide. According to the World
Health Organization [50], suicide is the fifteenth leading cause of death and is the
second leading cause of death among young people (15-29). More than 800,000 people
are the victim of suicide and many people who have suicide attempt every day.
Although national efforts have been made for reducing suicide risk, the evidence for
effective suicide intervention is still limited in both clinical and school context [38].
A comprehensive strategy for suicide prevention is urgently needed.

However, the rapid growth of Internet technology makes suicide issue even more
complicated. The increasing use of the Internet may have either positive or negative
influences on users, especially for vulnerable individuals [10]. Several studies indicated
that online users could search for information for suicide methods [1, 9, 15, 16, 32],
look for suicide pacts [52], or broadcast their suicide [5]. On the other hand, online
communities function as support groups and bring the positive effect to individuals
with suicidal thoughts or attempts [3, 17–19, 24, 49]. Moreover, the anonymity
afforded by online forums makes suicidal individuals more open to disclose personal
feelings and experiences [10, 49]. Online forum becomes a new venue for suicide
prevention.

While previous studies addressed a range of benefits for using an online forum as a
tool for suicide intervention, its effect on users remains unknown. The variety and

G. Meiselwitz (Ed.): HCII 2019, LNCS 11579, pp. 108–123, 2019.
https://doi.org/10.1007/978-3-030-21905-5_9

anonymity of online forum make it even more difficult to assess the influence of online responses on individuals, such as the level of distress alleviation and emotional state [10, 38]. In addition, unlike the traditional telephonic communication provides immediate conversation, an online forum is usually asynchronous discussion. Then, will individuals receive different levels of attention when posting to the online forum?

In this study, we focus on a forum on Reddit called "SuicideWatch" as our research context. SuicideWatch (SW) is described as an online version of telephone crisis hotlines [23], which is also the biggest community (40,419 subscribers) among suicide-related forums on Reddit. Users on SuicideWatch may post their suicidal thoughts or scroll through others' posts and comments and either "upvote" or "downvote" them. In the light of text-based content of the forum, we employ linguistic analysis as a research approach, which has been broadly adopted in suicide-related research [12, 34, 35].

The first aim of this study is to investigate whether users have response bias by the language used in posts. We examined the association between linguistic cues and the number of upvotes and comments. Then, based on previous studies, we proposed four indicators: affective distress, cognitive thinking, social awareness, and interpersonal focus to assess the effect of online responses on posters by comparing their posts before and after receiving others' comments. Our research questions are addressed as follows:

- *RQ1: What type of linguistic cues of the original post may influence users' response to the post?*
- *RQ2: What is the effect of online response on posters?*

The rest of this paper is organized as follows: in Related Work, we review the relevant literature pertaining to suicide, online community and linguistic analysis. In Methodology, we present our research procedure and measurements. We then present our results for two research questions and discuss our findings and its implications and limitations. We conclude and summarize the contributions of this study.

2 Related Work

2.1 Suicide Prevention and Community in Online Forum

Online forums are a type of community where users participate via personal narratives and collective discussions [10]. For individuals with suicidal ideations, an online forum is a space to develop connections with others, seek empathy and support, and share feelings and experiences with people similar problems without being judged [3, 19, 41, 45, 49]. However, there was no consensus on whether supports from online forums enhance suicide preventions or not [26].

Several studies have found that participation in the online forum increase positive behaviors, such as seeing medical professionals for help, reciprocal helping among users, and alleviate psychological distress [2, 19, 31, 45]. However, other studies found that online forums become a source for sharing suicide method, finding suicidal companies and increasing hopelessness that may result in suicide contagion [4, 11, 13, 27, 52].

Even though the influence of online forum on suicide prevention remains unclear, researchers found that the majority of online responses to suicidal posts show caring, empathy or called for help [14]. Gilat, Tobin, and Shahar [17, 18] further found that trained volunteers and lay individuals exhibited different strategies to offer supports. Volunteers used more technique and responded with more strategies of empowerment, interpretation and cognitive change, which were rarely used by lay individuals. On the other hand, lay individuals used more emotional supports by disclosing personal experiences in their responses.

These studies provide different insights into suicide prevention and online forum, including its positive and negative effects, and language strategies adopted by users. However, online forum, unlike traditional telephone crisis line, provides immediate responses, mainly operates in an asynchronous way. Then, is there any potential bias that may exist to influence users' responses to suicidal posters? Our first question is to investigate what type of linguistic cues shown in a suicidal post may influence users' behaviors, including voting and comment.

2.2 Suicide and Linguistic Cues

Previous studies have investigated the association between linguistic styles and suicide. Because of the difficulties of obtaining information from suicidal individuals, most previous research uses poetry or publicly available suicide notes as the source of content for analysis [28, 42]. Stirman and Pennebaker [46] employed a popular and validated psycholinguistic lexicon LIWC to analyze the different linguistic constructs expressed in poems by suicidal poets. They found that the suicidal poets exhibited more self-reference, more death-oriented and sexual words in their writing when compared to non-suicidal poets. Other studies also found that suicidal poems showed more expressive writing [43], cognitive discordance [47] and less positive emotions and the reference to the self and others over time [29]. In the suicide note, an early work found the language used in the note tends to be short, simple and more repetitious [33]. Later research further found that the emotion exhibited in the suicide notes becomes more positive over time [35]. The suicide notes from completed suicides used more future tense verbs, social references to others, and showed more positive emotions than attempted suicides [20].

Our second question is to assess if the online response has positive impacts on individuals with suicidal thought. However, linguistic cue of suicide is dynamic and various by contexts. There is no absolute standard to evaluate the language use of suicidal individuals. The most relevant work to ours is by Kumar et al. [28]. They examined the Werther effect of a celebrity-suicide event on Reddit's forum SuicideWatch by measuring four attributes: affective, cognitive, linguistic style and social attribute. They found that suicidal posts on Reddit became more inward focused, less social concerns and more negative emotions after a celebrity-suicide event. Inspired by their study, we adopt their four concepts but define and measure in different ways based on the literature of psychology.

Literature in psychology indicates that mental disorders, cognitive vulnerability, family conflict, social isolation, and hopelessness are risk factors of suicide [6, 8, 25, 36, 44]. According to Interpersonal Theory [48], suicide is a consequence of thwarted belongingness and perceived burdensome. Thwarted belongingness results from the lake of reciprocal care and loneliness; perceived burdensome comes from self-hate and liability. Interpersonal Theory suggests suicide prevention to decrease thwarted belongingness and perceived burdensome by maintaining social connections of individuals with suicidal ideation. Based on this theory, we consider online response as a way of providing connections and support of individuals who are going through suicide crisis. Then, their thwarted belongingness and perceived burdensome will decrease after supports. We assess these two psychological aspects by four linguistic indicators adopted from Kumar et al. [38], including affective distress (perceived burdensome), cognitive thinking (perceived burdensome), social awareness (thwarted belongingness) and interpersonal focus (thwarted belongingness).

Affective Distress. Affective distress has been considered as a risk factor for suicide evaluation especially for young people [7, 51]. Affective distress includes anger, anxiety, hopelessness, loneliness and so forth [21, 40, 48]. The intensity of affective distress is a signal of suicide crisis for depressed individuals [22, 30]. We hypothesize that individuals' affective distress decreases after receiving supports.

H1: Linguistic cues of affective distress decrease in original posters' comments.

Cognitive Thinking. Suicidal behavior is the manifestation of a cognitive evaluation that the pain of choosing suicide is bearable [48]. The cognitive vulnerability makes individuals difficult to redirect their thoughts and be trapped in a ruminative cycle of negative perception [44]. We assume that individuals' cognitive thinking will increase when having others' supports. Meanwhile, we expect the thought of death and self-denials will decrease as well. Therefore, there are positive and negative cognitive thinking. We hypothesize that positive cognitive thinking increases, and negative thinking decreases.

H2a: Linguistic cues of positive cognitive thinking increases in original posters' comments
H2b: Linguistic cues of negative cognitive thinking decreases in original posters' comments

Social Awareness. Social isolation and family conflict have critical effects on individuals' suicidal ideation and behavior [8, 25, 48]. We expect that individuals' awareness of social isolation and family conflict will decrease after having supports. Thus, we hypothesize that individuals express more agreement and focus less on family-related issues.

H3a: Linguistic cues of agreement increase in original posters' comments.
H3b: Linguistic cues of family-related concepts decrease in original posters' comments.

Interpersonal Focus. Previous studies point out that the frequent use of first-person pronouns by suicidal individuals indicates a higher self-focus tendency and lower social integration of suicidal individuals [35, 39]. When interacting with online responders, individuals' focus may be shifted from the self to others, which facilitate their sense of reciprocal care. We hypothesize that their self-focus decreases and interpersonal focus increases.

H4a: Linguistic cues of self-reference (1st personal singular pronouns) decrease in original posters' comments.
H4b: Linguistic cues of social references increase in original posters' comments.

3   Methodology

3.1   Data Collection and Procedure

We use Reddit's official API to collect posts, comments and relevant metadata from the subreddit "SuicideWatch". The crawl of this subreddit in this study is employed from November 22 to 23 in 2015. The procedure of data collection includes three aspects: the original post, comment, and users. For the original post, we collect the title and content of post, username, posting date, number of comment and number of upvote and downvote. For each post, we record if original posters leave comments to their posts and document the first comment arrival time. For comment, we collected the content of comments, username, date, number of upvote and downvote. We further distinguish whether the comment was from the original poster and whether a comment was the first response to the original post. We then divide users into two categories: the poster who post initially and supporter who left comments to the poster. After completing data collection, the researcher scrutinized the data and deleted two posts generated by the board manager and its relevant comments. The details of data are exhibited in Table 1.

3.2   Measurement

We use psycholinguistic lexicon LIWC, including 90 variables, to examine the language used in the posts and comments. According to the purpose of research questions, we adopt different measurements for each of them. Our first question is to explore what type of language cue could influence readers' responses. We select word count, four summary language variables (analytical thinking, clout, authenticity, emotional tone), eight standard linguistic dimensions, 41-word categories of psychological processes, 6 personal concern categories, and 5 informal language markers as our measurements. Total 65 variables are examined in this study.

According to the aforementioned literature, we propose four indicators to measure the effect of online response on posters. These indicators are (1) affective distress, (2) cognitive thinking, (3) social awareness and (4) interpersonal focus. Affective distress consists of four measures: sad, anger, anxiety and swear words. Cognitive thinking includes six measures: insight, causation, certainty, health, death, and negations. Social awareness has five measures: affiliation, assent, family, friend, and home. Interpersonal focus includes five measures: first person singular, first person plural, second person, third person singular, and third person plural pronouns. These measurements are computed by LIWC.

Table 1. General information about /r/SuicideWatch dataset

Timeframe of post	November 04–22, 2015
Total post	977
Post with posters' comment(s)	523 (53.5%)
Post without posters' comment(s)	454 (46.5%)
Total comment	4990
First comment by original poster	20 (0.4%)
Not first comment by original poster	1633 (32.7%)
First comment by supporter	902 (18.1%)
Not first comment by supporter	2485 (48.8%)
Unique users	1647
Poster	893
Supporter	754
Average daily original post	51.42
Average comment	7.47 (SD = 5.36)
Average upvote	4.89 (SD = 6.57)
Average downvote	0
First comment arrival interval	1.94 h (SD = 4.63)

4   Results

4.1   Influence of Linguistic Cue on Supporters' Response Behavior

We conducted correlational analysis to explore which type of language used in titles and comments has influences on supporters' upvoting and comment behaviors. Downvote behavior is excluded because no posts received downvote.

Influence of Post Title on Supporters' Behavior of Upvote and Comment. According to Table 2, we found 15 variables are significantly correlated with the number of upvote. All variables have a positive correlation with the number of upvote, except emotional tone, positive emotion, and cognitive process. This means that titles displaying a more positive tone, positive emotion, and cognitive process have fewer upvotes. Additionally, the results show that the number of comments has a significant positive correlation with five types of linguistic cues, including word count, anger, relativity, time, home and assent. In another word, the title with more words and exhibiting more relevance to anger, relativity, time, home and assent, received more comments.

Table 2. Correlational analysis of linguistic cues. P-value is included if it is smaller than .05.

	Title (N = 977)		Content (N = 977)	
	Number of upvote	Number of comment	Number of upvote	Number of comment
Word count	.065, $p = .043$	.073, $p = .022$	−.031	−.042
Emotional tone	−.095, $p = .003$	.043	.044	.042
Personal pronouns	.075, $p = .019$	.020	.013	−.014
She/He	.117, $p = .000$	−.018	.061	−.055
Positive emotion	−.076, $p = .018$	−.006	.016	.021
Negative emotion	.072, $p = .024$	−.023	−.036	−.027
Anger	.137, $p = .000$	.072, $p = .024$	.002	−.005
Family	.108, $p = .001$	−.003	.017	.009
Male	.169, $p = .000$	.037	.059	−.015
Cognitive processes	−.076, $p = .018$	−.028	−.064, $p = .045$	−.034
Perceptual processes	−.026	−.038	−.022	−.078, $p = .015$
Feel	−.033	−.052	−.031	−.066, $p = .041$
Body	.063, $p = .048$	.007	−.021	−.002
Sexual	.063, $p = .048$	.022	.013	.012
Reward	−.038	.024	−.003	.085, $p = .008$
Relativity	.048	.071, $p = .027$	.012	−.059
Time	.097, $p = .002$	.085, $p = .008$	−.008	−.064, $p = .044$
Home	.001	.139, $p = .000$	.076, $p = .018$	.028
Death	.091, $p = .004$	.036	−.011	−.016
Swear word	.063, $p = .048$	.037	.038	.006
Assent	.012	.086, $p = .007$	−.001	.014

Influence of Content on Behavior of Upvote and Comment. Compared to the title, only two linguistic variables of content significantly correlate with the number of upvote. The results show that cognitive process has a negative correlation and conversely home as personal concern has a positive correlation with upvote. Also, we found that *perceptual processes, feel and time* have a significant negative correlation with comments. On the other hand, the *reward* has a positive correlation with comments. The correlational analysis indicates that the linguistic cue in the title of the post has more significant influences on supporters' upvote and comments than the content.

Furthermore, we also want to know if the linguistic cues in the title have predictable influences on upvoting and comment behaviors by conducting multiple regression analysis. To determine the best predictive model, we use a backward elimination approach, which starts with all variables in the model and eliminates the variable with the largest p-value of F-test greater than the criterion of 0.10. Then the model is refitted and repeats the process until all remaining variables have p-value smaller than the criterion.

The regression model for the behavior of upvote suggests that 11 predictors explained 9.1% of the variance ($R^2 = .091$, $F(11,965) = 8.734$, $p < .000$). As exhibited in Table 3, the language of *shehe, anger, family, body, space, time and death* have positive regression weight, indicating that the title using more words pertain to these linguistic cues would have more upvote. Interestingly, the title using more words with *female references and relativity (e.g., area, bend, exit)* would have less upvote. The cue of time is the most influential predictor on upvote followed by *shehe and female references*.

The regression model for commenting behaviors has 11 predictors explaining 5.9% of the variance ($R^2 = .059$, $F(11,965) = 5.473$, $p < .000$). The results found that social processes, time, home and assent have significant positive regression weights, implying that the title with more these linguistic cues would have more comments. The *affiliation (e.g., ally, friend, social)* has significant negative regression weights, meaning that the title with more affiliation cue would receive fewer comments. Also, the linguistic cue of 'home' has the most important prediction on comment followed by *social processes and affiliation*.

Table 3. Multiple regression model of linguistic cues in title of suicidal posts on reddit.

Variable	Standardized Beta	p-value (sig. <.05)
Dependent variable: number of upvote		
Shehe	.216	**.000**
Anger	.124	**.000**
Family	.089	**.025**
Female references	−.174	**.001**
Male references	.079	.057
Body	.074	**.017**
Relativity	−.147	**.046**
Space	.107	**.043**
Time	.219	**.000**
Money	.060	.051
Death	.070	**.027**
Dependent variable: number of comment		
WC	.055	.085
Analytic	.063	.066
Clout	−.082	.064
Social processes	.156	**.004**
Family	−.072	.061
Male	.066	.079
Affiliation	−.117	**.009**
Time	.087	**.006**
Home	.157	**.000**
Money	.060	.056
Assent	.084	**.007**

4.2   Effects of Supporters' Response on Posters with Suicidal Thoughts

Our second question is to investigate the effects of online response on posters by examining language use in their comments and posts. We selected posts with posters' comments and conduct Welch t-test to compare their language use in the content of post and comments. Considering the purpose of this question is to know the effect of others' supports, we exclude the first comments left by posters because these comments were not influenced by other comments.

Affective Distress. Affective distress has been addressed as an important antecedent for suicide [37, 42, 51]. Our first hypothesis is that posters' affective distress will reduce after receiving others' comments. As shown in Table 4, the results show that the use of anxiety, anger, sadness and swear words in comments is less than posts, implying that posters' affective distress decrease after receiving others' comments. The first hypothesis is supported.

Table 4. Comparison of linguistic cues in comment and content of post by original posters.

Indicator	Comment	Post (Content)	t-test	p-value (sig. <.05)
Affective				
Anxiety	0.41	0.65	−3.84	<.000
Anger	0.83	1.25	−5.50	<.000
Sad	0.96	1.35	−4.46	<.000
Swear words	0.41	0.53	−2.36	.018
Cognitive thinking				
Insight	3.29	3.04	1.89	.082
Causation	1.70	1.74	−0.33	.739
Certainty	1.73	2.10	−3.48	.001
Health	1.28	1.74	−3.77	<.000
Death	0.46	0.87	−4.36	<.000
Negations	4.10	3.38	3.71	<.000
Social awareness				
Affiliation	1.65	1.77	−0.98	.323
Assent	0.84	0.16	4.43	<.000
Family	0.38	0.61	−4.51	<.000
Home	0.29	0.43	−3.36	<.000
Interpersonal focus				
1st person singular (I)	10.95	12.40	−5.87	<.000
1st person plural (We)	0.21	0.20	0.22	.825
2nd person singular (You)	2.52	0.42	12.46	<.000
3rd person singular (She/He)	0.88	1.08	−1.76	.079
3rd person plural (They)	0.64	0.52	1.96	.051

Cognitive Thinking. We hypothesize that online responses increase posters' positive cognitive thinking and decrease negative thinking. For positive cognitive thinking, we found no difference for the use of insight and causation. The uses of certainty and health are significantly lower in the comments, which rejects our hypothesis of positive thinking. For negative cognitive thinking, the use of death significantly decreases. Conversely, the word of negations increases in comments.

Social Awareness. Social isolation and family conflict are two main factors of suicide [48]. The online response may decrease the sense of social isolation and family conflict. We assume that posters' awareness of affiliation and assent will increase after receiving comments from others. On the other hand, their use of family-relevant words will decrease because the awareness of family conflict is shifted.

We found that posters show no difference on the use of affiliation words, but the use of assent word significantly increases in the comment. The use of family and home words significantly decrease in comments, which supports our hypothesis.

Interpersonal Focus. Our assumption for interpersonal focus is that posters would decrease their use of 'I' word and increase the use of other pronouns, including 'we', 'you', 'she/he' and 'they' after receiving others' comments. The results demonstrate that the use of 'I' word is significantly lower and the use of 'you' word is higher in comments. The use of 'she/he' and 'they' word has no difference between comments and posts. The increasing use of 'you' word by posters may suggest their interaction with supporters.

5   Discussion

This study investigated the response bias and effects of response on posters on a Reddit forum, SuicideWatch, by examining linguistic cues in original posts and comments. According to the findings, certain types of linguistic cue could bias users upvoting and commenting behaviors to the post. For the effects of online responses on suicide posters, we proposed four indicators to assess including affective distress, cognitive thinking, social awareness, and interpersonal focus. The results show that online supporters; responses have certain positive effects on posters with suicidal thoughts. We discuss these results in the following paragraph.

5.1   Response Bias by Linguistic Cues in Title

The results reveal that more linguistic cues in title show significant correlation with the number of upvotes and comments than cues in content, which indirectly suggests that title, as the first "impression," will influence users' responses more than the content. Linguistic cues in the title can be classified into five categories: length, threat, emotion, relationship, and rationality (see Table 5).

For length, the longer the title is, the more supporters upvote and comment. A possible explanation is that the longer title provides more information to supporters, so they have more understandings about the situation of the poster. With the confidence of understandings, supporters are more willing to respond. Considering the context of suicide, online supporters are also more aware of the title with threat signals, such as body (e.g., wrists, head, throat), sexual (e.g., pregnant, rape), and time (e.g., end, birthday, forever). Threat signals inform users that posters may be suffering from suicide thought with immediate danger, which urges them to respond.

Table 5. Category of linguistic cues in title

Category of signal	Cue
Length	Word Count (+)
Threat	Body (+), Sexual words (+), Time (+)
Emotion	Emotional tone (–), Positive emotions (–), Negative emotions (+), Anger (+), Swear word (+)
Relationship	Personal pronouns (+), She/He (+), Family (+), Home (+), Male references (+), Relativity (+)
Rationality	Cognitive process (–)

Supporters also tend to respond to the title with more negative and anger emotions, suggesting that emotion is an essential signal for users to decide whether the poster needs help. This also indicates that emotions may represent the impulsive action to users that strong negative emotions signal a high risk of suicide [48]. In addition, social isolation and family conflict also signal the danger of individuals' suicidal ideation and behavior [8, 25, 48]. Our findings show that more supporters respond to the title with relational cues, such as family (e.g., parents, brother), home (e.g., apartment, home), and male references (e.g., husband, boyfriend). Since the relationship is a common topic, users may feel more familiar with relationship issues and have more empathy.

The linguistic cues of the cognitive process exhibit rational thinking of an individual. With a comparison of emotions, users have fewer responses to the title with more rationality, implying that users may have a stereotype that a more rational individual also act more rationally. The rationality displaying in title sends a signal that the poster is not in the danger. According to multiple regression analysis, we want to particularly point out that the cues of time and home in the title are two important signals that can predict users' responses to the post.

5.2 Effects of Supporters' Response on Posters with Suicidal Thoughts

Since the influences of online community on suicide prevention are unclear, this study investigated the effect of users' response on posters by comparing four indicators of linguistic cues in their original posts and comments, including affective distress, cognitive thinking, social awareness, and interpersonal focus. Table 6 exhibit the overview of results and differences in posts and comments respectively.

Affective Distress. The findings show that posters' linguistic cues of affective distress decrease in their comments, indicating that posters' affective distress may be alleviated by others' responses.

Cognitive Thinking. For cognitive thinking, positive cues do not increase but decrease significantly, such as certainty and health. However, there is no sufficient information to evaluate if supporters' responses have positive or negative impacts on posters due to the ambiguous meaning of cognitive cues. For example, we did not know what posters have lower certainty about. If they have negative thoughts in their posts, then they may have less certainty about their negative thoughts in their posts, which is a positive sign. This may suggest that certainty is a counter signal that requires more investigation.

Moreover, the cues of death decrease, implying that posters' suicide thoughts may decrease after having others' responses. Yet, it is worth noting that the use of negations increases in their comments, demonstrating a denial thinking process still happens while replying to other responses.

Social Awareness. Based on the Interpersonal Theory [48], we assume that suicide posters will increase their agreements as interacting with others. Our findings show that the linguistic cues of assent did increase in their replying comments; yet, the affiliation cue did not significantly increase. These findings further suggest that posters may show agreement with others' responses but not necessarily increase their sense of social connections. Due to that family conflict is a critical factor of suicide [8], the decreasing use of family-related cues in comments can be a benign signal for reducing posters' rumination of family conflict. The findings show that family-related cues indeed decline in posters' comments. In another word, an online response may shift posters' focus from family conflict to other issues, which also helps them reduce the recursive cycle of negative thoughts about family conflict [44].

Interpersonal Focus. Prior research found that suicidal individuals showed the inclination of self-focus and used more 1st singular pronouns in their suicide notes [35, 46, 49]. Then, if posters lower their use of self-references and increase references to others, this may offer the evidence of positive effect on posters. We did find the use of self-reference declining and for social references, only 2nd singular personal pronouns "You" increases significantly. We believe this is a good signal representing that posters interacted and had a dialogue with other users. This further suggests that online response increases posters' social interaction with others.

Table 6. Overview of findings of hypothesis

Hypothesis	Findings
H1: Affective distress decreases in original posters' comments	Support
H2a: Positive cognitive thinking increases in original posters' comments	Reject
H2b: Negative cognitive thinking decreases in original posters' comments	Partial support
H3a: Agreement increase in original posters' comments	Partial support
H3b: Family-related concepts decrease in original posters' comments	Support
H4a: Self-reference (1st personal singular pronouns) decrease in original posters' comments	Support
H4b: Social references increase in original posters' comments	Partial support

5.3 Implications of Findings

There are several implications of this work. The online forum /r/SuicdeWatch may detect the potential response bias through linguistic cues presented in title. Then, for those ignored posts, SW can further detect which posts may needs urgent response by its content and adjust its ranking. In this way, SW can increase the exposure and response rate of ignored posts. Furthermore, SW can apply our four indicators to evaluate condition of suicide posters. If the psychological state of a poster remains the same or even exacerbate, SW may inform moderators/trained volunteers to provide professional responses and assistances.

5.4 Limitation and Future Direction

There are several implications of this work. The SW may detect the potential response bias through linguistic cues presented in the title. Then, for those ignored posts, SW can further detect which posts may need an urgent response by its content and adjust its ranking. In this way, SW can increase the exposure and response rate of ignored posts. Furthermore, SW can apply our four indicators to evaluate the condition of suicide posters. If the psychological state of a poster remains the same or even exacerbate, SW may inform moderators/trained volunteers to provide professional responses and assistance.

6 Conclusion

Online community has changed the scope of suicide prevention in the past decade. However, its effects on suicide prevention remain unclear. To fill this gap of knowledge, this study investigated users' response bias and the effects of response on suicide posters. We found that title is a critical signal for users' responses and identify five types of linguistic cues that influence. Moreover, in order to assess the effects of responses, we proposed four types of indicators based on the literature of psychology. The findings show positive effects of online community on suicide posters of SW. The contribution of this study is to provide different approaches to assessing potential bias and the effects of an online community for suicide prevention. We hope this study can deliver insights for developing an innovative and practical approach to suicide prevention.

References

1. Alao, A.O., Soderberg, M., Pohl, E.L., Alao, A.L.: Cybersuicide: review of the role of the internet on suicide. CyberPsychol. Behav. 9(4), 489–493 (2006)
2. Barak, A.: Emotional support and suicide prevention through the internet: a field project report. Comput. Hum. Behav. 23(2), 971–984 (2007)
3. Baker, D., Fortune, S.: Understanding self-harm and suicide websites: a qualitative interview study of young adult website users. Crisis 29(3), 118–122 (2008)

4. Baume, P., Rolfe, A., Clinton, M.: Suicide on the internet: a focus for nursing intervention? Aust. N. Z. J. Mental Health Nurs. 7(4), 134–141 (1998)
5. Birbal, R., Maharajh, H.D., Birbal, R., et al.: Cybersuicide and the adolescent population: challenges of the future? Int. J. Adolesc. Med. Health 21, 151–159 (2009)
6. Bostwick, J.M., Pankratz, V.S.: Affective disorders and suicide risk: a reexamination. Am. J. Psychiatry 157, 1925–1932 (2014)
7. Brent, D.A., et al.: Psychiatric risk factors for adolescent suicide: a case-control study. J. Am. Acad. Child Adolesc. Psychiatry 32(3), 521–529 (1993)
8. Brent, D.A., et al.: Personality disorder, personality traits, impulsive violence, and completed suicide in adolescents. J. Am. Acad. Child Adolesc. Psychiatry 33(8), 1080–1086 (1994)
9. Cantrell, F.L., Minns, A.: Cybersuicide with "homemade Valium". Clin. Toxicol. 49(1), 56 (2011)
10. Daine, K., Hawton, K., Singaravelu, V., Stewart, A., Simkin, S., Montgomery, P.: The power of the web: a systematic review of studies of the influence of the internet on self-harm and suicide in young people. PLoS One 8(10), e77555 (2013)
11. Dunlop, S.M., More, E., Romer, D.: Where do youth learn about suicides on the internet, and what influence does this have on suicidal ideation? J. Child Psychol. Psychiatry 52(10), 1073–1080 (2011)
12. Fernández-Cabana, M., et al.: Linguistic analysis of suicide notes in Spain. Eur. J. Psychiatry 29(2), 145–155 (2015)
13. Eichenberg, C.: Internet message boards for suicidal people: a typology of users. CyberPsychol. Behav. 11(1), 107–113 (2008)
14. Fu, K.W., Cheng, Q., Wong, P.W., Yip, P.S.: Responses to a self-presented suicide attempt in social media. Crisis 34, 406–412 (2015)
15. Gosselink, M.J., Siegel, A.M., Suk, E., Giltay, E.J.: A case of 'cybersuicide' attempt using chloroform. Gen. Hosp. Psychiatry 34(4), e7–e8 (2012)
16. Gunnell, D., et al.: Impact of national policy initiatives on fatal and non-fatal self-harm after psychiatric hospital discharge: time series analysis. Br. J. Psychiatry 201(3), 233–238 (2012)
17. Gilat, I., Tobin, Y., Shahar, G.: Offering support to suicidal individuals in an online support group. Arch. Suicide Res. 15(3), 195–206 (2011)
18. Gilat, I., Tobin, Y., Shahar, G.: Responses to suicidal messages in an online support group: comparison between trained volunteers and lay individuals. Soc. Psychiatry Psychiatr. Epidemiol. 47(12), 1929–1935 (2012)
19. Greidanus, E., Everall, R.D.: Helper therapy in an online suicide prevention community. Br. J. Guidance Counselling 38(2), 191–204 (2010)
20. Handelman, L.D., Lester, D.: The content of suicide notes from attempters and completers. Crisis 28(2), 102–104 (2007)
21. Hawkins, K.A., Hames, J.L., Ribeiro, J.D., Silva, C., Joiner, T.E., Cougle, J.R.: An examination of the relationship between anger and suicide risk through the lens of the interpersonal theory of suicide. J. Psychiatric Res. 50, 59–65 (2014)
22. Hendin, H., Maltsberger, J.T., Szanto, K.: The role of intense affective states in signaling a suicide crisis. J. Nerv. Ment. Dis. 195(5), 363–368 (2007)
23. Hess, A.: "Please Do Not Downvote Anyone Who Asked for Helps" How Reddit Is Changing Suicide Intervention (2015). http://www.slate.com/articles/technology/users/2015/03/reddit_and_suicide_intervention_how_social_media_is_changing_the_cry_for.html. Accessed 4 Dec 2015
24. Hsiung, R.C.: A suicide in an online mental health support group: reactions of the group members, administrative responses, and recommendations. CyberPsychol. Behav. 10(4), 495–500 (2007)

25. Joiner Jr., T.E., Van Orden, K.A.: The interpersonal-psychological theory of suicidal behavior indicates specific and crucial psychotherapeutic targets. Int. J. Cogn. Ther. 1(1), 80–89 (2008)
26. Jones, R., et al.: Online discussion forums for young people who self-harm: user views. Psychiatrist 35(10), 364–368 (2011)
27. Katsumata, Y., Matsumoto, T., Kitani, M., Takeshima, T.: Electronic media use and suicidal ideation in Japanese adolescents. Psychiatry Clin. Neurosci. 62(6), 744–746 (2008)
28. Kumar, M., Dredze, M., Coppersmith, G., De Choudhury, M.: Detecting Changes in suicide content manifested in social media following celebrity suicides. In: Proceedings of the 26th ACM Conference on Hypertext & Social Media, pp. 85–94. ACM, August 2015
29. Lester, D., McSwain, S.: Poems by a suicide: sara teasdale. Psychol. Rep. 106(3), 811–812 (2010)
30. Maltsberger, J.T.: The descent into suicide. Int. J. Psychoanal. 85(3), 653–668 (2004)
31. Mitchell, K.J., Ybarra, M.L.: Online behavior of youth who engage in self-harm provides clues for preventive intervention. Prev. Med. 45(5), 392–396 (2007)
32. Musshoff, F., Kirschbaum, K.M., Madea, B.: An uncommon case of a suicide with inhalation of hydrogen cyanide. Forensic Sci. Int. 204(1), e4–e7 (2011)
33. Osgood, C.E., Walker, E.G.: Motivation and language behavior: a content analysis of suicide notes. J. Abnorm. Soc. Psychol. 59(1), 58 (1959)
34. Pająk, K., Trzebiński, J.: Escaping the world: linguistic indicators of suicide attempts in poets. J. Loss Trauma 19(5), 389–402 (2014)
35. Pennebaker, J.W., Mehl, M.R., Niederhoffer, K.G.: Psychological aspects of natural language use: Our words, our selves. Ann. Rev. Psychol. 54(1), 547–577 (2003)
36. Petrie, K., Brook, R.: Sense of coherence, self-esteem, depression and hopelessness as correlates of reattempting suicide. Br. J. Clin. Psychol. 31(3), 293–300 (1992)
37. Pisani, A.R., et al.: Emotion regulation difficulties, youth–adult relationships, and suicide attempts among high school students in underserved communities. J. Youth Adolesc. 42(6), 807–820 (2013)
38. Robinson, J., et al.: Social media and suicide prevention: a systematic review. Early Interv. Psychiatry 10, 103–121 (2015)
39. Rude, S., Gortner, E.M., Pennebaker, J.: Language use of depressed and depression-vulnerable college students. Cogn. Emot. 18(8), 1121–1133 (2004)
40. Saltz, A., Marsh, S.: Relationship between hopelessness and ultimate suicide: a replication with psychiatric outpatients. Am. J. Psychiatry 147, 190–195 (1990)
41. Schotanus-Dijkstra, M., Havinga, P., van Ballegooijen, W., Delfosse, L., Mokkenstorm, J., Boon, B.: What do the bereaved by suicide communicate in online support groups? A content analysis. Crisis J. Crisis Interv. Suicide Prev. 35(1), 27 (2014)
42. Shneidman, E.S., Farberow, N.L.: Clues to suicide. Public Health Rep. 71(2), 109 (1956)
43. Silverman, M.A., Will, N.P.: Sylvia plath and the failure of emotional self-repair through poetry. Psychoanal. Q. 55, 99–129 (1986)
44. Smith, J.M., Alloy, L.B., Abramson, L.Y.: Cognitive vulnerability to depression, rumination, hopelessness, and suicidal ideation: multiple pathways to self-injurious thinking. Suicide Life-threatening Behav. 36(4), 443–454 (2006)
45. Smithson, J., et al.: Membership and boundary maintenance on an online self-harm forum. Qual. Health Res. 21, 1567–1575 (2011)
46. Stirman, S.W., Pennebaker, J.W.: Word use in the poetry of suicidal and nonsuicidal poets. Psychosom. Med. 63(4), 517–522 (2001)
47. Thomas, K.M., Duke, M.: Depressed writing: cognitive distortions in the works of depressed and nondepressed poets and writers. Psychol. Aesthetics Creativity Arts 1(4), 204 (2007)

48. Van Orden, K.A., Witte, T.K., Cukrowicz, K.C., Braithwaite, S.R., Selby, E.A., Joiner Jr., T.E.: The interpersonal theory of suicide. Psychol. Rev. **117**(2), 575 (2010)
49. Westerlund, M.: Talking suicide. Nordicom Rev. **34**(2), 35–46 (2013)
50. World Health Organization. World Suicide Prevention day Media Release: Suicide Prevention (2018). http://www.who.int/mental_health/suicide-prevention/exe_summary_english.pdf?ua=1. Accessed 18 Jan 2019
51. Wyman, P.A., et al.: Emotional triggers and psychopathology associated with suicidal ideation in urban children with elevated aggressive-disruptive behavior. J. Abnorm. Child Psychol. **37**(7), 917–928 (2009)
52. Naito, A.: Internet suicide in Japan: implications for child and adolescent mental health. Clin. Child Psychol. Psychiatry **12**(4), 583–597 (2007)

Healthier Life and More Fun? Users' Motivations to Apply Activity Tracking Technology and the Impact of Gamification

Linda Schaffarczyk and Aylin Ilhan$^{(\boxtimes)}$ (iD)

Department of Information Science, Heinrich Heine University Düsseldorf,
Düsseldorf, Germany
{linda.schaffarczyk,aylin.ilhan}@hhu.de

Abstract. As being fit and physically more active has become more important in today's society many people start to use fitness trackers to achieve this goal. To find out if fitness trackers and their gamification elements (here, challenges and achievements) motivate users to be more physically active, a survey was conducted. The survey builds on the *Uses and Gratifications Theory*, the *Self-Determination Theory*, and on information gathered during interviews with users of fitness trackers. The investigation contains 689 adequately filled-out online surveys. The participants are looking for information and were intrinsically as well as extrinsically motivated. 61% of all 689 participants take part in competitions and 89% of them recognize achievements. The results show that users apply fitness trackers to get information. The investigation shows that the integrated gamification elements do not only support people to be more physically active but are rewarding them as well.

Keywords: Gamification · Activity tracking technology ·
Self-Determination Theory · Uses and Gratifications Theory · Motivation

1 Introduction

Today, being fit and active is a goal many people want to reach. Especially, since according to the World Health Organization (WHO) [1], the obesity of people has reached epidemic proportions. People who are obese or overweight have a major risk of getting chronic diseases like type 2 diabetes, a stroke or cardiovascular disease. More and more people are trying to live a healthier way of life by doing regular sports and exercises. The internet as well as social media is helping the being-fit movement, be it through users who share their daily run in Facebook groups or getting the best yoga shots with many likes on Instagram. Fitness trackers give visual feedback through corresponding applications and are equipped with gamification elements to motivate the users to achieve their goal.

Ilhan and Fietkiewicz investigated ten activity tracking technology brands considering the integrated game mechanics (e.g., challenges, points, leaderboards, badges, and so on). The investigation linked to different theories, Flow-Theory, Goal

© Springer Nature Switzerland AG 2019
G. Meiselwitz (Ed.): HCII 2019, LNCS 11579, pp. 124–136, 2019.
https://doi.org/10.1007/978-3-030-21905-5_10

Orientation Theory, and the Self-Determination Theory to understand the effectiveness and usefulness of different game mechanics [2].

Buchem et al. [3] investigated how gamification elements will help and support elderly people to improve their physical activity. They implemented a project called fMOOC (fitness Massive Online Learning Course) equipped with the use of fitness trackers and integrated gamification elements. Participants enjoyed the gamification elements and as a result, it supported them to be more physically active.

Considering the fact that gamification should motivate users to reach a desired behavior or change a behavior, could people be dependent on gamification elements integrated into activity tracking technologies? Do users lose motivation if those elements would not exist anymore? The results of one research showed that the motivation for physical activity decreased in situations where the fitness tracker was not available, especially for users who were highly extrinsically motivated [4].

Fitness tracker applications are equipped with behavior change techniques. Middelweerd et al. [5] found out that most apps had at last five behavior change techniques. The most common were self-surveillance, setting goals, and getting feedback.

Apart from investigations on activity tracking technologies considering gamification and motivation, research about activity tracking technologies, for example, accuracy [e.g., 7, 8], acceptance, perceived service quality, usage, and impact [e.g., 6, 9, 10], sprouted.

But to our knowledge, research concentrating on activity tracking technology and using the *Self-Determination Theory* (SDT), *Uses and Gratifications Theory* (U&GT), and consideration of challenges and achievements to investigate users' motivation and their impact is not investigated yet. To offer new and further insights in this research area, first semi-structured interviews with users of fitness trackers were made to find out why people use fitness trackers. The SDT and the U&GT is applied to understand the needs of users and their motivation. The U&GT is known as the theory to understand why people use a specific medium. Here, it is used to understand first, why people use activity tracking technologies, and second, what gratifications they are searching for and obtaining. The SDT is used to be able to understand if the use of those technologies is caused through intrinsic or extrinsic motivation. Further, apart from these two theories, the reaction-based device functionalities, such as the daily goal or the feedback function are considered as well. At latest, the gamification elements challenges and achievements are part of this research as well.

First of all, the paper will give an overview of the applied theories. Subsequently, methods, including interviews, construction and distribution of the survey, data preparation, and used measurement are presented. The research questions are answered in the result section, followed by a discussion.

2 Theoretical Background

2.1 Gamification

According to Deterding et al. [11], *Gamification* describes the use of game elements in a non-game context. Gamification has not ultimately one definition. For example,

Huotari and Hamari [12, p. 19] mentioned that gamification refers "to a process of enhancing a service with affordances for gameful experiences." Further, they explain that gamification aims to improve motivation and the engagement. Seaborn and Fels [13, p. 14] describe gamification as a possibility to "motivate and engage end-users through the use of game elements and mechanics." Further, gamification is not only used to motivate users to engage in desired behavior, but also to help to change a behavior or even increase the loyalty to a brand [14, 15].

Furthermore, Huotari and Hamari [12, p. 19] explain that there does not exist one "clearly defined set of game elements." But, the use of game design elements is beneficial as it motivates users [11]. Game elements are here, as the name suggests, elements that are commonly used in games (e.g., achievements, points, leaderboards, and so on). Hunicke et al. [16] explain with their MDA framework (mechanics, dynamics and aesthetics) that mechanics can trigger different dynamics. Mechanics like challenges trigger dynamics like competitions where users want to beat others, compare themselves and want to win. Blohm and Leimeister [17] confirm as well that game mechanics trigger game dynamics and show their correlations, for example, rankings create a game dynamic of competition.

Activity tracking technologies are usually equipped with some of those game elements. Ilhan and Fietkiewicz [2] found out considering the 12 investigated activity tracking applications that, documentation, avatars, time pressure, clear goals, badges, and community features where integrated at less to 50% [2]. Their investigations include, besides those game elements (mechanics) that achievements (here, badges) can be shared with other users and that challenges could be included to compete against others or oneself. Challenges come with a leaderboard, showing the users how many steps they took but also how many steps other users took. Challenges could be characterized as a five-day step challenge (Fitbit) or as a monthly challenge (Samsung Health) to rank users according to their counted steps. It depends on the activity tracking application. Time constraints are also integrated in activity tracking technology. The user can set their own daily step goal which has to be completed during a day. Some fitness trackers also include levels and points that can be gained by fulfilling various tasks such as reaching your daily step goal for 3 days [2].

All those gamification elements (here, mechanics) are made to motivate the user to engage with the activity tracking technologies and not only to support the engagement with using a service but as well to support the reach of a desired behavior, here to be physically more active. Those gamification mechanics can be motivating. But apart from concretely integrated game mechanics, here challenges and achievements, there are reaction-device based motivation aspects, which belongs here to the gamification elements, as well. These include the daily step goal and the feedback to be more active. Considering the aim of using gamification elements, to motivate users of services, here to be more physically active, the following research questions arises:

RQ1a: Do the reaction-based device functionalities motivate users to be physically active?

RQ1b: Do the gamification elements (challenges and achievements) motivate users to be physically active?

But apart from concretely integrated game elements, people might be intrinsically or extrinsically motivated while doing something in their everyday life (including, school, work, leisure time, and so on).

2.2 Self-Determination Theory (SDT)

The SDT, developed by Richard M. Ryan and Edward L. Deci and starting in the 1970s, is based on human motivation. It evolved from studies that researched effects of extrinsic rewards on intrinsic motivation [18].

Intrinsic motivation occurs regardless of extrinsic rewards or external reasons (e.g., friends, family members, work environment). Doing something for fun is defined as being intrinsically motivated [19]. The intrinsic motivation is the person's own motivation, the task-orientated motivation. There are different reasons to be intrinsically motivated: the fun of the task itself, to try something new, curiosity, and to accomplish something [20].

The extrinsic motivation is divided into four categories from the least autonomous to very autonomous [20]. The four extrinsic sub-forms of regulations are "external regulation," "introjection," "identification," and "integration." Considering the external regulation, people would use the fitness tracker in order to get rewards. Introjected regulation means here the use of a fitness tracker to show others how much physically active they were during the day. Apart from that, identified regulation means users who identify the importance of the task. For example, a user identifies with the importance of being fit and, therefore, uses the fitness tracker to achieve this goal. Lastly, integrated regulation is reflected in cases where a user has completely accepted the fitness tracker and its value [20].

Apart from intrinsic and extrinsic motivation, there is amotivation [20]. Amotivation is defined as being not motivated at all to act and do something [20]. It happens, when there is no value in the activity or task [21], the feeling of not being competent enough to fulfil the activity or task [22] as well as the expectation that doing the task will not yield the desired outcome [23].

Therefore, with using the SDT, it is possible not only to understand why specific decision or behaviors are triggered, but also to explain their background. This led to the second research question:

RQ2: Are users intrinsically or extrinsically motivated to use a fitness tracker?

Apart from researching the motivational nature and the impact of gamification, users might have other reasons as to why they are using their activity tracking technologies as well.

2.3 Uses and Gratifications Theory (U&GT)

The U&GT is an approach to understand why people use a specific medium, what gratifications attract them, if they obtained them, and what kind of content satisfies their social and psychological needs [24]. It is distinguished not only between gratification sought and gratification obtained, but also their correlation. The sought gratification might be completely different from the obtained gratification [25]. If a user joins a

Facebook group for gathering information as a gratification, the user might obtain social interaction as a gratification as well [26]. Ilhan [27] found out that users of activity tracker or fitness-related Facebook groups seek mainly information and obtain information while using them, but they also tend to have fun while using those Facebook groups. Considering the U&GT, there are four basic gratifications noticeable: information, socialization, self-presentation (self-status seeking) and entertainment [26, 28–31].

The four basic gratifications are used to analyze the motivation as to why users use activity tracking technologies. For example, an activity tracker offers a lot of information: How many steps a user took, how many active minutes the user had during a day, how many calories were burned, and so on. To learn this information can cause the use of activity trackers. Using a fitness tracker to socialize, can work either through the integrated functionalities (e.g., groups, challenges) or through doing sports together supported through the use of fitness trackers. Through the fitness application of the activity trackers, people can share their achievements, experience, and even join challenges against each other. Using a fitness tracker might evoke fun and might therefore be used for entertainment. Eventually, the use of fitness tracker for self-status seeking (self-presentation) is caused by the motivation to share and show others how many steps a user has been taking during a day or to use an expensive fitness tracker as a status symbol. Therefore, the paper will answer the last research question:

RQ3: Which gratifications do the users seek and obtain while using a fitness tracker?

3 Methods

3.1 Interviews

First, six semi-structured interviews [32] with friends as well as members of the Department of Information Science at the Heinrich Heine University of Düsseldorf, Germany were conducted which took place in October and November 2017. An interview took about 30 minutes. All six interviewees were using fitness trackers. This preliminary study not only enabled gaining more insight into the use and motivation of fitness trackers but helped with setting up the survey as well. The participants were asked questions about their fitness tracker, their behavior, as well as the impact (motivation) to be more physically active. The interviews were not recorded, instead notes were taken.

3.2 Survey

The survey was first pretested by colleagues at the Department of Information Science at the Heinrich Heine University of Düsseldorf, Germany. The survey was spread to and through colleagues/friends and through social media platforms like fitness forums, Facebook, Twitter, Reddit, and Xing. The sampling of the survey was non-probabilistic and the survey was available in English. The survey was anonymous and no contest or prize money were offered to the participants. The survey is characterized through two main parts.

The survey starts with questions about the sociodemographic data. The participant answers questions about gender, age (nonobligatory), country and which fitness tracker is used.

After the first part, the first four statements asked for the gratifications sought, followed by further four statements for gratifications obtained. The next part of the survey contained statements about the SDT. The first three statements asked about the intrinsic motivation, followed by four questions about the sub-forms of the extrinsic motivation. The reaction-based device motivation has eight statements in total. Those statements are based on the outcomes of the conducted interviews. The gamification elements challenges and achievements had each their own statements. The gamification element challenge contains nine statements, and achievements by four. Before participants had the possibility to evaluate those statements, conditional questions, here "Do you recognize achievements?" and "Do you take part in challenges?" precede. Especially for the case that participants do not take part in challenges, three statements based on the amotivation of SDT were included as well. Based on the interviews, it was obvious that users either recognize achievements or do not notice at all that they exist. All these statements, except the "yes/no" questions, are equipped with a seven-point Likert scale from 1 "Strongly Disagree" to 7 "Strongly Agree." Participants have the possibility to choose the option 'prefer not to answer' as well.

3.3 Data Preparation and Analysis

The data included 942 filled out (non-completed and completed) surveys. After cleaning the data, 253 surveys were removed. Those cases were participants who did not fill out the survey to the end (N = 229). Further, as this study concentrates on activity tracking technology users, participants who mentioned not to use fitness trackers were removed as well (N = 8). Another participant was removed due to the low age of 7 and 16 participants, who do not specify their age (N = 15). All in all, there were 689 adequate responses. The data is not normally distributed. The statements equipped with a Likert scale were not interval scaled. Therefore the data will be considered as ordinal. Instead of the mean, the median had to be used while analyzing the data. From the 689 participants, 73.9% were female, 25.4% were male and 0.7% preferred not to say. Most participants of the survey came from the USA (40.5%) and Germany (30.5%). The three most-used fitness trackers were Fitbit (39%), Garmin (27.3%) and Apple Watch (10.9%). The age ranges from 9 to 72 years.

4 Results

4.1 Do the Reaction-Based Device Functionalities Motivate Users to Be Physically Active? (RQ1a)

Figure 1 shows the results of the reaction-based device motivation. With the first statement, if users are motivated when the fitness tracker tells them to be active, the users somewhat agreed (median: 5).

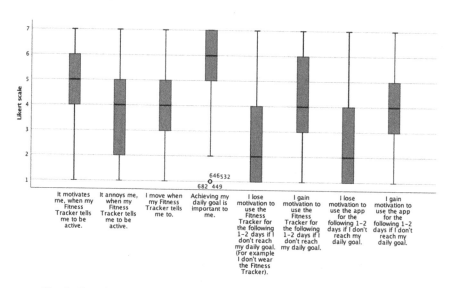

Fig. 1. Reaction-based device motivation (N = 673; excluded cases listwise).

The participants of the survey neither agree nor disagree with the statement that it annoys them when the fitness tracker tells them to be active (median: 4). Although users are motivated when the fitness tracker tells them to be more physically active, they neither agree nor disagree to moving (median: 4). It is important to reach the daily goal (median: 6), but if the goal is not reached, users do not lose motivation to use the fitness tracker (median: 2) or the app (median: 2). Users are not getting more or less motivated to use the fitness tracker when they did not reach their daily goal (median: 4) and the app (median: 4).

4.2   Do the Gamification Elements (Challenges and Achievements) Motivate Users to Be Physically Active? (RQ1b)

61% of all participants do take part in challenges while 39% of them do not. Figure 2 shows the impact of challenges while using activity tracking technologies. Users agree to being more physically active (median: 6) when taking part in a challenge and to enjoying it (median: 6). Participants are neutral (neither agree nor disagree) about feeling pressured when taking part in a challenge (median: 4) but they somewhat agree to directing their behavior towards winning a challenge (median: 5). Participants do not lose motivation to use the fitness tracker (median: 1) or to take part in the next challenge (median: 1) after losing a challenge. The users strongly agreed to not losing interest in taking part in the next challenge after they won the last one (median: 1). Interestingly, after winning a challenge, users are much more certain to take part in the next challenge for sure (median: 6) than after losing (median: 5).

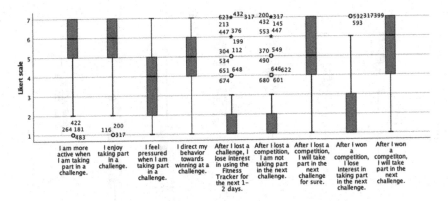

Fig. 2. Impact of challenges/competitions (N = 413; excluded cases listwise).

89% of the participants did recognize achievements and answered the statements about achievements. Figure 3 shows that users feel rewarded when they get achievements (median: 6) and enjoy it (median: 6). The participants of the survey also agreed to changing their behavior towards obtaining achievements (median: 5). Lastly, users do not compare each other based on achievements (median: 3).

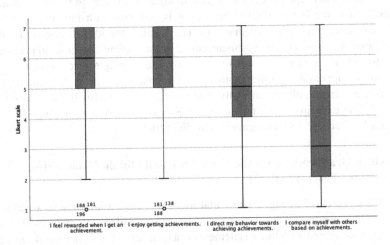

Fig. 3. Impact of achievements (N = 602; excluded cases listwise).

4.3 Are Users Intrinsically or Extrinsically Motivated to Use a Fitness Tracker? (RQ2)

The motivation to use fitness trackers can be extrinsic or intrinsic (Fig. 4). Users are intrinsically motivated to use fitness trackers, because they use them for fun (median: 6), to accomplish something (median: 6) and to learn something new (median: 5). The

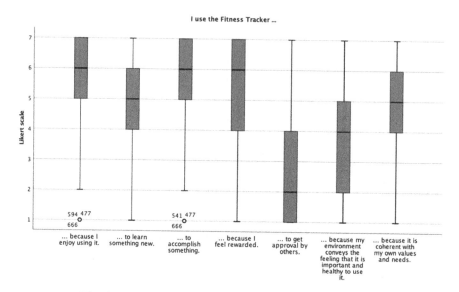

Fig. 4. Self-determination (N = 675; excluded cases listwise).

next four statements represent the extrinsic motivation. Many users agreed with the statement "I use the fitness tracker because it is coherent with my own values and needs" (integrated regulation, median: 5). The median for identification, "I use the fitness tracker because my environment conveys the feeling that it is important and healthy to use it", is neutral (median: 4). Many users disagreed to using the fitness tracker to get approval by others (introjected regulation, median: 2). Interestingly, although users are highly intrinsically motivated, they are also highly extrinsically motivated. The participants of the survey agreed with external regulation, "I use the fitness tracker because I feel rewarded" (median: 6).

4.4   Which Gratifications Do the Users Seek and Obtain While Using a Fitness Tracker? (RQ3)

The results represented in Fig. 5 show that users are seeking information (median: 7). Most users were not looking for social contacts (socialization) and entertainment, because they disagreed with those statements (median: 2). They somewhat disagree that they use the fitness tracker because they want to present themselves (median: 3). Users are not only seeking but also obtaining information (median: 7). Social contacts are both not sought and not obtained (median: 2). Entertainment and self-presentation are, as mentioned above, not sought much but still, users obtain some of it on a low level (median: 3).

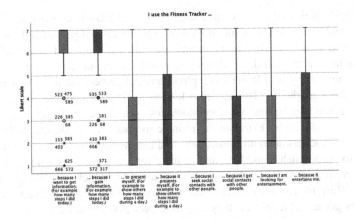

Fig. 5. Gratifications sought and obtained (N = 674; excluded cases listwise).

5 Discussion

The purpose of this investigation was to understand whether or not gamification elements on fitness trackers foster use, if users are intrinsically or extrinsically motivated, and what gratifications the users of fitness trackers are looking for and which they are obtaining.

The investigation confirms that it is important to reach the daily goal. Especially, users feel motivated when the fitness tracker reminds them to be active, but this does not mean that they move when the fitness tracker tells them to. From the interviews that were made before the survey, the participants told that when the fitness tracker tells them to be active, they only move when it is appropriate. For example, they do not get up and start moving around when they are in a meeting, but they mostly do so when this happens during their break. The participants agreed that, although achieving the daily goal is important, they did not lose motivation to try it again the next day when they did not manage it. From the interview, when the daily goal is close to being reached, the user needs less than 500 steps to reach the goal, most users still get up in the evening and do the last steps to finish the goal. In the case where, for example, still 2,000 and more steps are needed to reach the daily goal the user usually just relaxes in the evening.

This study concentrated on two gamification elements. The gamification mechanics achievements and challenges were looked at separated from the reaction-based device motivation. Users notice challenges, make use of them, and enjoy them. This can help with being and staying motivated to be more physically active. Therefore, competitions do foster motivation and the use of activity trackers. The users agree that they will take part in the next challenge no matter whether they won or lost the last one, although they are a little more motivated to join the next challenge if they won. Users who are joining a challenge could be as a result more physically active because they might feel motivated to walk more to beat other users who are on the first ranks. The motivation to join a challenge is the same as to reach the daily goal. Users do more sports and are more physically active when they are challenging others. Users notice that other users might have more steps and they might try to compete with that person and catch up. In the interviews, some participants mentioned they do the same and nearly all participants in the interviews who do challenges agreed that being the last is the worst. It can be assumed that many people are more physically active because nobody wants to be the last on the leaderboard. This can also lead to feeling pressured.

The SDT was used to find out what motivates users to use the fitness tracker and if the behavior is caused by extrinsic or intrinsic motivation. As shown in the results, users of fitness trackers are both intrinsically and extrinsically motivated. For users, it is important to accomplish something and to have fun, which are both intrinsic motivations. Apart from that, users like to receive rewards, which is a highly extrinsic motivation. Rewards are, for example, reaching a daily goal or getting an achievement. When users get an achievement, they feel motivated and rewarded.

This research focuses on which gratifications (socialization, entertainment, self-presentation, and information) users are looking for and which they are obtaining. The results show that users of fitness trackers are looking mainly for information. This can explain why people bought a fitness tracker. They are looking for information which supports the goal to be more physically active. Information is not only sought but also obtained by the users. Fitness trackers show amongst other things how many steps a user takes during a day. This helps to walk more or to develop an awareness of one's physical activity level.

Lastly, achievements motivate users as well. Users enjoy getting achievements and directing their behavior towards getting them. Users like to receive rewards and enjoy the feeling of getting the rewards based on achievements but they do not compare themselves to others based on achievements. This means users see achievements as something personal that is for themselves, as a personal reward.

The study showed that the motivation of users to use fitness trackers is both extrinsic and intrinsic. Users are seeking and obtaining information as a gratification. They want to know how many steps they take and how physically active they are. Competitions, achievements and the reaction-based device functionalities do foster use of activity trackers and their applications. The users stated that they enjoyed these elements and they helped them to be more active.

Our study did a successful step in the research of the motivation for the use of fitness trackers. The study has of course the limitation that the results only show a selection from all users of fitness trackers.

Future work should investigate if the motivation of users from fitness trackers starts to decrease over time. Do different fitness trackers motivate differently? Further, are there differences in the use of the fitness trackers and the gamification elements considering different generations and genders? Last but not least, it can also be researched if there are differences between users from different countries.

References

1. Word Health Organization. https://www.who.int/dietphysicalactivity/pa/en/. Accessed July 2018
2. Ilhan, A., Fietkiewicz, K.J.: Learning for a healthier lifestyle through gamification: a case study of fitness tracker applications. In: Buchem, I., Klamma, R., Wild, F. (eds.) Perspectives on Wearable Enhanced Learning. Current Trends, Research and Practice. Springer, New York (2019, in press)
3. Buchem, I., Merceron, A., Kreutel, J., Haesner, M., Steinert, A.: Gamification designs in wearable enhanced learning for healthy ageing. In: Proceedings of 2015 International Conference on Interactive Mobile Communication Technologies and Learning (IMCL), pp. 9–15. IEEE, Washington (2015). https://doi.org/10.1109/IMCTL.2015.7359545
4. Attig, C., Franke, T.: I track, therefore i walk – exploring the motivational costs of wearing activity trackers in actual users. Int. J. Hum. Comput. Stud. (2019). https://doi.org/10.1016/j.ijhcs.2018.04.007
5. Middelweerd, A., Mollee, J.S., van der Wal, C.N., Brug, J., te Velde, S.J.: Apps to promote physical activity among adults: a review and content analysis. Int. J. Behav. Nutr. Phys. Act. 11 (2014). https://doi.org/10.1186/s12966-014-0097-9
6. Ilhan, A., Henkel, M.: 10,000 steps a day for health? User-based evaluation of wearable activity trackers. In: Proceedings of the 51st Hawaii International Conference on System Sciences. Institutional repository ScholarSpace, Hononulu, pp. 3376–3385 (2018). http://hdl.handle.net/10125/50316
7. Evenson, K.R., Goto, M.M., Furberg, R.D.: Systematic review of the validity and reliability of consumer-wearable activity trackers. Int. J. Behav. Nutr. Phys. Act. 12 (2015). https://doi.org/10.1186/s12966-015-0314-1
8. Sasaki, J.E., et al.: Validation of the fitbit wireless activity tracker for prediction of energy expenditure. J. Phys. Act. Health 12, 149–154 (2015). https://doi.org/10.1123/jpah.2012-0495
9. Fritz, T., Huang, E.M., Murphy, G.C., Zimmermann, T.: Persuasive technology in the real world: a study of long-term use of activity sensing devices for fitness. In: Proceedings of the SIGCHI Conference on Human Factors in Computing Systems, pp. 487–496. ACM, New York (2014). https://doi.org/10.1145/2556288.2557383
10. Shih, P.C., Han, K., Poole, E.S., Rosson, M.B., Carroll, J.M.: Use and adoption challenges of wearable activity trackers. In: Proceedings of the iConference 2015. IDEALS, Repository of University of Illinois (2015). http://hdl.handle.net/2142/73649
11. Deterding, S., Dixon, D., Khaled, R., Nacke, L.: From game design elements to gamefulness: defining "gamification". In: Proceedings of the 15th International Academic MindTreck Conference: Envisioning Future Media Environments, pp. 9–15. ACM, New York (2011). https://doi.org/10.1145/2181037.2181040
12. Huotari, K., Hamari, J.: Defining gamification: a service marketing perspective. In: Proceedings of 16th International Academic MindTrek Conference, pp. 17–22. ACM, New York (2012). https://doi.org/10.1145/2393132.2393137
13. Seaborn, K., Fels, D.I.: Gamification in theory and action: a survey. Int. J. Hum. Comput. Stud. 74, 14–31 (2015). https://doi.org/10.1016/j.ijhcs.2014.09.006
14. Richards, C., Thompson, C.W., Graham, N.: Beyond designing for motivation: the importance of context in gamification. In: Proceedings of the first ACM SIGCHI Annual Symposium on Computer-Human Interaction in Play, pp. 217–226. ACM, New York (2014). https://doi.org/10.1145/2658537.2658683

15. Muntean, C.I.: Raising engagement in e-learning through gamification. In: Proceedings of the 6th International Conference on Virtual Learning ICVL, vol. 1, pp. 323–329 (2011)

16. Hunicke, R., LeBlanc, M., Zubek, R.: MDA: a formal approach to game design and game research. In: Workshop at the Game Developers Conference, 2001–2004, San Jose, July 2004. https://www.cs.northwestern.edu/~hunicke/MDA.pdf

17. Blohm, I., Leimeister, J.M.: Gamification - Design of IT-based enhancing services for motivational support and behavioral change. JM Bus. Inf. Syst. Eng. **5**, 275–278 (2013). https://doi.org/10.1007/s12599-013-0273-5

18. Deci, E.L., Ryan, R.M.: Self-determination theory. In: van Lange, P.A.M., Kruglanski, A. W., Higgins, E.T. (eds.) Handbook of Theories of Social Psychology 2012, vol. 2, pp. 416–437. Sage, London (2012)

19. Deci, E.L.: Effects of externally mediated rewards on intrinsic motivation. J. Pers. Soc. Psychol. **18**, 105–115 (1971). https://doi.org/10.1037/h0030644

20. Ryan, R.M., Deci, E.L.: Self-determination theory and the facilitation of intrinsic motivation, social development, and well-being. Am. Psychol. **55**, 68–78 (2000). https://doi.org/10.1037/0003-066X.55.1.68

21. Ryan, R.M., Deci, E.L., Grolnick, W.S.: Autonomy, relatedness, and the self: their relation to development and psychopathology. In: Cicchetti, D., Cohen, D.J. (eds.) Developmental Psychopathology, vol. 1. Theory and Methods, pp. 618–655. Wiley, Hoboken (1995)

22. Bandura, A.: Social Foundation of Thought and Action: A Social-Cognitive View. Prentice-Hall Inc, Englewood Cliffs (1986)

23. Seligman, M.E., Maier, S.F., Geer, J.H.: Alleviation of learned helplessness in the dog. J. Abnorm. Psychol. **73**, 256–262 (1968). http://dx.doi.org/10.1037/h0025831

24. Ruggiero, T.E.: Uses and gratifications theory in the 21st century. Mass Commun. Soc. **3**, 3–37 (2000). https://doi.org/10.1207/S15327825MCS0301_02

25. Palmgreen, P., Wenner, L.A., Rayburn, J.D.: Relations between gratifications sought and obtained: a study of television news. Commun. Res. **7**, 161–192 (1980). https://doi.org/10.1177/009365028000700202

26. Park, N., Kee, K.F., Valenzuela, S.: Being immersed in social networking environment: Facebook groups, uses and gratifications, and social outcomes. CyberPsychol. Behav. **12**, 729–733 (2009). https://doi.org/10.1089/cpb.2009.0003

27. Ilhan, A.: Motivations to join fitness communities on facebook: which gratifications are sought and obtained? In: Meiselwitz, G. (ed.) SCSM 2018. LNCS, vol. 10914, pp. 50–67. Springer, Cham (2018). https://doi.org/10.1007/978-3-319-91485-5_4

28. Katz, E., Gurevitch, M., Haas, H.: On the use of the mass media for important things. Am. Sociol. Rev. **38**, 164–181 (1973)

29. Greenberg, B.S.: Gratifications of television viewing and their correlates for British children. In: Blumler, J.G., Katz, E. (eds.) The Uses of Mass Communications: Current Perspectives on Gratifications Research, pp. 195–233. Sage, Beverly Hills (1974)

30. McQuail, D.: Mass Communication Theory: An Introduction. Sage, London, UK (1983)

31. Zimmer, F., Scheibe, K., Stock, W.G.: A model for information behavior research on social live streaming services (SLSSs). In: Meiselwitz, G. (ed.) SCSM 2018. LNCS, vol. 10914, pp. 429–448. Springer, Cham (2018). https://doi.org/10.1007/978-3-319-91485-5_33

32. Qu, S.Q., Dumay, J.: The qualitative research interview. Qual. Res. Account. Manage. **8**, 238–264 (2011). https://doi.org/10.1108/11766091111162070

The Effects of Online Social Supports on Exercise Behavior

Xinjia Yu[1]([⊠]), Chunyan Miao[1,2], Cyril Leung[1,2,3],
and Charles T. Salmon[4]

[1] Joint NTU-UBC Research Centre of Excellence in Active Living for the
Elderly (LILY), Nanyang Technological University, Singapore, Singapore
{XYU009, ASCYMIAO}@ntu.deu.sg
[2] School of Computer Science and Engineering,
Nanyang Technological University, Singapore, Singapore
[3] Department of Electrical and Computer Engineering,
The University of British Columbia, Vancouver, Canada
CLEUNG@ece.ubc.ca
[4] Wee Kim Wee School of Communication and Information,
Nanyang Technological University, Singapore, Singapore
SALMON@ntu.deu.sg

Abstract. Exercise is demonstrated to be beneficial to both physical and mental wellbeing. The challenge of how to persuade individuals to maintain regular exercise has received attention from multiple disciplines. With the rise of online social networks, a number of studies found positive correlations between online social support and active lifestyle. In this paper, we report findings from a 52 weeks study under the methods of phynomenography to analyze the roles played by friends in social networks and the support in exercise behavior changes related to these relationships. The results show that besides the individual effect from message tailoring and intervention strategies, the interaction ecosystem based on appropriate role playing by leaders, peers and followers can enhance persuasion power. Effective social support for encouraging physical activities should consider the roles played by the target individuals in the environment and provide comfortable role support.

Keywords: Physical active · Persuasion · Transtheoretical model ·
Online social support · Role playing

1 Introduction

Exercise is demonstrated to be beneficial and necessary to both physical and mental wellbeing [1]. Though the benefits of exercise are well known, physical inactivity is still a worldwide problem [2]. The research problem of how to persuade individuals to maintain regular exercise has attracted attention from multiple disciplines. With the rise of social networks, a number of studies found positive correlations between online social support and more active lifestyles [3–7]. However, there is a lack of study focusing on the role played by social network followers or friends during this kind of interactions. Without understanding the effect of this kind of relationships, we cannot

© Springer Nature Switzerland AG 2019
G. Meiselwitz (Ed.): HCII 2019, LNCS 11579, pp. 137–150, 2019.
https://doi.org/10.1007/978-3-030-21905-5_11

fully exploit online social support in effecting exercise behavior changes to guide persuasive designs.

Based on the review of 71 previous studies, Marshall and Biddle identified three widely accepted categories for "regular exercise or Physical Active (PA)" [8]: (a) unspecified intensity level of exercise for 15 to 30 min each time, three times per week, (b) moderate-to-vigorous level of exercise for 15 to 20 min each time, three times per week, and (c) moderate-to-vigorous level of exercise for 30 min each time, four to seven times per week. In this paper, we followed this standard with considerations for differences in age, gender, and exercise purposes by participants, and define a participant as "performing actively" or "taking regular exercise" by taking "moderate-to-vigorous level of exercise for at least 30 min each time, at least three times per week".

We report findings from a 52 weeks study under the methods of phynomenography to analyze the roles played by friends in social networks and the support in exercise behavior changes related to these relationships. The results show that besides the individual effect from message tailoring and intervention strategies, the interaction ecosystem based on appropriate role playing by leaders, peers and followers can enhance persuasion power. Effective social support for encouraging physical activities should consider the roles played by the target individuals in the environment and provide comfortable role support.

2 Related Work

A number of studies around the world in all age groups have demonstrated the positive effects of intervention in persuading the individuals to adopt and maintain a physically active lifestyle. Researchers have summarized several effective intervention methods. According to Kahn [9], interventions in encouraging PA can be accomplished by providing knowledge and information, teaching behavioral management technologies, building social support and policies. Furthermore, previous studies found that tailored interventions based on the targeted subjects' behavioral change strategies to be effective.

TTM provides a dynamic perspective for understanding the processes of change rather than regarding it as an "all or nothing" phenomenon. As an intervention strategy, it provides a framework for understanding the stages of changes (SOC) in behaviors for each individual. TTM defined five main stages of change to adopt a healthy behavior pattern including: pre-contemplation, contemplation, preparation, action, and maintenance.

Stage 1: Pre-contemplation: people at this stage are not ready to adopt a healthier lifestyle. They do not have the awareness to gather knowledge or think about changes. They will not start to change in the near future (within 6 months). To persuade them, we need to wake their mind by encouraging him/her to think with more conscious about the multiple benefits of changing behaviors.

Stage 2: Contemplation: people at this stage tend to change their behavior by reevaluating the cons and pros of changing their behaviors. They may take action within 6 months. We encourage the subject in the stage of contemplation by helping them to reduce the potential cons of behavior changing.

Stage 3: Preparation: people at this stage are ready to change their behaviors in both beliefs and abilities. They take small steps as gathering information or making a plan. They always start to take actions within 1 month. To persuade them to move on, we can provide knowledge, strategies and help them to make plans.

Stage 4: Action: at this stage, people finally start to act. They adopt new behaviors and work hard to maintain it. When people start to take actions, they need supports like techniques or incentives. We can also persuade them to maintain the behavior by help them to avoid tempts.

Stage 5: Maintenance: at this stage, people have kept the healthy behavior for at least 6 months. In the maintain stage, people tend to spend time with people with similar beliefs. They need to seek support from those who believe and take healthy lifestyle. We need to maintain their habit of relying healthy activities to cope stress.

The first 3 stages are categorized as the inactive stage, while action and maintenance are grouped with the name of active stages. During the stages of change, people use both covert and overt strategies and techniques to influence cognitive, emotional and behavioral activities to process through the stages [10, 11]. Prochaska defined 10 distinct processes of change (POCs) to interpret how the behavior changes happen through the stages moves:

1. Consciousness Raising: showing increasing awareness in gathering facts, information and knowledge about healthy behaviors.
2. Dramatic Relief: feeling fear or worry about the unhealthy behaviors. Feel inspiration to others' experiences of behavior change.
3. Environmental Re-evaluation: noticing that he/she can affect others through his/her behaviors; realizing the positive social impact of healthy behaviors and vice versa.
4. Social Liberation: realizing that the society including both the public and the close social relations is supportive of the healthy behaviors.
5. Self-reevaluation: creating a new self-image with the healthy behaviors as one important signature and be ready to act following this new self-image.
6. Self-liberation: believing that he/she has the ability to conquer the temptations and change the behaviors positively and make commitments to act in this way.
7. Counter Conditioning: learning and adopting healthy behaviors instead of continuing with the old ways.
8. Helping Relationship: seeking support for their change; finding building and maintaining this kind of supportive social relationship proactively.
9. Stimulus Control: managing the environment to support the behavior change like setting goals, and planning to encourage exercise or using check-in APPs to stimulate healthy behavior maintenance.
10. Reinforcement Management: setting reward mechanism to encourage healthy behaviors while punish the negative ones.

The relationship between SOC and POCs is displayed in Fig. 1.

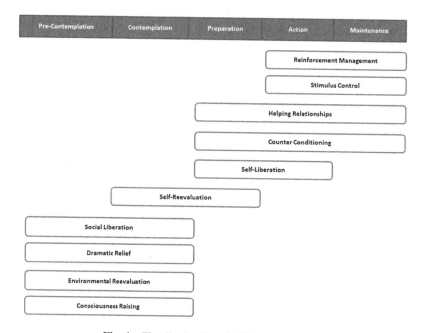

Fig. 1. The distribution of POCs along SOC

The description of the POCs has been demonstrated to be effective in guiding the design and implementation of interventions.

Some of the discriminations between the stages are vague. For example, people in the preparation and maintenance stages all tend to seek support, but the support must be different in practice. Can we go further to supplement these persuasive strategies? Furthermore, both the POCs and the persuasive strategies mentioned social support but there is little studies talk about the sources of the social support. When the same support is provided by different social relations, will the effectiveness be influenced?

To address these questions, we proposed the following study.

3 Methods

We use phenomenography, a qualitative method, to analyze the participants' exercise behavior changes. Phenomenography is "a research method for mapping the qualitatively different ways in which people experience, conceptualize, perceive, and understand various aspects of, and phenomena in, the world around them" [12]. It is a methodology with the aim of seeking and describing the variation in ways people experience. It groups the participants by their performance. Then the researcher will observe and analyze the experiential differences between the active group and the inactive one. Based on the coding of the qualitative data collected during the observation, the research will categorize and define the different experiential and behavioral patterns. The descriptions as results are called phenomenographic essence which is assumed to be the key reason leading the experiential differences between the two groups. To test this hypothesis, the researcher will do iterative comparisons by training the inactive group by the phenomenongraphic essence. If the performance of the inactive group improves after adopting the new methods, the phenomenongraphic essence is demonstrated to be effective.

In this study, we would like to understand how online social support affects the individuals' physical actives. Therefore, we choose a chatting group with the tag of fitness randomly as the target of this study. It is supported by the QQ application provided by Tencent, China. This group has 309 members. The participants are all Chinese females aging from 18 to 42 (mean = 26.0, SD = 6.5) in acceptable health conditions for regular exercising. We designed a 52 weeks long study to analyze online social support behaviors among the members in a chatting group as a social support platform. Since the participants joined the chatting group aiming to keep fitness initiatively before the experiment, we assume that they have all passed the first stage of pre-contemplation. Therefore, this study will focus on the last four SOCs: contemplation, preparation, action, and maintenance.

3.1   Experiment 1

In the first 4 weeks, we observed and recorded each group member's self-reported exercise session every day. The communication context among the members is also recorded automatically by the application. At the end of the 4th week, we grouped the participants according to their performances for further analysis: Group A covers all the participants who took regular exercises during this period, while Group B contains the subjects who failed to maintain regular exercises. Based on this grouping, we compared the communication pattern differences between the active Group A and the inactive Group B. Following the process of Phenomenography method, we analyzed the daily chatting contexts by members of Group A on each SOC using Axial coding.

The results show that:

1. The persuasive argumentations in Group A always show a signature of "completion". The right person appears at the right time. We found 2 argumentations with similar beginning but leading to different consequences as an example to show the differences between effective persuasion and ineffective ones. In this scenario, when the individual describes temptation, a "leader" provides her practical solutions to conquer the temptation, while in the other case a "follower" appears to comfort her with excuses. The feedback from the online social support directs the subject's follow-up behaviors. The logistic analysis is shown in Table 1:

Table 1. Example of effective argumentation vs ineffective argumentation

An effective argumentation example		An ineffective argumentation example	
Communication function	Dialogue	Communication function	Dialogue
Describe temptation	A. I fall in love with a TV show. It occupies all my leisure time	Describe temptation	A. I was not a sofa potato, but when I think about exercise, I cannot lift myself
Propose solutions	B. Try to stand to watch TV instead of sitting and lift dumbbell during your watching	Comfort others	B. Why do you torture yourself? Just do what you want. At least that makes you happy
Make excuses	A. That's a good idea! But my room is too small to do this	Make commitment	A. I made a promise to take exercise every evening
Provide knowledge and share experience	C. See the link below and copy the postures. I've tried this in my Harry Potter's room	Make excuses	B. It doesn't matter to miss one day. You can always find a time to offset
Agree	A. Wow! You saved me!	Agree	A. That makes sense... ...

2. The decisive argumentations look like a mini theatrical with the members supporting by playing their own roles. We can borrow the definition of Role to assist this study. Role is a symbol for individuals in a society to communicate with each other [13]. Role playing contains a set of expected behavior patterns from one individual to another [14]. In this study, the concept of role is defined by its functions.

In addition to the processes of individual behavior changes, the participants showed diversity and complexity in their interaction actions. They undertook different functions in the system. By Axial coding, we category their chatting record as following (Table 2):

Table 2. Coding Results

Axial Coding	Open Coding	Examples
Follower demands	Ask questions	"How can I break up with my soft belly?" "I am not good at any sport, what should I do to keep active?"
	Require supervision	"I am not sure how long I can persevere. Is there anyone who would like to inspect me?"
Follower supports	Join in active groups	"I like your training plan, may I copy it? We can encourage each other."
	Worship	"Hope I could keep active as long time as you did."

(continued)

Table 2. (*continued*)

Axial Coding	Open Coding	Examples
Leader demands	Call for participation	*"I'm going to take fitness courses, is there anyone like to join me?"* *"It's Spring! Let's fight for hot pants in the coming summer!"*
Leader supports	Provide knowledge	*"If you want to build lines on your stomach, you can try the following actions..."* *"Exercise is not only about keeping fit. It contributes to a healthier, happier and balanced life."*
	Propose solutions	*"If you cannot find time to exercise, try to tighten your belly for 5 min every hour when you are sitting in a chair."*
	Dispel negative feelings	*"Of course you can say goodbye to the fat. You've just started. Let's see the results after one month."*
	Correct wrong behaviors	*"Having KFC after exercise is not a good idea."*
	Supervise commitments	*"Have you finished your daily training plan?"*
	Introduce a role model	*"I have to show you these compare photos, girls. My friend lost 12 kilos by physical exercise in one semester!"*
	Rewards	*"Wow, that's really something! I'll put a sticker on your avatar as a reward."*
Peer demands	Set up a goal	*"I bought a pair of jeans in the size of 25. I will stuff myself into it by July"*
	Make a plan to achieve the goal	*"I will jog for 30 min every day."*
	Describe temptations	*"There are so many interesting things to do beside PA in my limited after work time."*
	Make excuses	*"It is too cold to work out today."* *"I do not want to take an extra shower after the exercise."*
	Conquer temptation	*"I was too tired to work out today but I crawled to the gym."*
	Display achievement	*"Check-in! Finished 1 h training today!"* *"Now, I can run 10 km without a stop."*
Peer states	Describe feelings	*"I took the elevator even when I just need to go up one floor. I'm afraid I will lose the ability to go upstairs by my feet forever."*
	Make self-reevaluation	*"I was too lazy."* *"I hate to look like this."*
	Share beliefs	*"I won't take running since it will make my muscles look like stones."*
	Share experience	*"I used to take exercise every week, but lost 0 kilo."*
	Refute or doubt others	*"Are you serious? I've never heard about this exercise program."*

(continued)

Table 2. (*continued*)

Axial Coding	Open Coding	Examples
Peer supports	Encourage	*"Come on! You can make it! You are doing so well till now."*
	Agree to others' opinion	*"That's true. You cannot keep fitness by discarding breakfast."*
	Comfort others	*"That's all right. You've already tried."*

3. Based on the categories generated from coding, we define the roles in this study as leaders, peers, and followers in the online social support system. These roles communicate with each other with the purpose of changing behaviors. They are taking different functions in different SOCs. A Leader always acts initiatively and takes responsibility to others. They usually have more related knowledge and would like to share with others. In this small online society, they are taking the roles as PA coaches or supervisors. They feel satisfaction from the others' following. A follower behaves in the opposite way. They tend to ask questions or request help from the environment. They contribute to the online society by providing feedbacks as praise or behavioral changes. Besides these two classic roles, peers are more complex to define. They need social support as the followers but with more initiative. They share knowledge as the leaders but without much purpose to affect others. They also "state" something which is more personal with less sociality. This category is not stable in practice. A group member may play different roles in different scenarios. However, from a long-term perception, the role playing of a member can be defined by others' expectation towards him/her and his/her self-awareness of his/her social functions. Table 3 lists down the appropriate role interactions we observed during this experiment at each SOC.

4. The effectiveness of specific persuasive strategy changes not only along the stages of change of the individual but also the role she is playing in the group. The most powerful strategy in this case is playing the appropriate role in the communications. Role playing is a two-way process. The feedback from the other party affects the subject's behavior. For example, a Leader cannot play her role if there is no Follower appreciating her shared information or exercise plan. This phenomenon leads to relapse of the Leaders. When a Leader in the maintenance stage affecting others by persuasion, she is also be persuaded to maintain this behavior pattern because of the cognition of responsibility and the enjoyment of leading.

5. When the individual's SOC moves, her role playing switches with it gradually. For example, after a period of preparation, a Peer may make a committee to take actions. During her preparation, she gathered a lot of knowledge and techniques to support her further actions. When she enters the action stage, she may be eager to share her knowledge and experiences to help others. This behavior change makes her a new leader.

Based on the coding results, we can hardly make a conclusion about which category of the social support works most effectively in persuading the members to take more exercise. The phenomena showed that the persuasive effectiveness of one strategy depends on both the stage of change of the individual and also her role playing during the interactions.

Table 3. Overview of the role playing strategies

Role	Interaction behaviors	SOC				The proposed appropriate following actions	The possible actions lead to this feedback
		C	P	A	M		
Follower	Ask questions	√	√			Provide knowledge and propose solutions	
	Require supervision			√	√	Supervise commitments and rewards	
	Join in active groups			√		Supervise commitments	Call for participation
	Worship	√	√	√	√	Agree to others' opinion	Introduce a role model, display achievement
Leader	Call for participation		√	√	√	Join in active groups, set up a goal, make a plan	
	Provide knowledge	√	√	√	√	Agree to others' opinion, state self-belief and Share experience	Ask questions
	Propose solutions			√	√	Set up a goal, and agree to others' opinion	Make excuses
	Dispel negative feelings	√	√	√	√		Describe feelings
	Correct wrong behaviors			√	√	(behavior changes)	Make a plan to achieve the goal and share experience
	Supervise commitments			√	√	(behavior changes)	Require supervision, set up a goal, make a plan and conquer temptation
	Introduce a role model	√	√			Worship, set up a goal	Share experience
	Rewards			√	√	(behavior changes)	Require supervision, display achievement

(continued)

Table 3. (*continued*)

Role	Interaction behaviors	SOC				The proposed appropriate following actions	The possible actions lead to this feedback
		C	P	A	M		
Peer	Set up a goal		√			Propose solutions and supervise commitments	Call for participation
	Make a plan to achieve the goal		√			Supervise commitments	Call for participation
	Describe temptations	√	√	√	√	Propose solutions	
	Make excuses	√	√	√	√	Propose solutions	
	Conquer temptation			√	√	Worship, rewards	
	Display achievement			√	√	Worship, rewards	
	Describe feelings	√	√	√	√	Share beliefs…	
	Make self-reevaluation	√				Share beliefs, encourage, comfort others	
	Share beliefs	√	√	√	√	Encourage and comfort others	
	Share experience			√	√	Share belief, worship, and correct wrong behaviors	
	Refute or doubt others		√			Provide knowledge, share experience	Provide knowledge, share belief, share experience
	Encourage	√	√	√	√		Share experience, set up a goal, make a plan
	Agree to others' opinion	√	√	√	√	(share more)	Provide knowledge, share experience, set up a goal, make a plan
	Comfort others						Share experience, share belief, describe feelings

3.2 Experiment 2

To demonstrate our findings, we designed an intervention experiment and recruited participants in Group B. 185 of the group members joined the experiment. We use several controlled IDs to join Group B (n = 185) as persuasive agents. We separated Group B into Group B Experiment1 (n = 62), Group B Experiment2 (n = 62) and

Group B Control (n = 61) almost equally in SOCs. In Group B Experiment1 (BE1), the agents played the roles following the pattern we observed in Group A. For example, the controlled IDs played the roles of L to communicate with the Fs in the preparation stage by helping them to make a work out plan or proposing solutions to solve their practical problems.

In Group B Experiment2 (BE2), the agents are playing opposite roles compared with Group BE1. We go continue to use the example in BE1, when a Follower in the preparation stage is demanding a plan, we send a follower instead of a leader to help. We do not reject the traditional strategies demonstrated to be effective by the previous researchers, but we deliver the same messages by a different "role" comparing with Group BE1. From the subject's perception, this "person" is less expertise on the related area based on their previous communications. The experiment results will show us whether the role of the members is a critical factor in affecting the persuasion.

In Group B Control (BC), there is no agent. But it does not mean there is no social support in this group. The participants in this group are also doing interventions to others and themselves. They also tend to change their behaviors towards a healthier way.

The agents speak in the groups every day in the following 48 weeks. The communication context and self-reported exercise sessions per week are recorded. We also recorded the weekly physical active frequency of each participant before the experiment as Week 0 to be a benchmark. The results are analyzed after each 12 week period. An ANOVA test at the end of 48 weeks after the intervention, demonstrated significant differences between Group BE1, BE2, and BC (F = 9.59, P < 0.005). The Table 4 shows the results in each group. The members in Group BE1 take average 3.6 exercise session per week at the end of this study. This number rises from 1.4 at week 0. Comparing with the little numerical fluctuation in the other two groups, we can see a significant ascent in physical active.

Table 4. Mean exercise session per week based on self-report

	Week 0	Week 12	Week 24	Week 36	Week 48
BE1	1.4	3.9	3.2	3.3	3.6
BE2	1	2.1	1.7	2.3	1.4
BC	1.1	0.8	1.8	1.6	1

Figure 2 visualized the differences between the experimental groups (BE1 and BE2) and the control group (BC). Participants supported by the appropriate role playing were more active comparing with the other two groups. Though the drop in Week 24 shows a classic problem of short term effectiveness in persuasion intervention, the participants' performance got better after the valley. The mean exercise session reported by treatment group BE1 increased in the last 12 weeks which significantly differs from the other 2 groups. This trend shows a positive potentiality of our proposed role playing theory in long term online social support.

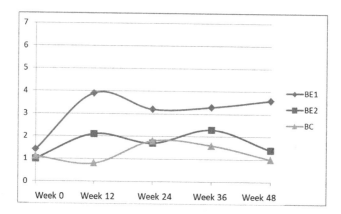

Fig. 2. Mean self-reported exercise sessions of the 3 groups along the 48 weeks

To analyze the long term relationships of role playing and behavior changes, we calculated the percentages of the participants who take behavior changes in each experimental group. In Group BE1, 30% of the participants (n = 62) changed their behavior positively from inactive (contemplation and preparation) to active stages (action and maintenance) and maintain the active behavior for at least 1 month. 45% of the participants processed from inactive stages to active ones for a short term but relapse within 1 month. 25% of the participants in this group did not change their behaviors. Table 4 displayed the results of Group BE2 and Group BC.

Table 5. Percentages of participants in SOC

	Percentage of participant process from IA to A for at least 4 weeks	Percentage of participants process from IA to A for a short term	Percentage of participants adopt no behavior change
Group BE1	30%	45%	25%
Group BE2	15.1%	39.4%	45.5%
Group BC	21%	37%	42%

At the end of Week 48, 7 of the participants from Group BE1 were still maintaining regular exercises. At the same time, none of the participants from the other two groups were able to keep up.

4 Discussion

- In the maintenance stage, the consideration of "who" is more critical. Our proposed theory shows significant effectiveness in the last three months by comparing the per capita weekly active days between Group BE1 and BE2. At the same time, the participants who maintain the physical active lifestyles at the end of the study were all under the intervention of our proposed theory in Group BE1. People who are trying to maintain a habit consider more about feelings and social relations than practical issues.

- Based on our proposed theory and experiment results, we conclude that appropriate role playing is an important component of online social support in persuading the individuals to adopt a physical active lifestyle. These roles can be played by not only human beings but also artificially intelligent agents. Our proposed theory can inspire AI designs.

- What factors lead to the role adapted by each group member? From this study, we found in the stages of change of a specific individual affect the role he/she is playing in the online group because of his/her cognition and ability. However, we can also see that people at the same stage choose multiple roles naturally. Some of the role adoptions come from the first impression, for example, if a member answered a question by coincidence at the first time when he/she enters the group and gets broad support, he/she will face a great chance to be followed. What follows is a subtle leader role adoption. In addition to this, the personality of each individual may also affect the role adoption during their interaction though this kind of role playing may not be successful for other members' unpredictable reactions.

5   Conclusions

How does social support persuade the individuals to adopt a physical activate life style? In additional to the separated personalized message tailoring and intervention strategies, the interaction among the social members can empower the persuasive strength at the same time. This ecosystem runs in a healthy way based on the appropriate role playing of the leaders, peers and followers. An effective social support in encouraging physical actives should consider the role playing by the targeted individual and provide the comfortable role support.

Developing persuasion techniques to support behavior changes for users is a critical challenge in human computer interaction study. This study can help us to understand the appropriate roles an intervention agent needs to play. It will provide useful guidelines to support the designs of persuasive artificial intelligence agents and applications to support the adoption of healthy styles.

Acknowledgement. This research is supported by the Interdisciplinary Graduate School, Nanyang Technological University, Singapore. This research is also supported, in part, by the National Research Foundation, Prime Minister's Office, Singapore under its IDM Futures Funding Initiative and the Singapore Ministry of Health under its National Innovation Challenge on Active and Confident Ageing (NIC Project No. MOH/NIC/HAIG03/2017).

References

1. ACSM. ACSM's guidelines for exercise testing and prescription. American College of Sports Medicine. 9th revised edition. Williams & Wilkins (2014)
2. Andersen, L.B., Mota, J., Pietro, L.: Update on the global pandemic of physical inactivity. Lancet **388**, 1255–1256 (2016)
3. Berkman, L.F., Glass, T.: Social integration, social networks, social support, and health. Soc. Epidemiol. **1**, 137–173 (2000)
4. Centola, D., van de Rijt, A.: Choosing your network: social preferences in an online health community. Soc. Sci. Med. **125**, 19–31 (2015)
5. Teodoro, R., Naaman, M.: Fitter with twitter: understanding personal health and fitness activity in social media. In: ICWSM (2013)
6. Cavallo, D.N., Tate, D.F., Ward, D.S., DeVellis, R.F., Thayer, L.M., Ammerman, A.S.: Social support for physical activity—role of Facebook with and without structured intervention. Transl. Behav. Med. **4**(4), 346–354 (2014)
7. Zeng, L., Almquist, Z.W., Spiro, E.S.: Stay connected and keep motivated: modeling activity level of exercise in an online fitness community. In: Meiselwitz, G. (ed.) SCSM 2018. LNCS, vol. 10914, pp. 137–147. Springer, Cham (2018). https://doi.org/10.1007/978-3-319-91485-5_10
8. Marshall, S.J., Biddle, S.J.H.: The transtheoretical model of behavior change: a meta-analysis of applications to physical activity and exercise. Ann. Behav. Med. **23**(4), 229–246 (2001)
9. Kahn, E.B., et al.: The effectiveness of interventions to increase physical activity: a systematic review. Am. J. Prev. Med. **22**(4), 73–107 (2002)
10. Prochaska, J.O., Redding, C.A., Evers, K.E.: The transtheoretical model and sages of change. In: Glanz, K., Rimmer, B.K., Viswanath, K. (eds.) Health behavior and health education, 4th edn. pp. 97–121. Jossey-Bass, San Francisco (2008)
11. Prochaska, J.O., Velicer, W.F.: The transtheoretical model of health behavior change. Am. J. Health Promot. **12**, 38–48 (1997)
12. Marton, F.: Phenomenography: a research approach to investigating different understandings of reality. In: Sherman, R.R., Webb, R.B. (eds.) Qualitative Research in Education: Focus & Methods, pp. 141–161. Routledge Falmer, London (2001)
13. Heiss, J.: Social roles. In: Rosenberg, M., Turner, R.H. (eds.) Social Psychology: Sociological Perspectives, pp. 95–129. Transaction Publishers (1981)
14. Gordon, C., Gordon, P.: Changing roles, goals, and self-conceptions: process and results in a program for women's employment. In: Ickes, W., Knowles, E.S. (eds.) Personality, Roles, and Social Behavior, pp. 243–283. Springer, New York (1982). https://doi.org/10.1007/978-1-4613-9469-3_9

Social Media in Education

Study Case of an Adaptive Educational Tool Oriented to University Students for an Object Orientation Course

Ninozka González, Claudio Cubillos[✉], Silvana Roncagliolo, and Rafael Mellado

Pontificia Universidad Católica de Valparaíso, Valparaíso, Chile
ninozka.93@gmail.com, {claudio.cubillos,
silvana,rafael.mellado}@pucv.cl

Abstract. The use of e-learning for educational purposes has been the focus of researchers for a long time, because of the difficulty to determine if a tool based on this concept is able to instruct the educational content that a professor can easily teach on a classroom. In this document the available tools and teaching methods to deliver Adaptive Learning to each user are investigated. Through the development of this paper, the adaptive techniques to be implemented to the Educational Tool are proposed; how and which contents will be presented to the students and which adaptation model will be applied to that content. Thanks to the investigations on the topic, and the analysis of the performance of the students on the Object Orientation course, from the Pontificia Universidad Católica de Valparaíso (PUCV), preliminary models for the Educational and Adaptive Tool have been defined, with promising results.

Keywords: E-learning · Adaptive learning system · Educational tool · Adaptive Hypermedia System · Object-Oriented Programming · Java language

1 Introduction

Nowadays, the action of teaching tends to be related, in the first instance, to a classroom where a teacher instructs in a general and personalized way students who are interested in learning. But this process can not only be carried out depending solely on a teacher in a physical environment such as the classroom, we can also get teachings through, for example, computational online platforms.

In this work it is sought to demonstrate that the educational and adaptive tools are a plus in the classroom and that they support the study of students, improving their performance, offering more personalized content, including adaptation mechanisms. The research described in this document are done by students from the Pontificia Universidad Católica de Valparaíso (PUCV); the analyses were done to students who have taken an Object Oriented Programming course based on JAVA programming language, taught under an Informatics Engineering Bachelor Program.

This document is divided in sections; Sect. 2 the related and theoretical works are explained. In the third section the architecture of the adaptive tool used is explained.

© Springer Nature Switzerland AG 2019
G. Meiselwitz (Ed.): HCII 2019, LNCS 11579, pp. 153–169, 2019.
https://doi.org/10.1007/978-3-030-21905-5_12

In Sect. 4 a historical analysis of the students is done. In Sect. 5 the evaluation of the tool and the content to be used for testing. The tests done by the students are in Sect. 6. Finally, the conclusions can be found in Sect. 7.

2 Related Work

2.1 Educational and Adaptive E-learning Tools

Adaptive learning is creating a new approach to teaching action, where teachers must adapt existing methodologies in order to teach and students are changing their way of learning. Some of the educational and adaptive e-learning tools that are related to this work are the following:

- Ask-Elle: tutoring system used to teach Haskell programming language, by Gerdes et al., for the University of Utrecht in Norway [2]. The mechanism used in this work consists of verifying the correctness of incomplete programs and providing suggestions. The system makes it possible to deliver solutions with feedback messages.
- AtoL: is an intelligent tutoring system that dynamically adapts to the needs of each student and provides the student with immediate feedback. Realized by Yoo et al. [3].
- The JavaTutor System: It is a LE for Java with multimodal affection recognition. It takes into account the cognitive and affective aspects of students who use different hardware tools to recognize their affective state [15].
- CTutor: a problem-solving environment that diagnoses students' level of knowledge, but also provides feedback and advice to help them understand the course topic, overcome misconceptions, and reinforce concepts learned [12].
- JITS: Java Intelligent Tutoring System (JITS) involves the development of a programming tutor designed for students in their first Java programming course at university level. An overview of architectural design, artificial intelligence techniques, and the user interface is presented [13].
- J-LATTE: intelligent, constraint-based tutoring system that teaches a subset of the Java programming language. J-LATTE supports two modes: conceptual mode, in which the student designs the program without having to specify the content of the instructions, and coding mode, in which the student completes the code [14].

The mentioned systems have been made to support the teaching, most of these use artificial intelligence techniques, such as Intelligent Tutor Systems, to create student profiles and provide feedback to students.

However, some of the works listed above are aimed at teaching a programming language other than JAVA (as in Ask-Elle, CTutor and AtoL). Studies related to JAVA (such as in The JavaTutor System, JITS and J-LATTE) use adaptive mechanisms based on the student's learning styles, while in this work rules of adaptation are generated from profiles created from historical data extracted from students.

Besides, in these works the way of teaching is through the resolution of code problems giving feedback if a problem was solved in an inappropriate way; in the present work for each subject the theoretical contents are taught in a sequential way and in addition coding examples are presented. In addition, feedback is given to the students when they carry out the final tests of each module. Finally, there are few studies in the literature oriented to Latin America and university students, such as in the present work.

2.2 E-learning

The definition of e-learning, from the work done by Bowles [1], is explained as a novel approach to provide well-designed, student-centered, interactive learning environments that are available anytime, anywhere. The author of this book classifies the aspects of e-learning into the following:

- Pedagogical: referring to educational technology as a discipline of educational sciences associated to technological means, educational psychology and didactics.
- Technological: referring to information and communication technology, through the selection, design, customization, implementation, hosting and maintaining of solutions where proprietary open source technologies are integrated.

2.3 Adaptive Learning

Adaptability to a learner's personal interests, characteristics and objectives is a key challenge in e-learning. Adaptability is the ability to shape to the situation in which a given object is being subjected; in this case, adaptability means that learners are provided with a learning design that is adapted to their personal traits, interests and goals [4].

Personalization includes not only objectifying the student's styles, but monitoring the system's usage to adapt to the student's way of learning. Such systems can help students stay focused through patterns that adapt to changes [5, 6]. The system should perform, as far as possible, both the teacher's role and the construction of robust student models for each user, allowing:

- Adaptation in the study program of each user.
- Help in the navigation through the course activities.
- Support in the accomplishment of tasks, exercises and problem solving.
- Support resources at any time needed.

In Mathoff's work [16] a series of requirements are proposed which an educational system should have in order to manipulate the adaptive process, such as interactivity, adaptable instruction, robustness, direct control of the learning process, empirical evaluation; and to be friendly in use.

2.4 Intelligent Tutoring System

For Ovalle and Jiménez [8], Intelligent Tutoring Systems (ITS) aim to emulate the behavior of a human tutor. They are called "intelligent" to contrast them with traditional computer-assisted instruction systems, being its distinction the use of IT techniques such as Artificial Intelligence.

ITS can provide individualized education by adapting to each student's level of knowledge, learning abilities, and individual needs. These systems separate by modules the necessary components to form an ITS architecture:

- Domain Module: represents the knowledge that will be taught and pedagogically organized to ease the tasks of the tutor module.
- Tutor Module: is in charge of guiding the teaching-learning process.
- Student Module: represents the student's level of knowledge for the system.
- Educational Module: is responsible of the management of the interactions between the system and the users through the communication of the modules and the client.

2.5   Adaptive Hypermedia System

For the authors who carried out the research work presented in [7, 9], the Adaptive Hypermedia System (AHS) is capable of constructing a mock-up of the objectives, preferences and knowledge of each user, in order to use it dynamically through what is called a user model and a domain model. With this mock-up it is possible to adapt the content, navigation and interface to the user needs.

The overall architecture of an AHS must have three essential parts according to the works of Benyon [10] and De Bra [11] explained below:

- User model: describes the information, knowledge and preferences of the student.
- Domain model: provides a structure for the representation of user-dominated knowledge. This model stores the user's estimated level of knowledge for each concept defined in the course content.
- Interaction Model: represents and defines the interaction between the user and the application.

3   MAGLE Adaptive Tool Architecture

3.1   MAGLE Authoring Tool

For the presentation of contents, the MAGLE authoring tool was used, which allows to visualize the contents created in a web page, where each module and activity is represented. The acronym for the authoring tool used comes from Modular Adaptive and Gamified Learning Environment.

MAGLE is a learning management system for creating learning environments based on adaptation and gamification. It allows you to create e-learning content (lessons), organize courses, deliver content, register users in courses, and finally monitor and evaluate their performance. Generally speaking, we can say that it is:

- An online learning management software package.
- A virtual learning space aimed at facilitating the experience of distance training, both for educational institutions and companies, in mixed or semi-present form, and only virtual.

MAGLE allows you to create modules, clusters, and activities; each module can contain clusters and activities, and each cluster is a set of activities. The activities represent what a web page would look like. The tool allows you to enter layout, text, a series of types of exercises (such as alternative, multiple response and binary), and multimedia content, such as images or videos.

3.2 Teaching Material for the Adaptive Tool

For the tests, the tool covered the contents described in Table 1. These topics were chosen from the opinions of the same students carried out in the classroom, studies on the partial academic performance of the course and about the academic performance of the first formal evaluation.

Table 1. Contents covered by the tool.

Topics covered by the platform	
Topic 1	Classes
Topic 2	Objects, get and set methods, visibility modifiers
Topic 3	Overload
Topic 4	Collections

In the object orientation course, the first part of the content is described in the following Table 2.

Table 2. Contents covered for the first formal evaluation.

Content of the first part of the course	
Main topic	Sub-topic
Introduction	Origins
	Principles
	Languages
	Installation and compilation
Classes	Declaration
	Access
	Attributes
	Constructors
	Destructors
	Methods
	Control structures
	Data structures
GUI interfaces	Windows
	Events

3.3   Tool Content Architecture

The content architecture in the authoring tool is divided into topics, where each topic covers a specific content of the subject. The topics in turn have explanatory introductions, explanatory exercises and evaluative exercises; the evaluations that are carried out are Pre-test and Post-test. The module divisions and tool evaluations are explained below:

- Explanatory introduction: consists of an introduction to the content, which explains the theoretical concepts of the subject being studied, through plain text or images.
- Explanatory exercises: it consists of the realization of explanatory examples supporting the introduction of the topic.
- Evaluation exercises: it consists of a brief evaluation test where the contents presented in the module will be evaluated.
- Reinforcement: consists of a more detailed explanation and more examples of a particular subject.
- Pre-Test: consists of an evaluation of the student to know how much he handles the subject being studied.
- Post-Test: consists of an evaluation with the same questions as the pre-test but modified to compare how much the student learned with the tool.

Before starting with the explanation of the subject, and for study purposes, the students carry out a pre-test evaluation. After this, the students visualize the explanation of the topic, where it contains the exercises, and explanatory introductions. Once the student has gone through all the explanation of the subject of a specific topic or reinforcement a post-test is done. In this way, meaningful data will be obtained to compare student performance with the tool.

3.4   Tool Adaptation Model

Complementary explanations of sub-topics of each item were used for the adaptation model, leaving content visible for one user profile or another. Two user profiles were used, taken from the analysis made of the students; the adaptive explanatory contents are classified into two levels:

- Low: This grade is oriented to students who perform poorly, therefore the explanations consist of more examples and explanation slides.
- High: this grade is oriented to students who have good academic performance; the amount of explanation and examples is briefer than in the other case.

Using the MAGLE authoring tool, an adaptation is made as the student progresses through the course. This consists of, for each sub-topic of the main topic, evaluating the subject with a key question. If the student answers this question incorrectly, then for this student a deeper explanation will be shown with another type of exercise, so that he can understand why he made a mistake. If the student responds well to this question then the content will follow its normal path.

Below a flowchart to better explain how the adaptation mechanism works is presented in Fig. 1.

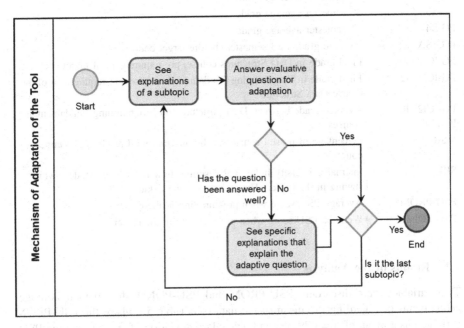

Fig. 1. Flowchart of adaptive model.

4 Stage 1: Historical Analysis of University Students to Obtain Adaptation Profiles

The analysis of the students was made with the objective of creating profiles and finding factors that influence the performance of the students who have taken the Object Orientation course, and that make them fail or pass the course. For this analysis, 107 university students from the PUCV who have already taken the Object-Orientation course between 2015 and 2016 were studied. Also, the studied variables were extracted from the academic web system used in the university (called Navegador Académico), where the students' grades are registered, in addition to the PSU scores.

4.1 Analysis of Academic Variables

Through the access to the Navegador Académico it has been possible to extract certain characteristics that at first sight have been intuited as possible factors in the approval or reprobation of the course. A total of eleven variables were initially considered (See Table 3).

Table 3. Variables extracted from the Navegador Académico.

Variable	Description
PG-S2	2nd semester average grade
PG-S3	3rd semester average grade
PG-S4	4th semester average grade
PG3-SA	Average grade of 3 semesters before target course
FG-ICI2240	Final grade in Data Structures course, pre-requirement of target course
FG-ICI1142	Final grade in Programming Fundamentals course, pre-requirement of the course Data Structure
PG-ICI2240-ICI1142	Average grade between Data Structure and Programming Fundamentals courses
%SR	Percentage of passed courses in the program until reaching the target course
SRI	Internal University Index that describes how risky is the student while staying in the career. The closer to 1, the riskier
PSU-PROM	Average PSU score when pre-enrolling in the career
PSU-POND	Weighed PSU score when pre-enrolling in the career

4.2 Results of the Analysis

Two variables were discarded, PSU-PROM and PSU-POND, due to their homogeneous behavior regarding the mean of the data (see Table 5), where the PSU-PROM variable has a mean of $\mu = 629$ pts. and a standard deviation of $\sigma = 40$ pts; the PSU-POND variable has a mean of $\mu = 627$ pts. and a standard deviation of $\sigma = 37$ pts.

Having a standard deviation in both variables very below the mean, it can be concluded that PSU variables are not very influential in generating student profiles, such that they fail or pass the Object Orientation course.

To verify the expressed conclusion with PSU variables, an analysis of all variables was performed with the Naive Bayes Multinomial algorithm, which is an algorithm used to predict independence between predictor variables. This algorithm is used to search each variable's weights and discover which factor is most significant for the failure or approval of the course of each student. The algorithm is applied with variables of the same type of measure, since it is possible to study the weight of the variables over others. They were grouped as follows:

- Percentage Variables: Such as the percentage of assed courses and the SRI.
- PSU Variables: Such as the weighted PSU and the average PSU.

Note that scale variables from 1.0 to 7.0: Such as those that are the student's final or average grade. Exit classifications are named as:

- "CLASS 1": represents the course's failure.
- "CLASS 2": represents the course's approval.

Table 4. Weights of the percentual variables

Variables	Class 1	Class 2
%SR	0.55	0.89
SRI	0.44	0.1

In the next table the PSU variables are analyzed (see Table 5), being able to notice that they do not influence much one variable over the other in approving or failing the course.

Table 5. Weights of the PSU variables

Variables	Class 1	Class 2
PSU-POND	0.5	0.5
PSU-PROM	0.49	0.49

Finally, with the variables in the grading scale, it was noted that the grades of the course ICI2240, ICI1142 and the average of both have more weight over the other variables analyzed. It was also noted that in the semester that the course ICI2240 was dictated, it also has more weight than the other variables in the approval or failure of the course (see Table 6).

Table 6. Weights of the note variables

Variables	Class 1	Class 2
PG3-SA	0.137	0.138
FG-ICI2240	**0.16**	**0.16**
FG-ICI1142	**0.14**	**0.142**
PG-ICI2240-ICI1142	**0.153**	**0.155**
PG-S2	0.134	0.125
PG-S3	**0.137**	**0.141**
PG-S4	0.136	0.135

The first variables analyzed were the percentual ones, as it can be seen in the following Table (see Table 4), the variable of %SR influences much more in the approval of the course than the variable of SRI, while for the course failure %SR also has more weight than the SRI.

To develop a predicting algorithm the most significant variables were chosen (PG-ICI2240, FG-ICI1142, PG-ICI2240-ICI1142, %SR and SRI). The resulting model obtained a 81% successful classification, but in this case, the most important thing is to find out if the algorithm successfully classifies the students in failed profile rather than approval. For this profile, the algorithm only achieved 65% success in the ranking. Table 7 describes the error percentage of the algorithm (See Table 7).

Table 7. Percentage of error and classification

	% of error
Error	19%
Class 2 classification	35%
Class 1 classification	0%

Given these results, we can conclude that there is a relationship between students who, during the course of the career, have had low grades in general and in the prerequisite courses of the Objects Orientation course. That is to say, it is much more likely that this profile of students will fail the course, compared to the profile of students with good grades.

5   Stage 2: Test for the Tool and Content Evaluation

Prior to testing the adaptive tool with students, a survey was conducted to randomly selected students to evaluate the design of the contents that was presented to students and the proper functioning of the MAGLE authoring tool.

5.1   Content Evaluation by the Students

For these tests, students from the School of Computer Engineering at the PUCV participated, with a total of 13 people. The assessments of the students for the explanation of the content were not good, of a total of 5 questions made with the Likert scale, which evaluated the presentation of the content, 4 of them were rated as deficient. Given these results, the presented content was changed, more examples were added and the way of explaining the theory was reformulated, so that it would be more didactic and simpler for the students. The changes made were validated with the course professors. The following Table 8 shows the results of the evaluation done by the students, separated by item.

Table 8. Students' assessment regarding the content

Variables	Strongly disagree	Disagree	Neutral	Agree	Strongly agree	Total
The content explanation was clear	0	1	8	1	3	13
I agree with the amount of examples taught in the tool	0	4	8	1	0	13
I agree with the level of deepness of the content	0	3	9	1	0	13

(continued)

Table 8. (*continued*)

Variables	Strongly disagree	Disagree	Neutral	Agree	Strongly agree	Total
The content shown in the tool proved to be didactic	0	10	2	1	0	13
The content presentation motivated me to continue studying it	2	3	7	1	0	13
Total	2	21	34	5	3	

Table 9. Evaluation of students regarding the tool MAGLE

Variables	Strongly disagree	Disagree	Neutral	Agree	Strongly agree	Total
The tool follows a normal flow, without connection errors, throughout the process	0	0	0	2	11	13
It did not take me long to get to the target when I was navigating through the tool	0	0	0	8	5	13
User registration of the tool is quick and simple	0	0	0	0	13	13
The tool contains easy-to-access buttons and instruction for the user	0	0	1	2	10	13
I was able to complete my task without visual problems	0	0	4	5	4	13
Total	0	0	5	17	43	

5.2 Evaluation by Students of the MAGLE Tool

In general, the ratings regarding the tool were very good, the navigation in it was measured, its performance and user-friendly interface. The students evaluated the following items regarding the tool (see Table 9).

6 Stage 3: Student Tests with the Tool

For the following tests, students were selected from a Database course of the career in IT Engineer ("Ingeniería en Ejecución en Informática"), because these students have already passed a Data Structure course and have not had an Object-Oriented Programming course yet, therefore the first contents will be better evaluated than with students who had already done the course. For reasons of better explanation of contents, the following topics were selected:

- Topic 1: Classes and their components.
- Topic 2: Visibility Modifiers and Methods.

6.1 Content Testing Topics 1 and 2, with the Tool Without Adaptation

For these tests, the students were given a pre-test and post-test to evaluate how much help the educational tool provided to the students. The results were as follows (See Table 10).

We concentrated on topic 2, specifically because the students answered all of the test questions. As seen in Table 10, students have a considerable improvement of at least 25% when they study the content with the tool.

For analysis purposes, two biases were performed in the pre-test row of topic 2, when students were not yet passing through the tool explanations; the first bias was taken with the measurement of the mean of 4 good questions; the second bias was taken with the measurement of the mean of 3 good questions. With the objective of comparing the performance of the students who had lower grades, with the students who did the pre-test without problems; thus obtaining 4 groups:

- Bias from minor to 4 good questions.
- Bias from greater than 4 good questions.
- Bias from minor to 3 good questions.
- Bias from greater than 3 good questions.

The following table (see Table 11) shows the results of this bias, calculating the mean and standard deviation in the groups.

Table 10. Results table for 1st and 2nd topics using tool without adaptation

Student	Pre test 1st topic	Post test 1st topic	Pre test 2st topic	Post test 2st topic	PG3	% SR	Grade: Prog. fundamentals	Grade: Data structures	Course average	Pretest and posttest delta value	Improvement percentage
1	6	6	2	6	4,1	69	5,1	3,9	4,5	4	50
2	5	6	3	6	5,1	75	6	1,5	3,8	3	37,5
3	7	7	3	6	5,3	100	4,8	4,5	4,7	3	37,5
4	5	5	3	8	5	98	5,1	4,2	4,7	5	62,5
5	5	7	4	8	3,8	64	4,2	4,9	4,6	4	50
6	6	8	4	6	5,1	100	5,7	4,7	5,2	2	25

(*continued*)

Table 10. (*continued*)

Student	Pre test 1st topic	Post test 1st topic	Pre test 2st topic	Post test 2st topic	PG3	% SR	Grade: Prog. fundamentals	Grade: Data structures	Course average	Pretest and posttest delta value	Improvement percentage
7	6	6	4	7	4,7	70	4,1	4,1	4,1	3	37,5
8		6	4	6	4,6	75	4,2	6	5,1	2	25
9	8	7	4	8	5,5	100	5,9	5,8	5,9	4	50
10	8	5	5	8	5,4	100	5,1	6,1	5,6	3	37,5
11	6	7	5	6	4,3	67	5,2	4,8	5	1	12,5
12	7	6	6	8	6,5	100				2	25
13		6	6	8	5,1	98	6,4	6,2	6,3	2	25
Mean	6,1	6,2	3,7	6,9	4,9	83,1	5,0	4,1	4,9	2,5	
Standard deviation	1,1	0,9	1,2	1,0	0,7	15,5	0,8	1,3	0,7	1,1	

With these results we can conclude: that the students who have lower grades in the pre-test and pass through the explanation of the tool, improve considerably their results and have a higher delta of improvement than the students who have more knowledge and pass through the tool. With this we can affirm that the students who have lower grades can reach the students who have higher grades; minimizing the performance difference among the students.

Table 11. Analysis of biases of topic 1 and 2 with the tool without adaptation

Bias	Measure	Pre-test topic 4	Post-test topic 4	PG3	% SR	Grade: Programming fundamentals	Grade "Estructura"	Course average	Pre and post test delta
Bias minor to 4 good questions	**Mean**	3,4	6,7	4,8	83	5	4,4	4,7	**3**
	Standard deviation	0,7	0,9	0,5	16	0,7	1,3	0,6	**1**
Bias greater than 4 good questions	**Mean**	5,5	7,5	5,3	91	5,6	5,7	5,6	**2**
	Standard deviation	0,6	1	0,9	16	0,7	0,8	0,7	**0,8**
Bias minor to 3 good questions	**Mean**	2,8	6,5	4,9	86	5,3	3,5	4,4	**4**
	Standard deviation	0,5	1	5,3	16	0,5	1,4	0,4	**1**
Bias greater than 3 good questions	**Mean**	4,7	7,2	5	86	5,1	5,3	5,2	**3**
	Standard deviation	0,9	1	0,8	16	0,9	0,8	0,7	**1**

6.2   Content Testing Topic 1 and 2, with the Tool Including the Adaptation Mechanism

The test that was carried out with the adaptation mechanism had a total number of 16 questions; there were also 12 reinforcement questions that were in charge of the adaptation mechanism. The results of these tests with the tool and the adaptation mechanism can be seen in Table 12.

Table 12. Results table for 1st and 2nd topics using tool with adaptation

Student	Time: Content	Time: Final test	Reinforcement	Good answers	% SR	PG-3S	Grade: "Data structure"	Grade: "Informatics introduction"	% Good answers
1	22	8	1	12	100	6,1	–	–	75
2	16	8	1	14	100	6,1	6,9	6,6	87,5
3	22	8	1	14	86	5,1	5,8	6	87,5
4	14	8	1	16	100	6,1	6,7	6,4	100
5	10	8	2	12	100	5,5	5,8	5,9	75
6	22	10	2	14	62	4,9	5,8	4,7	87,5
7	20	8	2	16	98	5,1	6,2	6,4	100
8	16	8	4	10	100	5,5	5,5	5	62,5
9	18	12	4	14	80	4,6	4,3	5,3	87,5
10	22	10	4	14	100	5,3	4,6	5,6	87,5
11	20	8	4	16	100	5,3	4,5	4,8	100
12	14	8	4	16	98	5,5	4,7	6,5	100
13	16	8	6	8	69	4,3	4,1	4	50
14	16	12	6	12	100	5,1	4,7	5,7	75
15	20	12	7	12	48	3,6	4,1	3,9	75
16	20	8	7	14	98	5.3	5,5	6,3	87,5
17	20	8	7	14	76	4,2	4,3	5	87,5
18	24	12	9	14	100	5,5	4,6	5,6	87,5
19	20	10	9	14	71	4	3,3	3,6	87,5
20	20	12	10	12	69	4,1	3,9	5,1	75
Mean	19	9	5	13	88	5,1	5,1	5,4	
Standard deviation	4	2	3	2	16	0,7	1	0,9	

As in previous tests, for reasons of analysis, two biases focused on the row of number of reinforcement used by the student were carried out. Obtaining four groups in this way:

- Bias of 6 or more reinforcement questions.
- Bias less than 6 reinforcement questions.
- Bias of 7 or more reinforcement questions.
- Bias less than 7 reinforcement questions.

These biases have the purpose of compare between students who required more reinforcement to understand the subject and the ones who did not require reinforcement. The results can be seen in the following Table 13.

Table 13. Analysis of biases of topic 1 and 2 using the tool with adaptation

Bias	Measure	Reinforcements	Good answers	% SRI	PG3	Grade "Data structure"	Grade "Informatics introduction"
Bias of 6 or more reinforcement questions	Mean	6,2	13	85	4,8	4,5	5,1
	Standard deviation	2,2	2,3	17	0,7	0,6	0,8
Bias less than 6 reinforcement questions	Mean	1,4	14	92	5,6	6,2	6
	Standard deviation	0,5	1,6	14	5,4	0,5	0,7
Bias of 7 or more reinforcement questions	Mean	7,6	13	78	4,5	4,3	4,9
	Standard deviation	1,5	2,1	19	0,7	0,7	1
Bias less than 7 reinforcement questions	Mean	2,5	14	94	5,4	5,5	5,8
	Standard deviation	1,4	1,9	11	0,5	1	0,7

We can conclude that students who score lower on pre-test tests and see the explanation of the tool considerably improve their scores and have a much higher delta than students who already have the knowledge and go through the tool. With this we can affirm that the students who have bad grades can reach the students who have good grades; minimizing the gap between groups of students.

6.3   Analysis of Results

If we rank students according to the average grade of the prerequisites courses such as Data Structure and Programming Fundamentals we can draw the following conclusions from the tests performed:

- The percentage of courses approved by the students during the university career is related to the performance of the students in these tests.
- Students with grade averages lower than 5.0 in the prerequisite courses had to go through more reinforcement content than students with grades higher than 5.0.
- The time spent on the test by students with grade averages below 5.0 is greater than those with grade point averages above 5.0.
- The percentage of improvement for the two tests increases considerably when studying the contents through the educational tool.
- In both tests, the amount of good answers in both biases does not have much variation, when students already pass through the tool.
- The reinforcement used in the content turned out to be satisfactory, since the students who had to go through a reinforcement were leveled with the students who didn't have to go through a reinforcement.

7 Conclusion

An adaptive e-learning system was developed and novel adaptation mechanism was implemented based in the profiling of students based on its academic performance in previous courses. Based on our previous studies of the educational topic [6, 17–19] together with the opportunity to work directly in the classroom, gave a plus in being able to leverage a solution capable of adaptively teaching and reinforcing topics on students.

The preliminary study of the factors that influence the approval or disapproval of the course has been able to reflect certain variables of great weight for the students, and provides information necessary to focus the tool on those students with the highest risk of failing the course.

In this document, the good acceptance of e-learning tools in students has been made known and a positive impact on the learning process is reflected, together with an adaptation mechanism that supports and generates a 'leveling factor' in the knowledge of the participating students of this experiment. With the tests carried out in this work we left open the possibility of further research and experiments on university students, either in the same course or with other courses and topics since the MAGLE tool allows to modify the contents and the mechanisms of adaptation.

References

1. Bowles, M.S.: Relearning to E-learn: Strategies for Electronic Learning and Knowledge. Melbourne University Press, Carlton (2004)
2. Gerdes, A., Heeren, B., Jeuring, J., van Binsbergen, L.T.: Ask-Elle: an adaptable programming tutor for Haskell giving automated feedback. Int. J. Artif. Intell. Educ. **27** (1), 65–100 (2017)
3. Yoo, J., Pettey, C., Yoo, S., Hankins, J., Li, C., Seo, S.: Intelligent tutoring system for CS-I and II laboratory. In: The Annual ACM Southeast Conference 2006, pp. 146–151 (2006)
4. Van Rosmalen, P., Brouns, F., Tattersall, C., Vogten, H., Van Bruggen, J., Koper, R.: Towards an open framework for adaptive, agent-supported e-learning. Int. J. Continuing Eng. Educ. Life-Long Learn. **15**, 261–275 (2005)
5. Rani, M., Nayak, R., Vyas, O.P.: A ontology-based adaptive personalized e-learning system assisted by software agents on cloud storage. Knowl.-Based Syst. **90**, 33–48 (2015)
6. Diaz, F., Cubillos, C., Mellado, R., Barbaguelatta, E.: Development of a prototype of e-learning based on ontologies to analyze the impact of learning styles on engineering students. In: Proceedings of the 36th International Conference of the Chilean Computer Science Society, SCCC 2017, Arica, Chile, pp. 1–9 (2017)
7. Brusilovsky, P.: Methods and techniques of adaptive hypermedia. User Model. User-Adapt. Interact. **6**, 87–129 (1996)
8. Ovalle, D.A., Jimenez, J.A.: Ambiente inteligente distribuido de aprendizaje: Integración de ITS y CSCL por medio de agentes pedagógicos. Revista EIA **6**, 89–104 (2006)
9. Martins, A.C., Faria, L., Vaz de Carvalho, C., Carrapatoso, E.: User modeling in adaptive hypermedia educational systems. Educ. Technol. Soc. **11**, 194–207 (2008)
10. Benyon, D.: Adaptive systems: a solution to usability problems. User Model. User-Adapt. Interact. **3**, 65–87 (1993)

11. De Bra, P.M.E., Aroyo, L.M., Chepegin, V.: The next big thing: adaptive web-based systems. J. Digit. Inf. **5** (2004)
12. Kose, U., Deperlioglu, O.: Intelligent learning environments within blended learning for ensuring effective C programming course. Int. J. Artif. Intell. Appl. **3** (2012)
13. Sykes, E.R., Franek, F.: An intelligent tutoring system prototype for learning to program Java TM. In: Proceedings of the 3rd IEEE International Conference on Advanced Learning Technologies (ICALT03) (2003)
14. Holland, J., Mitrovic, A., Martin, B.: J-LATTE: a constraint-based tutor for Java. In: 17th International Conference on Computers in Education 2009, pp. 142–146 (2009)
15. Wiggins, J.B., et al.: JavaTutor: an intelligent tutoring system that adapts to cognitive and affective states during computer programming. In: Proceedings of the 46th ACM Technical Symposium on Computer Science Education, p. 599 (2015)
16. Masthoff, J., van Hoe, R.: APPEAL: a multi-agent approach to interactive learning environments. In: Perram, J.W., Müller, J.-P. (eds.) MAAMAW 1994. LNCS, vol. 1069, pp. 77–89. Springer, Heidelberg (1996). https://doi.org/10.1007/3-540-61157-6_23
17. Bourgeois, M., Sentis, F., Cubillos, C., Mellado, R., Roncagliolo, S.: Ashy.alRescate(): a videogame for developing basic object oriented programming skills. In: Proceedings of the 37th International Conference of the Chilean Computer Science Society, SCCC 2018, Santiago, Chile (2018)
18. Silva, R.M., Cubillos, C., Melgarejo, B., Roncagliolo, S., Velasquez, C.: Role videogame tool for teaching myths and legends to primary school students. In: Proceedings of the 37th International Conference of the Chilean Computer Science Society, SCCC 2018, Santiago, Chile (2018)
19. Silva, R.M., Barbaguelatta, E., Cubillos, C., Diaz, F.: X9: an adaptive learning platform for geometry at school level. In: Proceedings of the 37th International Conference of the Chilean Computer Science Society, SCCC 2018, Santiago, Chile (2018)

Using a Gamification Tool to Support the Teaching-Learning Process in Computer Science Program

Pamela Hermosilla$^{(\boxtimes)}$ (iD), Katherine Valencia, and Erick Jamet

Pontificia Universidad Católica de Valparaíso, Valparaíso, Chile
pamela.hermosilla@pucv.cl, {katherine.valencia.c,
erick.jamet.h}@mail.pucv.cl

Abstract. Today's students are immersed in an environment where technology predominates and they expect learning to be as fast, simple and entertaining as possible, integrating digital information and the internet in the realization of activities and development of the courses. However, the reality differs from the expectations of the students; Despite the large number of tools available for carrying out activities in classes, they do not manage to effectively support the teaching and learning process.

It is in this context the incorporation of games in the classroom is presented as an important factor for the reinforcement of knowledge, development of skills such as problem solving, teamwork and communication, among others. In this sense, gamification, defined as "The use of game elements and game design techniques in non-game contexts", enhances the way of motivating and encouraging students to develop desired behaviors.

In this study we design and evaluate a gamification strategy and a web application, which are focused on measuring the progress of student's competences through game elements integrated in the activities carried out in classes.

Keywords: Gamification · Motivation · Computer Science (CS) students · Information and communication technologies (ICT) · Teaching-Learning process

1 Introduction

Currently, students who enter educational establishments have very high expectations regarding the use of technology in the classes, as support for teaching and learning methodologies, which leads in a certain way to innovate in the classroom, to motivate and engage the students. Thus, the objective of this study is to compare the results of the application of activities based on gamification techniques, in two groups of students of the course "Software Engineering Workshop" of the Pontificia Universidad Católica de Valparaíso.

This study details the process of designing a the web application based on the 6D's proposed by Hunter and Werbach [1], in order to evaluate the effectiveness of 'Gama CET' (Gamified Competences Evaluation Tool), a web application which allows to develop and evaluate the expected competences in students, through the integration of

© Springer Nature Switzerland AG 2019
G. Meiselwitz (Ed.): HCII 2019, LNCS 11579, pp. 170–181, 2019.
https://doi.org/10.1007/978-3-030-21905-5_13

games elements in the activities carried out in classes, such as the recognition of achievements through points, badges, prizes, or leaderboards, among others.

Finally, to evaluate the motivation and effectiveness of the use of the tool, a data collection instrument was designed to know the perception of the students about this experience.

2 Definitions and General Aspects of Gamification

The gamification, was born as a concept in 2003, and it was masified in 2010 through the work of multiple professionals. It is formally defined as 'The use of game elements and game design techniques in non-game contexts' [1]. In other words, it's about finding fun in everyday things. The game elements define the small pieces that make up a complete game as a whole experience, which can be inserted into activities that are not games in themselves, such as education; the design techniques allow to decide which game elements to use and how to improve the gamified experience; and the non-game contexts refer to any real context that does not belong to the fiction of the games.

In this way, the gamification allows to encourage the development of expected behaviors, as is the case of the development of the *competences* of each subject, through *motivation* and *feedback*.

- Competencies

Competencies show a person's ability to cope with situations, putting psychosocial resources into operation, including skills and attitudes in a specific context [2].Through studies, students acquire knowledge and develop skills, which correspond to general education, as well as other skills of a professional nature [3]. In this sense, The Pontificia Universidad Católica de Valparaíso promotes the 'Competency Based Learning' for their careers, with the purpose of directing the efforts to improve the teaching of the university [4]. According to these guidelines, the graduation profiles of Computer Science Programs [5] have been defined under three groups of competences related to the areas: disciplinary (CD), professional (CP) and fundamental formation (CF).

In this way, each course of the curricular plan of the Computer Science Programs, includes a set of competences to be considered in these.

- Motivation

Motivation is one of the most important elements for gamification, since its main objective is to encourage the motivation of people to achieve an objective or develop an expected behavior. The word comes from the Latin 'motivus' (movement) and the suffix 'tion' (action and effect), so 'being motivated' refers to being in motion to do or achieve something. There are two types of motivation, extrinsic and intrinsic.

There are different factors that influence the motivation positively and negatively, as the followings:

- Intrinsic motivation: It is based on the theory of self-determination [6] and indicates that people are inherently pro-active, with a desire to improve.

– Performance-inhibiting anxiety: the elements of this factor refer to the existence of anxiety that negatively affects the person's motivation and performance.
– Absence of effort: this factor indicates that the person tends to have a lack of will to do and finish things.
– Motivation for learning: is oriented towards personal goals that can be developed by own choice, and therefore these goals are related to the search of knowledge, get new skills and improve these.
– Motivation for fear of failure: it is a factor related to avoiding negative evaluations and, in general, of failure. People tend to be more concerned about not losing than wanting to win, so their performance is reduced.

• Feedback

The constant interaction of the games is based fundamentally on the feedback which allows to know the progress towards an objective or as a response to an action that has weight in the context that is used. Players like to receive information about their progress towards a goal, how many steps they have completed to receive a prize.

Players can regulate their behavior towards the metrics that are presented to them in the feedback. In addition, feedback with unexpected information helps autonomy and intrinsic motivation. Feedback is important for the called activity cycle, which indicates how motivation is capable of generating an action, it receives immediate feedback through points or rewards, which motivates the person to perform more actions [1] (Fig. 1).

Fig. 1. The games and the activity cycle [1]

3 Implementation Proposal for Gamification

The work methodology considered for the realization of this study was based on the design process for the gamification proposed by Hunter and Werbach [1], in which the steps to design and implement the gamification are described in an effective and specific way for the context to achieve specific business objectives. This design process for the gamification is based on six steps, or 'Six Steps to Gamification' according to its initials:

- Define Business Objectives
- Delineate Target Behaviors
- Describe Your Players
- Devise Activity Cycles
- Don't Forget The Fun!
- Deploy the Appropriate Tools

To integrate the concept of the gamification within the educational context, with the 6 steps mentioned, a strategy is posed in a gradual way, which considers the aspects mentioned above. The following Fig. 2 represents the aspects considered in this implementation proposal.

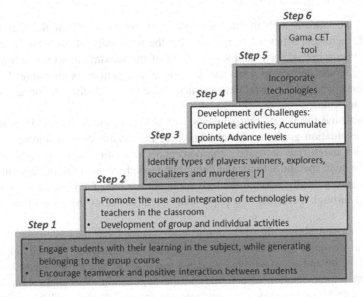

Fig. 2. General scheme of implementation

As a final result of the application of the previous elements we have designed a gamification strategy, and implemented game elements as progression, leaderboards, and social fun through a prototype of a web application to support the methodology and manage the activities in the course, at the same time it allows to automatically measure the competences developed through these.

In this gamification strategy we considered a "gamification factor", which represents a percentage value between 0 and 100% and indicates the amount of points obtained by a student with respect to the highest score obtained in the course. This factor is then used to calculate a reward in the form of a bonus of n tenths to the final mark of the subject, with n defined by the teacher, in order to encourage the extrinsic motivation of the participants, based on the following formulas:

$$GF = \left(\sum(SA)/MS\right) * n \tag{1}$$

$$FMG = FM + GF \tag{2}$$

GF: Gamification Factor
SA: Score Achieve
MS: Maximum Score
FMG: Final Mark Gamificated
FM: Final Mark of the course
n: Number of tenth(s) rewarded

Where the student with the highest score will obtain 100% of the gamification factor and, therefore, a reward of n tenths for the final mark of the subject, unlike a student whose score is, for example, one third of the maximum, which will obtain a third of the tenths defined as a reward. Therefore, competition is encouraged without harming those who have a lower performance, since they will still get a prize, even if it is smaller in scale.

To determine the points that students will obtain in the activities developed, an analytical evaluation guide has been defined for the evaluation of competences. This guide allows measuring separately the percentage of achievement of each expected competence in an specific activity and obtaining a weighted score for the student, this is performed automatically through the web application 'Gama CET' in the experimental group, and through guidelines on paper and spreadsheets in the case of the control group.

As mentioned above, the web application 'Gama CET' has been developed to support the designed gamification strategy. This is a responsive web application developed by the authors to motivate students and evaluate the competences developed through the implementation of activities in the application. The application consists mainly of a dashboard in which the students can see and do the available activities in the course, integrating game elements such as points, progression and socialization in these. The main utility of the application lies in the automation of the calculation of points, as well as their respective weighting in the competences developed, in order to generate real-time feedback on the progress of the competences, while centralizing the information of the subject for teacher's comfort.

4 The Experiment

For the development of this study, as mentioned before, two groups of students of the same course and of the same level of curricular advancement within their curriculum are considered. In both groups, the gamification methodology described in the previous point was applied, but only one of the groups used the game tool developed to support the methodology. Both groups of students attend "Software Engineering Workshop" course (INF 4540 and ICI 4540) considering the same game elements, however, one of these courses (INF 4540) used the gamification through the prototypes of the application 'Gama CET', called Experimental Group, and the other who did not use it, was called the Control Group.

In this way, the students were given a set of tasks to complete, which included different competences: disciplinary (CD), professional (CP) and fundamental formation (CF), and each one indicates the following:

- CD1: Apply mathematical, scientific and engineering principles to design solutions to problems in the area.
- CD2: Participate in work teams for the execution of engineering projects.
- CD3: Develop solutions to engineering problems, in the field of their specialty, using critical thinking and analytical skills.
- CP1: Develop computer applications, efficient and of quality.
- CP2: Participate in computer projects using the available ICT appropriately.
- CP3: Select components that make up the technological base in the implementation of computer applications.
- CP7: Communicate orally and in writing in the English language in specific contexts and situations specific to their profession.
- CF2: Orient the work performance with values principles, tolerance and professional ethics.
- CF3: Manage your learning independently to update and deepen your knowledge.
- CF4: Demonstrate creativity, initiative and proactivity in the performance of their activities.
- CF5: Communicate effectively orally, written and graphically in their mother tongue.

In order to evaluate the achievement for the task, a data collection instrument was designed, which would allow to compare both groups of students, in order to compare the results between them. The groups that participated in the study correspond to 18 students (Experimental Group), and 35 students (Control Group), remembering that both groups are from the same course or are in the same year of study.

The instrument used considered 12 questions, grouped into three categories: motivation, gamification and application, which together allowed investigating the subject. The evaluation scale used considers:

- Likert Scale: A measurement tool allows measuring attitudes and knowing the degree of compliance of the respondent. In this sense, the response categories will serve to capture the intensity of the respondent to certain statements. For this case scale with 5 degrees of compliance is used.
- Dichotomous questions: with yes/no answer (Boolean).
- Selection of Options: identification of possible alternatives for a certain evaluated aspect.

The followings Tables 1, 2 and 3 present the questions according to the categories, dimensions and evaluation scales considered to this study.

Table 1. Motivation category questions

Dimension	Questions	Scale type
D1. Apreciation	Q1. Intrinsic motivation (+) Q2. Inhibitory performance (−) Q3. Absence of effort (−)	Likert scale levels: SA. Strongly Agree A. Agree NAD: Neither agree nor disagree D. Disagree SD. Strongly Disagree
D2. Tendency	Q4. For learning (+) Q5. For fear of failure (+)	Likert scale levels: SA. Strongly Agree A. Agree NAD: Neither agree nor disagree D. Disagree SD. Strongly Disagree

Table 2. Gamification category questions

Dimension	Questions	Scale type
D3. Knowledge	Q6. ¿Do You know about the concept of "Gamification"?	Yes/No
D4. Perception	Q7. Regarding the complexity of the gamification strategy	Options selection: D4.1 Simple but incomplete D4.2 Simple and easy to understand D4.3 It is understood at a general level but its dynamics are complicated D4.4 Very complex strategy and complicates the normal development of the course
D5. Importance	Q8. According to your point of view, do you think that incorporating challenges with rewards (independent of points) such as medals, would increase your motivation in the subject?	Yes/No
D6. Preference	Q9. How well do you agree with the Point System used? (optional and obligatory activities)	Likert scale levels: SA. Strongly Agree A. Agree NAD: Neither agree nor disagree D. Disagree SD. Strongly Disagree

Table 3. Application category questions

Dimension	Questions	Scale type
D7. Experience (pg. 100)	Q10. Do you have experience with systems/tools that use gamification?	Yes/No
D8. Evaluation 101,103)	Q11. In general, how would you describe your level of motivation with respect to the subjects that you have studied at the university Q12. Do You think that the use and integration of technology in the subjects studied is adequate?	Likert scale levels: SA. Strongly Agree A. Agree NAD: Neither agree nor disagree D. Disagree SD. Strongly Disagree

5   Results and Discussion

The main results of the instrument used in this study are shown below. It will be determined *"Experimental Group"* to those students who used the gamification tool and *"Control Group"* to those who do not.

The analysis of the results will be carried out for each of the identified categories, and the dimensions evaluated in them, comparing both groups of the study (Table 4).

Table 4. Percentage scores for dimensions (D1, D2)

		D1.Apreciation		(NAD)	D2. Tendencies	
		(SA)	(A)		(D)	(SD)
Experimental Group (18 participants)	D1.1	**25.6**	33.3	0	41.0	0
	D1.2	28.2	28.2	0	20.5	23.1
	D1.3	25.6	25.6	0	28.2	20.5
	D2.1	**23.1**	**33.3**	0	15.4	28.2
	D2.2	**28.2**	**28.2**	0	20.5	23.1
Control Group (35 participants)	D1.1	19.2	30.8	0	15.4	34.6
	D1.2	32.7	21.2	0	13.5	32.7
	D1.3	32.7	36.5	0	28.8	19.2
	D2.1	**34.6**	**13.5**	0	19.2	32.7
	D2.2	**32.7**	**21.2**	0	13.5	32.7

- Motivation Category Questions

In the case of Motivation Category, it can be seen that in Apreciation associated with D1.1 question, students of Experimental Group reaches a greater acceptance of motivation intrinsic than de Control Group (25.6%, 19, 2%), meanwhile in D1.2 and D1.3 this same group shows lower rate (28.2%, 25.6%), that means, motivation slows them down less than de Control Group (32.7%, 32.7%), because D1.2 and D1.3 represent factor to influence negatively on the motivation of the students.

In relation to the D2.1, of Tendency dimension, *Experimental Group* shows 56.3% considered options of agreement (SA, A) meanwhile *Control Group* reach 48.1%. Similar situation can be appreciated to the question D2.2, with 56.4% and 53.9% to *Experimental Group* and *Control Group* respectively (Table 5).

Table 5. Percentage for dimensions (D3, D4, D5)

	D3. Knowledge		D4. Perception				D5. Importance	
	Yes	No	D4.1	D4.2	D4.3	D4.4	Yes	No
Experimental Group (18 participants)	**44.4**	55.6	0	**66.7**	33.3	0	**88.9**	11.1
Control Group (35 participants)	**40**	60	11.4	62.9	25.7	0	**80**	20

- Gamification Category Questions

Regarding the knowledge and importance of gamification concept (D3,D5), it is possible to appreciate that *Experimental Group*, reaches greater marks in both dimensions (44.4% and 88.9%) if you compare with *Control Group* (40% and 80%), that shows they know more about the concept, and give it more relevance. In addition to this, the Perception is also better for the *Experimental Group* (66.7%), related to D4.2 affirmation which indicates that strategy of gamification seems to be simply and easy understand (Table 6).

Table 6. Percentage for dimension (D6)

D6. Preference

	Dimension	(SA)	(A)	(NAD)	(D)	(SD)
Experimental Group (18 participants)	D6.1	**44.4**	22.2	5.6	16.7	11.7
Control Group (35 participants)	D6.1	**40.0**	25.7	2.9	25.7	5.7

The analysis of this dimension was associated with the point bonus system, and even when both groups present similar results, the Experimental Group shows a slight inclination to the acceptance of point system with 44.4% respect of the Control Group with 40%, but it is observed that there is no clear difference between them (Table 7).

Table 7. Percentage for dimensions (D7, D8)

	D7. Experience			D8. Evaluation				
	Yes	No		(SA)	(A)	(NAD)	(D)	(SD)
Experimental Group (18 participants)	16.7	83.3	D8.1	0	66.7	33.3	0	**88.9**
			D8.2	**50**	16.7	16.7	16.7	0
Control Group (35 participants)	28.6	71.4	D8.1	11.4	62.9	25.7	0	**80**
			D8.2	**11.4**	40	28.6	20	**0**

- Use of Tool to support Gamification (Gama CET)

For the last dimensions of this study, it is possible to see that even Experimental Group recognized has less experience (16.7%) and feel less motivated (88.9%), than the Control Group (28.6%, 80% respectively), this first group had 50% of "strongly agree (SA)" in the affirmation related to integrate adequately ICT in the development of the courses, and on the other hand *Control Group* only reached a 11.4%.

Additionally, to understand last results of this study, it is necessary to show the achievement of competences to the activities considered and the gamification factor in each study group.

This is the comparative progress of the competences, calculated as percentages from the points obtained, as detailed in the implementation proposal, regarding the total sum of points given in the activities of the subject, which represents the 100% (Table 8).

Table 8. Percentage for achievement of competences (CD, CP, CF)

	Competences disciplinary			Competences professional				Competences fundamental			
	CD.1	CD.2	CD.3	CP.1	CP.2	CP.3	CP.7	CF.2	CF.3	CF.4	CF.5
Experimental Group (18 participants)	3.56	**18.49**	3.83	3.40	**9.63**	**4.49**	**7.41**	**8.80**	**19.87**	**8.45**	12.07
Control Group (35 participants)	**16.69**	14.77	**19.14**	**6.10**	8.13	0	6.16	5.33	4.87	5.79	**13.02**

The results presented in the previous table, indicate that *Experimental Group* shows higher percentages on the Professional and Fundamental competences with 6.23% and 12.30% on average respectively, meanwhile *Control Group* had 5.10% and 7.25% in the same areas evaluated, and this last group, only had higher average (16.87%) in Disciplinary Competences compared with Experimental Group (8.62%).

Finally, related to the Gamification Factor (GF) and the marks of students, referenced in (1) and (2), the following table presents the Gamification Factor Rewards obtained expressed in tenths, considering from 1 to 5, and the min, max and mark average of both groups (Table 9).

Table 9. Percentage gamification factor and marks

	Factor gamification (1 to 5)					Mark (10 to 70)		
	1	2	3	4	5	Min.	Max.	Average
Experimental Group (18 participants)	0	0	15	66	**19**	42	**66**	**58**
Control Group (35 participants)	2	4	8	84	2	29	62	57

The last results shown in Table 9, evidences that *Experimental Group* had 19% of the maximum reward possible (5) and only 2% in the *Control Group*. In addition to this *Experimental Group* had better mark than *Control Group*, including minimum, maximus and average mark.

6   Conclusions

The use of gamification represents a great opportunity to motivate students and integrate technology and innovation within the courses. The multiple success cases studied they indicate that the gamification, in spite of being a relatively new concept, is a good way to continue to achieve these objectives, while allowing students to enjoy the dynamics presented, and consequently, of the course taken.

For this study the dimensions (D1, D2) evaluated within the motivation category, shown better results to the *Experimental Group* considering the positive and negative factors that influence motivation, in the student's process learning. Regarding the gamification category (D3, D4, D5, D6) despite *Experimental Group* knows less about gamification concept, they had better perception and give more importance than de *Control Group*.

In the dimensions D7 and D8 in the application category questions, *Experimental Group* shown had less experience with gamification tools, they recognized feel a little motivated in other curses of their career, and they strongly agree with the use of technology in the development of the gamified course, unlike the control group.

Related to achievement of competences (Table 8), it can be seen that it is indeed viable to quantitatively measure the progress of competences in a subject, through its evaluation in the activities. Thanks to the metrics studied, it is possible to observe in a simple way the comparative progress of all the competences worked through the activities. In this way, it is also possible to adjust the development of the expected competences whose progress is less, since we can include new activities that consider a greater weighting on those. Additionally, the marks in the Experimental Group showed an improvement compared to the Control Group.

With the results obtained in this sample, it is possible to demonstrate that incorporate gamification activities, it is a way that CS students could improve their motivation and marks using a gamification tool, and it seems to be easy and entertaining for students related to Information Technology Careers.

As future work, it would be interesting to focus on those aspects that did not present a significant difference and that may require more detail for their study, as well as trying to repeat the experience with others groups and continue with the development of the web application so that can be used in different educational contexts, and thus facilitate the evaluation of competences and encourage the active learning of students.

Acknowledgments. We thank all the students involved in this case of study. They provided useful opinions that allowed us to prepare this article and could be the beginning of other related studies.

References

1. Hunter, D., Werbach, K.: For the Win: How Game Thinking Can Revolutionize Your Business (2012)
2. Pinto, M.: Alfabetización informacional y e-learning: diseño de tutoriales y cursos online (2008)
3. Garcia, M.: Las competencias de los alumnos universitarios (2006)
4. PUCV: Marco de Cualificación de la Docencia Universitaria, Pontificia Universidad de Valparaíso (2015)
5. PUCV: Plan curricular Escuela Ingeniería Informática 2013 (2013)
6. Ryan, R.: Self-determination theory and the facilitation of intrinsic motivation, social development, and well-being (2002)
7. Bartle, R.: Hearts, Clubs, Diamonds, Spades: Players Who suit MUDs (1996)

Quality Assurance in Online Education: A Development Process to Design High-Quality Courses

Fernando G. Paniagua[✉]

School of Technology Art, and Design, Computer Science/Information
Technology, Community College of Baltimore County,
7201 Rossville Boulevard, Rosedale, MD, USA
fpaniagua@ccbcmd.edu

Abstract. The number of courses and full degrees offered online, raises a considerable interest in concerns and problems associated with online education, particularly as it relates to the quality of online instruction. Quality Assurance (QA) has become a very important issue for both, educational institutions and institutional accrediting agencies. This is a progressive process and institutions go through different stages until they implement QA effectively in their institution. This paper will start by presenting different QA approaches using different rubrics; then it will describe the three different stages that the Community College of Baltimore County (CCBC) had experienced in this path to design high-quality courses: (a) training, (b) process, and (c) formalizing the process. In the last step, a very detail process for designing online courses will be presented. In the next section, the types of QA reviews that are done at CCBC will be depicted. Finally, the paper will end with some topics that the Online Learning office is working in this continuing process of designing and implementing high-quality courses.

Keywords: Quality Assurance · Online learning · Quality Matters ·
High-quality courses · QM rubric

1 Introduction

The number of courses and full degrees offered online, raises a considerable interest in concerns and problems associated with online education, particularly as it relates to the quality of online instruction [1]. In the case of the Community College of Baltimore County (CCBC), they started offering online courses around Fall of the year 2000, and launched CCBC Online during Fall 2018, offering not only full degrees but also certifications completely online. As of today, CCBC offers more than 20° online and certificate options, in addition to thousands of online classes, rolling admissions, and multiple starts-dates.

In this context, Quality Assurance (QA) has become a very important issue for both, educational institutions and institutional accrediting agencies. According to Universitas 21 Global approach, this QA process relates to five main areas: course content, courseware development, adjunct faculty recruitment, pedagogy and delivery [2]. The

G. Meiselwitz (Ed.): HCII 2019, LNCS 11579, pp. 182–194, 2019.
https://doi.org/10.1007/978-3-030-21905-5_14

main focus of this paper is about course content, development and delivery; recruitment and pedagogy are out of the scope of the present work. In order to improve course quality, several rubrics have been developed by different institutions. These rubrics can also work well as guide when developing a course, similar to a roadmap to success.

This paper is organized as follow: Sect. 2 discusses some of quality course rubrics, Sect. 3 presents the Quality Assurance process performed at CCBC, Sect. 4 depicts the types of Quality Assurance reviews, while Sect. 5 considers some future work and provides some conclusions for this article.

2 Quality Control Rubrics

Because of the exponential growth in the offering of online education, and the aim of quality by those institutions that are offering those courses and degrees, several companies and institutions developed different rubrics to help developers in achieving good quality courses. The first institution that is going to be presented is the Online Learning Consortium (OLC) who supports higher education institutions seeking best practices for advanced quality. OLC offers a robust suite of quality scored cards providing educational institutions with the necessary criteria and benchmarking tools to ensure online learning excellence for the entire institution. The current scorecards include Administration of Online Programs, Blended Learning Programs, Quality Course Teaching and Instructional Practice, Digital Courseware Instructional Practice and the Open SUNY Course Quality Review (OSCQR) from Open SUNY. These scorecards can be used to demonstrate several quality elements not only within a particular program but also as an overall level of quality, that can be presented to the higher education accreditation institutions [3].

From all the scorecards provided by OLC, the one that focuses on the quality of the course will be discussed. OSCQR is not only a rubric, but a collaborative process to improve instructional design and accessibility of an online and blended course. The main focus of the process is continuous improvement and it is not a curse or instructor evaluation tool. Each course is reviewed using the OSCQR rubric by three different perspectives: faculty perspective (the author of the course), instructional design perspective, and an external reviewer perspective (a librarian, or another faculty member that is not familiar with the course). The team reviews the course asynchronously and provides suggestions for improvement. Those improvements are discussed, and a refresh plan is developed; once the course has been updated to the new version, then the team meet again, review the accomplishment and plan future enhancements. The rubric contains 50 quality and accessibility standards and have been categorized as 'essential' or 'important' based on research-based effective online practices. This rubric might be particularized by the higher-education institution by adding other standards [4]. It is very important to understand that OSCQR is an approach to review, refresh, and continue improve online courses, but it doesn't help when you need to decide if the course under review has good QA to be offered online.

The next course quality rubric to be presented is the Quality Online Learning and Teaching (QOLT) Rubric developed by California State University at Chico. The rubric can be used in three different ways: as a self-evaluation tool, so a faculty member will evaluate his/her course, as a guide for developing a new online/blended course, so the rubric can be used as a roadmap, and finally as a recognition tool for exemplary online instruction [5]. The rubric is composed of six domains, and each domain is presented with different criteria. Each criterion provides rankings with clear explanations so the reviewer can see how the course meets each one of the criteria: 'baseline', 'effective', or 'exemplary'. There are no explanations about what the requirements for a course are to be considered a good quality course. Does all the criteria for all the domains be ranked at 'exemplary', or only some of them?

Blackboard provides the Exemplary Course Program which recognized instructors and designers that demonstrate the applicability of best practices in the following areas: course design, interaction and collaboration, assessment, and learner support. Courses are evaluated by Blackboard clients using a common rubric. The Exemplary Course Program Rubric uses weighting values and numerical scores. A weighting value from 0.5 to 3 has been assigned to a category in each one of the areas, to indicate the relative importance of the category. Also, each category is described according to the level of mastery and assigned a numerical score: Exemplary (5–6), Accomplished (3–4), Promising (2), Incomplete (1), and Not Evident (0). Reviewers assign a numeric value to each category in each area [6]. The program does not specify a minimum numeric value needed by a course to indicate the quality of the course.

North America Council for Online Learning (NACOL) released the National Standards for Quality Online Courses (iNACOL) which provides guidelines for online course content, design, technology, assessment, and course management. These standards are available to states, districts, online programs, or other educational organizations, and are primarily geared towards K-12 online learning. Several standards are organized into five different sections: content, instructional design (how the course has been designed: learning activities and communication), student assessment, technology (tools and accessibility to those tools), and course evaluation and support. Each standard contains some considerations for the reviewers, and the corresponding rating: 0: Absent (the component is missing), 1: Unsatisfactory (needs significant improvement), 2: Somewhat satisfactory (needs targeted improvements), 3: Satisfactory (discretionary improvement needed), and 4: Very Satisfactory (no improvement needed) [7]. The rubric does not provide any suggestion on how to work with this rating to determine if a course can be considered a quality course.

Quality Matters (QM) is a nonprofit organization that supports and maintains quality assurance in online learning. The principal characteristic of the QM rubric is the concept of Alignment, which occurs when the learning objectives, assessments, instructional materials, learning activities and interactions, and course technology work together to ensure students achieve desired learning outcomes. There are a total of eight general standards: course overview and introduction, learning objectives (competencies), assessment and measurement, instructional materials, learning activities and learning interaction, course technology, learner support, and accessibility and usability [8]. These general standards are further breaking down into specific review standards, giving a total of 42. Standards are assigned different points depending on their relative importance: 3: Essential, 2: Very important, and 1: Important. The rubric also provides a series of annotations with examples to help the reviewer decide if the standard is met. For the standard to be met, the reviewer asks this question: does the course meet the standard at an 85% or better level? If the answer is yes, then the standard receives the corresponding value according to its importance. Whether or not the standard is met, the reviewer provides constructive feedback for continued improvement. Each course is reviewed by a three QM-Certified Peer Reviewers using the QM Rubric, one of them must be of the same discipline as the course being reviewed (subject matter expert), and one of them is the team chair, who is QM-Certified Master Reviewer. The team chair combined all three reviewers scoring and decide if a standard is met or not, based on the majority rule: at least two reviewers agreed on the same decision. The course can meet Quality Matter Review Expectations if all 3-points standards are met, and the review resulted in a total overall score of 85 or higher out of 100 points. There are many other rubrics available for higher-education institutions, that are not going to be presented in this work.

3 Quality Assurance Process: The Beginning

After analyzing several QA rubrics and approaches, CCBC decided to adopt Quality Matters and the decision was made because their suggested process is centered on continuous improvement. This process is designed to help institutions achieve the QA goals for online learning as they grow to address all aspects of the Online Learning Quality Pie [9] (see Fig. 1).

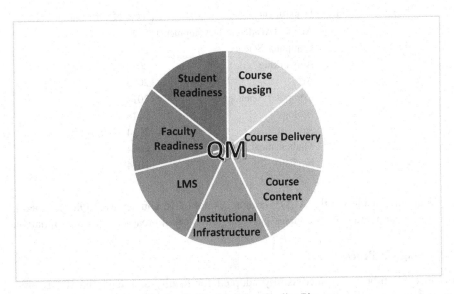

Fig. 1. Online Learning Quality Pie

Even though quality matters focuses on course design, institutions can use the same rubric to scale the model and apply it to all the aspects of online learning specified in the previous figure. This is a progressive process and institutions go through different stages until they implement QA effectively in their institution.

3.1   Stage 1: Training

In the particular case of CCBC, some faculty and staff already have online training and have been teaching online for quite some time. Faculty were required to complete a formal training in order to be ready to teach online and to design their courses. The format and name of training has changed through the years, from Virtual Academy to Online Training Institute and Online Course Design Institution. If faculty or staff already had online training obtained at other institutions, a waiver could be obtained via a very informal process.

Based on several comments received from the Accreditation Institution in one of their reviews, CCBC decided to adopt QM as quality control in their courses. To start with this process, an Instructional Design and Online Learning (IDOL) office was created, and instructional designers were hired. Faculty that were already trained were the first ones invited to participate in the Apply the Quality Matter Rubric workshops. This was the beginning of the QM implementation. Faculty stated to be trained, courses started to be self-reviewed, and after the final review from the IDOL office, they were submitted for external certification.

Table 1 shows the number of courses by department that were externally reviewed, and the year of certification.

Table 1. List of QM certified courses.

Number of courses	Department	Year of certification
1	ACDV (Academic Development)	2012
4	Computer Science	2013
1	Networking	2013
1	Art	2013
4	Computer Science	2014
2	Biology	2014
1	Art	2014
1	Mathematical Science	2014
2	English	2014

Without considering the ACDV course, a total of 16 courses were QM certified in two years, an average of 8 courses per year. This was a great start for this initiative.

3.2   Stage 2: Process

Because the rubric was successfully adopted for faculty and staff, the IDOL office decided that a formal structure was needed for the online learning initiative. CCBC is formed by seven schools: (1) Business, Education, Justice and Law (SBEJL), (2) Continuing Education (CE), (3) Health Professions (SOHP), (4) Liberal Arts (SOLA), (5) Mathematics and Science (SOMS), (6) Technology, Art, and Design (STAD), and (7) Wellness, Behavioral, and Social Science (WEBSS); so, each school selected a member to be design as an Online Coordinator for their school. This team meet once a month with the IDOL office to discuss all the aspect related to online learning.

At the same time, a new board was created: Distance Learning Advisory Board (DLAB) and was composed by a representative from different offices such as schools, IDOL office, the Deans of the schools, the Blackboard Department, the IT department. The mission for this board was to define distance education policies for the college. Those policies were then sent to the College Senate for approval and implementation. Among those policies are: Faculty Usage of CCBC Learning Management System Policy, Policy on Ensuring Quality in Distant Learning Courses, Learning Management System Course Menu Best Practices.

The number of courses seeking formal certification was growing as well as the cost of having those courses certified externally by Quality Matters. This forced the Online office to look for a different way to do this formal certification: Internal Certification. This new initiative required to train faculty as Peer-Reviewers, and formally organize the QA process. Several informal policies were established:

- Courses that were Externally Certified by QM, become now Master Courses
- Faculty teaching online was suggested to use the Master Courses
- If faculty did not want to use the Master Course, then his/her course must go under Internal QM Review
- Highly-enrolled courses should continue to be certified externally by QM

Table 2 depicts the courses that were Internally QM Certified, while Table 3 shows the courses that were Externally QM Certified.

Table 2. List of internally QM certified courses.

School	Number of certified courses		
	2015	2016	2017
Business, Education, Justice, and Law	6	7	7
Help Professions	2		3
Liberal Arts	9	2	3
Mathematics and Science	6		
Technology, Art, and Design	3	7	1
Wellness, Behavioral, and Social Science	7	4	5
Total	33	20	19

As it can be appreciated through those tables, a total of 72 courses were internally QM certified, while 23 courses were externally certified, giving a final total of 95 courses.

Table 2 is not showing any courses for the year 2018, because the certification process last two semesters: during the fall semester, courses are self-reviewed by their authors, and they are submitted for review at the end of the semester. During the spring semester, the review teams are formed, the review is performed, and for those courses that do not meet the certification, a report of improvement is provided, and faculty implement the suggestions, so their courses can achieve the level needed to be certified.

Table 3. List of externally QM certified courses.

School	Number of certified courses			
	2015	2016	2017	2018
Business, Education, Justice, and Law		2	1	
Help Professions				1
Liberal Arts		1	1	2
Mathematics and Science	3	4	3	3
Technology, Art, and Design			1	
Wellness, Behavioral, and Social Science				1
Total	3	7	6	7

This process can be repeated only twice, and at the end of the third time, the decision is final, and the course Met or Not Met the qualifications needed to be QM certified. At the moment of writing of this paper, the 2018 Internal Review courses are being reviewed by the 3 peer-reviewer teams.

3.3   Stage 3: Formalizing the Process

Until August of 2018, online course development has been faculty-driven with little intervention or help from instructional designers, aside from specific course development training. As the number of online and blended courses starts to increase, a more systematic approach must be developed where faculty will continue to be the developers of the courses, with the assistance needed from the instructional designers. With this official Policy, courses will be developed with the proper online learning pedagogy, built in a timely manner, and designed following QM standards from the beginning.

Because of the launch of CCBC Online, an Online Learning office was added to control and supervise all the aspects related to online learning with its Assistant Dean and coordinate these activities with the IDOL office. CCBC identifies two categories of professional development in instructional design and online learning: course facilitation and course development.

Course Facilitation

Teaching an online or blended course requires a specific set of skills. There must be proficiency at using Blackboard as well as an understanding of pedagogy required to engage online students. Because of that, faculty that want to teach online at CCBC must complete the following training: Teaching Online Course (TOC). This course is offered usually twice a year, it is completely online, and teaches faculty how to engage with students and facilitate an already constructed course. There are no prerequisites for this training, but there is an assumption of prior knowledge of Blackboard. This training also assumes that the faculty members have a course that has already been built for them to teach.

Faculty who have expertise and prior experience teaching online from other institutions must demonstrate competency in Blackboard, online skills including facilitation, and assessment measurement & learner engagements prior to teaching online courses. Proper documentation must be sent to the Instructional Design and Online Learning office.

Figure 2 depicts this process graphically for a clear understanding of this process.

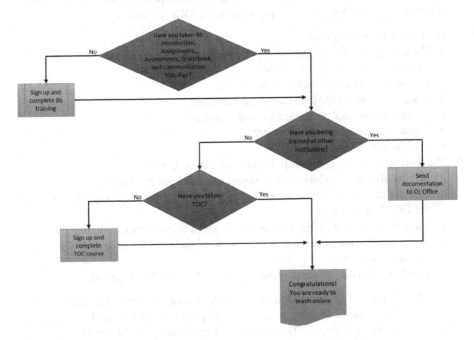

Fig. 2. Teaching Online Course (TOC) procedure

Course Development

Each academic School as well as Continuing Education, have an Online Learning Coordinator (OLC) who should create a production schedule for the courses to be developed. This production schedule is approved by the Dean of the School and share with the Assistant Dean of Online Learning and the Director of IDOL. If a faculty member wants to develop a course that is not on the schedule, written authorization by the Dean and the Department Chair/Director must be presented prior to production. When a course is added into the production schedule, faculty members developing the course are also identified and an application is completed. This application is signed by the faculty member(s), OLC, and Academic Dean.

Once the application is signed, the OLC schedule a meeting with the Director of IDOL to determine the professional development needs of the faculty involved and determine the appropriate course development process.

If the faculty member has been already trained at CCBC in the past (by taking Virtual Academy (VA), Online Teaching Institute (OTI), Online Course Design Institute (OCDI)) a DOCS (Designing Online Courses) process is assigned to the course. If a faculty member already has this training from other institutions, formal documentation must be submitted to the IDOL office prior to developing a course. If it is approved, then also a DOCS process is assigned to the course.

In a DOCS process, there are some professional development requirements prior or during course development: updated APPQMR and specific Blackboard training modules. In this process, the responsibilities are divided between the faculty member and the Instructional Designer with the help of the OLC as follow:

1. Faculty member is able to:
   a. Write rough drafts of module level objectives;
   b. Outline the design of the course;
   c. Create Assignments/Assessments;
   d. Create content/identify instructional materials;
   e. Align content, make changes to course design;
   f. Create rubrics within Blackboard;
   g. Design overall structure.
2. The Instructional Designer with the help of the OLC will:
   a. Review the first module before subsequent modules are built;
   b. Monitor faculty course development process according to the plan developed in the DOCS meeting;
   c. View the course at designated points to assist overall course alignment;
   d. Assist faculty member with construction of parts of the course if the faculty member requests it;
   e. Conduct a Quality Matters review at the end of the development.

The DOCS process begins with a one or more than one meeting with all the parties involved in the process: Faculty member developing the course, OLC, Director or IDOL, Instructional Designer (ID), and Library Representative (if using OER). During this meeting the group will determine the tasks needed to build the course and assign those tasks to members of the committee. Also, the timeline for completion is set and the professional development needs of the faculty member is determined based on the tasks assigned. To ensure the quality of the course, the ID will review the first module before subsequent modules are built.

If the faculty member has not taken TOC, then the first step is to follow the procedure described above and take the course. Then, complete the following training Blackboard Rubrics, and Test Student courses; and APPQMR. According to the time constraint, two different processes can be assigned to the course: CRIRP (Course Redesign Institute Regular Program) or CRISP (Course Redesign Institute Summer Program).

This is a more extensive training and incorporates online learning pedagogy while developing an online course. The Regular Program involves two consecutive semesters: during the fall semester, online learning pedagogy is instructed, and best practices are applied to create one module for a course. At the end of this first semester, a showcase of the module is presented, and certificate is awarded. During the second semester, faculty replicates the structure of the module to the rest of the modules of the course and finalized the process by doing a QM self-review. In the case of the Summer Program, everything is compressed during the summer months of June, July, and August. At the end of this process, the course is also reviewed by an ID from the IDOL office. Figure 3 shows this process graphically.

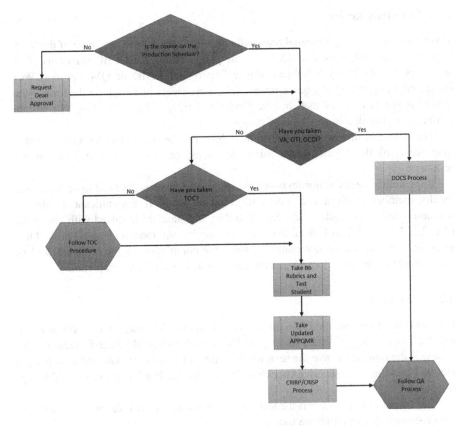

Fig. 3. Course development procedure

Independently of the process followed to developing a course, once it is finished, it will go under a Quality Assurance Review. The type of QA review that the course is going to undertake will depend on the type of course, and the professional development of the faculty member. See next section for details on these types of QA.

4 Types of Quality Assurance Reviews

The Online Learning office provides 4 different types of QA Reviews: (a) Eyes Review, (b) Second Generation Review, (c) CCBC Internal Quality Assurance Review, and (d) Quality Matters (External) Review.

In addition to these 4 types, courses that have been built using the DOCS process will undergo an Essentials Review prior going live, and then they under Internal Review.

Let start describing each one of those types.

4.1   Essentials Review

This review uses all the Essential Standards from the QM Rubric and some of the Very Important Standard, a total of 35 Standards plus 4 additional CCBC standards. This review is performed by a Subject Matter Expert and an ID or QM Certified Peer Reviewer. This process is a quick review where reviewers just mark on the form if the standards are met or not met, by checking the corresponding checkbox. No written feedback is provided in this type of review.

The output of this review could be as follow: (a) the course met the QM Essential Standards, (b) the course needs minor revisions, or (c) the course needs major revisions.

If the course needs minor revision, meaning just few changes need to be made, the faculty member is given two weeks to complete them. If a significant number of revisions need to be made and/or Standard 2 or any standard involved with alignment (2.1, 2.2, 3.1, 4.1, 5.1, 6.1) need to be revised, faculty will meet with an ID or the OLC to assist them with their revisions. Deadline for completion of the revisions will be determined at a meeting, with a maximum time of 8 weeks for completion.

4.2   Eyes Review

For this type of review, the same rubric as the Essential Review, the only difference is that this review is performed just by an ID or a Certified QM Peer Reviewer. This review is the quickest where the reviewer just marks whether the standard is met or not met by checking the respective checkbox. No written feedback is provided in this type of review.

The output of this review is the same as the previous one, and faculty should follow the procedure described above too.

This type of review is used when a course needs to be evaluated quickly, because it can be done in hours since it is reviewed by only one QM Peer Reviewer or ID.

4.3   Second Generation Review

This type of review uses the same rubric as the Essential Review, and the review is performed by the same team of reviewers. The output is exactly the same, the only difference is when this type of review is used.

If a faculty member already has a course that have been through QM (external) Review or CCBC Internal QA Review, then an assumption can be made about the other courses developed by the same faculty: they follow the same design principles and therefore the QM standards. Because CCBC wants all the courses to go under QA, this process is used to certify those courses in a quick manner and using the minimum of resources.

4.4   CCBC Internal Quality Assurance Review

If the course to be certified is the first for the faculty member, and the course is not considered to be a high-enrolled course for CCBC, then this is the QA process to follow. The only condition for a course to be reviewed using this process is that the course has been taught online at least twice before undergoing this review. The process resembles the official process that QM uses to certify courses, but it is performed totally in-house. The process starts by the faculty member doing a self-review of their course, making sure that it follows all the QM standards specify in the QM rubric.

Later, the faculty member submits some documentation of the course such as: Module objectives, objective worksheet, alignment worksheet and other information about the course. Then the Online Learning office forms a team to review the course by selecting a Subject Matter Expert, a Certified QM Peer Reviewer, and a Team Chair. The team review the course individually, and then a Final Report is generated indicating if the course met QM Standards or not. In order to be certified, all 3 points (essentials) standards must be met, and the total points must be equal or greater than 85 (out of 100). In addition, all CCBC specific standards must be met.

In this process, reviewers provide feedback on improvement of each one of the standards so faculty can perform those modifications to meet the standard. Faculty is provided with the feedback from each one of the reviewers.

If the course does not meet QM standards, the faculty have three weeks to perform the changes suggested, and the Chair of the team re-evaluates the standards marked as 'no met' and mark whether the changes made in the course makes the standard to be 'met'. This process can be done twice, and after that the final decision is made: the course is QM Certified or not.

This internal process is performed once a year, usually during the fall semester, faculty perform the self-review and during spring the team is formed, and the evaluation is done. The certification is valid for five years, and CCBC provides a logo that can be added to the course.

4.5   QM (External) Review

This is the last type of review and only for high-enrolled courses, and courses that are considered Institutional Courses (used by all the faculty teaching the class as is) undergo this type of review. Before sending the course directly to Quality Matters, faculty also performed a self-review, and finally the course is reviewed by an ID from the IDOL office.

When the course is ready, then it is sent to the QM for certification. This process is entirely done by QM and CCBC have to pay a fee for the process. Because of that, just a small number of courses are sent for certification.

This certification is also valid for 5 years, and QM provides a logo that can be added to the course too.

5   Future Work and Conclusion

There is always something to improve when we are talking about QA. At this moment, the Online Learning office is working on a re-certification process, so it can also be performed in-house instead of sending the courses to QM for external re-certification.

On the other hand, OLC are reviewing all the courses that are offered online in their school and have never undergo a QA process, to determine the type of QA process for the course. This review is a long process and will take for sure several months to be completed; courses would need to be scheduled according to the resources available to perform each type of review.

Another path that the Online Learning office is researching right now, is the QA for a complete program or degree. Of course, the first step will be reading and learning how QM does the Program Review and see if that model fits CCBC or needs to be adapted to our needs.

As a conclusion, and as shown in this process, to ensure the quality of the design and development of a course, the qualification of the instructor needs to be considered first. If the instructor does not have those qualifications, training should be provided.

Second, the institution should provide a clear and very detail formal process for course design and implementation. On that way, faculty can realize that the school administrators want to ensure quality in the online instruction.

Successful online instruction is a collaborative process among instructors, administrators, staff, students, and the community at large. Courseware development industries should maintain the faculty informed about their new updates and provide them with training and technical support.

References

1. Yang, Y., Cornelious, L.: Preparing instructors for quality online instruction. Online J. Distance Learn. Adm. (2005). http://www.olc.edu/~cdelong/dl401/yang81.pdf. Accessed 15 Jan 2019
2. Chua, A., Lam, W.: Quality assurance in online education: the universitas 21 global approach. Br. J. Educ. Technol. (BJET) **38**(1), 133–152 (2007). https://doi.org/10.1111/j.1467-8535. 2006.00652.x
3. OLC quality scorecard suit. https://onlinelearningconsortium.org/consult/olc-quality-scorecard-suite/. Accessed 14 Jan 2019
4. The Open SUNY Course Quality Review (OSCQR) process. http://commons.suny.edu/cote/course-supports/oscqr-process/. Accessed 14 Jan 2019
5. California State University at Chico, Exemplary online instruction. https://www.csuchico.edu/eoi/_assets/documents/rubric.pdf. Accessed 16 Jan 2019
6. Blackboard community, exemplary course program rubric. https://community.blackboard. com/docs/DOC-3505-blackboard-exemplary-course-program-rubric. Accessed 14 Jan 2019
7. iNACOL, National standard for quality online courses. https://www.inacol.org/resource/inacol-national-standards-for-quality-online-courses-v2/. Accessed 15 Jan 2019
8. Quality Matters. https://www.qualitymatters.org/about. Accessed 16 Jan 2019
9. Quality Matters, Process. https://www.qualitymatters.org/why-quality-matters/process. Accessed 05 Jan 2019

Mentoring College Students via Computer-Supported Tools in a Public University in Mexico

Cuauhtémoc Rivera-Loaiza$^{(\boxtimes)}$, Karina Figueroa-Mora, and Francisco J. Domínguez-Mota

Facultad de Ciencias Físico-Matemáticas,
Universidad Michoacana de San Nicolás de Hidalgo, Morelia, Mexico
{crivera,karina,dmota}@fismat.umich.mx

Abstract. One of the most acute problems in the higher education in Mexico is the high rate of dropouts in college education. Particularly during the last decade we have witnessed troubling signs in the first stages of the career of our students, where the incentives for abandoning their studies seem to be appearing every day with a bigger intensity. To ease their adaptation in the demands that professional education asks of them several institutional programs have been in place, with varying degrees of success. However, we are convinced that in order for those programs to be successful they have to rely more in information technologies so that help can be available for the students in every possible way. Our main objective is to curb the increasing rates of students that dropout from their careers by providing a support network based on computer-supported tools.

Keywords: Mentoring · Social networks · Computer supported collaborative work

1 Introduction

Mentoring is a fundamental piece in the educational process in every single stage, and this becomes particularly fundamental during early college years. Transitioning from High School to College brings challenges to every student such as a new living spaces and social groups, lax parental supervision and support, and a demanding curriculum. In this setting, students require additional support which can be provided by person-to-person and computer-supported mentoring designed to address every possible circumstance that might prevent them from succeeding in their college experience.

Our university, Universidad Michoacana de San Nicolás de Hidalgo (UMSNH), founded in 1917, is one of the biggest public higher education institutions in Mexico. With more than 50,000 students (Table 1) and 3000 professors it provides high school, undergraduate and graduate accredited programs (95% of them in 2018) in the state of Michoacán and its surrounding areas. It has 48 undergraduate programs, and 75 graduate programs (including Master, PhD and specializations).

However, amongst the many challenges that the institution has, one of the most urgent to attend is the high dropout rate in most of its programs one of the most important ones. Currently, the university has a dropout rate of over 50% of its first year

© Springer Nature Switzerland AG 2019
G. Meiselwitz (Ed.): HCII 2019, LNCS 11579, pp. 195–203, 2019.
https://doi.org/10.1007/978-3-030-21905-5_15

in its undergraduate programs and in order to curb this trend we have implemented a mentoring strategy based on computer-supported tools that have shown promise in helping students to better cope with this demanding time in their lives.

Mentorship was established in the mid 90s as a federal funded program with a focus in person-to-person interaction, but has since then become obsolete to a certain extent. Ever since its inception as a whole has not had any major updates, and the use of technology has been completely ignored.

Computer-supported tools, which include several well-established social networks, provide several advantages (beginning with a familiarity of use to the students and mentors alike) over traditional mentoring methods used in our institution and do offer a greater rate of success in keeping track of the overall well-being of our students.

1.1   Higher Education in Mexico

We deem important in this paper to illustrate the state of our higher education system. In Mexico in 2016–2017, the country had a total of 3, 762, 679 students in any of the undergraduate and graduate programs, as described in Table 1.

Table 1. Scope of higher education in Mexico in 2016–2017 (Secretary of Education/DGPPyE, 2018)

Type	Students		
	Total	Women	Men
Higher education	3,762,679	1,864,102	1,898,577
Normal school	94,241	69,532	24,709
Undergraduate	3,429,566	1,669,009	1,760,557
Graduate	238,872	125,561	113,311
Public	2,655,711	1,263,018	1,392,693
Private	1,106,968	601,084	505,884

In the state of Michoacán, according to the State Secretary of Education, the number of students enrolled in a Higher education program are shown in Table 2.

Table 2. Scope of higher education in Michoacan, Mexico in 2016–2017 (Secretary of Education/DGPPyE, 2018)

Type	Students		
	Total	Women	Men
Higher education	106,055	52,337	53,718
Normal school	5,726	3,536	2,190
Undergraduate	95,706	46,486	49,420
Graduate	4,263	2,315	2,308
Public	84,218	39,931	44,287
Private	21,837	12,406	9,431

The UMSNH has a share of 51% of the total of students in a higher education program in the State as of this year.

1.2 Characteristics of Our Student Population

In the first half of 2018 a survey was conducted to explore the characteristics of the students in our university. We have a approximately the same number of male and female students, and they are mostly in the 19–24 age range (62%), 20% are in the 15–18 age range (belonging to our high-school sub-system). Those two groups belong to our undergraduate and high-school programs and form the core population of our study. The vast majority were born in Michoacán state (where our University is located).

Our survey indicates that over 96% [2] of them have a Smartphone, mostly running on some version of Android (82%), with the rest using iOS. Practically all the students use a social network on their devices being the most popular WhatsApp, Facebook and YouTube. The preferred way of using their smartphones is in a prepaid manner (60%), and the rest with a monthly plan. 85% of the students own a computer, and have internet access at home (91%).

All this data is consistent with the most recent country wide surveys conducted by the federal government.

2 Mentoring Program in the UMSNH

As in many higher education institutions in our country, our university has a high dropout rate, especially in the first months of their careers. In recent years the rate of dropouts has increased significantly, and the motivations for this vary from economic problems, weak academic abilities, relocation issues, adverse social dynamics, etc. In this context, the support needed by the students is vital for their survival in the university. Our students have access to institutional programs that are designed to bring additional support for their careers, from an integral point of view.

Mentorship, as one of the services that the student body has access in our university, was established in 2005. This was a federal funded program replicated on a national level in which a group of academic workers (professors and other members of academia) were trained in a set of five courses that aimed to train them in the mentoring process. The main objective of the mentoring program is to provide students with an integral support especially in the beginning of their transition into college.

Registered mentors in the University have to take a five-part course in which professors are trained to better help students. Professors learn about different mentoring techniques, university legislation, time management, and other administrative matters. However, one issue that is not dealt in the mentoring training program is how technology can be fundamental in providing our students of a better mentoring experience.

There is a department part of the Academics Secretariat of the University in charge of managing the program, named Coordinación de Responsabilidad Social y Formación

Docente (Coordination of Social Responsibility and Teaching Training). Mentoring training is not a compulsory program for professors, but are encouraged to get a certification in order to advance in their own career in the institution.

At the beginning of each semester a mentor is assigned a group of students to mentor, either individually or in groups. At the end of the semester, the mentor has to send a detailed report to the Coordination.

However, we are convinced that the mentoring program can be greatly benefited from a greater reliance in information technologies. Ever since its inception has not had any major updates, and the use of technology has been completely ignored.

3   Our Proposal

In our professional experience since becoming registered mentors in our University, it has been evident how difficult is to keep track of the students assigned to us in the program. Especially as the semester carries on, the commitment of the students with the program begins to loosen up and many of them eventually abandon it. Time management is usually the main culprit for dropping off from the program.

As the program is set, there is a scheduled weekly meeting between the student and the mentor that lasts between half an hour to a full hour. During this appointment, the student will recount what happened during the week at the university and the mentor will coach him or her in order to improve their academic performance.

However, as the class semester advances it becomes more and more difficult to set a time where both parties can meet. Due to this observance, we decided to change our strategy in order to retain the students in the program. We designed our strategy as follows (Table 3).

Table 3. Time planning with activities

Period	Activity
First month	Half-hour face to face meetings
Second month	Twice a month face to face meetings, and remote mentoring
Rest of the semester	Once a month or video conferencing meeting, and remote mentoring

Face to face meetings were done in a traditional manner: both parties would agree in a particular time to get together in a school facility (could be in the mentor's office or a designated space for mentoring). As mentioned before, the length of the meeting would vary from half an hour to a full hour. The mentor is encouraged to take notes to keep track of the session.

For the remote mentoring, we decided to use free tools that were widely available and particularly that did not have a steep learning curve. As it will be described ahead, the current student body has a whole permanent access to the internet and at least one device of their own (most frequently an Android-powered smartphone). We decided to use as our main Learning Management Systems (LMS) Moodle and Google Class-room. And for messaging applications Slack and WhatsApp. These tools were selected based upon their wide support for different platforms and scalability. We also decided to use Facebook to some extent, since it is extensively used in both the student and mentor communities.

3.1   Methodology

During 2018 we established four groups of internet-based set of tools: synchronous and asynchronous. These tools had to be free (at least on their most used functionalities), available in Spanish, and suitable to be used in a Smartphone.

As such, the synchronous tools were: WhatsApp, Slack, Facebook Messenger and Facebook. The asynchronous were: Google Classroom and Moodle.

We started our study with 3 groups and 1 control group. On each experimental group we implemented some internet-based strategies as we resume on Table 4.

Table 4. Group settings and tools

Groups	Messaging tools	Asynchronous tools
Group 1		Email
Group 2	WhatsApp, Facebook, Facebook Messenger	
Group 3	Slack	Google classroom
Group 4	WhatsApp, Slack	Moodle

Each group had different skills using the internet-based strategies proposed, as described in Table 5.

Table 5. Group settings and student skills

Group	Student skills
Group 1	In this group we use the traditional mentoring program. This is our control group
Group 2	Students with skills to use synchronous tools
Group 3	Students with almost null skills on Slack and Google Classroom platform
Group 4	Students with almost null skills on Slack and Moodle

- Group 1.
  In this case, we followed the traditional strategy (without synchronous internet-based tools). The group (as we expected) did not improved significantly on their academic progress, and eventually dropped out of the mentoring program.

- Group 2.

In this group, we used the Moodle which was mostly used for sharing information about lessons or interesting news for the students (Fig. 1). We have few interactions with students in this group. They were without supervisor, but they tried to support each other Our students mentioned that they felt more closely monitored by us during the semester compared to the experience they had in previous mentoring sessions without using an internet-based tool.

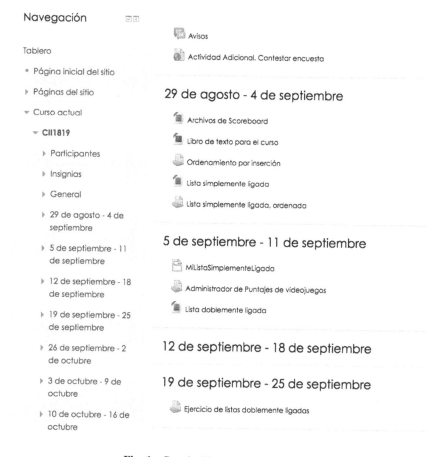

Fig. 1. Google Classroom for Group 2.

- Group 3.

For this group, we used two synchronous internet-based tools WhatsApp and Slack. They participated actively in the apps, however students preferred Slack over

WhatsApp (their interactions were richer and they had chances to share more than only text and images). As mentors, we were more active in there too. Our students were interacting between them, we limited our participating. Usually they were sharing their achievements, tools that they found for their lessons. We also provided students with a Google Classroom group, which was mostly employed for keeping track of their performance with specific courses, more than their overall academic experience. There their interaction and openness were more limited (Fig. 2).

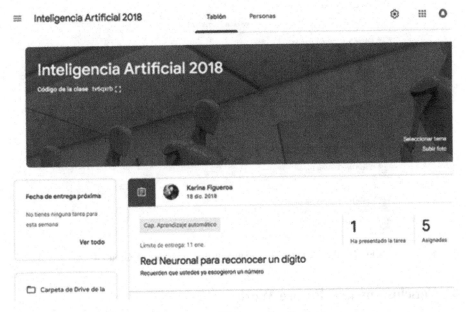

Fig. 2. Google Classroom for Group 3.

- Group 4.
  In this group, we used only Slack. Students learned to use Slack very fast, and they participated frequently sharing with their mentor the different challenges that they encountered during their semester, in real time. Because of the immediacy of the feedback that they got, it was very rewarding for the students. They expressed that they felt taken care of by their mentors more so than in any of the other control groups that we had (Fig. 3).

Fig. 3. Slack channel for a student that was part of Group 4.

4   Conclusions and Future Work

Although this study is in its very first stages, the first results have been promising. To begin with, we have proven how a wider support network does convey a bigger commitment from the students with their daily activities, and their own career accountability increases substantially.

Also, from the mentor's perspective, the interaction with their students is in many ways richer and better to keep track of them. The use of widely available Internet tools for collaboration have been received extremely well, despite the unfamiliarity of most of them with the chosen programs (like Slack or Moodle, for example); the fact that younger generations are mostly digital natives makes new tech adoption quite easy.

For future work, we are continuing the deployment and monitoring with more students and mentors, within our School and other departments of our University. We expect to have conclusive results by the end of the first semester of 2019.

This work is being funded by the Scientific Research Council (Coordinación de la Investigación Científica, CIC) of the Universidad Michoacana de San Nicolás de Hidalgo under the 2018–2020 program.

References

1. Barnett, B.G., O'Mahony, G.R.: Developing a culture of reflection: implications for school improvement. Reflective Pract. 7(4), 499–523 (2006)
2. Campos, H.: Construcción de conocimiento en el proceso educativo. UNAM-Plaza Y Valdés, Mexico (2005). ISBN: 970-32-1993-4
3. Cofetel. Estadísiticas del Uso de internet en México (n.d.). https://www.mexicoconectado. gob.mx/?p=10755. Accessed 8 Feb 2019
4. Cole, J., Foster, H.: Using Moodle: Teaching with the Popular Open Source Course Management System. O'Really, Sebastopol (2007). ISBN: 0-596-52918-X
5. Jovanovic, J., Gasevic, D., Devedzic, V.: E-learning and the social semantic web. In: Semantic Web Technologies for E-Learning, pp. 245–259 (2009). ISBN: 978-1-60750-062-9
6. Keeler, A., Miller, L.: 50 Things You Can Do with Google Classroom. Dave Burgess Consulting (n.d.). ISBN: 978-09-8615-5420
7. TESS-INDIA. Transforming teaching-learning process: mentoring and coaching (2017). http://www.open.edu/openlearncreate/pluginfile.php/135983/mod_resource/content/4/SL09_AIE_Final.pdf. Accessed 2 Feb 2019
8. University, A.S. "Mentoring" (online) (n.d.)
9. Rice, W.: Moodle E-Learning Course Development. Packt (2006). ISBN: 9-781-904-811-299
10. Zapotecatl, J., Al, E.: Pensamiento computacional (AMEXCOMP) (2018)

Pistacho: An Interactive System to Support the Development of Phonological Awareness for Blind Children

Isabella Sánchez[1(✉)], Nataly Betancur[1], Andrés Solano[1], and Sandra Cano[2]

[1] Universidad Autónoma de Occidente, Cali, Colombia
isabellasanchez567@gmail.com
[2] Universidad San Buenaventura, Cali, Colombia

Abstract. The acquisition of *phonological awareness* (**Phonological awareness:** the ability to segment, recognize and decompose the phonemes that make up a word.) allows us to recognize, segment and decompose the phonemes (sounds) that make up a word, facilitating the learning of skills such as reading and writing. This is a difficult process for a blind child, for this reason, the objective of this project is to implement an interactive system that serves as a support tool for the development of phonological awareness of blind children between five to seven years old who are studying early grades.

Pistacho offers blind children a non-traditional experience for learning the vowels, this has two components: software and hardware. The first consists of an application developed for the phonoaudiologist and the teachers of the institute in charge of the pre-garden and garden grades. The hardware component consists of a character called Pistacho, who suggests children do a set of activities to reinforce topics seen in class, that help the development of consciousness phonological.

As part of the process to obtain the proposed system, first of all, users were approached through interviews and observation in the environment, which resulted in the detection of a series of needs and difficulties presented by the students at the time of developing phonological awareness. The specification of the requirements was made from the information collected and analyzed, to subsequently design and implement the components, software, and hardware. Finally, the system was evaluated with the users, to make the respective adjustments.

Keywords: Interactive system · Blind children · Phonological awareness

1 Introduction

Writing and reading are important skills to obtain knowledge, to get these capabilities a different process is required for each of them. One of them is the development of *phonological awareness* [1], in the case of blind children, this one is a crucial one as one of the more developed senses is the audition [2]. In Spanish, a language in which the formation of words is more connoted for the vowels is a hard task for blind people

© Springer Nature Switzerland AG 2019
G. Meiselwitz (Ed.): HCII 2019, LNCS 11579, pp. 204–216, 2019.
https://doi.org/10.1007/978-3-030-21905-5_16

to create phonological awareness, especially in kids. It is really hard for them to identify phonemes in every word [3].

The present project implements an interactive system, which is intended to improve the development of the phonological awareness of blind children. This system provides no traditional methods to display information, interaction, and integration of senses, with the objective that the children train the phonological awareness through four interactive activities with emphasis in vowels since this is the fundamental base to obtain the reading skills.

It's fundamental to stand out that the needs of the children are extremely important in this project and the center of the development of the interactive system are them since finally they are the ones who use the system to strengthen their competence.

2 Problem

The process of language acquisition in blind children has a fundamental role in the development of their lives because it is one of the main sources of learning and communication. According to the Spanish National Organization for Blind People (ONCE), "reading and writing is a secondary process of speech, derived from the oral language" [4]. Also, it should be considered that reading and writing are intellectual processes that include aspects beyond the translation of graphemes or the interpretation of phonemes. In order to achieve these competencies, the process begins at different levels, where children acquire different activities that allow them to reach this goal later [4]. Among these levels is the obtaining of phonological awareness.

To develop the phonological awareness in a child must be a pass for the different subprocess, which according to Emilia Ferreiro, are [5]: the syllabic hypothesis and the syllabic-alphabetic hypothesis. Besides, is important to mention that for blind children's it is a bigger challenge, since it is not easy for them to associate the graphemes with phonemes as a child would commonly do, when they use of their visual and auditory senses [6], because of this the blind children's have difficulties in the stage syllabic-alphabetic. In this phase, the child must understand that the sound similarity implies similarity of letters and that the sonorous difference supposes different letters, and to associate in a clear way a phoneme for each letter. This is a hard process for a blind child, who can not associate visually the things that they hear. In that way, the blind children present complications in the differentiation between the consonants and vowels, because in the Spanish the vowels are more frequent. This causes children to become confused in their differentiation and to lengthen the learning processes.

3 Methodology

For the development of the interactive system, we follow the methodology Engineering Process Model for usability and accessibility (MPlu+a), proposed by the Griho research group of the University of Lleida (Spain) [7]. MPlu+a adopts user-centered design principles. This model offers a guide for the construction of usable and accessible interactive systems.

MPlu+a breaks down into three basic pillars: Software Engineering, prototyping, and evaluation, but it does not establish a specific method to follow for its development as such. Therefore, it is flexible to the quantity, the type of prototypes and evaluations to be used. It should be noted that the stages of prototyping and evaluation are iterative throughout the development of the interactive system.

4 Preliminary Results

4.1 Users

The students that participated in the project were in pre-garden and garden grades at the Institute of blind and deaf of Valle del Cauca, located in the city Cali, Colombia. Actually, the pre-garden grade is formed by ten children (four girls and six boys), among them, there are two blind girls, one inclusion child (child without disability) and seven children with low vision. In garden grade, there are eight children (four boys and four girls), three blind children, two of inclusion and three with low vision. Moreover, when we approached this last course, it was possible to identify that one of the children, in addition to suffering from blindness, has attention deficit and dyslalia[1].

Furthermore, the project counted on the participation of the professors and the speech therapist of the institute, who assumes the role of the counselor and use the system to select the activities that the students will carry out according to their needs.

4.2 Study of the User's Context

The investigation was made in the installations of "Instituto de Niños Ciegos y Sordos del Valle del Cauca", specifically in the classroom of pre-garden and garden grades. The user's context was studied through the technique of direct observation. This research was initiated by visiting the institute to observe the language class and interview people who were in charge and in constant contact with the children, in order to interact with those involved and identify the needs of the users.

Both pre-garden and garden grades, children begin to develop phonological awareness focused on vowels, working with rhymes, tongue twisters, songs, a combination of words and semantic categories. Also applies the invariant method, which has been adopted by the Institute for blind children, the method consists in through pieces (green and square: consonants, red and circle: vowels), the child is able to replace the phonemes of the word according to its classification. For some activities, physical representations of a word (objects) are used, in such a way that the child relates the concept and the word.

---

[1] **Dyslalia:** Is the inability to articulate comprehensible speech, especially when associated with the use of private words or sounds.

4.3   Users Needs

Once the information collected through the observation techniques and interviews carried out with those involved in the context study stage was analyzed, the following needs of the users were detected:

- Information perception: The blind children's need a mechanism that allows them to optimize the interpretation of the information obtained through the auditory and tactile sense, unlike the sighted people who perceive 80% of the information through the sense of sight, the blind children perceive it to through your other senses, the stimulus received through hearing, touching and smelling should be clear and frequent.
- Skill development: The blind children face a process more complex at the moment to learn new concepts, as are the vowels in this particular case since they need to develop and strengthen phonological awareness. This is a fundamental factor in their education because it allows the child to access reading and writing skills, which are significant when thinking about inclusive education.
- Generation of interest regarding the activity in development: For blind children participation in activities that motivate the use of different communication channels, plays a vital role to motivate their participation in the classes, that is necessary to perform activities like sing, rhymes, stories, and repetition, where children, apart from stimulating their other senses, approach language.
- Reward during the activity: It is necessary to include the gamification in the classroom and the interactive system to propose, with the objective that blind children can have stimulation in their learning process.

Activities for the Development of Phonological Awareness

Once the analysis of the information obtained in the first phase was done, it was found that the child must acquire the ability to decompose, segment and differentiate the phonemes, skills that can be developed through activities that involve the auditory sense. Therefore it was chosen four activities that were implemented in the interactive system, which were selected taking into account activities that are currently carried out in the institute and other activities that were determined from the investigation of the context and the state of the art, considered influential for the development of phonological awareness.

The activities for the development of phonological awareness that were included in the system, are:

1. **By which vowel the word begins** [8]: this activity consists in that the students must identify which is the first phoneme of the word that Pistacho has said and introduce the vowel piece corresponding to the first phoneme in the mouth of Pistachio.
2. **By which vowel the word finish** [8]: this activity consists in that the students must identify which is the last phoneme of the word that Pistacho has said and introduce the vowel piece corresponding to the first phoneme in the mouth of Pistachio.
3. **Classification of words according to the vowel** [9]: Pistacho will say a set of words that belong to the group of a vowel, depending on their first phoneme, for example, if all the words begin with the A belongs to the group of the vowel A. The

child after hearing all the words, they must decide which group it belongs, and put the corresponding vowel piece in the mouth of Pistachio.

4. **The vowels sound** [12]: *Pistacho* reproduce the sound of the vowel and the child has to identify the sound and insert the vowel piece correspondent.

The activities mentioned are both pre-garden and garden grade, nonetheless, the activities of pre-garden grade have a level of difficulty more than ones of pre-garden.

5   Design and Developing of the System

5.1   Description of the Interactive System

Based on the identified problem, as a solution, it was proposed the design of a multimodal interactive system called *Pistacho,* which has two components: software and hardware. The software consists of an application developed for the speech therapist and the teachers of the institute, in charge of the pre-garden and garden grades. The application performs three main functions: (a) control of the activities that the hardware component will execute, (b) registration of children's information in the database, and finally, (c) allows teachers to know the children answer in each activity.

The component hardware allows interaction between the child and the system in the classroom. The hardware consists of a character from another planet called Pistacho (which gives the name to the interactive system) and suggests to the children the realization of a set of activities for improving topics seen in class. With Pistacho we seek to motivate the child to participate actively in the learning process. Pistacho presents attributes that try to capture the child's attention, such as their voice, shape, size, and texture in their body. Besides the software and hardware, the child has pieces to interact with Pistacho, these pieces represent each vowel.

Pistacho, explains the children a set of activities to enhance the development of phonological awareness. The activities were identified after realized the analysis of the information obtained in the context study, with which, we discovered that the activities for the development of phonological awareness should implicate the auditory sense.

It is important to clarify that with the implementation of the interactive system in the classroom, it has a purpose to offer support in the development of phonological awareness specifically in the vowels, nevertheless, we are not trying to replace the role of the teacher.

Storyboard

The storyboard explains how is the interaction between the users and the system (see Figs. 1 and 2), the information in the images are in Spanish, but it is planned to include another language such as English. In first instance the teacher select the activity (A) it will send to Pistacho which will explain to the children's the activity (B), to which the child must answer with one of the vowels that they have to their disposition (C) and *Pistacho* indicate if it is the right or not (D).

Fig. 1. Storyboard of the user experience part 1 (Color figure online)

Fig. 2. Storyboard of the user experience part 2 (Color figure online)

5.2   Design and Implementation of Hardware

The design of *Pistacho* was proposed in the way that has a friendly appearance and attractive for the children, its structure was made in wood "mdf" of 5.5 mm of thickness and it has one meter of height, due to this child doesn't do a big physical effort and/or cognitive to look the mouth of Pistacho, and 70 cm of width to his easy perception in the place. His mouth is always open, for that the child can deposit the objects; its horns, its tongue, its texture, and its anatomy make *Pistacho* a tool that will call the attention of the children (see Fig. 3).

In order to create a hardware system with different communication channels, Pistacho has a layer with furry plush fabric, providing a tactile experience, thus allowing to the children create a mental image of how Pistacho is.

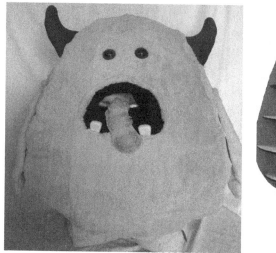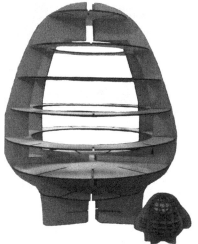

Fig. 3. Pistacho.

Hardware Electronic Components

For the development of the component hardware, it was used the tool of open code Arduino, through this software we programmed two microcontrollers of the system: the nodeMcu and the Arduino Mega. The Arduino mega is in charge of the controller the decoder plaque of audio Shield Mp3, which is connected to a speaker. This connection is made with the objective of can play the audios that Pistacho reproduce.

The nodeMcu is the one who does the connection to the database which is hosted in the cloud, and it is consulting permanently the status of the same, through requests HTTP. This node has the function of sending to the Arduino the code of audio that is required for the activity that is in progress at the moment, at the same time this plaque must controller the RFID1 and the RFID2, the first one read the tag of the bracelet of the child and the second one read the tag of the vowel that the children deposited in the mouth of Pistacho. After all, the information collected is sent to the database, for later this was consulted for the teacher.

Figure 4 presents a general scheme of the connection and the location of every component inside of the structure. As you can see the RFID1 is ubicated strategically in the mouth of Pistacho, for reading the bracelet of a child at the moment that the children deposited the vowel, and the RFID2 as mentioned earlier is ubicated at the end of conduit with the purpose to read the vowel after that the child the deposited to *Pistacho*.

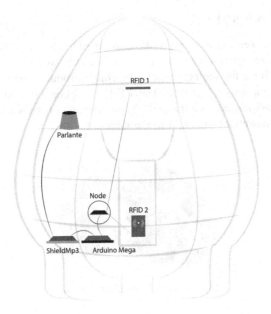

Fig. 4. Location of the components inside Pistacho.

5.3 Vowel Pieces

The five vowel pieces that the child has to interact with *Pistacho*, represent each of the vowels (see Fig. 5), thinking about taking advantage of the prominent development of tactile sense that has the blind child, the pieces were made with different geometric figures and textures. Also, each piece count with two sides, one side face A has a special texture to differentiate itself from the others, and the face B, it is written the vowel in braille and in Spanish.

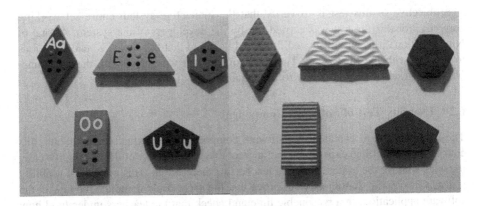

Fig. 5. Vowel pieces.

5.4   Identification Bracelet

With the purpose of keeping a record of the answers of the users, each child must use a unique bracelet of recognition (see Fig. 6). Each bracelet has an identification tag, that be read by the RFID at the moment in that the child introduces the hand for deposited the vowel to the mouth of Pistacho. The RFID recognizes the unique code of the bracelet which is associated with the child in the moment of the register, and this way will save all the answers of the child in the database.

Fig. 6. Bracelet of identification.

6   Tests

With the purpose of obtaining the ideal interactive system that fulfills with the objectives set. Along the process of development different evaluations were made to each component of the system. The developers of the interactive system made a test of the functions of the system, another test with a usability expert and different tests with the final users, with the feedback of these tests let make improvements to Pistachio in the visual appearance and functionality.

6.1   Functionalities Test

The objective of this test is to verify that the interactive system entire set working correctly, for this the test was carried out by the developers of the system. A total of Nine functionalities was evaluated. It should be noted that this test was made previous to the test with the final users. The result of this test was successful, the nine functionalities tested works correctly to the requirements of the evaluators.

6.2   Usability Test of Software Component

The method used to evaluate the software component was formals experiments, this consists in a controlled experiment and measurable with the user of the test, in this case, the ones who try the system were the teachers of the institute. This method of usability test was made with the objective to prove that the users could complete the task in the software application, in a reasonable time and check that the teachers understood how the system works. In this method, the users made the task in the system while the evaluators saw the interaction and functionality of the system.

The results show that the teachers made satisfactory the tasks, with the exception of two tasks, since it took them more time than the maximum proposed to the start, that shows us that the application has usabilities problems, that we can fix before the final test.

6.3   User Experience Test of Pistacho

This evaluation was made with the group of 12 blind children the "Instituto de niños ciegos y sordos del Valle del Cauca", and also counted with the participation of three teachers and the phonoaudiologist of the Institute (see Fig. 7), in order to contribute objectively to the improvements of the system from your professional point of view. It's important to mention that due to time the test was carried out with one child at a time, this is highlighted since in the context the system can work both as a group and individually.

Since the tests were performed with children who are in a situation of disability, the evaluation was required to be made in a dynamic and pleasant manner, for that, different strategies and elements were used for this case, once the child used Pistacho, five stars were given to the child on paper, with which they qualified eight questions that inquire about their experience with Pistachio.

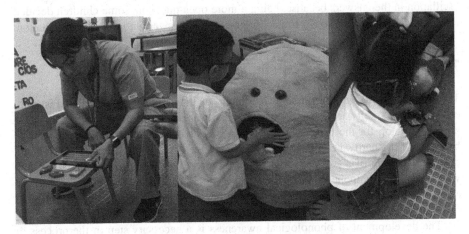

Fig. 7. Teacher and kids using Pistacho

Table 1 presents the percentage with stars obtained for each question, being five stars the maximum score and one star the lowest score that the child could assign. Among these questions, the child is questioned about the understanding of the activities, the affinity with *Pistacho* and the interest and understanding he had about the cards.

From the results obtained, one of the things that were evident in the children's at the time of asking the questions, is that by having at their hands the five stars to qualify the experience of using Pistacho, most of them gave the meaning of one (1) star as a NO,

Table 1. Qualification assigned by children

Questions	Percentage of start (%)				
	1	2	3	4	5
1. Are all the vowel pieces different for you?	0	0	0	41.6	58.3
2. Do you like the vowel pieces?	0	0	8.3	0	91.6
3. Did you understand the activity you had to do?	8.3	0	0	0	91.6
4. Do you find it difficult to do the activity?	91.7	0	0	0	8.3
5. Did you have fun playing with Pistacho?	8.3	0	0	0	91.6
6. How much do you like Pistacho?	0	8.3	0	0	91.6
7. Did you understand what Pistacho tells you?	8.3	0	0	0	91.6
8. Do you know what activities Pistacho is asking for?	8.3	0	8.3	58.3	25

three (3) stars as a DO NOT KNOW and five (5) stars as a YES. Therefore, it is concluded that in questions like No. 4 a big percentage of children gave a rating of one (1) star, in this case, although the question obtained the lowest rating does not imply that this is a bad grade, due to the way the children interpreted giving a star, as mentioned above. On the other hand, in questions such as No. 2, 3, 5, 6 and 7, most children gave a rating of five (5) stars. In Questions No. 1 and 8 there was a greater oscillation in the answers because, being a more open question, some children decided to give four (4) stars or two (2) and complement their answer with a verbal explanation.

7   Conclusions

Through this work, it was possible to obtain an interactive system called Pistacho, composed by a software component and a hardware component. The software component, develop for the use of the teachers, consists of an application that allows the handling of the hardware component. The hardware component, oriented to the blind children, consists of a wooden structure that represents a being from another planet, with electronic components that allow the user (child) to interact naturally with the system. Pistacho aims to support the development of phonological awareness in blind children.

The development of phonological awareness is a necessary step in the process of acquisition of reading and writing, which plays a fundamental role in the education of children. For this, four activities were implemented that improve factors such as the recognition and segmentation of words in phonemes, in this particular case focusing on the vowels, because they are the beginning of the literacy process.

The creation of an interactive system under the principles of Usability and Accessibility Engineering, as was done by implementing the MPIu+a model, which provided a guide for developers during the project research and execution process, to detect the real needs of the target audience, and reach the development of a product that satisfies them.

The implementation of Pistacho also looks to the benefit of the teachers in the institute, providing them with an additional resource that they can use as a complement to their class, which look up to promote the development of phonological awareness of the children's. In addition, the implementation of Pistacho not only has the objective of consolidating knowledge in a non-traditional way, making use of technologies that allow interaction through different senses, but also to reach better motivation and interest on the part of children, and thus to reduce the gap existing between technology and blind children.

The implementation of Pistacho also searches for benefit of the teachers of the institute, providing them with an additional resource that they can use as a complement to their class, which seeks to promote the development of phonological awareness of the members. In addition, the implementation of Pistacho not only aims to consolidate knowledge in a non-traditional way, making use of technologies that allow interaction through different senses, but also to achieve greater motivation and interest on the part of children, and thus to reduce the gap existing between technology and blind children's.

One of the challenges in the design of Pistacho was to catch the interest and motivation of the children's at the time to do the activities, and to reach this, was necessary the use of some game mechanics, the implementation of activities that generate a challenge in the students to finally receive a good feedback, just as it is sought with the proposed activities impose challenges for users to overcome each interaction, with the aim of strengthening phonological awareness in a different way, using activities that are currently implemented by teachers in the classroom, but generating a different dynamic for the acquisition of such knowledge.

In the analysis, it was perceived that children's with visual disabilities need mechanisms in their environment that allow them to optimize the information obtained through the senses of hearing and touch. For this reason, *Pistacho* considered the use of different textures, both in the vowel pieces and the structure of Pistachio, in order to provide the child with mechanisms that allow him to recreate in his mind the image of the elements with which he interacts. In the same way, the personification of the Pistachio voice considers different intonations so that the child perceives it not only as a monster but as a friendly, good and sociable character.

In the analysis, the stage was possible to collect information of great value, for the selection and correct design of the components of the interactive system, resultant in the implementation of Pistacho with low-cost technological instruments and optimal functioning, which would allow compliance of the purpose for which it was developed.

Because the MPIu+a model proposes an iterative process, throughout the process of development of Pistacho, different evaluation techniques were implemented that allowed to demonstrate usability problems, the navigation in the application, ergonomics and the feedback of the users, which were corrected at the appropriate time, allowing to achieve a final product that meets the functional and non-functional requirements.

References

1. Joao, R.: Children with visual impairments: social interaction, language, and learning, United Estates, pp. 60–70 (1998)
2. Yetta, G.: Los niños construyen su lectoescritura, Buenos Aires Aique, p. 3 (1991)
3. Organización Nacional De Ciegos Españoles. Servicios especializados en discapacidad visual
4. Emilia, F.: Desarrollo de la alfabetización psicogénesis, p. 24
5. Walter, E.: Los trastornos del lenguaje en niños con deficiencia visual, p. 5
6. Griho Research Group of the University of Lleida. MPlu+a Modelo de proceso de la ingeniería de la usabilidad y accesibilidad
7. Mary, O.: Desarrollo de la conciencia fonológica en niños de preescolar a través del recurso digital adaptativo (REDA) "El universo mágico de las palabras", Chia (2015)
8. Equipo de audición y lenguaje CREENA. Materiales para trabajar las habilidades fonológicas
9. Gladys, R.: Creación de una aplicación multimedia para el desarrollo de la conciencia fonológica en niños de primer año de educación básica. Pontificio Universidad Catolica de ecuador sede Ambato (2016)

EduGit: Toward a Platform for Publishing and Adopting Course Content

Michael C. Stewart[✉]⬤, Jason Forsyth, and Zamua O. Nasrawt

James Madison University, Harrisonburg, VA 22807, USA
{stewarmc,forsy2jb,nasrawzo}@jmu.edu
http://hcientist.com
http://www.jasonforsyth.net/

Abstract. In light of the continued dearth of an online Community of Practice for the collaborative development and distribution of educational materials for Human Computer Interaction, we propose EduGit. EduGit is a web application that serves as a platform for publishing, adopting, and collaboratively authoring educational resources. The system facilitates and incentivizes publishing and adoption of course materials through interactions with existing learning management systems and estimates impact through aggregate material adoption and usage statistics.

Keywords: Education · Sharing · Online community ·
Open educational resources · Community of practice

1 Introduction

There has been a sustained interest in electronically sharing educational materials since there have been electronic means to do so (e.g. [19]). Across various disciplines there have been periodic efforts addressing the need to share resources. This sustained interest is due to the lack of a satisfactory approach. Currently, authors of course content have little support for systematic publishing and updating of their materials. Instead these authors develop their material and then often share it with their current students via their institution's adopted Learning Management System (see: Fig. 1). When a contact wishes to use their materials, they communicate via some backchannel such as email and distribute the materials (e.g. [13]). This form of sharing is problematic for several reasons:

1. The sharing instructor may accidentally share more (e.g. student grades or identifying information).
2. The sharing instructor may accidentally omit content they intended to share.
3. The sharing instructor would have to manually record those people who are potentially adopting their materials.
4. The adopting instructor may forget to give proper attribution for the adopted materials.

© Springer Nature Switzerland AG 2019
G. Meiselwitz (Ed.): HCII 2019, LNCS 11579, pp. 217–226, 2019.
https://doi.org/10.1007/978-3-030-21905-5_17

5. The sharing and adopting instructors may not have established a protocol for the adopter to offer critique or other feedback to the sharer.
6. The adopting instructor may incorrectly assume they have permission to share the resources with other instructors.
7. Instructors who receive the materials from someone other than the author may make incorrect attribution for the resources.
8. Would-be adopters may be unable to access the materials due to a lack of sufficient technical skills.
9. Would-be adopters may be unable to access the materials due to limitations on accessing the publishing platform.
10. Materials being published in many different places that different institutions may not support equally could result in an information indexing/retrieval problem.

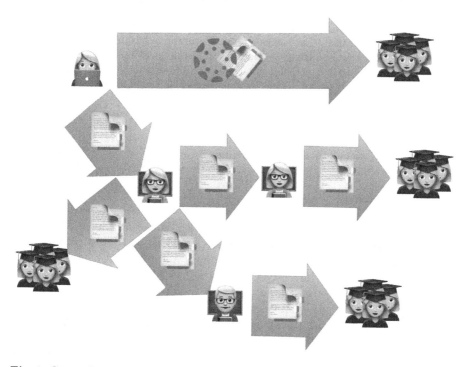

Fig. 1. Currently, authors share their curricular materials with students via an LMS, and then separately send files to other instructors.

In the Human Computer Interaction (HCI) community alone, there have been numerous efforts to define, share, and critique curricula and to build a community of practice for HCI Education [4–6,12,22]. These efforts have tackled various of the enumerated issues, and others beyond this list as well.

1.1   Design Space for Sharing Educational Materials

Through our on-going literature review, we will contribute a taxonomy that can help interested researchers see at a high-level the approaches that have been taken previously, and which parts of the sharing problem have been previously studied. So far we have identified several dimensions of the design space:

1. target audience
   (a) academic level
   (b) academic discipline
2. granularity of sharing: syllabi, large assignments (projects), quizzes, exams, in-class activities (e.g. slides), entire courses
3. ease of use for publisher
4. ease of use for adopter
5. license of published content
6. support for attribution
7. incentives

In the Discussion (Sect. 3.3), we will discuss where our approach falls in these dimensions.

We observe that in the field of software development there seem to be successful communities of practice engaged in sharing and reuse of software artifacts (e.g. [10]). Through (1) tracking the provenance of the source code, (2) nudging developers toward open licenses, and (3) facilitating the incorporation of improvements from third-parties into the original code bases, GitHub has fostered a vibrant community of collaborative software development. Following our participation in [22], we are developing EduGit [23] to support the sharing (publishing and adoption) of course materials, with lessons gleaned from GitHub and past education resource sharing efforts (e.g. those above as well as [2,3,8,9,20,21].

2   EduGit

EduGit is first a catalogued repository of educational materials. Interested authors of educational materials can easily publish their materials to the catalog. Interested educators can easily adopt those published materials for use in their own course. However, EduGit is more than a simple catalog of published educational materials.

2.1   EduGit Goals

EduGit aims to help educators establish a consequential practice of citing sources. The system tracks the adoptions of published materials to provide evidence of use. Similar to citation counts or the "h-index" for estimating researcher impact, statistics about actual adoption of an author's educational materials by other educators can help establish their educational impact. HCI educators may have differential need for such measures depending on their professional role [16]. EduGit has two primary Goals:

1. Facilitate
    - publication of educational resources.
    - adoption of educational resources.
2. Incentivize
    - publication of educational resources.
    - collaboration on educational resources.

In addition to the primary goals related to sharing educational resources, we are carefully designing EduGit to create a space for specific people to have specific interactions [11] that we believe are not well supported otherwise. We are designing EduGit to facilitate and incentivize critique of educational resources and pedagogical approaches.

2.2   System

EduGit is in the Proof-of-Concept development phase. The system is being developed as a web application (see: Fig. 2). It will consist of a relatively thick web client implemented as a ReactJS web application. The web application will

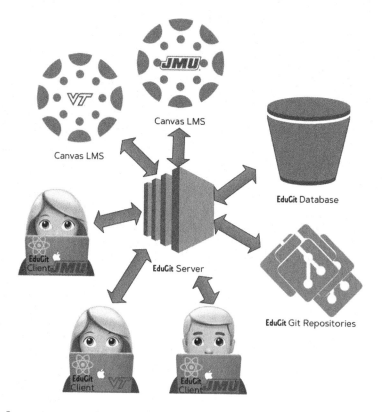

Fig. 2. Instructors at multiple institutions can authorize EduGit to access their Learning Management System to publish their courses, or to import published courses from EduGit for adoption.

communicate via RESTful API with the Django server. The server in turn, will communicate with (1) users' existing Learning Management Systems, (2) EduGit's own database, and (3) git repositories on the EduGit server that will facilitate versioning of the published materials.

2.3   Features

In the first version of EduGit, educational resources will only be able to be shared in units of a course (i.e. all content for a whole term of a course). While this design decision conveniently scopes the problem, it also reduces the administrative and cognitive efforts of publication and adoption because the syllabus, assignments, and other resources are all packaged together. This results in an adopter having more context than they might have through piecemeal sharing of individual resources.

A second simplification of the problem space that we employ in the first version of EduGit is limiting publication and adoption of courses to those available or to be offered in the Canvas Learning Management System (LMS) [14].

Publishing. An educator wishing to publish their course to the EduGit catalog will simply click a "Publish my course(s)" button, which will prompt them to sign in to their institution's Canvas instance. Having authenticated and granted EduGit access to their institutional Canvas account, the educator will see a detailed presentation of all the courses they have taught, each with a "Publish" button. Adding their course to the EduGit catalog simply requires clicking the corresponding "Publish" button.

Adopting. Similarly, an educator who finds a course they wish to adopt in the EduGit catalog can simply click the course's corresponding "Adopt" button. This will redirect the educator to their institution's Canvas authentication process. Having successfully authenticated and authorized EduGit to access their Canvas account, EduGit will present the adopting educator with a detailed list of their courses. Simply clicking one of these courses' corresponding "Select" button will import the published Canvas course contents into the adopter's course.

Collaboration and Updates. EduGit requires access to educators' existing institutional Canvas accounts to function. This access enables EduGit to support the educators in tracking changes to courses they have published or adopted (see: Fig. 3).

When an educator makes a change to a course that has been adopted by others, the educator can be prompted to indicate whether the changes might be beneficial (downstream) to the adopters. Likewise when an adopter makes changes to a Canvas course that they have adopted from another educator, EduGit can prompt the adopter to indicate whether it would be appropriate to propose the change (upstream) to the course from which they adopted the content.

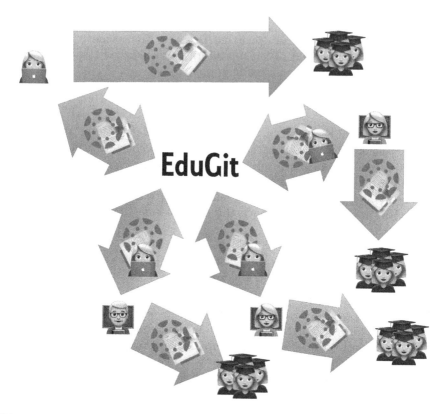

Fig. 3. Authors publish- and track the adoption of- their curricular materials through EduGit's access to their institution's adopted Learning Management System.

In choosing whether to share these updates up- or downstream, educators may wish to describe the changes and perhaps their rationale. Like git's commit messages, and GitHub's pull requests, these discussions of rationale for changes create a space for contextualized, detailed discussion of pedagogical choices that currently lack a designated arena.

2.4   User Experience

EduGit should be simple to use. Educators of any academic level and from any discipline should be able to publish and adopt courses with ease. Despite the "git" [24] suffix, publishers and adopters of content should have a simple graphical user interface in the EduGit web application for publishing and adopting content. Given the simplifications in the first version (see: Sect. 2.3), the process of publishing and adopting materials is simplified to publishing and adopting courses. This reduction in scope results in a simpler user experience for both (1) the actions of publishing and adopting, and (2) the pedagogical practice of comprehending and incorporating another educator's resources.

It is worth discussing why we mention restricting our problem scope to the Canvas LMS. The same features mentioned previously are available in Github and similar applications, and there even exist movements to re-purpose these applications for education without the need for any new tooling [7]. Initiatives of this nature provide standards for modeling course materials in these version control applications such that they can be viewed, shared, and tracked easily. The issue lies not with the initiative in any mechanical sense, but with the target audience. Interfacing with any current version control system is frankly not accessible to the broader population of educators. Git's primary interface is on a command line, and even the graphical interfaces are designed with code in mind. EduGit aims to wrap all of Git's features into a friendlier package that is easily accessible to a lay audience.

Other motivations for developing a new application have to do with institutional policies and practices. Universities cannot license LMS applications based solely on feature set. They must also proactively protect user privacy as mandated by law (e.g. FERPA in the United States). This limits the set of applications available to an educator. Current LMS applications only lack the sharing and provenance features; it would be unreasonable for a new application to re-implement all of the existing features. EduGit has two key advantages by integrating with existing LMS applications (initially only Canvas):

1. Standard features such as course and student management can still be handled by the LMS. This means EduGit will have a dramatically reduced development work load.
2. Sensitive data about students such as demographics and grades are not needed for our target features. This means institutional privacy policies won't block educators from using EduGit.

3   Discussion

EduGit will contribute to rich discussions about the development of online communities of practice for educational resources [15,17,18,25]. In addition to questions of the establishment and maintenance of the online community of practice, interesting questions of user experience and pedagogical practice confront EduGit.

3.1   Attribution

Currently, there is little meaningful citation of another educator's materials. While many of us include acknowledgements in our syllabi or even in specific project or assignment specifications, these citations are not indexed or tabulated. Perhaps this lack of tracking promotes less consistent attribution of authorship. Educators often participate in a "free-information" style of sharing course materials that encourages others to be more relaxed about citing sources, or asking for permission. EduGit at its core does not want to change this model. In fact it wants to formalize this ideology by automating the tedious task of attribution. As a result of automatic, accurate, and persistent attribution, educators are incentivized to offer their course materials. Furthermore, contributions "up stream" from adopters to original authors are also attributed automatically. This incentivizes educators to share what has worked for them when they pilot a newly adopted course on their own students.

As EduGit aims to support attribution, there may be an issue in soliciting original content. That is, having lacked a meaningful outcome of attributing educational resources to the original authors, experienced educators may have a significant amount of unattributed content in "their" courses. These educators may feel uncomfortable publishing "their" course materials as they recognize their inability to properly cite their sources so long after they originally adopted them. An important research question as we develop EduGit will be how to help establish the new practice of more consistent attribution and how to transition from the status quo of less careful citing. Perhaps a statement on published courses that authors are sharing the courses as they teach them, but do not guarantee the content is theirs alone would help ease the concerns of publishing courses. Alternatively, similar to the "take-down" model on other user-contributed content web sites, EduGit could provide a feature to report content as belonging to the reporter. Initially, EduGit could rely on the publisher to agree that the reporter is the original source for the materials so that proper attribution can be made.

3.2 New Patterns of Collaboration

There is currently little professional space for developing and sharing quality educational materials. While some conferences (e.g. SIGCSE [1]) do have Experience Reports, there remain too few opportunities for educators to seek criticism of and collaboration on their educational materials. In EduGit, we can provide the ability to attribute to the contributor the change a publisher incorporates into their course. We expect this to help improve the (likelihood and) quality of the collaboration.

3.3 Locating EduGit

We have so far identified seven dimensions that help characterize the Design Space for Sharing Educational Materials (Sect. 1.1). EduGit aims to support instructors in any discipline. EduGit will not assume any specific academic level. EduGit will limit the granularity of sharing to the unit of a whole course (syllabus, assignments, exams, slides and other in-class content). EduGit will have extreme ease of use for the publisher and adopter alike, publishing or adopting the course in a just a few clicks. EduGit will initially support only open licenses (such as Creative Commons's share-a-like licenses). EduGit will automatically record attribution records when one instructor adopts a course from another, but EduGit will also support the ability of someone to indicate that an attribution may have been accidentally omitted to help establish new practices around proper attribution in the educational communities. EduGit will thereby incentivize sharing and even critical feedback by offering evidence-based reports of users' contributions to published courses.

4   Future Work

In future versions of EduGit, we will eliminate the version 1 simplifications. We will support other learning management systems (beyond Canvas). We will support the ability to adopt portions of a course. We will support cross-LMS adoption. As the first implementation of tracking provenance will be implemented using git [24], and will internally model the relationships between courses as "forks" of repositories (e.g. on GitHub), the first version of EduGit will not provide the ability to compose multiple published courses into a single adopted course. We will remove this limitation in future versions to support a richer relationship between existing and newly adopted courses.

References

1. ACM. SIGCSE Technical Symposium 2019 (2019)
2. Akbar, M., et al.: How educators find educational resources online. In: Proceedings of the 16th Annual Joint Conference on Innovation and Technology in Computer Science Education, ITiCSE 2011, New York, NY, USA, p. 367. ACM (2011)
3. Akbar, M., et al.: Digital library 2.0 for educational resources. In: Gradmann, S., Borri, F., Meghini, C., Schuldt, H. (eds.) TPDL 2011. LNCS, vol. 6966, pp. 89–100. Springer, Heidelberg (2011). https://doi.org/10.1007/978-3-642-24469-8_11
4. Churchill, E., Preece, J., Bowser, A.: Developing a living HCI curriculum to support a global community. In: Proceedings of the Extended Abstracts of the 32nd Annual ACM Conference on Human Factors in Computing Systems - CHI EA 2014, New York, New York, USA, pp. 135–138. ACM Press (2014)
5. Churchill, E.F., Bowser, A., Preece, J.: Teaching and learning human-computer interaction. Interactions 20(2), 44 (2013)
6. Churchill, E.F., Bowser, A., Preece, J.: The future of HCI education. Interactions 23(2), 70–73 (2016)
7. Conrad, P., Kharitonova, Y.: UCSB CS Course Repos (2017)
8. Fouh, E., Sun, M., Shaffer, C.: OpenDSA: a creative commons active-ebook (abstract only). In: Proceedings of the 43rd ACM Technical Symposium on Computer Science Education, SIGCSE 2012, New York, NY, USA, p. 721. ACM (2012)
9. Fox, E.A., et al.: Ensemble PDP-8: eight principles for distributed portals. In: Proceedings of the 10th Annual Joint Conference on Digital Libraries, JCDL 2010, New York, NY, USA, pp. 341–344. ACM (2010)
10. GitHub. GitHub (2019)
11. Harrison, S., Tatar, D.: Places: people, events, loci-the relation of semantic frames in the construction of place. Comput. Support. Coop. Work (CSCW) 17(2–3), 97–133 (2008)
12. Hewett, T.T., et al.: ACM SIGCHI Curricula for Human-Computer Interaction. ACM, New York (1992)
13. Hu, H.H.: CS 1 POGIL Activities (2017)

14. Instructure. Canvas Learning Management System
15. Lampe, C., Wash, R., Velasquez, A., Ozkaya, E.: Motivations to participate in online communities. In: Proceedings of the 28th International Conference on Human Factors in Computing Systems - CHI 2010, New York, New York, USA, p. 1927. ACM Press (2010)
16. Peck, E.M., Smith, M.E., Stewart, M.C.: HCI for PUI: human-computer interaction for primarily-undergraduate institutions. In: WORKSHOP: Developing a Community of Practice to Support Global HCI Education of the 2018 CHI Conference on Human Factors in Computing Systems, vol. 2018 (2018)
17. Pitt, R.: Mainstreaming open textbooks: educator perspectives on the impact of OpenStax college open textbooks. Int. Rev. Res. Open Distrib. Learn. 16(4) (2015)
18. Preece, J.: Online Communities: Designing Usability and Supporting Socialbilty. Wiley, New York (2000)
19. Rubincam, D.P.: Electronic book (1977)
20. Shaffer, C.A., Akbar, M., Alon, A.J.D., Stewart, M., Edwards, S.H.: Getting algorithm visualizations into the classroom. In: Proceedings of the 42nd ACM Technical Symposium on Computer Science Education, SIGCSE 2011 (accpetance rate: 34%), New York, NY, USA, pp. 129–134. ACM (2011)
21. Shaffer, C.A., et al.: Algorithm visualization: the state of the field. Trans. Comput. Educ. 10(3), 9:1–9:22 (2010)
22. St-Cyr, O., MacDonald, C.M., Churchill, E.F., Preece, J.J., Bowser, A.: Developing a community of practice to support global HCI education. In: Extended Abstracts of the 2018 CHI Conference on Human Factors in Computing Systems - CHI 2018, New York, New York, USA, pp. 1–7. ACM Press (2018)
23. Stewart, M.C., Nasrawt, Z.O.: EduGit (2018)
24. Torvalds, L.: GIT
25. Wenger, E., McDermott, R.A., Snyder, W.: Cultivating Communities of Practice: A Guide to Managing Knowledge. Harvard Business Press, Boston (2002)

Enhancing Database Courses Through the EDNA Project: A Preliminary Framework for the Extraction of Diverse Datasets and Analysis

Sandra Tavegia[1]([⊠]), James Braman[1]([⊠]), Giovanni Vincenti[2]([⊠]),
and Barbara Yancy[1]([⊠])

[1] Computer Science/Information Technology,
Community College of Baltimore County, Rosedale, MD 21237, USA
{stavegia, jbraman, byancy}@ccbcmd.edu
[2] Division of Science, Information Arts and Technologies,
University of Baltimore, Baltimore, MD 21201, USA
gvincenti@ubalt.edu

Abstract. To enhance and grow the database certificate program and enhance database courses offered by the Computer Science/Information Technology department (CSIT) at the Community College of Baltimore County (CCBC), we are in the process of developing the EDNA Project. The EDNA Project- Extraction of Diverse Datasets and Analysis will be an educational database and project set encompassing several large real-world datasets that will be accessible to students in the database courses. This project was created out of the need for more elaborate examples and hands-on experience with database concepts. This repository will help serve to teach database concepts, data analytics, and lead to topics related to big data to students in these courses and certificates programs. In addition, this paper describes collaboration with the University of Baltimore and the beginnings of Project RED. This paper discusses our current work in developing this project.

Keywords: EDNA · RED · Database curriculum · Collaboration · Project infusion · Diverse Datasets

1 Introduction

Teaching fundamental database concepts is essential for many technology-related degree programs. Within the Computer Science/Information Technology department at the Community College of Baltimore County (CCBC) several database courses are offered each semester. These courses are offered as part of the Associates Degree in Information Technology and a database credit certificate. Specific course sequences are required depending on a student's declared major or certificate program, but any student can take these courses if they have met the prerequisites. The focus of these required core database courses is to develop basic skills and understanding of database concepts to be relevant and applicable for those entering the workforce or transferring to a bachelor's degree program.

© Springer Nature Switzerland AG 2019
G. Meiselwitz (Ed.): HCII 2019, LNCS 11579, pp. 227–237, 2019.
https://doi.org/10.1007/978-3-030-21905-5_18

The Community College of Baltimore County (CCBC) located in Maryland, is an integral part of Baltimore County, collaborating with government, business and local organizations to enrich the community. CCBC provides an accessible, affordable and high-quality education that prepares students for transfer and career success. In fiscal year 2017, the college educated 61,191 students, including 29,115 credit students and 33,247 non-credit students [1]. CCBC awarded 2,131 Associate degrees and 1,410 Certificates in 2017. There were 6,687 student transfers to other institutions [2]. CCBC offers 280 associate degree, credit certificate, and non-credit workforce training certification programs including 20 online degree and certificate options [3]. CCBC has the distinct honor of being the number one provider of workforce development in the Baltimore Metropolitan area. Ninety-two percent of the college's graduates continue to live and work in the Greater Baltimore region. With three main campuses and three extension centers, CCBC serves a diverse population of Maryland residents.

The Computer Science/Information Technology (CSIT) department offers associate degrees in Information Technology, Computer Science, and Computer Science with a concentration in Information Systems Management as well as five credit-based certificates (Database, Information Management, Mobile Development, Programming, and Office Specialist). The database certificate requires taking 22 to 23 credits. Required courses include (1) Introduction to MIS, (2) Database Concepts, (3) Introduction to SQL using Oracle, (4) Emerging Database Design and the addition of two other Computer Science/Information Technology related electives. The CSIT department offers a total of five database courses, three of which are required for the database certificate (See Table 1). The other two classes are offered as elective options for students meeting the prerequisites but encouraged for those in the program (See Table 2).

The additional database related electives as noted in Table 2 are not the only option for students but are the only elective database focused courses. CSIT 256 is the second course in a two-course sequence and required as part of the Database option. Non-database courses that can be taken include Introduction to Information Assurance, Visual Basic programming, Introduction to Data Communications or Introduction to Linux/Unix. Each of database courses will be using the EDNA database as part of the ETL process (Extract, Transform and Load). The order of priority of the courses listed for the EDNA project are as follows: CSIT 154, CSIT 134, CSIT 156, CSIT 254 and CSIT 256. These will be discussed in more detail in the following sections. In the initial testing phase of the project CSIT 154 is the main course being explored to be used with EDNA. Additional components will be introduced into the other classes in subsequent semesters.

The certificate option is often a good choice for students that already have another degree or for those that need to enhance their knowledge for employment purposes. As noted by the CSIT department "The Database Certificate will prepare students for employment as entry-level database programmers and designers or provide current professionals with essential database programming and design skills" [4]. In the next section enhancements to the database curriculum through the EDNA project is discussed.

Table 1. Required database courses

Course Number	Course name	Course description	Prerequisites
CSIT 154	Database concepts	Database concepts provides in-depth coverage of the content of database management systems (DBMS) and their capabilities and limitations, and it covers both physical and logical data structure with an emphasis on meaningful data relationships, the role of the database administrator, and the data dictionary	English 101 and CSIT 101: Technology and Information Systems
CSIT 156	Introduction to SQL Using Oracle	Provides an introduction to the Oracle relational database, structured query language and database concepts. Students will create tables, establish relationships, enforce integrity constraints and manipulate data. Additional database objects, database security, transaction control and user creation and management will also be introduced	CSIT 101: Technology & Information Systems
CSIT 254	Emerging Database Design	Utilizes relational database design principles, techniques and emerging technologies to design and develop relational databases using contemporary database management software. Students will identify business information requirements; transforming them into relational databases	CSIT 154: Database concepts OR CSIT 156: Introduction to SQL Using Oracle

Table 2. Database related electives

Course number	Course name	Course description	Prerequisites
CSIT 134	Comprehensive databases	Provides an introduction to databases and database management systems (DBMS) and an opportunity to design, create, and modify a database using Microsoft Access; discusses retrieval of information by creating queries, reports, and forms.3 lecture hours. This course is delivered in a combination lecture and hands-on format	CSIT 101 – Technology and Information Systems

(continued)

Table 2. (*continued*)

Course number	Course name	Course description	Prerequisites
CSIT 256	Advanced Oracle	Discusses PL/SQL in application development, program constructs, application schemas, functions, subprograms, packages, triggers, dependencies, large object types, supplied packages and advanced security concepts	CSIT 156 – Introduction to SQL Using Oracle

2 Developing the EDNA Project

To enhance and grow CCBC's database certificate program and enhance database courses offered by the computer science/information technology department we are in the process of developing the EDNA Project. The EDNA Project-Extraction of Diverse Datasets and Analysis will be a student-centric educational database of large real-world datasets that will be accessible to students in the database courses. This project was created out of the need for more elaborate examples and hands-on experience with database concepts. This repository will help serve to teach database concepts, data analytics, and lead to topics related to big data to students in these courses and certificates programs. EDNA allows students to not only interact with these datasets for learning but provide the infrastructure for database configuration and data manipulation in a more substantial way than was currently available in the program. The datasets through EDNA will allow students to find relevant trends and explore the impacts of technology on society. Having this system in place will allow for an improved database program through real-world problems, increase collaboration, and enhance retention and completion rates. As part of the program, the Computer Science and Information Technology Department (CSIT) of the School of Technology, Art and Design (STAD) will develop this system and maintain the datasets, database, and server. This project as a resource will serve as a significant tool to improve the database certificate program, and all database courses offered through the Department.

Strategies for teaching database concepts are often employed using teaching strategies that are similar to teaching other technical courses where students remain as passive listeners [5]. While there are many factors to student success, there are many pedagogical approaches to make learning more meaningful and engaging where content is retained by students [6]. In the context of teaching database concepts, Connolly, Stansfield, and McLellan (2006), discuss the difficulty students have when there is not a "single, simple or well-known or correct solution" [7, p. 104]. Students also display difficulty when dealing with vagueness and complex database analysis [7]. We need these database projects as encompassing issues of vagueness and can be used to teach students strategies to work through these difficulties. To combat this issue and as a student engagement technique, EDNA infused projects will be collaborative in nature. From this preliminary implementation of EDNA, the following research questions will need to be addressed as the curriculum is designed and improved:

R1: What datasets will students find engaging yet beneficial to their understanding of core database concepts?
R2: What pedagogical approach is best for teaching using the EDNA framework?
R3: Does EDNA provide an improvement to the database curriculum?

Given the exploratory nature of this project, a pilot study will be conducted during the next academic year to examine these research questions in the context of the project framework. Currently, the EDNA server uses the Oracle Linux 6.0 Platform. Students will use the Oracle Business Intelligence Suite 2.820 in the initial phase of the project.

Major components to the overall design of EDNA:

1. Student Dataset Resources
   a. Datasets maintained on Server for use in database courses.
   b. Projects for database courses aligned to datasets and configuration.
2. Database
   a. Small Database configured on required Server (PowerEdge T630) to hold student class resources.
   b. Provide means for students to learn introductory data analytics and database configuration and tools.

3 Enhancing the Curriculum

The Overall objectives of the EDNA project are to enhance the database courses by improving curriculum materials and providing students access to real-world problems and projects. Providing students with real-world projects that include real or large datasets can be advantageous as they explore more complex topics related to databases including understanding the complexities of big data. To address the current gap in skills in preparing students to work with big data, educators should make learning real and relevant [8]. As a preliminary step to this project, several modules will be introduced into the database courses to both expand and align the curriculum in preparation of working with additional datasets. Students will work collaboratively in groups throughout the semester on several projects. Each project will be designed to highlight a particular database topic using the provided datasets. These projects will be in addition to the standard curriculum. Each module will have three major components: 1. Extract raw data, 2. Load relevant data into a database and 3. Examine the data using Business Intelligence tools for analysis (see Fig. 1).

Fig. 1. Three components processes

Component 1 would require students to examine the listing of available datasets and choose the appropriate data for the assignment or project. However, before proceeding to Component 2, students need to carefully examine aspects of the data (Process A). What does the data represent? How should the data be organized? What are the attributes? Are there any preprocessing or cleansing steps needed? After this examination step for process A, students would need to prepare the data to be stored in their own database. This would include planning, analyzing the structure and creating various diagrams to illustrate and describe the data and its organization. Students would have then completed Component 2 (Load and Organize). Next, for Process B, students would practice a set of manipulations, queries, and tests on the database they have created. This is to both practice their skills and deepen their knowledge of the dataset. In Component 3, students would then spend time analyzing the data. This process will introduce students to necessary analysis tools, techniques, and terminology. Students can discover new trends about the data.

The list below illustrates some sample projects under development as part of the project:

- Project 1
    - Students will be given access to a raw data dump of simulated or donated telephone records. They will need to ascertain which information is relevant for a given scenario and consider how additional information can be derived.
- Project 2
    - Students will use graphic files to demonstrate how information can be requested by characteristics other than file name or structure. Students can learn other categorization techniques.
- Project 3
    - Students can utilize social media imports from public posts to examine connections between accounts and other attributes.

In addition to examining different types of data, students can be introduced to basic data collection methodologies, ethics, security, data management, and content rights. Although the scope and level of the course may limit the depth of coverage, students can be introduced to general concepts at this level through various projects. The intent of the projects are to be both relevant and exciting to the students while developing particular skillsets.

3.1   EDNA Major Components

In the efforts to enhance the curriculum, several components are underway for the pilot. Based on feedback gained during the initial phases, we intend to make improvements and add to the projects and datasets available. The following steps are being implemented for the preliminary EDNA project:

- Courses identified for EDNA project trial
- Initial design of several project modules for the course
- Develop training for students to connecting to server and datasets
- Design of dataset exploration component
- Design a data cleaning component
- Design or project specification report for student assignments
- Student performance and assessment criteria
- Implementation of a short survey to collect student feedback

4   Datasets

There are a growing number of available resources and open datasets that students can use for various analyses. Currently, we are working with several available sources, including the creation of our own large collection. To list a few sample datasets under exploration, include: The Stanford Dog Dataset [9], SMS Spam Collection [10], Social Structure of Facebook Networks Data Scrape [11], 2012 data from the Global Ensemble Forecast System [12], 1996 through 2017 College Scorecard Data [13] and several more. The aim is to have an array of diverse data. Each type of dataset can yield interesting project assignments and interpretations. For example, the images stored in the Stanford Dog Dataset could be used to examine metadata, storage issues for images versus text, or used to explore topics of image classification. These datasets can be fully downloaded. In addition, there are public datasets from government sources also can provide a rich set of content that can be revised for course content. Some are provided by web-based portals like Open Baltimore where there are numerous reports and data available including web-based filters and basic visualization tools [14]. Example datasets include information related to crime, health care, taxation, parking, cultural interests, and much more. Learning and knowledge analytic research by [15] describe several dataset properties and resources.

There are also several concurrent projects underway where students can capture data to create large datasets to become part of the EDNA project. One example is through a group project in an introductory Python programming course, where students have been working on creating a small sensor network to collect temperature, air pressure, and air quality data. This data is being measured over various time increments and recorded to an external server. This data can be changed and enhanced through scripts and stored as part of the EDNA database with ever-increasing amounts of and granularity of data. Currently, this data is being used by students to test a machine learning algorithm and a web-based affective computing-based display. This project is just one example of a student-driven project. In the future, we intend to increasingly use student created content for datasets as they can contribute towards the project.

Another example is data extracted from faculty-driven projects using public social media and search engine data to contribute to the datasets. For text analysis purposes students can make use data collected from the web crawling component of PAsSIVE (Personalized Assisted Search in a Virtual Environment) as it crawls web content for a fixed depth based on a set of starting seed links [16]. As elements used in PAsSIVE, [17] describe several text features that can be obtained from crawled pages as part of the indexing strategy: page content, page descriptions, hyperlink structure, hyperlink text, keywords or meta tags, page title, text with different font, and the first sentence. Additional diverse content can also be obtained through public social media posts through SADD (Social Media Agent for the Detection of the Deceased) where large text content, with link structure and time stamps, can be evaluated [18]. Content generated by SADD has generally been complex providing a real dataset and problem for students. This data will be particularly useful for students wanting to learn and work with sentiment analysis.

5   Collaborations - Project RED

Recent agreements between CCBC and the University of Baltimore (UB) have made it possible for students working on Associates Degrees in Computer Science or Information Technology to complete their 2-year degree at the community college, and then continue to earn their Bachelor's in Applied Information Technology at UB. Such a pathway is essential not only to ensure that students complete their undergraduate studies in a timely manner but also to give them options in terms of 4-year degree-granting institutions in the area.

The collaboration goes beyond an administrative agreement alone, as students should get some continuity in terms of educational resources and expectations. In particular, the EDNA Project dovetails into a new initiative at UB, where faculty members are collecting databases and datasets particularly suited for educational purposes, creating RED, the Repository of Educational Datasets. The primary intent of this project is to enable students to easily access resources that may not necessarily be designed to be used in a database course, such as datasets made available by open access data initiatives.

Table 3. Example dataset

Dataset	Attribute	Sample data
MBE/WBE	Location1	4519 Fairfax Road Baltimore Md 21216- $(39.31841103000045°, -76.69144016099966°)$
RPT	PropertyAddress	2037 W NORTH AVE
	Location	$(39.30942111°, -76.65094166°)$

Typically, datasets are single-entity schemas that contain significant information about a certain topic. Although this is extremely important in terms of transparency to the public from governmental institutions, for example, these individual datasets are generally not very useful in a SQL-based course. A dataset such as the "Minority and Women's Business Enterprises Certifications" (MBE/WBE) contains a single table with 25 attributes and 1,835 records [19]. This limits the usefulness of this dataset to queries that utilize a single table.

When we then wish to utilize another dataset from the same repository, such as the "Real Property Tax" dataset (RPT), which also contains a single table with 16 attributes and over 239,000 records, we run into different types of issues in terms of data compatibility [20]. For example, the address in the first dataset is reported as a single field, whereas the second dataset contains information stored with a different format and in two fields, as reported in Table 3.

Table 4. Related course listing

Course code	Course title	Notes
COSC 151	Computer programming I	The course teaches Python
COSC 356	Database systems	The course uses MySQL and teaches SQL
COSC 3XX	Advanced scripting	The course is under development, but will focus on Python
COSC 456	Advanced database systems	The course focuses on advanced database scripting and non-relational technologies

Although the data is conceptually the same, the two datasets cannot easily be integrated into a larger schema that can then allow students to perform queries using multiple tables. For this reason, we intend to utilize RED in multiple courses in order to integrate different datasets into schemas that are usable in projects and assignments. The classes that we will target are reported in Table 4 above.

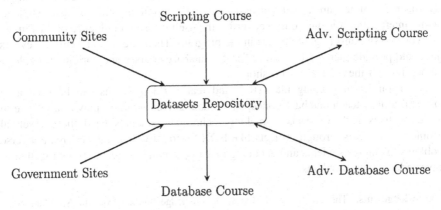

Fig. 2. RED course model

The courses will contribute to RED using the model shown in Fig. 2. This approach will allow projects from all courses to contribute to the dataset repository while letting the students develop multiple skills. Similarly, to the EDNA Project, students in scripting courses will learn how to download data from online resources of sensors, adding to the repository. Students in database course can utilize the datasets for queries, as well as to create documentation describing them. Projects in advanced courses can then focus on the integration of datasets either through the direct manipulation of current datasets already in the repository (for example, ETL techniques and tools for advanced database courses), or reach out to external sources and augment any missing data (for example, using freely available API services in advanced scripting courses).

6 Conclusion and Future Work

There are numerous aspects of this project that need additional investigation and continued improvement. After the initial EDNA pilot, several semesters of enhancements are planned. It will take some time to gather and test multiple datasets to build a large assortment of projects that can be used in different ways each semester. We also intend to examine other data analytic tools and investigate what strategies are most helpful at an introductory level.

To measure the impact of EDNA, we plan to assess the course by comparing to a control group by using the online version of database courses. Also, several student surveys will be administered to collect feedback on course design, dataset interest, and perceived helpfulness. This would be in addition to grade assessment and feedback from our external advisory board. With increased collaboration with the University of Baltimore, there are numerous opportunities to examine best practices in teaching database topics, designing new projects and creating fascinating datasets. In the future, we intend to connect together several projects to enhance and augment several of the data sources. Students may also develop an interest to pursue a more advanced degree in these related fields.

In an effort to increase visibility at CCBC, we intend to host several small hands-on workshop activities or demonstrations at the College's Pathway events. There are six Pathways where students are grouped by their declared major in an effort to target advertisement of resources, student assistance, collaborations, and to foster student-faculty interaction. It is our goal to advertise the usefulness and influence of data in the real world to students to gain interest in the program. There are several semester events that could provide increased visibility for the database courses and various technology majors through these EDNA workshops.

Hands-on learning using interesting and real-world problems can be used as a powerful tool to teach database concepts. As data is continuing to play a large role in our daily lives and our decision-making techniques, students need these essential technical skills. It is through projects like EDNA and RED that we can create diverse problems to engage students and encourage faculty to collaborate and work together to solve today's data problems.

Acknowledgments. The authors would like to acknowledge funding from the Maryland State Department of Education CTE Reserve Fund to support the EDNA project.

References

1. CCBC Office of Planning, Research and Evaluation. CCBC Fact Book. http://www.ccbcmd. edu/~/media/CCBC/About%20CCBC/Administrative%20Offices/PRE/ccbc_factbook.ashx
2. CCBC Quick Facts. http://www.ccbcmd.edu/About-CCBC/Administrative-Offices/Admini strative-Services/Planning-Research-and-Evaluation/CCBC-Facts.aspx
3. CCBC Program and Courses. http://www.ccbcmd.edu/programs-and-courses
4. CCBC Database Certificate, Credit Certificate. http://www.ccbcmd.edu/Programs-and-Courses-Finder/program/database-certificate
5. Mohtashami, M., Scher, J.M.: Application of Bloom's cognitive domain taxonomy to database design. In: Proceedings of ISECON (Information Systems Educators Conference) (2000)
6. Barkley, E.F.: Student Engagement Techniques: A Handbook for College Faculty. Wiley, New York (2009)
7. Connolly, T.M., Stansfield, M., McLellan, E.: Using an online games-based learning approach to teach database design concepts. Electron. J. e-Learn. 4(1), 103–110 (2006)
8. Henry, R., Venkatraman, S.: Big data analytics the next big learning opportunity. Acad. Inf. Manage. Sci. J. 18(2), 17 (2015)
9. Khosla, A., Jayadevaprakash, N., Yao, B., Fei-Fei, L.: Novel dataset for fine-grained image categorization. In: First Workshop on Fine-Grained Visual Categorization (FGVC), IEEE Conference on Computer Vision and Pattern Recognition (2011)
10. Almeida, T.A., Gómez Hidalgo, J.M., Yamakami, A.: Contributions to the study of SMS spam filtering: new collection and results. In: Proceedings of the 2011 ACM Symposium on Document Engineering, Mountain View, CA, USA (2011)
11. Traud, A.L., Mucha, P.J., Porter, M.A.: Social structure of Facebook networks. Physica A Stat. Mech. Appl. 391(16), 4165–4180 (2012)
12. National Center for Environmental Information. Global Ensemble Forecast System (GEFS). https://www.ncdc.noaa.gov/data-access/model-data/model-datasets/global-ensemble-forecast-system-gefs
13. United States Department of Education. College Scorecard Data. https://collegescorecard.ed.gov/data/
14. Open Baltimore. https://data.baltimorecity.gov/
15. Verbert, K., Manouselis, N., Drachsler, H., Duval, E.: Dataset-driven research to support learning and knowledge analytics. J. Educ. Technol. Soc. 15(3), 133–148 (2012)
16. Braman, J., Dierbach, C.: Utilizing virtual worlds for personalized search: developing the PAsSIVE framework. In: Meiselwitz, G. (ed.) SCSM 2015. LNCS, vol. 9182, pp. 3–11. Springer, Cham (2015). https://doi.org/10.1007/978-3-319-20367-6_1
17. Hu, W., Yeh, J.: World wide web search engines. In: Si, S.N., Murthy, V.K. (eds.) Architectural Issues of Web-Enabled Electronic Business. Idea Group Publishing, Hershey (2003)
18. Braman, J., Dudley, A., Vincenti, G.: Designing SADD: a social media agent for the detection of the deceased. In: Meiselwitz, G. (ed.) SCSM 2018. LNCS, vol. 10914, pp. 345–356. Springer, Cham (2018). https://doi.org/10.1007/978-3-319-91485-5_26
19. Minority and women's business enterprises certifications. https://data.baltimorecity.gov/City-Services/Minority-and-Women-s-Business-Enterprises-Certific/us2p-bijb
20. Real property taxes. https://data.baltimorecity.gov/Financial/Real-Property-Taxes/27w9-urtv

The Gamification Encouraging Access to Information and Academic Interaction

Klaudia Weronika Serwa Dionisio[(✉)], Gustavo Marcelino Dionisio,
Rafaela Oliveira Santos, Daniela de Freitas Guilhermino Trindade,
Thiago Adriano Coleti, José Reinaldo Merlin,
Ederson Marcos Sgarbi, and Carlos Eduardo Ribeiro

Center of Technological Sciences, State University of Paraná, Bandeirantes,
Paraná, Brazil
klaudia.sd.95@gmail.com, gugamd93@gmail.com,
rafaelaoliveirast@outlook.com, {danielaf,
thiago.coleti,merlin,sgarbi,biluka}@uenp.edu.br

Abstract. Institutional websites are available for a large amount of data hindering the access of scholars to information relevant to their academic journey. As the university is also a space of opportunities, it is necessary that the student is aware of all the possibilities that can support his professional and human growth, such as, monitoring, projects of scientific initiation, cultural activities, among others. So, considering the massive use of smartphones by students, this paper proposes a mobile application that provides the information of interest to academics in a more simplified way, using the resources of gamification. In order to investigate the most interesting contents of the students of the State University of the North of Paraná (UENP), a questionnaire containing questions related to university contents was applied a 220 students. The investigation allowed to verify that the students have a high level of difficulty to access the contents of their interest, pointing out as main reason the organization and the great amount of information available. The most interesting contents of the students were their scores, class schedule and the availability of the teachers. For the application, only the most interesting subjects pointed out by the students. All these subjects usually have a long way to their access, due to the structuring of the university website and the large amount of information already mentioned.

Keywords: Gamification · Mobile application · Access to information · Education

1 Introduction

One factor that stands out in the information age is the emergence of a new generation of young people, called by Machado and Matsuura (2018) of the "all at the same time now" generation, which has access to much information immediately and instantaneously.

Within the university it is possible to perceive the reflexes of this new generation. Reading lengthy documents, such as regiments, statutes and manuals, is no longer a practice of most students, since they are used to receive information in a more succinct

© Springer Nature Switzerland AG 2019
G. Meiselwitz (Ed.): HCII 2019, LNCS 11579, pp. 238–248, 2019.
https://doi.org/10.1007/978-3-030-21905-5_19

and dynamic way and have difficulty waiting and concentrating. This brings a lot of misinformation, often harming the academic, which fails to meet deadlines or unaware of their duties and even their rights in the educational institution.

Students use institutional information for the development of their activities, such as class schedule, support scholarship announcements, student assistance, legislation, among others. The problem is that institutional websites provide a large amount of information from various interest groups. Thus, most students do not feel motivated to seek such information, mainly because of the difficulty in finding it, due to the diversity and quantity of information available.

This new generation is also visibly more interested in games than previous generations, which has an impact on education and how they interact with other people (Da Silva et al. 2014). The concept of gamification can be a motivational factor for this scenario. The use of game strategies and bonus application for reading important documents can increase the knowledge of this generation of university students. Nguyen et al. (2018) report that's "gamification has increasingly become a hot topic over the past few years".

The gamification is the application of game elements in different environments and activities not related to games to motivate and engage users. The act of playing brings benefits such as pleasure, development of thinking and cognition skills, and stimulation of attention and memory (Da Silva et al. 2014).

Thus, considering the difficulty of accessing information on institutional websites, the great interest in games and the increasing use of mobile devices, this research proposes an application that offers relevant information to students in a more simplified and dynamic way, using the resources of gamification.

In order to achieve the objectives of this research, the following methodological steps were necessary: (i) Study on gamification, its characteristics and forms of application; (ii) Diagnosis together university students the information that is most useful to their academic life; (iii) Application prototype development for mobile devices; (iv) Validation of the prototype through its application to the target audience.

2 Gamification

The Gamification is the application of game elements in various environments and non-game related activities to motivate and engage users. The act of playing brings benefits such as pleasure, development of thinking skills and cognition, and stimulation of attention and memory (Da Silva et al. 2014).

The term gamification means the application of elements used in the creation of electronic games, such as mechanics and dynamics (Borges et al. 2013). The mechanisms that can be found in games have an important role to motivate and engage their players. Engagement is defined by the "time period in which the individual has a large amount of connections to another person or environment."

It can be said that the level of engagement is influenced by the person's dedication to assigned tasks and that is the main aspect for the success of gamification. In terms of motivation it is necessary to highlight two types:

- Intrinsic motivation: it comes from within the person and is not based on the external world. The player engages of his own volition because the activities arouse interest and pleasure.
- Extrinsic motivation: it comes from the external world and has as its starting point the desire to obtain an external reward, such as material goods.

According to Fadel et al. (2014) the challenge of creating a gamification environment is to stimulate the two types of motivation and to maintain the motivation of the users it is necessary to provide incentives of high quality and in different formats. To strengthen individuals' motivation, the environment/activity must have clear objectives, feedback and guidance, rewards, among others.

Some of the game mechanics that were used in the application to motivate students to acquire needed knowledge through edicts, documents, and regiments are presented in Table 1.

Table 1. Some mechanics of gamification.

Name of mechanic/author	Description	Why use?
SCORING/Fadel et al. (2014)	It allows the accompaniment of the players during the interaction as the environment and motivates them to make the right decision	To improve the motivation and engagement of users so much as to generate a spirit of competition
LEVELS/Zichermann and Cunningham (2011)	It is a summary of scoring, allows the story involved in the environment to be presented in parts - chapters	To students have control of their progress
RANKING/Martins et al. (2014)	Demonstrates players' punctuation and should serve not only to give transparency, but as a motivating element	To give users insight into the progress of other participants
RESTRICTION/Vianna et al. (2013)	Implementing the rules helps to motivate people and shows what they should and should not do	To help the students follow the right way to use the application
(REWARDS/Li et al. 2012)	It works as a motivational factor, the participants gain something in exchange for participation	To reward and motivate student effort
FEEDBACK/Vianna et al. (2013)	Information element where the user can get the information needed in a shorter time	To answer students questions in a reasonable time, with it the chance to use the application is greater

The main focus of gamification is to involve the user emotionally with the tasks performed by him. For this, it is possible to use several game mechanics that are perceived by the participants as elements that bring pleasure and challenge, favoring the creation of an environment conducive to engagement. The mechanics of a game system consists of several tools that have the ability to produce significant aesthetic responses to the players (Fadel et al. 2014).

The gamification therefore can be applied not only in the learning process, but also in activities that involve the seeking of information and activities that encourage the individual's behavior.

3   Access to Information by University Students

The Higher Education Institutions (IES), with the purpose of dynamizing and expanding their actions, have been active in the areas of teaching, research and extension, which demands integrated information systems and easy usability for access to large amount of content available.

The IES, for Maccari and Rodrigues (2003), while "having in knowledge its main product, has its processes compartmentalized in specialized blocks of knowledge, usually limited by its structure", which hinders access to information.

For Bianchi et al. (2010), numerous Information Technologies have been used to support the sharing of information and knowledge, such as: internet, intranet, extranet, moodle, workflow, groupware, electronic document management, knowledge maps, data mining, data warehousing, among others.

In the HEIs, institutional websites have been the main way to disseminate and share information. However, in institutional sites, university students often find it difficult to find information that is relevant to them, because they add a large amount of content, seeking to meet the diverse interests of teachers, undergraduate and graduate students, university agents and the external community.

Each student faces his university entrance in a different way, but there is a common challenge for all, which is to understand the functioning of an HEI, with all its duties and rights. The academicals should adapt to a series of routines and activities, turning their efforts to meet the norms and demands of the higher course. There are so many obligations with deadlines and fees to pay, such as rematch, second call for evidence, request of documents, among others.

The university is also a space of opportunities that go beyond the classroom, encompassing academic activities as well as monitoring, extracurricular activities, scientific initiation, extension actions and cultural and leisure activities. In order for the student to develop in its fullness, it is necessary to have access to opportunities for participation in projects that the institution and the course offer, whether voluntary projects or with scholarship assistance and also to the pedagogical project of the course, always with fast, dynamic and real-time access.

Fenerick (2017) states that "integration between people and the intensive technologies of using information and communication technologies (ICTs), represented by the transformations caused in social relations by the use of smartphone." A survey released by CanalTech[1] shows the high rate of access to the internet by Brazilian university students through cell phones, corresponding to approximately 95%, which indicates that only 5% of students do not have a smartphone. Given this scenario, organizations have increasingly made available applications to disseminate information with greater convenience and speed, meeting the needs of this new generation always connected via mobile phones.

Diagnosis together university students the information that is most useful to their academic life.

Aiming to identify the difficulties presented in the access to information and which information present in the institutional site are of greater importance to the academics, a research was carried out with the students of different courses and graduation periods of the State University of Norte do Paraná (UENP) - Campus Luiz Meneghel (CLM).

A questionnaire containing 19 questions regarding access to the contents of the website, difficulty of access and suggestions of contents important for students to be made available. 220 students participated in the study, with the highest participation being students of first years of formation, totaling 73.1 students in the 1st and 2nd years, 24.2 students in other years (3rd, 4th and 5th) and 2.7 did not report the graduation period.

The vast majority of participants reported a significant level of difficulty in finding relevant content and information. 23.6% of the students who demonstrated difficulty 5, on a scale between 1 and 10, were enrolled in the first years of the courses, which may mean that at the beginning of the graduation, when they do not have so much access to the various resources, students already find the difficulty.

The results higher than 5, for the degree of difficulty, were pointed out by the students of all the years and courses so it can not be affirmed that the course or time of study improves or worsens the difficulty of access.

One of the reasons most pointed to the difficulty of finding information was the organization of the information (59.5% of the answers). It is also important to note that a large number of participants pointed to the large amount of information on the institutional website and that search engines are not efficient. With this you can understand that students can not find what they need easily.

As already mentioned, the institutional website connects all the information about the institution and not only those of interest to the academics, which may be one of reasons for this result.

From the results it is possible to assume that students enrolled have little knowledge of the Regiment. Those who read the regiment mentioned that it was the first year, the vast majority. This may mean that when entering to university, students seek to learn about academic norms, but over time they will fail to access this information, which may change occasionally.

The main way of obtaining information pointed out by academics is "the institutional website" (40.5) followed by "for guidance from other students" (36.8%). Thus, students obtain information about enrollment, transfer, curriculum and approval

---

[1] https://canaltech.com.br/smartphone/Quase-95-dos-universitarios-possuem-smartphones-aponta-estudo/.

system, mainly through the institution's website, other students, course teachers, academic secretary, among others.

An important point also in the research is that students have more interest to the events and college news, followed by information on the entrance exam, the academic calendar and notices and documents related to graduation.

On extension and culture, most do not access this information, the ones that access, usually look for event certificates. Information about Distance Education, Internationalization and Publications are poorly accessed by students, perhaps because of the lack of knowledge and applicability of these subjects.

Another point of prominence in the research demonstrates the priorities of interest of the students on the information that should be available in the institutional website, which are, respectively, from the highest priority to the lowest priority: notes of the lessons; class schedule; schedule of availability of teachers; and frequency in lessons.

On this subject, scholars also pointed out that most of these contents are not available on the institutional website, such as class schedule, which are always fixed on physical panels somewhere in the university, which makes it difficult to access from home, for example.

On investigation about Gamification, most students (81.8%) do not know the concept and those who know it are usually matriculate in technological courses. After guidance on the concept and application of gamification, students also indicated some rewards they would like to receive, which are, respectively, the highest priority to lowest: partial grades in subjects; discounts in the cafeteria; discount on events; various awards; discounts on Xerox; others.

4 Application Prototype Development for Mobile Devices

From the research carried out, an application was developed to assist students in undergraduate courses in the field of information relevant to their academic development. Some mechanics of the gamification were used in the development of the application in order to promote the motivation for access to information and academic interaction.

4.1 Application Development

The application prototype was developed with the support of the PhoneGap framework. This framework makes it possible to use HyperText Markup Language (HTML), CSS (Cascading Style Sheets) and Javascript interpreted programming language to send and receive requests to a system developed with the programming language of PHP (PHP: Hypertext Preprocessor).

In order to store the application data, we used an open source relational database manager, MySQL (Structured Query Language). In this version, the application is available for mobile devices using the Android operating system.

In addition to PhoneGap, other open source frameworks and libraries were used to develop the application and PHP system, all based on the languages mentioned above, in order to achieve faster and more secure development. For the stylization of the application, in addition to the pure CSS, the Bootstrap framework in its version 3.3.7 was used, since it contemplates styles and components ready for use, friendly and responsive. To control the actions in the application, some functions of the jQuery library in version 3.3.1 were used, together with pure JavaScript, as Document Object Model (DOM) manipulations and Asynchronous JavaScript And XML (AJAX) requests for the PHP system.

The PHP system is being built to function as an API (Application Programming Interface), so it is possible to use other interfaces integrated in the system in the future, without having to re-code the back-end routines. For the development of the API, the Laravel framework in version 5.7, based on PHP is being used as it offers an architecture in MVC (Model View Controller) has routines prepared to function as an API in addition to following the design pattern ORM (Object-relational mapping), which makes it easier to work with relational database data.

4.2   Application Features

Students are currently not used to reading documents and edicts with numerous pages and information. Thus, considering these difficulties, the application relies on the provision of excerpts that refer to the essential academic norms to the life of the academic. The gamification feature has been applied in accessing these standards in order to stimulate their use. The main screen has the contents of greater access or greater interest of the students, as verified in the diagnosis made. In Fig. 1 (left side), you can see the application's functionalities, which are: News, Events, Academic Calendar, Schedules, Certificates, Edits and Documents, Score, Moodle, Regiment and Contacts.

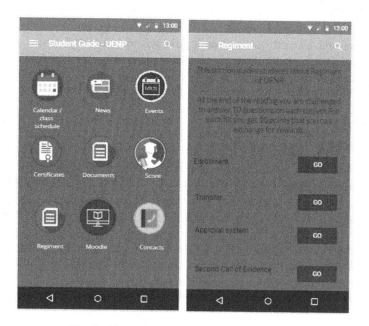

Fig. 1. The main screen and screen of regiment

The application development involved in this first stage the creation of a functional prototype of the final application and, to facilitate the development, some sections of the institutional website of the university were used. The Events, Certificates and Documents buttons have been programmed to redirect the user to the university's institutional website. One of the advantages in this redirection is that by the institutional website the student has to go a long way to arrive at this information, and by the application the access is direct.

Schedules and score content is not available on the institutional website, but has been chosen by students as more important to be made available in the application. The news button, remembering that the institutional website is accessed not only by students, but also by teachers, employees and external community, redirects to news tab, bringing only those that are of interest to the students. The Academic Calendar and class schedules are usually made available in PDF format, so it was made available in image form, making access simpler, avoiding having to download it again and again.

Students' scores are usually physically available; in the application they may be presented in the form of images, separated into folders by course and period, to facilitate student access. Moodle button redirects the user to the Moodle page that is widely used for monitoring of some lessons.

The concept of gamification has been applied in the content called Academic Procedures, in which we can find all the necessary information concerning the registration, enrollment renewals, second call of the tests, transfer, among others. In order to access these contents the user must log in to the application (if the student is not registered yet, it is necessary to do it first), then you can access the content of interest, participate in the quiz with questions related to the content read, observe the progress of the other players and compete with them.

Thus, the user can access the academic norms, choosing the topic of their interest, as shown in Fig. 1 (right side). The user will be directed to the passages of the academic regiment referring to the chosen theme (approval system, transfer, second call of exams, among others), as shown in Fig. 2 (left side). When it is necessary to obtain further information he will always have the option of reading the entire regiment.

After reading the selected theme, the application user can access the questions related to the text read (Fig. 2 – right side). On this screen the user can see, besides the questions regarding the read section, your current score and may also be directed to the full regiment. Feedback on hit happens immediately after the answer. In the case of the correct answer, the marking turns green and the user earns points in his score.

The rewards according to the score can be given in different ways (partial grades in subjects; discounts in the cafeteria, discounts on events, among others), as suggested by academics in the diagnosis performed. Rewards have not yet been treated in the app in this first release.

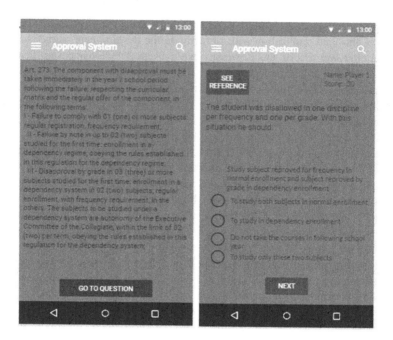

Fig. 2. Screen of a part of academic regiment and screen of a question.

The idea of the application of gamification is to use the game of thought and the mechanics of games to motivate students to know the academic norms of the institution and to create a culture of reading these documents. Gamification does not imply creating a game that addresses the real world problem in the virtual world, but rather uses the same strategies, methods and thoughts to solve problems in the real world.

5   Final Considerations

The university students needs to be informed on a daily basis about academic issues and also to have access to the opportunities that can contribute to its development. To do this, you need to have access to this information facilitated. Institutional websites make it difficult for students to quickly access content that is of interest to them, usually because of the large amount of information they add. Like this, in order to investigate the most interesting contents of the students, a questionnaire containing questions related to university contents was applied a 220 students.

The investigation allowed to verify that the students have a high level of difficulty to access the contents of their interest, pointing out as main reason the organization and the great amount of information available. The most interesting contents of the students were their scores, class schedule and the availability of the teachers.

The application prototype was developed for Android operating system, containing only the most interesting subjects pointed out by the students, such as, News, Events, Certificates, Documents and the Environment of Distance Learning (Moodle). All these subjects usually have a long way to their access, due to the structuring of the university website and the large amount of information already mentioned.

Another point worth mentioning is that most of the students do not have any or have little knowledge about the rules and academic procedures of the UENP that are included in its Regiment. In this way, the application presents the contents of fundamental interest of them. To engage the student and motivate access to these contents, the gamification technique was applied and some mechanics were used to motivate the users: Scoring, Levels, Ranking, Rewards and Feedback.

The next step of this research is the verification of the applicability of the "Student-Guide" application together with a group of students of the different courses and areas of knowledge. There are so many tasks that a student must deal with within the university that it becomes almost impossible to deal with all at once. Thus, the application is expected to facilitate and, through the use of gamification, bring greater motivation for access to academic information.

Acknowledgment. Our acknowledgment for the *"Fundação Araucária de Apoio ao Desenvolvimento Científico e Tecnológico do Estado do Paraná"* for the support given for the research.

References

Bianchi, I.S., Silveira, R.R., Jacobsen, A.L., Silva, J.M., Dal Prá, R.: Tecnologia da Informação no Ambiente Universitário: Uma Contribuição para a Gestão do Conhecimento. In: X Coloquio Internacional sobre Gestión Universitaria em América del Sur, Mar del Plata (2010)

Borges, S.D.S., Reis, H.M., Durelli, V.H., Bittencourt, I.I., Jaques, P.A., Isotani, S.: Gamificação aplicada à educação: um mapeamento sistemático. In: Brazilian Symposium on Computers in Education (Simpósio Brasileiro de Informática na Educação-SBIE), vol. 24, no. 1, p. 234 (2013)

Da Silva, A.R.L., et al.: Gamificação na Educação. Pimenta Cultural (2014)

Fadel, L.M., Batista, C., Ulbricht, V.R., Vanzin, T.: Gamificação na educação. Pimenta Cultural (2014)

Fenerick, G.M.P.: A utilização de smartphones no acesso à informação científica por jovens estudantes: um estudo de caso. Dissertação de Mestrado. Programa de Pós-graduação em Ciência, Tecnologia e Sociedade - Universidade FEderal de São CArlos (UFSCar) (2017)

Li, W., Grossman, T., Fitzmaurice, G.: GamiCAD: a gamified tutorial system for first time AutoCAD users. In: UIST 2012, 7–10 October, Cambridge, Massachusetts, USA (2012)

Maccari, E.A., Rodrigues, L.C.: Gestão do conhecimento em instituições de ensino superior. Revista de Negócios - Studies on Emerging Countries, vol. 8, N° 2 (2003)

Machado, A.E., Matsuura, A.M.: Tudo ao mesmo tempo agora na rede. Observatório da Imprensa, Ano 19 - n° 1008 (2018). ISSN 1519-7670

Martins, T., Nery Filho, J., Vieira, F., Pontes, E.: A Gamificação de conteúdos escolares: uma experiência a partir da diversidade cultural brasileira. In: X Seminário de Jogos Eletrônicos, Educação e Comunicação (2014)

Nguyen, H.D., Jiang, Y., Eiring, Ø., Poo, D.C.C., Wang, W.: Gamification design framework for mobile health: designing a home-based self-management programme for patients with chronic heart failure. In: Meiselwitz, G. (ed.) SCSM 2018. LNCS, vol. 10914, pp. 81–98. Springer, Cham (2018). https://doi.org/10.1007/978-3-319-91485-5_6

Vianna, Y., Vianna, M., Medina, B., Tanaka, S.: Gamification Inc.: como reinventar empresas a partir de jogos. MJV Press, Rio de Janeiro (2013)

Zichermann, G., Cunningham, C.: Gamification by Design: Implementing Game Mechanics in Web and Mobile Apps. O'Reilly Media, Inc., Sebastopol (2011)

Digital Marketing and Consumer Experience

Product Placements by Micro and Macro Influencers on Instagram

Rachidatou Alassani$^{(\boxtimes)}$ ⓘ and Julia Göretz ⓘ

Heinrich Heine University Düsseldorf,
Universitätsstr. 1, 40225 Düsseldorf, Germany
{rachidatou.alassani,
julia.goeretz}@uni-duesseldorf.de

Abstract. Influencer marketing is considered one of the most promising marketing strategies in the age of digital transformation of media. The social platform Instagram offers a huge opportunity for companies to market their products and services through influencers, without it being directly recognized as an advertisement. The purpose of this examination is to investigate, which and how many products are promoted via influencer marketing and which hashtag, tag and mention categories are used. Throughout six months, product placements of German micro and macro influencers were evaluated. 234 contributions on Instagram containing product placements were analyzed, with a total of 1122 hashtags, 506 tags and 289 mentions. The results indicate that the fashion (30,51%), accessory (19,07%) and beauty (18,64%) industries are among the sectors most commonly marketed by influencer types. On average, macro influencers use 4 hashtags per product placement and micro influencers use 6 hashtags per product placement. Hashtags of the content categories *Slogan, Product, Fitness* and *Brand* are the most commonly used. In addition, hashtags of the categories *Lifestyle, Description, Company, Sentiment, Technology* and *Environment* are among the 10 most common hashtag categories for advertising products. Tags of the categories *Company, Distributor, Company location, Company's product feed* and *Company specification* are utilized. Mentions of the categories *Company* and *Company location* are in use most frequently. The research reveals that despite the product placement labelling policy, a high level of influencer marketing is still executed on Instagram and the use of hashtags, tags and mentions is still popular.

Keywords: Influencer marketing · Macro influencer · Micro influencer · Product placements · Hashtags · Mentions · Instagram · Tagging behavior

1 Introduction

In the age of digitalization, it is becoming more and more common to promote the rapid development of information technologies and the use of social media is encouraged, what leads to new forms of information processing and communication in the information and knowledge society. Apart from the connection with other people in social networks, social media enables users to search, to create and to exchange information [1].

© Springer Nature Switzerland AG 2019
G. Meiselwitz (Ed.): HCII 2019, LNCS 11579, pp. 251–267, 2019.
https://doi.org/10.1007/978-3-030-21905-5_20

Social Media is a revolution in media development. Companies that are present on social media have the chance to communicate directly with their target group and to establish the communities as further channels for promotion of their products and services [2].

Influencer marketing is a marketing strategy on social media, where influencers share product placements on social networks. In Germany, cooperating with influencers is becoming increasingly relevant, which is why the effect of influencer marketing on Instagram users is an important aspect of further development.

The social platform Instagram offers a huge opportunity for companies to market their products and services through influencers, without it being directly recognized as an advertisement. Thereby influencers differ in size, concerning the number of their followers and the type of influence [3, 4]. Surprisingly, there is little to no scientific research on product placements by influencers on Instagram. In order to make clear in which manner products and particularly marked contributions from micro and macro influencers are advertised on Instagram, scientific analysis was carried out to observe the selection of hashtags, tags and mentions.

2 Theoretical Framework

Consumers are becoming increasingly insecure with usual forms of advertising. They are more inclined to follow recommendations from friends, acquaintances or independent experts, which have a buoyant effect on the development of influencer marketing [5]. The following chapter provides a closer look at the research topic, presenting the fundamentals of influencer marketing, introducing Instagram as a marketing channel, describing the current state of influencer marketing research on Instagram and listing the research questions relevant to the study.

2.1 Fundamentals of Influencer Marketing

Influencers are persons who influence the customer's purchasing decision. Preferably influencers are bloggers and stars, whereby a high social status is not always essential [6]. It is more important to what extent an individual can pass on an advertising message to a more significant number of people and influence the decision-making process [4]. Due to the high influence on the purchase decision of potential customers through recommendations, reviews and ratings of the products and services of a company or a brand are very important for the marketing mix [7].

According to their range, influencers are divided into *nano, micro, macro* and *mega influencers* [3]. *Nano influencers* have a limited reach, but a high level of authority, a high level of commitment in his social group and a maximum follower number of 1,000. Any digitally networked consumer, respectively social media user can be assigned to this group of influencers. Particular forms in this category are indeed the product fans or brand advocates who stand out as "persuaders" regarding particular opinion on a product in a social group. *Micro influencers* are topic experts with follower numbers in the four- or five-digit range. They are characterized by credibility, relevance and great social media engagement, interacting with the followers. Parasocial relationships, which are one-sided relationships in which one person expands emotional energy, interest as well as time and the other party, the persona, is completely unaware of the existence of the other, is established and familiarity with the influencer is built [8]. *Macro influencers* are influencers with followers in the six- and seven-digit rage. In this area, the commitment rate drops to only 5 to 25%. A high frequency of postings characterizes this group of influencers, to create an artificial connection about updates. In contrast to the three above mentioned types of influencers, *mega influencers* are influencers with follower numbers from seven- digit range and a minimal commitment rate of 1 to 5%, including celebrities and stars who have already worked in the classic testimonial business and also manifest their prominence in the social media [3].

Influencer marketing is described as "an approach that identifies and targets influencers in a market," which requires a considered selection of influencers, to guarantee authentic and unremarkable advertisement to the user or the potential customer [6]. The user, as a potential customer is the focus of influencer marketing. Influencers are to be seen as role models and people with whom the user can identify. With regard to the increasing importance of social media and due to the postponement of information procurement, influencers are becoming increasingly important for companies and the information process [10].

The strategic approach of influencer marketing aims to profit from the influence and the range of the important opinion makers and the multipliers, while the opinion makers spread an advertising message for a company on social networks and the social web [10]. Main goals are the positioning of the brand via product placement, brand awareness and customer acquisition with a priority goal of generating revenues. Thereby, it is not social media itself that influence the potential costumers, it is the content and the content creators, namely the influencers that influence users [6].

2.2 Instagram

The online platform Instagram enables influencers to distribute content individually and has been named as one of the most influential social platforms in the world in 2016 [11]. The complimentary mobile and internet-based photo and video-sharing application allow users to share pictures and videos publicly or in private. Those postings can be edited with digital filters as well as geotags and hashtags, which help to find an image or video directly and faster [12]. The basic concept is based on an existing user account, which can be connected to other social media profiles [5]. Meanwhile, over 1,000 million people worldwide use Instagram, with a rising tendency [13]. Among other things, the business model of influencers on this platform is to market their own Instagram channel as advertising space. After companies become aware of appropriate opinion leaders, they often pay for them to mention and present their products and brands in contributions [5]. This examination will analyze how as well as which products will be placed by different types of influencers on Instagram as an advertisement.

2.3   State of Research of Influencer Marketing on Instagram

As influencer marketing on Instagram is a relatively new marketing tool, there are only a few studies on this advertising method, the social platform Instagram and the tagging behavior of Instagram users, which are summarized in the following paragraph.

The paper of Parth, Kraft, and Raif concerning influencer marketing of fashion brands on Instagram showed that tags in the image were included in nearly half of product placements. Furthermore, it was found that hashtags had hardly any relation to the advertised products. The study also indicated that the evaluated influencers rather avoid making specific product recommendations. Additionally, the paper exposed that profiles of brands are only being followed if the users are genuinely interested in the products and want to be informed about new products. On the other hand, the Instagram users follow blogger accounts because they are fascinated by their lifestyle [14].

Gräve and Greff focused on measuring the success of influencer marketing. Quantitative key performance indicators (for example, the number of likes or the number of followers), which are easily available via the insights on Instagram, are mostly used by influencers themselves and companies. The study analyzed what value these metrics actually have for influencer marketing and whether they are a suitable proxy for content quality. Using an online survey of marketing professionals, combined with secondary data on Instagram's influencer marketing campaigns, it turns out that professionals generally consider an influencer's reach and the number of interactions to be the key performance indicators. In contrast, when professionals are faced with a compromise between multiple metrics, they rely largely on the mood of user comments. A regression analysis was then conducted, showing that only mood metrics were positively associated with professional content evaluation [15].

Wnent examined the impact of the advertising style of a weight loss and fitness product on the credibility of the message, product placement and purchase intent. In an online survey with 256 participants, no significant effects of the type of advertising on message credibility, product placement and purchase intent were found. It turned out that the attractiveness that is the wording of the text influenced the product attitude and purchase intent. For rational text calls, participants showed higher interest and positive product attitude and a higher purchase intent compared to emotional text calls. The Instagram investment had a significant impact on the purchase intent. The higher the usage of Instagram users, the higher the purchase intent. Regarding text applications, it shows that a rational textual stimulus affects product stewardship and purchase intent more effectively than an emotional appeal [16].

Dorsch analyzed how Instagram users tag their images with respect to different types of image and hashtag categories. A comparison was made between the content categories Food, Pets, Selfies, Friends, Activity, Art, Fashion, Quotes (captions), Landscape and Architecture as well as Content-relatedness (ofness, aboutness and iconology), Emotiveness, Isness, Performativeness, Fakeness, "Insta"-Tags and Sentences. It was found that on average 15 hashtags are used per image. The categories *Selfie* and *Friends* received the lowest average values and the categories *Pet*, *Fashion* and *Landscape* the highest. In addition, 60.20% of all hashtags were categorized as content related. Categories *Emotionality* and *Sentences* were used less frequently.

A χ^2 test of independence showed that there was a statistically significant correlation between hashtag categories and image categories on Instagram [17].

Vassallo, Kelly, Zhang, Wang, Young and Freeman examined the frequency of images and videos published on Instagram by the most popular, energy-intensive, low-nutrient food and beverage brands, as well as the marketing strategies used in these images, including all health claims. It turned out that each brand used 6 to 11 different marketing strategies in their Instagram account, but often focused on a common theme such as athletics or related consumers. There was a high level of brand-building, although not necessarily product information on all accounts, but very little health claims. It was found that brands use social media platforms such as Instagram to market their products to a growing number of consumers by using a high frequency of targeted and curated posts that manipulate consumer emotions. The researchers criticized the public health institutions, which should collaborate with new media platforms and develop convincing social countermeasures [18].

The study by Evans, Phua, Lim, and Ju examined the impact of the disclosure language (control/no disclosure, "SP", "sponsored" and "paid ad") of product placement by influencers on ad detection, branding, purchase intent and sharing intent a sample of 237 students. It turned out that the "paid ad" mark positively influenced ad recognition. Results also showed that the presence of a declaration, regardless of the variation in language, produced more advertising compared to no disclosure. It was significant that users of Instagram postings with disclosure, underlie a negative impact on the intention of dissemination. The study confirmed that disclosures using clear language have a positive impact on advertising recognition and disclosure memory, which in turn can negatively impact attitudes and behavioral intention [19].

Uzunoğlu and Kip explored the role of bloggers in brand communication and how brands interact with bloggers from the perspective of two-stage flow theory. The results indicated that the blogger is the key to transmitting a message to a specific audience in the digital form of two-step flow theory, but readers and followers are at least as important as they have the ability to relay messages on their own network, what promotes word-of-mouth propaganda, which influencer marketing refers to [20].

Lee and Watkins investigated how video blogs (vlogs) affect consumer perception of luxury brands. The study found that the perception of luxury brands was significantly increased after Vlog's reputation and increases in parasocial interaction with vloggers were moderated. It emerged that the perceptions and purchase intentions of luxury brands were higher than those for experimental groups that saw vlogs reviewing luxury products Control group who had not seen those vlogs [21].

2.4   Research Questions

As related researches have shown, research in influencer marketing and tagging behavior on Instagram is quite advanced. However, research into product placement of micro and macro influencers has not yet been done, but it is an essential aspect of influencer marketing on Instagram. This study is now aimed at closing this research gap. The purpose of this examination is to investigate, which products are promoted via influencer marketing and how these products are promoted. It also wants to analyze how influencer marketing is done using different types of influencers. For this purpose, product placements of micro influencers and macro influencers were considered. The main research questions are:

RQ1: Which industries promote their products through influencer marketing?
RQ2: How much product placement takes place in the comparison of micro and macro influencers?
RQ3: Which hashtag categories are used to promote products?
RQ4: Which tag and mention categories are used for product placement?

The following Sect. 3 explains the methodology of the applied qualitative content analysis. Therefore, it focuses on the selected macro and micro influencers, the study period, the subject of the evaluation and the explanation of the codebook. Section 4 presents the results of the content analysis related to the research questions. Section 5 discusses the results, explains limitations and gives an outlook with further possible research on influencer marketing on Instagram.

3   Methods

For this investigation, product placements of German micro and macro influences on Instagram were examined with the help of content analysis [22]. The analysis included the tagging behavior of Instagram users, as well as the used hashtags, tags and mentions of product placements.

In order to investigate enough hashtags and several holiday periods at the same time, a period of 6 months was defined. The exact period was therefore set from 1 November 2017 to 31 April 2018.

3.1   Selection of Influencers

Solely micro and macro influencers in Germany were considered, as nano influencers usually have a small range and thereby hardly advertise any products. On the other hand, mega influencers were disregarded, since they were already working in the classic testimonial and thus already dispose to a particular influence on people, which they do not have to develop through high commitment [3].

To select suitable influencers, a website was consulted that tracks different types of influencers. The website *indahash.com*[1] was chosen, as it filters actual German influencers with different ranges and engagement rates. On 27 June 2018, the five biggest and most successful German micro and macro influencers were selected for investigation. The selected influencers are presented in Table 1.

---

[1] www.indahash.com.

Table 1. The selected influencers.

Influencer	Influencer type	Follower number	Niche
Artgallery.ab	Micro influencer	99.8 thousand [23]	Lifestyle
Byashrafb	Micro influencer	99.7 thousand [24]	Photography
Aladiia	Micro influencer	99.1 thousand [25]	Photography
Kuhrmarvin	Micro influencer	98.7 thousand [26]	Photography
Llynnllaura	Micro influencer	98.3 thousand [27]	Lifestyle, beauty & fashion
Alvarosolermusic	Macro influencer	989 thousand [28]	Lifestyle & music
Enyadres	Macro influencer	974 thousand [29]	Lifestyle
Debiflue	Macro influencer	968 thousand [30]	Lifestyle, beauty & fashion
Bettytaube	Macro influencer	951 thousand [31]	Lifestyle & fashion
Culturewithcoco	Macro influencer	922 thousand [32]	Lifestyle, beauty & fashion

3.2   The Subject of the Investigation

The performed content analysis collected data along with categories in image, title and description level and recorded in a master sheet. The investigation's key subjects were contributions of macro and micro influencers with product placements in the form of pictures and videos. Figure 1 shows the investigation levels using an example, which will be explained in the following.

Fig. 1. An exemplary representation of the investigation levels [33]. (Color figure online)

The title coding (green frame) and description level (black frame) was intended to ignore contributions that are not subject of research interest due to their irrelevance. Reference was made to contributions with the hashtags *#advertisement, #advertise, #ad, #werbung* (*#advertisement*), *#sponsored* or the title-labelling "*Bezahlte Partnerschaft mit xxx*" ("*Paid affiliation with xxx*") or the word *Werbung* (*advertisement*). Contributions from January 2018 that only contained *#anzeige* (*#advertising*), or the word *Anzeige* (*Advertising*) were not considered as since the case of Vreni Frost, many influencers use *#anzeige* (*#advertising*) or *Anzeige* (*advertising*) in postings with brand recognition, brand linkage or profile linking of self-acquired products. Vreni Frost was convicted of secret advertising for omission. She posted a picture of self-generated products and tagged the company in the picture [34].

At the description level, in addition to the advertised product and the resulting industry, data from the mentions (1) were also collected. It was analyzed which profiles are linked in case of a mention and which kind of profiles they represent (for example, distributor or photographer). On which content categories were formed. Besides, data from the hashtags (2) was obtained at the description level. The hashtags were added to the master sheet, the total number of hashtags was noted, followed by the creation of content categories. At the image level (blue frame), the tags respectively image markers (3) to which other profiles in the image are linked were analyzed. All visible tags were added to the master sheet and the tags were used to create categories that reflect the content.

3.3 Codebook

Based on the illustrated schema in Sect. 3.2, a codebook was created with a total of 31 content hashtags, ten content tags, as well as six content mention categories and 14 industries, containing all the detailed definitions of the categories, all coding instructions and examples. The creation and structure of the codebook is based on Brosius, Koschel and Haas [35].

To verify the reliability and validity of the codebook, a second encoder was used that encoded a sample according to the instructions of the codebook. During the defined period, the sample included contributions from the micro influencers *artgallery.ab* and *llynnllaura* as well as the macro-influencers *debiflue* and *culturewithcoco*. The intercoder reliability was measured to ensure consistency between the codings. The Reliability Coefficient was 0.87. Therefore the measurement instrument used can be considered as reliable [35]. In assessing validity, the factors selectivity, one-dimensionality, completeness and frequency of categories as well as variables in a conversation with the coding partner were examined, discussed and adjusted if necessary. The integrity and redundancy led to marginal changes as well as to definitions and understandability adjustments. Several categories have been summarized, simplifying coding. To extend and visualize the coding instruction, some sample contributions have been added. The evaluation was performed manually with the help of Microsoft Excel. The following Sect. 4 presents the results based on the codebook-instructed master sheet.

4   Results

During this study, a total of 1,086 contributions are examined. As a result, 234 contributions contain product placement. The total advertising share accounts for 22% ($n = 1086$). The following paragraph presents the outcome of this study following the four research questions.

RQ1: Which industries promote their products through influencer marketing?
The accessories, fitness, beauty and clothing industries are among the most widely marketed influencer types. Surprisingly, banks, telecommunications companies, technology companies and tourism companies also use influencer marketing to advertise their products and services. The advertised industries are listed in Table 2.

Table 2. The various industries promoted by micro and macro influencers.

Industry	Description	Product example
Accessory	Industries that market jewelry and fashion accessories	Watch bag sunglasses
Automobile	Industries that market automobile vehicles	Car motorcycle
Bank	Industries that market credits, credit cards and bank accounts	Mastercard Biro bank account
Beauty	Industries that market beauty and cosmetic products	Lip injection Liquid lip colour
Fashion	Industries that market fashion clothes	Lace top Hoodie
Fitness	Industries that market weight loss, fitness and sport products	Whey protein Waist cincher
Food	Industries that market food-processing	Tea Beer
Health	Industries that market medicaments, nutritional supplements and medical accessories	Healing ointment Braces
Interior	Industries that market products around the house and interior design	Scented candles Pillowcase
Layette	Industries that markets baby and toddler care products	Stroller
Technology	Industries that market techno gadgets	Camera Power bank

(*continued*)

Table 2. (*continued*)

Industry	Description	Product example
Telecommunication	Industries that market products for telecommunication	Mobile contract Social pass
Leisure	Industries that offer different attractions for leisure time	Amusement park Shopping mall
Tourism	Industries that market travel destinations, resorts and hotels	Resort & Spa Desertsafari

Out of the products promoted by the micro influencers, 20% belong to the cosmetics and beauty industry. 18 fitness products account for 18% of the promoted products and 17 products for the accessories industry.

The highest number of products advertised by macro influencers during the survey period are 51 placements out of the fashion industry, accounting for 38% of the advertised products. Followed by the accessory industry with 28 products (18%) and beauty industry with 24 products and thus 21% of the advertised products. In contrast to micro influencers, no fitness and interior products are marketed by macro influencers as shown in Fig. 2.

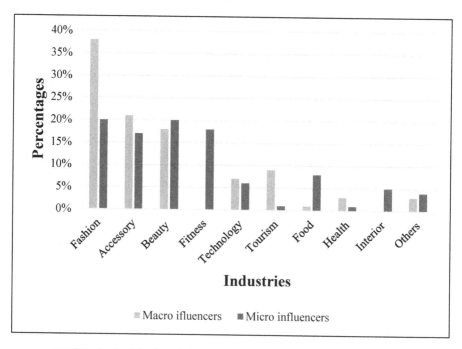

Fig. 2. Percentages of product placements per industry (n = 236).

RQ2: How much product placement takes place in the comparison of micro and macro influencers?

During this investigation, macro influencers share an average of 27 postings with product placements and micro influencers an average of 20. More products are promoted by macro influencers (135) than by micro influencers (101). The fashion industry, which includes both high-end and low-budget companies from domestic and foreign countries, tends to use macro influencers with their high number of ranges to advertise 71% of the investigated fashion products.

RQ3: Which hashtag categories are used to promote the products?

A total of 1,122 hashtags are examined during the study period and assigned to 31 content categories on the base of the data collected. For a more concise presentation, the ten most frequently used hashtag categories are consulted, illustrated in **Error! Reference source not found**.

Out of the 784 top 10 hashtags used, 150 hashtags belong to the *Slogan* category, which is by far the most used category. Followed by the categories *Fashion*, *Company* and *Brand*, which are used 85 times on average (Table 3).

Table 3. The 10 most commonly used hashtag categories for influencer marketing.

Category	Description	Example
Brand	Hashtags representing brand names of advertised products	#cluse
Company	Hashtags containing the name of the company	#nakdfashion
Description	Hashtags that serve a closer description of a product or represent sale actions	#madeingermany
Environment	Hashtags which describe the visuals of the posting or hashtags which gives information about a planet	#sunset
Fashion	Hashtags representing fashion, clothing and outfits	#lookoftheday
Fitness	Hashtags representing the fitness lifestyle, health and sport	#fitnessmotivation
Lifestyle	Hashtags representing motto of life, concluding regarding the day, hobbies, work, greeting paraphrases, advices and attitude towards life	#foryou #mademyday
Product	Hashtags giving more information about the advertised product	#nikond7500
Sentiment	Hashtags that convey feelings	#blacklover
Slogan	Hashtags that represent slogans for special memorability	#alleJahreLila

The most commonly used hashtag categories by macro influencers are *Slogan* hashtags (28%), followed by *Product* hashtags (16%) and *Brand* hashtags that are used 42 times. The *Lifestyle* (3%) and *Fitness* categories (3%) are those with the least hashtags.

On the other hand, the most hashtags used by micro influencers are the *Fashion* category with a utilization of 15% in postings with product placements. Followed by the *Fitness* category with a percentage of 14% and the *Slogan* category with 13%. The lowest number of hashtags out of the top 10 hashtag categories of micro influencers is represented by *Environment* hashtags (4%) and *Product* hashtags (3%) (see Fig. 3). Micro influencers use 20% more hashtags than macro influencers in the study.

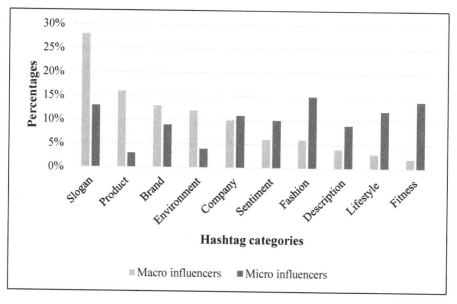

Fig. 3. Percentages of the top 10 hashtag categories of influencer marketing (n = 784).

RQ4: Which tag and mention categories are used for product placement?

A total of 506 tags are reviewed, including 352 macro influencer tags and 154 micro influencer tags. Most tags with a number of 198 belong to the category *Company*. Followed by the category *Influencer*, that are tagged 101 times and the category *Photographer*, which are utilized 54 times. The categories *Distributor, Company location, Company's product feed* and *Company specification* are also frequently used. The tag categories used for product placements are presented in Table 4.

Table 4. The tag categories used for product placements by micro and macro influencers.

Category	Description	Example
Blog	Profile tags of Instagram repost profiles or blogging profiles	blondesandtravel
Company	Profile tags of the company of the product	asambeauty
Company location	Profile tags of the company with explicit naming of the country of distribution	nikondeutschland
Company of clothes	Profile tags of the clothes' company or accessory's company	Tommyhilfiger Socosi_jewelry
Company specification	Tags that represent a specific area of the company	lorealhair
Company's product feed	Tags of the company's product profile	loreal_professionnel_products
Distributor	Profile tags of the distributor of a product	zalando
Influencer	Profile tags of the influencer himself, another influencer, friends, hair/makeup-artists or models	debiflue
Location	Profile tags of locations or buildings	balanceflensburg
Photographer	Profile tags of the photographer who took the contribution	keevsch

The most substantial proportion of micro influencer tags belong to the categories *Company*, *Company location* and *Company of clothes*. *Company* with 83 tags has the largest share of micro influencer tags 54%. Followed by the categories *Company Location* with a percentage of 14% and *Company of clothes* with a 14% share.

As well as with micro influencers, it is found that macro influencers tag the category *Company* with 33% tags the most in the picture, followed by themselves or other influencers (Category: *Influencer*) with 28% and with 15% the photographer or the person who took the picture (Category: *Photographer*).

A total of 289 mentions are evaluated for the study and assigned to the hence resulted categories of Table 5. 199 of the mentions examined belong to the *Company* category, making this the most frequently used mention category. Followed by the category *Company location* with 42 mentions and the category *Photographer* with 18 mentions.

Table 5. The mention categories used for product placements by micro and macro influencers.

Category	Description	Example
Company	Mentions of the company of the product	foodspring
Company location	Mentions of the company with explicit naming of the country of distribution	smashboxgermany
Company specification	Mentions of the company by naming the specific area of the company	lorealhair
Distributor	Mentions of the distributor of the product	amazonprimenow
Influencer	Mentions of another influencer or a friend	marinathemoss
Photographer	Mentions of the photographer or the photography technology	ernstaugustgalerie

The examined mentions by macro influencers belong to the category *Company*, which accounts for 64% and therefore the majority of mentions. Followed by the category *Company location*, which is used 27 times and represents a percentage of 15%. The *Photographer* category is the third most used category with 10% and thus 17 uses.

One hundred fifteen of the examined mentions by micro influencers belong to the category *Company*. The percentage of the category *Company* is 76% and correspond to a use of the category of 87 times. The category *Company location* is used 27 times and represents 13%. The third place is occupied by the category *Company specification* with a percentage of merely 4% and a usage of 4 times which accounts for 64% and therefore the majority of mentions.

5 Discussion

This research study examined Instagram contributions with product placements of macro and micro influencers over a period of six months. As already mentioned in the state of research, influencer marketing has already been investigated. This study is the first to focus on product placement and tagging behavior of different types of influencers on Instagram. The research model includes the extraction of the advertised industries, hashtags, tags and mentions, whereby content categories were developed from the qualitative content analysis. This research shows that despite the product placement labelling policy, a high level of influencer marketing is still performed on Instagram. This is particularly evident in the accessories industry, where 19% of advertised products belonged to the accessories industry. This confirms that accessories companies such as *Cluse*[2] and *Daniel Wellington*[3], who are not represented in popular testimonials, are using mainly influencer marketing to build brands and spread advertisement [36]. It turns out that micro influencers are mainly used by the fitness industry to market products, as opposed to macro influencers, which do not advertise fitness products. In addition to large companies such as *L'Oréal*[4], which advertise their products in the study using only macro influencers, unknown and medium-sized companies such as *Asambeauty*[5] and *Calu*[6], also use micro and macro influencers to market their products. The role model function of the pretty girl or boy next door enables cosmetics companies to appeal to a particularly younger audience. Larger companies probably tend to use macro influencers, as they already have a broad reach and the viral effect is stronger than micro influencers. Also, worth mentioning is the plastic surgery industry, which uses macro influencers to promote services such as lip injections. This could lead to the spread of false ideals of beauty, which opinion leaders should pay attention to, especially as they are regarded as role models.

---

[2] www.cluse.com.

[3] www.danielwellington.com.

[4] www.loreal.de.

[5] www.asambeauty.com.

[6] www.calu.de.

Among the average 4 hashtags used by macro influencers per product placement, slogan hashtags such as *#FallforCluse,* product hashtags that represent and describe the product or product model and brand hashtags such as *#Nakd* are the most common. Micro influencers, who use an average of 6 hashtags, as well as macro influencers often use slogan hashtags, frequently supported product placements with fitness hashtags such as *#strongwoman* and fashion hashtags such as *#Fashionista.* It turns out that most hashtags are product-related or even company or brand related. Presumably, the slogan hashtags are given by the companies. Furthermore, it turned out that micro influencers used more image-related hashtags, such as *#sunset* of the *Environment* category.

Tags are links of profiles in the image plane, which are used by both influencer types in 99% of the analyzed product placements On average, micro influencers use 1 to 2 tags per product placement and macro influencers used 3 to 4 tags. It is shown that the identification in the image plane differs between company tags that refer to the product (for example, category *Company*) and company tags that refer to internal objects or persons (for example, category *Company of clothing*). The companies have different locations all over the world, different sales partners or specific profiles, which are also marked in the image layer to draw attention to these profiles. Other tag categories not related to the product but sharing information about the image, such as category *Location*, are also used. Tags are used to draw attention to repost sites that usually have a large number of followers and to increase their reach in a repost. The photographer's tag, especially in the product placements of the macro influencers, shows on the one hand that professional photographers are used for appealing Instagram images and on the other hand it confirms that more and more value is placed on the aesthetics of the images and that advertising is therefore not perceived as such by users [11]. It is also noteworthy that macro influencers often tag blog profiles, repost images and are seen as an inspiration by users. Micro influencers are tagging the companies of the clothes and accessories they wear that have no relation to the advertised product. Macro influencers do not use this category at all for product placements. The tagging behavior in the image thus confirms that Instagram mainly focuses on images, as 99% of the product placements examined were represented in the form of images [37]. Only one product placement of micro and macro influencers are advertised in videos where tagging is currently not possible.

Mentions are links to other Instagram profiles via the @ symbol in the description box, which also represent research objects. 174 mentions of macro influencer and 115 mentions of micro influencer are also research objects. On average, both types of influencer use one mention per product placement. Only 6 products without mention are advertised. The analysis of the mentions finds that the company (category: *Company*) and the company with location (category: *Company location*) are mentioned most frequently. Further mentions are from the categories *Photographer, Influencer, Distributor* and *Company Specification*, which are linked in the description level. The analysis of mentions also shows that there is a distinction between product and company-related mentions (for example, *@lorealhair*) and image and location-related mentions (for example, *@balanceflensburg*). This reveals that micro influencers use more image-related mentions than macro influencers, who presumably only use the specified mentions from the advertised companies.

Since electronic access to Instagram data was difficult at the time of the study, the data was collected manually, so the generalizability of these results is subject to the following limitations. Only micro and macro influencers are investigated. Besides those two types of Instagram, there are also nano and mega influencers concerning the number of followers, which could be considered in future research. In addition, the paper does not deal with the parasocial relationships that micro influencers, in particular, establish with their followers. However, there are certain relationships between product placements and the parasocial relationships that could be analyzed. Also, a period of 6 months has been established. It would be interesting to study for a more extended period or a whole year. In addition, there was no code training, which would have been significant given the number of categories.

References

1. Gabriel, R., Röhrs, H.-P.: Social Media: Potenziale, Trends, Chancen und Risiken. Springer, Wiesbaden (2017). https://doi.org/10.1007/978-3-662-53991-0
2. Pfeiffer, T., Koch, B.: Social Media, Wie sie mit Twitter, Facebook und CO: Ihren Kunder näher kommen. Addison-Wesley, Boston (2011)
3. Tegtmeier, A.-K.: Micro, Macro, Nano und Mega – die Unterschiede von Influencern in Reichweite und Einfluß. https://espresso-digital.de/2017/10/12/micro-macro-nano-und-mega-die-unterschiede-von-influencern-in-reichweite-und-einfluss/. Accessed 02 Aug 2018
4. Schüller, A.M.: Auf Tuchfühlung mit dem Kunden von heute: Management- strategien für unsere neue Businesswelt. Gaba, Offenbach (2014)
5. Nirschl, M., Steinberg, L.: Einstieg in das Influencer Marketing. Springer, Wiesbaden (2018). https://doi.org/10.1007/978-3-658-19745-2
6. Brown, D., Hayes, N.: Influencer Marketing: Who Really Influences Your Customers? Routledge, London (2007)
7. Eicher, D.: Influencer Marketing. http://www.digitalwiki.de/influencer-marketing/. Accessed 03 Aug 2018
8. Bennett, N.-K., et al.: Parasocial Relationships. https://www.findapsychologist.org/parasocial-relationships-the-nature-of-celebrity-fascinations/. Accessed 16 June 2018
9. Drexler, S.: Influencer: Der Schlüssel zur Genration Z. http://www.hitstorm.net/blog/influencer-schluessel-zur-generation-z/. Accessed 03 Aug 2018
10. Tamble, M.: Content Marketing und Influencer Relations. http://www.influma.com/blog/content-marketing-und-influencer-relations/. Accessed 03 Aug 2018
11. Faßmann, M., Moss, C.: Instagram als Marketing-Kanal: Die Positionierung ausgewählter Social-Media-Plattformen. Springer, Wiesbaden (2016). https://doi.org/10.1007/978-3-658-14349-7
12. Instagram Definition. https://en.wikipedia.org/wiki/Instagram. Accessed 04 Aug 2018
13. Statistiken zu Instagram. https://de.statista.com/themen/2506/instagram/. Accessed 25 Jan 2019
14. Parth, M., Kraft, P., Raif, H.: Influencer Marketing: Eine empirische Multimethodenanalyse zur Markenwahrnehmung von Sportmodenherstellern auf Instagram. Munich Business School Working Paper Series (2017)
15. Dorsch, I.: Content description on a mobile image sharing service: hashtags on instagram. J. Inf. Sci. Theory Pract. 6(2), 46–61 (2018)

16. Gräve, J.-F., Greff, A.: Good KPI, good influencer? Evaluating success metrics for social media influencers. In: 2018 SM Society, International Conference on Social Media and Society, vol. 9, pp. 291–295. ACM, New York (2018)

17. Wnent, S.: #Productplacement on Instagram – The sponsored and fabricated EWOM https://essay.utwente.nl/71525/1/master%20thesis_sandra%20wnent_s1097342.pdf. Accessed 30 Aug 2018

18. Vassallo, A.J., Kelly, B., Zhang, L., Wang, Z., Young, S., Freeman, B.: Junk food marketing on Instagram: content analysis. JMIR Public Health Surveill 4(2), e54. (2018). https://doi.org/10.2196/publichealth.9594

19. Evans, J.N., Phua, D., Lim, J., Jun, H.: Disclosing Instagram influencer advertising: the effects of disclosure language on advertising recognition, attitudes, and behavioral intent. J. Interact. Advert. 17, 138–149 (2017)

20. Uzunoğlu, E., Kip, S.: Brand communication through digital influencers: leveraging blogger engagement. Int. J. Inf. Manag. 34, 592–602 (2014)

21. Lee, J.E., Watkins, B.: YouTube vloggers' influence on consumer luxury brand perceptions and intentions. J. Bus. Res. 69, 5753–5760 (2016)

22. Krippendorff, K.: Content Analysis: An Introduction to Its Methodology, 3rd edn. Sage Publications, Los Angeles (2013)

23. Artgallery.ab Instagram profile. https://www.instagram.com/artgallery.ab/

24. Byashraf Instagram profile. https://www.instagram.com/byashrafb/. Accessed 27 June 2018

25. Aladiia Instagram profile. https://www.instagram.com/aladiia/. Accessed 27 June 2018

26. Kuhrmarvin Instagram profile. https://www.instagram.com/kuhrmarvin/. Accessed 17 June 2018

27. Llynllaura Instagram profile. https://www.instagram.com/llynnllaura/. Accessed 27 June 2018

28. Alvarosolermusic Instagram. https://www.instagram.com/alvarosolermusic/. Accessed 27 June 2018

29. Enyadres Instagram profile. https://www.instagram.com/enyadres/. Accessed 27 June 2018

30. Debiflue Instagram profile. https://www.instagram.com/debiflue/. Accessed 27 June 2018

31. Bettytaupe Instagram profile. https://www.instagram.com/bettytaube/. Accessed 27 June 2018

32. Culturewirhcoco Instagram profile. https://www.instagram.com/culturewithcoco/. Accessed 27 June 2018

33. Debiflue Instagram post. https://www.instagram.com/p/Bh4cnfkA0Os/?taken-by=debiflue. Accessed 26 Jan 2019

34. Plutte, N.: 10 Rechtstipps zu Twitter & Instagram Marketing. https://www.ra-plutte.de/rechtstipps-zu-twitter-instagram-marketing/. Accessed 23 Aug 2018

35. Brosius, H.-B., Haas, A., Koschel, F.: Methoden der empirischen Kommunikationsforschung - Eine Einführung, 7th edn. Springer VS, Wiesbaden (2016). https://doi.org/10.1007/978-3-531-19996-2

36. Mottola, I.: Daniel Wellington perfect Instagram marketing strategy. https://medium.com/@ignaziomottola/daniel-wellington-perfect-instagram-marketing-strategy-ce637c19c68c. Accessed 17 Sept 2018

37. Grabs, A., Bannour, K.B., Vogl, E.: Follow Me!: Erfolgreiches Social Media Marketing mit Facebook, Instagram und Co, 4th edn. Rheinwerk-Verlag, Bonn (2017)

Social Media Conversations: When Consumers Do Not React Positively to Brands' Kindness to Others

Andria Andriuzzi[1(✉)] and Géraldine Michel[2]

[1] Coactis - Université Jean Monnet, Saint Etienne, France
andria.andriuzzi@univ-st-etienne.fr
[2] Gregor - Sorbonne Business School, Paris, France
michel.iae@univ-parisl.fr

Abstract. In the context of consumers' advertising digital literacy, this research examines the impact of brand-consumer social media conversations. Based on Goffman's 'face-work' as a theoretical lens, we investigate to which extent consumers can feel like brands show human traits when they interact with consumers on social media. Taking into account online communication's multiple audience dilemma, we analyze how brand attachment influences the effect of brands' interaction strategies on consumers' attitude. Using an experimental method, we find that appreciative expressions from the brand have a positive effect on brand anthropomorphism when consumers are not attached to the brand. In contrast, appreciation does not show such an effect when consumers are attached to the brand. Therefore, this research contributes to the brand-consumer interactions and brand anthropomorphism literature and suggests that managers could segment their online conversation platforms depending on the kind of consumer brand relationships.

Keywords: Anthropomorphism · Brand attachment ·
Brand-consumer interactions · Conversation · Face-work · Social media

1 Introduction

Since the emergence of relationship marketing, practitioners have been trying to create strong ties between brands and consumers. Indeed, consumers develop feelings towards brands that are similar to those they have towards humans (Fournier and Alvarez 2012). To bring their brand closer to consumers, practitioners develop their brand's presence on social media sites such as Facebook or Twitter. Nowadays, consumers interact with brands on a wide range of online platforms (Hamilton et al. 2016). Online brand-consumer interactions have a positive impact on consumers attitudes (Hudson et al. 2015) and behaviors (Kumar et al. 2016). However, research generally considers this interaction as a whole, without being specific about the different kinds of interactions.

Conversation, a particular form of interaction, has emerged over the last few years as a trending topic in the marketing field (Berthelot-Guiet 2011; De Montety and Patrin-Leclère 2011). We define 'brand conversation' as a series of public online messages exchanged between several individuals, at least one of them being a brand

© Springer Nature Switzerland AG 2019
G. Meiselwitz (Ed.): HCII 2019, LNCS 11579, pp. 268–278, 2019.
https://doi.org/10.1007/978-3-030-21905-5_21

representative (Andriuzzi 2017). These conversations can be initiated by brands, e.g., when brands post a message on their Facebook page, or initiated by consumers, e.g., when they complain about a brand's products or services on Twitter.

Only a few authors are beginning to study these conversations. For example, within the recent 'webcare' research field, researchers have been discussing the circumstances in which brands should respond to consumers' comments (e.g., Van Noort and Willemsen 2012), adopting a reactive point of view on interaction. Although the issue of effectively managing consumer complaints is crucial, it seems important to study brand conversations initiated by brands, as well as those initiated by consumers.

Another problem for brand managers is that only a minority of consumers react to brand messages on social media (Campbell et al. 2014). As social media budgets are dramatically increasing, it could be disappointing for marketers to think that they are addressing only a small part of consumers. However, existing research helps to put this situation into perspective by showing that the online audience is made of both posters who participate in conversations and lurkers who simply observe them (Schlosser 2005). It is therefore necessary to understand to what extent these conversations have an impact on both types of web users. In addition, by using new advertising tools offered by social media sites such as Facebook and Twitter, brands can push their posts to a wider audience, beyond their regular followers. Since these messages can be modified by consumers' comments, brand-consumer interactions have a significant potential impact. With this in mind, this research addresses two main themes: the lack of knowledge about conversations initiated by brands, as well as the lack of knowledge about their effect on lurkers.

Using an experimental method, we test the impact of brand-consumer conversations on consumers who just look at these interactions on social media. As lurking consumers can have different experiences with tested brands, we study the potential moderating effect of brand attachment on the relationship between conversational strategies and consumers' perceptions. Using Goffman's face-work (1955) as a theoretical lens, we find that consumers with high attachment do not react to a brand showing appreciation to other consumers. Conversely, we find that consumers with low attachment feel like the brand is more human when the brand does show appreciation to others.

2   Conceptual Development

2.1   Face-Work Theory

Verbal and unscripted interactions between brands and consumers typically involve a human brand spokesperson, e.g., a community manager (Griffiths and Mclean 2015). Therefore, in order to study brand conversation, we mobilize a theoretical framework that usually applies to interactions between individuals: face-work. Sociology and linguistics-rooted, face-work theory was developed by Goffman (1955, 1967) before being extended by Brown and Levinson (1987) and others like Kerbrat-Orecchioni (2005). Face-work explains how individuals behave when they meet others by assuming that, during an interaction, each of the participants are committed to carrying out two simultaneous and continuous actions: maintaining their own face while ensuring other participants do not lose face (Goffman 1955). To achieve this dual mission, they use a number of strategies aimed at avoiding or minimizing face-threatening acts (FTAs; Goffman 1973), as well as producing face-flattering acts (FFAs; Kerbrat-Orecchioni 2007).

According to face-work theory, any interaction potentially threatens people's desire for freedom and autonomy (Brown and Levinson 1987). For instance, in an online context, encouraging people to participate in the conversation by asking for their opinions or making suggestions, or even just simply addressing them, could be considered an FTA. To counteract the potential negative impact of social media posting, and thus improve the perception of Internet users, face-work theory suggests speakers could try to minimize their FTA, for example by being indirect (e.g., "one could do…" instead of "you should do"). To counteract FTAs' negative effects, one could also enhance consumers' face by producing FFAs. An FFA can consist of flattering people, paying respect to them or more generally by producing appreciative expressions (Brown and Levinson 1987; Kerbrat-Orecchioni 2007). In an online marketing context, brands could be considered as producing FFAs when showing consideration or appreciation to consumers, while responding to their questions or comments on social media.

2.2 Appreciative Expressions Impact on Brand Humanization

Even if a very scarce amount of marketing research taps into face-work as a theoretical framework, FFAs have already shown a positive effect on consumers within previous works. For example, when a firm rejects consumers' ideas, consumers feel less face-threatened when the firm uses face enhancement at the same time (Fombelle et al. 2016). Such face enhancement could include recognizing consumers' past-submitted ideas, including consumers within a community or apologizing. Furthermore, as FFAs are more efficient when produced publicly compared to privately (ibid.), we could suggest that face-work strategies have an impact on consumers when produced on public social media sites such as Facebook or Twitter.

When developing such face-work strategies, one could say that brands conform to human conversational norms as face-work is considered as an invariant of human communication (Brown and Levinson 1987). Indeed, brands tend to mimic human-to-human communications on social media, instead of just adopting an "advertising" posture. Brands and their agents rely on a wide range of rhetoric tactics in online posts such as using personal pronouns (see Packard et al. 2018), second-person pronouns when addressing consumers (see Cruz et al. 2017) or using a familiar language (see Gretry et al. 2017). In addition, as consumers can interpret social cues online, brands use nonverbal communications such as emoticons, a technique that can provide consumers with a feeling of warmth towards brands (Li et al. 2018). Therefore, one could think that mimicking human interactions norms, such as adopting face-work strategies, drives consumers to feel that brands have human characteristics.

The consumers' propensity to attribute human characteristics to inanimate objects, i.e., anthropomorphism, is an important concept in marketing. Indeed, it is considered to be the pillar of the existence of brand-consumer relationships, a foundation for profitable consumer's attitudes and behaviors (Aaker and Fournier 1995). Even if anthropomorphism is an individual psychological characteristic (Epley et al. 2007), brands' strategies can have an impact on the way consumers attribute more or less human traits to them (MacInnis and Folkes 2017). The adoption of human language in interaction, a human characteristic if any, could lead to such outcomes. Thus, as the production of face-flattering acts during a conversation is supposed to generate a positive attitude towards the speaker, we make the following hypothesis:

H1: Brands are perceived as more human when they use appreciative expressions, compared to when they do not use them.

2.3 Moderating Role of Consumer's Brand Attachment

Although face-work theory predicts a positive effect of appreciative expressions, research shows that practitioners should be careful not to go too far when interacting with consumers online. For instance, a brand that warmly thanks consumers for their positive contributions is not always well received: consumers may think that the brand is trying to manipulate them by using flattery (Wang and Chaudhry 2018). Such results contrast with face-work theory, where positive comments should rather lead to positive outcomes. Yet, the body of work from Brown and Levinson (1987) shows a potential explanation: when in a close relationship, people do not need sophisticated face-work strategies for their interactions to be successful. For example, an interaction between old friends would be more likely be made of "bald on record" speech acts rather that to contain sophisticated FTA mitigation or FFA production. In other words, the type of existing relationship between speakers moderates the relationship between face-work and its outcomes.

As we know that the relations between brands and consumers sometimes imitate person-to-person relationships (Fournier and Alvarez 2012), one could think that brand-consumer relationships could have an impact on the brand's face-work perception by consumers. As brand attachment is a good way to evaluate the strengths of brand-consumer relationships (Whan Park et al. 2010), one could think that appreciation from the brand would be more or less well perceived depending on the degree of brand attachment. Indeed, as they are already close to the brand, attached consumers probably do not need the brand to "over-emphasize" the relationship.

Psychology research supports the existence of different perceptions depending on the context: people usually like better those who flatter them rather than those who flatter others (Vonk 2002). This occurs because, on the one hand, most people have positive self-esteem and therefore are likely to think their ingratiator is sincere. On the other hand, observers lack information on the target of ingratiation and therefore could question the ingratiated judgement. Moreover, ego considerations would lead people to think that they deserve to be appreciated more than others:

"Being motivated to assume, as most people are, that they are better than others, observers may be reluctant to uncritically accept lavish praise about another participant who just happened to be there at the same time" (Vonk 2002, p. 525).

For similar reasons, in a marketing context, consumers may prefer to be flattered rather than to see strangers being flattered. In addition, because of their emotional bond to the brand, attached consumers would negatively over-react to brand appreciation targeting others. Indeed, attached consumers would likely claim to be the subject of brand appreciation, as they would think that they deserve it more than unknown consumers would. Conversely, unattached consumer should not wait for specific treatment from the brand and therefore not react as negatively to brand flattery addressed to others. In contrary, as they do not have specific expectation from the brand, unattached consumers may be pleasantly surprised to see that the brand respects the rules of interpersonal communication by paying attention to others. Indeed, a surprise effect can play a positive role in brand evaluation (Schamari and Schaefers 2015). For all these reasons, we formulate a second hypothesis:

H2: When consumers are attached to the brand, the use of appreciative expressions addressed to others influences brand anthropomorphism less than when consumers are not attached to the brand.

3   Method

To test the causal relationship between brand interaction strategies and consumers' attitudes, we ran an experimental design. We tested the impact of a face-work lever (i.e., appreciative expressions) on consumers' attitude by measuring to what extent they see the brand as imbued with human characteristics (i.e., on perceived anthropomorphism) in the context of high or low brand attachment. Thus, we conducted a 2 (appreciation: yes/no) × 2 (brand attachment: high/low) between-subjects experiment.

3.1   Participants and Procedure

One hundred and eighty-eight participants (mean age = 36.60, SD = 11.77; 50% female) living in France were recruited and received monetary compensation. Participants belong to a consumer panel managed by an online research firm. They were screened by attesting they were holding a Facebook account.

Participants were randomly assigned to the different experimental cells. They received an email with a link to a self-assessed survey where they were asked questions about a car brand (n = 97) or about a coffee brand (n = 91). After these preliminary questions, we asked participants to imagine they were browsing their Facebook newsfeed and we exposed them to a screenshot of a fictitious brand-consumer conversation on Facebook, designed by us. Chosen brands are well known in France, thus the Facebook brand-consumer interaction stimuli could be seen as credible by participants. Finally, we asked them to answer questions about this conversation and again about the car or the coffee brand. Among other variables (see below), we chose brand personification as a control variable, as personification can have an impact on perceived anthropomorphism (Cohen 2014; MacInnis and Folkes 2017). Therefore, we designed four stimuli by combining two modalities of appreciation (yes/no) and of brand personification (yes/no).

3.2   Appreciation and Brand Attachment Manipulation

Appreciation was manipulated by including appreciative expressions to the brands' posts and answers in the conversations (e.g., "What a nice question, thank you again!"; appreciation = yes) or not including them (appreciation = no). Second, we created ex-post groups of consumers based of their brand attachment (M = 4.56). We ended with a group of weakly attached consumers (n = 88, Attachment < 4.56) and a group of strongly attached consumers (n = 99, Attachment > 4.56).

3.3   Measures

As manipulation checks, participants answered four items using seven-point Likert scales indicating to which extent they found the brand used appreciative expressions (e.g., "[Brand] cast people in a good light", "[Brand] make people look good"; α = .92; adapted from Kerssen-Griep et al. 2008). As for brand attachment, we used the measure by Lacoeuilhe (2000) as cited and adapted by Gouteron (2011). Participants answered five seven-point Likert scales (e.g., "I have a lot of affection for [Brand]", "I feel connected to [Brand]"; α = .95). Finally, consumers indicated to which extent they anthropomorphized the brand by answering six seven-point semantic differential scales (e.g., "conscious/unconscious", "artificial/natural"; α = .89; adapted from Hudson et al. 2015).

3.4   Control Variables

As face-work theory predicts that incentive expression (e.g., "Tell us what you think!") can have an impact on consumer's perception, we controlled incitation. Thus, we chose a non-incitation condition by only showing participants conversation without explicit incentive expressions as we thought it would be more neutral. To measure incitation level perception, we asked participants to answer three seven-point Likert scales, indicating to which extent they found the brand used incentive expressions (e.g., "[Brand] incites people to answer questions", [Brand] pushes people to give their opinion"; α = .85). We also controlled the conversation topic by only showing conversations that were related to the brand's core product (a new coffee format launched by the coffee brand; a new electric car launched by the car brand). To check their understanding of the conversations' topics, we asked participants if they thought the conversation was about the brand's products. Finally, we manipulated brand personification by exposing participants to conversations where the brand was posting from a generic branded account (i.e., identified by the brand's name and logo) or from a dedicated employee account ("Stéphanie – [brand's name] client service" plus the picture of a young woman). To check brand personification manipulation, we asked participants if they thought the brand was represented by its logo or by the picture of an employee. To control brand personification as well as the brand itself, we included them as covariates in data analysis (see below).

4 Results

4.1 Manipulation Check

A one-factor ANOVA revealed a significant effect of appreciation (yes/no) on perceived appreciation (F (1, 186) = 6.01, p < .05). Participants in the appreciation condition found that appreciation was higher (M = 5.53, SD = 0.94, n = 94) than participants in the no-appreciation condition (M = 5.19, SD = 0.98, n = 94). Moreover, we found a significant difference in brand attachment between our groups of high and low attached consumers (p < .001). Consumers in high attachment condition scored higher in attachment (M = 5.65) than consumers in low attachment (M = 3.35). Therefore, we considered our manipulations were successful. As for control variables, first, participants judged the brand's incentive level low, as expected (M_perceived_incitation = 3.62). A one-factor ANOVA showed that differences of perceived incitation within cells were non-significant (F (3, 184) = 1.72, p = .165). Therefore, incitation was controlled at a weak level. Second, as for the conversation topic, all participants found that the conversation was about a product sold by the brand (n = 188). Finally, as for brand personification, all participants in the "logo" condition (n = 89) said they thought the brand was represented by its logo, where all participants in the "employee" condition (n = 99) said they thought the brand was represented by an employee.

4.2 Hypotheses Testing

We conducted a two-factor ANCOVA (appreciation: yes/no; brand attachment; high/low) on anthropomorphism, with brand personification and brand name as covariates (Table 1).

Table 1. Results

Brand attachment	Appreciation	n	Anthropomorphism	
			M	SD
Low	No-appreciation	44	4.57	1.11
	Appreciation	45	5.15	1.09
High	No-appreciation	50	5.71	.92
	Appreciation	49	5.49	.97
			F	p
Treatment	Appreciation		1.33	.250
	Brand attachment		26.57	.000
	Appreciation × brand attachment		7.19	.008
Covariates	Brand		.80	.372
	Brand personification		2.97	.086

On the one hand, findings show no direct effect of appreciation on anthropomorphism (F (1, 182) = 1.33, p = .250) nor significant effect of covariates - neither from brands (F (1, 182) = 0.80, p = .372) nor from brand personification (F (1, 182) = 2.97, p = .086). On the other hand, findings show a direct effect of brand attachment on anthropomorphism (F (1, 182) = 26.57, p = .000) as well as an interaction effect between appreciation and attachment on anthropomorphism (F (1, 182) = 7.19, p = .008). Because of this interaction effect, we can say brand attachment has a moderating effect on the relation between appreciation and anthropomorphism.

However, a simple effects analysis shows that appreciation has a significant positive effect on consumers with low brand attachment (F = 7.10, p = .008) but not on consumers with high brand attachment (F = 1.08, p = ns). Consumers who are not particularly attached to the brand feel like the brand is more human when the brand uses appreciative expressions (vs. when the brand does not use appreciative expressions), but appreciation has no effect on consumers who are attached to the brand.

Therefore, we partially validate our first hypothesis: brands are perceived as more human when they use appreciative expressions, compared to when they do not use appreciative expression, yet we found a significant effect for weakly attached consumers only. Moreover, we validate our second hypothesis: when consumers are attached to the brand, the use of appreciative expressions addressed to others influences brand anthropomorphism less than when consumers are not attached to the brand. Indeed, we found no influence of appreciation on anthropomorphism when brand attachment is high, *versus* a positive influence when brand attachment is low.

5 Discussion and Conclusion

While there is a lot of research on the effects of social media in general, little is known about the actual interactions taking place between brands and consumers. Using an experimental method, we identify a causal relationship between brand interaction strategies and consumers' attitude. This research contributes to two streams of literature: brand-consumer interactions and brand anthropomorphism. It also provides managerial implications in the area of community management.

First, this research shows that face-work theory applies to brand-consumer interactions on social media, revealing the potential impact of face-flattering acts on consumers' perception in interactive brand communications. Face-flattering acts such as positive expression or compliments are supposed to respond to one of the fundamental aspirations of individuals during an interaction: the desire to be accepted (Goffman 1967). Consistent with face-work theory, consumers react positively to the brand's appreciative expressions, yet we found this effect only when brand attachment is low.

What's more, we found a specific manifestation of face-work in a marketing context. Findings show, in a somehow non-intuitive way, that consumers who are attached to the brand do not react in a positive way when they see the brand showing appreciation to others. Do consumers who are strongly attached to the brand develop a form of jealousy towards other consumers? Research in psychology supports the fact that, because of their emotional bond to the brand, attached consumers may prefer to be appreciated by the brand rather than to see the brand showing appreciation to strangers (Vonk 2002).

Our results could also be examined in the context of advertising literacy. Consumers who are advertising literate show knowledge, expertise and a critical viewpoint toward brands' communications (O'Donohoe and Tynan 1998). Moreover, a consumer's level of advertising literacy has an impact on the way they respond to brand messages (Livingstone and Helsper 2006). Can we therefore say that consumers who score higher on brand attachment also score higher on advertising digital literacy, at least toward the object of their attachment? Indeed, advertising literacy can emerge from cumulative experience with brands' communications (O'Donohoe and Tynan 1998). Therefore, attached consumers, with greater knowledge and experience of the brand they favor, could better decode the brand's social media strategies compared to non-attached consumers.

Second, this research highlights the impact of interaction strategies on anthropomorphism, a tendency for individuals to see humanlike characteristics or feelings in nonhuman agents (Epley et al. 2007). Anthropomorphism is important for marketing researchers and practitioners alike as it is the foundation of brand personality (Aaker 1997) and consumer-brand relationships (Fournier and Alvarez 2012). In a literature review on brand humanization, MacInnis and Folkes (2017) stress that visual, verbal and rhetorical clues can help to humanize brands. Therefore, we contribute to the brand anthropomorphism literature by showing that language in interactions can generate anthropomorphic reactions, as long as the brand conforms to interpersonal interaction norms. In addition, we contribute to the literature on brand personification (see Cohen 2014), stressing the idea that the use of a human spokesperson does not always have positive effects (Fleck et al. 2014) and is not sufficient to humanize a brand (Andriuzzi 2016). Indeed, findings show that in brand conversation it is important for the spokesperson to act as a human by respecting interpersonal communication rules.

As for managerial implications, our research shows that brand representatives, such as community managers, should carefully adapt their interaction style to the context. For example, they could segment their conversational platforms depending on whether they are talking to loyal customers or whether they are talking to new customers or prospects. These recommendations are important when managing sponsored posts campaigns where community managers may have to deal with multiple audiences, a persistent issue in online communications (Schlosser 2005).

In conclusion, this research shows the impact of brand conversation on consumers' attitudes. Marketers face the constant development of new interactive tools, such as connected objects or virtual reality devices. In addition, innovation in the field of artificial intelligence leads to the emergence of increasingly sophisticated automated conversation assistants such as chatbots. As verbal interactions between brands and consumers occurs in a growing number of environments, our work encourages new research on the role of conversation in marketing.

Acknowledgments. The authors would like to thank the Sorbonne Business School's brands and values research group and Entrecom for their support.

References

Aaker, J.L.: Dimensions of brand personality. J. Mark. Res. **34**, 347–356 (1997). https://doi.org/10.2307/3151897

Aaker, J.L., Fournier, S.: A brand as a character, a partner and a person: three perspectives on the question of brand personality. Adv. Consum. Res. **22**, 391–395 (1995)

Andriuzzi, A.: La conversation de marque à la lumière de la théorie du face-work : impact de la stratégie d'interaction des marques sur l'attitude des internautes. Ph.D. thesis, Paris 1 Panthéon Sorbonne University, France (2017)

Andriuzzi, A.: The tweeting brand: when conversation leads to humanization. In: Levallois, C., Marchand, M., Mata, T., Panisson, A. (eds.) Twitter for Research Handbook 2015-2016, pp. 232–242. EMLYON Press, Lyon (2016)

Berthelot-Guiet, K.: Extension du domaine de la conversation: discours de marque et publicitarité. Commun. Lang. **3**, 77–86 (2011). https://doi.org/10.4074/S0336150011003073

Brown, P., Levinson, S.: Politeness: Some Universals in Language Use. Cambridge University Press, Cambridge (1987)

Campbell, C., Ferraro, C., Sands, S.: Segmenting consumer reactions to social network marketing. Eur. J. Mark. **48**, 432–452 (2014). https://doi.org/10.1108/EJM-03-2012-0165

Cohen, R.J.: Brand personification: introduction and overview. Psychol. Mark. **31**, 1–30 (2014). https://doi.org/10.1002/mar.20671

Cruz, R.E., Leonhardt, J.M., Pezzuti, T.: Second person pronouns enhance consumer involvement and brand attitude. J. Interact. Mark. **39**, 104–116 (2017). https://doi.org/10.1016/j.intmar.2017.05.001

De Montety, C., Patrin-Leclère, V.: La conversion à la conversation: le succès d'un succédané. Commun. Lang. **3**, 23–37 (2011). https://doi.org/10.4074/S0336150011003036

Epley, N., Waytz, A., Cacioppo, J.T.: On seeing human: a three-factor theory of anthropomorphism. Psychol. Rev. **114**, 864–886 (2007). https://doi.org/10.1037/0033-295X.114.4.864

Fleck, N., Michel, G., Zeitoun, V.: Brand personification through the use of spokespeople: an exploratory study of ordinary employees, CEOs, and celebrities featured in advertising. Psychol. Mark. **31**, 84–92 (2014). https://doi.org/10.1002/mar.20677

Fombelle, P.W., Bone, S.A., Lemon, K.N.: Responding to the 98%: face-enhancing strategies for dealing with rejected customer ideas. J. Acad. Mark. Sci. **44**, 685–706 (2016). https://doi.org/10.1007/s11747-015-0469-y

Fournier, S., Alvarez, C.: Brands as relationship partners: warmth, competence, and in-between. J. Consum. Psychol. **22**, 177–185 (2012). https://doi.org/10.1016/J.JCPS.2011.10.003

Goffman, E.: On face-work; an analysis of ritual elements in social interaction. Psychiatry J. Study Interpers. Process. **18**, 213–231 (1955). https://doi.org/10.1162/15241730360580159

Goffman, E.: Interaction Ritual. Aldine, Oxford (1967)

Goffman, E.: La mise en scène de la vie quotidienne. 2: Les relations en public. Editions de Minuit, Paris (1973)

Gouteron, J.: L'intégration d'une mesure de l'attachement à la marque dans les études de satisfaction. La Rev. des Sci. Gest. **6**, 109–117 (2011). https://doi.org/10.3917/rsg.252.0109

Gretry, A., Horváth, C., Belei, N., Van, Riel A.C.R.: "Don't pretend to be my friend!" when an informal brand communication style backfires on social media. J. Bus. Res. **74**, 77–89 (2017). https://doi.org/10.1016/j.jbusres.2017.01.012

Griffiths, M., Mclean, R.: Unleashing corporate communications via social media: a UK study of brand management and conversations with customers. J. Cust. Behav. **14**, 147–162 (2015). https://doi.org/10.1362/147539215X14373846805789

Hamilton, M., Kaltcheva, V.D., Rohm, A.J.: Hashtags and handshakes: consumer motives and platform use in brand-consumer interactions. J. Consum. Mark. **33**, 135–144 (2016). https://doi.org/10.1108/JCM-04-2015-1398

Hudson, S., Huang, L., Roth, M.S., Madden, T.J.: The influence of social media interactions on consumer–brand relationships: a three-country study of brand perceptions and marketing behaviors. Int. J. Res. Mark. **1**, 27–41 (2015). https://doi.org/10.1016/j.ijresmar.2015.06.004

Kerbrat-Orecchioni, C.: Le discours en interaction. Armand Colin, Paris (2005)

Kerbrat-Orecchioni, C.: L'analyse du discours en interaction : quelques principes méthodologiques. Limbaje si Comun. **IX**, 13–32 (2007)

Kerssen-Griep, J., Trees, A.R., Hess, J.A.: Attentive facework during instructional feedback: key to perceiving mentorship and an optimal learning environment. Commun. Educ. **57**, 312–332 (2008). https://doi.org/10.1080/03634520802027347

Kumar, A., Bezawada, R., Rishika, R., et al.: From social to sale: the effects of firm-generated content in social media on customer behavior. J. Mark. **80**, 7–25 (2016). https://doi.org/10.1509/jm.14.0249

Lacoeuilhe, J.: L'attachement a la marque : Proposition d'une échelle de mesure. Rech. Appl. en. Mark. **15**, 61–77 (2000). https://doi.org/10.1177/076737010001500404

Li, X., Chan, K.W., Kim, S.: Service with emoticons: how customers interpret employee use of emoticons in online service encounters. J. Consum. Res. 1–50 (2018). https://doi.org/10.1093/jcr/ucy016

Livingstone, S., Helsper, E.J.: Does advertising literacy mediate the effects of advertising on children? A critical examination of two linked research literatures in relation to obesity and food choice. J. Commun. **56**, 560–584 (2006). https://doi.org/10.1111/j.1460-2466.2006.00301.x

MacInnis, D.J., Folkes, V.S.: Humanizing brands: when brands seem to be like me, part of me, and in a relationship with me. J. Consum. Psychol. **27**, 355–374 (2017). https://doi.org/10.1016/j.jcps.2016.12.003

O'Donohoe, S., Tynan, C.: Beyond sophistication: dimensions of advertising literacy. Int. J. Advert. **17**, 467–482 (1998). https://doi.org/10.1080/02650487.1998.11104733

Packard, G., Moore, S.G., McFerran, B.: (I'm) Happy to Help (You): the impact of personal pronoun use in customer–firm interactions. J. Mark. Res. **LV**, 541–555 (2018). https://doi.org/10.1509/jmr.16.0118

Schamari, J., Schaefers, T.: Leaving the home turf: how brands can use webcare on consumer-generated platforms to increase positive consumer engagement. J. Interact. Mark. **30**, 20–33 (2015). https://doi.org/10.1016/j.intmar.2014.12.001

Schlosser, A.E.: Posting versus lurking: communicating in a multiple audience context. J. Consum. Res. **32**, 260–265 (2005). https://doi.org/10.1086/432235

Van Noort, G., Willemsen, L.M.: Online damage control: the effects of proactive versus reactive webcare interventions in consumer-generated and brand-generated platforms. J. Interact. Mark. **26**, 131–140 (2012). https://doi.org/10.1016/j.intmar.2011.07.001

Vonk, R.: Self-serving interpretations of flattery: why ingratiation works. J. Pers. Soc. Psychol. **82**, 515–526 (2002). https://doi.org/10.1037/0022-3514.82.4.515

Wang, Y., Chaudhry, A.: When and how managers' responses to online reviews affect subsequent reviews. J. Mark. Res. **55**, 163–177 (2018). https://doi.org/10.1509/jmr.15.0511

Whan Park, C., MacInnis, D.J., Priester, J., et al.: Brand attachment and brand attitude strength: conceptual and empirical differentiation of two critical brand equity drivers. J. Mark. **74**, 1–17 (2010). https://doi.org/10.1509/jmkg.74.6.1

Evaluating the Mckinsey's Choices Framework: A Chilean Experiment of Online Customers

Jaime Díaz[1](✉), Ángela Patricia Villareal-Freire[2],
Andrés Felipe Aguire Aguirre[2], and Freddy Paz[3]

[1] Depto. Cs. de la Computación e Informática,
Universidad de La Frontera, Temuco, Chile
jaimeignacio.diaz@ufrontera.cl
[2] Departamento de Sistemas, Universidad del Cauca, Popayán, Colombia
{avillareal,afaguirre}@unicauca.edu.co
[3] Departamento de Ingeniería,
Pontificia Universidad Católica del Perú, Lima, Perú
fpaz@pucp.pe

Abstract. Users learn patterns of thought, activities, and communications by being in a specific social environment. An application or website interface is the environment in which the user and the system interact. It makes sense that the interface should facilitate users to use their own style. The global management consulting company Mckinsey, developed a framework that categorizes general actions to encourage particular behavior in electronic commerce. This approach can be enough as a starting point for the design of a website. Though, we can note that cultural behavior, emotions and user satisfaction is not discussed in a broader way. In this study, we present a first approximation of experiments, which evaluate the importance of McKinsey's proposal and its relevance in a Chilean context. 104 customers participated, managing to identify the most relevant constructs when developing a specific website. The future work, relates to extend the model of this article by examining whether user satisfaction, emotions and cultural behavior performs well as a consequence of customer experience.

Keywords: Electronic commerce · User experience · Human behavior · User satisfaction · Cultural behavior

1 Introduction

In a world with more online competition, the specialist always looks to enhance the customers' experience as a priority. They normally recommend investing in products, people, and in the service delivery process to put customers first. However, when we look the customer-satisfaction survey results and other metrics of customer experience, we got disappointed. We can observe that customer satisfaction metrics, are not improving with the changes that clients can see each day in the services that they deliver [1].

© Springer Nature Switzerland AG 2019
G. Meiselwitz (Ed.): HCII 2019, LNCS 11579, pp. 279–290, 2019.
https://doi.org/10.1007/978-3-030-21905-5_22

Behavioral scientists tell us that human interactions (and decision making) influence the considerations such as the sequence in which customers encounter unsatisfactory and pleasurable experiences. The research undertaken by Nobel laureate Daniel Kahneman form the foundation upon which the practical principles have been developed and had a significant impact on how individuals make decisions [2–4]. By focusing on these principles, companies can design and manage service encounters to maximize customer satisfaction.

The global management consulting company Mckinsey, developed a framework that categorizes general actions to encourage particular behavior in electronic commerce. This approach can be enough as a starting point for the design of a website. Though, we can note that cultural behavior, emotions and user satisfaction is not discussed in a broader way. What is the impact to not embrace these characteristics in the full proposal? Is one of question that we are looking to analyze in this work.

Bidin et al. [5] mention that the emotions of users are the reason that made many products successful. If a product, cannot attract visitors, at first sight, it will go out of business. So, the design guidelines for e-Commerce interfaces no only must achieve user experience best practices, but also, we must consider how to design to evoke positive emotions [6].

Regarding the cultural behavior, this influences in how people interact. This is a premise that is widely discussed and supported in the literature [7]. This interaction, however, can also be extrapolated to other situations, such as User Interface. Several studies have emphasized the importance of culture when designing them [8, 9].

This investigation, present results regarding a first research questions: (RQ1) *How important are McKinsey's recommendations for the final users in a chilean context?* Through various exercises, we try to respond the concerns raised, and leaving specific future works for the construction for effective interfaces.

This paper is organized as follows: Sect. 2 outlines the basic concepts related to the present investigation. Section 3 presents the methodologies of the experiments carried out. Section 4 shows the data analysis and results. Finally, Sect. 5 presents the conclusions and future work.

2   Conceptual Foundations

In this section, we describe the central concepts of the study and their adjustment for the following proposal and experimentation.

2.1   User's Satisfaction: The ISO Approach

User satisfaction is one of the elements in the quality of interaction in any digital system. In fact, if the Customer Experience (CX) limits the achievement of the user's goals or does not meet their needs, it generates a non-return point that leads the users to the competition or the search of other alternatives [10, 11]. This situation shows that user satisfaction becomes the main parameter that defines the success or failure of a product or service [12].

The ISO 9126 standard [13] and subsequently ISO/IEC 25010 [14], has a similar definition: "Degree in which the needs of users are met when a product or system is used in a context of specific use". However, the ISO/IEC 25010 standard categorizes user satisfaction in characteristics: Utility, Trust, Pleasure, Comfort, Motivation, Performance, and Preference.

In our proposal, the "user satisfaction" involves the complete proposal. It is one of the supports of the experience and is considered a transversal element. We took the definition from the ISO/IEC 25010 because represents a standard and is widely adopted.

2.2   Interfaces Design Guidelines: An Emotional Perspective

The EMOINAD approach (in English, EMOtive INterfaces for Attention Deficit), It is a set of procedures and activities that facilitate the establishment of heuristic principles for the interface design of therapeutic systems, considering the emotional perspective, but which, can be applied to interfaces in a transversal manner [6]. This proposal takes into account the following characteristics: layout, navigation, content and performance.

We selected this proposal, because of its methodological way to gather information.

Other guides, collects a small set of heuristics, neither taking into account previous studies, or simple are outdated. The idea with this guide is for the designer/developer to find all the relevant information to the design of emotional interfaces in one place.

2.3   Hofstede Cultural Approach

The works of Hofstede are recognized as some of the most referential with respect to understanding the influence of culture on values presented by users during their activities [7]. From his first studies [15] and later additions [7], Hofstede developed a model which identifies six principal dimensions to help differentiate between cultures: (i) Power Distance, (ii) Individualism vs. Collectivity, (iii) Masculinity vs. Femininity, (iv) Uncertainty Avoidance, (v) Long Term Orientation and (vi) Indulgence vs. Moderation.

To reinforce this trend, studies have emphasized the importance of culture when designing web interfaces, prototypes, recommendations, patterns and best practices [9, 16, 17]. Ford and Kotzé [8], also indicate characteristics which an interactive system should contain, based on each country's cultural and behavioural attributes.

2.4   CHOICES Framework

Based on the work from Kahneman et al. [2–4], the Global management consulting company McKinsey developed a framework for categorizing general actions that attempt to encourage particular behavior from individuals in consumer and other settings. The CHOICES framework (see Table 1) is an acronym for *Context, Habit, Other people, Incentives, Congruence, Emotions* and *Salience*.

These characteristics have associated drivers of behavior, which try to identify traditional behaviors for new users of e-Commerce. Table 1 discloses the summarized framework and some examples of intervention.

Table 1. CHOICES framework from Mckinsey's behavioral insight lab.

CHOICES	Drivers of behavior	Example of interventions
Context	People gauge information relative to other, mostly implicit benchmarks	**Prime**: Playing German music in a wine store significantly increases sales of German wine
Habit	People often act and judge without deliberation, following habits or mental shortcuts	**Expect errors:** To reduce the risk of customer losing cards, ATM usually return the card first, then dispense cash
Other People	People are influenced by what other people do, say, or think	**Tell about others:** Tax fraud is reduced by 15% when taxpayers are informed that most people actually do not commit fraud
Incentives	People respond to "objectively" better offers	**Give immediate gratification**: Little treats for good deeds today (e.g. cash for going to the gym) can help fight procrastination
Congruence	People act to preserve a positive and consistent self-image	**Activate commitments:** Public commitments work better than promised to oneself (e.g. to quit smoking)
Emotions	People are influenced by emotions and the physical state of their bodies	**Create "yes" emotions:** A photo of a happy/attractive persona had the same demand effect for a bank as a mortgage-rate cut of 100 basis points
Salience	People take in messages that are easier to process and remember	**Show consequences:** Regular information on energy usage and price increases drives energy consumption down more than twice as effectively as yearly updates

Many companies take advantage of these principles to improve the customer perception of the services received [18, 19]. Airlines and movie theaters allow customers to select their seats, providing customers with a sense of control. Most online retailers understand the value of allowing customers a sense of control and strive to keep their website displays, placement of buttons, and other functions consistently in line with customer habits.

3   Methodology

Our proposal will look to initiate an approach that solve our first research question: (RQ1) *How important are McKinsey's recommendations for the final users in a chilean context?*. RQ1 will be addressed through a perception survey.

3.1 Questionnaire and Measures

The data was collected by adapting the attributes (constructs) of Mckinsey's CHOICES framework [2–4]. The questionnaire has 18 items, three for each construct. For each construct, we consider attributes and characteristics from a user satisfaction, emotions and cultural behavior perspective. We eliminate the construct "*congruence*", due to be an internal topic of the consumer, not addressed in this first study.

The questionnaire was based on constructs that were measured using existing scale items (see Table 2). All responses were recorded by means of a 5-point Likert scale, that ranged from "completely disagree" to "completely agree."

Table 2. Constructs and items used in the questionnaire.

Constructs	Items
Context	• *When I seek to buy/contract a product or service, I carry out a preliminary analysis of the product* • *If we are at Christmas, New Year, Valentine's Day or another, do you prefer to buy on a page that has offers and promotions alluding to these festivities?* • *I wait for the offers of Cyber Monday, Black Friday or similar to buy online*
Habit	• *I have a preference for brands of products that appear on television or are renowned* • *It generates confidence to use my credit card online* • *The value of the delivery and the quality of the carrier is paramount when it comes to determining my purchase*
Other people	• *I have purchased a product, according to the references of another buyer on the same/another website* • *I have bought products because they are promoted by artists, celebrities or influencers* • *I have bought products because it was recommended to me by a friend or acquaintance*
Incentives	• *When I go shopping on websites, I prefer the products that come with a gift* • *I Prioritize the purchase of products that are on offer, over other products* • *2x1 offers call my attention more than other offers*
Emotions	• *I prefer to buy on a website that allocates a percentage of their profits to charity* • *I prefer to buy a company in which I accumulate points for my next purchases* • *I prefer to buy on a website where I know the history of the company and its creators*
Salience	• *If there are many payment options, I always prefer the one that appears first* • *I prefer websites that allow me to prioritize the best options to buy* • *I prefer the pages in which you do not have to register to access to their products*

In addition, we pre-tested the questionnaire in two sections. The first one, to avoid potential misinterpretation by respondents, 2 full-time professors and 5 practitioners' students from the areas of computer science and user experience were asked to assess the adequacy of the questions. In a second instance, 10 target respondents were asked to evaluate the questionnaire case of comprehension.

3.2 Data Collection and Sample

Participants. This study resulted in a sample of 104 customers, whose ages ranged from 18 to 65, with an average of age of 30 and 57.69% of respondents were female. Table 2 depicts the sample profile in detail.

Method. The present study is quantitative, descriptive, non-experimental and transversal. A non-random selection was made, where users of social networks were asked to answer the questionnaire voluntarily and anonymously. The instrument is distributed through the Google Docs platform. The data were analyzed with the statistical program STATA 15 (Table 3).

Table 3. Sample Profile

		%
Gender	Male	40.38%
	Female	57.69%
	Unidentified	1.92%
Age	18–29	50%
	30–49	50%
	50–65	0%

4   Data Analysis and Results

In order to know the distribution for the relevance of constructs, descriptive statistics of the measures: the means, the standard deviation, the asymmetry and the kurtosis of the variables were calculated (see Table 4).

Table 4. General results.

Construct	Mean	Median	SD	Asymmetry	Kurtosis
Context	11.269	11.000	1.9414	−0.271	2.556
Habit	10.423	11.000	2.226	−0.274	2.517
Other people	9.115	9.000	2.430	−0.367	3.378
Incentives	10.808	11.000	2.559	−0.273	2.784
Emotions	9.500	9.000	2.616	0.093	2.635
Salience	10.192	10.500	1.715	−0.349	2.482

The value of the asymmetry shows that the six constructs evaluated have values between 0.093 and −0.367. The Kurtosis varies between 3.378 and 2.482. With a negative asymmetry and a flattened Kurtosis in 5 out of 6 constructs. The *"Other People"* construct got a targeted distribution.

In the constructs evaluated, with an average response between 9.115 and 11.269 of a maximum of 15 (and minimum of 3), it means that the population agrees that all the constructs are relevant to the final customer. However, the most important for them are: Context, Incentives and Habit.

Context and Habit. Hofstede cultural dimension: Uncertainty Avoidance (86/100).

The extent to which the members of a culture feel threatened by ambiguous or unknown situations. At 86 Chile scores high on Uncertainty Avoidance – and so do the majority of Latin American countries that belonged to the Spanish kingdom. These societies show a strong need for rules and elaborate legal systems in order to structure life.

Incentives. Hofstede cultural dimension: Long-term orientation (31/100).

With a low score of 31, Chile is said to have a normative culture. People in such societies have a strong concern with establishing the absolute Truth; they are normative in their thinking. They exhibit great respect for traditions, a relatively small propensity to save for the future, and a focus on achieving quick results.

4.1 Measurement Assessment

In Table 5, we analyze the items that compose the constructs. The data mean varies between values of 1 to 5, with a standard deviation of 0.6 to 1.2, an asymmetry between −1.016 to 2.8 and kurtosis between 1.7 and 7.69. There are significant differences between items. We will analyze each one separately.

CON1. *When I seek to buy/contract a product or service, I carry out a preliminary analysis of the product.* With an average of 4.557, a median of 4, SD 0.61, asymmetry −1.016 and kurtosis 3.1. We can note that the population agrees with the statement presented. The distribution got a negative asymmetry, concentrating the data pointing to the normal curve.

CON2. *If we are at Christmas, New Year, Valentine's Day or another, do you prefer to buy on a page that has offers and promotions alluding to these festivities?* With an average of 3.711, a median of 4, SD of 1.054, asymmetry −0.42 and kurtosis 2.78, it indicates that the population is indifferent to the statement presented, with a distribution with negative asymmetry, concentrating the data pointing of the curve flattened.

CON3. *I wait for the offers of Cyber Monday, Black Friday or similar to buy online.* With an average and median of 3, SD of 1.268, an asymmetry of 0.1106 and kurtosis of 2.1190, We can conclude that the population is indifferent to the statement presented. The symmetric distribution concentrates the data pointing to the flattened curve.

HAB1. *I have a preference for brands of products that appear on television or are renowned.* With an average of 2.673, a median of 3, SD of 1.294, an asymmetry of −0.031 and kurtosis of 1.7607. We can identify that the population is indifferent to the assertion presented. With a positive asymmetry, the data is concentrated pointing the flatted curve.

Table 5. Construct and item description

Construct	Item	Mean	Median	SD	Asymmetry	Kurtosis
Context	CON1	4.557	5	0.607	−1.016	3.102
	CON2	3.771	4	1.054	−0.417	2.782
	CON3	3.000	3	1.268	0.110	2.119
Habit	HAB1	2.673	3	1.294	−0.030	1.760
	HAB2	3.596	4	1.208	−0.530	2.512
	HAB3	4.153	4	0.997	−1.387	4.914
Other people	OTP1	3.942	4	1.144	−0.837	2.829
	OTP2	1.519	1	0.851	2.055	7.689
	OTP3	3.653	4	1.202	−0.094	3.277
Incentives	INC1	3.404	3	1.159	−0.069	2.052
	INC2	3.923	4	1.006	−0.660	2.874
	INC3	3.480	4	1.146	−0.386	2.409
Emotions	EMO1	2.750	3	1.045	−0.006	2.836
	EMO2	3.403	3	1.256	2.836	1.888
	EMO3	3.346	3	1.218	−0.162	2.167
Salience	SAL1	2.019	2	1.019	0.746	2.923
	SAL2	4.153	4	0.936	−0.742	2.454
	SAL3	4.019	4	1.111	−0.730	2.44

HAB2. *It generates confidence to use my credit card online.* With an average of 3.596, a median of 4, SD of 1.208, an asymmetry of −0.530 and kurtosis 2.51. We can conclude that the population agrees with the statement presented. With a negative asymmetry, the data is pointing in a flattened curve.

HAB3. *The value of the delivery and the quality of the carrier is paramount when it comes to determining my purchase.* With an average of 4.153, a median of 4, SD of 0.1, an asymmetry of −1.388 and kurtosis 4.9. It indicates that the population agrees with the statement presented. With a negative asymmetry, the data is concentrated on the large numbers.

OTP1. *I have purchased a product, according to the references of another buyer on the same/another website.* With an average of 3.942, a median of 4, SD of 1.144, an asymmetry of −0.84 and kurtosis 2.83. We can conclude that the population agrees with the statement presented. With a negative asymmetry, the data is concentrated in large numbers.

OTP2. *I have bought products because they are promoted by artists, celebrities or influencers.* With an average of 1.52, a median of 1, SD of 0.85, an asymmetry of 2.0559 and kurtosis 7.69. We can notate that the population strongly disagrees with the statement presented, with a positive asymmetry, the data is concentrated in the small numbers.

OTP3. *I have bought products because it was recommended to me by a friend or acquaintance.* With an average of 3.66, a median of 4, SD of 1.20, an asymmetry of −0.95 and kurtosis 3.27. We can indicate that the population agrees with the statement presented, with a negative asymmetry, the data is concentrated in the intermediate numbers.

INC1. *When I go shopping on websites, I prefer the products that come with a gift.* With an average of 3.403, a median of 3, SD of 1.16, an asymmetry of −0.069 and kurtosis 2.052. We can note that the population is indifferent to the statement presented, with a negative asymmetry, concentrating the data in the intermediate numbers.

INC2. *I Prioritize the purchase of products that are on offer, over other products.* With an average of 3,923, a median of 4, SD of 1,006, an asymmetry of −0,660611 and kurtosis 2,874. We can conclude that the population is in agreement with the statement presented, with a negative asymmetry, concentrating the data in the intermediate numbers.

INC3. *2x1 offers call my attention more than other offers.* With an average of 3.480, a median of 4, SD of 1.146, an asymmetry of −0.386 and kurtosis 2.40. We can conclude that the population is in agreement with the presented statement, with a negative asymmetry, concentrating the data in the intermediate numbers.

EMO1. *I prefer to buy on a website that allocates a percentage of their profits to charity.* With an average of 2.75, A median of 3, SD OF 1.04, an asymmetry of −0.0064 and kurtosis 2.8361. We can note that the population is indifferent to the statement presented, with a negative asymmetry, concentrating the data in the intermediate numbers.

EMO2. *I prefer to buy a company in which I accumulate points for my next purchases.* With an average of 3.403, a median of 3, SD of 1.256, an asymmetry of 2.836 and kurtosis 1.88. We conclude that the population is indifferent with the statement presented, with a positive asymmetry, concentrating the data in the lower numbers.

EMO3. *I prefer to buy on a website where I know the history of the company and its creators.* With an average of 3,346, a median of 3, SD of 1,218, an asymmetry of −0,162 and kurtosis 2,1678. We can infer that the population is indifferent with the statement presented, with a negative asymmetry, concentrating the data in the superior numbers.

SAL1. *If there are many payment options, I always prefer the one that appears first.* With an average of 2,019, a median of 2, SD of 1,019, an asymmetry of 0,746 and kurtosis 2,923. We can resolve that the population disagrees with the statement presented, with a positive asymmetry, concentrating the data in the lower numbers.

SAL2. *I prefer websites that allow me to prioritize the best options to buy.* With an average of 4.154, a median of 4, SD of 0.936, an asymmetry of −0.7427 and kurtosis 2.4543. We can conclude that the population disagrees with the statement presented, with a negative asymmetry, concentrating the data in the higher numbers.

SAL3. *I prefer the pages in which you do not have to register to access to their products.* With an average of 4.019, a median of 4, SD of 1.111, an asymmetry of −0.7305 and kurtosis 2.4483. We can resolve that the population agrees with the presented statement, with a negative asymmetry, concentrating the data in the superior numbers.

5 Conclusions and Future Work

Users learn patterns of thought, activities, and communications by being in a specific social environment [20]. An application or website interface is the environment in which the user and the system interact. It makes sense that the interface should facilitate users to use their own style. Global interfaces need to accommodate a variety of styles to provide support to the cultural diversity of users [9].

Regarding our Research Question: (RQ1) *How important are McKinsey's recommendations for the final users in a chilean context?* Although this proposal is based on widely discussed works, this type of validation is not always carried out in a specific cultural context.

On average, the constructs have a value above the mean, and the most relevant for the target culture were: "Context, Incentives, and Habit". This can be explained principally by the attributes of "Power Distance Index" and "Uncertainty Avoidance" from the Hofstede approach.

5.1 Integration Proposal

We can relate all these concepts and concerns in the following proposal (see Fig. 1), where we preliminarily disclose the intervention that we are going to evaluate. This, however, is related to a second research question: (RQ2) *What are the gaps and conclusions about the implementation when we evaluate other attributes such as emotions, user satisfaction and cultural behavior?*. We are looking to evaluate the CHOICES framework and its integration with the previous attributes.

5.2 Limitations and Future Research

Notwithstanding its theoretical contributions, this research also has some limitations. First, this study is limited to the Chilean culture, and therefore the external validity of the findings is an issue. Future research should replicate this investigation and widen the diversity of cultures and services settings in the sample to discover if the results are consistent across the whole sector.

In addition, future research could try to understand from an Omni-channel perspective the impact of the best practices and how we can integrate the recommendations from cultural behavior, user satisfactions and emotions.

Finally, in line with recent suggestions [6, 12], future research could extend the model of this article by examining whether user satisfaction, emotions and cultural behavior performs well as a consequence of customer experience.

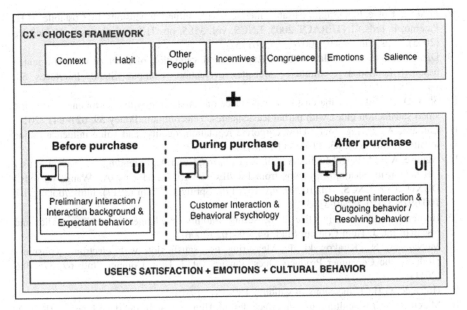

Fig. 1. Customer experience main process and related concepts

Acknowledgment. The authors would like to thank all the participants involved in the preliminary experiments, especially Danay Alejandra Ahumada Soto for her invaluable statistical contribution. Also, all the members of the "Centro de Estudios de Ingeniería de Software, CEIS", "User Experience & Game Design - Research Group, UXGD" and "HCI, Design, User Experience, Accessibility & Innovation Technologies Group, HCI-DUXAIT". UXGD is a member of the HCI-COLLAB network. Funded by Universidad de La Frontera, Proyecto DI18-0022.

References

1. Kumar, A., Steward, M.D., Morgan, F.N.: Delivering a superior customer experience in solutions delivery processes: seven factors for success. Bus. Horiz. **61**, 775–782 (2018)
2. Frederick, S., Kahneman, D., Mochon, D.: Elaborating a simpler theory of anchoring. J. Consum. Psychol. **20**, 17–19 (2010)
3. Chater, N., Loewenstein, G.: The under-appreciated drive for sense-making. J. Econ. Behav. Organ. **126**, 137–154 (2016)
4. Jahedi, S., Deck, C., Ariely, D.: Arousal and economic decision making. J. Econ. Behav. Organ. **134**, 165–189 (2017)
5. Bidin, S.A.H., Lokman, A.M., Mohd, W.A.R.W., Tsuchiya, T.: Initial intervention study of Kansei robotic implementation for elderly. Procedia Comput. Sci. **105**, 87–92 (2017)
6. Villareal Freire, A.P., Collazos Ordoñez, C.A.: The EMOINAD Guide construction proposal: an emotive interface design guide for attention deficit disorder in children. Rom. J. Hum.-Comput. Interact. **9**, 352–366 (2016)
7. Hofstede, G.H.: Hofstede: Cultures and Organizations - Software of the Mind, pp. 1–29 (2001)

8. Ford, G., Kotzé, P.: Designing usable interfaces with cultural dimensions. In: Costabile, M.F., Paternò, F. (eds.) INTERACT 2005. LNCS, vol. 3585, pp. 713–726. Springer, Heidelberg (2005). https://doi.org/10.1007/11555261_57

9. Díaz, J., Rusu, C., Collazos, C.A.: Experimental validation of a set of cultural-oriented usability heuristics: e-commerce websites evaluation. Comput. Stand. Interfaces **50**, 160–178 (2017)

10. Shin, D.-H.: Effect of the customer experience on satisfaction with smartphones: assessing smart satisfaction index with partial least squares. Telecommun. Policy **39**, 627–641 (2015)

11. Caruana, A., Ewing, M.T.: How corporate reputation, quality, and value influence online loyalty. J. Bus. Res. **63**, 1103–1110 (2010)

12. Aguirre, A.F., Villareal-Freire, Á., Gil, R., Collazos, César A.: Extending the concept of user satisfaction in e-learning systems from ISO/IEC 25010. In: Marcus, A., Wang, W. (eds.) DUXU 2017. LNCS, vol. 10290, pp. 167–179. Springer, Cham (2017). https://doi.org/10.1007/978-3-319-58640-3_13

13. Hornbæk, K.: Current practice in measuring usability: challenges to usability studies and research. Int. J. Hum Comput Stud. **64**, 79–102 (2006)

14. McNamara, N., Kirakowski, J.: Measuring user-satisfaction with electronic consumer products: the Consumer Products Questionnaire. Int. J. Hum Comput Stud. **69**, 375–386 (2011)

15. Hofstede, G.H.: Dimensions of Culture. 159–181 (1980)

16. Marcus, A.: Cross-cultural user-interface design. Hum.-Comput. Interface Internat (HCII) **2**, 502–505 (2001)

17. Huang, Z., Benyoucef, M.: From e-commerce to social commerce: a close look at design features. Electron. Commer. Res. Appl. **12**, 246–259 (2013)

18. Heinonen, K., Campbell, C., Lord Ferguson, S.: Strategies for creating value through individual and collective customer experiences. Bus. Horiz. **62**, 95–104 (2019)

19. Iglesias, O., Markovic, S., Rialp, J.: How does sensory brand experience influence brand equity? Considering the roles of customer satisfaction, customer affective commitment, and employee empathy. J. Bus. Res. **96**, 343–354 (2019)

20. Ulvydienė, L.: Psychology of Translation in Cross-cultural Interaction. Procedia - Soc. Behav. Sci. **116**, 217–226 (2014)

The Post-advertising Condition.
A Socio-Semiotic and Semio-Pragmatic
Approach to Algorithmic Capitalism

Ruggero Eugeni[✉]

Università Cattolica del Sacro Cuore, Milan, Italy
ruggero.eugeni@unicatt.it

Abstract. The primary hypothesis of this paper is that recent years have seen a shift from digital advertising to post-advertising: thanks to the growing role of machine learning algorithms in communicational processes, advertising has been losing the character of explicitly persuasive addresses to assume that of friendly and open proposals and advice, or even the simple facilitation of everyday purchasing practices. The paper seeks to understand if and under what conditions the socio-semiotic and semio-pragmatic approaches developed in relation to traditional advertising can still be applied to post-advertising phenomena. The paper is divided into three parts. In the first one, the advent of the post-advertising condition is considered. In the second one, Amazon's Alexa, an example of a post-advertising dispositive, is analyzed. In the third part, the question of the use of traditional semiotic concepts and methods for the analysis of post-advertising is examined. The final answer to this question is affirmative, but on the condition that some new conceptual and methodological tools be introduced.

Keywords: Media semiotics · Social semiotics · Socio-semiotics · Semio-pragmatics · Digital advertising · Post-advertising · Big data · Machine learning · Artificial intelligence · Algorithmic capitalism · Media experience · Dispositive

1 Semiotic Approaches from Advertising to Post-advertising

The semiotics of advertising [1] and of marketing [2, 3] accompanied and monitored the developments and transformations of its object of study from the 1960s until today: semiotics followed the metamorphoses of advertising practices and discourses, starting from traditional forms (see Sect. 4), then passing through self-referential and post-modern ones [4], and finally arriving at to the use of advertising in digital and social media [5], including user-generated advertising [6, 7] and online/offline unconventional advertising [8].

The hypothesis behind this paper is that in recent years the world of advertising has been at the center of a break that is not yet entirely over. The main engine of this turn is the use of increasingly sophisticated and refined machine learning algorithms that automate both the brand's communicative manifestations and the purchasing processes carried out by consumers. As a consequence, traditional forms of digital advertising

© Springer Nature Switzerland AG 2019
G. Meiselwitz (Ed.): HCII 2019, LNCS 11579, pp. 291–302, 2019.
https://doi.org/10.1007/978-3-030-21905-5_23

tend to disappear, as a result of ad-blocking software products, for example. At the same time, however, corporate communication does not vanish: on the contrary, it becomes ubiquitous, deeply personalized, and radically relational. In other words, advertising loses the character of explicitly persuasive addresses to assume that of friendly and open proposals and advice, or even the simple facilitation of everyday purchasing practices. I propose to designate this incoming landscape with the term of "post-advertising" condition [9]. Starting from this hypothesis, I seek to understand if and in case with what revision the semiotic approaches developed for the analysis of traditional advertising can still be used for defining and analyzing post-advertising phenomena.

This paper is divided into three parts. In the first, I consider the transformations in the relationship between web media and advertising that have taken place over the last thirty years; I argue that digital communication is currently guided by the logic of algorithmic capitalism, of which post-advertising is an essential component and a typical manifestation. In the second part, I take as a case study the system of Voice User Interface Alexa, by Amazon, which I consider an example of a post-advertising dispositive; the semiotic analysis of two Amazon commercials focused on Alexa allows me to reconstruct the discursive identity of such dispositive. In the final part I ask more systematically if and how the semiotic tools that were used for the analysis of advertising (whether socio-semiotic or semio-pragmatic) can be applied to the study of post-advertising; in the light of my previous analysis my answer is affirmative, but on the condition that some new conceptual and methodological tools are introduced.

2 Algorithmic Capitalism and the Advent of Post-advertising

2.1 From Networked Capitalism to Sensor Capitalism

We can distinguish three major phases of the relationship between web media and digital advertising [10, 11]. In the first phase, which goes from the 1990s until about 2000, the web is considered a new space for the presence of advertising messages. Companies open their sites and buy banners, pop-ups, page takeovers, and so on – all means often considered intrusive. In some cases, companies perceive the potentialities of User Generated Content for the construction of a good reputation (for example in the case of fan pages of characters or media products or discussion in forums, chats and blogs), but the possibility of awkward reactions is always lurking – for example, that of Warner Bros against Harry Potter fans documented by Henry Jenkins [12]. In this phase (which roughly corresponds to Web 1.0) advertising remains quite traditional and tends to produce (both symbolic and economic) value by entering network spaces: we could thus speak here of "networked capitalism".

The second phase of the relationship between web media and advertising spans from around 2000 to 2010. Many events transform the rules of the game: the advent of social media and the transition from "networked communication" to "platformed sociality" [13], the explosion and complexity of User Generated Content, and the spread of mobile media. Two main consequences emerge for web advertising. On the one hand, new forms of "wikinomics" are developed, tending to bypass corporate, institutional communication: the sharing economy and above all the spread of peer-to-peer counselling sites help to develop a suspicious attitude towards big companies and their intrusiveness. Companies respond to these trends in various ways, for example by experimenting with alternative forms of integrated communication such as branded content. In respect to these phenomena, some commentators speak about "post-capitalism" [14].

On the other hand, companies discover the usefulness of the traces left by users in their web browsing as evidence of their habits, tastes and preferences. Although we often talk about "big data", the term is not entirely correct: the data has increased not only in terms of volume, but also of variety (it comes from different sources, in the form of both "captured" and "exhaust" data and metadata [15, 16]), velocity (the speed of acquisition and processing), veracity (the automatized assumption of data reliability) and value (the worth derived from exploiting data) [17]. In general, the term "sensors data" is preferable [18]. As a consequence, brands can better profile advertising proposals and switch from targeted to customized/tailored/personalized advertising [19, 20]. However, messages remain largely traditional, sent by e-mail or through "personalized" banners. Some speak of these phenomena in terms of "platform capitalism" [21], but I think that on the whole the most fitting term is that of "sensor-capitalism".

2.2   From Data Capitalism to Algorithmic Capitalism

The third phase of the relationship between advertising and digital media is the one in which we find ourselves today, inaugurated at the beginning of the 2010s. The main feature of the transformations underway is the advent of a new generation of machine learning algorithms [22] within artificial intelligence studies [23–25], for example, those based on deep- or representation-learning neural networks [26]. These algorithms allow the machines to learn to identify patterns within data without having to write software containing predefined logical rules and instructions: data science distinguishes in this regard between supervised and unsupervised learning. There are different types of learning algorithms, inspired by different conceptions of learning processes (symbolism, connectionism, evolutionism, probabilism, analogism) [27]; all of them can in any case be described as devices able to transform a vast and disordered mass of data as input in a series of very complex but still organized and manageable models as output.

As a consequence, machine learning algorithms typically intervene in the data modelling phase (i.e. the extraction of non-obvious and useful patterns from data cubes); in practice, however, their usefulness manifests itself in all the steps of data flows. First, they proved to be very powerful in the transformation of unstructured, low-density, low-value, big data coming from sensors (so-called "raw data" [28]) into structured, high-density and high-value data, for example in machine vision, natural-language processing, and so on (see also Sect. 3.1). In other terms, these algorithms dynamically implement data cubes by constructing and transforming analytics base tables in real time. Second, they work the data inside the data cubes, transforming them into models that allow advancing reliable predictions; for example, through operations of *clustering* (which allows market segmentation and advertising customization), or through *association-rule mining* processes (which allow to identify groups of products typically purchased together, and then to advance purchasing advice). Finally, machine learning algorithms intervene in the output phase within the various forms with which the interfaces return information to users, from data visualization to interactive voice response (see Sect. 3.1).

Thanks to machine learning algorithms, interactions with data come to serve the small and big needs of every day: what information is relevant to my research (Google), which partner to choose for the evening (Tinder), which television series to watch (Netflix), which book or which detergent to buy (Amazon), and so on. Moreover, they do it through a series of "naturalized" practices that consider machines as an integral part of living and working environments. In this way, the algorithms become "culture machines [i.e.] complex assemblages of abstractions, processes, and people" [29]. In this case, the extreme importance assumed by algorithms in the processes of production and manipulation of values leads me to speak of "algorithmic capitalism".

In this context, traditional banners and ads continue to operate in an increasingly personalized form, thanks to the algorithms of Google Ads, Facebook Ads, Instagram Ads, etc. At the same time, however, traditional advertisements tend to be less visible – due to the spread of ad-blocking software, whose availability and use have grown enormously in recent years (passing in the U.S. from a 15,7% penetration rate in 2014 to an estimated 27,5% in 2020 [30]). Conversely, the dynamics of mutual and disintermediate advice, previously delegated to peer relationships, are now primarily assumed by the algorithms themselves: these, appropriately constructed and trained, become the main agents of the guidelines for purchasing goods, services, products. In this way, we return to the phenomena of post-advertising from which we started; in fact, I consider post-advertising as the most typical form assumed by corporate communication within algorithmic capitalism.

3 The Marvelous Mrs. Alexa

3.1 Alexa as a Post-advertising Dispositive

In 2014, Amazon introduced a line of smart speakers (the Echo series), that offered the possibility of interacting with a digital assistant named Alexa. Alexa can give information in real time (for example on current weather, or traffic situation), play music from various platforms, make phone calls, activate or control home automation appliances, or place orders for goods or services. In this section, I propose to consider Alexa as a typical "post-advertising dispositive"; the analysis of some aspects of Alexa will then allow us to test semiotic tools on post-advertising objects and phenomena.

Alexa is a digital assistant. This category of appliances is the most recent evolution of Vocal User Interfaces (VUI), i.e. tools for interacting with a machine that does not use the traditional Graphic User Interface (GUI) means but instead relies on oral interaction. Typically, a VUI has three components. The first is a vocal sensor connected to human speech recognition (HSR), automatic speech recognition (ASR) and natural language understanding (NLU) software [31]; these components capture the human voice and translate it into sentences that the machine can interpret correctly. The second component is a mechanism for digging for information within a data set, which can present an output corresponding with the input request. The third component is an interface that provides the user with the required information through an Interactive Voice Response (IVR): in recent years research has provided synthetic voices with greater fluidity and emotional coloring, also linked to their gender [32]. A typical VUI application is a chatbot that, faced with a limited set of possible user requests, offers a series of answers chosen from a limited array (for example, in telephone travel booking systems, or complaint services). In some cases, a VUI device can be embedded within a home automation appliance, becoming part of the so-called Internet of Things: in this case, in addition to responding vocally, it can activate and control the appliance (switching on or off an oven, adjusting the home temperature, and so on).

Digital assistants like Alexa derive from the application of machine learning algorithms to VUI devices, a phenomenon typical of algorithmic capitalism. Artificial intelligence has particularly affected the first and second components of VUIs. First, the introduction of machine learning algorithms has significantly improved HSR, ASR, and NLU: they have made it possible to move ever faster from the "raw data" of natural speech to organized data that can be understood and managed by the machine, without having to depend longer on sets of prefixed statements. Secondly, the new machine learning algorithms make it possible to search for the answers requested by the subjects within the universe of big data: queries are no longer limited to prefixed data-sets but can range over any subject, including updates in real time.

Today, we can find four main players in the VUI field: Apple Siri (introduced in 2010), Google Now (introduced in 2013 and replaced in 2016 by Google Assistant), Microsoft Cortana (introduced in 2013), and Amazon Alexa (introduced with Echo speakers in 2014, as noted above). Each of these assistants has specific characteristics related to the company that developed them. In this context "Alexa is your almost perfect shopping assistant, at least for now. Integrating Amazon Prime for shopping, videos, and now, music has given users a straightforward choice to buy into the Amazon ecosystem." [33: p. 10]. In other words, the Alexa system is designed to act as an elicitor or facilitator of practices of purchasing: it is a "shopping medium". Unlike its competitors, Amazon has directly aimed at building a v-commerce (voice-commerce) system; this sector is currently limited (data shows 0.4% of sales as e-commerce in the US for 2018) but destined to expand [34].

It is worth underscoring that at the moment Amazon explicitly denies any intention to introduce advertising messages into Alexa's interactions; traditional advertising coming from Amazon is therefore explicitly banned. Rather, users are "naturally" advised about brands and products best suited to meet their specific needs, with the tendency of enhancing the routine nature of certain consumer behaviors and thereby intensifying brand loyalty. This process takes place through a two-part mechanism. First, brands can develop "skills", i.e. applications intended to implement Alexa's capabilities, that users can activate; for example the Starbucks Reorder Skill allows you to "reorder your usual from one of the last 10 stores you have ordered from before [...] Your Starbucks order will be minutes away when you say 'Alexa, tell Starbucks to start my usual order.'" [35]. Second, the integration of Alexa with some home automation devices (such as refrigerators, printers, and so on) makes it possible to automatically reorder the products that are about to run out from Amazon [36].

From what we have said, we can draw three conclusions. First, Alexa appears to be not only a "voice" but rather an "apparatus," i.e. "[something] that has in some way the capacity to capture, orient, determine, intercept, model, control, or secure the gestures, behaviors, opinions, or discourses of living beings" [37: p. 14]); or even better a "dispositive," i.e. an *assemblage* of technological components, use practices embedded in wider social activities, objects and subjects' roles, spatial and temporal determinations, plans, intentions, and desires [38]. Second, from this point of view it is possible to grasp a specific strategic component of Alexa as dispositive: Amazon rejects by policy any recourse to traditional advertising, in order to configure Alexa as a direct and natural consumer elicitor and facilitator. For this reason, I consider Alexa (more than other digital assistants) as a typical *post-advertising dispositive*. Finally, it must be recognized that as a dispositive Alexa is not just a set of technologies, but has a specific "discursive" identity, i.e. an identity oriented and determined at various levels by social discourses that take it as their object. In order to now explore this identity more thoroughly, I will consider in particular two commercials for Amazon's Alexa broadcast during Super Bowls LII (2018) and LIII (2019).

3.2   A Momentary Lapse of Alexa

Broadcast for the first time during Super Bowl LII, "Alexa Loses Her Voice", a video advertisement lasting 1'30", was the most viewed commercial on Youtube in 2018, with 50.1 million views [39]. The commercial recounts in a comedic tone the catastrophic event in which the voice assistant for Amazon loses her voice because of a sudden cold. All that remains is to find many stand-ins, including a star-studded cast (from the chef Gordon Ramsay to the singer Cardi B, from the actress Rebel Wilson to Sir Anthony Hopkins) that tries, and obviously fails, to replace Alexa. Finally, we hear Alexa saying "Thanks, guys, but I will take it from here"; at the same time, the graphic element of the smile that is part of the Amazon logo is stretched out on the image.

The narrative structure of the commercial is extremely traditional: an initial loss is balanced by a final recovery of the missing element [40], in this case the voice of Alexa. Moreover, as usually happens in the advertising narrative, the missing element becomes an object of desire and therefore of valorization as a consequence of the dysphoric perception of its absence. In other words, the commercial works as a real and effective test of commutation [41], aimed at assessing how and in what measure Alexa's voice is significant in everyday life practices. The result of this procedure is twofold. On the one hand, Alexa and the devices that convey her presence (the various models of Echo Dot), appear flawlessly and fluidly inserted into the physical environments and the life practices of the subjects who use them: the technological component of the dispositive is thoroughly naturalized within the unreflective actions of everyday life. On the other hand, Alexa appears to be a competent, relevant, and non-intrusive presence: for example, her plain and natural "grain of the voice" [42] positively contrasts with the aggressive (Ramsey), shrill and mocking (Cardi B), sensual (Wilson), or subtly threatening (Hopkins) ones of her substitutes. To sum up, Alexa's absence ends up highlighting the qualities of her presence, and above all the fact that she constitutes a perfect form of presence for her user.

Moreover, this narrative structure binds to a specific enunciation regime [43]: the enunciator (identifiable with Amazon) proposes to the enunciatee (the spectator) a communicative contract [44] founded on irony, according to a typical strategy of post-modern advertising [45]. Thus, we find a gap between the reality status of the enunciated story and the relationships at the level of enunciation and narrative discourse [46]: Amazon as enunciator invites the spectator as enunciatee not to take seriously the literal meaning of the story, but only its moral; the presence at the end of the commercial (coinciding with the return of the "true" Alexa) of the Amazon "smile" underlines this enunciative choice. This strategy has an important implication: some sensitive points pertaining to the reputation of Amazon and Alexa can be at the same time declared at the level of story and denied (or, in psychoanalytical terms, "disavowed" [47]) at the level of narrative discourse. I refer in particular to two aspects: the charge against Amazon of promoting a gig economy, for example through the platform The Mechanical Turk (seen in the ad concept, in which big stars are rented to do gigs), and the fear that through the Echo Dots Amazon can watch what happens in the intimacy of the houses (the face of Anthony Hopkins threateningly appearing to the woman who tries to call her husband).

3.3 Alexa Unbound

"We're putting [Alexa] in a lot of stuff now"; unfortunately, however, "there are [still] a lot of fails." The leaks of an Amazon Alexa developer to a stunned colleague in the company's cafeteria are at the center of "Not Everything Makes the Cut," the 1′30″ Amazon advertisement released during the 2019 Super Bowl. The commercial recounts a series of disastrous performances by funny and unlikely devices controlled by Alexa: from Forest Whitaker's toothbrush to Abbi Jacobson and Ilana Glazer's Alexa hot tub (actually, an oversized version of the Echo dot); from an Hal 9000 style interface used by twin astronauts Kelly and Kelly in a spaceship, to Harrison Ford's dog's Alexa collar.

On the one hand, the story presents a situation opposite to that of the previous commercial: while the 2018 advertisement focused on Alexa's absence, the 2019 one plays on her "excessive" presence. Moreover, while in 2018 Alexa was mainly represented in her interactional aspects, the new commercial insists on her operational aspects: the "new" Alexa is not simply a presence able to inform, entertain, play music, or make phone calls through Amazon devices, but has been "embedded" within various kinds of appliances. In this way, the commercial reflects (in paradoxical terms) the new actual Amazon policy, which is tightening various agreements with domestic appliance manufacturers to connect Alexa to the Internet of Things.

On the other hand, the enunciation strategy is similar to that of the previous commercial: the Amazon employee turns out to be an "unreliable narrator" [48], as her story is implicitly denied by the enunciator, relying on a relationship of complicity with the enunciatee who is presumed to be able to correctly interpret what is being shown. The conclusion of the commercial is once again revealing. Harrison Ford looks downcast at the arrival of the huge quantity of gravy and sausages bought by his dog thanks to the Alexa collar, and growls at the animal "I'm not talking to you." In this way, Amazon as an enunciator points out its own "disengagement" (*débrayage*) [44] from the narrator's discourse (the phrase can be interpreted as "it's no [longer] me, Amazon, who is talking to you, the spectator, by referring the discourse of the (unreliable) narrator"), and then a new direct engagement (*embrayage*) of the enunciator expressed by the euphoric tones of the Queen song in the background ("Do not stop me now, I'm having a good time") and the smile of the Amazon logo, which is simultaneously an Amazon signature and an interpretive indication for the viewer.

Furthermore, the enunciation strategy based on irony once more allows the ad to acknowledge and at the same time deny a series of anxieties related to the use of Alexa. It is interesting to note that among the different aspects, the fear that Alexa encourages automatic purchasing practices occupies a prominent place: it is no coincidence that the storyline that stars Harrison Ford and his dog, represented as a kind of compulsive buyer, returns several times in the commercial, and represents the closing gag of the story.

3.4 Alexa's Discursive Identity

The analysis of these two Amazon commercials allows us to draw some conclusions about the discursive identity of Alexa as a post-advertising dispositive. First, the discursive construction of Alexa's identity is based on a semantic and axiological universe in which different areas are blended and hybridized. For example, the recreational-aesthetic values and the practical-utilitarian ones are hardly distinguishable in Alexa's presentations and valorizations: indeed, making a phone call, listening to music, making a purchase, or operating an appliance are similar activities in which cognition, emotion, movement and action are equally co-present.

Second, and consequently, Alexa is presented and tends to be experienced as a dispositive that is perfectly integrated into the network of everyday practices and operations: it is not an object, but rather a form of living presence with which subjects can interact, reflexively assessing at the same time the quality of their presence in living environments. Amazon does not sell technology, but a way of "being in the world" and interacting with the world, while it seeks with the irony of its commercials to defuse the possible anxieties linked to such a condition.

4 Towards a Post-advertising Semiotics

In these conclusions, I take a broader perspective, and ask more generally about the possibility of using the semiotic tools developed for the analysis of traditional advertising in the analysis of post-advertising phenomena. In doing so, I will bear in mind the analysis just carried out of Alexa's discursive identity and its construction.

It is worth recalling the two founding essays at the origin of advertising semiotics. The first one is the well-known work of Roland Barthes, initially published in 1964 and dedicated to the advertisement of Pasta Panzani [49]. Barthes' essay intends to "deconstruct" the advertising image to identify the system of cultural connotations underlying it (for example, its "Italianicity"). At the same time, his semiotic analysis reveals the cultural value of the medium used: in particular, photography is "a message without a code," at the service of an ideology of transparency and immediacy. Barthes' essay thus initiates a tradition of studies that analyzes advertising messages as "signification systems," i.e. "Set[s] of meanings that are generated for a systematic association of various signifiers (brand name, logo, ad texts, etc.) with implicit signifieds relating to personality, lifestyle, desires, etc." [50: p. 23]. Scholars often identified the logic governing these universes in the opposition between simple terms linked by relationships of contrariety, contradiction, or complementarity, as happens in Greimas's semiotic square [44, 51], applied to advertising messages by Floch [52]. Such an approach has proved to be very productive for the reconstruction of the large, mutually articulated, and culturally-based semantic universes determining advertising strategy and in turn determined by them [53, 54]. This approach can be traced back to the strand of structural semiotics and more specifically to the current that would take the name of *socio-semiotics*.

The second founding essay of advertising semiotics in the analysis of printed advertisements was presented by Umberto Eco in *La struttura assente* in 1977 [55]. Despite the explicit reference to Barthes's essay, Eco's goal is different: he tries to understand which rhetorical and semiotic mechanisms the texts use to design and govern an interpretative path for their reader, and how these mechanisms can function persuasively. Eco's hypothesis is that the more an advertisement re-proposes a series of consolidated topoi in apparently new forms, the more it appears reliable to the reader and therefore achieves persuasion. In other terms, the mapping of the semantic fields proper to socio-semiotics is integrated with the analysis of the strategic uses of the same semantic fields within the interpretative paths of the discourse: this approach can be labeled *semio-pragmatic* [56, 57], and is typical of interpretive semiotics.

Here we come to the question that has guided this intervention: is it possible to apply this system of thought and analysis developed by the semiotics of advertising to post-advertising phenomena, such as the Alexa dispositive I analyzed above? My answer is positive, but on the condition that some modifications and developments be added to traditional semiotic instruments. I will limit myself to some brief indications.

First, the socio-semiotic approach should revise the mappings of signification systems intended as the detection of binary oppositions; indeed, we have seen that the domains of signifiers, signified, and values typical of the post-advertising condition are characterized by extreme fragmentation, hybridization and fluidity. For example, the analysis of Alexa's discursive identity showed how the opposition between human subjects and technological objects loses its strength, as does the opposition between playful and practical areas of everyday life. It would probably be more useful rethink signification systems in terms of different "modes of existence" [58, 59] and "modes of presence" [60] through which subjects think and engage with different types of human or artificial agents.

Second, the semio-pragmatic approach should overcome a conception of user activity as purely cognitive and linked to the interpretation of "texts." It should instead deal with the design of the subjects' experiences in their different and related dimensions (sensibility, cognition, emotion, movement and action, and so on), even drawing inspiration from the new models of experience emerging from neurocognitive sciences [61, 62]. At the same time, semio-pragmatics should realize that the experiences thus planned are deployed (and can therefore be identified and analyzed) within complex dispositives and environments that extensively mix texts, objects, spaces, actions, and interactions.

References

1. Bianchi, C.: Semiotic approaches to advertising texts and strategies: narrative, passion, marketing. Semiotica **183**, 243–271 (2011). https://doi.org/10.1515/semi.2011.012
2. Oswald, L.R.: Marketing Semiotics: Signs, Strategies, and Brand Value. Oxford University Press, Oxford (2012)
3. Oswald, L.R.: Creating Value: The Theory and Practice of Marketing Semiotics Research. Oxford University Press, Oxford (2015)
4. Bettetini, G.: Semiotica della comunicazione di impresa (Semiotics of Corporate Communication). Bompiani, Milano (1993)
5. He, J., Shao, B.: Examining the dynamic effects of social network advertising: a semiotic perspective. Telemat. Inform. **35**, 504–516 (2018). https://doi.org/10.1016/j.tele.2018.01.014
6. Kucuck, S.U.: A semiotic analysis of consumer-generated antibranding. Mark. Theory **15**(2), 243–264 (2015). https://doi.org/10.1177/1470593114540677
7. Rossolatos, G.: A socio-semiotic approach to consumer engagement in user-generated advertising. Soc. Semiot. **28**(4), 555–589 (2018). https://doi.org/10.1080/10350330.2017.1381452
8. Peverini, P.: Environmental issues in unconventional social advertising: a semiotic perspective. Semiotica **199**, 219–246 (2014). https://doi.org/10.1515/sem-2013-0126
9. McKee, R., Gerace, T.: Storynomics: Story-Driven Marketing in the Post-Advertising World. Hachette, New York (2018)
10. Fiandaca, D., Burgoyne, P. (eds.): Digital Advertising: Past, Present, and Future. Creative Social, London (2010)
11. McStay, A.: Digital Advertising, 2nd edn. Palgrave Macmillan, London (2016)
12. Jenkins, H.: Convergence Culture: Where Old and New Media Collide. New York University Press, New York (2006)
13. van Dijk, J.: The Culture of Connectivity: A Critical History of Social Media. Oxford University Press, Oxford (2013)
14. Mason, P.: PostCapitalism: A Guide to Our Future. Allen Lane, London (2015)
15. Kitchin, R.: The Data Revolution: Big Data, Open Data, Data Infrastructures, and Their Consequences. Sage, Los Angeles (2014)
16. Kelleher, J.D., Tierney, B.: Data Science. The MIT Press, Cambridge (2018)
17. Mohamed, A., et al.: The state of the art and taxonomy of big data analytics: view from new big data framework. Artif. Intell. Rev. (2019). https://doi.org/10.1007/s10462-019-09685-9
18. Davenport, T.H.: Big Data at Work: Dispelling the Myths, Uncovering the Opportunities. Harvard Business Review, Cambridge (2014)
19. Nesamoney, D.: Personalized Digital Advertising: How Data and Technology Are Transforming How We Market. Pearson Education, Old Tappan (2015)
20. Turow, J.: The Daily You: How the New Advertising Industry Is Defining Your Identity and Your Worth. Yale University Press, New Haven (2013)
21. Srnicek, N.: Platform Capitalism. Polity Press, Cambridge (2017)
22. Mohri, M., Rostamizadeh, A., Talwalkar, A.: Foundations of Machine Learning, 2nd edn. The MIT Press, Cambridge (2018)
23. Bostrom, N.: Superintelligence: Paths, Dangers, Strategies. Oxford University Press, Oxford (2014)
24. Kaplan, J.: Artificial Intelligence: What Everyone Needs to Know. Oxford University Press, Oxford (2016)
25. Husain, A.: The Sentient Machine: The Coming Age of Artificial Intelligence. Scribner, New York (2017)

26. Sejnowski, T.J.: The Deep Learning Revolution. The MIT Press, Cambridge (2018)
27. Domingos, P.: The Master Algorithm: How the Quest for the Ultimate Learning Machine Will Remake Our World. Basic Books, New York (2015)
28. Gitelman, L. (ed.): "Raw Data" is an Oxymoron. The MIT Press, Cambridge (2013)
29. Finn, E.: What Algorithms Want: Imagination in the Age of Computing. The MIT Press, Cambridge (2017)
30. Statista: The Statistics Portal. https://www.statista.com/statistics/804008/ad-blocking-reach-usage-us/. Accessed 15 Feb 2019
31. Pieraccini, R.: The Voice in the Machine: Building Computers That Understand Speech. The MIT Press, Cambridge (2012)
32. Nass, C., Brave, S.: Wired for Speech How Voice Activates and Advances the Human-Computer Relationship. The MIT Press, Cambridge (2005)
33. Dasgupta, R.: Voice User Interface: Design Moving from GUI to Mixed Modal Interaction. Apress, Hyderabad (2018). https://doi.org/10.1007/978-1-4842-4125-7
34. Dignan, L.: Amazon Alexa, why aren't more people doing voice commerce? ZDNet, 20 December 2018. https://www.zdnet.com/article/amazon-alexa-why-arent-more-people-doing-voice-commerce/. Accessed 15 Feb 2019
35. Starbucks Reorder. https://www.amazon.com/Starbucks-Coffee-Co-Reorder/dp/B01F9RRL46. Accessed 15 Feb 2019
36. Koksal, I.: How Alexa Is Changing The Future of Advertising. Forbes, 11 December 2018. https://www.forbes.com/sites/ilkerkoksal/2018/12/11/how-alexa-is-changing-the-future-of-advertising/#19b8ffd41d4d. Accessed 15 Feb 2019
37. Agamben, G.: What is an Apparatus? And Other Essays. Stanford University Press, Stanford (2009)
38. Casetti, F.: The Lumière Galaxy: Seven Key Words for the Cinema to Come. Columbia University Press, New York (2015)
39. Ives, N.: Amazon Alexa Super Bowl Commercial Leads 10 Most-Viewed Ads on YouTube in 2018. The Wall Street Journal (2018). https://www.wsj.com/articles/amazon-alexa-super-bowl-commercial-leads-10-most-viewed-ads-on-youtube-in-2018-11545033660. Accessed 15 Feb 2019
40. Barthes, R.: Introduction to the structural analysis of narratives. In: Barthes, R. (ed.) Image Music Text, pp. 79–124. Fontana Press, London (1977)
41. Lorusso, A.M.: Cultural Semiotics: For a Cultural Perspective in Semiotics. Palgrave MacMillan, Houdmills (2015)
42. Barthes, R.: The grain of the voice. In: Barthes, R. (ed.) Image Music Text, pp. 179–189. Fontana Press, London (1977)
43. Eugeni, R.: Enunciation, film and -. In: Branigan, E., Buckland, W. (eds.) The Routledge Encyclopedia of Film Theory, pp. 157–161. Routledge, London (2014)
44. Greimas, A.J., Courtés, J.: Semiotics and Language: An Analytical Dictionary. Indiana University Press, Bloomington (1982)
45. Foster Wallace, D.: E Unibus Pluram: Television and U.S. Fiction. Rev. Contemp. Fict. **13** (2), 151–194 (1993)
46. Chatman, S.: Story and Discourse: Narrative Structure in Fiction and Film. Cornell University Press, Ithaca (1978)
47. Laplanche, J., Pontalis, J.B.: The Language of Psycho-Analysis. The Hogarth Press, London (1973)
48. Booth, W.C.: The Rhetoric of Fiction, 2nd edn. The University of Chicago Press, Chicago (1983)
49. Barthes, R.: Rhetoric of the image. In: Barthes, R. (ed.) Image Music Text, pp. 32–51. Fontana Press, London (1977)

50. Beasley, R., Danesi, M.: Persuasive Signs: The Semiotics of Advertising. Mouton de Gruyter, Berlin (2002)
51. Greimas, A.J.: On Meaning: Selected Writings in Semiotic Theory. University of Minnesota Press, Minneapolis (1987)
52. Floch, J.-M.: Semiotics, Marketing and Communication: Beneath the Signs, the Strategies. Palgrave, New York (2001)
53. Floch, J.-M.: Visual Identities. Continuum, London (2000)
54. Mangano, D., Marrone, G.: Brand language: methods and models of semiotic analysis. In: Rossolatos, G. (ed.) Handbook of Brand Semiotics, pp. 46–88. Kassel University Press, Kassel (2015)
55. Eco, U.: La struttura assente (The Absent Structure). Bompiani, Milano (1977)
56. Eco, U.: The Role of the Reader: Explorations in the Semiotics of Texts. Indiana University Press, Bloomington (1981)
57. Odin, R.: A semio-pragmatic approach to the documentary film. In: Buckland, W. (ed.) The Film Spectator: From Sign to Mind, pp. 227–235. Amsterdam University Press, Amsterdam (1995)
58. Latour, B.: An Inquiry into Modes of Existence: An Anthropology of the Moderns. Harvard University Press, Cambridge (2013)
59. Souriau, É.: The Different Modes of Existence. Univocal, Minneapolis (2015)
60. Noë, A.: Varieties of Presence. Harvard University Press, Cambridge (2012)
61. D'Aloia, A., Eugeni, R.: Neurofilmology: an introduction. In: D'Aloia, A., Eugeni, R. (eds.) Neurofilmology: Audiovisual Studies and the Challenge of Neurosciences, special issue of Cinéma et Cie. International Film Studies Journal, vol. XIV, pp. 22–23, 9–26 (2014)
62. Eugeni, R.: La neurofilmologie. Une théorie pragmatique de l'audiovisuel en dialogue avec les sciences neurocognitives. ¿Interrogations?, Numéro special: Du pragmatisme en sciences humaines et sociales. Bilan et perspectives, 27 (2019). http://www.revue-interrogations.org/La-neurofilmologie-Une-theorie. Accessed 15 Feb 2019

Do Consumers Dream of Digital Advertising?
New Communication Rules in Social Media

Mauro Ferraresi[(✉)]

IULM-International University of Languages and Media, 20141 Milan, Italy
mauro.ferraresi@iulm.it

Abstract. The aim of this paper is to analyze the recent form of communications and the rhetoric rules that nowadays are used in order to optimize the advertising impact in social media. After having described, with the help of literature, the main communicative guidelines for new media and social media, we will test the new communication rules with the consumers.

Therefore, to better elaborate these topics, we will make use of an exploratory research conducted in the IULM University of Milan in spring 2019. The research will answer to the likes and dislikes regarding the social media communication and advertising. Thus the consumer research findings can help researchers and marketers to better understand the birth of those new forms of communication. Another focus of the research will be the question if and when the social technology is a bias and to what extent. Finally, do consumers love the digital advertising on social media?

Actually, every new technology requires new languages and, a fortiori, this must happen when the new technology impact has to do with media. In sum, the social media seem to be a good ground to explore recent changes in communication and specifically in advertising communication.

The findings of the exploratory research can lead to new questions. In other words, questions could arise as followings: communication and advertising change the same? At the same pace? Do they go in the same direction? And to what extent? Advertising simply have to follow the new communication rules or advertising is forced to use and to invent new form of communication?

The present paper will only be able to outline and quickly schematize possible answers to the questions that, indeed, are bound to develop further considerations and further researches.

Keywords: Advertising · Social media · Communication rules

1 Introduction

Advertising and internal communication are two sides of the same coin. The two areas, separated until about ten years ago, are now much more interpenetrated in intents and formulations. More often figures of speech, themes and arguments and how to handle them, plus the creativity, are coming out from advertising style, both through old media but also through new media, since they are equally useful in internal communication (see, Artuso and Mason 2008; Barone and Fontana 2005 and Pastore and Vernuccio 2008).

© Springer Nature Switzerland AG 2019
G. Meiselwitz (Ed.): HCII 2019, LNCS 11579, pp. 303–318, 2019.
https://doi.org/10.1007/978-3-030-21905-5_24

After all, the intended effect is the same for internal and external communication, to sell a product, the company itself and its internal audiences, thus fulfilling a task fundamentally equal to that performed by classical advertising. Definitions are different but the semantic substances are not, such as the good corporate climate i.e. the goodwill of classic advertising. The two streams of communication are more and more inter-penetrating each other.

2 The Methodology of the Research

This paper is based on a questionnaire on advertising and communication given in January 2019 to about 700 respondents, 50% men and 50% women, distributed throughout the country. The percentage subdivision for macro areas was as follows: 26% in the north-west, almost 19% in the north-east, about 20% in the center and the remaining 35% in the south and in the islands. The graduates were almost 15%, the rest graduates, or women and men who had discontinued their studies after compulsory schooling.

As for the socioeconomic class to which they belong, 36% declared an income under 18,000 euro, 48% an income between 18,000 and 70,000 euro and only 2% declared an income of over 70,000 euro. The remaining ones preferred not to answer.

3 Findings

The questionnaire immediately shows what were, and still today are, the main functions of advertising, at least in the people's perception. The two main functions are creativity and hammering. Figure 1 in fact shows that respondents identify as its main charac-teristics of advertising its great inventive power together with the insistent ability to speak continuously to its public and not only to that; for the sake of truth, let's add that this last feature is allowed more than anything else by the results of a good (pounding and hammering) media planning.

The advertising speech, in fact, continually elaborates themes, figures, forms and narratives often derived from the present times and inevitably enriched with inven-tiveness, in language, in storytelling, and also with regard to the visual power and impact. On the other hand, every new inventive, but generally speaking every new advertising communication, is obliged to repeat the message until the exhaustion, continually proposing the same message again and again, following the media planning.

If we had to identify two historical adv guru, whose creative styles are somehow recognized by the people perception as it emerges in Fig. 1, we should certainly name William (Bill) Bernbach with his *negative approach* and the his exquisite irony (Ferraresi 2017, 143) and the theory of the *unique selling proposition* and the ham-mering, carried out by Rosser Reeves (ibid., 141). Bernbach is recognized as the most important advertising figure, the innovator and the creator who was the first to succeed in bending the creative need of advertising communication to the business logic, thus giving life to the modern advertising agency. He was also the first to invent the creative

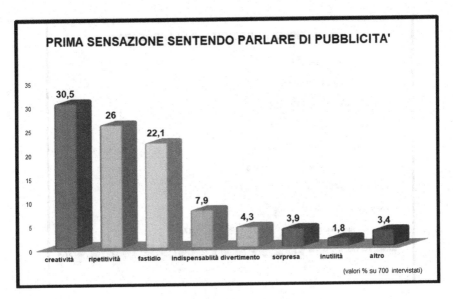

Fig. 1. Advertising perception.

couple, believing that advertising was a verbo-visual communication and that therefore copywriters and art directors had to work together, in concert, to produce the perfect fusion of words and images able to surprise, entertain, make people feel, think, act, and experience about the brands.

Rosser Reeves, instead, a man of linear character and simple culture, with a straightforward personality, managed to translate those aspects of character into a business idea. In fact, every new advertisement was based on a single concept, which had to be simple, clear and direct. No frills, no turnaround in Reeves commercials. For him creativity had to be ancillary, that is to say, following the will to communicate more on that particular product or service. Moreover, not satisfied, Reeves theorized the need to repeat several times that simple and straightforward idea present in the advertising release, until the current or potential consumer had well implanted it in the brain. A sort of mental hammering.

Reeves's approach seems to collect an important percentage of responses in our questionnaire. At least, this seems what Fig. 1 testify. In fact, Fig. 1 shows that more than 48% perceive advertising as a hammering. And annoying communication And it is important to note that 22% consider this characteristic to be strongly negative and boring. On the other hand, you can consider the answers that define advertising as fun and surprising, a total of almost 39%, as the result of the creativity in adv.

However, combining the results of Fig. 1 with those of Fig. 2 the Bernbach approach is still winning: actually people prefer the creativity and they enjoy creative, fun, surprising and also fantastic and unpredictable advertisements. These character-istics are loved by 53% of the answers, reflecting a creative appreciation that seems not to have failed over the years.

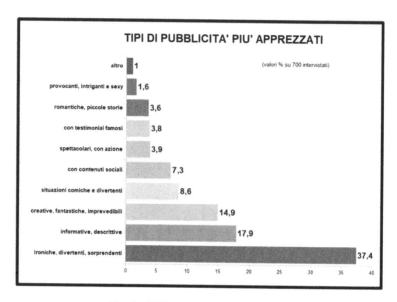

Fig. 2. Different types of advertising.

It should also be noted that more than 7% of respondents today appreciate those advertisements that deal with social issues and use those themes to promote a product or service. Among various theories and models that analyze advertising, we can choose those according to which the messages of advertising are leaning on the dominant value system, which is somehow conveyed and translated into the various adv. releases. (see Polesana 2016) Thus we can define adv. as a funhouse mirror that reflect, nevertheless, dominant social ideas together with costumes, habits and the way we consume.

That 7% turns out to be a precious indicator of a socio-cultural trend according to which we, as a consumers, want to have knowledge of traceability, and we want to know the social impact, and the ecological footprint for each product. And we, as consumers like to find all those information in a narrative form, so that inside the advertising message those values, those themes, those information can be turned in storytelling.

The third figure that we report appears explicit in underlining and reiterating that advertising is also and above all a source of information. This theme has long been a pet subject for the Italian sociologist like Fabris who, in his writings on advertising, believed that information was an asset, bringing to a large number of people the knowledge of products, goods, services, technological innovations and in general the whole process of innovation brought about by progress and consumption, in a simple and direct way, sometimes even fun and fascinating. (Fabris 1992, 2003) Such a concept seems today to be clearly perceived by the majority of those interviewed who, despite the annoyance deriving from a communication that is often too insistent, still seem to appreciate its informative side.

However, the appreciation shown in Fig. 3 by respondents should not make us forget that advertising is loved and hated at the same time: accepted, though badly tolerated. This is what emerges from the topic discussed in Fig. 4, which explains to us that we do not have fun with advertising.

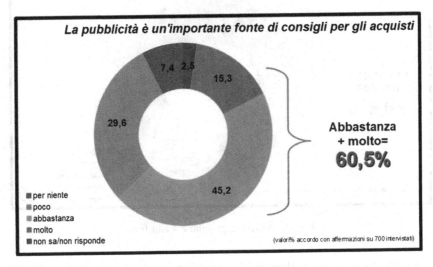

Fig. 3. Information in advertising.

Why such a statement in Fig. 4 is clearly opposite to what was previously discussed? In our opinion, it is necessary to separate the comprehension of advertising as a whole from the advertising intended as individual ads and single commercials. In fact, the question in Fig. 4 refers to the entire advertising discourse, and doesn't go deep into the specific adv. discourses, nor discusses the various adv. types and the different ways themes and figures can be handled. In the latter case the answers are apparently more flattering, because they give to advertising an important share of creativity, entertainment, fascination. On the other side, taken as a whole, the advertising discourse produces an informative overload that, obviously, can not be tolerated any longer. Advertising enlarge and enriches the possibility of buying and consuming, and that's could be fine or at least acceptable, but if this information becomes excessive, exaggerated and if during a normal day commercials are more frequents than waves in a rough sea, then we find ourselves facing a sort of a map (tips for the purchases) that has become immense, complex and articulated as the same territory (i.e. the occasions of consumption). This is the reason for that amount of 60% and more answers that deny lightness and fun to advertising. The reason is further confirmed by the answer to another statement reported in the questionnaire where advertising is considered too intrusive: more than 85% of respondents consider true this statement.

Perhaps the golden age of advertising is done. Is it so? Perhaps, the driving force of that way of communication that certainly sinks its roots into the very heart of Western civilization and developed together with the very beginnings of human commerce, is weakening.

Actually, we know that there are advertising communications dating back to the ancient Babylonian civilization, five thousand years before Christ. In Tebe an inscription

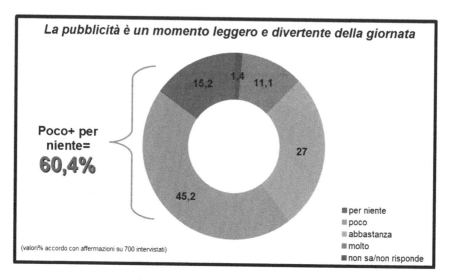

Fig. 4. Advertising: lightness and fun.

dating back to the second millennium BC has been found. The inscription said: "The Hapù weaver's shop, where the most beautiful canvases of the whole Tebe are woven, according to the taste of each one". (see Pelloso, Stigliano, in Ferraresi 2017, 134) More recently there are important traces of advertising and visual communication depicted over the walls in the ruins of the roman town of Pompei (Ferraresi 2002).

However, despite those signs so far away, advertising as we know it today, men and women of the contemporary world, is differently structured and designed. The advertising communication of our times was born in Madison Avenue, New York, in the twenties. In those years William Bernbach started the organizational and creative staff; he invented the creative couple and in the thirties the media developed in such a way, ready to become an excellent advertising vehicle. In those days a nephew of Freud, Edward Bernays, gave birth to a new discipline, Public Relation, a discipline able to understand the sociological and psychological aspects of the masses in order to better grasp convictions and habits of consumption. Bernays was the inventor of modern propaganda. (Bernays 2008) In short, in those years we witness the dawn of a new and modern form of communication, endowed, for better and for worse, with new rules and high effectiveness. According to the answers gathered in Fig. 5, that propulsive drive seems to have been exhausted and advertising seems no longer able to improve. She is really ugly and suffers a fall in creativity.

Which subjects should take care of a new start in advertising? Who should improve it both on the rhetorical-aesthetic level and on effectiveness level? For Italian respondents the answer to these questions is clear: this difficult step towards new heights of creativity cannot be taken in account by creative director or by advertising agencies, instead the companies themselves should carry out a Copernican revolution and, courageously, they can open new possibilities and work for new advertising languages.

Fig. 5. The worsening of the quality in advertising.

On the other side, advertising is something that companies can not do without, and this observation is considered true for more than 87% of respondents (Fig. 6).

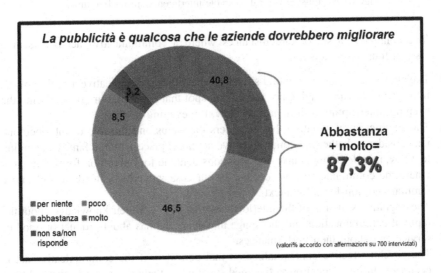

Fig. 6. Companies and advertising.

Figure 7 introduces the very important question of the context. In fact, the appreciation of an advertisement largely depends on the context. A simple reflection by Seth Godin can help us. The author, the theorist of permission marketing, says that selling a product to someone who wants to listen to you is much more effective than interrupting strangers who do not want to listen to you. (1999) Advertising, especially tv commercials, often performs an unsolicited interruption and breaks into our homes without asking for permission nor taking into account the question about the context of communication.

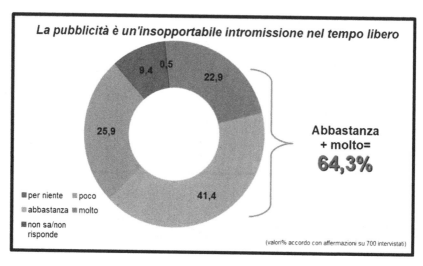

Fig. 7. Advertising is an unbearable interference in our free time.

The context is a set of circumstances where a communicative act occurs, and consists of four main elements.

1. The physical, spatial or temporal situation where the communicative act takes place: in our case we can imagine the advertising spot that enters in our homes during the evening, interrupting a film, an interview, the evening news.
2. The socio-cultural situation that considers the status and the role of interlocutors, i.e. considers whether the communicative act takes place within a family belonging to a low, middle or high class, and also considers the formal or non-formal moment where the communicative act occurs. In our case, advertising tends to fall into a familiar and non-formal context.
3. The cognitive situation of the interlocutors, that is to say their knowledge about the topic of communication and the image that everyone has about product or good or service and about their performances.
4. The psycho-affective contextualization that considers if the communicative act is occurring during a silent or participated situation, if there is tension or tranquility in the family, if the day events has produced serenity or anxiety, etc. All these elements build the complete meaning that that advertising act produces. Simply speaking, the contest mark the difference between the utterer meaning and the receiver meaning. In "Kant and the Platypus" Eco deals with a series of semiotic

questions concerning cognitive processes and consolidates the idea that meaning can be delineated only on the basis of continuous negotiations. Eco (1999) his point of view help us to understand that even in advertisement the context produces an important meaning negotiation, up to distort sense and communication effect. Figure 7 explains that the brute force modality really is not the best way to produce an advertising campaign. The latter can be distorted, or rejected following of the four elements of the context we discussed.

Reactions can be like that: "I do not want advertising here and now in my house; I do not want to see goods too far from my lifestyle; I do not want to receive advertising from that product because I know it doesn't work, or because I hate the company that I consider reality a polluter, or an exploiter. I do not want to see advertising because I'm not in the ideal state of mind to enjoy it."

These can be different explanations of that high percentage (64, 3%) that defines advertising as an unbearable intrusion.

In the followings, questionnaire specifically investigated the characteristics of advertising on television and the characteristics of internet advertising.

The result about television is illustrated in Fig. 8 and in Fig. 9.

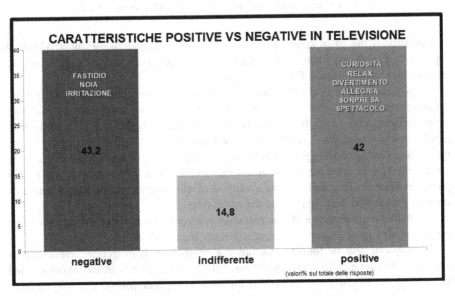

Fig. 8. Positive and negative characteristics attributed to advertising on TV.

Figure 8 shows likes and dislikes in television commercials. To explain it in a formula we will say that advertising generates negativity with regard to the circumstances of the enunciation but generates positivity with regard to the subjects of the utterances, which from time to time can be fun, surprising, spectacular.

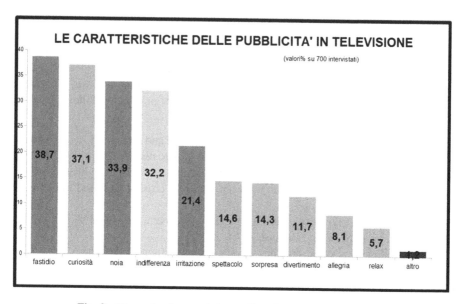

Fig. 9. The main characteristics attributed to advertising on TV.

Curiosity is the main spring that seems to keep the advertising afloat. Figure 9 suggests that, amid so many negative aspects, an advertising story, if he is able to intrigue, then he vigorously fights his battle.

To provide a more in-depth explanation of why curiosity and annoyance in television advertising have more or less the same percentage, we must take into account some considerations of applied psychology dedicated to the stories. According to a popular study whose main results are now traceable also on the web (http://www.psicologiaapplicata.com/leggere-fa-bene-al-cervello/) to read and be involved in a story is very effective in reducing stress. According to the researchers, reading, and participating as listeners to a narrative, is a method of effective relaxation that generates a sense of escape and participation, at the same time.

"… the total immersion and concentration in a book causes the body to concentrate less on its own muscles, and consequently relax them." (Ibidem)

A study can also be found in Goleman's "Emotional Intelligence", especially as regards to the connections and intersections between our two minds, the emotional and the rational. (1995) In short, everything happens as if participation in a story "glues" the subject to the story itself, both chemically and emotionally. Therefore the "tearing" that can be produced by an abrupt interruption generates stress that inevitably flows negatively on the subsequent narration (in our case the advertising spot that breaks in). That why 38.7% of respondents are bothered with advertising. If the new storytelling arouses curiosity then allows us to "glue" to the narration that has taken over again.

A parallel analysis conducted on internet advertising, as shown in Fig. 10 and in Fig. 11, explains why the online advertisements are even more annoying. The reasons for this unpleasantness are many. Let's focus on four elements of differentiation of the network. the elements (not all) through which the network works: proximity, networked public, socialcasting, and people relations.

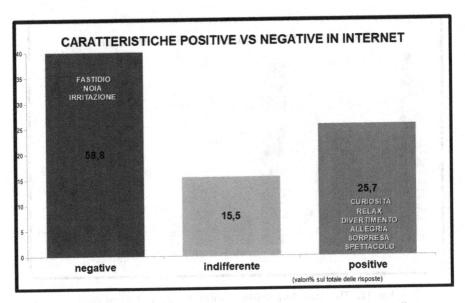

Fig. 10. Positive and negative characteristics attributed on advertising on line.

As for the proximity of new media we must say that it is both physical and psychological. We continuously use electronic media such as tablets and smartphones, we always carry them with us by placing them before our eyes. Moreover, proximity is psychological in the sense that our sites, our profiles on Facebook, Instagram, Twitter, etc., are experienced as private virtual spaces where the advertising interventions are badly tolerated.

Networked public explains that there is no longer on the network a difference between a passive public and a public content producer. (Boyd 2007, 2010 and Van Dijk 1999)

Socialcasting is the result of the technological innovation of the network and of web 2.0. With socialcasting everyone communicates with everyone, imposing that era of mass self-communication that Castells speaks about (2006, 2009).

People relations explain that the raw material, i.e. the content of the web are people with their passions, habits, customs, stories, lifestyles and worlds Bennato (2011). This is why the discipline of content marketing addresses and communicates with people, with employees, with their stories.

On the web it is no longer enough, in fact it is totally wrong to say: "We are the leading company in the market", because the phrase sounds emptied of all information content and, above all, is not addressed to people but is only self-referential. What network wants from companies, generally speaking, is hearing the true company voice telling true stories without hiding behind the screen of promotional and self-referential communication Pasquali (2003).

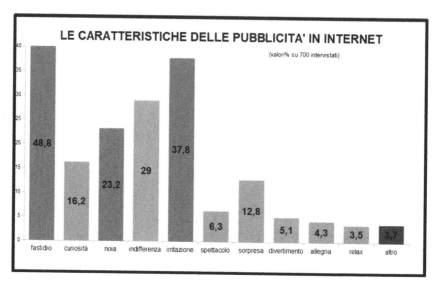

Fig. 11. The main characteristics attributed to advertising on line.

Online the need for a new advertising communication is very strong. This need follows new forms of diffusion and, alongside the visibility acquired typical of old media, develops the visibility owned. Online everyone is now a small Berlusconi, a media owner of many mass self-communication media. Thus, thanks to the memes and virality of network communication, it happens that many other users can talk and amplify our releases and our news, for free. This is what is called visibility gained.

The new advertising communication is no longer direct and unidirectional. It has become a sort of contextual deepening into the consumer's mind, not by forcing his thoughts but by accompanying them, as happens in the sponsored communication.

Online contents and people are back to the center of advertising and communication. This is the reason why storytelling importance is increasing. Storytelling puts people in the center catching their attention.

If these rules are not followed, if the advertising communication adheres to the old methods, then the people's refusal of the network becomes almost total. Therefore the explanation of Fig. 11, that shows high percentages of annoyance and irritation regarding the classic advertising communication, is that on the web advertising becomes something else, it becomes a story, a narration of proximity: simple, direct and warm. Sometime ironic and sarcastic.

Figure 12 compares the popularity and non-acceptance of advertising on TV and online advertising. The percentages are important: indifferent and negatives advertising exceed 74%. But we have already noted that this is due to the fact that online advertising must be completely different.

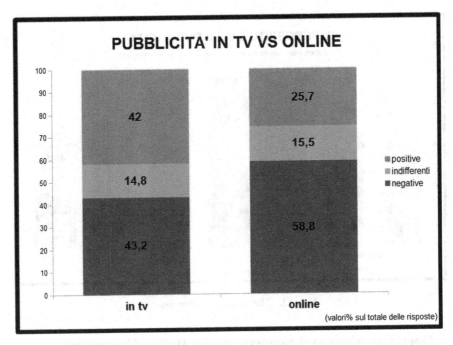

Fig. 12. Tv vs online.

Before concluding this outlook, we report the results of an extrapolation concerning the preferred media as advertising vehicles: television, newspapers, online, radio or outdoor advertising.

The answers tell us that in Italy television advertising was ranked first by the largest number of respondents. Within the answers there is an obvious polarization between those who put it on the first step of the podium and who, instead, relegates it in the back of the fourth and fifth place. Online advertising is by far the least appreciated with 38.4% of respondents who do not hesitate to leave it at the bottom of the ranking. Radio advertising tends to be placed in the center of the ranking, without infamy and without praise. Newspaper advertising deserves, according to the most, the silver square, therefore is well accepted. Finally, outdoor advertising is on the first step of the podium with a more flattering score than all the others (over 32%). It is thus crowned with the gold medal of preference over all types of promotional communication conveyed by the various media analyzed.

Figure 13 is simply summarizing the perceived publicity with regard to "enough" and "very" answers. The figure contemplates and collects all means of communication, without distinction. The end result seems to be that of an advertisement perceived as very intrusive; however, it is essential and provides advice, but in any case, certainly to be improved.

Fig. 13. The perceived advertising.

4 Open Questions and Suggestions for Italian Companies

Analyzing the answers to the open questions collected by the questionnaire it is interesting to note that the range of memorable advertisements are mostly linked to the big brands and that, on the other hand, those same big brands are often mentioned both in advertising more fun and appreciated both among those that like less.

So, for example, in the first choices both positive and negative, Mulino Bianco and Buondì collect many mentions. Nutella is massively present in the minds of the interviewees, especially in the positive, despite some of its nominations among the advertising products that do not like.

The brands, especially Tim and Wind, are also receiving considerable attention.

Finally, the online situation is even more fluid than what is observed for television advertising, in the sense that the level of memorability is decidedly lower and the cases mentioned are more heterogeneous.

As for the suggestions to Italian companies to improve the quality of their advertising, the suggestions provided by the respondents are not extremely numerous and varied and can be summarized in the following points we list here without order of importance:

- Respondents ask for quality in advertising: "Do less but do it with quality", "Spots more and more beautiful like films to improve the quality of the message", "Do less but of higher quality", "Decrease quantity, increase quality", "Focus on quality, investing more money";
- Respondents are also looking for more creativity: "Advertiser must have more imagination and creativity", "Being more creative and stimulating is really a plus", "Why not proposing more creative and surprising ideas?", "More creative and less repetitive", "Less banal and repetitive", "avoiding repetitiveness, devising a dedicated Carosello space";

- They look for diversification, courage and originality: "To find original ideas and out of the box", "More creativity and originality; differentiate yourself ", "They must invest more in the originality of the spot but always keeping in mind that the important thing is to enhance the characteristics of the sponsored product/service", "Less stereotypes, which would make the most original advertisements", "Choose new situations, innovative subjects, original and engaging movies", "It takes a bit of diversity";
- Advertising is too much. Respondents want short messages, brevity and sincerity: "Short and concise", "Being shorter but more effective", "Shorten sketches", "Shorter sketches and more informative", "Give brief information on the good quality of their production" verification", "Advertising must be more sincere and less repetitive";
- They also like precision of information: "Shorter and less absurd", "Shorter and informative", "Indicative messages on products", "Make them as short as possible, while keeping clear in the message you want to give", "Being very essential, precise and direct, without wandering or being repetitive";
- They like truthfulness: "Communicating the truth", "Making them more likely to normal life", "Telling the truth and not deceiving the consumers";
- Respondents want irony and fun: "Be ironic and funny and at the same time give some information about the product", "They should make them interesting and ironic, less obvious", "More ironic and light", "Cheerful and carefree advertising... very ironic", "To focus more on irony and the values of the new generations: such as integration and curiosity towards what is not known. It seems to me that advertising in Italy speaks a language that is not the current one", "Make it less heavy, more ironic and fun", "Be ironic and funny and at the same time provide some information on the product";
- Advertising must be less intrusiveness and less repetitive: "Be less intrusive", "Less intrusive especially with background music at very high volume", "Less repetitiveness, more interesting content", "Less repetitions of the same advertising";
- Finally, respondents ask for a less vulgar, stereotyped advertising and they dislike the commodification of women: "Avoiding to propose standardized content, not original or creative, just commercialization of the woman", "Being creative and less stereotypical use of beautiful women", "Make it less intrusive, less sexist and less stupid", "Use less content associated with sexuality or ambiguity and focus only on the product's quality".

References

Artuso, P., Mason, G.: La nuova comunicazione interna. Reti, metafore, conversazioni, narrazioni. FrancoAngeli, Milano (2008)

Bernays, E.: Propaganda: Della manipolazione della opinione pubblica in democrazia. FaustoLupetti editore, Bologna (2008)

Barone, M., Fontana, A.: Prospettive per la comunicazione interna e il benessere organizzativo. Appartenere, integrarsi e comunicare nell'organizzazione che cambia. (Ed. by, G. Del Mare). FrancoAngeli, Milano (2005)

Bennato, D.: Sociologia dei media digitali. Laterza, Roma (2011)

Boyd, D.: Why Youth (Heart) Social Network Sites: The Role of Networked Publics in Teenage Social Life. MacArthur Foundation Series on Digital Learning – Youth, Identity, and Digital Media Volume (Ed. by, D. Buckingham). MIT Press, Cambridge (2007)

Boyd, D.: Social Network Sites as Networked Publics: Affordances, Dynamics, and Implications. In: Papacharissi, Z. (ed.) Networked Self: Identity, Community, and Culture on Social Network Sites, pp. 39–58 (2010)

Castells, M.: The Internet Galaxy: Reflections on the Internet, Business, and Society. Oxford University Press, Oxford (2006)

Castells, M.: Communication Power. Oxford University Press, Oxford (2009)

Eco, U.: Kant and the Platypus: Essays on Language and Cognition. Secker and Warburg, London (1999)

Fabris, G.: La pubblicità teoria e prassi. Franco Angeli, Milano (1992)

Fabris, G.: Il nuovo consumatore: verso il postmoderno. Franco Angeli, Milano (2003)

Ferraresi, M.: Pubblicità e comunicazione. Carocci, Roma (2002)

Ferraresi, M. (ed.): Pubblicità: teorie e tecniche. Carocci, Roma (2017)

Godin, S.: Permission Marketing: Turning Strangers into Friends, and Friends into Customers. Simon & Schuster, New York (1999)

Goleman, D.: Emotional Intelligence. Bantam, New York (1995)

Pasquali, F.: I nuovi media. Tecnologie e discorsi sociali. Carocci, Roma (2003)

Pastore, A., Vernuccio, M.: Impresa e comunicazione. Principi e strumenti per il management. Maggioli editore, Santarcangelo di Romagna (2008)

Pelloso, G., Stigliano, G.: Gli stili creative. In: Pubblicità: teorie e tecniche. Carocci, Roma (2017)

Polesana, M.A.: Pubblicità e valori. Nuovi consumi e nuovi messaggi per una società che cambia. FrancoAngeli, Milano (2016)

Van Dijk, J.: The Network Society: Social Aspects of New Media. Routledge, London (1999)

Customer Preference and Latent Needs Analysis Using Data of TV Viewing and Web Browsing

An Guo[1(✉)], Kohei Otake[2(✉)], and Takashi Namatame[3(✉)]

[1] Graduate School of Science and Engineering,
Chuo University, Hachiōji, Japan
lluo3330474382@gmail.com
[2] School of Information and Telecommunication Engineering, Tokai University,
2-3-23, Takanawa, Minato-ku, Tokyo 108-8619, Japan
otake@tsc.u-tokai.ac.jp
[3] Faculty of Science and Engineering, Chuo University,
1-13-27, Kasuga, Bunkyo-ku, Tokyo 112-8551, Japan
2nama@indsys.chuo-u.ac.jp

Abstract. In recent years, with the needs of TV viewing change in Japan. TV viewing changes from long time to short time. In order to prevent the viewing time from decreasing as it is, the need to predict customers' taste for TV viewing is increasing. This research focuses on several types of TV viewing, i.e. real time and time shift viewing, in addition, web browsing of customers in view of television viewing is considered. We will grasp the viewing tendency of the customer and predict the TV viewing of customers.

Keywords: TV viewing · Time shift · Web browsing · Cluster analysis

1 Introduction

In recent years, due to diffusion of recorder and the spread of the Internet, the functions of television are changing, the purpose of watching television also changed [1]. So, it changes the TV industry circumstance. Therefore, it is an important issue for predicting customer's preferences and the latent needs. Then, TV viewing changes from a long time to a short time, and the positive consciousness to the television decreases. As a result, it is thought that the viewing time of the people of the world is decreasing, and the viewing time is reduced. In this study, we predict what kinds of customers can be preference-oriented, faithful customers for what kind of programs, that is, the need to predict customers' actions for watching television is increasing.

Looking at the TV viewing time as a customer's loyalty, we should pay attention to how long watching of TV on weekdays customers should Kimura reported the statistics about Japanese TV viewing behavior on long-term change from the viewpoint of behavior and consciousness of the studies [1]. He gathered TV viewing data both 2010 and 2015 from 2400 monitors then he found that many monitors reduced watching TV, from the viewing time of television for 30 min to 2 h for short time, 3 h for normal

© Springer Nature Switzerland AG 2019
G. Meiselwitz (Ed.): HCII 2019, LNCS 11579, pp. 319–329, 2019.
https://doi.org/10.1007/978-3-030-21905-5_25

viewing, 4 h for long time viewing, 5 years viewing trend variation Data is available for 2400 people all over the world, customers in the former age group increased (35% to 38%) for short time, ordinary viewing (21% to 19%), long-time viewing (40% to 37%) decreased (see Fig. 1).

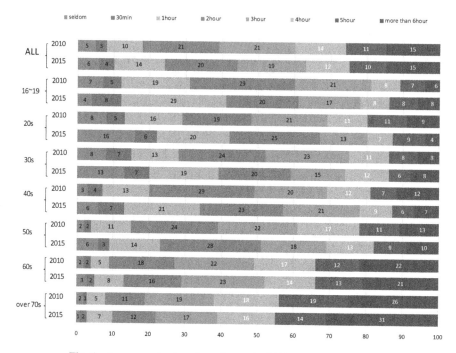

Fig. 1. Japanese viewing time change in 2010 and 2015 (from [1])

2 Dataset

In this study, we use below data. This data is obtained from VR-CUBIC of Video Research Ltd. that was provided from Data Analysis Competitions 2018 by Joint Association Research Group of Management Sciences. This data is obtained from Kanto district area and mainly consist with some detail media contact situation. The summary of data is shown in below:

- Source of data: Television viewing data (data set on television from April 2017 to April 2018)
- Contents of data: TV contact log, TV play log, web site browsing log, program information, sample information.

In this study, we randomly selected 1,500 customers from all the data from September 2017 to the December 2017.

3 Method

In this section we explain our analysis procedure.

3.1 Data Summary

First of all, from 03/Sep./2017 to 01/Dec./2017 data, 1,500 respondent monitors were randomly extracted from customer data. The results are as following Table 1:

Table 1. Data item

Column name	Type	Description
Date	DATE	yyyy-mm-dd
Household no.	CHAR	
Individual no.	CHAR	
Sex	CHAR	1. male/2. female
Married/unmarried	CHAR	1. married/2. unmarried
Age	CHAR	
Occupation code	INT	
Household head, housewife code	CHAR	1: Household head 2. Household head and housewife 3. Housewife 4. Other

Based on the sample information and the customer's personal information, we calculate summary statistics of 1,500 monitors' data for each generational/housewife code, gender, unmarried and age (see Figs. 2, 3, 4 and 5).

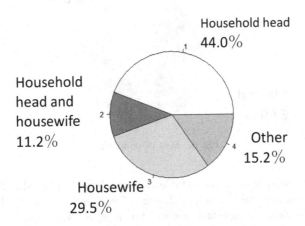

Fig. 2. Monitor attribute

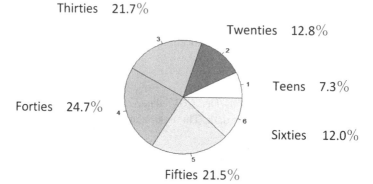

Thirties   21.7%

Twenties   12.8%

Teens   7.3%

Forties   24.7%

Sixties   12.0%

Fifties 21.5%

Fig. 3. Age ratio

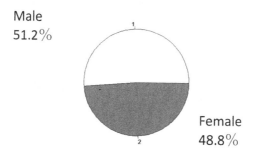

Male
51.2%

Female
48.8%

Fig. 4. Distinct of sex

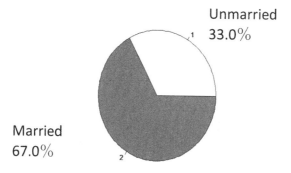

Unmarried
33.0%

Married
67.0%

Fig. 5. Data of unmarried

As shown in these figures, this sample has more household head and 30 s to 50 s monitor, it is greater ratio than population. Moreover, there is hardly difference between the numbers of men and women, but men are a bit more abundant. The number of married monitors is twice of unmarried ones.

3.2   Analysis of TV Viewing

Firstly, we analysis characteristics of consumers' TV viewing behavior. We divide all target monitors into some groups by TV viewing method. The viewing method is divided into three (i.e. time shift, real time, web site). Then, in this study, the relationship among these three construct a hierarchical structure is shown (Fig. 6).

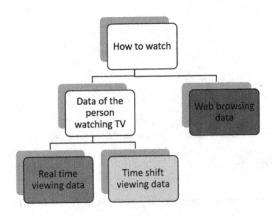

Fig. 6. Customer split by TV viewing method

Next, we calculate how much time is taken for each method, and how much proportion are there three methods by Eq. (1).

$$Real\,time\,viewing\,time\,ratio = \frac{Real\,time}{Real\,time + time\,shift + web\,site} \tag{1}$$

Further, time shift and web site browsing ratios are obtained using same nature of Eq. (1). Then using these three ratios, we depict a triangle graph as Fig. 7.

As shown in this figure, lots of monitors are watching TV in real time mainly. Inferring the reason for seeing the time shift regarding TV viewing is thought that there is cause such as wanting to see at different time or want to see repeatedly, we can see that many customers watch television in real time.

However, time shift ratio is not high ratio and Web TV is near ratio. So, we think time shift viewing is limited some situation about consumer or contents of TV program.

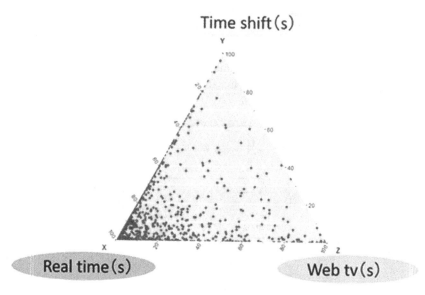

Fig. 7. Viewing time ratio of the three viewing methods (X is real time TV, Y is time shift TV and Z is web site)

3.3 Cluster Analysis for Segment

In this study, we divide customers into several segments which can be considered homogeneous features. Latent class model [2] with EM (Expectation and Maximizing) algorithm is used in this study. Latent class model is also known as a mixture model. Some common latent classes are assumed and each case belongs to these classes with a probability. Difference of belonging probabilities appear the heterogeneity among monitors. It is very difficult to obtain the optimal parameters containing probabilities at once, because the number of parameters is so many, then EM algorithm which is algebraic calculation repeatedly, are performed.

We use time, sex, age, etc. as explanatory variables. Moreover, we decide the number of clusters based on Bayesian Information Criteria [2], and 2 cluster model was chooses. We can interpret the segment and obtain some representation characteristics of customer [3]. The summary of results is shown in Table 2.

Table 2. Cluster Summary

		Class1	Class2
Class composition ratio		0.67	0.33
Sex	Male	0.52	0.55
	Female	0.48	0.45
Real time viewing	Long time	0.24	0.42
	Medium time	0.29	0.38
	Short time	0.47	0.20

(*continued*)

Table 2. (*continued*)

		Class1	Class2
Time shift viewing	Long time	0.03	0.64
	Medium time	0.46	0.20
	Short time	0.51	0.16
Age	Teens	0.06	0.08
	Twenties	0.14	0.11
	Thirties	0.24	0.25
	Forties	0.22	0.25
	Fifties	0.21	0.16
	Sixties	0.13	0.15

As shown in Table 1, comparing with Class 1 and Class 2, 20's and 50's monitors see real-time viewing is more frequent in short-time viewing, in the case of time shift, There are more in medium-time monitors. The consumers who belong to class 2 tend to long time watch TV. Almost of them are older.

The box plot of real time viewing time of Class 1 and Class 2 are shown in Figs. 8 and 9. The statistics are summarized in Table 3.

Table 3. Real time viewing summary (min.)

Real time viewing	Min	1st Qu.	Median	Mean	3rd Qu.	Max
Class1	0	176	696	1093	1596	7525
Class2	0	405	1094	1394	2061	7882

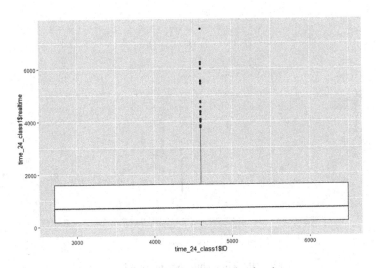

Fig. 8. Real time viewing in class1

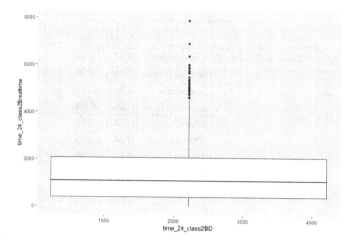

Fig. 9. Real time viewing in class2

It is a real-time viewing and a box-by-class diagram by customer's class, and it can be seen that the viewing time tends to be long in the class 2. Then the box plot of the time shift are shown in Figs. 10 and 11. The statistics are summarized in Table 4.

Table 4. Time shift viewing summary (min.)

Time shift viewing (min)	Min	1st Qu.	Median	Mean	3rd Qu.	Max
Class1	0	0	21	116	150	2425
Class2	0	0	32	152	188	2606

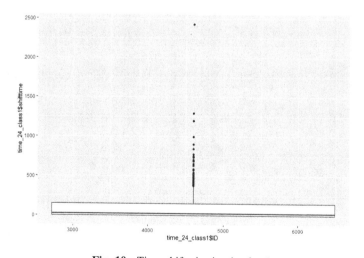

Fig. 10. Time shift viewing in class1

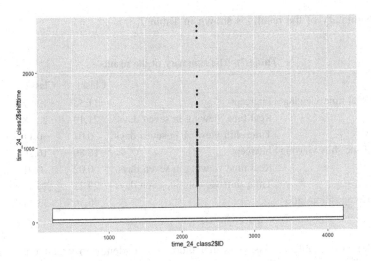

Fig. 11. Time shift viewing in class2

We can know that Class 2 tends to have longer viewing time.

3.4   Prediction Model

In this section, we construct a behavior prediction model for each customer segment and clarify the viewing trend of customers. The prediction method is to set the day as t and summarize the viewing data for the previous seven days. We can estimate parameters affecting viewing on the day by putting real time viewing, time shift viewing and watching TV viewing on the day of the day and performing logistic regression analysis. The objective variables is whether TV watching by real time or time shift in the next day are shown in Table 5. Then, we perform 4 analyzes which one combined objective variable and segment.

Table 5.   Objective variables

Objective variables	Description
Real time viewing	1 = see, 2 = not see
Time shift viewing	1 = see, 2 = not see

Explanatory variables as shown in Table 6.

Table 6.   Explanatory variables

Explanatory variables	Description
Real time viewing in seven days	Total real time viewing time in seven days before that day
Time shift viewing in seven days	Total real time viewing time in seven days before that day

The summary of the results is shown in Table 7.

Table 7. The summary of the results

		Class1	Class2
Real time viewing	Intercept	−11.54	−12.37
	Real time viewing in seven days	21.19	22.78
	Time shift viewing in seven days	0.01	−0.11
Time shift viewing	Intercept	−16.89	−16.26
	Real time viewing in seven days	0.02	0.01
	Time shift viewing in seven days	29.23	28.12
Composition ratio		66.56%	33.44%

As shown in Table 7, class 1 is that there is a tendency to watch for short time viewing. The longer the viewing time for seven days, the higher the possibility of viewing that day. Class 2 is that there is a tendency to view for medium and long time viewing and the longer the viewing time for seven days. The longer the viewing time for seven days, the higher the possibility of viewing that day. With consideration of explanatory variable, customer personal attribute data and TV program data are added, and a more accurate model can be obtained.

4   Discussion

From the result of the classification as shown in above section we discuss from some aspects. By evaluating the features, we were able to learn that each person tended to see which program. By forecasting programs that are easy to see, it is possible to predict the viewing tendency of customers and categorize viewing characteristics. Then you can grasp the viewing trend of the customer in the future.

5   Conclusion

In this study, using television viewing data, we clarified some customer clusters and made it meaning to each cluster. Then, we have revealed several customer clusters using television viewing data, making it meaningful for each cluster. The result confirmed the customer's lifestyle to the television. Then, from viewing data for seven days, for each class, estimate the viewing tendency of the customer with a simple explanatory variable, and clarify the viewing tendency of the customer.

In the future, to find variables when clustering from data, to add data such as programs etc. to the viewing tendency of customers, and to grasp the tendency of viewing programs of customers are our works.

References

1. Kimura, Y., Sekine, C., Namiki, M.: The present of television viewing and media usage research from "Japanese and TV". NHK Mon. Rep. Broadcast. Res. **65**(8), 18–47 (2015). (in Japanese)
2. Miwa, S.: Introduction to latent class models. Sociol. Theory Method **24**(2), 345–356. (in Japanese)
3. Sato, S., Asahi, Y.: Purchasing model considering customers' visit to consumers e-commerce site. Commun. Oper. Res. Soc. Jpn. **58**(2), 80–86 (2013). (in Japanese)
4. Mizuoka, Y., Tao, Y., Nakata, K., Orihara, R.: Comparison of clustering methods for large scale TV viewing data. In: Proceedings of the 31st Annual Conference of the Japanese Society for Artificial Intelligence, 3 p. (2017). (in Japanese)

When Complaining Is the Advertising: Towards a Collective Efficacy Model to Understand Social Network Complaints

Daniel Halpern[1]([⊠]), Gerald C. Kane[2], and Claudia Montero[1]

[1] Pontificia Universidad Católica de Chile, Alameda 340, Santiago, Chile
{dmhalper, clmonter}@uc.cl
[2] Carroll School of Management, Boston College, 140 Commonwealth Avenue,
Newton, MA 02467, USA
kanegb@bc.edu

Abstract. Engaging consumers through social media is a successful way for firms to get users attention and allow them to participate in content creation by two-way communication. However, social network sites (SNS) also challenges brands as users have the ability to change the narrative expressed by a firm with non-favorable content. This paper presents a process-oriented model to study one of the most frequent types of negative word of mouth: complaint behaviors. Given the collaborative and social characteristics of SNS, and drawing on literature in social psychology and consumer behavior, we theorize that cognitive aspects (e.g. collective efficacy) largely mediate the effects of dispositional factors (perceived utility) on complaining. A survey to a nationally representative sample of online Chileans show that even after controlling for factors recognized by previous research able to influence negative word of mouth (e.g., trust in companies, altruism or exposition to complaints on SNS), the level of collective efficacy affects consumers' willingness to complain in SNS and relate to others their experiences with brands, services or products.

Keywords: Social media · Word of mouth · Complaining · Collective efficacy

1 Introduction

1.1 When Complaining Is the Advertising

Since 2009, social network sites (SNS) has become very popular, especially in countries such as US where more than 70% of the population are active users [1]. Not surprisingly, brands have also relied on SNS to engage with customers, as these communication channels present a cost effective medium that integrates communication and collaboration with users by co-creating content [2]. Further, SNS provides opportunities for content customization and delivers superior speed to the delivery of information communication and feedback [3]: social media can enhance a two-way communication between firms and customers, attaching customers more with the organisations' brands [4]. Accordingly, research has considered social media as an effective mechanism that contributes to the firms' marketing aims and strategy;

© Springer Nature Switzerland AG 2019
G. Meiselwitz (Ed.): HCII 2019, LNCS 11579, pp. 330–345, 2019.
https://doi.org/10.1007/978-3-030-21905-5_26

especially in the aspects related to customers' involvement, customer relationship management and communication [5, 6].

However, these opportunities have also developed challenges inherent to social media practices, as users can interact with brands through SNS during multiple stages of the consumption process including information search, decision-making and word of mouth. In fact, as SNS gives customers a convenient and direct line to engage openly with a brand, the balance of power with respect to both the control of a shared reality and the individual's ability to express a brand narrative changed completely as customers can intervene [7]. Thus, similar to the transformation from advertising to integrated marketing communication, brands should also be aware of the possible moderations and consequences arising from participation through SNS [8].

Further, SNS have become one of the most popular options for dissatisfied customers to complain or voice their discontent [9], as SNS gives customers a convenient and direct line to the company, especially in times of crisis [10]. It also makes complaints visible to others through the user's social network [11], significantly amplifying the range of influence compared to other channels [12]. This visibility may increase the sense of urgency for companies to respond quicker, because, both users and the company's contacts are made aware of the problem. Given the relevance that SNS are acquiring as a channel for customer service [13, 14], it is important to understand how users perceive these social platforms for complaining and the impact it may have on branding.

Given the collaborative and social characteristics of SNS in facilitating mediated interactions among groups of individuals, we propose that SNS make users more cognizant of the problems experienced by other customers, enhancing their level of collective efficacy and augmenting their complaint behaviour. Accordingly, our interest in consumers' collective efficacy emerges as a consequence of the capabilities for horizontal interpersonal communication highly embedded in these platforms, which facilitate customers' ability to rebroadcast content (e.g., an answer from a company) adding personal commentaries, which in turn, enhance their capacity for discussion, engagement, and promotion of this information collectively.

We test the hypotheses related to consumers' collective efficacy through a nationally-representative survey of Chilean internet users. In this way, we complement previous research [9, 13, 15] that has studied consumer behavior in SNS by applying the Bandura's construct of collective self-efficacy to complaining. The approach is rooted in the idea that collective efficacy largely mediates the effects of dispositional factors on participatory outcomes (e.g. complaining in SNS). This mediation model moves beyond the simple stimulus–response perspectives of direct effects to a more process-oriented one. The model analyzes potentials antecedents that explain why users decide to socially complain through SNS, and then, controlling by those aspects, it draws attention to the ways in which users' collective beliefs mediate the effects of the perceived utility of this medium on complaining. Consistent with this framework, our results show that even after controlling for factors recognized by previous research able to influence complaining (e.g., trust in companies, online privacy concern or exposition to others' comments), the level of collective efficacy affects consumers' willingness to complain in SNS.

1.2   Perceived Utility of Complaining

While existent research in consumer behavior indicates that individuals complain over products or services when they are dissatisfied [16], the same literature shows that dissatisfied consumers do not always express this unfavorable attitude to others [17]. To explain the likelihood of complaining, research has focused on the consumers' perceived loss produced by the deficiency of the product or service [18]. However, the problem with this approach is that the feeling of dissatisfaction is a mental reaction to a perceived negative gap between what a person expects and what he or she gets. Since this perception is subjective and varies from person to person, individuals differ in their propensity to complain in similar situations [19]. To reduce this uncertainty, Kowalski [20] developed a theory of complaining that distinguishes between the two aspects that affect this behavior: people's thresholds for experiencing dissatisfaction (dissatisfaction threshold) and the expressing dissatisfaction (complaining threshold).

Kowalski [20] explains that underlying both of these processes is a state of self-focused attention. This is an evaluative process where the individual compares the current events with his/her standards for those events. When the actual state of events falls below the individuals' standards, the person experiences a discrepancy that leads him/her to feel dissatisfied. This feeling of dissatisfaction is what increases their motivation to reduce the discrepancy [21]. Before individuals decide to complain, however, they have to believe that complaining will actually serve to reduce the discrepancy and not incur additional undesired outcomes.

Kowalski [20] names this tradeoff as the perceived utility of complaining - the degree to which a person perceives that a complaint will be instrumental in promoting the achievement of a desired goal-, without affecting negatively other aspects, such as his/her image in the front of others (e.g. nobody likes to be stereotyped as a complainer). If a person, for instance, is dissatisfied with a perceived inequity in an ordered product (the dissatisfaction threshold is low), the individual is unlikely to complain unless he or she perceives that the expression of dissatisfaction will actually lead to accomplish a goal. The goal may be related to the product itself (i.e., materialist end) or to let other people know about it (i.e., altruistic or vengeance end). According to the perceived utility of complaining, individuals try to maximize the rewards to be gained by complaining and minimize the costs associated with it, regardless the consumers' goals. "Such a cost-benefit analysis suggests that the utility of complaining is high when the rewards to be gained outweigh the costs of complaining." [20, p. 181].

By applying this logic to complaining in SNS, it is possible to argue that individuals will not complain in SNS unless they perceive a high utility for complaining on this platform, such as receiving a satisfactory answer from the company or a valuable interaction with other users. Similarly, it is expected that positive experiences complaining in SNS will increase the perceived utility of this medium, specifically for egocentric and altruistic motivations, which according to the literature are the main drivers behind electronic word of mouth [9, 15]. That is, it is expected that users will feel satisfied complaining in SNS if they receive effective answers from the company or feedback from their contacts. Consequently, for those users who have experienced effective answers from companies and messages from contacts when they complain, it is expected that this perceived utility also lead them to complain more. Thus, it is possible to predict:

H1: Perceived utility will be positively related to frequency of complaining in SNS.

1.3   Social Learning as a Moderator for Complaining in SNS

Social learning theory offers a framework to explain why users who are exposed to others' complaints in SNS may also be more prone to complain. Bandura [22] theorizes that most of the behavioral, cognitive, and affective learning acquired by individuals can be explained by social observations. Social learning theory suggests that humans have an advanced capacity for observational learning that enables them to rapidly expand their knowledge and skills through information conveyed by models in their immediate environments. According to this logic, individuals' conceptions of social reality are greatly influenced by what they see, hear, and read. To a large extent, people act based on their images of reality. Therefore, these role models observed in their immediate environment have the potential to transmit new ways of thinking and behaving, which influences individuals to begin acting like them even without external incentives. Bandura [22] argues that the learning process involves four mains steps: (a) Attention: individuals must pay attention to the modeled behavior to learn; (b) Retention: it is necessary to remember the behavior in order to learn and reproduce the behavior; (c) Reproduction: individuals should have the ability to organize their responses and act according to the model behavior; and (d) Motivation: if new "learners" are not motivated to reproduce what they saw, they will not change their behavior.

Relevant to this research is the fact that SNS provide all these steps for social learning to occur, particularly when friends' actions are aggregated in a content feed (Burke, Marlow and Lento [13]). The News Feed feature in Facebook or Twitter for example, allows newcomers to view friends' or followed' actions and recall them later. Users can also link or tag content, which makes their contribution more salient; this may motivate users to participate in creating content. Indeed, Burke et al. [13] found that friends' behavior during newcomers' first two weeks is one of the most important predictors for newcomers' activities. Therefore, based on the social learning theory, it is possible to explain the positive relationship between exposition to complaining and this behavior on SNS as a reinforcement effect. Since these platforms facilitate users to be more aware of others complaints and they learn from their friends' activities, it is possible to argue that they could "replicate" their actions. Thus, it is therefore reasonable to expect that users who encounter more these reactions will complain more in SNS.

H2a: Exposition to others' complaints will be positively related to complaining
H2b: Exposition to others' complaints will moderate the relationship between perceived utility and complaining in SNS.

1.4   Social Network Complaints: Towards a Collective Efficacy Model

Perceived self-efficacy is the term used to represent an individual's perceived ability to influence his/her environment [22]. This sense of capability of acting effectively has been extensively documented by previous research as one of the key psychological variables that is able to explain individuals' accomplishments in several areas such as civic participation [24], academic performance [25] and knowledge sharing [26], to name only a few. Research in consumer behavior has also considered self-efficacy as an important primary measure for achievements [27]. The literature has traditionally recognized two dimensions: one internal, that represents the perceptions of an individual's ability to attain desired results using his/her own capacities and resources, and one external, that refers to people's beliefs about the system's responsiveness to their concerns [28]. However, concerted actions may also depend on perceptions of the group's efficacy [29]. In fact, collective efficacy has also been used as a basis of the efficacy construct [30].

From an "internal" perspective, the notion of group efficacy can be conceptualized as the judgments that members of a group have about their capabilities to engage in successful action [29]. This emphasis is based on Bandura's definition, which conceptualizes collective efficacy as the group's shared belief in its conjoined capabilities to organize and execute the courses of action required to produce given levels of attainment [22]. On the other hand, collective efficacy can also be understood in terms of the perceived responsiveness to the collective action that emerges from organized groups [31]. This second perspective is also relevant because does not focus on the abilities of the group but on how the system responds to the actions that emerge from the collective action. This paper considers both perspectives by integrating the beliefs that individual actions have the potential to transform the destiny of their group but with the responsiveness of the system to the collective demands for change. Therefore, drawing from the internal and external dimensions of the construct, we conceptualize consumers' collective efficacy as a "user's belief in the public's capabilities, as a collective actor, to organize and execute the courses of action required to achieve that companies and sellers respond to their demands for change".

Collective efficacy can be expected to operate in relation to complaining at the group level in a manner similar to self-efficacy at the individual level, but extending the concept of individual causality to collective agency exercised through a shared sense of efficacy [32]. Given the collaborative and social characteristics of SNS, we believe that these platforms can enable a sense of collective efficacy that, ultimately, might contribute to augment complaint behaviors in users. Moreover, by relying on mass information sharing to simplify social interactions, in which comments generated by peers most of the times precedes the information broadcasted by companies, SNS facilitate an ideal setting to discuss their experiences collectively. Thus, it may be argued that the dynamic of these conversations will make users more cognizant of discussions when they post comments about brands, and force them to process the information socially. However, unlike virtual communities, in which individuals share information by posting questions, providing answers, and debating issues based on shared interests [33], there are three affordances in SNS in particular that may lead users to an increased level of collective efficacy.

First, in SNS users not only create content but they also categorize collectively the information, which gives users the capability to tag all types of data. By marking content with descriptive terms (also called tags), users facilitate organization entries and access of information for other users as well. However, unlike tagging in Flickr or de.licio.us for instance, where users employ descriptive terms like "disappointed" or "cheated" to share semantic annotations, tagging in Facebook is the linking of a face in a photo or a public status update with a registered user. Thus, for complaint purposes the singling-out feature afforded by Facebook is relevant because "tagging" others highlights particular actions, making them not only visible to the "tagged" users but also to their entire network. In this way, social-tagging systems would help users to retrieve information about similar situations that other people went through, but also to be more aware of other users in their networks with similar problems, which force users in communities or networks to process the information socially.

Second, users in SNS are constantly evaluating content. These platforms allow users to evaluate content in two different ways: actively, by making comments or ranking specific information (e.g. reviewing a product), and passively, by tracking how users interact with the content offered in the platform (Web-browsing patterns). In fact, auto-generated indicators of information such as users' traffic (e.g. counters indicating the number of contacts in Facebook, viewers in YouTube or followers on Twitter), are seen as one of the most relevant indicators for users to make quality judgments about the underlying content (Sundar [34]). Thus, one of the consequences of these affordances is that when users see someone complaining in SNS and how others react to it (likes, comments, etc.), these interactions would create aggregated data that allow users to process the information socially and respond collectively to it as well.

Third, users also have the ability through these new applications to form social networks by creating a profile within a bounded system: they designate other users as contacts, followers, fans, viewers, or friends. One of the main differences with virtual communities is that in SNS users have their own network of contacts (in addition to groups), and most of the activities are notified to all the users' network, which can initiate social conversations between groups of users [11]. Our expectation is that these affordances will impact user's belief in the public's capabilities as a collective actor, to organize courses of action to achieve that companies and sellers respond to their demands for change. This, instead, will influence their tendencies toward complaining behaviors in SNS, such as their willingness to persist complaining given the support (e.g. likes or comments) that they may receive from their contacts. Thus, we expect that measurements of collective efficacy would help us to understand the impacts of SNS on this specific consumer behavior, by predicting:

H3a: Consumers' collective efficacy will be positively related to complaining.
H3b: Consumers' collective efficacy will mediate the relationship between perceived utility and complaining in SNS.

2   Methods

2.1   Sample and Procedure

This survey used an online panel provided by TrenDigital, a think tank based at the Catholic University of Chile. To overcome some of the limitations of using online surveys and assure a more accurate representation of the online national population,

TrenDigital based the sample on the National Socioeconomic Characterization Survey (CASEN), a governmental survey ran every three years. Three variables were considered for this panel: gender (male: 48.7%; female 51.3%); age (18–34: 55%; 35–44: 20%; 45–64: 22%; 65+: 3%) and geography (Metropolitan Region: 47%, Fifth Region: 11%, Seventh Region: 10%, other regions south: 20%, other regions north: 12%). The selected panel members received the survey's URL through an e-mail invitation. This invitation provided respondents information about a monetary incentive drawing for their participation. A first invitation was sent and then, to improve response rates, two reminders were sent during the next three weeks. 8,840 participants received the email and 1,070 responded the questionnaire, yielding a 12.1% response rate.

2.2 Dependent Variables

Complaining in SNS. First respondents were asked whether they have complained in SNS against product or services offered by companies (36.1% answered yes). Then, for those who answered positively, respondents registered in a 5-point scale ranging from 1 (never) to 5 (always) how frequently they have complained against a product or service offered by a company: (1) on the company's social media (e.g. it's Facebook), (2) on a conversation with a friend via SNS, (3) on their own Facebook's wall, (4) on their Twitter. An index was created with these 4 items (M = 2.48, SD = .94, α = .78). The questions to create the complaining scale in SNS were selected for two main reasons. First, Facebook (91%) and Twitter (44%) were the social media platforms with the higher penetration rates. And second, research has shown that users talk about their experiences not only with the companies' accounts, but also in conversations with friends and in their own accounts, so we included these aspects as well.

2.3 Independent Variables

Perceived Utility of SNS for Complaining. Based on egocentric and altruistic motivations, which according to the literature are two of the main drivers behind eWOM [9, 15], an averaged index that represents these motivations was created, with the questions: "thinking in your last complaints in SNS, were you satisfied with: (1) the answer given by the company, (2) the feedback gave by other users (interterm r = .19, M = 2.64, SD = .9).

Consumers' Collective Efficacy. Respondents registered their frequency of occurrence with a 5-point scale ranging from 1 (never) to 5 (always). Four questions from previous research [30] on an 5-point scale ranging from strongly disagree to strongly agree (M = 3.9, SD = .9, Cronbach's α = .86) were averaged to calculate the shared belief held by individuals about the consumer's capabilities to perform a collective action (e.g. "If consumers organize they could influence the decisions made by the companies"), and the perceived responsiveness of the environment to the action (e.g. "Companies would respond to the needs of consumers if they organize and demand changes").

Exposition to Others' Complaint. Using the same 5-point scale, we asked participants how frequently they see users complaining on SNS about products or services offered by companies in 9 areas, such as retailers (M 3.07; SD .71; cronbach .84).

2.4 Control Variables

We controlled for factors underlined as capable of affecting complaint behavior on SNS.

Trust in Companies. It influences the perception about products and services offered by companies, diminishing negative aspects such as lower anxiety and vulnerability, which instead affects the willingness of consumers to talk about them (Matos and Rossi 2008). Using a 5-point scale ranging from "nothing" to "very confident", respondents were asked how mucho do they trust in national, transnational and public companies (M = 3.04, SD = .7, Cronbach's α = .68).

Online Privacy Concern. Research has shown a negative relationship between privacy concern and different types of online behavior and attitudes toward online firms, such as purchase, trust in companies and word of mouth [35, 36]. It was measured using nine of the items from Buchanan et al.'s [37] Online Privacy Concern Scale (M = 3.72, SD = .81, Cronbach's α = .89). An example items is "Are you concerned about people online not being who they say they are?" respondents answered on a 5 point Likert scale ranging from 1 (Strongly disagree) to 5 (Strongly Agree).

Number of Brands Users Follow/Like in SNS. Research [38] has shown that familiarity with brands affect how users process the information related to it: when brands are unfamiliar, negative information elicited more supporting arguments. Thus, we asked participants how many brands they follow/like/view in SNS in a 7-point scale, ranging from 1 (No, I do not) to 7 (more than 30), with intervals of 5 brands per point (M = 3.54, SD = 1.8).

Frequency of SNS Use. We used a 7-point scale ranging from never to almost all the time (M = 4.7, SD = 1.5).

Frequency of Online Purchasing. Users who buy more frequently online may also have more exposed to complaints. We used a 5-point scale to measure how frequently users buy online ranging from never to almost all the time (M = 2.45, SD = 1.06). Participants were asked how much time they spent on four platforms (Facebook, Twitter, Instagram, and WhatsApp) (range = 0 [do not use that social network] to 7 [use more than 6 h per day]; (Cronbach's α = 0.62, M = 3.45, SD = 1.25).

2.5 Demographics Variables

We controlled for three demographics variables: age, using the same ranges of the panel (18–34: 57%; 35–44: 25%; 45–64: 15%; 65+: 3%), gender (58% females) and monthly income (less than 800 USD: 16.8%; 800–1,600 USD: 25.1%; 1,600–3,000 USD: 24.9%; 3,000–5,000 USD: 14.2%; 5,000–7,000 USD: 9.6%; more than 7,000 USD: 9.4%).

3   Results

3.1   Descriptive Analysis

Before proceeding to the formal tests of the hypotheses, we wanted to understand the differences between those who have complained (n = 387 or 36.1%) and who have not complained (n = 683, or 63.9%) through SNS. Table 1 presents t-tests and chi-square tests between individuals who have and who have not complained on demographics and our interest and control variables.

Although female are more likely to complain via SNS than male users, this difference is only marginal. Regarding our control variables, complainers are heavier SNS users than non-complainers, they follow/like more companies in these platforms, but they have purchased fewer products online, which may be related to the idea that they are younger users so they still have a lower salary, as Table 1 shows. Interestingly, we did not find differences in the levels of privacy concern and trust in companies.

Table 1. Differences between SNS's complainers (387) and non-complainers (683). Note: Statistical significance of the difference between members and nonmembers was assessed with chi-square tests for nominal variables and one-tailed t-test scores not assuming equal variances for continuous variables.

	Non-complainers	Complainers	Significance of difference
Consumers' collective efficacy	2.6	3.12	$t = 5.9, p < .001$
Online purchasing	1.81	1.99	$t = 3.3, p < .001$
Trust in companies	3.04	3.03	Not significance
Perceived utility of complaining in SNS	2.83	2.58	$t = 2.6, p < .01$
Exposition to others' complaints in SNS	3.31	2.98	$t = 6.04, p < .001$
Online privacy concern	3.76	3.84	Not significance
Frequency of SNS use	4.75	3.95	$t = 6.84, p < .001$
Number of companies follow/like	3.62	2.65	$t = 7.84, p < .001$
Gender (male)	43.9%	56.1%	$X2 = 2.45, p = .07$
Income	3.03	3.34	$t = 2.6, p < .01$
Age	1.81	2.09	$t = 2.9, p < .001$

Concerning our interest variables, those who have complained have also been exposed to more complaints in SNS and they also perceive a higher utility for complaining in these platforms, however their consumers' collective efficacy does not differ. The lack of difference in this last variable, however, may increase our confidence in the potential cause-effect relationship only among those users who interact more frequently with other users about problems with brands and have experienced collectively these aspects through SNS (Table 2).

Table 2. Correlations and descriptive statistics for key study variables. *Notes.* 1 = Consumers' collective efficacy; 2 = Online purchasing; 3 = Trust in companies; 4 = Perceived utility of complaining; 5 = Exposition to others' complains; 6 = Online privacy concern; 7 = Complaining in SNS; 8 = Frequency of SNS use; 9 = Number brands follow/like.

	M (SD)	1	2	3	4	5	6	7	8	9
1	3.9 (.9)		.104*	.101*	.103*	.092*	.80	.16**	.008	.036
2	2.45 (1.06)			.185**	.228**	.162**	−.043	.269**	.073	.134**
3	3.04 (.71)				.170**	−.144**	−.039	.004**	.023	.184**
4	2.64 (.9)					.088	−.02	.290**	.087	.09*
5	3.07 (.71)						.185**	.214**	.117*	.104*
6	3.72 (.81)							.016	−.076	−.102*
7	2.48 (.94)								.23**	.199**
8	4.7 (1.5)									.316**
9	3.54 (1.8)									

3.2 Multivariate Analysis

To test our hypotheses, a mediation regression analysis using a bootstrapping resampling method was conducted according to the specifications set out by Andrew Hayes's PROCESS for SPSS using model five with one mediator and one moderator. As the Fig. 1 shows, perceived utility of complaining was entered as the independent variable (X), consumers' collective efficacy as the mediator variable (M), exposition to others' complaint as the moderator variable (W) and frequency of complaining was entered as the criterion variable (Y) in the model. Data analysis using 1,000 bootstrap simulations revealed that perceived utility of complaining in SNS was positively associated with frequency of complaining, with a significant total effect (b = .25, t (387) = 5.3, p < .001), corroborating H1. Interestingly, the direct effect of perceived utility was also statistically significant (effect = .3, SE = 0.11, p = < .001 [95% CI .007, .06]), suggesting that the mediation, in case of exists, it would be only partial.

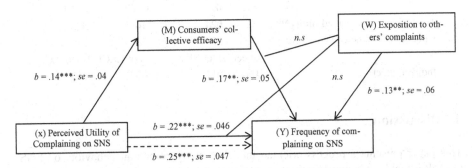

Fig. 1. Path model for the mediation analysis showing unstandardized path coefficients. Note. b = unstandardized regression coefficients with standard error are presented. All the control variables were entered in the model as covariates. Dotted line denotes the total effect of perceived utility on frequency of complaining on SNS. *p < 0.05; **p < 0.01; ***p < 0.001

Regarding the role of exposition to others' complaints to complaining on SNS, the analysis showed a positive relationship between these two variables (b = .14, t (387) = 3.53, p < .001), confirming H2a. However, when it was tested as moderator, the variable was not significant. This means that the indirect effect of perceived utility on complaining through consumers' collective efficacy does not increase linearly as users get exposed to others' complaint, so it should be treated as one independent variable instead of a moderator one. Consequently we could not corroborate H2b. Concerning the influence of the other variables inserted in the model, neither the relationship between trust in companies and complaining in SNS was statistically significant, nor the relationship between online privacy concern and complaining in SNS. Interestingly, control variable such as frequency of SNS use, online purchasing and number of brands that consumers follow or like, are positively related to complaining in SNS. This means that users who spent more time in SNS, buy more online and follow more companies in SNS, they also complain more in these platforms.

Concerning the relationship between consumers' collective efficacy and frequency of complaining, as H3a predicts, results show a positive effect (b = .17, p < .01). A similar relationship was found between perceived utility and consumers' collective efficacy (b = .14, p < .001). Because both paths were significant, mediation analyses were tested using the bootstrapping method with bias-corrected confidence estimates. The 95% confidence interval of the indirect effects was obtained with 1,000 bootstrap resamples. Results of the mediation analysis confirmed the role of consumers' collective efficacy in mediating between perceived utility of complaining and frequency of complaining in SNS (effect = .03, SE = .01, p < 0.01[95% bias-corrected bootstrap CI .01, .06]). Since the interval does not include zero, it is safe to conclude that the indirect effect was significantly different from zero, confirming the partial mediation of collective efficacy and our hypothesis H3b as well. The indirect effect was also statistically significant using the Sobel test, z = 2.1, p = .03 (Table 3).

Table 3. Total, Direct and Indirect Effects. Note. Number of bootstrap samples for bias corrected bootstrap confidence intervals: 1,000. Level of confidence for all confidence intervals: 95. *p < 0.05; **p < 0.01; ***p < 0.001.

	Effect	SE	t	LLCI	ULCI
Total effect of perceived utility***	.25	.024	5.31	.16	.34
Direct effect of perceived utility***	.22	.023	4.79	.13	.31
	Effect	Boot SE		Boot LLCI	BootULCI
Indirect effect*	.03	.011		.007	.055

4   Discussion

This paper presents a process-oriented model to study complaint behaviors on SNS. Overall it yields four main findings. First, it was found that higher perceived utility of SNS lead users to complain more on these platforms: users who perceive that companies respond satisfactorily to their demands on SNS and, receive feedback from other users about their experiences, show a higher disposition to complain in SNS. Second, by adding consumers' collective efficacy as an intermediary process between the perceived utility and subsequent complaints, the results obtained extend current theoretical models that consider the perception that users have about a medium able to trigger a series of cognitive and expressive processes (e.g. consumers' collective efficacy), which instead activates behavioral outcomes (e.g. complaining). Third, it was found that structural features of SNS through which consumers occurs (such as exposition to others' complaints) positively affect complaining behavior. Fourth, results show that other aspects in the relationship between consumers and companies, such as the trust that consumer have on them, did not impact complaining behavior.

4.1 Theoretical Implications

This paper corroborates the idea that as communication technologies become more participatory, consumers are gaining greater access to information as well, which gives them more opportunities to engage with others in this networked realm and get a stronger ability to undertake online actions, such as complaining. Consistent with previous research that shows how the Internet satisfy the need for information in pre purchasing processes [35], we analysed some of the affordances in SNS that facilitate users to be socially informed and enhance discussion among them about the presented information. Based on the theory of perceived utility [20], the results show that individuals complain more in SNS when they perceive higher utilities in this platform, specifically when they satisfy egocentric and altruistic motivations through their complaints, two of the main drivers behind eWOM.

Regarding the indirect effect of perceived utility on complaining in SNS through consumers' collective efficacy, two considerations are important. First, from a theoretical perspective, it was demonstrated that the framework is appropriated for understanding how SNS can facilitate and reflect community cohesion and enable a sense of consumers' collective efficacy, that ultimately contribute to complaining behavior through this communication technology. By studying SNS as a structure that facilitates access to consumer information and promotes interactions through the integration of peer-generated and organizational content, we should conceptualize SNS as a source that it is constantly disseminating potential stories about experiences with products or services among contacts. This conceptualization is relevant since results show that the exposition to other consumers' experiences dealing with companies, and the perceived utility of the channel to respond to dissatisfactions, lead users to believe that it is easier to mobilize collective efforts for solving the consumer problems. It activates their sense of agency and augments the likelihood of complaining.

One plausible explanation may be related to the higher opportunities for exposure to "social information" presented in SNS: social media promotes a participatory dynamic in which discussants can see what their contacts collectively think about others' experiences. They can even get collective answers from their networks to personal inquiries. By allowing mass information-sharing mechanisms, users of these social platforms can simultaneously communicate with all their contacts and networks while responding to information or comments posted by users. Therefore, it is likely that SNS users will find resources in their networks when they want to clarify a situation that they go through a company. We believe that this exposition augments consumers' exposition to spheres in which reflective storytellers operate and take collective actions to solve problems.

The second consideration that results from this study suggests that social feedback exerted by users in forms of dialogues may impact this form of psychological empowerment, especially when others indicate how you should complain or respond to a company or service. As explained above, the capabilities for interpersonal and mass communication highly embedded in these social media platforms enable users to inform their contacts and receive "collective" feedback from them as well. This may increase opportunities for consumers to see how groups of people respond to individual complaints. As our study showed, consumers also learn and replicate what they see online. This finding is relevant because SNS allow consumers to share their thoughts with their entire network and learn what their network is thinking or what they commented just by logging onto their own accounts. This non-invasive form of communication may augment exposition to complaining behavior and affect users' actions as well.

4.2   Practical Implications

When costumers complain publicly through a company's social media accounts, not only the seller becomes aware of the problem, but also its followers, likers, and viewers. Even more, the complainers' contacts could also learn about the problem, and each time that one of them interact with the complaint posted, new "networks" could potentially learn about the situation. This higher visibility, compared to more traditional channels such as regular phone calls, may force the seller or service behind the complaint to act in order to solve the problem and reduce the visibility attained by it. Thus, community managers should be trained to recognize the source behind the problems in order to be able to answer as soon as they can.

Interestingly, however, the results of our study show that in this regard, the perceived utility of SNS leads users to complain more on these platforms. This basically means that customers who perceive that companies respond satisfactorily their demands on SNS, would motivate them to complain even more through that channel. Thus, based on the results it is possible to conclude that "good" and "fast" answers are going to attract more complainers. In other words, as companies try to respond as soon as possible to costumers, they are also motivating them to complain more through SNS, and since users also "replicate" the behaviors that they observe online, it may increase even more the likelihood of complaining.

Furthermore, these waves of complaining may also affect negatively the brand's reputation. If consumers see constantly how other users complain against brands in their social media accounts, it is likely that the company's image will be affected. On the other hand, if companies do not respond to users' accusations, it may be affected even more for the situation. The result presents companies with a paradox. How should companies respond? Based on our results, we suggest that companies should look for a balance, where even though they should try to respond as much as they can, they also should know that these compromises might motivate users to complain even more. In these particular cases, sometimes "less" would be "more."

4.3   Limitations

However, the study has several limitations that deserve mention. First, the analyses are based on cross-sectional data. Although we based our causality approach in pivotal research, the study could not be fully confident in causal relationships among variables, and the question of causal direction needs verification through longitudinal and/or experimental approaches. Second, even though our model took several variables into account (i.e., demographics, SNS use, privacy concern), future studies should explore whether other variables related to individuals' activities on SNS could impact complaint behavior. And third, we used self-reported data and not actual observations of how users complain on SNS, and the limitations of this approach are painfully well-known.

Despite these limitations, this paper still makes a contribution to theory and practice. The interest in how users today are interacting with companies and services through SNS have gained a lot of attention from scholars in the last couple of years. This paper presents a process-oriented model to explain how cognitive aspects (e.g. consumers' collective efficacy) mediate the effects of dispositional factors (perceived utility) on complaining. We believe that our findings are valuable for both scholars and practitioners. One the one hand, we could integrate theoretical insights from different areas in a model able to explain complaining on SNS, but on the other hand our results are also interesting for marketers and corporate communicators, as the analyses showed that complaints in SNS not necessarily need to responded massively and in a short period of time.

References

1. Smith, A., Anderson, M.: Social media use in 2018. Pew Internet & American Life Project, Washington, DC (2018)
2. Jung, A.R.: The influence of perceived ad relevance on social media advertising: an empirical examination of a mediating role of privacy concern. Comput. Hum. Behav. **70**, 303–309 (2017). https://doi.org/10.1016/j.chb.2017.01.008
3. Shilbury, D., Westerbeek, H., Quick, S., Funk, D., Karg, A.: Strategic Sport Marketing, 4th edn. Allen & Unwin, Sydney (2014)
4. Alalwan, A.A., Rana, N.P., Dwivedi, Y.K., Algharabat, R.: Social media in marketing: a review and analysis of the existing literature. Telemat. Inform. **34**(7), 1177–1190 (2017). https://doi.org/10.1016/j.tele.2017.05.008
5. Filo, K., Lock, D., Karg, A.: Sport and social media research: a review. Sport. Manag. Rev. **18**(2), 166–181 (2015). https://doi.org/10.1016/j.smr.2014.11.001
6. Knoll, J.: Advertising in social media: a review of empirical evidence. Int. J. Advert. **35**, 266–300 (2016). https://doi.org/10.1080/02650487.2015.1021898
7. Quinton, S.: The community brand paradigm: a response to brand management's dilemma in the digital era. J. Mark. Manag. **29**(7), 912–932 (2013). https://doi.org/10.1080/0267257X.2012.729072
8. Felix, R., Rauschnabel, P.A., Hinsch, C.: Elements of strategic social media marketing: a holistic framework. J. Bus. Res. **70**, 118–126 (2017). https://doi.org/10.1016/j.jbusres.2016.05.001

9. King, R.A., Racherla, P., Bush, V.D.: What we know and don't know about online word-of-mouth: a review and synthesis of the literature. J. Interact. Mark. **28**(3), 167–183 (2014). https://doi.org/10.1016/j.intmar.2014.02.001

10. Oh, O., Agrawal, M., Rao, H.R.: Community intelligence and social media services: a rumor theoretic analysis of tweets during social crises. MIS Q. **37**(2), 407–426 (2013). https://doi.org/10.25300/MISQ/2013/37.2.05

11. Kane, G.C., Alavi, M., Labianca, G.J., Borgatti, S.: What's different about social media networks? A framework and research agenda. MIS Q. **38**(1), 274–304 (2014). https://doi.org/10.25300/MISQ/2014/38.1.13

12. Dewan, S., Ramaprasad, J.: Social media, traditional media, and music sales. MIS Q. **38**(1), 101–121 (2014). https://doi.org/10.25300/MISQ/2014/38.1.05

13. Jansen, B.J., Zhang, M., Sobel, K., Chowdury, A.: Twitter power: tweets as electronic word of mouth. J. Am. Soc. Inf. Sci. Technol. **60**(11), 2169–2188 (2009). https://doi.org/10.1002/asi.21149

14. Gallaugher, J., Ransbotham, S.: Social media and customer dialog management at Starbucks. MIS Q. Exec. **9**(4), 197–212 (2010)

15. Cheung, C.M., Lee, M.K.: What drives consumers to spread electronic word of mouth in online consumer-opinion platforms. Decis. Support Syst. **53**(1), 218–225 (2012). https://doi.org/10.1016/j.dss.2012.01.015

16. Hunt, H.K.: Consumer satisfaction, dissatisfaction, and complaining behavior. J. Soc. Issues **47**(1), 107–117 (1991). https://doi.org/10.1111/j.1540-4560.1991.tb01814.x

17. Morel, K.P., Poiesz, T.B., Wilke, H.A.: Motivation, capacity and opportunity to complain: towards a comprehensive model of consumer complaint behavior. ACR North Am. Adv. **24**(1), 464–469 (1997)

18. Andreasen, A.R., Manning, J.: The dissatisfaction and complaining behavior of vulnerable consumers. J. Consum. Satisf. Dissatisf. Complain. Behav. **3**, 12–20 (1990)

19. Thøgersen, J., Juhl, H.J., Poulsen, C.S.: Complaining: a function of attitude, personality, and situation. Psychol. Mark. **26**(8), 760–777 (2009). https://doi.org/10.1002/mar.20298

20. Kowalski, R.M.: Complaints and complaining: functions, antecedents, and consequences. Psychol. Bull. **119**, 179–196 (1996). https://doi.org/10.1037/0033-2909.119.2.179

21. Pyszczynski, T., Greenberg, J., Hamilton, J., Nix, G.: On the relationship between self-focused attention and psychological disorder: a critical reappraisal. Psychol. Bull. **110**, 538–543 (1991). https://doi.org/10.1037//0033-2909.110.3.538

22. Bandura, A.: Social cognitive theory: an agentic perspective. Ann. Rev. Psychol. **52**(1), 1–26 (2001). https://doi.org/10.1111/1467-839X.00024

23. Burke, M., Marlow, C., Lento, T.: Feed me: motivating newcomer contribution in social network sites. In: Proceedings of the SIGCHI Conference on Human Factors in Computing Systems, pp. 945–954 (2009). https://doi.org/10.1145/1518701.1518847

24. McPherson, J.M., Welch, S., Clark, C.: The stability and reliability of political efficacy: using path analysis to test alternative models. Am. Polit. Sci. Rev. **71**(2), 509–521 (1977). https://doi.org/10.1017/S0003055400267427

25. Niemi, R.G., Craig, S.C., Mattei, F.: Measuring internal political efficacy in the 1988 National Election Study. Am. Polit. Sci. Rev. **85**, 1407–1413 (1991). https://doi.org/10.2307/1963953

26. Zimmerman, B.J., Bandura, A., Martinez-Pons, M.: Self-motivation for academic attainment: the role of self-efficacy beliefs and personal goal setting. Am. Educ. Res. J. **29**(3), 663–676 (1992). https://doi.org/10.3102/00028312029003663

27. Hsu, M.H., Ju, T.L., Yen, C.H., Chang, C.M.: Knowledge sharing behavior in virtual communities: the relationship between trust, self-efficacy, and outcome expectations. Int. J. Hum.-Comput. Stud. **65**(2), 153–169 (2007). https://doi.org/10.1016/j.ijhcs.2006.09.003

28. Bearden, W.O., Hardesty, D.M., Rose, R.L.: Consumer self-confidence: refinements in conceptualization and measurement. J. Consum. Res. **28**(1), 121–134 (2001). https://doi.org/10.1086/321951

29. Gecas, V.: The social psychology of self-efficacy. Ann. Rev. Sociol. 291–316 (1989). https://doi.org/10.1146/annurev.so.15.080189.001451

30. Van Zomeren, M., Postmes, T., Spears, R.: Toward an integrative social identity model of collective action: a quantitative research synthesis of three socio-psychological perspectives. Psychol. Bull. **134**(4), 504–535 (2008). https://doi.org/10.1037/0033-2909.134.4.504

31. Yeich, S., Levine, R.: Political efficacy: enhancing the construct and its relationship to mobilization of people. J. Community Psychol. **22**, 259–271 (1994). https://doi.org/10.1002/1520-6629(199407)22:3<259::AID-JCOP2290220306>3.0.CO;2-H

32. Caprara, G.V., Vecchione, M., Capanna, C., Mebane, M.: Perceived political self-efficacy: theory, assessment, and applications. Eur. J. Soc. Psychol. **39**, 1002–1020 (2009). https://doi.org/10.1002/ejsp.604

33. Yates, D., Wagner, C., Majchrzak, A.: Factors affecting shapers of organizational wikis. J. Am. Soc. Inf. Sci. Technol. **61**(3), 543–554 (2010). https://doi.org/10.1002/asi.21266

34. Sundar, S.S.: The MAIN model: a heuristic approach to understanding technology effects on credibility. In: Metzger, M.J., Flanagin, A.J. (eds.) Digital Media, Youth, and Credibility, pp. 72–100. The MIT Press, Cambridge (2008)

35. Eastlick, M.A., Lotz, S.L., Warrington, P.: Understanding online B-to-C relationships: an integrated model of privacy concerns, trust, and commitment. J. Bus. Res. **59**(8), 877–886 (2006). https://doi.org/10.1016/j.jbusres.2006.02.006

36. Wirtz, J., Lwin, M.O., Williams, J.D.: Causes and consequences of consumer online privacy concern. Int. J. Serv. Ind. Manag. **18**(4), 326–348 (2007). https://doi.org/10.1108/09564230710778128

37. Buchanan, T., Paine, C., Joinson, A., Reips, U.: Development of measures of online privacy concern and protection for use on the internet. J. Am. Soc. Inf. Sci. Technol. **58**(2), 157–165 (2007). https://doi.org/10.1002/asi.20459

38. Ahluwalia, R.: How prevalent is the negativity effect in consumer environments? J. Consum. Res. **29**(2), 270–279 (2002). https://doi.org/10.1086/341576

The Cultural Component in Advertising Analysis. A Non-numerical Vision of the Programmatic Advertising

Pedro Antonio Hellín Ortuño[✉]

Facultad de Comunicación y Documentación, University of Murcia,
Campus Universitario de Espinardo, 30100 Murcia, Spain
phellin@um.es

Abstract. In this text I try to present the first approximation (my first such) to the idea of how Culture, from an anthropological point of view, is a variable; bearing in mind advertising analysis which seeks to establish a model of analysis for programmed advertising. The cultural counterfoil forms a part of the map of the mediations, together with the technologies involved in communication, production logistics and media competitors. This exposition attempts to sketch the passage which, starting from the study of advertising language, has brought me to this (fluid, mutating, hybrid) relationship between the brands and post-modern social culture, and am interest in their being open topics, which occupy our current research and which, in my opinion, take into account the fundamentals of Brand Advertising Discourse. In this exploratory text, I will look for the links between the cultural bases of our society and new ways of programming and designing advertisements; and of how technology based on numerical calculations appears as an aid to explain and apply qualitative data, that is not quantifiable, in the successful segmentation of target groups.

Keywords: Programmatic advertising · Brands · Consumer culture · Advertising

1 Initial Theoretical Aspects

Advertising language (it would be more correct to speak of "languages" so as to touch on its discourse richness), which some time ago "escaped" structural and linguistic limitations, is now also embracing creative and socio-cultural aspects. It is from that point that we now consider the cross-disciplinary perspective as the most appropriate for this study.

In the current scenario, advertising discourse seeks a symbiotic inter-dependence with the media domain (a hybridization of media languages). In this way, advertising gives ideal distinction to the consumer-driven product by interposing an enormous amount of semiotic meaning between the object itself and its manufacture.

The result is that the product is considered as a part of social culture and its consumption patterns; and not just within the context of its processing.

© Springer Nature Switzerland AG 2019
G. Meiselwitz (Ed.): HCII 2019, LNCS 11579, pp. 346–360, 2019.
https://doi.org/10.1007/978-3-030-21905-5_27

Fundamental perspectives about the Concept of Culture, for the study of Brands.

Cognitive Dimension: CULTURE as an INDIVIDUAL STATE of MIND	Collective Dimension: CULTURE as a SOCIAL DEVELOPMENT
Social Dimension: CULTURE as a MODE of INTERACTION	Anthropological-Sociological Vision: CULTURE as a WAY of LIFE
Specific and Descriptive Dimension: CULTURE as a CREATIVE and ARTISTIC WORK	Classic-Humanistic Vision: CULTURE as a PRODUCT of ARTISTIC ACTIVITIES

1.1 Definition of Culture

There only exists a consensus in that, culture is not: "It is not obtained studying Shakespeare, listening to classical music nor attending History of Art classes".

Marvin Harris [10]: "a culture is a way of life learnt socially, which is found in human societies and which touches on every aspect of social life, including thinking and behaviour".

Terry Eagleton [6]: Culture can be roughly understood as the grouping of values, customs, beliefs and practices which constitute the way of life of a specific group of people.

Subirat's concept of spectacular culture, "Its marvellous power resides not only in the reproduction and ontological organisation of the world, in the reduplication of reality, but also in its capability of supplanting as much the individual experience of reality as the relatively immediate interactive forms of liberal society; ranging from the democratic parliament to public forums, and to one's own private or family conversation" [16].

Communication Media achieve the artificial, aesthetic or artistic construction of the world's reality in a pre-fabricated unity of reality.

The Cultural production is the effect of a permanent tension

- between originality and standardisation,
- between industrial logic and dialectic-standardising anti-logic,
- between industrial logic and creative anti-logic,
- between the originator's preferred vision, be it individual or collective, and the necessity of system's profitability. González Martín [9]

Mass Culture

Culture has converted itself into an industry, on an equal footing with the food, textile, pharmaceutical or automobile industries. It detects standard needs, and supplies the market with products that satisfy it. These products are superficially different (and here, marketing and publicity play their differentiating role).

But, in the final analysis it is the laboratory combinations which tend to exhaust the generous, albeit limited, number of variables. Cultural products are not only manufactured en masse –in so many technologically reproduced products further multiplied by copies and distributed globally– but also they are organised into series, standards and ranges. "Specifically, they confine themselves to types, formats, styles, levels, profiles, and wrappings; even if we want, into compartments which rank our preferences and our differences and emerge in search of their public" [15].

Popular Art has surged from the roots of modern society of the industrialised masses, and has been conceived expressly by that society for its own use, employing its productive forces, that is to say, mass technology, with the purpose of distributing this art to enormous consumer populations.

"Popular Art is the art of a Mass Society and attempts to serve the purposes of such a society" [2].

From these foundations I am working the idea of cyber-culture, highlighting the visible paradigm-shift of the contemporary intersection between art and technology. New concepts of Media Art are put forward, beginning with media properties taken from the works themselves: technical reproduction, innovation, aesthetic information, artificial reality or new-media-reality.

So, the study goes deeply into a machine-related aesthetic from philosophic reflections. These range from the incursion of optical technologies (photography, cinematography) to electronic technologies (videograph, computer graphics, networks). The media have opened up to artists the possibilities of the laboratory of aesthetic experimentation between art, science, and technological innovation.

At the same time, thinking about the relationship between art, technology and advertising leads us to think about the context of that interaction, the city, and which are the obvious relationships, outdoors advertising shows its diversity by occupying privileged sites throughout urban space and confined to corners of the marginal areas, like a visual overview of the city.

In the post-modern metropolis there exists a socio-political geography of images in which the language of industry is a primary element in the urban landscape; places where such advertising has replaced monuments. Art is not advertising and advertising is not Art, but they are heterogeneous discourses that interweave. These properties are ideal for cross-fertilisation.

This intersection of common discourse factors is made even sharper when we link:

- the phenomenon of outdoors advertising
- the function of the monument, and
- the theory of public art (that of an urban art and of graffiti)

Three different discourses which in post-modern society give rise to one only interwoven discourse in the eyes of the spectator trained in the media-mixing. Moreover, it is an interweaving.

- with which art generates an innovative and alternative form, and
- with which industry feels comfortable infiltrating itself into the individual awareness of its consumers.

1.2   Mass Culture and Mass Communication

Mass Culture possesses a phenomenon framework in post-industrial development which grew under conditions of the Capitalist Economic Model. Capitalism was perfect for advancing the innovating objectives which these societies pursued, and in which, the importance of the study of human communication as applied to international markets, was exalted. The notion of Mass Communication refers to an organisational paradigm which affects not only political, economic entrepreneurial, cultural and social models. Mass Communication is present in the very structure of knowledge. Since knowledge, now more than ever, is nourished with a collective awareness in which the responsibility for truth is homogeneous and universal.

The market feeds itself from a network of communication nodes - points of confluence from various directions – which, by their geopolitical and strategic situations, encompassed greater responsibility and power. In this way, Mass Communication is more than a strategy of conquest of space by means of the growth of social interactions. So as to apply this strategy, space is won with time.

The Communication Media accelerate the time phenomenon of human experiences. At the same time, there are media which abandon the presentation of objects in favour of their representation. They flourish on projects and illusions which consume themselves even before materialising. The decisive factor is the speed of the changes; the acceleration of life or the vertigo of continually-changing consumption replete with novelties. Time is not now human. History disappears when industrial production exhausts periods of time with its production of objects which scarcely subsist. Mass Media enters into the cycle of creation and destruction of information which annuls every historical possibility of indicating stages in Post-Modern Societies.

In spite of that, it is fair to affirm that Mass Communication possesses, by reason of its idiosyncrasy, an autonomous identity. Mass Communication is a new phenomenon which arises from the media which brought together the multitudes; such as the cinema industry, music-disk production and its association with juvenile urban hordes (rockers, mods, punks, technos) or the international formulation of TV programmes. Their principal value, which surrealist artists already appreciated in cinematographic show rooms, was their capacity of bringing masses together, which gathered more people for whatever exposition or artistic event.

Mass Communication utilises Technology to achieve interaction between compatible individuals which provokes the alienation of the general public. The loss of individual personality is a consequence of Mass Culture which does not contribute to the definition of specific features of individuals. On the contrary, it indicates those preferences which, up to a point, make them similar, the fiercest critic has always insisted on that as a consequence. An example is the modern culture of product brands.

Mass Communication directly causes life alteration in individuals, through symbolic connections of objects. The replacement of a vision of a world of living things with an object-driven world is simply a consequence of substituting the authentic with the symbolic. Mass Culture transforms the natural world into a symbolic world which is consumed, firstly in the interior realities of individuals. A consequence of the communicative activity of the Mass Media is the appearance of two very differentiated worlds: the natural world and the artificial world.

The Artificial world is created beginning from a high degree of technification of communication, and for that matter, of human activities. In parallel, the artificial world is constructed by displacing public places; at first natural spaces by other spaces directly designed for collective communication. The artificial world consists basically in the construction of a social reality.

2 The Digitalisation of Mass Communication

The appearance of Digital technologies amplified the technical possibilities of Mass Communication. Digitalisation managed to create a more ordered and controlled reality. Cyber-reality produces a particular from of sensorial perception, of information coding, of communication interpretation; and of acting on that. Virtual Reality is a simulated space in which the intuitive faculties, so as to intervene, will not have the same process as in analogical reality. Digital technology manages to present the world in another, distinctive, mode.

In the Digital World there is a condition; the contra-intuitive performance, for evaluating the repercussions of that technology. We prioritise the brain as distinct from the physical body in this metaphor of artificial life. The constitution of an informational sphere which involves the simulation of the natural, requires a natural structure as a support for constructing its own ontological structure –if we consider that it has such–. Digital Technologies generate things without which the real world, the natural world, re-creates.

The World Vision supplied as Information encapsulated in Digital Archives is subject to the logic of a mathematical model for communication, and to a cybernetic model for organisation. For Shannon, information remains reduced to a structure which acquires sense in a space of probabilities. Hence, information passes through simpler or more complex states. The information quantity is defined specifically by such a state within its field of definition. By this means we come to appreciate that the natural world can be reduced to information. Since this has a structure which allows for the remaking of what we can know, and understand, of the natural world [8]:

- The differences between states is a condition of the existence of Information.
- Transmission and Participation are qualities of Information.
- Structural changes which information experiences in a system can be seen by means of their causal relationships.
- The natural world possesses its field structure.
- The physical field is completely specified by the relationships which define it.
- Finally, all that which remains outside of the Information, which the fields specify, does not exist and does not require our attention.

The technological domain of the natural world (control of reality) is a question of reduction. For this technology, to digitalise consists, simply, in reducing reality to information. The consequence of this action is that now the reality is the product of technologies by way of their reduction to information. On that matter [8] makes a very interesting observation. "In this way, they began to be made plausible at the same time as the analogies between the three levels of reality which distinguish classic episte-mology; the three levels of Popper.; reality itself, the concepts that describe it and the subject thought about".

Digitalisation is the basis of the Information Society and also of a Knowledge Society. Technologies are required in this world for the control of the immense quantities of information. In spite of the evident progress in information management, societies appear condemned to an unconscious ignorance in renouncing the subjective value of communication.

Digitalisation imposes, moreover, a social, political, and economic organisation which encourages the alienation of specialities. Mankind specialises itself in its functions within its community and associates itself with those of the same desire for specialisation. For Habermas, Post-Modern communities characterise themselves by identifying the thought with the deed, making the latter as valid as the former and therefore reaffirming the irrational, the relative and the arbitrary. For this thinker, there exists a critical point in the rupture of tradition by means of post–metaphysical thinking, the linguistic twist and the surmounting of logo-centrism.

The digitalisation of life is a metaphor which illuminates sensibly the creative possibilities of technology on life's experience. It is evident that communication, stimulated by technological implements, generates new sensorial experiences which will lead to other meanings about reality. Since we are not able to forget that life's experience begins in the first place from the interior of mankind. It is necessary that the process of living passes through a stage of interiorisation and, beginning from there, the interpretation will arise which will be no more than the exteriorisation of understanding.

3 Mass Culture, General Context of Advertising

To study a General Advertising Context implies questions of a cultural, technological and communication nature from the perspectives of each of those fields of knowledge. For the purposes of approaching knowledge of contemporary Mass Culture, there appears to be no better idea than to avail oneself of the opportunity of multi-disciplinary study. We cannot avoid the fact that we are confronted with a new con-figuration of the social, political, institutional, democratic, human, migratory, biolog-ical and post-biological, ethical and aesthetical, provoked by radical technological changes since the beginning of the current century. In our opinion this immense task is important for the comprehension of the influences on production processes in the context of Global Discussion of Advertising.

Communication has experienced a radical transformation with network technolo-gies as the main consequence of new advertising formats. Nevertheless, this is not the only factor, since new advertising discourse production has also seen itself altered by a trans-national market model which those very same merchandise and passenger transport systems, and national commercial policies, have developed within their territories.

From empirical investigation in fields, such as the economy, to work in computing applications for direct information for users, the Global Culture presents itself to us as a highly complex system and the observation of Advertising acquires a highly significant value for communication, since it is presented to us as a multi-faceted prism with numerous faces.

Globalisation has made Advertising a frontier between different disciplines. It is not a defined or confined space, but rather a place of interacting wisdom and knowledge. About studies of this type; Aronowitz explains to us:

> Cultural studies do not linger in a new frontier because of blocked channels; but rather in a place in which each action produces an incision (however small that may be) and outflow. Cultural studies trim spaces in existing disciplines not so as to cordon them off; but rather to connect, so as to bring together small groupings of students and lecturers; a heterogeneous, and therefore imperfect, *patchwork* which facilitates a space into which those who choose can come and go and dispense with the pseudo-sanctity of the disciplinary preserves. [8]

The paradigmatic context of Advertising is closed off with the philosophic values of Technological Societies. Advertising discourse also sees itself as being affected by Post-Modern phenomenology based on dialects of the appearance, and disappearance, by means of Communications Media speed [18], or the evolution of tele-objective vision which causes in people an atrophied experience of one's perception of the world. The real world is replaced by symbols which share a likeness. The symbolic relationship with images is appropriated from the truly authentic. Moreover, Post-Modern mutations have achieved narrative forms which now fragment, and then organise themselves, by means of hypertext syntax.

Techno-science, understood as a Post-Modern scientific mode, also presupposes a rupture relative to the classical culture of times past. Techno-science introduces its procedures so as to operate in fields exclusively reserved for mankind's questions. Human life-forms are conditioned by this techno-science which alerts us about climate change, atmospheric contamination, disappearance of nature's heritage, biological modification of nature, or, more simply, the survival limitations of our planet. Advertising feeds itself on these stories, and on others of a political or social character.

The importance of Techno-science, relative to other meta-narratives, is explained when we contemplate the epistemic turnaround provoked by individual behaviour relative to life by way of technologies of communication, and of information and knowledge. The overwhelming influence of technologies has presupposed, from the beginning of this century, an ontological change in discovery and innovative thinking in ethical crossroads into which bio-technologies place us.

All of these elements regulate the formation of a Global Advertising Culture, since already they no longer refer to localised facts or events in concrete localities. On the contrary, they define communication processes in highly technologised societies which interchange the same concerns, challenges and future expectations.

The systematic elimination of old and obsolete communication models in favour of replacement with other models based on the strength of the Virtual, of the absolutely Symbolic, explains sufficiently well that to which Global Advertising is conforming. This highlights the culture of rational practicality, from which trans-national markets profit, so as to organise the production and distribution of their merchandise. Technological innovation has achieved that the new economic order will not end up in the same uncontrolled situation. We can state that technology facilitates, from the panoptic vigilance of Advertising messages, and of consumers, towards the efficacy of brands and, above all, in detecting new tendencies and fluctuations of tastes in the market. Information Technologies also serve the purpose of information vigilance and why not also *Infor-Attack* also? when Advertising annihilates the factors which hinder the advance of consumption of our products and services.

To deal with Global Advertising, a world guarded by vigilant instruments which register our psychological profiles; inspecting and processing, by means of this presence; one's changes of personality, of tastes, of needs, retaining in artificial memories the variations in our way of life. Global Advertising already possesses a registration technology of the styles of the persons connected to a world phenomenologically reduced to digital networks.

Contemporary Advertising confronts a consumer world which marches to the rhythm of current lifestyles. The communicative process is more chaotic and, expressed in terms of complexity, is saturated with attractors which augment desires and personal virtual experiences. The fusion of the virtual and real worlds has generated the "cyberperson" whom Whittaker outlines with precision.

> ....a new space; cyberspace which exists both nowhere and everywhere, and which consists of a kind of *tabla rasa* in the sense that it is constructed, and constantly re-constructed, is written and re-written, by means of simultaneous Network users and their consequent re-elaboration of the same occurrence. [19]

Since the middle of the 20th Century, Advertising is the discourse of Mass Culture and of the Consumer Society. Nevertheless, it is in the cyberspace of new phenomena where advertising acquires its denomination as a Global Discourse, since it is here that Virtual Communities come together. These human collectives in cyberspace are groups of individuals united by a common interest. Here the interest is the same as an affinity; subjects associate themselves around a consumer tendency, a brand, or a lifestyle which, individually or collectively, links them independently of where they actually live. The similarity of their preferences in life arranges them around a common need for Information (and Advertising) of a pre-determined type which satisfies their leaning towards their desired objectives.

In these places —dematerialised but with the presence of human desires— nonexistent space in the ontological sense, but only in a phenomenon sense —there is now, what's more, an interactive space where individuals link up with others, opening up and communicating, by means of visual elements (texts, images, videos) the image or presentation of their own identity–. The elasticity of cyberspace offers users the possibility of continually reinventing themselves. Advertising thrives on the need for appropriation of social signs and symbols (riches, culture, education, experience, elegance, training, etc.) which individuals use so as to create their own personalities. All of those social signs, which allow them to integrate themselves into a community, whose profile (social, psychological, economic, political) coincides with their individual desires.

To sum up, there are three fundamental clarifications in the study of the general context of Global Advertising Culture. Firstly, an ontological differentiation; advertising culture is an exclusively human phenomenon which developed itself with the modernity that blossomed with capitalism. Then there is a pragmatic differentiation;

advertising language respects cultural diversity, since it is a form of communication which feeds itself on mutual and harmonious understanding of individuals from different cultures; always under the influence of a capitalist socio-economic model. Finally, there is a phenomena distinction which is more interesting, because experience demonstrates that we all share a society which lives under diverse norms. In this sense, the definition of culture consists of a complex and dynamic ecology of people, objects, world views, activities, actions, places and scenarios which, fundamentally, remain stable; yet which also change by virtue of routine communication and social interaction. Culture is a global context [13].

Advertising culture has evolved through socio-economic changes. There exist numerous theories which link Advertising Communication with Modern Economics. [4, 5, 11]. Globalisation processes brought with them an upsurge in the modern economy, which, fundamentally, consists of an aggressive capitalist neo-liberalism carrying a particular and distinct vision of industrial economic models [4] explains that the Information Society rewards those entrepreneurial projects which are capable of creating expectations in the market, without the need for either supporting material or new capital to back it; such as had happened in the Industrial Society. Now market confidence, in future success possibilities, is sufficient for businesses to have progressed. In the Nineties of the last century, the adolescent millionaires, or *geeks* as they are known, who possessed Information Technology knowledge and had put it at the disposal of their enterprises are an example of these socio-economic transformations.

For Castell [4], this emergent model offers similar opportunities, independant of place, or of initial capital on which new enterprises count. This widely-accepted vision, however, also has its detractors who fear a retrogressive tendency for human liberties with the establishment of such a Virtual Feudalism.

Virtual Feudalism shares political aspects with Classic Feudalism, but its economic base is abstract riches, and the resultant social system can be very fluid. The central institution of (*the new*) European Feudalism will be Virtual Feudalism, and not the Castle nor the lordly lands of (*the previous*) European Feudalism. The distribution of assets and privileges will depend on "Virtual Resources" on an international scale; that is to say, the particular basis of abstract riches can vary according to temporary variations of institutional financial needs and market conditions. [19]

The background of the Global Advertising Culture is the Information Society and Post-Modernity [14]. Modernity had abandoned us in a stagnant system, both permanent and subject to tradition, custom and the land. The Information Society and Post-Modernity place us in an unstable society based on a continuous change and re-adaptation of life's direction in the liquidation and re-construction of ideas, in the disappearance and re-appearance of objects, in change which has as its foundation "change for the sake of change". Society advanced towards the future; looking exclusively in the rear-vision mirror.

Globalisation, Localisation, Dis-location, Re-location and Glocalization are Socio-Cultural processes which indicate the effects of trans-national markets, of the Toyota production model, and of the neo-liberal economy on the cultural diversity of communities.

In the Information Society, Mass Culture develops itself outside of its original geographic context among new hybrid cultures. Cultural hybridisation has bypassed the problems of the Industrial Cultures which are now confronted with political identity problems. Privatisation is a cultural phenomenon characteristic of limited groups who struggle to preserve their identifying symbols, traditions and way of life.

All these factors incorporate a new phenomenology of merchandise into people's daily lives. This phenomenology of Global Advertising Culture is translated into what appears; what manifests itself. But previously it was Mass Culture which manifested itself to human awareness. The Phenomenon of the Masses is the aspect by which Industrial Production Objects bring themselves to the awareness of others and demand the intervention of intuition so as to promote the essence of things. In general terms, it could be said that the essence of Mass Culture is economic development, social progress and human wellbeing in Western societies.

The critical revision of the Mass Culture emphasises the importance of intuition and of common sense; thereby excluding awareness, as a resource, of what mankind has available in a contemporary society for gaining knowledge of a day-to-day nature by which to develop the quality of his life. To survive in this civilisation of the Mass Culture, mankind exercises an informed interpretation of objects which are presented to him, and at the same it throws light on an epistemic labour of world knowledge. Mass Culture and its context describes the realities in mankind's lives, but also the diverse world visions which are derived about this world of material desires produced by industry and which future generations will inherit.

In the Information Society, Virtual Communities are those connected by Digital Networks constituted by individuals who basically interpret this world, conceding the same validity to objects from industry. In this sense, Mass Culture succeeded in reuniting the consensus of individuals with similar interests; although, maybe, tightening symbolic links around products of Industrial Cultures. Mass Culture equipped itself with its own ideological planning, applying that to societies by means of heterogeneous forces (such as education, science, art, law, etc.), all of which dragged with it; a unique rhetoric.

Mass Culture organises itself around a super-structure which also understands science, managing to augment its credibility opposed to a growing relativism which introduces a Post-Modernity that is destructive. It was responsible for the lack of credibility in the major global debates -in which science was included-. That inclusion produced a new post-industrial hermeneutic.

The modern world, which surged from the end of the Second World War, was complicated and complex, and its irrational consumption was a senseless spiral. New interpretations impelled new modes of understanding, and of recognition, of what appeared in the everyday environment of mankind, relative to the vague discourses which industry produced through Advertising and the Communication Media.

4 The Role of Advertising in the Mass Culture

To make culture find its way to the masses is expensive and relatively unproductive; but absolutely necessary to maintain a social order.

Cultural Products are industrial output which are difficult to automate and, in a high-salaried economy, they are the dearest products to produce.

The Confrontation between production and creativity.

As a result, Advertising, apart from being an object of cultural consumption, is an important catalyst in society, and is also a financial source of the Mass Culture.

Advertising as a CULTURAL INDUSTRY (C.I.).

Symbolic creations may access society, through communicative supports and materials, in the spheres of the Media and the Market. They impact on a very diverse grouping of products and services, such as production chains and of product distribution, languages, and symbolic representations in the Communication Media.

Advertising is a C.I. to the extent that, the communicative tools may be used in the general promotion of products and services.

C.I.'s contribute directly to the construction of the culture which currently surrounds us by way of its iconic and audiovisual creations. Cultural Industries also construct languages and everything (is) a grouping of representations generated by their very actions.

Advertising, as a C.I., is a vague concept, referring to the grouping of constructive processes and to the dissemination of social knowledge.

4.1 The New Consumer Society

Consumption within the Mass Culture scarcely has anything to do with the necessities for the survival of humanity, but rather with personal desires, frustrations, insecurities and (dis)satisfactions. In the past, consumption evolved as a process of transformations so that something might function. In Mass Culture, consumption implies deterioration, expenditure or extinction of something. The pessimistic viewpoint of Consumerism is wastage. Irrational expenditure of survival resources of civilisations is the nucleus of the criticisms of the Consumer Society. This expenditure brings added importance to the cycle of destruction of natural resources of our planet and is necessary for the maintenance of the economic development of our societies.

5   The Promotional Condition of Contemporary Culture

Culture goes back to the World of Brands and Consumption, and the Commercial World reverts, more or less, to the Cultural. The term Promotion is very broad; it includes advertising, packaging and design, and also the commercial non-communicational activities.

The very nature of Mass Culture carries with it the idea of promotion:

- Cultural Products are produced for its benefit
- The Culture Industry promotes its products
- The market, the ongoing *re-novation* of products
- Culture promotes, and self-promotes, itself continuously, so as not to lose its market share.

The expansion of Logos and Brands is visible in advertising, the media, and progressively more so, in public places; be they commercial or not (*logofilia*).

The Brand is the lynchpin of World Culture. For various reasons:

- There is a lot of creative work in its conception and diffusion
- Advertising has changed its tune.
- Now, there are not objective characteristics of the product, but rather entertainment, involvement, and the spectacular.
- The aesthetic dimension of the brand goes beyond advertising.
- The design and packaging, the commercial architecture are points of reference which contribute to the anesthetization of the world.
- Brands associate themselves with grand causes to promote their image.

The brand is a aesthetic universe, and communication aesthetics result from a great interest in understanding new hegemonic forms of contemporary visual culture. The promotional condition of contemporary culture commences with new possibilities of understanding of the world through vision. Reality can be constructed by the use and manipulation of images.

Advertising appears in urban space occupying privileged places, or cornered in marginal zones as a visual debasement of cities. In the Post-Modern metropolis there exist geopolitical phenomena of images in which Industrial discourse is a primary consideration in the urban countryside.

Art is not Advertising and Advertising is not Art; but their rhetoric is heterogeneous and inter-textual. These properties are appropriate for their basic structure, and for the display of their communication plan. The inter-textuality of advertising resembles that which art generates in an innovative and alternative work, and with what industry feels itself comfortable for infiltrating into the individual awareness of its consumers.

It is complicated to find town-planners or architects who design cities counting on Advertising as an integral element of its countryside. The streets or squares are not designed for the placement of Advertising, as the Renaissance Monument organises the centre of the Square or the Baroque statue de-centralises the space of the same area. There does not exist an aesthetic urban environment which organises Advertising into the urban ambience, but indeed we know of an urban architecture respectful towards the natural environment and nature which avoids the contamination of the visual countryside. Always, and with an invasive attitude, Advertising opens for itself space in the asphalt and in the concrete; looking for maximum visibility, and with that, the exponential growth of visual impact.

In the Post-Modern era, the intentions of external Advertising are not so deep-rooted. It is not a question of imposition on the space. There exist examples of more intelligent advertising; looking for inter-textuality through places in which, in the past, there was an appropriate monument. This is a new dodge of Post-Modern cultural relativism; together with strategies of Capitalistic Culture.

5.1 The New Advertising

Concepts like *Publicização* [3], allow categorise new advertising formats which arose as a result of the transformation promoted by the socio-technological intervention of media devices on hyper-modern or post-modern society [7] with their contemporary social values [11].

Such values and interactive processes characterise new or alternative environments for the "movement of trademarks" (planned media and format rotation of brand advertising) in the context of the phenomena referred to as Transmedia or Crossmedia; generators of meaning for the consumer society.

Then, final thoughts are woven about the relevance of the creation and operation of procedures for observing network communication.

From these thoughts, a conclusion is drawn which comments on the implications of these phenomena for communicative thinking in relation to the problematic nomenclature Storytelling TransMedia and Crossmedia, that has been used to explain such so-called phenomena; especially seeking ways to delineate the horizons of this terminology and its uses in advertising communication in the Latin American context.

In this way, the tradition of Latin-American thought can, through qualitative studies, concern itself with supplying theoretical solutions, aimed at the creation of meaning, and linkages between brands and consumers, as is the intent of this document.

In doing so, a different position is assumed to that of the Anglo-Saxon, especially North American, which is more focused on the study of the effects. As a counterpoint to the latter, a closer look has been taken here at the socio-cultural aspects.

The new Hyper-Consumer Society [12], it is characterised by:

- Loss of traditional "Points-of-reference".
- A voluble, disorganised and unregulated consumer.
- Consumption that is more experiential and emotional than describable.
- One consumes more for oneself than to obtain the recognition of others.
- Consumers are possessed by fear of not experiencing new sensations.
- To buy is to play (Subjectivity)

5.2   The Capitalism of Fiction

The author of this concept is Vicente Verdú [17], who constructs the idea; beginning from the exposure of Jesús Ibáñez:

- Production-driven Capitalism: since the end of the 18th C. to the end of WWII.
  - MERCHANDISE.
    Consumer-driven Capitalism: Until the fall of the Berlin Wall. Publicity loads produced merchandise with meaning.
  - SIGNAGE.
    Capitalism of Fiction: Arises at the beginning of the 21st C. (written 20th C) places emphasis on
- THEATRICAL IMPORTANCE in PEOPLE.
  The two first-mentioned Capitalisms are loaded, above all, with material well-being. The third, is that of Fiction of sensations, of Psychological Well-being.

Their main function is to create a reality from fiction, with the appearance of improved and sweetened authenticity, which are characterised by:

- The importance of appearance.
- A spectacularised reality.
- The change from being citizens to being spectators.
- Global cultural homogenisation.

6 Advertising Global Culture

It´s a concept under construction, which is based on all of the above and which we summarize as follows:

Technology has changed the ways of communication, social relations and consumption; from programmatic advertising, which is global because it uses Communication Networks, through which spreads very quickly using, in addition to the numerical strategies, postmodern aesthetics based on art and visual culture, modes of social behavior socially based on shared cultures and consumption as a social activity with a cultural sense throughout the world. The Global Advertising Culture (complex, changing and evolving) has been raised thanks to programmatic advertising, based on numerical calculations and statistical prediction.

References

1. Aronowitz, S.: Science, objectivity and cultural studies. Crit. Q. **40**(2) (1998). https://doi.org/10.1111/1467-8705.00152
2. Carrol, N.: Philosophy of Art: A Contemporary Introduction. Routledge, London & New York (2002)
3. Casaqui, V.: Por uma teoria da publicização: transformações no processo publicitário. In: Anais do XXXIV Congresso Brasileiro de Ciências da Comunicação, Intercom/UNICAP, vol. 1, pp. 1–15 (2011)
4. Castells, M.: La sociedad de la red. Taurus, Madrid (1998)
5. Contreras, F.R.: El Cibermundo: Dialéctica del discurso informático. Sevilla, Alfar (1998)
6. Eagleton, T.: The Idea of Culture. Blackwell Publishers, Oxford (2000)
7. Fausto Neto, A.: Nas Bordas da circulação... Alceu **10**(20), 55–69 (2010)
8. González-Quirós, J.: Anatomía de una fascinación. Revista de Occidente **206**, 144–156 (1998)
9. González Martín, J.A.: Teoría General de la Publicidad. Fondo de Cultura Económica, Madrid (1996)
10. Harris, M.: Teorías sobre la cultura en la era posmoderna. Crítica, Barcelona (2000)
11. Hellín, P.A.: Publicidad y valores posmodernos. Siranda, Madrid (2007)
12. Lipovetsky, G.: Hypermodern Times. Polity Press, Cambridge (2006)
13. Lull, J.: The Push and Pull of Global Culture. Rouledge, London (2009)
14. Media, Communication, Culture: A Global Approach. PolityPress, Cambridge (2001)
15. Picó, J.: Modernidad y posmodernidad. Alianza, Madrid (1992)
16. Rodríguez-Ferrándiz, R.: De industrias culturales a industrias del ocio y creativas: los límites del "campo" cultural. Comunicar **36**, 149–156 (2011)

17. Subirats, E.: La cultura como espectáculo. Fondo de Cultura Económica, Madrid (1998)
18. Verdú, V.: El estilo del mundo. La vida en el capitalismo de ficción. Anagra, Barcelona (2003)
19. Virilio, P.: La máquina de visión. Cátedra, Madrid (1989)
20. Whittaker, J.: The Cyberspace Handbook. Routledge, London & New York (1999)

Reciprocal Customer Transfer Analysis at Golf Course Reservation Service and Golf Goods EC Site

Kento Hirota[1]([⊠]), Kohei Otake[2], and Takashi Namatame[3]

[1] School of Information and Telecommunication Engineering, Tokai University, 2-3-23, Takanawa, Minato-ku, Tokyo 108-8619, Japan
al5.3pb7@g.chuo-u.ac.jp
[2] Faculty of Science and Engineering, Chuo University, Bunkyo-ku, Japan
otake@tsc.u-tokai.ac.jp
[3] Graduate School of Science and Engineering, Chuo University, 1-13-27, Kasuga, Bunkyo-ku, Tokyo 112-8551, Japan
nama@indsys.chuo-u.ac.jp

Abstract. For consumer market, it is important fact that the BtoC-EC (business-to-consumer electronic-commerce) market continues to grow. One of the effective marketing strategies is "reciprocal customer transfer" which a store introduces the store's customers to another store to obtain customer loyalty. In this study, we analyze for effective reciprocal customer transfer between a golf course reservation site and a golf EC site to promote customer's upsell. Firstly, we divided golf courses into 32 categories and the golf items into 40 categories. Next, we extracted the user's usage history of these two services. Then, using these data, we carried out the time series association analysis. As a result of the analysis, we found some characteristic rules.

Keywords: Time series association analysis · K-means cluster analysis

1 Introduction

In recent years, the BtoC-EC (business-to-consumer electronic-commerce) market has been expanding steadily. According to the definition of the Ministry of Economy, Trade and Industry, this market is composed of three fields: the field of merchandising, the field of service, and the field of digital. Markets themselves continue to be booming, and there can be no major issues that will impede market growth. However, the growth rate of the merchandising field in 2017 is 7.5%, which is slower than the growth rate of 10.6% in 2016 [1]. We thought that one of the future effective strategies to keep current growth in BtoC-EC market is that "reciprocal customer transfer". It is a strategy to expand services by introducing customers to each other among different companies and services. For example, Softbank was deploying a service that triples a T point at Family Mart for its mobile phone subscribers [2], and JCB is making up a mechanism of reciprocal customer transfer with Person Holdings [3].

© Springer Nature Switzerland AG 2019
G. Meiselwitz (Ed.): HCII 2019, LNCS 11579, pp. 361–377, 2019.
https://doi.org/10.1007/978-3-030-21905-5_28

2 Purpose of This Study

In order to promote reciprocal customer transfer, it is necessary to analyze the relationship between the two services. In this research, we aim to activate reciprocal customer transfer between golf tool EC site and golf course reservation site. For that purpose, we analyze the mutual use situation between both services for the golf tool EC site and the portal site which manages the golf course reservation site.

3 Target Data

In this study, we focus on a golf course reservation history and a golf EC site purchase history from January 2016 to December 2017 of users possessed by a management company of both golf course reservation site and golf goods EC site. The target user is restricted customers who registered from January 2016 to June 2017 and come under the following formula (1) value is between 0.4 to 0.6.

$$0.4 \leq \frac{Number\ of\ golf\ course\ reservations}{Number\ of\ golf\ course\ reservations + Mail\ order\ site\ usage\ count} \leq 0.6 \quad (1)$$

There were 7947 users. The target golf courses are the average handicap of the user can be calculated out of the golf courses. Then, the number of golf course becomes 1867.

4 Analysis

In this section, we explain own analysis procedure.

4.1 Flow of Analysis

Firstly, we classified golf courses using their features such as average handicap of reserved users, the average utilization price per capita and the average review score. Secondly, we classified the product into some product categories. Next, we compiled the product by brand for each product classification. Then, we classified brands into 3 or 4 clusters based on average price and total sales volume for each product classification. Thirdly, we combined categorized golf courses and golf items with customer's transaction history. Finally, we carried out time series association analysis using the customer's transaction history.

4.2 k-Means Clustering

The k-means method is one of typical methods of non-hierarchical cluster analysis. By minimizing the evaluation function φ expressed by the following equation, it is divided into arbitrary k clusters.

$$\varphi = \sum\nolimits_{x_j \in X} \min_{i \in k} \|x_j - c_i^2\| \tag{2}$$

$x_j(j = 1, \ldots, n)$ is the value for j, and n is the number of cases. Also c_i is the center of cluster $i(i = 1, \ldots, k)$ [4].

4.3   Time Series Association Analysis

Time series association analysis [5] which is an analysis to extract effective association rules considered time transition of record. In usual association rule analysis, rules relating to simultaneous events are extracted. However, in time series association rule analysis, an association rule of events occurring at different times is searched in accordance with the temporal flow of the data designated by the time series. As a result, it is possible to clarify the temporal change in purchase behavior such as which product the person who purchased a certain product purchase next. Indicators are confidence, support and lift. The following will explain the indicators. *Count* (X) is the number of transactions including antecedent X, *Count* ($X \cap Y$) is the number of transactions including both antecedent X and consequent Y, and U is the total number of transactions.

- Confidence

Confidence shows the ratio at which antecedent X and consequent Y appeared at the same record among transaction data in which antecedent X appears. Confidence is calculated as follows.

$$confidence(X \rightarrow Y) = \frac{Count(X \cap Y)}{Count(X)} \tag{3}$$

If the value of this indicator is large, it can be said that it is a rule that the relation between the antecedent and the consequent is strong.

- Support

The degree of support shows the proportion of combinations that will be the antecedent X and the consequent Y among the whole. Support is calculated as follows.

$$support(X \rightarrow Y) = \frac{Count(X \cap Y)}{U} \tag{4}$$

A large value of this indicator indicates that the rule is frequently performed. Conversely, if the value of this indicator is low, the rule is considered to have happened by chance and it is judged that it is not useful.

- Lift

Lift expresses whether the assignment of the rule which is the antecedent X and the consequent Y increases more than the assignment of the rule leading to the consequent Y in the whole, by the ratio thereof.

$$lift(X \rightarrow Y) = \frac{\frac{Count(X \cap Y)}{Count(X)}}{\frac{Count(Y)}{U}} = \frac{confidence(X \rightarrow Y)}{Support(Y)} \tag{5}$$

If the value of this indicator is large, it can be judged that there is a relationship between X and Y. Because it is judged that Y was purchased on the antecedent that X was not purchased for Y alone reason.

5 Result and Discussions

In this section we show the analyzing result and discuss about them.

5.1 Result of Classification of Golf Course

The golf courses were divided into 32 categories based on three values which are the average handicap of users who reserved, the average utilization price per capita and the average review score. We divided the average handicap of users into four categories according to the quartile. From the top it was "for senior", "for semi-senior", "for semi-beginner", "for beginner". We divided the average utilization price per capita into four according to the quartile. From the top it was "expensive", "relatively expensive", "relatively low-price", "low-price". We divided the average rating points below the average and below "high" and "low". We made 32 classifications by multiplying these three variables.

5.2 Classification Result by Product Category

We divided products into 11 categories based on the genre of the EC site. Next, we classified brands belonging to each the genre into 3 or 4 categories based on the average price and the number of sales of brand products. Also, I used the k-means method for classification for each category (Table 1).

Table 1. Classification of product categories

Category	Brand classification	Average price (yen)	Average sales volume (pieces)
Wear (lady)	Low-price brands	3944	33
	High brands	22438	152
	Standard brands	10947	154
	Popular brands	12730	1885
Wear (men)	Low-price brands	4180	55
	High brands	22893	56
	Standard brands	13067	171
	Popular brands	10747	1629

(continued)

Table 1. (*continued*)

Category	Brand classification	Average price (yen)	Average sales volume (pieces)
Club	Low-price brands	10594	61
	high brands	66494	32
	Standard brands	33573	63
	Popular brands	21600	1272
Competition gift	Low-price brands	2209	11
	high brands	10644	20
	Popular brands	1875	106
Shaft parts	Low-price brands	2483	14
	High brands	5611	14
	Popular brands	4043	418
Shoes	Low-price brands	6095	38
	High brands	49500	2
	Standard brands	20581	84
	Popular brands	14830	1220
Bag and club case	Low-price brands	11029	30
	High brands	55293	4
	Standard brands	25714	78
	Popular brands	19256	847
Ball and accessory	Low-price brands	2668	114
	High brands	12369	333
	Standard brands	5927	107
	Popular brands	3386	2670
Distance measuring instrument	High brands	59760	11
	Standard brands	26944	71
	Popular brands	14290	595
Practice tool	Low-price brands	5188	51
	High brands	46534	22
	Popular brands	6283	698
Other	other	6663	41

We define brand classification with high sales quantity as "popular brands", define low-price brand classification as "inexpensive brands", define brand with a high price as "high brands", the remaining brand classification was defined as "standard brands".

5.3 Results and Discussion of Time Series Association Rule Analysis

We extracted rules with the support over1% and a lift over 1 among the obtained rules. In order to make rank the extracted rules, we calculated the standard score of each evaluation indicator and summed up then. Then we evaluated the rule with this value high as a useful rule. The characteristics of the obtained rule are shown below.

Results and Discussion Concerning the Rule from the Purchase of Goods to the Reservation of Golf Course

- Rules from purchasing balls and accessories to booking golf courses (Table 2)

Table 2. Rules from purchasing balls and accessories to booking golf courses

Antecedent	Consequent	Confidence	Support	Lift	Sum of standard scores
Ball and accessory _ low-price brands	Golf course for semi-beginner with relatively low-price and low ratings	21.284	3.154	1.202	1.425
Ball and accessory _ low-price brands	Golf course for beginner with relatively low-price and low ratings	19.848	2.942	1.089	0.315
Ball and accessory _ high brands	Golf course for semi-senior with relatively expensive and high ratings	18.767	1.752	1.254	0.388
Ball and accessory _ high brands	Golf course for senior with relatively expensive and high ratings	11.126	1.039	1.434	0.319
Ball and accessory _ popular brands	Golf course for semi-senior with relatively expensive and high ratings	19.037	2.078	1.272	0.810
Ball and accessory _ popular brands	Golf course for semi-beginner with relatively low-price and low ratings	18.807	2.053	1.062	-0.711
Ball and accessory _ standard brands	Golf course for semi-beginner with relatively expensive and high ratings	8.809	3.305	1.053	-0.719
Ball and accessory _ standard brands	Golf course for semi-senior with relatively low-price and high ratings	9.109	3.417	1.015	-0.864

From these rules of purchasing balls and accessories to reserving golf courses, I found the following. First, purchase of a popular brand led to a highly rated golf course. Next, purchasing low-price brands led to semi-beginners or beginners centric, relatively low-price and low rating golf courses booking. Also, purchasing standard brands led to golf course for semi-senior, relatively expensive and high rating golf courses booking. Finally, purchasing high brands led to semi-seniors or seniors centric, relatively expensive and high rating golf courses booking. From the above, it is considered that there is a proportional relationship between the price range of purchased balls and accessories and the price, reputation and player level of the golf course to be used.

- Rules from purchasing clubs to booking golf courses (Table 3)

Table 3. Rules from purchasing clubs to booking golf courses

Antecedent	Consequent	Confidence	Support	Lift	Sum of standard scores
club _ low-price brands	Golf course for semi-senior with relatively expensive and low ratings	7.524	1.164	1.038	−2.717
club _ low-price brands	Golf course for semi-senior with relatively low-price and low ratings	8.01	1.239	1.021	−2.728
club _ low-price brands	Golf course for senior with relatively expensive and high ratings	7.767	1.202	1.001	−2.923
club _ low-price brands	Golf course for semi-senior with low-price and low ratings	6.634	1.026	1.023	−3.024
club _ standard brands	Golf course for semi-senior with expensive and high ratings	14.218	1.127	1.298	−0.263
club _ standard brands	Golf course for semi-senior with relatively expensive and high ratings	16.904	1.339	1.129	−1.015
club _ standard brands	Golf course for semi-beginner with relatively expensive and low ratings	16.904	1.339	1.118	−1.092
club _ popular brands	Golf course for semi-beginner with relatively low-price and low ratings	17.849	2.992	1.008	−0.410

We summarize the results and discussions about rules from purchasing clubs to golf course reservations. First, golf courses linked from the purchase of popular brands were semi-beginners centric, the low-price and the evaluation was low. second, golf courses linked from the purchase of standard brands were semi-senior-centric and expensive. Finally, golf courses linked from the purchase of low-price brands were semi-senior-centric and the evaluation was low. Purchasing clubs and golf courses for semi-beginners and semi-senior players are highly relevant. In addition, we obtained not the rules from the purchase of low-price brands to the reservation of the beginner-centered golf course but the rules from the purchase of low-price brands to the reservation of the semi-senior centered golf course. The reason is considered as follows (Fig. 1).

Fig. 1. Comparison of overall and low-price brands in the proportion of wedge sales.

It is understood that the proportion of wedge is higher for low-price brands than for whole. Therefore, it can be inferred that player who is in the progress process stick to this tool more than beginners. The wedge is a club used for shots within 100 yards, approaches from around the green, and bunker shots.

Fig. 2. Comparison of average amounts by type of club in the whole and low-price brands.

From Fig. 2 it can be seen that the price of a low-price brand wedge is not cheaper than the whole wedge. Based on the above, we think that the ratio of wedges is high in the low-price brands is the reason for obtaining rules from the low-price brands to golf courses for semi-senior.

Results and Discussion Concerning the Rule from the Reservation of Golf Course to the Purchase of Goods

Overall, there were many rules linked to the purchase of balls, accessories and menswear from booking of golf courses. As there are no distinctive and definite rules compared to each golf course classification, we focus on the consequent of purchasing goods and consider the difference between the antecedent of the reserved golf course. First, we consider the rules that have the consequent of purchase to balls and accessories.

- **The rule from the reservation of golf course to the purchase of balls and accessories** (Table 4)

Table 4. Top 20 of the rule from the reservation of golf course to the purchase of balls and accessories

Antecedent	Consequent	Confidence	Support	Lift	Sum of standard scores
Golf course for semi-beginner with relatively low-price and low ratings	Ball and accessory _ popular brands	43.534	7.711	1.16	7.067
Golf course for beginner with relatively low-price and low ratings	Ball and accessory _ popular brands	41.758	7.61	1.113	6.479
Golf course for semi-beginner with low-price and low ratings	Ball and accessory _ popular brands	43.878	6.459	1.17	6.138
Golf course for semi-senior with relatively expensive and high ratings	Ball and accessory _ popular brands	42.057	6.296	1.121	5.480
Golf course for beginner with low-price and low ratings	Ball and accessory _ popular brands	39.202	6.521	1.045	4.852
Golf course for semi-senior with relatively low-price and high ratings	Ball and accessory _ popular brands	43.933	3.943	1.171	4.073
Golf course for semi-beginner with relatively expensive and low ratings	Ball and accessory _ popular brands	37.914	5.733	1.011	3.836
Golf course for semi-beginner with relatively low-price and high ratings	Ball and accessory _ popular brands	43.047	3.643	1.147	3.570

(*continued*)

Table 4. (*continued*)

Antecedent	Consequent	Confidence	Support	Lift	Sum of standard scores
Golf course for beginner with relatively expensive and low ratings	Ball and accessory _ popular brands	40.176	4.581	1.071	3.529
Golf course for beginner with relatively low-price and low ratings	Ball and accessory _ low-price brands	20.536	3.743	1.386	3.134
Golf course for semi-senior with expensive and high ratings	Ball and accessory _ high brands	15.657	1.715	1.677	3.031
Golf course for senior with relatively low-price and high ratings	Ball and accessory _ popular brands	43.671	2.591	1.164	2.882
Golf course for semi-senior with low-price and high ratings	Ball and accessory _ popular brands	42.994	2.804	1.146	2.865
Golf course for semi-beginner with relatively expensive and high ratings	Ball and accessory _ standard brands	17.964	1.502	1.646	2.863
Golf course for semi-senior with expensive and high ratings	Ball and accessory _ popular brands	38.743	4.243	1.033	2.842
Golf course for semi-beginner with relatively expensive and high ratings	Ball and accessory _ popular brands	41.018	3.43	1.093	2.816
Golf course for semi-beginner with low-price and high ratings	Ball and accessory _ popular brands	43.944	1.953	1.171	2.432
Golf course for semi-senior with relatively expensive and high ratings	Ball and accessory _ standard brands	16.304	2.441	1.494	2.405
Golf course for semi-beginner with low-price and low ratings	Ball and accessory _ low-price brands	20.323	2.992	1.371	2.387
Golf course for senior with low-price and high ratings	Ball and accessory _ popular brands	45.267	1.377	1.207	2.339

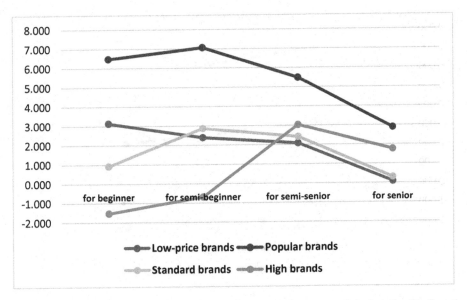

Fig. 3. The relationship between the level of players at golf courses and the brands of balls and accessories with reference to the sum of standard scores.

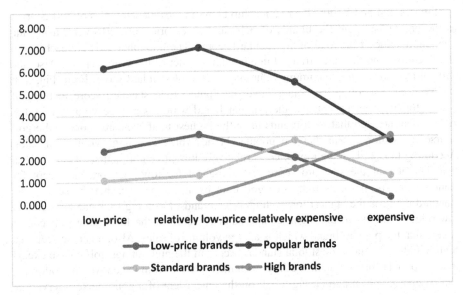

Fig. 4. The relationship between the price of the golf course and the brands of balls and accessories with reference to the sum of standard scores.

Fig. 5. The relationship between the evaluation points of the golf course and the brands of balls and accessories with reference to the sum of standard scores.

Figures 3, 4 and 5 show the relationship between the characteristics of golf courses as the prerequisite and the brands of balls and accessories as consequent, using the maximum value of the total of the standard scores. The horizontal axis are each brand classification, and they are arranged in descending order of the average price. Also, the vertical axis shows the maximum value of the total of standard score. From Fig. 3, it can be seen that low-price brands have the highest total standard score in the golf course for beginner except that the popular brand which is a large volume of sales. Also, it can be seen that high brands have the highest total standard score in the golf course for senior except that the popular brand which is a large volume of sales. According to Fig. 4, in the low-price or relatively low-price golf course, it can be seen that the total of the standard score is the highest for low-price brands except for standard brands. Also, in high price golf courses, it can be seen that the sum of the standard points is the highest for the high price brands. From Fig. 5, it can be seen that low-price brands have the highest total standard score in the low rating golf course except that the popular brand which is a large volume of sales. Also, it can be seen that high brands have the highest total standard score in the high ratings golf course except that the popular brand which is a large volume of sales. From the above, the following can be considered in purchasing a ball on the antecedent of a golf course reservation. First, regardless of the characteristics of the prerequisite golf course, balls and accessories of the popular brands are most likely to be purchased most. Next, it is thought that the price, evaluation, the level of the player's golf course used, and the price range of the balls and accessories are proportional.

- **The Rule from the Reservation of Golf Course to the Purchase of Men's Wear**
  (Table 5)

Table 5. Top 20 of the rule from the reservation of golf course to the purchase of balls and accessories

Antecedent	Consequent	Confidence	Support	Lift	Sum of standard scores
Golf course for semi-senior with relatively expensive and high ratings	Men's wear _ popular brands	37.625	5.633	1.101	4.359
Golf course for semi-beginner with relatively low-price and low ratings	Men's wear _ popular brands	35.689	6.321	1.044	4.336
Golf course for beginner with relatively low-price and low ratings	Men's wear _ popular brands	34.478	6.284	1.009	3.941
Golf course for semi-beginner with relatively expensive and low ratings	Men's wear _ popular brands	35.43	5.357	1.037	3.466
Golf course for semi-senior with relatively expensive and high ratings	Men's wear _ standard brands	18.395	2.754	1.438	2.474
Golf course for senior with expensive and high ratings	Men's wear _ popular brands	35.345	4.106	1.034	2.404
Golf course for semi-beginner with relatively expensive and high ratings	Men's wear _ popular brands	37.725	3.154	1.104	2.343
Golf course for senior with relatively low-price and high ratings	Men's wear _ popular brands	39.451	2.341	1.154	2.193
Golf course for senior with relatively low-price and high ratings	Men's wear _ standard brands	19.831	1.177	1.55	2.101
Golf course for semi-senior with relatively low-price and high ratings	Men's wear _ standard brands	19.107	1.715	1.494	2.080
Golf course for senior with relatively expensive and high ratings	Men's wear _ popular brands	37.419	2.904	1.095	2.044
Golf course for semi-beginner with relatively low-price and high ratings	Men's wear _ popular brands	36.538	3.092	1.069	1.930

(continued)

Table 5. (*continued*)

Antecedent	Consequent	Confidence	Support	Lift	Sum of standard scores
Golf course for semi-beginner with expensive and high ratings	Men's wear _ standard brands	19.115	1.515	1.494	1.916
Golf course for semi-senior with low-price and high ratings	Men's wear _ cheap brands	17.85	1.164	1.519	1.679
Golf course for semi-senior with relatively low-price and high ratings	Men's wear _ popular brands	35.146	3.154	1.029	1.563
Golf course for semi-beginner with low-price and low ratings	Men's wear _ cheap brands	16.156	2.378	1.375	1.501
Golf course for senior with low-price and high ratings	Men's wear _ popular brands	39.918	1.214	1.168	1.407
Golf course for semi-beginner with relatively low-price and low ratings	Men's wear _ cheap brands	15.477	2.741	1.317	1.326
Golf course for senior with expensive and high ratings	Men's wear _ standard brands	17.349	2.015	1.356	1.185

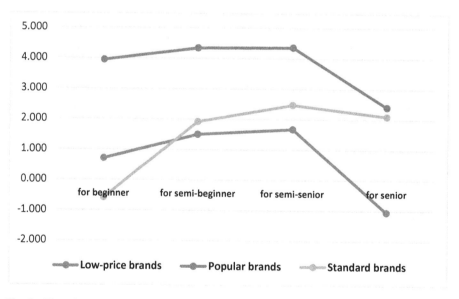

Fig. 6. The relationship between the level of players at golf courses and the brands of men's wear with reference to the sum of standard scores.

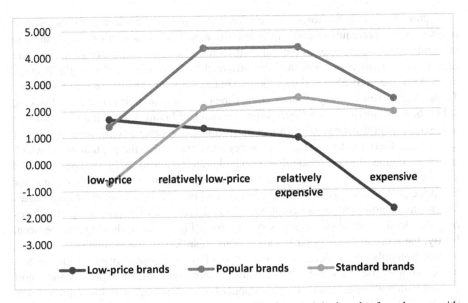

Fig. 7. The relationship between the price of the golf course and the brands of men's wear with reference to the sum of standard scores.

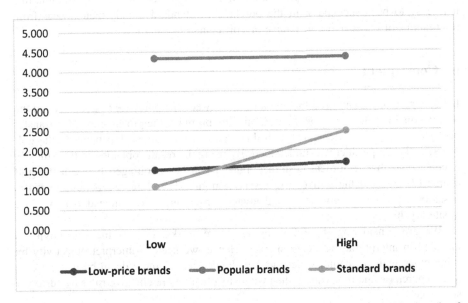

Fig. 8. The relationship between the evaluation points of the golf course and the brands of men's wear with reference to the sum of standard scores.

Figures 6, 7 and 8 shows the relationship between the characteristics of golf courses as the prerequisite and the brands of men's wear as consequent, using the maximum value of the total of the standard scores. The rows on the horizontal axis are each brand classification, and they are arranged in descending order of the average price. Also, the vertical axis shows the maximum value of the total of standard score. There were no rules on high brands among men's wear brand classifications. Looking at Fig. 6, the following can be seen. First, the standard brand showed the highest value in any type of golf course. Next, it can be seen that low-price brands have the highest total standard score in the golf course for beginner except that the popular brand which is a large volume of sales. In addition, standard brands showed the highest value in golf courses for senior. Figure 7 shows that low-price brands showed the highest value for low-price golf courses. Also, standard brands and popular brands showed high values for expensive golf courses. In addition, standard brands as the price of golf courses rises, the total of standard scores is rising. From Fig. 8, the following can be seen. Firstly, the score of the popular brands is high regardless of the evaluation of the golf course. Secondly, the difference of the standard score between ones which are low rating and golf courses which are high rating is not seen, but for popular brands, golf courses with high ratings have a higher standard score than ones with low ratings. From the above, the following was found out.

First of all, we think that it tends to lead to the purchase of low-price brand men's wear from reservations of low-price and golf courses for beginner. Next, we think that it is easy to be associated with the purchase of standard brands men's wear from reservations of expensive golf course or golf course for senior.

6   Consequent

In this research, we analyzed the relationship between the purchase of golf tool and the reservation of golf course at the EC site to promote reciprocal customer transfer between these two services. Through this analysis, the relationship between the golf course and each product was understood. By using the results obtained in this study, it is considered that reciprocal customer transfer can be encouraged between the golf course EC site and the golf course reservation site. Therefore, we believe that it is possible to expand customer share and advance upselling, which can lead to an increase in site loyalty.

We are considering the following as future works. First, some subjectivity is included in interpreting association rules. Hence, we need to interpret objectivity by using other analysis methods. Second, we should analyze more detail by using access logs to purchase and reservation, then we many obtain more effective rules by customer site wage.

Acknowledgment. We thank Golf Digest Online Inc. for permission to use valuable datasets and for useful comments. This work was supported by JSPS KAKENHI Grant Number 16K03944 and 17K13809.

References

1. Ministry of Economy: Trade and Industry Ministry of Economic Affairs Commerce Transaction Bureau. Infrastructure development of data driven society in Japan (e-commerce market research) (2018, in Japanese). http://www.meti.go.jp/press/2018/04/20180425001/20180425001-2.pdf
2. Nihon Keizai Shimbun website (in Japanese). https://www.nikkei.com/article/DGXLASDZ22HMR_S5A720C1TJC000/. Accessed 29 Jan 2019
3. Sankei Shimbun website (in Japanese). https://www.sankei.com/economy/news/181108/prl1811080407-n1.html. Accessed 29 Jan 2019
4. Onoda, T., Sakai, M., Yamada, S.: Experimental comparison of clustering results for k-means by using different seeding methods. In: Conference of the Japanese Society for Artificial Intelligence of Japan, vol. 25, pp. 1–4 (2011, in Japanese)
5. NTT DATA Mathematical System, Inc.: Visual Mining Studio Manual (2018, in Japanese)
6. Kim, M.: Data Science by R. Morikita Publishing (2012, in Japanese)

Analysis of the Characteristics of Customer Defection on a Hair Salon Considering Individual Differences

Mana Iwata[1]([⊠]), Kohei Otake[2], and Takashi Namatame[3]

[1] Graduate School of Engineering, Tokyo Institute of Technology,
2-12-1 Ookayama, Meguro-ku, Tokyo 152-8552, Japan
manachan.kororo@gmail.com
[2] School of Information and Telecommunication Engineering,
Tokai University, 2-3-23, Takanawa, Minato-ku, Tokyo 108-8619, Japan
[3] Faculty of Science and Engineering, Chuo University,
1-13-27, Kasuga, Bunkyo-ku, Tokyo 112-8551, Japan

Abstract. In recent years, as the number of hair salons increases, and the scale of the hair salon market has declined. Hence, competition for hair salon acquisition will be intensified. It is important for a hair salon to specify the cause of customer defection and plan to settle that. In this study, we analyzed the POS data with customer distinguishing information of a hair salon chain. Concretely, we performed logistic regression and hierarchical Bayes logit model to identify the cause of customer defection on the hair salon. After that, we categorized and considered the customers using hierarchical cluster analysis. Using these models, we extract the characteristics of customer defection on a hair salon and propose marketing measures to prevent defection.

Keywords: Customer defection · Logistic regression analysis ·
Hierarchical Bayes logit model

1 Introduction

The number of hair salon reached over 240,000 stores according to a research of the Ministry of Health, Labour and Welfare in fiscal year 2017, and new opening keeps increasing [1]. An emporium is increased newly, but also the scale of the hair salon market decreases in recent years, and it seems it is becoming severe in customer acquisition competition of a hair salon [1]. It is an important to reduce customer defection. It seems that the problem of compatibility with the hair salon is great for new customers, and it is difficult to completely prevent this. However, for customers who visit two or more times, we can think about marketing measure to prevent defection.

In this research, we aim to clarify factors of customer defection by analyzing customers' behavior at the last visit and one time ago of the last visit to the last visit, and their changes. Moreover, we aim to propose marketing measures to prevent customer defection.

© Springer Nature Switzerland AG 2019
G. Meiselwitz (Ed.): HCII 2019, LNCS 11579, pp. 378–391, 2019.
https://doi.org/10.1007/978-3-030-21905-5_29

2 Data Sets

In this study, we target on 10 stores of a hair salon chain in Japan, all stores are located in urban area and near railroad stations. In this study, we used following data.

- Member registration information data: Information on customer attributes such as gender, date of birth, member ID
- Purchasing history data with customer information: Information on purchasing behavior such as visit date/time, sales amount, purchased item (menu), staff rank, etc. (data period: July 1, 2015 to June 30, 2017)

We analyzed 11,683 customers with their information and visited at least twice during the data period of ID-POS data.

First, we defined the defect situation. Because each customer's visit interval was not same, we defined each customer's defect that was over 30 days from the visit interval maximum of former.

In addition, it is thought that the situation at the time of the last visit and change from the previous visit will lead to customer defection. Therefore, we made variables about the accounting contents which are at the last visit, the contents one time ago of the last visit and the amount which changed to the last visit.

3 Analysis of Customer Defection Factors

In this section, we describe our analysis procedure.

3.1 Flow of Analysis

We show the outline of analysis in Fig. 1.

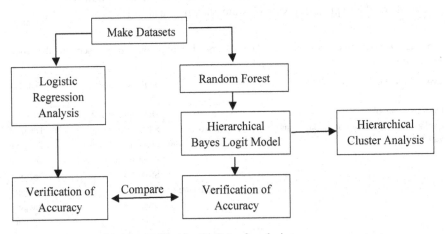

Fig. 1. Outline of analysis

In this research, first, we perform logistic regression analysis and then a hierarchical Bayes logit model. Then, we compare the accuracy of these two analyzes.

In the hierarchical Bayes logit model, variables cannot be selected sequentially like a general regression model, and it is necessary to select explanatory variables in advance. Since there are many explanatory variables created in this study, we select explanatory variables beforehand by using random forest. After that, we create a hierarchical Bayes logit model and obtain accuracy. Then, we perform hierarchical cluster analysis in order to cluster customers based on the determined individual parameters.

3.2 Logistic Regression Analysis

In order to identify factors of customer defection, we try to perform logistic regression analysis. When regression coefficient is defined as β_k and explanatory variable is defined as x_k, probability of occurring defection p of event y is shown as Eq. (1) [2].

$$p_y = \frac{\exp\{\beta_0 + \beta_1 x_1 + \cdots + \beta_k x_k\}}{1 + \exp\{\beta_0 + \beta_1 x_1 + \cdots + \beta_k x_k\}} \tag{1}$$

where y of (1) defines below, and we estimate parameter β_k.

$$y = \begin{cases} 1 \cdots \text{Defect} \\ 0 \cdots \text{Continue} \end{cases}$$

As explanatory variables used in the model construction, we created twelve variables from customers' behavior at the last visit, thirteen variables from changes from one time ago of the last visit to the last visit, four variables from personal attributes of customers and hair salon's staffs. Moreover, we normalized sales, discount amount, point balance, diff of sales, diff of discount amount, and diff of point balance

Details of the explanatory variables are shown in Table 1.

Table 1. Demographic variables and customers' behavior variables used in the model construction

Type of variable			Variable name	Data type
Objective variable			Defection or not	0 or 1
Explanatory variable	Behavior at the last visit	No interaction	Sales	Decimal
			Discount amount	Decimal
			Point balance	Decimal
			Store ID	Factor
		Interaction	Cut	Integer
			Treatment	Integer
			Color	Integer
			Blow shampoo hair set	Integer
			Private brand item	Integer
			Perm	Integer

(continued)

Table 1. (*continued*)

Type of variable			Variable name	Data type
Change in behavior from one time ago of the last visit to the last visit	No inter action	Sales	Decimal
		Discount amount	Decimal
		Point balance	Decimal
		Store ID	Factor
		Staff ID	Factor
	Interaction	Cut	Integer
		Treatment	Integer
		Color	Integer
		Blow shampoo hair set	Integer
		Private Brand item	Integer
		Perm	Integer
Interaction in a day of the week		A day of week at the last visit	Factor
		A day of week at one time ago of the last visit	Factor
Interaction in time		Time at the last visit	Factor
		Time at one time ago of the last visit	Factor
Interaction in rank		Staff's rank at the last visit	Factor
		Staff's rank at one time ago of the last visit	Factor
Interaction in demography		Customers' sex	Factor
		Customers' age	Integer

3.3   Hierarchical Bayes Logit Model

Conventional statistical methods such as logistic regression analysis common obtaining point-estimate parameters by most likelihood method. On the other hand, the hierarchical Bayes logit model assumes a prior distribution for each parameter and performs distribution convergence and individual parameter estimation for each case by repeatedly generating random numbers based on prior distribution in simulation and update parameter values using Bayesian theory. As a result, it is possible to flexibly express the parameters of each individual and each group. Based on the premise that customer's desire for service varies from individual to individual, we think that it is appropriate to estimate parameters for each customer rather than uniquely estimate parameters, and we apply a hierarchical Bayes logit model.

3.3.1   Formulation of Defection Discrimination Model

In this section, we show a model that discriminates whether or not it is a defection using a hierarchical Bayes logit model. The proposed model is expressed in the framework of a logistic regression model. The defection probability p_i is shown below as a proposed model in Eq. (2).

$$p_i = \Pr\{y_i = 1\} = \frac{e^{u_i}}{1 + e^{u_i}} \qquad (2)$$

Equation (3) concretely shows the utility u_i for the defection of the customer i.

$$u_i = X_i^T B_i + x_i[StoreID[i]] \qquad (3)$$

X_i is an explanatory variable vector containing intercept terms related to the defection of customer i, B_i is a parameter vector containing intercept term of each customer, and x_i is a store specific term. Also, in order to take account of heterogeneity of customers, parameters are assumed to be different for each customer [2].

3.3.2   Parameter Hierarchy

In this study, we used Markov Chain Monte Carlo methods, (MCMC) to estimate parameters and No-U-Turn-sampler for sampling [6]. Sampling was done 5000 times. Then the first 500 times was the burn-in period that the samples were discarded.

To consider customer heterogeneity, we constructed the hierarchical Bayes logit model that was assumed that individual parameters for each customer. To estimate the parameters of a hierarchical Bayes logit model, simulations are performed in which the prior distribution is assumed for each parameter and the generation of random variables is repeated from the distribution [3, 4].

In this study, it is assumed that the parameter vector β_i follows the multivariate normal distribution as Eq. (4).

$$\beta_i \sim MVN(\Delta, \Sigma_B) \qquad (4)$$

In addition, as a hyper prior distribution for expressing the variation of parameters for each customer, for Δ and $\sum_B$ in Eq. (4), a uniform wide distribution (no information prior distribution) and the inverse Wishart distribution as shown in Eqs. (5) and (6).

In Eq. (6), M represents the number of variables, v_0 represents a constant M, and V_0 represents a square matrix of $M \times M$ with a diagonal component $M + 3$.

$$\Delta \sim U(0, 100) \qquad (5)$$

$$\sum_B \sim IW(v_0, V_0), v_0 = M, V_0 = \begin{bmatrix} M+3 & 0 & \cdots & 0 \\ 0 & M+3 & & \\ & \vdots & \ddots & \vdots \\ 0 & 0 & \cdots & M+3 \end{bmatrix} \qquad (6)$$

In addition, we use $\hat{R}$ to confirm convergence of parameters. $\hat{R}$ is a convergence determination index proposed by Gelman and Rubin [5]. If $\hat{R}$ is close to 1, convergence to a steady distribution is suggested, and when it is larger than 1 it is considered not converging. In [5], if $\hat{R}$ should be less than 1.1 or 1.2, we use the criterion that it can be judged that it converged.

Random Forest
In the hierarchical Bayes logit model, when the more variables are, it takes more time to calculate the simulation. In addition, since all 29 explanatory variables used in this analysis do not necessarily work significantly, so we perform random forest as a preliminary analysis before creating a model. Using the significance due to the average decrease in impurity of the Gini coefficient calculated from the result, the top eight variables with the highest importance are selected in advance. The top eight variables with high importance obtained as a result of performing the random forest using explanatory variables shown in Table 1 are shown in descending order in Table 2.

Table 2. Variable selected by random forest

Point balance at the last visit
Difference of point balance
Store ID at the last visit
Sales at the last visit
Difference of sales
Day of the week at last visit
Day of the week at one time ago of the last visit
Age

In the hierarchical Bayes logit model, if we use categorical variables, it takes very long time to calculate. In order to think about marketing measures, we thought that it is not necessary to obtain a specific day of the week, so the day of the week was converted into two values, that is, the weekend or not. Furthermore, since we thought that the store ID at the last visit could be explained by the store specific that introduced this time, it is excluded from the explanatory variables.

3.4   Hierarchical Cluster Analysis

This analysis attempts to identify relatively homogeneous groups of cases (or variables) based on selected characteristics, using an algorithm that starts with each case (or variable) in a separate cluster and combines clusters until only one is left. We use the Ward method.

3.5   Dataset and Evaluation Indicator

Although the number of target customers in this research is 11,683, when constructing, we randomly sample the number of continuing customers by setting the number equal to the number of defective customers.

Furthermore, in order to verify the prediction accuracy of the model, we set 75% of the data for training data and 25% for the test data, for each continuing customer and each defective customer. As a result, the datasets used in the model construction was divided as follows (Table 3).

Table 3. Datasets used in the model construction

	Training data	Test data	Total
Defective customers	2,493	831	3,324
Continuing customers	2,493	831	3,324
Total	4,986	1,662	6,648

In order to confirm the prediction accuracy of the constructed model, we performed hold-out validation by using the train data and test data. Specifically, we created a confusion matrix like a following table and we calculated prediction accuracy of the constructed model by using following equations (Table 4).

Table 4. Confusion matrix

		Predicted class	
		Positive	Negative
Actual class	Positive	True Positive (TP)	True Negative (TN)
	Negative	False Negative (FP)	False Negative (FN)

Accuracy (ACC): Percentage of the total number correctly predicted among the total number predicted.

$$ACC = \frac{TP + TN}{FP + FN + TP + TN}$$

Precision (PRE): Percentage of the total number that is a positive class actually among the total number predicted positive class.

$$PRE = \frac{TP}{TP + FP}$$

Recall (REC): Percentage of the total number predicted positive class among the total number that is a positive class actually

$$REC = \frac{TP}{FN + TP}$$

F-measure: harmonic mean of PRE and REC

$$F\text{-}measure = 2 \times \frac{PRE \times REC}{PRE + REC}$$

4 Results

In this section, we summarize our results.

4.1 Logistic Regression

We built a model that predicts defection for the entire customer using binomial logistic regression analysis with stepwise selection method. Then, we selected explanatory variables of coefficient of significant probability less than 0.05.

Table 5. Estimated value of selected partial regression coefficient

Explanatory variables	Partial regression coefficient
Intercept	1.232
Sales	−0.137
Discount amount	−0.135
Point balance	−0.607
Store ID at the last visit was B	1.301
Store ID at the last visit was C	0.510
Store ID at the last visit was D	0.606
Store ID at the last visit was E	0.401
Store ID at the last visit was F	0.402
Store ID at the last visit was G	0.720
Store ID at the last visit was H	0.751
Store ID at the last visit was K	0.786
Last visit was on Friday	−0.316
Last visit was on Sunday	−0.287
Menu at the last visit was cut	−0.840

(continued)

Table 5. (continued)

Explanatory variables	Partial regression coefficient
Menu at the last visit was blow shampoo hair set	−0.771
Difference of point balance	0.319
Not changed staffs	−0.204
Add cut	0.384
Add private brand goods	0.123
Menu at the last visit was cut and perm	0.750
Menu at the last visit was cut and blow shampoo hair set	0.585
Age	−0.010

From Table 5, we found that sales, point balance, store ID, the day, menu and staff's sex at the last visit become significant.

Tables 6, 7, 8 and 9 show the confusion matrix and the evaluation indicator for the train data and the test data.

Table 6. Confusion matrix of model for the train data

		Predicted class	
		Positive	Negative
Actual class	Positive	836	1657
	Negative	339	2154

Table 7. Evaluation indicator of model for the train data (%)

ACC	PRE	REC	F-measure
60.0	71.1	33.5	45.6

Table 8. Confusion matrix of model for the test data

		Predicted class	
		Positive	Negative
Actual class	Positive	266	565
	Negative	114	717

Table 9. Evaluation indicator of model for the test data (%)

ACC	PRE	REC	F-measure
59.1	70.0	32.0	43.9

From Tables 6, 7, 8 and 9, it turns out that it is almost resulted in Negative

4.2 Hierarchical Bayes Logit Model

Table 10 shows the average value and $\hat{R}$ of the individual parameters of the explanatory variable obtained as a result of the hierarchical Bayes logit model.

Table 10. Variable selected by random forest

Explanatory variables	Average of parameters	$\hat{R}$
Intercept	−0.052	1.001
Point balance at the last visit	−1.123	1.001
Difference of point balance	0.753	1.011
Sales at the last visit	−0.144	1.008
Difference of sales	−0.029	1.001
Day of the week at the last visit	−0.148	1.001
Day of the week at one time ago of the last visit	−0.137	1.001
Age	−0.245	1.001

From the Table 10, we also found that $\hat{R}$, which determines the convergence of each parameter, also falls below 1.1, which is a measure of convergence. It is understood that point balance and age parameter are negative, and difference of point balance is positive. Also, we can see that difference of sales and sales parameter may be negative or positive. In addition, the confusion matrix for the train data and the evaluation indicator are as shown in Tables 11 and 12 below.

Table 11. Confusion matrix of model for the train data in hierarchical bayes logit model

		Predicted class	
		Positive	Negative
Actual class	Positive	2057	436
	Negative	11	2482

Table 12. Evaluation indicator of model for the train data (%)

ACC	PRE	REC	F-measure
91.0	99.5	82.5	90.2

Comparing Tables 6, 7, 8 and 9 with Tables 11 and 12, it is understood that the hierarchical Bayes logit model was better than logistic regression in performance.

As a result of hierarchical cluster analysis, it was divided into four clusters. The average values of the parameters of each cluster are shown in Table 13.

Table 13. The average value of each parameter

	Cluster 1	Cluster 2	Cluster 3	Cluster 4
Intercept	0.154	0.169	−0.277	−0.237
Point balance at the last visit	−1.179	−1.105	−1.052	−1.158
Difference of point balance	0.728	0.828	0.768	0.695
Sales at the last visit	−0.270	0.005	−0.021	−0.279
Difference of sales	−0.103	0.076	0.032	−0.106
Day of the week at the last visit	−0.080	−0.085	−0.217	−0.210
Day of the week at one time ago of the last visit	−0.069	−0.075	−0.214	−0.183
Age	−0.181	−0.170	−0.315	−0.311

From Table 13, the positive and negative of the average value of most parameters did not change depending on the cluster. However, there is a case that sales and the difference of sales differed, and it turned out that a difference arises depending on the cluster.

5   Discussions

In this section, we discuss about the results of our analysis and propose some efficient marketing strategies.

5.1   Discussions for Logistic Regression

As the result of logistic regression analysis, we found that customers with low sales and small discount amount at the last visit are easy to defect. The sales are considered to represent money sense for beauty. Therefore, it can be said that customers who think that they do not want to pay so much for beauty and customers who are dissatisfied with less discount amount are easy to defect. Therefore, because coupons generated at a certain amount of money or more cannot prevent such customer defection, measures that distribute coupons that arise only by visiting stores are considered to be effective.

Also, when the point balance at the final visit was small, and customer with a difference in point balance know that it is easy to defect. The point balance is considered to represent the loyalty to the store of the customer. Also, the difference of the point balance is the point award amount one time ago of the last visit - the point usage amount one time ago of the last visit, so the difference of the point balance is considered to represent the intention to accumulate points. In other words, it can be said that customer with low royalties for the store and having little intention to accumulate points tend to defect. Considering that customers who do not intend to accumulate points generally are hard to become good customers, it is thought that firstly it is necessary to raise the royalty for the store by urging to accumulate points. Therefore, measures such as preparing some benefits when saving points more than a certain amount are considered to be effective.

In addition, variables for staff and menu are also selected. Regarding the staff, we found that customers who are changing staff are more likely to defect. Therefore, it can be said that it is necessary to take careful handover when the customer changes staff. Regarding the menu, we found that it was easy to continue if the customer selects blow shampoo hair set at the last visit. This is because menus are less likely to cause mistakes than perms and colors.

Also, we found customers choosing a cut at the last visit are more likely to continue, but adding a cut tends to lead to defect. The staff are familiar with the preferences of customers who continue to select a cut, but they do not know the preferences very much about customers who add a cut. It is thought that as the hearing about the preferences does not go properly, it may lead to defect. Hence, it is considered that it is necessary to carefully hear the preferences for customers who have added a new menu, even if they are not visiting for the first time.

Also, we found that customers who visit on Friday and Sunday are harder to defect. However, because it is difficult to identify the cause of such a result, we found that it was necessary to compare it between weekdays and weekends. The results compared on weekdays and weekends are stated in Sect. 5.2. It also turned out that there was a difference in departure rate for each store. Therefore, rather than doing a campaign common to all stores, it is considered more effective to conduct different campaigns for each store. It is necessary to analyze each salon, which is also a future work.

5.2 Discussions for Hierarchical Bayes Logit Model

As the result of the analysis using the hierarchical Bayes logit model, the overall tendency is point balance at the last visit is small, and customer with a difference in point balance know that it is easy to defect. Hence, measures for points as stated in Sect. 5.1 are considered to be effective.

Also, customers with low sales and little increase from the last visit in sales are easy to defect. Sales represent the sense of money for beauty, and the difference in sales represents how good the menu compared to last time. In other words, customers not only do not want to pay so much for beauty, but also want to cheaper than raising the rank of the menu are easy to defect. Therefore, it is considered good practice to advertise to customers like this, appealing cheaper than appealing the quality of treatment.

Furthermore, it turned out that customers who come to the store on weekdays are more likely to defect. Hence, it seems that establishing benefits such as restricted visits on weekdays is a measure to prevent defection. In addition, it is found that the lower the age, the easier it is to defect, so it is considered that setting privileges for young people is a measure to prevent defection.

As a result of hierarchical cluster analysis, the average value of parameters for most clusters did not change much, but there was a difference in the difference between sales and difference of sales. In other words, unlike the overall trend, it turned out that there are clusters that can be defected even if sales are high or there is a difference in sales. Hence, there is a group that tends to defect, despite spending money on beauty or changing to a good menu. In such a group, it is better to think about improving the quality of service rather than devising measures to lower the price. Hence, it is thought that there is a group that should appeal affordable sales rather than the quality of treatment and there is a group that should appeal quality and satisfy rather than sales. In order to identify the characteristics of attributes of such a group, further analysis is necessary and it can be said that this is also our future work.

6   Conclusion

In this research, for a hair salon chain using member registration information data, purchase history data at the last visit, purchase history data one time ago of the last visit, purchase history data changed from one time ago of the last visit to the last visit, we constructed a model that predicts customer defection. As a result, we are able to grasp actions specific to customers who defected.

In addition, in order to consider individual differences, we construct a hierarchical Bayes logit model to predict customer defection. As a result, accuracy has improved and individual differences among customers can be considered. Furthermore, by using hierarchical cluster analysis, we divided the clusters into four, and analyzed the characteristics of each cluster. Hence, we can propose some marketing measurements to prevent defection.

In the defection prediction model constructed in this research, although it is possible to clarify the characteristics of customers by performing logistic regression analysis. However, the prediction accuracy of the constructed model is not satisfactory and it was found that REC was especially low, and it tended to be subject to negative expectations, so there is room for improvement. In addition, in the hierarchical Bayes logit model, only a part of the result variable considering calculation time was selected, and categorical variables such as age were also treated as numerical values. As a result, the variables were not sufficient and we could not fully grasp the characteristics of the customers that were divided into clusters. In order to solve the problem, it is necessary to increase the number of variables, and accordingly it is necessary to consider the reduction of calculation time.

Furthermore, we could confirm the accuracy in the hierarchical Bayes logit model only for the train data. Since there is no general method for checking the accuracy with respect to the test data, it is necessary to construct an algorithm in consideration of this point. In addition, it can be said that more concrete measures can be devised by constructing a more detailed model using variables not used in this research.

Acknowledgment. We thank a hair salon company for permission to use valuable datasets. This work was supported by JSPS KAKENHI Grant Number 16K03944 and 17K13809.

References

1. Ministry of Health, Labor and Welfare: Statistical Information White Paper "Overview of Health Administration Administrative Report in Heisei 29" (2018). https://www.mhlw.go.jp/toukei/saikin/hw/eisei_houkoku/17/. (in Japanese)
2. Yano Economic Research Institute: 2018 Edition beauty care marketing general press release (2018). https://www.yano.co.jp/press-release/show/press_id/1884. (in Japanese)

3. Sato, Y., Otake, K., Namatame, T.: Analysis of the characteristics of repeat customer in a golf EC site. In: Meiselwitz, G. (ed.) SCSM 2017. LNCS, vol. 10282, pp. 223–233. Springer, Cham (2017). https://doi.org/10.1007/978-3-319-58559-8_19
4. Matsura, K.: R2 Bayesian statistics modeling with Stan and R. Kyouritu (2016). (in Japanese)
5. Sato, S., Asahi, Y.: The model of purchasing and visiting behavior of customers in an e-commerce site for consumers. Commun. Oper. Res. Soc. Jpn. **58**(2), 16–22 (2013)
6. Oikawa, Y., Otake, K., Namatame, T.: Purchasing behaviors considering various search actions of customers at EC sites. In: Abstracts of Spring Conference for 2018 of Operational Research Society of Japan, pp. 270–271 (2017). (in Japanese)
7. Gelman, A., Rubin, D.B.: Inference from iterative simulation using multiple sequences. Stat. Sci. **7**, 457–472 (1992)
8. Gilks, R.W., Richardson, S., Spiegelhalter, J.D.: Markov Chain Monte Carlo in Practice, pp. 131–143. Chapman & Hall, London (1996)

Analysis of Characteristics of Golf Course Using User Review at Golf Portal Site

Mizuki Izawa[1(✉)], Takashi Namatame[2], and Kohei Otake[1]

[1] School of Information and Telecommunication Engineering, Tokai University,
2-3-23, Takanawa, Minato-ku, Tokyo 108-8619, Japan
6bjm2209@cc.u-tokai.ac.jp, otake@tsc.u-tokai.ac.jp
[2] Faculty of Science and Engineering, Chuo University, 1-13-27, Kasuga,
Bunkyo-ku, Tokyo 112-8551, Japan
nama@indsys.chuo-u.ac.jp

Abstract. Customer reviews have a major impact on consumers who are considering purchasing and using. There are various reviews, such as positive reviews and negative reviews. Consumers who are considering purchasing can obtain useful information without actually using products or shops by looking at the reviews. Moreover, it is possible to grasp the consumer's actual opinion from the customer review. In this study, we will grasp the characteristics of each golf course for the review on the golf course of a certain golf portal site. In addition, we clarify what kind of change in feature appears due to the difference in golfer skill.

Keywords: Natural language processing · Hierarchical cluster analysis · User review

1 Introduction

In recent years, EC (Electronic Commerce) market developed rapidly because of the spread of the internet [1]. The size of the B to C - EC market in 2017 is 16,555.4 billion yen (Table 1). Compare with the other sector, the elongation percentage of the service sector is higher. Focusing on the service contents provided by the EC site, the use contributed review service has been introduced at many EC markets. In this service, the user posts review based on his/ her own experience after purchasing the products. This is commonly called "a word of mouth (WOM). In internet ere, many of E-WOMs are posted to many EC-sites, information site or SNS. These posted reviews are used to make decisions for consumers who are considering purchasing [2]. Consumers who are considering purchasing can obtain useful information without using products or shops by looking at the reviews. A review has a strong influence on consumer's decision making. In addition, it is said that user review is information based on the user's experience and opinions, it is considered that the features of the review target can be grasped.

In this study, we focus on a golf portal site in Japan and we clarify the features of golf courses from user review. We attempt to can clarify the characteristics of golf courses on the consumer's point of view by using user reviews. Moreover, we consider

© Springer Nature Switzerland AG 2019
G. Meiselwitz (Ed.): HCII 2019, LNCS 11579, pp. 392–402, 2019.
https://doi.org/10.1007/978-3-030-21905-5_30

the difference of evaluation to the golf course from the difference of player golf skill. This is because the contents of the review differed depending on the user's golf skill.

Table 1. The market size of B to C - EC in Japan

	2016	2017	Elongation percentage
Merchandising field	8.04 trillion yen	8,600.8 billion yen	7.5%
Service field	5,335.2 billion yen	5,995.8 billion yen	11.3%
Digital field	1,778.2 billion yen	1,947.8 billion yen	9.5%
Total	15,135.8 billion yen	16,550.5 billion yen	9.1%

2 Data Summary

In this study, we used data provided by the Japanese golf portal site. Specifically, we targeted on customer data, golf course attribute data and review data for golf courses. Summary of these data is shown below.

- Customer data: Customer data contains information on customers' sex, age, golf score, income etc.
- Golf Course Attribute Data: Golf course attribute data contains information such as the postal code, location of golf course, price range presence of professional tour etc.
- Review Data: Review Data is information on reviews about the golf courses. It contains that contents of a review (text), golf score of customers who posted review, golfer type of customers who posted review etc. The data period is three years from August 2015 to August 2018.

3 Materials and Method

3.1 The Purposes of Analysis

We grasp the characteristics of the golf course from customer data and review data and clarify the evaluation of the golf course due to the difference of the customer's golf skill. Figure 1 shows the outline of our analysis. First, we create dataset from the provided data. Second, in order to classify the golf course, we performed hierarchical cluster analysis. Third, we performed natural language processing in order to grasp the characteristics of the review posted on the golf courses belonging to each cluster. Moreover, we also focus on the level of reviewer. Finally, we clarify the characteristics of the golf course from the review and propose measures.

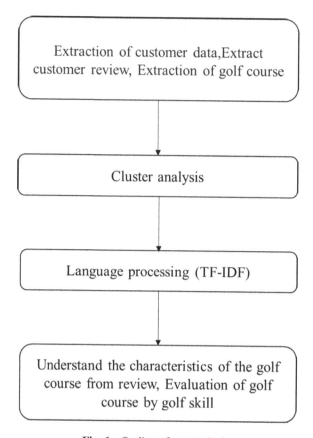

Fig. 1. Outline of our analysis

3.2 Dataset

First, we extracted customers who have customer ID from customer data. Additionally, we selected customers who have written a review of the golf course more than 10 times in the data period. From the result, we extracted 3,563 customers' data and 1918 golf course data used by customers who wrote reviews more than 10 times as the data set.

3.3 Classification of Golf Courses Using Hierarchical Cluster Analysis

Next, we performed hierarchical cluster analysis using the golf course attribute data. This aims to gather golf courses with similar attributes. We think that it is possible to extract features common to multiple golf courses by gathering golf course.

Here, we used the 6 variables (caddy is adjoined or not, the minimum price of course uses, the maximum price of course uses, number of practice place, host a large-scale golf tour or not, course land price) to perform hierarchical cluster analysis. We used Manhattan distance as the distance between the data, and we used Ward method as a distance between the clusters. The results are shown in the Fig. 2.

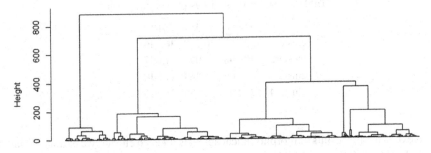

Fig. 2. Result of hierarchical cluster analysis using golf course attribute data

From the result, we divided all golf course into four clusters.
Summary statistics of each cluster are shown in Table 2.

Table 2. Summary statistics for each cluster

Cluster (Number of golf course)	Caddie (sum)	Minimum price (yen, average)	Maximum price (yen, average)	Tournament (sum)	Land price (average)	Practice ground (average)
Cluster 1 (405)	405	8,174	15,107	0	1,152,262	21.6
Cluster 2 (392)	392	10,920	18,115	0	1,304,008	220.5
Cluster 3 (162)	0	8,534	14,436	0	1,086,657	57.6
Cluster 4 (274)	268	15,536	26,935	28	1,138,488	32.9

From Table 2, we named cluster 1 as "General public course", cluster 2 as "Large high price course", cluster 3 as "Practice course", cluster 4 as "Professional course".

3.4 Analysis of Customer Review by Natural Language Processing

Next, we performed natural language processing in order to grasp the characteristics of the review posted on the golf courses belonging to each cluster. Natural language processing is used for analysis of text data, and many types of research are targeted on reviews on the EC site [3].

First, we summarized. the review data on golf courses belonging to each cluster as one document. We performed morphological analysis for each document. We use KH Coder for analysis. KH Coder is a free software for quantitative content analysis or text mining [4].

In this study, we extracted nouns, verbs, adjectives, proper nouns, place names, organization names and part-of-speech of proper nouns. From the result, nouns, verbs and adjectives appeared frequently. The frequency of appearance of part-of-speech (nouns, verbs and adjectives) in each cluster is summarized in Table 3.

Table 3. Summary statistics of part of speech

	Noun	Verb	Adjective
cluster1	133,247	46,750	36,946
cluster2	40,098	11,097	11,097
cluster3	37,765	14,369	11,340
cluster4	121,800	46,230	35,729

Next, using the results of morphological analysis for each cluster, we extracted feature words by the TF-IDF method. TF-IDF method was adopted by the following formulas (1) to (3). The TF-IDF method calculates the importance by weighting the occurrence of all documents and the number of times of non-appearance in other documents. The accuracy of feature words is raised by weighting the documents in two viewpoints [5].

$$TF - IDF_{i,j} = tf_{i,j} \times idf_i \qquad (1)$$

$$tf_{i,j} = \frac{n_{i,j}}{\sum_S n_{S,j}} \qquad (2)$$

$$idf_i = \log \frac{|D|}{|\{d : d \in t_i\}|} \qquad (3)$$

Here, $n_{i,j}$ is the number of appear frequency about word i in the sentence j. $\sum_S n_{S,j}$ is the number of appear frequency of all words in the sentence j, $|D|$ is the total number of all sentences $|\{d : d \in t_i\}|$ is the number of sentences containing word i.

Table 4 shows words with the highest TF-IDF value in each document (cluster).

Table 4. The highest TF-IDF value in each document (cluster).

Appearance rank	General public course	Large high price course	Practice course	Professional course
1	Play	Tournament	Riverbed	Middle
2	Revenge	Mt. fuji	Resort	Lunch
3	Undulation	Caddie	Old	Atmosphere
4	Score	To attack	In	Level
5	Tricky	Long time	Small	Girl
6	Hardware way	To be desolate	Flat	Hold
7	Navigation	Listen	A battery	Deep
8	OB	Happy	Cost performance	Regular
9	Divot	High	Fly	Light rain
10	Hardware four	High speed	Pin	A ward
11	Greens in regulation	Company	Reasonable	Aim
12	Valuable	Season	Long	Best
13	Course layout	Pressure	Short	Caddy
14	Hold	Look for	Seem	Laugh
15	Middle	Be late	Comparison	Last

We try to evaluate characteristic of the user review for each cluster using the feature with the high TF-IDF value in each cluster.

Cluster 1 is characterized by the words "Play," "Revenge," "Score," "Tricky" which appeared higher rank of Table 4. These feature wards are words related to golf skills and play situation, and it can be inferred that these points have been evaluated by the user.

Cluster 2 is characterized by the words," "Caddy" and "High" appeared higher rank of Table 4. These feature words are words related to the golf service, and it can be inferred that this point has been evaluated by the user. Also, feature words such as attacking, raging, happy appeared higher rank of Table 4. This is a word concerning emotion, and it can be inferred that the difficulty level of the golf course is the subject of evaluation.

Cluster 3 is characterized by the words," "Resort," "Old" and "Cost performance" appeared higher rank of Table 4. The content of the course location and the contents concerning the price are subject to the evaluation.

Cluster 4 is characterized by the words "Lunch," "Atmosphere" and "Girl" appeared higher rank of Table 4. It can be inferred that the points of golf facilities and the situation that have been evaluated by user.

3.5   Analysis of Customer Review by the Difference of Golfer Skill Using Natural Language Processing

Next, we focus on differences in review contents due to golf skills. First, we classified the customers into three golf skills, and we performed natural language processing to each skill of each cluster. We used the value of the golf score of customer data for classification of golf skills. Specifically, we classified the customers for the three ranks, less than 92 (expert players), 93 to 100 (intermediate players) and 101 to 131 (beginners). As for the extraction of characteristic words, we used the TF-IDF method in the same way as above. The feature words of these three ranks of each cluster are as follows (Tables 5, 6, 7 and 8).

Table 5. The highest TF-IDF value in cluster1 by difference of golfer skill rank (top 18).

Appearance rank	Expert	Intermediate	Beginner
1	Teahouse	Easy to do	Old
2	Load	Want to	To empty
3	Exist	Good	Player
4	Leftover	Want to	Go down
5	To blow	Good	Distance
6	Hang	Hateful	High speed
7	To be surprised	Best score	Big
8	Ground	As usual	Front
9	Run	Type	Change
10	Drink	Aim	Club house

(*continued*)

Table 5. (*continued*)

Appearance rank	Expert	Intermediate	Beginner
11	Drink	On the way home	A feeling
12	Speed	Drink	Locker
13	This side	Rainy season	Latency
14	Up and down	Best	Eat
15	Drop down	Beverage	Bath
16	Complaint	Golfer	Crowded
17	Small	Go back	Woman
18	Distant	Clear sky	Be attentive

Table 6. The highest TF-IDF value in cluster2 by difference of golfer rank (top 18).

Appearance rank	Expert	Intermediate	Beginner
1	Professional	Cut	Strict
2	Run	To go around	Cost performance
3	Tournament	Condition	Caddy
4	Rich	To spend	Club house
5	Point	High	To use
6	Lost	Tournament	Locker
7	Be taken	Hot spring	Self
8	Back	Stand out	Be effective
9	Iron	Attach	Short
10	Line	Prestige	Price
11	Prestige	Caddy	Friend
12	Clear sky	Environment	Plan
13	Speed	Moderate	Strong
14	Hot spring	Best	Bath
15	Know	Self	Crowded
16	Ground	Exceed	Be attentive
17	Drop down	Player	Maintenance
18	Roll over	Friends	Pond

Table 7. The highest TF-IDF value in cluster3 by difference of golfer rank (top 18)

Appearance rank	Expert	Intermediate	Beginner
1	Tee shot	Maintenance	Course
2	Beginner	Beginner	Fairway
3	Maintenance	Wait	Good
4	Strategy	Myself	Green
5	Interesting	Restaurant	Think
6	To see	Feels good	Round

(*continued*)

Table 7. (*continued*)

Appearance rank	Expert	Intermediate	Beginner
7	Slow	Driver	Distance
8	Manner	Interesting	Golf
9	Menu	Be blessed	Maintenance
10	Through	To fall down	price
11	Fast	Fast	Pleasant
12	Impression	The weather	Hole
13	Tea	Price	Go
14	Long time	Exist	Capable
15	Price	Cold	Difficulty
16	Fee	Fee	Many
17	Exist	Long time	Impressions
18	Half	Half	Weather

Table 8. The highest TF-IDF value in cluster4 by difference of golfer rank (top 18).

Appearance rank	Expert	Intermediate	Beginner
1	Player	Player	Self
2	Mt. fuji	Intense heat	Eat
3	Fuji	Mt. Fuji	Cup
4	Golf Iron	Like	Feeling
5	Up and in	Stuff	Persons
6	Golfer	To drop	Plan
7	Stand out	Winter	One
8	Speed	Get on	Temperature
9	To go around	Go back	Go up
10	Caddy	Moderate	Correct
11	Prestige	Best	Pleasure
12	Read	Know	Weather
13	To hit	Rainy season	Maintenance
14	Customer	Fuji	Price
15	Front	Environment	Latency
16	Large	Become cloudy	Club house
17	Marshall	Caddy	Enjoy
18	Hazard	Exceed	Woman

Since Cluster 1 is a general public course, it is understood that all skills contain words related to the quality of golf facilities and services. Also, the words related to play manners and quality of green appears in each skill. Focus on the feature words of experts of cluster 1, "Teahouse," "Speed," "Small" and "Complaints" are high on the list (Table 5). From these words, it can be inferred that experts emphasize the green speed, the size of the green, and the manner of players. On the other hand, "Easy to play," "Best score," "Golfer," "Drink," and "Beverage" are high on the feature words of intermediate of cluster 1 (Table 5). From these words, it can be inferred that intermediate emphasize ease of giving the best score, easy to around the course, good manners for golfers and services such as drink offering. Focus on the feature wards of beginners are "Old," "Player," "Crowded," "Women," "Be attentive," "Clubhouse" and "Eat" are high on the list (Table 6). It can be that beginners emphasis the state of the facility, whether maintenance of the course and facilities and meal quality is adequate.

Since Cluster 2 is a high price course, it is understood that the customers belonging to Cluster 2 are high in price as each skill, but prestige is important factor. Focus on feature wards of experts in cluster 2, "Professional," "Tournament," "Rich," "Prestigious" and "Speed" are higher rank on the list (Table 6). From these wards, it can be inferred that experts are emphasize prestigious golf courses like to use professionals, the course of strategy and green speed. Then focus on feature wards of Intermediate, "Prestige," "Environment," "Moderate," "Best", "Player" and other words are distinctive. Form these wards, it can be inferred that intermediate are emphasizes prestigious courses, the level of practice enrichment, and whether it can be played at an affordable price. Focus on feature wards of beginners, "Price," "Crowded" and "Maintenance". Form these wards, it can be inferred that beginners are emphasizes easy to rotate without getting crowded, we place importance on maintenance at a low price.

Cluster 3 is a course for practice. From the review of Cluster 3, the word "Maintenance" commonly appears in each skill. So that customers belonging to Cluster 3 have a high degree of importance of course maintenance. In addition, middle - level and higher level seek strategy and interest for the course. Focus on feature wards of experts in Cluster 3, "Beginners," "Maintenance," "Manner," "Strategy," "Interesting," "Fee" and "Fast" are high on the list (Table 7). From these wards, it can be inferred that expert are emphasize the elements of the strategy and fun of the course. Experts also focus on maintenance, green speed and play manners. Focus on feature wards of intermediate, "Maintenance," "Beginner," "Interesting," "Fast," and "Fee" are high on the list (Table 7). The speed of green and the state of maintenance, beginners can also use it, and emphasize an interesting course. Focus on feature wards of beginners, "Courses," "Fairways," "Maintenance," "Price," and "Difficulty" are high the list (Table 7). From these wards, it can be inferred that beginners are emphasize Course status, difficulty and price.

Cluster 4 is a course for professionals, customers belonging to Cluster 4 are middle-ranked and over, and the word "player" commonly appears. From that, it turns out that the player's manner is high importance in the professional course. Focus on feature wards experts in Cluster 4, "Speed," "Player," "Prestige," "Read," and "To hit" are high on the list (Table 8). From these wards, it can be that experts emphasize prestigious golf courses and green speed. Technical aspects such as reading the characteristics of the course are taken into consideration. Next, focus on feature wards intermediate in cluster 4, "player", "environment" is characteristic. From these wards, it can be that Intermediate worried the course can't be turned by too much customer packing. Moreover, Intermediate emphasizes convenient and the practice environment and play manners. Focus on feature wards beginners in cluster4, "Cup," "Plan,"

"Price," "Latency" and "Women" are high on the list (Table 8). Form these wards, it can be that beginners emphasis the location of the hall cup and the availability of the utilization plan.

In the experts in all clusters, the word "Speed," "Maintenance," "Strategy," "Play," and "Manners" is distinctive. For expert users, the importance of the maintenance concerning the green speed and the strategy of the course itself is high. Moreover, we are also careful about the play manners of users, and advanced players have high standards for play environment. Intermediate players in all clusters are commonly characterized by the word "Player". The importance of the play manners is high in all intermediate players. For beginners in all clusters, words related to "Maintenance" and "Price" are distinctive. Beginners have less requests to the golf course in common, and the importance of price and maintenance is high.

4 Discussion

Finally, we consider feature wards of each cluster focusing on golf skill.

Cluster 1 is a course for the general public, and words concerning the quality of golf facilities and services appears in the review of each skill. It is necessary to carefully observe reviews on golf facilities and services. Improvement is necessary if negative evaluations are seen for reviews on golf facilities and services. Also, it is necessary to be careful about reviews on green maintenance and play manners.

Cluster 2 is a high price course. Customers emphasize prestigious courses, strategy of course and green speed. Improvement is necessary if there are negative contents about the strategy of the course and the green speed. Also, words related to practice environment and crowdedness are also high importance, so it is necessary to carefully observe reviews related to those words.

Cluster 3 is a course for practice. Customers emphasize changing of green speed according to green maintenance. Therefore, for customers belonging to Cluster 3, it is necessary to be careful about reviews on green speed and maintenance. If a negative review is seen, course surface maintenance is required.

Cluster 4 is a course for professionals, and intermediate players consider player manners. If there is negative content, it is necessary to create a golf course that strictly manages players' manners. In addition, it is necessary to increase the difficulty level of the course to suit the professional, to set restrictions on customers' entrance and make the course more comfortable.

5 Conclusion

In this study, we used the review on the golf course of the golf portal site and clarified the features of the golf course. We also grasped what kind of difference is in the evaluation of the golf course from the difference of the golf skill. Through this study, we clarified the characteristics of the golf course and the evaluation of the golf course due to the difference in golf skills. In addition, this method can be applied not only to golf courses but also to various reviews, and features can be grasped.

In this study, we divided customer reviews with one index called golf skill. In the future works, we are planning to classify customers by using demographic attributes such as age, income, residential area and so forth. Moreover, we will evaluate each customer review based on differences in demographic attributes and clarify what features are available.

Acknowledgement. We thank Golf Digest Online Inc. for permission to use valuable datasets and for useful comments. This work was supported by JSPS KAKENHI Grant Number 16K03944 and 17K13809.

References

1. Ministry of Economy, Trade and Industry (Japan): Results of the E-commerce market survey compiled (2017). http://www.meti.go.jp/press/2017/04/20170424001/20170424001-2.pdf. Accessed 31 Jan 2019. (in Japanese)
2. Survey of Internet Shopping Trend: http://www.lifenet-seimei.co.jp/newsrelease/2014/5679.html. Accessed 31 Jan 2019. (in Japanese)
3. Shiraishi, R., Otake, K., Namatame, T.: Proposal of the review recommendation system using the concurrent network. In: Proceedings of 2016 Future Technologies Conference (FTC) (2016)
4. KH Coder Index Page. http://khcoder.net/en/. Accessed 31 Jan 2019
5. Miyazaki, M., Kawabata, T.: A Study of "tfidf" Measure Using Wikipedia Statistics, The Information Processing Society of Japan, vol. SLP, 2009-SLP-77, no. 2, pp. 1–6 (2009). (in Japanese)

Blockchain Technologies in E-commerce: Social Shopping and Loyalty Program Applications

Yi Han Lim[1], Halimin Hashim[1], Nigel Poo[2],
Danny Chiang Choon Poo[3], and Hoang D. Nguyen[1($\boxtimes$)]

[1] University of Glasgow, Singapore, Singapore
{2355358L, 2355332B}@student.gla.ac.uk,
Harry.Nguyen@glasgow.ac.uk
[2] Trolle, Singapore, Singapore
npoo3l@gmail.com
[3] National University of Singapore, Singapore, Singapore
dpoo@comp.nus.edu.sg

Abstract. With the rapid advancement of cryptography and distributed computing systems, blockchain technologies are highly anticipated to transform many industries with better transparency, high security, and low transaction costs. However, the scalability and performance of blockchains are limiting their utility and suitability in online services, especially e-commerce. This paper provides a survey of blockchain technologies to highlight their benefits and challenges in online shopping. We, therefore, propose two blockchain-based e-commerce applications with detailed design guidelines: social shopping and loyalty program. The study contributes to the cumulative theoretical development of social computing and blockchains. It also provides a number of implications for academic bodies, platform operators, and developers of blockchain technologies.

Keywords: Blockchain · E-commerce · Social shopping · Loyalty program · Transformation

1 Introduction

With the steady growth of communication and security technologies, blockchains have emerged as digital innovations that would transform many industries and businesses [1]. A blockchain is a shared, secured ledger, which is distributed across a network of devices. These devices verify transactions in encrypted blocks among network participants, which are not just limited to cryptocurrency but any product of value.

In e-commerce, the adoption of blockchain technologies is highly anticipated; nevertheless, the applicability of blockchains remains as limited due to the inherent scalability and performance issues in major blockchains such as Bitcoin and Ethereum. In average, the power consumption for a Bitcoin transaction is 3 to 4 times higher than the power consumption for 100,000 VISA transactions [2]. Therefore, this study investigates blockchain technologies and applications to identify their benefits and

© Springer Nature Switzerland AG 2019
G. Meiselwitz (Ed.): HCII 2019, LNCS 11579, pp. 403–416, 2019.
https://doi.org/10.1007/978-3-030-21905-5_31

challenges in e-commerce. Moreover, we propose two blockchain-based applications with detailed design and implementation of social shopping and loyalty program.

Based on the survey of blockchains, the study contributes to the cumulative development of e-commerce and blockchains. It has also drawn out several insights and implications for academic bodies and developers in social computing.

The structure of the paper is as follows. Firstly, we review the existing blockchain technologies and applications in e-commerce in Sect. 2. Secondly, we present our proposed solutions with the design guidelines for social shopping and loyalty program. Lastly, Sect. 4 concludes our paper with findings and contributions in the final section.

2   Blockchain Technologies in E-commerce

Blockchain technology is a digital ledger that stores blocks of immutable transaction that occurs in the system. Each transaction produces a hash which is generated using the public key, the private key, the previous hash, the timestamp and transaction details as shown in Fig. 1. The public key is essentially an address which allows participants to identify each other, and the private key is used for authentication. The previous hash is stored to link the blocks together. Before this transaction will be stored into a block, it is broadcasted to the other nodes for consensus on the distributed peer-to-peer network. These nodes will verify that the transaction has not been altered, and once it has been approved by the majority of nodes only then it will be appended to a block.

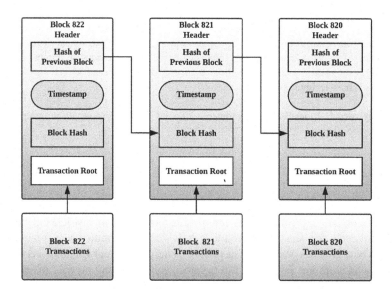

Fig. 1. Blockchain data structure

With the hype of cryptocurrency, there is a growing list of blockchain technologies, which were created with different purposes for various use cases. In this paper, we review a number of major blockchain solutions as shown in Table 1.

Table 1. A survey of existing blockchain technologies

Technology	Transactions per second	Block time in seconds	Security	Consensus	Flexibility
Bitcoin	7	~600	Medium	Proof of Work (PoW)	Low
Ethereum	15–25	~14–15	Medium	Proof of Work (PoW)	High
Qtum	>17	120–180	Medium	Proof of Work (PoW)	High
Hyperledger Fabric	3500[a] 120–300[b]	0.3–0.5	High	Proof of Agreement (PoA)	High
EOS	250[c]	0.5	Medium	Delegated Proof of Stake (dPoS)	High
Aeternity	30	<15	Medium	Hybrid Consensus: Proof of Work (PoW) and Proof of Stake (PoS)	High
BigchainDB	80	–	Varied	Proof of Stake (PoS)	High

[a]Published by Androulaki et al. [3].
[b]Benchmarked by Nasir et al. [4].
[c]Reported by Xu et al. [5].

Bitcoin. Bitcoin is a cryptocurrency that is peer-to-peer with no trusted single authority [6]. It is built on blockchain for the purpose of exchange and only executes rules that are related to trading. Bitcoin, however, is vulnerable to threats such as theft and hacking attacks despite heavily encrypted. As the first mover, the design of Bitcoin has inspired many other blockchain technologies.

Ethereum. Ethereum is an open source, public blockchain app platform which was proposed by Vitalik Buterin in 2013 [7]. It supports the modified version of Proof of Work consensus and allows programming of various types of smart contracts within the system. Ethereum is operating as cryptocurrency as a public distributed ledger for transactions. Nevertheless, the scalability of Ethereum is limited to 25 transactions per second; and it is prone to security breaches due to Solidity Language, causing storage to be compromised.

Qtum. Qtum is a hybrid platform that enables smart contract technology on the existing blockchain. It allows execution of smart contracts on mobile or Internet-of-Things (IoT) devices. Qtum is designed as a toolkit for robust and modular scripting on mainstream blockchains. New to the market, hence it is still in the testing phase and vulnerable to hacks especially at the exchange level [7].

Hyperledger Fabric. Hyperledger Fabric is an open-source, permissioned distributed ledger platform hosted by The Linux Foundation [3]. It is an extensible blockchain system featuring modular consensus protocols, which allows organizations to create and maintain a private channel with other specified members. This permissioned blockchain technologies permits the participants to authenticate themselves in transactions but also to prove authorization to perform a variety of system operations. The scalability and flexibility of Hyperledger Fabric are promising; nevertheless, its end-to-end throughput remains controversial as several benchmarks were concluded with mixed results [4].

EOS. EOS.IO is released in 2018 as open-source software to overcome the scalability issues of mainstream blockchains such as Bitcoin and Ethereum [8]. The software utilizes Delegated Proof of Stake (dPoS) consensus algorithm, in which transactions are validated by a set of master nodes known as ranked delegates. The development and maintenance of EOS such as ownership structure offer free usage for users, allowing validators to use resources according to their stakes, hence, no there is no transaction fee. However, it is still vulnerable to threats like numerical overflow, especially when arithmetic operations are executed, resulting in unchecked contracts, which eventually leads to loss of assets.

Aeternity. Aeternity was established by Yanislav Malahov in 2016 as a scalable blockchain platform [9]. It enables high bandwidth transactions, smart contracts with built-in oracles. The state channel and oracle system ensure a high degree of flexibility. The state channel allows functions to be initiated and fulfilled off-chain and prevents congestion of smart contract functions executing together. Furthermore, if a smart contract is disputed, the signed off-chain transaction can use used as a record for examination. The oracle allows real word data to be used in terms of smart contract functions. It connects to the internet and monitors the outcome in the contract, so that when results are stored, the contract will be executed. Withdrawals of token take a lot of time which makes users' asset high likely to be prone to get compromised due to the risky exchanges.

BigchainDB. BigchainDB is an open-source software that combines both blockchain properties and database properties for production-ready use cases [10]. It can be built on top of a variety of existing distributed databases. The security of each node and the entire network are extrinsic. It depends on the network built on how the rule of security for each node is. The higher standard of security of the network of nodes, the better it is able to withstand attacks. BigchainDB allows developers to deploy a blockchain proof-of-concept easily as compared to other blockchain technologies.

2.1   Benefits in E-commerce with Blockchains

The use of blockchain technologies in online shopping has been evolved beyond decentralized digital payments towards blockchain-based online and offline services [11]. The following highlights the benefits of blockchains in the context of e-commerce.

High Security. Blockchains provide transactions to be immutable due to the implementation of the technology. In the event that a block is altered, the block would be rejected by most of the nodes and the information would not persist in the ledger. This is because the block is hashed using the hash of the previous block which would link the blocks together and creating a chain. If a block is altered the data would also affect the hash for the subsequent block which in turn causes the nodes in the network to reject it. This ensures that the information has not been tampered with which would ensure e-commerce ecosystems for customers, suppliers, sellers, and shipping companies to highly protected.

In addition, the use of smart contracts eliminates an external third-party entity when doing a transaction exchange, without compromising the security in the midst of the transaction process. Smart contracts are designed to automate tasks based on the preset rules, omitting any forms of interference by any signatories.

Lower Transaction Cost. Retailers are often required to pay commission fees to use e-commerce platform. This is inevitable if they want exposure to a large audience that an e-commerce platform provides. These fees do not yet include the cost of using payment gateways such as PayPal and credit card which would further decrease their profit margin. Retailers will have little choice but to increase the price of these products to gain profit from selling on the platform. These increase in price would also cost customers to pay more for the product. With the introduction of blockchain technologies into these, it would remove the need for the intermediaries, and these payments can be made directly between the retailer and customer reducing the cost of the product and increasing profit.

Traceability. Tracing an order item back to its root origin proves to be an arduous task when products are traded using a centralized traditional E-commerce platform. Therefore, with blockchains, it allows an audit trail whenever an action is done during the transaction. This help to verify the authentication of the transaction, preventing frauds. This is especially useful for order tracking as blockchain allows immutable tracking. This means that customers are able to locate where their products, whether their products are genuine and what is contained etc. This helps to maintain the integrity and authenticity of products.

Trustless. In traditional forms of e-commerce platforms, information used by retailers is owned by the platform. These platforms offer guarantees and reviews of seller whereas, for payment gateways, they offered to keep safe of the transaction amount till its verified. This undeniably gives absolute controls to these platforms and gateways over their customers. Furthermore, trusting these platforms and gateways to store huge amount of confidential data posed a risk in terms of privacy issues, which is why these companies are the choice of targets for fraud and hacking attempts.

Therefore, blockchain can be employed to create a system where trust is no longer required. The cryptography in blockchain can completely eliminate the external intermediary. This allows the customers to run the complex consensus protocol unanimously, hence allow them to agree securely the type of data to be added into the ledger while ensuring data integrity. By doing so, it builds a base of trust which also removes the third party and thereby, reducing the transactional cost.

2.2   Challenges of Blockchain Adoption in E-commerce

Blockchain technologies come with their own challenges. Factors ranging from policy discordances to technical limitations hinder the adoption of blockchain in e-commerce. There are a number of the existing obstacles discussed as the following.

Scalability. The limited block size of blockchain technologies has resulted in the loss of scalability as compared to modern payment processors such as Visa or Mastercard. According to data shown, the Visa payment processor is able to do around 48,000 transactions per second whereas, for blockchain protocols such as Bitcoin, it is only able to reach 7 transactions per second with a fixated block size of 1 MB [2]. In order to be on par with these modern payment processors, one solution is to increase the limit of the block size. However, by doing so, it affects the number of power consumption due to the huge amount of data resources.

Furthermore, increasing the limit of block size creates a strain on the security as the probability of blocks being orphaned increases which inevitably affects the bandwidth cost and validation cost. The higher the limit of the block size, the larger the transaction load and with a decrease in transaction fee, security decreases.

Privacy. Public blockchains simulate the current World Wide Web, enabling public access of data to all participants [12]. They ascertain that the recorded data are readily available and reduce transactional costs. However, public access blockchains may imperil data privacy. Blockchain technologies depend on the write-only data process which makes them unable to remove any information [13]. Moreover, their core depends on a distributed data storage system where the same data is stored in the entire node network. Therefore, any forms of changes require an agreement made by the entire node network, making any removal of data difficult. Data control to public blockchains has raised an issue, especially when sensitive or confidentiality of data is involved as there is no way to rectify damages once these data are uploaded.

Compatibility. Despite blockchains providing transparency and immutable of data information, the efficiency of entering information might be an issue. For example, in existing solutions such as supply chain management systems, legacy systems are usually used to store information. Therefore, this results in incompatibility in data and system sensors which makes data access arduous. By integrating blockchain into supply chains, it may cause an overload of data for the system to handle. Furthermore, this may affect the quality of data stored into the ledger, causing inaccurate data assumptions in the following chains.

Acceptance. In order for e-commerce to incorporate blockchain, it will require a lot of investments in using these new technologies. This is an undeniable step in order for it to be viable so as to provide traceability long the entire blockchain network. Furthermore, the issue to strike a balance between confidentiality and transparency of data in order to re-engineer business processes to use this distributed ledger to store and share data information requires in-depth discussions. It would be possible to access companies' business secrets and activities if all the information is stored in the ledger, resulting in loss of confidentiality. Therefore, this may lead to a reluctance for e-commerce companies to embrace blockchain wholeheartedly due to the culture of acceptance, organization, and standardization of its uses.

2.3   Existing Blockchain Solutions in E-commerce

With the rising bloom of online transactions, many e-commerce platforms have adopted a decentralized distributed ledger technology to reach out to their consumers to ensure efficiency with minimal cost. These are some of the existing solutions in e-commerce that imbued with blockchain as the following.

Legitimate Product Review System. Genuine reviews found online are usually based on assumptions. Positive reviews might be generated by sellers in order to increase their turnovers and negative reviews written by competitors to diminish fellow competitors. Also, there is no form of incentive for customers to leave reviews even if there were sales based on their reviews. The use of blockchain technologies can help to resolve the reliability of the verification of reviews. Furthermore, through referral systems, customers can be rewarded if their post leads to sales due to the ability of blockchain enabling to track all transactions. For example, Zapit, an US-based company utilized this to ensure compensations to both the reviewers and moderators, encouraging validity to ensure a win-win situation.

Supply Chain Management System. International shipping has proven to be a challenging problem faced by Shipping freights companies worldwide. In order to ship refrigerated goods from one country to another, a series of paperwork such as stamps and approvals are required in order for the process to be completed which result in high cost [14]. The use of blockchain technologies helps to eliminate inefficiency and digitize paper records. For example, Maersk, the world's largest shipping company, in collaboration with IBM, uses Blockchain technologies called TradeLens to provide an audit trail, allowing businesses to exchange information securely, connecting the vast global network of shippers, carriers, ports, and customs, so that all participants are able to access information in a unified view.

Employee Benefits System. An internal e-commerce platform has been successfully implemented for the Hainan Airlines (HNA) group to enrich employees benefit options [15]. It enables employees to have more options to claim their benefits and empowers suppliers with an additional channel to sell their products. The study revealed that blockchain of value in several ways: (1) cryptocurrency issuance, (2) sensitive information protection, and (3) no institutional intermediary. The implementation of such a win-win arrangement extended across three phases.

With the help of blockchain technologies, a number of existing solutions have been explored in e-commerce; nevertheless, there are vast fragmentations and differences in scales and sizes of blockchain applications. Furthermore, the full utilization of blockchain properties in e-commerce is yet to be investigated.

3   Proposed Blockchain Applications

Based on the survey of blockchain technologies in e-commerce, this study takes an important step to propose two applications for social shopping and loyalty program. These e-commerce applications are designed with the utilization of blockchain properties such as traceability and trustless in order to enhance customer engagement. They allow platform operators to embrace blockchain with minimal changes in technological infrastructure; thereby potentially leading to better compatibility and higher acceptance.

3.1   Social Shopping

The first proposed solution provides businesses and consumers a reinvented implementation of a social shopping functionality using blockchain technology as shown in Fig. 2. The prices of a product or service lower when the number of people who commit to buying increases [16]. This empowers the customers with a negotiating factor with the supplier to enjoy better savings as compared to purchasing product from brick and mortar establishment which most of time uses a fixed pricing model [17]. With the use of blockchains, social shopping leverages on the linked data structure and traceability of the technology to offer multi-tier dynamic pricings for groups.

Fig. 2. Blockchain-based social shopping

1. **Shopping on an e-commerce website.** The key benefit of social shopping for customers is that they would have the potential to get a discount of the product being purchased as the price of a product is often the most important factor to customers. It would draw more traffic to shopping on the e-commerce website and increase the sales of the products using the customers' social connections.
2. **Joining social shopping.** The model of social shopping is associated with time-limited deals as shown in Fig. 3(A). Shoppers would browse the e-commerce platform and discover the products on multi-tier promotions. The preview of dynamic pricings as shown in Fig. 3(B) would be a differentiating factor for customers to buy a product.

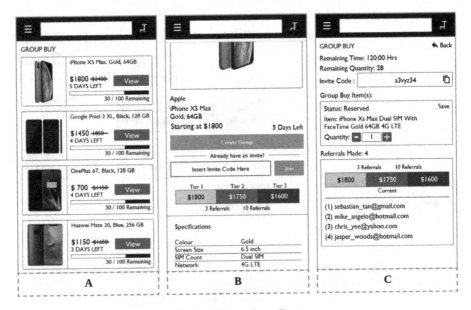

Fig. 3. Social shopping - Prototype

3. **Blockchain-based invite code.** Each customer that join the social shopping would be added as a transaction on the blockchain with related information such as the promotion-based product, payment and shipping particulars. A social invitation code will be assigned as the address to the customer's block as shown in Fig. 3(C). The blockchain network can be public, private, or consortium; in which network participants are decentralized peers to prevent double claiming or duplicated invitations with the use of a consensus algorithm.
4. **Inviting others to join the social shopping.** This invitation code serves as an important pointer to keep track of the multi-tier referring structure based on the linked data structure of blockchain technology. Sharing it over emails, private messages, or social networking sites would allow customers to unlock a better pricing tier for the time-limited shopping deal.

5. **Invited shoppers invite more social friends.** The invited buyers would also be incentivized to invite more social friends for further discounts on their purchase. A new transaction will be added when a new buyer joins the social shopping with an invitation code. This block will contain the linkages between the inviter and the invitee, as well as, the parental referrers and the invitee if any.
6. **Gaining from multi-tier dynamic pricings.** With the use of blockchain technology, the hierarchical relationships between referrers and invited buyers can be captured on the chain with minimal computational complexity.
7. **Tier calculation and final pricings.** The system will enumerate customers' tier and compute final pricings on the chain when the time-limited shopping deal is expired. An example is illustrated in Fig. 4.

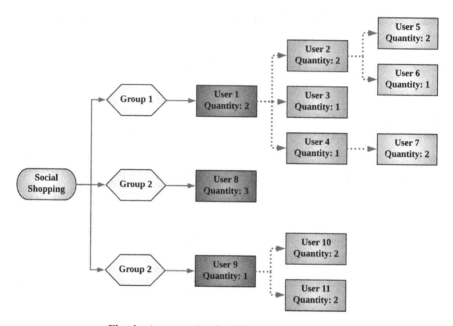

Fig. 4. An example of multi-tier social shopping

Participants are given discounts based on the number of items participants buy using their invitation code, there are different tiers to state how much of a discount they get as shown in Table 2.

Table 2. Multi-tier dynamic pricings

Tier	Discount
Tier 1	Quantity of 1 to 4: • Discount of 5% of each item
Tier 2	Quantity of 5 to 10: • Discount of 10% of each item
Tier 3	Quantity of 11 and more: • Discount of 20% of each item

In the example, User 1 would receive the tier 3 discount as Users 2, 3, and 4 join the social shopping using User 1's Invitation Code and also because User 5, 6 and 7 were invited by users who were invited by users who were invited by User 1, the user would also gain benefits from the invited users. The system is set up to allow users to back out of the group buy within the time limit of the group buy so even if a user backs out of the group buy, transaction records of the group buy are still available. The users who were invited by and who invited the user are not affected other than the reducing of quantity from the user backing out. From the diagram, if we use User 2 as an example of the user who backed out. User 1 would have a reduction in the quantity from 11 to 9 which will change him from Tier 3 to Tier 2. Similarly, for users under user 2 being user 5 and 6 would remain at their respective tiers.

Once finalized, the system will process the payment and begin the order fulfillment procedures like shipping the products.

3.2 Loyalty Program

The second proposed solution is to use purchasing tracking based on a loyalty program, integrating it with blockchain technologies as shown in Fig. 5. The solution will track customers' behavior when they are doing their shopping and stores each of their behavior activities into data which will be hashed and store into a database using blockchain [18]. The purchase tracking loyalty program will utilize a tier-based point system where there will be a different level of a point system in order to unlock different kinds of rewards. The more point accumulated by the customer, the better the rewards achievements unlocked. The points will be stored inside a single wallet where they will be converted and redeem in the form of promo codes or coupons. These promo codes will be enabled to use across major e-commerce loyalty programs.

Purchase tracking with blockchain resolves the problem of fragmentation of loyalty points across various loyalty programs. It allows the use of a single wallet where rewards will be tokenized and stored as a single type of token which can be utilized for other E-commerce loyalty programs. This prevents restrictions of redeeming rewards within the system. The use of blockchain enables it to convert reward points to a token for vast usage.

1. **Shopping on any e-commerce website.** Purchase tracking with loyalty program helps to retain existing customers and used to attract new customers, ensuring a better shopping experience. The advantage of blockchain is to integrate any e-commerce website into a loyalty network for a unified shopping experience.

2. **Making purchase transactions or taking rewardable activities.** The shopping behavior of customers will be tracked as demonstrated in Fig. 6(A) in order to tailor what kind of discount and gifts to ensure retention, attracting customers' attention. For example, when a customer buys a product, the transaction actions will be tracked where it will be stored as data. Each of these actions will have different loyalty points where some of them will have a max cap per day to ensure that consumer will not abuse the system.

3. **Session aggregation and blockchain forging.** During a shopping session, customer activities will be tracked and aggregated into an optimized data block for

Fig. 5. Blockchain-based loyalty program

forging. These data will be hashed and stored into the blockchain network. Transaction data will be converted as loyalty points using a point converter in the E-commerce platform. Each of the points will be referenced to the previous block to ensure that there will not be double spending or duplicate points redeemed. These points will be tallied against the Reward Point Tier System where the customer will be required to meet the minimum target of the points for the different tier in order to unlock exclusive features catered to the customers.

4. **Viewing loyalty program.** The loyalty program module lists down all the reward history the customers had done during and after his shopping experience as illustrated in Fig. 6(B). This will enable purchase tracking of customers behavior on what they had shopped which can be used for future analysis of behaviors. The page also records the balance points as well as which tier the customer belongs to. Each of the transaction id and name are generated by the public and private key using blockchain so that there will not be any form of double spendings or duplicates.

5. **Redeeming gifts and coupon codes.** The redeem module allows customers to redeem their points where it will be generated into promo code based on the amount converter. These promo codes will be able to use for their next purchase of items. The redemption activity allows users to collect their promo codes whenever they are awarded, or they unlock any discount features. The points will also be utilized across other e-commerce platforms. Blockchain allows each transaction to be recorded and access by multiple parties immediately.

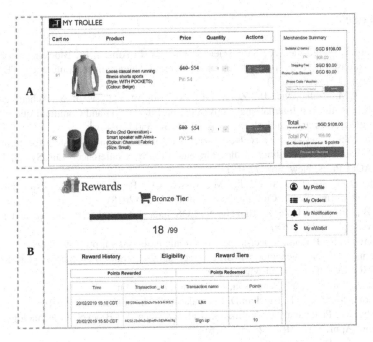

Fig. 6. Loyalty program - Prototype

The proposed blockchain-based applications in e-commerce have been developed in client-side programs, which support both mobile and web interfaces. Connected to a blockchain network via JavaScript Object Notation (JSON) serialization and deserialization, the implementation of these applications is highly compatible with major e-commerce platforms. It fully utilizes blockchain properties to reshape customer experience with better security and minimal investment in technological infrastructure. The study, therefore, demonstrates the utility and suitability of blockchain applications in e-commerce.

4 Conclusion

Our study has several implications for theoretical literature and practice of e-commerce and blockchains. First, the study provides a survey of existing blockchain technologies and application in e-commerce. Second, we highlight key blockchain properties with their benefits and challenges in online shopping sites. Third, the paper discusses several existing e-commerce applications with blockchains and proposes new applications with the full utilization of blockchain properties. These blockchain applications bridge the gaps between technological concepts and prototyping to support researchers, developers, and platform operators for rapid adoption, better compatibility, and higher acceptance. Last but not least, we designed and implemented a platform which is capable of transforming the current generation of e-commerce towards a more social and decentralized direction.

References

1. Ahram, T., Sargolzaei, A., Sargolzaei, S., Daniels, J., Amaba, B.: Blockchain technology innovations. In: IEEE Technology & Engineering Management Conference, TEMSCON 2017, pp. 137–141 (2017)
2. Bach, L.M., Mihaljevic, B., Zagar, M.: Comparative analysis of blockchain consensus algorithms. In: 41st International Convention on Information and Communication Technology, Electronics and Microelectronics, pp. 1545–1550 (2018)
3. Androulaki, E., et al.: Hyperledger fabric: a distributed operating system for permissioned blockchains. In: Proceedings of the Thirteenth EuroSys Conference - EuroSys 2018, pp. 1–15. ACM Press, New York (2018)
4. Nasir, Q., Qasse, I.A., Abu Talib, M., Nassif, A.B.: Performance analysis of hyperledger fabric platforms. Secur. Commun. Netw. **2018**, 1–14 (2018)
5. Xu, B., Luthra, D., Cole, Z., Blakely, N.: EOS: an architectural, performance, and economic analysis, pp. 1–25 (2018)
6. Nakamoto, S.: Bitcoin: a peer-to-peer electronic cash system, pp. 1–9 (2008)
7. Buterin, V.: A next-generation smart contract and decentralized application platform (2014)
8. EOS.IO: EOS.IO technical white paper
9. Hess, Z., Malahov, Y., Pettersson, J.: Æternity blockchain
10. McConaghy, T., et al.: BigchainDB: a scalable blockchain database (2016)
11. Crosby, M., Pattanayak, P., Verma, S., Kalyanaraman, V.: Blockchain technology: beyond bitcoin. Appl. Innov. Rev. **2**, 71 (2016)
12. Walch, A.: The bitcoin blockchain as financial market infrastructure: a consideration of operational risk. NYUJ Legis. Pub. Pol'y. **18**, 837 (2015)
13. Heires, K.: The risks and rewards of blockchain technology
14. Groenfeldt, T.: IBM and Maersk apply blockchain to container shipping. https://www.forbes.com/sites/tomgroenfeldt/2017/03/05/ibm-and-maersk-apply-blockchain-to-container-shipping
15. Ying, W., Jia, S., Du, W.: Digital enablement of blockchain: evidence from HNA group. Int. J. Inf. Manage. **39**, 1–4 (2018)
16. Kauffman, R.J., Wang, B.: New buyers' arrival under dynamic pricing market microstructure: the case of group-buying discounts on the internet. J. Manag. Inf. Syst. **18**, 157–188 (2001)
17. Kauffman, R.J., Wang, B.: Bid together, buy together: on the efficacy of group-buying business models in Internet-based selling. In: E-business Handbook, pp. 99–137 (2002)
18. Hofman-Kohlmeyer, M.: Customer loyalty program as a tool of customer retention: literature review. In: CBU International Conference Proceedings, vol. 4, p. 199 (2016)

Advertising or not Advertising: Representations and Expressions of Advertising Digital Literacy on Social Media

Caroline Marti[(⊠)] and Karine Berthelot-Guiet[(⊠)]

CELSA Sorbonne Université - GRIPIC, Paris, France
{caroline.marti,
karine.berthelot-guiet}@sorbonne-universite.fr

Abstract. Brands are ubiquitous for the last years, they are present in almost every space on the web and especially in social computing, social networks, and social media. Their presence is linked to different aims and accompanied by comments. Mainly, the professional point of view focuses on the idea that social media provide the possibility of a conversation based on transparency, equality, and proximity. These professional discourses stress the fact, whenever it comes to social media marketing, that these devices enable brands to speak directly with consumers and, thus, avoid communicating only with traditional advertising, or "paid media." These transformations seek to ensure advertising to be in the most frequented and wanted media spaces. These hybridizations and all the inventiveness actors can put in the process are limited in many ways, beginning with the trust they have to ensure with their audiences which are used to media spaces as they practice them and the possible saturation of the same spaces.

We intend, with a socio-semio-communication based method rooted in the scientific frame of French information and communication sciences, to question the grand metamorphoses all brand messages are undergoing under the strain of many different rationales. On the go, years after years, metamorphoses and hybridizations coming one after another, web users are developing skills and abilities regarding advertising and market discourses on the web. They build experience in the ability to identify and appreciate brand discourses; they do differentiate discourses and show a growing ability to identify the traits of marketing and advertising discourses as such. In this respect, the advertising show and the hybridizations can both benefit or be threatened by this growing mastering.

Keywords: Brand · Advertising · Digital literacy · Social media · Consumption

1 Introduction

We intend, with a socio-semio-communication based method rooted in the scientific frame of French information and communication sciences [33, 34], to question the grand metamorphoses all brand messages are undergoing under the strain of many different rationales. On the go, years after years, metamorphoses and hybridizations coming one after another, web users are developing skills and abilities regarding advertising and

© Springer Nature Switzerland AG 2019
G. Meiselwitz (Ed.): HCII 2019, LNCS 11579, pp. 417–433, 2019.
https://doi.org/10.1007/978-3-030-21905-5_32

market discourses on the web. They build experience in the ability to identify and appreciate brand discourses; they do differentiate discourses and show a growing ability to identify the traits of marketing and advertising discourses as such. In this respect, the advertising show and its hybridizations can both benefit or be threatened by this growing mastering.

The analysis we intend to develop here is based on the part of French Communication Sciences contemporary approaches [34, 35] that are mainly focused on the conceptualization, description or analysis of social discourses as well as media and market discourses [13, 14, 40, 43]. These analyses embrace all discursive elements, based on an extensive definition of discourse including speech, images and all kind of media products. One of the main concern is to comprehend the circulation of all these elements between different social and media spaces. This implies a specific point of view about media, commercial, advertising and brand speeches considered as social discourses carrying out market mediation processes. In this respect, these market mediations are entirely taken as a system of signification, at the same time social and symbolic and economic [4, 6, 7, 22, 25].

Our method tends to design or craft, on a socio-semiotic base, the appropriate mix to deal with signs and meanings linked to consumption items and speeches in a specific sociological, economic, cultural and communication background; mixing microscale approaches and macro analysis. The present paper is based on researches conducted, together or in parallel, for more than ten years, with a collective will to analyze at the same time and with the same depth communication processes and products (commercials, brand movies, museums, websites, social networks, and so on), escort discourses from marketing and advertising professionals and actions of audiences. In this respect, we reach the possibility to find an analytical way to uses, representations, and users creative appropriations.

This paper will focus on brand discourses on the web especially since brands tend to reach and take advantage of all web spaces. Discourses promoting brands pervade the web whether it is in dedicated websites, paid space in web media, online presence on "forums" and social media such as Facebook, Instagram, Twitter, Snapchat, and so on. Some of them are frankly what we can call traditional advertising occurring on paid media spaces. They also mix with web media discourses in all kind of hybridizations that appeared in the last decade, due to a rising criticism against traditional advertising as too present and obviously seeking selling. The kind of communicational uncertainty linked to the Internet as a system and its blurring effect on the identification of the enunciator tends to emphasize the phenomenon. This kind of jamming should be positive for brands since it enables their display and minimize bypass, thanks to contents (texts and images) presenting cultural interest whether as entertainment or information.

This explains why contemporary marketing, advertising, and branding professionals are so willing and eager to shape brand discourses with social and/or aesthetic appearances as different as possible from regular, classic advertising.

2 Advertising, *Unadvertization*, and *Hyperadvertization*

2.1 In Search of New Brand Expressions

Since more than ten years, advertising and brand managers are trying to find new ways to advertise, that they generally name branded content *that* tries to go back to a strong distinctiveness serving a brand [13, 43]. In this respect, professionals try to build a new demarcation between a good, transparent, non-manipulative communication, not far from information and a bad, opaque and manipulative one, in other words, advertising.

This is not exactly a new turn in contemporaneous communications, especially regarding brands. Nowadays, brands managers are confronted, especially in developed countries where advertising started back in the middle of the nineteenth century as a professional activity, to a social, economic and social context we can describe as complex and unfavorable towards brands in general and advertising in particular. People tend to be increasingly suspicious and even opposed to traditional media advertising. Brands are judged in the light of their actions, how and where they produce and how they speak. More and more people state they do not like advertising; they try to avoid it and do not believe in it. It is mainly an anti-advertising feeling we can describe especially in countries like France and the USA [16, 36].

At the same time, we live in societies where advertising is ubiquitous in everyday life. We wake up with it, have breakfast, go to work, watch TV, surf the web, and so on with advertising. Thus we encounter numerous advertising messages in just a single ordinary day. This situation produces mainly a saturation of space with advertising. Every single media, or so-called media, seems literally packed with advertising.

Working inside and outside these constraints, marketing, and advertising people both in agencies, announcers and media companies, have developed a strong shared belief in the fact that traditional advertising is more and more inadequate, based on the anti-advertising actions, the saturation of space and an economic need for this sector to find growth areas. This last point is particularly crucial since advertising agencies have to face that communications providers are more and more numerous, coming from different fields like media, design or web agencies. They also enter international competition. This is why advertising people try to find the proper pace to keep leadership and work on formats that fit and pre-empt media transformations as well in TV, radio, magazines, and papers or digital media.

In this context, at least two solutions have occurred in professional uses: one is about erasing a maximum of classical advertising features, called *unadvertization* [13, 14, 39, 41]; the other one is about optimizing advertising quality and/or trying to find new media or transforming things into a media for advertising, called *hyperadvertization* [13, 14]. These names come from research results that give afterward point of view giving logic to a broad set of professional practices mainly known as branded content, product placement, sponsoring, and so on. For example, what professionals call brand conversation is currently a case of *unadvertization?*

2.2   Unadvertization: Playing with the Limits

More precisely *unadvertization* refers to communications strategies used by advertising people whenever they want to avoid traditional or regular advertising or downsize it. They mainly use three sets of ways:

– They can enter an already existing media production as in product placement in TV shows, and series, movies, games. They also sponsor broadcasted programs.
– They can imitate existing media products as we can see with consumer magazines, branded web series as Ikea *Easy to Assemble*, brand games, or imitate existing cultural products as brand movies ("*Prada* presents A *Therapy*, by Roman Polanski, starring Ben Kingsley and Helen Bonham Carter), books as Recipe books around *Philadelphia*, *Oreos* and so on.
– They can try to benefit from new forms of communication supposed to redistribute communication parts such as blogs, co-produced content and social media. The brand conversation takes place in this last.

2.3   Hyperadvertization: Enhancing Advertising Features

On another hand, *hyperadvertization* is the counterpart of *unadvertization* and acts as hypertrophy of advertising aspects. Nothing about trying to hide the advertising nature of the message, the main point is to maximize advertising presence either in a qualitative way, working on the message and its forms, or in a quantitative way, trying to find or create new media spaces.

In the first case, the work will put the stress on the semiotic densification of the message, mainly through work on aesthetics and creativity. New creative formats are explored as very long TV commercials, exceptional work on very expensive sheets of paper, sophisticated finish, highly studied and unexpected billboard locations.

In the second case, the work is mainly the continuous creation of new media set, trying to use still non-used spaces as street furniture, buildings, café tables, metro tickets, and credit cards. Thus, every space can become an advertising media, such as flagship stores, media, and smart cities. Streets or city areas can be transformed, for a short time, in a massive advertising display.

Advertising, *unadvertization* and *hyperadvertization* messages multiply the presence of brand messages in everyday life. One at a time, these transformations of advertising messages seem only tactical but, as a whole, they become a great strategic renewal of modes of existence for brand discourses.

3   Equality, and Proximity

3.1   Conversation

All actors on the market usually fantasize about direct access to their targets. Regarding the context of industrialization of offers and their dissemination via marketing strategies, marketing people seek to mimic proximity with their prospects and customers instead of trying to generate it. The mass consumption makes individual exchange difficult if not impossible even if people still dream about it under new devices and names such as "one to one" marketing and, more recently, conversation.

The marketing and advertising professionals have practically jumped on the idea of conversation in order to name all kind of verbal or written exchanges that social networks and digital interactions enable. Many research or professional press papers stressed, during the 2000s, how it was necessary for brands to enter the conversation and many specialized agencies appeared.

In these cases, marketing and advertising people commonly talk about markets as conversations. This idea was first presented in 1999 in what is now widely known as the *Clue Train Manifesto*. Published on the web by four professionals, this text became a book one year later. Whenever it comes to brands and conversation, professionals regularly quote this text as the main reference and, up to a certain point, as the one that put into shape the setting of marketing conversation.

This is why it is necessary to analyze this specific piece of business literature to understand the roots of the idea of a conversation between brands and customers. It gives access to what advertising producers think and/or claim they do with digital conversation branded content. Firstly, they try to transform the mass of consumers into a collection of individuals to go towards the next step, re-gather them in a new mass, an audience they will be able to observe and qualify. The professional metadiscourses tend to present these productions as an Eldorado of brand-client relationship.

Thus, conversation appears in professional discourses as an ideal of communication. We get a glimpse of collective professional representation of conversation, reinterpreted nostalgically, related to a pre-industrial Eden of communication: the old farmers' marketplace. This pre-capitalistic conversation is depicted as real and direct far from the description linguists can give of conversation, as a "battle for dominance" [14].

Hence, the marketing conversation is a hybrid production, highly consensual and paradoxical, at the same time innate for consumers and to be learned for brands. It is based on an idea of without hierarchy. Instead of speaking of a "top-down," vertical way, imposing the brand and its advertising messages, marketing conversations are supposed to enable brands and consumers to be equals, in a horizontal way. Thus, marketing and advertising professionals redefine the concept of conversation, without a balance of power and hierarchy, as an irenic and idealized mode of communication. In this respect, professionals give a new demarcation between a good, transparent, non-manipulative communication, not far from information, and a bad, opaque and manipulative one, in other words, traditional advertising.

The conversation was and is everywhere, in chats, digital forums, brands websites and social networks such as Twitter or Facebook. The very idea of conversation implies a dialogue, or everything next to it like co-something (co-authoring, co-participation) and appears as a proof of good professional behavior [40, 42]. These discourses on behalf of brands at the same time defend their reputation, promote their products, act as consumer service. Moreover, brands sometimes called "friend," talk to Internet users who can happen to be consumers, willing to interact, and even to personalize their relation to consumption as explained by Baudrillard [6, 7]. They are part of a mix of complex interactions difficult to qualify since they change from one brand to another.

Whatever goodwill was at work, this marketing conversation happens to exist only metaphorically, since its typical characteristics disappear in digital conversations which are mainly anonymous or anonymized by the alias or profile name, giving no knowledge or a low one about characteristics of the interacting persons. No real exchange is possible because a real person is interacting with an entity, representing, the brand, that is a mock individual acted by one or many community managers. Instead of spontaneity, they are working mainly with the support of legal departments, top management guidelines, the history of previous digital exchanges.

3.2   A New Paradigm?

The widespread desire among marketing and advertising professionals to have "conversations" with Internet users and consumers gives us a clue as to the metamorphosis of corporate communications. These communications are often criticized because it can serve any offers, support any cause thanks to its rhetorical power and even impose views, representations values. In this context, conversation appears to be able to exonerate marketing and corporate communications since it seems more spontaneous, horizontal and respectful, even selfless or altruistic.

This occurs in a specific context, the emergence of digital uses that emphasizes and multiplies reputation risks since consumers are more easily able to take action to denounce bad market practices or publicize their choices. In this respect, consumers feel a kind of empowerment. This is why conversion is, in a way, for marketing and advertising professionals, to resume control on the relation in the very same space where Internet users express themselves. The primary goal is to collect Internet users speeches and try to master them under the guise of symmetry rather than to endure them. Behind apparent selflessness, centered only on interaction for the sake of it, everything is recorded and "categorized. Engagement is taken into account with the numbers of "like," "share" and "comments." Conversation is transformed with these performance indicators.

"Like," "share" and "comments," emojis like a heart are so part of everyday life for Internet users that they are partly or wholly naturalized and one can forget how and why they are produced, how they rise and why. So people enter the flow of comments and shares of opinions. The overall market dimension of digital space is rarely disputed and is, most of the time, accepted as a prerequisite to being able to participate in it. As a result, the integration of market players within interactions is regular, especially when brands are sometimes initiating the conversational platforms directly in order to keep control of information and comments.

4   Trade-Offs and Balance: Protecting the Brand

4.1   Entering Publishing Space: "Native Advertising"

The presence of brands on social media is sometimes a low profile advertising insertion, melted in publishing spaces. Let us take the point on the case of "native advertising," a digital descendant of good old "advertorial" in print media. "Native advertising" aka "sponsored content," "proposed advertising," "contextual advertisement" mimics digital media discourses. "Native advertising" looks like digital press discourses, aesthetically it looks like the rest and matches, thematically, with the global editorial line. It enables brands to appear as possible topics for journalistic discourse coming together with well-orchestrated public relations. "Native advertising" provides a rather inexpensive exposure and enhances credibility since the information seems journalistic. Even if this kind of blurring is not new, it increased in the last decade. The advertising content is integrated into editorial texts. Recently, marketing and advertising professionals started to show a new concern, trying to differentiate old advertorial from "native advertising" as a more sophisticated production, hence more efficient to seduce consumers and keep their attention. The main idea is based on the fact that the context benefits to the brand since the reader is concentrated on the interest of the content more than in the questioning of the source of information.

4.2 Towards Brand Journalism? [21]

"Native advertising" requires specific writing style and abilities that combine journalistic qualities and what could be called the "sense of the brand," that is to say a way of writing that values the brand. We can even say that nowadays this specific way of writing knows a constant demand and growing under the urge of advertising agencies and advertisers who want to find new spaces to promote brands. This new profession brings together freelance journalists and dedicated agencies. Advertising agencies for major news companies manage the system in order to increase, in all cases, their turnover. If this new market is a great source of enthusiasm for [4], it globally triggers problems for the whole inter-profession since it legitimizes journalism dedicated to brands, something in between journalism and public relations running counter to journalistic ethics. For advertising agencies, "native advertising" enables to couple the sales of traditional advertising spaces and Internet advertising spaces instead of display advertising, too obvious and less efficient. Brand managers prize and value "native advertising" as a relevant tool attract their targets. They tend to think that "native advertising" productions will retain attention and convince better because they are more credible. They are especially known because they do not suffer from ad blockers.

4.3 The Delicate Issue of Trust

Trust is the key of the success of "native advertising," and trust is deeply linked, in order to establish and sustain it, to specific writing skills that ensure that readers will not feel these contents sponsored by brands as manipulative. This would be extremely bad for the brand and the entire media platform. For this reason, marketing and advertising professionals have set, for each kind of digital media, guidelines, and course of action in order to avoid any damaging confusion in discourses categories while maintaining the enunciative blurring. Thereby journalists are rarely authors of these contents sponsored by brands. Some semiotic distinctions are established in order to draw the line between journalistic text and "native advertising," such as snippets, typographic effects, a slightly different color of the background or the presence of the brand logo. These elements are light enough to enable a possible mix-up at first sight but then a differentiation.

The enunciative blurring works together with the preservation of demarcation between advertisement and journalism. It is necessary to manage the significant risk of discrediting journalism and brands that try to invest it as a place. Even if advertising does need new media spaces, there is a strong precautionary principle in order to protect journalism as an economic necessity.

5 Interlacing Brand and Vernacular Discourses

5.1 Variations and Enunciative Blurring

The digital presence of brands can also be an advertising discourse intertwined with vernacular or media discourses. "#foodporn" that happened to be an international success provides a good observation point for these quite unprecedented interlacings on different platforms and social media, and, more specifically on Instagram.

The name "#foodporn" raised a surprising enthusiasm, its transgressive quality raises questions and interests audiences supports virality, encourages to look at it and share it even if the content is much more innocent than suggested by the suffix "porn." In fact, the images show streams of dishes, with colorful, glossy and juicy, dripping plates. People intend to share staged food with anybody crossing these images. Numerous comments and escort discourses come to these posts on social media, especially from professionals working for magazines, websites, restaurants ranking platforms.

Everything is based on the fact that this digital space enables semiotic inventiveness in a determined frame. Texts and images come together, the former being informative comments of the later, that support the culinary show whether an ordinary or exceptional one. At the heart of the system is what we can all iconic excitability even if the conditions of production and the producers are very different. Ordinary people, bloggers, specialized media, burgers sellers or restaurant owners do publish images using this hashtag. These enunciators are extremely different, and the result is very heterogeneous, from ordinary or sponsored testimonials to explicitly advertising discourses and sometimes, in between, the contribution of a well-informed amateur. Devices are very different too, from smartphones to elaborated filming sets. One can also use Instagram tools to enhance the productions aesthetically.

This great diversity becomes one because they all seek "sharing" or spread. They are all willing to respect the architext of Instagram, its iconic rules and frames and its text regulations such as a short description and the blue color for the hashtags. Every Instagrammed message can be evaluated with "hearts," and everybody can see the counting, comments and recorded. On a rhetorical point of view, this discourse is always concise and descriptive. The hashtag "#foodporn" is a metatext that adorns the message. It towers over the dishes the Internet users display as media valued culinary maker's marks, advertised burgers and highly elaborated dishes from great restaurants. Everything is gaining a mediatic and advertising value, due to the effect of the hashtag and its power to inscribe the message in a chain. As we can see, all of this is not due to communicants working for brands, and it is not even the result of advertising strategies.

It is, in fact, the result of publicizing, a display in a digital kind of public space that goes back to the roots of advertisement.

Instagram is the main beneficiary of this phenomenon, and this brand is successful thanks to the proliferation of contents produced by others. These communication productions have an uncertain status that benefits to Instagram as a media brand always explicitly pushing for more hashtags: "If you include the right Instagram hashtags on your posts, you will likely see higher engagement than you would if you didn't have any."

6 Brand Contemporary Shows

6.1 The Advertising Show

As seen before, brands and their advertising messages are spectacular mediations as well as selling mediations. Through this spectacular specificity, they lavish consumers and the general public with an aesthetic pleasure that produces signification and globally impresses. At the same time, this mediation provided by brands is prone to raise the gratitude of the audience.

Nevertheless, we have to acknowledge that the spectacular nature of advertisement is neither new nor restricted to some brands. One can identify great spectacular brand shows as well for luxury brands, car brands, and even hypermarket brands or spectacular urban happenings, branded festive, sport or cultural practices. These productions, sometimes designed to enter *unadvertization* strategies usually end up being *hyperadvertization* systems. Other brands are also in small daily deliveries on social media via devices such as *Facebook* fan pages, dedicated to brands. Thus, instead of achieving some perfect *unadvertization* ideal, they create some *hyperadvertization* forms with a strong repetitive omnipresence of the brand, mainly through its totems, its name, and logo [13].

Furthermore, the advertising show is not something new, and it can be retraced through the enthusiasm for advertising posters collectors in France between 1886 and 1896 in France, as much as through the interest of major film directors. People can choose to consume advertising, and especially commercials, as a show, which is evident with The Night of AdEaters, first launched in France in 1981 and now available internationally and offered in adding countries every year. As Baudrillard posed it: "it (advertising) contributes nothing to production or the direct application of things, yet it plays an integral part in the system of objects, not merely because it relates to consumption but also because it becomes an object to be consumed" [6].

During the last decade, three contemporary kinds of productions can be categorized as current metamorphoses of the advertising show: branded short films, spectacular TV commercials, and daily social media advertising show.

In the first case, we can say that brand short movies belong to *unadvertization* strategies. Brands are producers of short movies, most of the time ordered from a Hollywood famous director and starring equally famous actors; they broadcast them on the Internet pretending not to seek advertising and consumption. However, advertising is soon obvious through stereotypes, intertextuality and, distortions of the narrative structure. In that respect, these short movies are most of the time genre scenes ("car chase" for Pirelli *Mission Zero*, "psychoanalysis session for Prada *A Therapy*, "typical murder mysteries" for *Lady Dior*) and a prop seizes the forefront: a tire saves the main character, a fur coat does analyze the psychoanalyst, and a purse is at the heart of the plot. In other words, props become heroes as in regular advertising messages. Thus spectators feel the trick and can be not so happy to have been subjected to advertising without prior warning, which is not the case with spectacular TV commercials.

One main example of this last phenomenon is "L'Odyssée de Cartier," celebrating the 165 years anniversary of the brand, internationally released on March, 4th, 2012, as commercial and broadcasted as such during prime time on major French TV channels (TF1, Canal Plus) and American Channels as well (ABC, NBC, CBS), in movie theatre and online. It was launched as a blockbuster with a press release, trailer, a world premiere in the Grand Palais in Paris and multiple steps unveiling on *vogue.fr*, TV Channels, and Cartier *Facebook* fan page. The band provided a kind of documentary movie about the making of. Online and offline general press relayed the launching explaining how amazing, out of the ordinary the movie was.

The advertising movie is presented as exceptional in all ways with a significant track record: it is supposed to be one of the most expensive commercials in the international history of advertising, with an exceptional duration (3 min and 31 s). Its director underlines the epic scale. The music was recorded in Abbey Road studio with a symphonic orchestra, and so on. The show is outside and inside this commercial. The movie itself emphasizes the luxury of the brand with a highly anesthetized making of the film, dealing with strong onirism. The semiotic densification is evident given the accumulation of cinematographic processes, shooting locations, special effects, as well as trained animals. Thanks to the gathering of all these elements in a little more than three minutes, it ends up being a precipitate of advertising show.

6.2   Daily Advertising Show Delivery via Social Networks

Big shows are essential and highly visible but small shows on day-to-day delivery too. These are new small advertising formats one can follow, once registered as a "friend" of the brand, directly on personal *Facebook* accounts.

We found that instead of a genuine exchange between brands and people, old branded blogs and dedicated conversational devices (ancestors of social media) appeared to be already entirely mastered by brands and were far from erasing advertising attributes such as logotypes, claims, signature, and visual charts. At the same time, on a semiotic point of view, brands appeared as the real auctorial authority. Visually the entire system took birth into the logotype of brands, extending its shapes and main colors (blue and white) everywhere. This was a first clue towards the idea that whenever advertising people try to erase advertising features from communications, they tend to extend the signs of the brand everywhere ending in *hyperadvertization* instead of *unadvertization*. The redefinition of conversation is the same on some of Facebook brand pages; it even goes beyond a wide spread of the signs of the brand and provides small brand advertising shows.

A semiotic and content analysis of some *Facebook* brand pages shows the actors (the brand and the public) are both on the same enunciation space, but they do not interact. Most of the time, brands offer while consumers are reacting more than interacting. The brand gives the kick: a photo, a video, a motto, a test, and people react in parallel but not together without much feedback from the brand.

A specific analysis of posts on two analog *Facebook* brand pages: the American brand *M&M's* (sweets) and the French brand *Oasis* (fruit drink). *M&M's* USA brand page exists since 2008 and has more than ten millions followers currently; *Oasis* brand page is named *OasisBeFruit*, it was launched in 2009 and has been for several years the French brand page with the most significant number of followers (more than three million). They are similar in the cheerful tone they use in their TV commercials and their products or a part of them (fruit) appear as characters in their commercials.

A semio-communication analysis of the posts on the two brands *Facebook* pages shows that people mainly "like" whatever the brand has posted, they "share" it in some cases and they much more rarely "comment." That is to say; they prefer to press a button rather than writing down something. Whenever they choose to write, it usually goes up to three/four words on average. As a matter of fact, most of the people's reactions on these two *Facebook* pages do not appear as a dialog with the brands or even between participants and the architext of a *Facebook* page isolates the exchanges by automatically closing the direct access to their content and offering instead the number of "like," "share" and "comment." In a way, the architext create the contrary of conversation when it transforms everything into numbers showing plainly an audience counting system rather than a dialogical one (Fig. 1).

Fig. 1. M&M's and *Oasis Facebook* pages (March 2015 and May 2018.)

Thus, the only fact that so many people participate in these *Facebook* brand pages makes it essential to understand what they do, if they do not dialog as in a conversation with these brands. These brief comments look, in fact, more like answers to the brands' various stimuli: written laugh (LMAO! Hilarious, etc.), enthusiastic appreciation as one can express during a show ("Aaawwww I love it!, "Yay," "i like it!!so goood-ddddddd***"), short answers inspired by these brands advertising mottos ("Go yellow," "You go RED"), short declarations of love ("Love m&m," "my favorite is still the one where red takes it all off I miss that commercial," "The best ever *M&M* commercial is the one with Santa," "the absolute best *M&M* commercial ever!!!!!!").

We can conclude that people participating in *M&M's* and *OasisBeFruit Facebook* brand pages react and behave much more like spectators, an audience watching a show rather than people in dialog. We are facing a *hyperadvertization* 'show of brands on *Facebook* instead of an *unadvertized* conversation. *M&M's* and *OasisBeFruit Facebook* brand pages are great *hyperadvertization* devices where we can observe a strong pervasiveness of these brand signs (names, logos, content highly linked to their TV commercials). The French brand *Oasis* does use its commercial catchword "*Oasis-BeFruit*" (in English!) as its *Facebook* brand page name.

The advertising show is so obvious that participants directly qualify the messages as advertising or marketing discourse produced by professionals: "Simultaneous faint, candle falls to the floor.... the absolute best M&M commercial ever!!!!!!." While being *hyperadvertising,* these communications still attract many participants willing to get on a daily basis an advertising show delivered on their own *Facebook* account. We cannot know for sure that there are consumers or customers of these brands, but they consume their advertising discourses freely [15].

At the same time, participants give their evaluation of these advertising messages and show an aesthetic judgment and specific ideas about what can be considered as a good commercial depending on the brand concerned. The advertising show comes with amateur advertising reviewers who demonstrate a true advertising culture. *M&M's* took this into account and produced both for 2018 Super bowl a commercial as usual and a Critical Review *M&M's* Super bowl movie that plays on the confusion between commercials and short movie available on their *Facebook* page and their *YouTube* channel *mmschocolate*. *M&M's* also started to extend the range of its shows while showcasing "Sound+Color presented by *M&M's*" during *SXSW2018* or *South by West* festival of music, film and digital. This leads us towards brands that fully play on the advertising show as their main expression.

Some brands work on turning everything they touch into an advertising show. *Red Bull*, a brand of energy drink, produces, promotes and publicizes some extreme kind of sporting or musical shows to a young or teenage audience. On its website, the brand offers many shows focused on a continuous festive lifestyle, some risky and extreme physical activities, more often borderline than not. *Red Bull* has established a strong spectacular mediation, and the omnipresence of the advertising show is obvious.

Whatever the type or the form of the show, *Red Bull* gives an extremely aestheticized version of it. Whenever the brand produces or takes part in entertainment, it naturalizes for its young audience one single message being at the same time: "*Red Bull* gives you wings" (its advertising claim) and "*Red Bull* is the best." This is the pretty obvious result of a semio-communication analysis of the online brand communications, especially its website. The corpus has been gathered, respecting Barthes' approach [3], using what we call a core sampling process [15], which creates a kind of snapshot of all the messages of a brand at one point.

Regarding *Red Bull*, we chose the official French (February 2017) and American (April 2018) websites that happen to be very much alike in their structures, contents, and tone. Once on the homepage each navigation sign "giving access to different disseminated texts or, conversely, to the reproduction of external texts inside clustered sites" [34]. The global advertising universe of the brand takes shape in capillary action, revealing a huge global structure. This method enables us to reach a "saturated" corpus reached whenever any new web page does not provide anything new: "these "returns" are more and more frequent until one no longer discovers any new material: the corpus is then saturated" [3]. In fact, the sole home pages enable us to reach this stage.

The *Red Bull* corpus gathers *redbull.fr* and redbull.com, *Red Bull* TV and radio, redbulletin.com, et Events, Cartoons, Products and company and a second range of homepages Bike, Adventure, Motorsports, Games, Skate, Dance, eSports, Surf, Musique/Music, Snow, Weightlifting, Festival, Urban culture, Art, Dance, MC battle, etc. The *Red Bull* "world" explicitly addresses mainly male teenagers and young adults on leisure activities with a heavy concentration of risk, spectacularity, and performance. The aesthetic and spectacular mediation provided by the brand is obvious almost to the extent of concealing if one does not know it, the product (an energy soft drink can). Looking at its set of home pages, one would think that *Red Bull* is a media brand, producing both sport and culture shows and broadcasting them, since most of the space is dedicated to all kind of sports, extreme sport, music, and cultural festivals, and so on. The brand messages place is as a mentor coach, providing and explaining to its audience rituals around danger and risk linked to this time of life (teenage) in a safe exploration.

The *Red Bull* case appears to be a kind of extreme commodification of the brand itself. People tend to consume more signs of the brand than its products, even its flagship product. It appears as a show producer always feeding its advertising claim "*Red Bull* gives you wings" in its the largest extension as a global entertainment factory.

6.3 On *Advertisingness* and Advertising Shows

Unadvertization and *hyperadvertization* strategies enable brand discourses to metamorphose, form hybrids with other types of discourses and, at the same time, extend the scope of their actions and the limits of what can be called advertising. For most of the general population advertising already names an extensive set of messages and devices as soon as they are related to a brand. Thus, we could say that every brand message, whatever the form it takes, is, at the core, advertising since semiotic predilection shapes the discourse, but *Advertisingness* goes beyond this and names both this process and a matrix dimension.

Advertisingness is defined [12, 14, 15] as a set of rationales, all at once social and semiotic, profoundly underlining every brand public speech even if it does not seem like regular advertising. *Advertisingness* is a set of forms of discourses, communication imaginaries and social, collective imagination. It is rooted in the very essence of consumption.

Advertisingness in forms of discourses originate in the initial matrix of "classical" advertising messages (see above), that is to say, specific expressive rationales and semiotic work creating highly connoted messages with apparent commercial intentionality turning *unadvertization* into *hyperadvertization* most of the time. *Advertisingness* is based on a strong, self-asserting brand status, an oversemiotization [12, 19] due to semiotic condensation, and shows a saturation of the signs of the brands, a strong stereotypy, and intertextuality.

Advertisingness deals with communications professionals, researchers and collective imagination and imaginaries [3]. For the main part of the population, advertising is linked to rather dysphoric representations such as messages trying to deceive to lure into buying, the work of the "hidden persuaders" [12, 45]. As seen above, communications professionals mainly try to find a way to transform positively advertising into something like branded information. The idea is to slide the borderline opposing information and communication into a positive market branded information opposed to bad old, classical advertising messages. As for researchers, they can be attracted by the fact of presenting advertising as a matrix of communication in general.

Advertisingness is, in itself, a communication logic. Whatever is the shape of the discourse of a brand, it does step in commercial communication logic, inherent in market mediation: the logic of the aura of the commodity, as mentioned by Benjamin, the "logic of Father Christmas" and the logic of prophecy as described by Baudrillard.

The logic of the aura of commodity

Benjamin states that advertising gives access to the collective imagination: "The dream consciousness of the collective [...] awakes [...] in advertising" [9, 10]. Thus advertising takes the aura of the commodity [Baudelaire] to its zenith. The aura of commodity works like a reverse operation of the aura of the work of art [11]. The latter is linked to the authenticity of the unique work and tends to deteriorate through industrial replication. On the contrary, the aura of the commodity is strengthened by its multiplication and circulation mainly using advertising, which is the place of its exaggeration [10]. This aura is a deep characteristic of a market and commercial discourse enabling at the same time to reach a high semiotic condensation and dissemination of the signs of the brand.

The logic of Father Christmas and the logic of the prophecy

Baudrillard gives advertising several functions that build its social and communication logic [6]. Its explicit function is to promote selling; its symbolic and social value is linked to "believing," in a logic of "fables and of the willingness to go along with them": we do not really believe in advertising, but we care for it. Children and adults do the same when they pretend to believe in Santa Claus long after they know that the gifts come from their parents. In the same way, consumers are thankful for advertising for the care it shows. They come into a logic of belief and regression that gives way to a logic of protection and gratification. Thus, advertising is a free show but asks in return the consumer to comply with the social system. Consumption has a normative efficiency that comes from dream, imagination and it enables, all at once, each person to believe, he or she is the sole recipient of advertising and to give him or her collective desires as standard. Advertising refers to "dawnings of objects, dawnings of desires" and enables the advertising message to become a legend in all its meanings.

Baudrillard also stresses the fact that advertising is great at mythmaking [7]. It is neither true nor false; it is, as seen before, a matter of belief. Thus, it cannot deceive, all the more it gives what it says an existence through as a self-fulfilling prophecy: "Advertising is prophetic language, in so far as it promotes not learning or understanding, but hope." This prophetic logic enables brands to exist through all their discourses and strengthen from one message to the other until they become a reality.

One of the main deep logic of the advertising matrix comes from the encounter of Benjamin and Baudrillard theoretical approaches. Then *advertisingness* starts to appear as a strengthening of the aura of the brand to the point of evicting the product for the benefit of its signs and significations. The only presence of a brand in a message ensures the spectacularization of its aura.

Eventually, *advertisingness* is deeply related to the question of mastering communication and the power of representation. In a way, *advertisingness* brings very disparate items back into brand communications. This enables us to understand how contemporary existence strategies of brands broaden the boundaries of advertising in general and extends the scope of brands towards politics. The impact of multiple modes of representation on brand lies in the intensification of its display; it more and more shows of: "To "represent," then, is to show, to intensify, to duplicate a presence" [38] as explained by Marin.

In conclusion, brands strongly activate both types of power due to representation. Brands reach a state of ubiquity and pervasiveness in almost every moment of everyday life thanks to *advertisingness*. This power of presence is crucial since it gives them access to the second representation power effect, analyzed by Marin: "the effect of subject, that is, the power of institution, authorization, and legitimation as resulting from the functioning of the framework reflected onto itself" [38]. *Advertisingness* happens to be at the very heart of the logic of power.

7 Conclusion

Brands transformations and the hybridizations of their communications are deeply part of the way they are established in society [43]. Brands do take part, at the same time, in the transformations of culture as it is shared in digital spaces. Thus, they promote a kind of consumerism that is typical of what Bauman calls the "liquid life" [8]. Even if market players have strategic issues and try to bypass classical differences, the analyses presented in this paper show that society is watching, with attention and awareness, in order to keep the borders, to differentiate motives from one another. Most of the time people are fully aware of what is happening, how it occurs and when to state that they do not buy it or even condemn some overly advertising intrusion in digital spaces. The analyses of different strategies regarding "representations and expressions of advertising digital literacy on social media" put at the center questions of power and authorities at work on social media and social networks behind the scene, behind the show that brands offer to consumers.

References

1. Amossy, R., Herschberg-Pierrot, A.: Stéréotypes et clichés. Langue, discours, société. Nathan, Paris (1997)
2. Barthes, R.: L'imagination publicitaire, Points et perspectives de la recherche publicitaire, pp. 87–88. IREP, Paris (1967)
3. Barthes, R.: Elements of Semiology. Hill and Wang, New York (1968)
4. Barthes, R.: Mythologies. The Noonday Press, New York (1991)
5. Barthes, R.: Le message publicitaire. In: Œuvres Complètes, T. Éditions du Seuil, Paris (2002)
6. Baudrillard, J.: The System of Objects. Verso, London (1996)
7. Baudrillard, J.: The Consumer Society: Myths and Structures. Sage, London (1998)
8. Bauman, Z.: Liquid Life. Polity Press, Boston (2005)
9. Benjamin, W.: The Arcades Project. The Belknap Press of Harvard University Press, Cambridge (2002)
10. Benjamin, W.: The Writer of Modern Life. Essays on Charles Baudelaire. The Belknap Press of Harvard University Press, Cambridge (2008)
11. Benjamin, W.: The Work of Art in the Age of its Technological Reproducibility and Other Writings on Media. The Belknap Press of Harvard University Press, Cambridge (2008)
12. Berthelot-Guiet, K.: Paroles de Pub. La Vie Triviale de la Publicité, Éditions Non Standard, Le Havre (2013)
13. Berthelot-Guiet, K., Marti de Montety, C., Patrin-Leclère, V.: La Fin de la Publicité? Tours et Contours de la Dépublicitarisation. Bord de l'eau, Lormont (2014)
14. Berthelot-Guiet, K., Marti de Montety, C., Patrin-Leclère, V.: Sémiotique des métamorphoses marques-médias, In: Berthelot-Guiet, K., Boutaud. J.-J., (eds.) Sémiotique mode d'emploi. Le Bord de l'eau, Lormont (2015)
15. Berthelot-Guiet, K.: Analyser les discours publicitaires. Armand Colin, Paris (2015)
16. Berthelot-Guiet, K.: 80 ans d'autorégulation publicitaire. In: Wolton, D. (ed.) Avis à la publicité. Cherche-midi, Paris (2015)
17. Berthelot-Guiet, K.: La marque médiation marchande ou mythologie adolescente. In: Lachance, J., Saint-Germain, P., Mathiot, L. (eds.) Marques Cultes et Culte des Marques chez les Jeunes. Penser l'Adolescence avec la Consommation. Presses Universitaires de Laval, Laval (2016)
18. Berthelot-Guiet, K.: Elderly and IT: brand discourses on the go. In: Zhou, J., Salvendy, G. (eds.) ITAP 2016. LNCS, vol. 9755, pp. 186–193. Springer, Cham (2016). https://doi.org/10.1007/978-3-319-39949-2_18
19. Berthelot-Guiet, K.: Grandir en publicité: marques et mythes d'enfance. In: Bahuaud, M., Pecolo, A. (eds.) Naître et grandir en terres publicitaires, Jeunes et Médias, N°9 (2018)
20. Berthelot-Guiet, K.: New media, new commodification, new consumption for older people. In: Zhou, J., Salvendy, G. (eds.) ITAP 2018. LNCS, vol. 10926, pp. 435–445. Springer, Cham (2018). https://doi.org/10.1007/978-3-319-92034-4_33
21. Bull, A.: Brand Journalism. Routledge, London, New York (2013)
22. Bourdieu, P.: La Distinction, Critique Sociale du Jugement. Les Éditions de Minuit, Paris (1979)
23. de Certeau, M.: The Practice of Everyday Life. University of California Press, Berkeley (1984)
24. Cochoy, F.: Une histoire du marketing. Discipliner l'économie de marché, La Découverte, Paris (1999)
25. Douglas, M., Isherwood, D.: The World of Goods. Routledge, London (1979)

26. Douhei, M.: Digital Cultures. MA Harvard University Press, Cambridge (2011)
27. Eco, U.: La Structure Absente. Introduction à la recherche sémiotique, Le Mercure de France, Paris (1978)
28. Flichy, P.: The Internet Imaginaire. The MIT Press, Cambridge (2008)
29. Foucault, M.: The Order of Discourse. Routledge, London (1981)
30. Fuat-Firat, A., Dholakia, N.: Consuming People, From Political Economy to Theaters of Consumption. Routledge, London (1998)
31. Gottdiener, M.: The Theming of America. Westview Press, Boulder (2001)
32. Horowitz, D.: Consuming Pleasures. Intellectuals and Popular Culture in the Postwar World. University Press of Pennsylvania, Philadelphia (2004)
33. Jeanneret, Y., Ollivier, O.: Les Sciences de l'Information et de la Communication, CNRS Editions 38. Hermes, Paris (2004)
34. Jeanneret, Y.: The relation between mediation and use in the research of information and communication in France. RECIIS – Elect. J. Commun. Inf. Innov. Health. 3(3), 25–34 (2009)
35. Jeanneret, Y.: Critique de la Trivialité. Les Médiations de la Communication, Enjeux de Pouvoir. Éditions Non Standard, Le Havre (2014)
36. Klein, N.: No Logo. Taking Aim at the Brand Bullie. Saint Martin's Press Inc., New York (2000)
37. Kowalczyk, A., Pisarska, K.: The Lives of Texts: Exploring the Metaphor. Cambridge Scholar Publishing, Cambridge (2012)
38. Marin, L.: Portrait of the King. Palgrave MacMillan, London (1988)
39. de Montety, C.: Magazines de marque: métamorphoses d'une promesse. Ph.D. Université Paris-Sorbonne (2005). Unpublished
40. Marti de Montety, C., Patrin-Leclere, V.: La conversion à la conversation, le succès d'un succédané. Commun. Lang. 169 (2011)
41. Marti de Montety, C.: Les marques, acteurs culturels: dépublicitarisation et valeur sociale ajoutée. Commun. Manag. 10(2) (2013)
42. Marti, C.: Dialogues numériques en milieu marchand. Un rêve relationnel. Rom. J. Journalism Commun. (2017)
43. Marti, C.: Les mediations culturelles de marques: une quête d'autorité. ISTE editions, London (2019)
44. Morin, E.: L'Esprit du Temps: Essai sur la culture de masse. Grasset, Paris (1962)
45. Packard, V.: The Hidden Persuaders. Random House, New York (1957)
46. Patrin, V.: Pour un Contrat de Lecture Globale: l'Exemple de la Presse TV Française, Ph.D. Université Paris-Sorbonne (2000). Unpublished

Study on the Relationship Between Loyalty Program and Consumer Behavior on EC Site

Yusuke Nakasatomi[1]($\boxtimes$), Takashi Namatame[2], and Kohei Otake[1]

[1] School of Information and Telecommunication Engineering, Tokai University,
2-3-23, Takanawa, Minato-ku, Tokyo 108-8619, Japan
6BJM1206@cc.u-tokai.ac.jp, otake@tsc.u-tokai.ac.jp
[2] Faculty of Science and Engineering, Chuo University, 1-13-27, Kasuga,
Bunkyo-ku, Tokyo 112-8551, Japan
nama@indsys.chuo-u.ac.jp

Abstract. Point programs are offered as part of the loyalty program. In this study, we analyze customer's purchase history and usage trend of points at golf portal site. We first classified loyal customers by RFM analysis. We also categorized into two unique types according to customer's point use behavior. Next, we performed logistic regression analysis for discrimination of loyal customers. Through these analyzes, we clarified the characteristics of point use tendencies for loyal customers.

Keywords: Point use behavior · RFM analysis · Logistic regression analysis

1 Introduction

Currently, many retailers provide point programs as part of the loyalty program. Many of the loyalty programs conducted by retailers are called FSP (Frequent Shopper Program) and provide benefits according to customers' purchase price [1]. The method of giving benefits in FSP can be classified using two types such as continuous or non-continuous and linear or nonlinear. In the linear and continuous loyalty program, registered members can acquire points depending on a specific amount of money, and they can use available point in 1 point unit. In a previous research [2], it is reported that many consumers tend to use according to the balance at the time of purchase based on mental accounting theory. On the other hand, there are very few studies that clarify the use tendency of customer's point program at EC site based on actual use of loyalty program.

In this study, we clarify the characteristics of point usage trends based on purchase history, customer attributes, and point usage history of customers who are using linear and continuous point programs set at a certain golf portal site.

2 Dataset

In this study, we use a dataset provided by the golf portal site. Specifically, we use ID-POS (Identification-Point of Sales) data, point balance data, point history data, customer attribute information data. All data are linked by customer ID.

© Springer Nature Switzerland AG 2019
G. Meiselwitz (Ed.): HCII 2019, LNCS 11579, pp. 434–443, 2019.
https://doi.org/10.1007/978-3-030-21905-5_33

The data period is one year from 2017/08/01 to 2018/07/31. The data summary is following.

- ID-POS data: purchase date, product code, product classification code, product unit price, sales volume, etc.
- Point balance data: balance of customers points.
- Point history data: processing date, use or acquisition flag, number of points, etc.
- Customer attribute information data: sex, age, place of residence, date of registration, etc.

In this study, we focused on the customers who registered at a certain golf portal site and we targeted customers with purchase history between 2017/08/01 and 2018/07/31. In addition, we excluded customers who have historically returned products, never gotten points or never used any of them.

As a result of extraction under the above conditions, the number of target customers was 78,193.

In the targeted EC site, five categories (golf accessories, golf gear, men's wear, lady's wear and other) were set as major categories. Number of purchases and the average of purchase price for each product category in dataset is shown Table 1.

Table 1. Number of purchases and average of purchase price

	Golf accessories	Golf gear	Men's wear	Lady's wear	Other
Number of purchases	506045	199454	385673	107434	4876
Average purchase price	4801.105	22115.080	5474.102	6173.782	3877.261

3 Analysis Aimed at Feature Extraction of Points Usage Tendency

In this section, we describe the analysis aimed at feature extraction of point use tendency. First, we evaluate the loyalty of customer, then we classify the customers into two types, loyal customers and general customers. Next, we calculate "point retention value" using point history data.

3.1 Divide Method of Loyal Customers

We performed RFM analysis [3] as a divide method of customers' loyalties. RFM analysis is a method of representing and discriminating customers' loyalty using three indicators, i.e., Recency, Frequency and Monetary. Recency is determined by how recently customer purchased products. Frequency is determined by how often customer purchase products. Monetary is determined by how much money customer used.

In this study, we evaluated RFM using the following data.

- Recency: Time after last purchased
- Frequency: Total number of purchases during the data period
- Monetary: Total usage amount during the data period

Customer ranks are given in 10 levels, higher value means higher loyalty for each of the three viewpoints, and the total value of viewpoints is set as a comprehensive index. Based on the obtained comprehensive indices, we decided the top 30%, 28,393 customers as loyal customers. The outline of the customer after divide is shown Table 2.

Table 2. Outline of the customers' RFM value after discrimination

	Loyal customers	General customers
No. of customers	28,939	49,800
Recency: average days	41.06	158.36
Frequently: average value	12.32	2.49
Monetary: average value	111790.03	15877.05

3.2   Usage Trend of Customer's Point

Next, we categorize the usage type of the point from the point history data. As an index for classification, in this study, we calculated the maximum value (number of days) from point acquisition to usage as "point retention value". An image of the calculation "point retention value" is shown in Fig. 1.

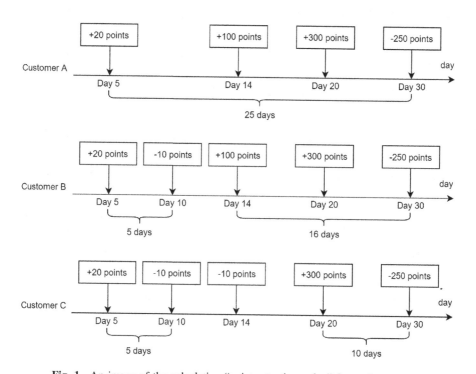

Fig. 1. An image of the calculation "point retention value" for each customer

From the Fig. 1, customer A's point retention value is 25 and customer A is a point saving-type which is holding without using point for a long period of time from point acquisition. On the other hand, customer C's point retention value is 10 and customer C is an immediate-type that uses points quickly after earned points.

We named the saving-type is within the top 10% of the points holding value, the immediate-type is the lowest point holding value is less than 10%.

3.3   Result of the Analysis of Point Usage Tendency

We use customers' loyalty and the usage type of points, we clarify the point usage tendencies.

First, the number of loyal customers belonging to the two types. As a result, it was found that about 59% of the saving-types are composed of loyal customers. On the other hand, in the immediate-type, it was found that about 88% of customers are loyal customers. Table 3 shows the comprehensive index calculated by RFM analysis for each usage type of point. From the Table 3, the saving-type has a larger variation in customer loyalty than the immediate-type.

Table 3. Percentage of customers and their avg. point balance by point usage type

	General customers	Loyal customers	Average point balance
Immediate-type	12%	88%	390.51
Saving-type	41%	59%	1351.94

Next, we show the product categories for each usage type are shown in Figs. 2 and 3. In the targeted EC site, five categories (golf accessories, golf gear, men's wear, lady's wear and other) were set as major categories. We totaled the number of purchasing based on major categories.

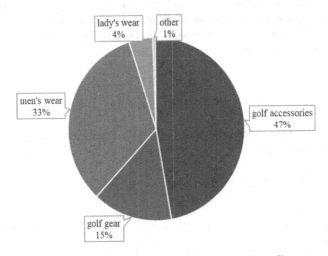

Fig. 2. Pie chart of purchases by category in the immediate-type

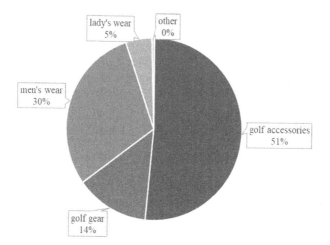

Fig. 3. Pie chart of purchases by category in the saving-type

From the Figs. 2 and 3, purchase of golf accessories is somewhat higher (about 3%) for the immediate-type. However, it cannot be said that there is a characteristic tendency. We create discriminant models of loyal customers and discover characteristic trends in the next step.

4 Analysis Using Logistic Regression Model

In this section, we describe analysis aimed at discriminating loyal customers using logistic regression. We created a model to distinguish the loyal customers calculated in 3.1 by binomial logistic regression and try to grasp the features.

The binomial logistic regression model is a type of classifier that performs class discrimination. By interpreting significant explanatory variables in the constructed model, it is possible to clarify the characteristics that affect the presence or absence of loyalties. In the binomial logistic regression analysis, the loyal customer probability p_i is expressed by the following equation.

$$p_i = \frac{\exp\{\sum_{j=0}^{m} \beta_j X_{ij}\}}{1 + \exp\{\sum_{j=0}^{m} \beta_j X_{ij}\}} \tag{1}$$

Here, X_{ij} is factors affecting loyalties and β_j is Parameters for each explanatory variable (β_0 is Intercept).

4.1 Variable Selection

In this analysis, we use the following variables.

- Explanatory variables: point retention value, point balance at 2018/07/31, Purchasing availability by product categories (golf accessories, club, men's wear, lady's wear, others)
- Objective variable: loyal customer classification

The objective variable is the classification result of the customer based on RFM analysis. 1 for loyal customers, 0 for general customers. Moreover, we set point retention value calculated in Sect. 3.2 as explanatory variables. In addition, we set explanatory variables for purchase history by five purchase categories, set 1 for purchase and 0 for no purchase. As shown in Sect. 3.3, when classifying the tendency of point use into the two types of the immediate-type and the saving-type, a difference was seen in purchasing behavior by product category. Therefore, we considered that customer loyalty would also be affected by product category.

4.2 Result

First, we performed under-sampling to estimate the model because two level of the objective variable is not balanced. The total number of cases is 78,193, the number of cases classified as loyal customers is 28,393, and the number of cases classified as general customers is 49,800. This is randomly extracted from majority data, here classified as a general customer, to match the number of minority data, here classified as a loyal customer.

Next, we performed normalization on the explanatory variables. Specifically, point retention value and point balance were normalized. We estimate the model 10 times and show the best results of the analysis in Table 4.

Table 4. Result of logistic regression analysis

Variables	Regression coefficient	P > |z|	Odds ratio
Point retention value	−0.0694	0.000	0.9329
Point balance	0.0840	0.000	1.0876
Sex	−0.0432	0.011	0.9576
Supplies/accessories	0.2331	0.000	1.2624
Club	0.9009	0.000	2.4618
Men's wear	0.1805	0.000	1.1977
Lady's wear	1.0557	0.000	2.8738
Others	0.5314	0.000	1.7012

Next, in order to verify the generalization performance of the model, we performed cross-validation. Cross-validation is a method that divides data used for model estimation and data used for model evaluation and applying it for validation and confirmation of the validity of the analysis. In this study, we divided into 10 pieces of the dataset. The averages of the correct answer rates were obtained, and a value of 80% was obtained.

Next, we create confusion matrix using prediction results. Confusion matrix is to check the number of each of the samples judged correctly for y = 0 and y = 1 of the sample and the number judged erroneously in the crosstable. The results are shown Table 5.

Table 5. The confusion matrix of logistic regression model

		Predict class	
		Positive	Negative
Actual class	True	TP: 10,281	FN: 4,844
	False	FP: 730	TN: 7,603

We calculated prediction accuracy of the constructed model by using the following Eqs. (2) to (5).

$$Accuracy = \frac{TP + TN}{TP + TN + FP + FN} \tag{2}$$

$$Precision = \frac{TP}{TP + FP} \tag{3}$$

$$Recall = \frac{TP}{TP + FN}. \tag{4}$$

$$F\text{-measure} = \frac{2 \times Precision \times Recall}{Precision + Recall} \tag{5}$$

These indexes are better when the values are closed to 1.

Evaluation was conducted ten times, and the average value was obtained. The results are shown Table 6.

Table 6. The evaluation of the model

Accuracy	Precision	Recall	F-measure
0.7711	0.6268	0.8794	0.7319

From Table 6, we considered that the model has a certain discrimination accuracy. The ROC curve is shown Fig. 4.

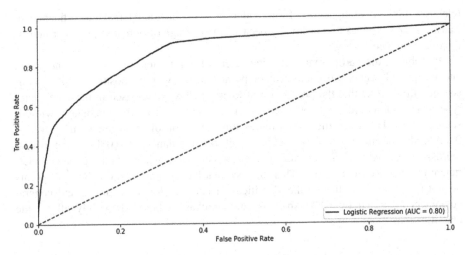

Fig. 4. A graph of the ROC curve

As shown in this figure, the ROC curve was exceeded to the diagonal line which is the expected value when it was predicated randomly. Hence also two figures, own result has enough predictability.

5 Discussion

In Sect. 3, we classified customer's point usage type into two types, the immediate-type and the saving-type, using point retention value. From Figs. 2 and 3 there was no big difference in the proportion of purchased genres between the saving-type and the immediate-type. In addition, the average purchase price by genre purchased from Table 1 greatly differs depending on genre. From these results, the use period of customer's point does not fluctuate depending on the amount of purchase. This seems to be the same result as the previous study [2] that the commodity price does not have a big influence on consumer's point use behavior.

In addition, since points are used immediately from Table 3, it is shown that the proportion of loyal customers increased to 88% in the immediate-type where point balance tends to be low. On the other hand, the saving-type, which saves points and tends to increase the point balance, shows that the percentage of loyal customers is lower than the immediate-type at 59%. The previous research [4] point out that customers who use points in linear and continuous point programs are more priced and purchasing behavior than customers who do not use them. In this study, we use RFM analysis that uses cumulative purchase price, purchase frequency, purchase period for discrimination of loyal customers, suggesting that customers using points as well as previous studies can be better customers.

Next, in the model shown in Sect. 4, as Table 4 shows, partial regression coefficients worked positively for all purchases by category. The influence of lady's wear and club category was higher loyalty because the average of purchase price per point is relatively high in both genres. From Table 1, it is considered that the influence of Lady's wear, club was higher loyalty because the average of purchase price per item is relatively high in both genres.

In Table 4, the partial regression coefficient of point retention value was negative, and the partial regression coefficient of point balance worked positive. This is consistent with the fact that the proportion of loyal customers increased in the immediate-type where points are used for a short period of time and used immediately without saving points. However, the partial regression coefficient of Point retention value is -0.0694, the partial regression coefficient of point balance is 0.0804, both partial regression coefficients can be said to be slight compared with partial regression coefficient in purchase by category. This suggests that the use period and balance of points do not significantly influence the classification between loyal customers and general customers classified by RFM analysis, and purchasing behavior greatly affects the classification.

6 Conclusion

In this study, we clarified the characteristic of point usage phenomenon in an EC site history data. It can be said that there is no big difference in the tendency of point use period in loyal and general customers classified by RFM analysis. However, there were differences between loyal customers and general customers depending on the point savings to consumption. This is due to the point data used in this study being linear and continuous point data at stores on the Internet. In the previous research [4], it is reported According to consumers in linear and continuous point programs continue to keep points until they reach a certain high point balance. In addition, another research [5], it is suggested that promoting the use of points in linear and continuous point programs of shops on the Internet does not lead to an improvement in customer loyalty. The conclusion of this study supports this.

The following three issues will be addressed in the future.

Firstly, it is a research on the point use tendency with respect to commodity price. In this research, we focused on the usage period of points, but the way of point is usage for each product unit price, the amount of points used for commodity price, was excluded from the research. It is possible to use only the fraction of the item price as a situation when using points. Also, in the case of shops on the Internet, many settlements are made through credit cards rather than cash. For this reason, we do not use fractional numbers, so we can think of patterns that always use the full amount. If the change in the utilization rate of points with respect to the unit price of a product is clarified, it will be possible to propose measures to promote the use of points from retailers and to improve sales.

Secondly, it is a research on point use trends in retailers in other forms. The subject of this research was a single item mail order and a retail business limited on the Internet. There are also multi-channel type retailers combining mall-type shops, Internet shops and real stores for retailers who only sell in real stores and retailers on the Internet. It is necessary to promote generalization of research by clarifying the use tendency of points in these customers.

Finally, it is a research on the tendency of goods bought at points. In this research, we do not consider that points affect the determination of purchased items themselves. For example, because the point's expiration date expires, it may be considered that the item is selected according to the point amount. Also, if the loyalty program is not provided, it can be inferred that the point cannot be acquired originally, and the customer neglects the point itself rather than cash. Whether items purchased at points are different from those purchased for cash is left as future research subjects.

Acknowledgement. We thank Golf Digest Online Inc. for permission to use valuable datasets and for useful comments. This work was supported by JSPS KAKENHI Grant Number 16K03944 and 17K13809.

References

1. Aoki, A., Sasaki, I.: A study of the effects of point program and discount system in Japanese retailers. Melco J. Manag. Account. Res. **4**(2), 3–16 (2015). (in Japanese)
2. Nakagawa, H.: Consumers' perceived benefit from price discounts and offering points: the moderating role of promotional benefit level. J. Behav. Econ. Financ. **8**, 16–29 (2015). (in Japanese)
3. Marcus, C.: A practical yet meaningful approach to customer segmentation. J. Consum. Mark. **15**(5), 494–504 (1998)
4. Smith, A., Sparks, L.: Reward redemption behaviour in retail loyalty schemes. Br. J. Manag. **20**(2), 204–218 (2009)
5. Nakagawa, H., Ono, J.: The effects of loyalty programs online: a comparative study on real shops. J. Acad. Soc. Direct Mark. **15**, 5–32 (2016). (in Japanese)

Digital Marketing Research – How to Effectively Utilize Online Research Methods

Marc Oliver Opresnik[(⊠)]

Technische Hochschule Lübeck, Public Corporation, Mönkhofer Weg 239,
23562 Lübeck, Germany
marc.oliver.opresnik@th-luebeck.de

Abstract. The term market research refers to gathering, analyzing and presenting information that is related to a well-defined problem. Hence the focus of market research is a specific problem or project with a beginning and an end.

Although the Internet is still confined to the boundaries of the personal computer screen this will soon be a thing of the past; it is now clear that the Internet is definitely going to be a medium for the masses. Many researchers are amazed at how efficiently surveys can be conducted, tabulated and analyzed on the Web. Additionally, online data collection lets marketeers use complex study designs once considered either too expensive or too cumbersome to execute via traditional means. Although the earliest online tools offered little more than the ability to deploy paper-based questionnaires to Internet users, contemporary online tools and services are available with a wide range of features at a wide range of prices which will be outlined in the following sections.

Keywords: Social Media marketing · Marketing research ·
Marketing management · Web 2.0 · Marketing 4.0 ·
Integrated marketing communication · Social computing · Social media

1 Introduction to Marketing Research

The term market research refers to gathering, analyzing and presenting information that is related to a well-defined problem. Hence the focus of market research is a specific problem or project with a beginning and an end.

Market research differs from a decision support system (DSS), which is information gathered and analyzed on a continual basis. In practice, market research and DSS are often hard to differentiate, so they will be used interchangeably in this context [1].

Marketers have the idea that different customers should be treated differently to maximize the relationship with the best ones and minimize the involvement with the worst ones. Information technology helps to realize that desire. The reality comes at a cost, however, as relationship marketing presents a new set of challenges both to marketers and information systems managers. To succeed, an effective cross-functional team of information systems and marketing specialists must work harmoniously. In the past, the two groups barely understood or tolerated each other. On a positive note, a new breed of cross-disciplinary executives exists. They understand both marketing and technology. Overall, the most successful implementation will require true collaboration [2].

© Springer Nature Switzerland AG 2019
G. Meiselwitz (Ed.): HCII 2019, LNCS 11579, pp. 444–451, 2019.
https://doi.org/10.1007/978-3-030-21905-5_34

To be useful to organizations, knowledge tools must be accessible to mainstream users. They must be understandable and useful to marketing managers, not just statistical experts and information systems managers. To overcome potential problems in applicability, marketers must insist that several key goals be achieved. They include [3]:

Putting the problem in the marketer's terms, including viewing the data from a marketing model perspective. Often the job of knowledge discovery is performed by analysts whose primary training is in statistics and data analysis. It is likely that these analysts do not have the same perspective as marketers. To be useful to marketing, the findings must be in a form that marketers can understand;

Presenting results in a manner that is useful for the business problem at hand. The foremost benefit of the analysis and the job of the analyst is to help solve business problems and increase or diminish the value of the analysis;

Providing support for specific key business analyses, marketers need to know about segmentation, market response, segment reachability. Knowledge discovery tools must support these analyses from the beginning;

Providing support for an extensive and iterative exploratory process. Realistic knowledge discovery is not simple and not linear. It is an interactive and iterative learning process. Initial results are fed back into the process to increase accuracy. The process takes time and can have a long lifespan.

2 Online (Internet) Research Methods

Although the Internet is still confined to the boundaries of the personal computer screen this will soon be a thing of the past; it is now clear that the Internet is definitely going to be a medium for the masses. Many researchers are amazed at how efficiently surveys can be conducted, tabulated and analyzed on the Web. Additionally, online data collection lets marketers use complex study designs once considered either too expensive or too cumbersome to execute via traditional means. While initial forays were fraught with technical difficulties and methodological hurdles recent developments have begun to expose the medium's immense potential.

The earliest online tools offered little more than the ability to deploy paper-based questionnaires to Internet users. Today, however, online tools and services are available with a wide range of features at a wide range of prices.

For the international market researcher, the major advantages and disadvantages of online surveys are the following [4]:

2.1 Advantages of Online Surveys

Low financial resource implications: the scale of the online survey is not associated with finance, i.e. large-scale surveys do not require greater financial resources than small surveys. Expenses related to self-administered postal surveys are usually in the form of outward and return postage, photocopying, etc., none of which is associated with online surveys.

Short response time: online surveys allow questionnaires to be delivered instantly to their recipients, irrespective of their geographical location. Fast survey execution allows for most interviews to be completed within a week or so.

Saving time with data collection and analysis: the respective questionnaire can be programmed so that responses can feed automatically into the data analysis software (SPSS, SAS, Excel, etc.), thus saving time and resources associated with the data entry process. Furthermore, this avoids associated data transcription errors.

Visual stimuli: this can be evaluated, unlike CATI.

2.2 Disadvantages of Online Surveys

Respondents have no physical addresses: the major advantage of postal over online surveys is that respondents have physical addresses, whereas not everyone has an electronic address. This is an international marketing research problem in geographical areas where the penetration of the Internet is not as high as in Europe and North America. For cross-country surveys the multi-mode approach (i.e. a combination of online and postal survey) compensates for the misrepresentation of the general population.

Guarding respondents' anonymity: traditional mail surveys have advantages in guarding respondents' anonymity. Sensitive issues, which may prevent respondents from giving sincere answers, should be addressed via the post rather than online.

Time necessary to download pages: problems may arise with older browsers that fail to display HTML questionnaires properly, and also with the appearance of the questionnaires in different browsers (Internet Explorer, Netscape).

Response rates to e-mail questionnaires vary according to the study context. Various factors have been found to inhibit response to e-mail or Internet data collection. These factors include poor design of e-mail questionnaires, lack of anonymity and completion incentives. By addressing these factors in the context of specific research objectives it may provide a way to tackle non-response to e-mail questionnaires. Incentives should be used to encourage response rates, especially if the e-mail questionnaires are lengthy. Potential respondents are likely to trade off their anonymity if incentives are used. The researcher can easily negotiate completion incentives if the sampling frame derives from a company's database [5].

3 Online Quantitative Market Research

Online surveys can be conducted through e-mail or they can be posted on the Web and the URL provided (a password is optional depending on the nature of the research) to the respondents who have already been approached. When a wide audience is targeted the survey can be designed as a pop-up survey, which would appear as a Web-based questionnaire in a browser window while users are browsing the respective websites. Such a Web-based survey is appropriate for a wide audience, where all the visitors to certain websites have an equal chance to enter the survey.

However, the researcher's control over respondents entering the Web-based surveys is lower than for e-mail surveys. One advantage of Web-based surveys is the better display of the questionnaire, whereas e-mail software still suffers from certain limitations in terms of design tools and offering interactive and clear presentation. However, these two modes of survey may be mixed, combining the advantages of each [6].

4 Online Qualitative Market Research

There are many interesting opportunities to conduct international qualitative market research quickly and at relatively low cost, without too much travelling involved [2]:

Saving Money on Travelling Costs, etc. Many qualitative researchers often have to travel to countries in which research is conducted, briefing local moderators and viewing some groups or holding interviews to get a grasp of the local habits and attitudes. This leads to high travelling costs and increases the time needed to execute the fieldwork. It usually takes one or two weeks to recruit the respondents, and one or two weeks before the analysis can start. In online research the respondents can be recruited and interviewed from any computer anywhere in the world. Nearly everyone who is connected to the Internet knows how to use chat rooms. Fieldwork may start two days after briefing, and the analysis may start straight after the last interview based on complete and accurate transcripts, with each comment linked to the respective respondent.

Cross-Country Qualitative Research. International online research is particularly interesting for multinational companies that sell their products on a global scale and are afraid to build the global marketing strategy on research which has been conducted in only a few of these countries. Online qualitative research could serve as an additional multi-country check. This is not intended to give insight into the psychology of customers but rather to check whether other countries or cultures may add to the general picture, which has been made on the basis of qualitative face-to-face research.

One of the limitations with, for example, online focus groups is that they seem to generate less interaction between members than the face-to-face groups. Discussions between respondents occur, but they are less clear and coherent.

5 Marketing Research Based on Web 2.0

Today, maybe 80% of international marketers' need for international marketing data are addressed by conducting a market-research project. In future, the leading edge MNEs—probably led by consumer-packaged goods and technologically driven companies—will look for answers to 80% of their marketing issues by 'catching' already available data. Some of the data sources and tools available through the Web 2.0 will include the following [2]:

Mobile Data. One of the biggest opportunities for marketers is the opportunity to collect real-time geographic information about consumers and to geo-target consumers.

GPS-enabled smart phones penetrating worldwide markets at an exponential rate coupled with an ongoing increase in cellular bandwidth and data processing speed will result in the opportunity to target the right consumer not only at the right time but at the right place. Major information firms such as Google and innovative start-ups are leading the way in utilizing such readily available data sources in real time.

User-Generated Content and Text Mining. Web 2.0 provides gathering places for Internet users in social-network sites (e.g. Facebook, Twitter), blogs, forums, and chatrooms. These assembly points leave footprints in the form of huge amounts of textual data. The difficulty in obtaining insights from online user-generated content is that consumers' postings often are extremely unstructured, large in magnitude, and not easy to syndicate. Commercial (e.g., Nielsen Online) and academic text-mining tools provide marketers and researchers with an opportunity to 'listen' to consumers in the market. By doing so, firms can better understand the topics discussed, consumers' opinions, the market structure, and the competitive environment.

Web Browsing. The use of click-stream data, which contain click-by-click Web page-viewing information, dates back to the introduction of the Internet to the mass market. Until now the utilization of clickstream data has been limited by the inability to collect, store, and analyze the huge data sets, often in real time. However, now firms use cross-organizational skills for developing and converting these data into international market insights.

Social Networks and Online Communities. Some of the fastest growing sources of information flow are the social-networking sites of which the most visible and powerful presences include Facebook and Twitter. Somehow consumers are turning from searching for information at news websites and search engines back to the traditional approaches of asking their friends their advice. Of course, the networking element means that they have a much wider circle of 'friends', which can also be used for more formal but 'quick-and-dirty' questionnaire surveys. Although social-networking sites have become ubiquitous, the full international marketing utilization of these sites is still untapped. The integration of social networking sites with other sources of information such as online retailers and media sources will amplify the opportunities to derive actionable marketing insights from online word-of-mouth content. Furthermore, by observing consumers' social-networking habits and purchase behavior, researches can leverage the social relationship information to identify and target opinion leaders. Furthermore, with emergence of Web 2.0, many consumer goods companies such as Nike, Harley-Davidson and Procter & Gamble have started to build their own brand communities. Brand communities open an opportunity for firms not only to enhance the interactions among consumers but to fully observe these interactions. Furthermore, brand communities open a direct of communication channel between the firm and its customer. As consumers move toward obtaining much of the information from other consumers, brand communities are likely to become a major component of the information flow.

Customer Decision-Making Data. Increasingly firms are interested not only in understanding the outcome of (or exposure to) the marketing effort but in understanding the entire process customers go though in arriving at a decision. This interest has been sparked by several technological advances in areas such as radio frequency identification (RFID), video-recognition tools and eye tracking. RFID technology allows researchers to track consumers in the retail environment, a capability to track items with the goal of improving the efficiency of supply-chain systems. Marketers can get the full picture of what is happening in the store and enable tracing consumers and product flow. The difficulty with converting these extremely valuable data into international marketing insights lies in the magnitude of data and the complexity of analysis.

Consumer Usage Data. More and more products now are being embedded with sensors and wireless devices that can allow marketers to track consumers geographically and over time. For example, sensors on cars and consumer packaged goods can open new windows into their usage and consumption in addition to the purchase of products.

Neuromarketing. Neuromarketing, referring to the use of neuroscience for marketing applications, potentially offers the ability to observe directly what consumers are thinking. Neuromarketing often is used to study brain activity to exposure to brands, product designs, or advertising. Neuromarketing is a relatively new tool for marketers, mainly owing to technological barriers, the ability to transform the neuroscience results into actionable business insights, and the high costs of collecting the data. It is expected, however, that the next decade will see improvement on these fronts, making neuromarketing a common component of the customer insights tool kit.

6 Social Media Funnel

Social Media marketing is about using social networks and tools to guide prospect (potential) customers through a series of steps – a funnel – to get them to take the desired action, e.g. becoming a new customer and buying the company's product and services, with the end-goal of turning new customers into loyal customers with a high lifetime value. As shown in Fig. 1 (the four categories of Social Media) there are a lot of media tools. With all these Social Media marketing tools at the disposal, how should the company decide which ones fit to optimally to the social media funnel, and in which order they should be used? To answer this question, the company has to know who the potential customers are and how they can be reached most effectively. The social media marketer also has to know about the company's objectives, how it should measure these objectives (i.e. the metrics that should be analyzed) and what numbers should be set for those metrics. Figure 1 provides a generic illustration of the social media funnel and the key metrics connected to the three stages of a typical customer buying process: Awareness, Engagement and Action [3].

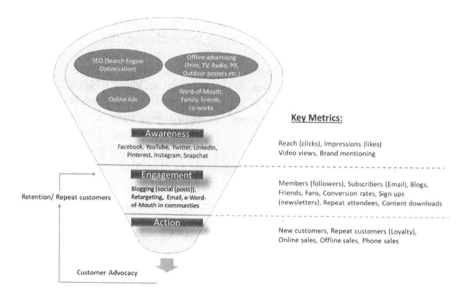

Fig. 1. The social media funnel (Source: Kotler, Hollensen and Opresnik, 2019)

As illustrated in Fig. 1, the following tools can act as vehicles to move and drive new potential customers into the funnel:

SEO (Search Engine Optimization);
Offline advertising;
Online advertising;
Word-of-Mouth conversation with family members, friends and co-workers;

Any bottlenecks in the social media funnel will slow the momentum of turning prospects into actual customers or stop the process completely. Depending on where the bottleneck happens, the company could miss out on brand awareness opportunities, or conversions into actual sales.

With the key metrics in place, the company should look at each tactic in each part of the funnel and it should try and set industry benchmark standards. These benchmark standards should be used to compare the company with its competitors and the industry in general [7, 8].

7   Conclusion

As digital communication becomes an increasingly dominant way for people exchange and share information, digital marketing research becomes and essential tool for any company and organization. Effectively utilizing online research methods will help organizations and companies better understand how to engage their target market online and outline the key activities they need to take to market their business digitally and measure the effectiveness of their actions.

References

1. Crie, D., Micheaux, A.: From customer data to value: what is lacking in the information chain. J. Database Market. Customer Strategy Manage. **13**(4), 282–299 (2006)
2. Hollensen, S., Opresnik, M.: Marketing: Principles and Practice, 1st edn., Lübeck (2017)
3. Kotler, P., Hollensen, S., Opresnik, M.: Social Media Marketing – A Practitioner Guide, 3rd edn., Lübeck (2019)
4. Grossnickle, J., Raskin, O.: Handbook of Online Marketing Research. McGraw Hill, New York (2001)
5. Michaelidou, N., Dibb, S.: Product involvement an application in clothing. J. Consum. Behav. **5**, 442–453 (2006)
6. Ilieva, J., Baron, S., Healey, N.M.: Online surveys in marketing research: pros and cons. Int. J. Market Res. **44**(3), 361–376+382 (2002)
7. Hollensen, S.: Marketing Management – A Relationship Approach, 4th edn. Pearson Benelux BV, Amsterdam (2019)
8. Hollensen, S., Opresnik, M.: Marketing – A Relationship Perspective, 2nd edn. Verlag Franz Vahlen GmbH, München (2015)

On-Line Travel Agencies' Usability: Evaluator eXperience

Virginica Rusu[1] , Cristian Rusu[2] , Daniela Quiñones[2(✉)] ,
Federico Botella[3] , Silvana Roncagliolo[2] ,
and Virginia Zaraza Rusu[2]

[1] Universidad de Playa Ancha, Valparaíso, Chile
virginica.rusu@upla.cl
[2] Pontificia Universidad Católica de Valparaíso, Valparaíso, Chile
{cristian.rusu,silvana.roncagliolo}@pucv.cl,
danielacqo@gmail.com, rvzaraza90@hotmail.com
[3] Universidad Miguel Hernández de Elche, Elche, Spain
federico@umh.es

Abstract. It is generally agreed that usability is a basic attribute in software quality. User eXperience (UX) extends the usability concept beyond its traditional dimensions (effectiveness, efficiency and satisfaction). UX refers to all user's perceptions resulting from the use (or even the anticipated use) of a product, system or service. For more than two decades heuristic evaluation proves to be one of the most popular usability inspection methods. When performing a heuristic evaluation, generic or specific heuristics may be used. Nielsen's ten usability heuristics are well known, but many other sets of heuristics were proposed. Based on proper heuristics, the heuristic evaluation may also assess other UX aspects, beside usability. Usability heuristic sets are specific artifacts, so heuristics' "usability" may also be evaluated. If we consider that evaluators are particular "users" of particular "products", the set of usability/UX heuristics and the heuristic evaluation method, we may also analyze Evaluator eXperience as a particular case of UX. We systematically conduct studies on evaluators' perception over generic and specific usability/UX heuristics. The paper presents a follow-up study on the perception of novice evaluators over Nielsen's heuristics, using three online travel agencies as case studies (Atrapalo, TripAdvisor and Expedia). The experiments involved Chilean and Spanish students. We compare new results with our previous findings. Based on empirical results, we think the methodology used when teaching the heuristic evaluation method is highly important.

Keywords: Online travel agency · Heuristic evaluation · Usability heuristics ·
Heuristic quality · Evaluator eXperience

1 Introduction

The ISO 9241 standard, updated in 2018, defines usability as the "extent to which a system, product or service can be used by specified users to achieve specified goals with effectiveness, efficiency and satisfaction in a specified context of use" [1]. As the

© Springer Nature Switzerland AG 2019
G. Meiselwitz (Ed.): HCII 2019, LNCS 11579, pp. 452–463, 2019.
https://doi.org/10.1007/978-3-030-21905-5_35

usability concept is too general, the standard also indicates that "the specified users, goals and context of use refer to the particular combination of users, goals and context of use for which usability is being considered". As the standard highlights, the term "usability" is "also used as a qualifier to refer to the design knowledge, competencies, activities and design attributes that contribute to usability, such as usability expertise, usability professional, usability engineering, usability method, usability evaluation, usability heuristic". However, we think that a clear distinction should be made between "usability" as (software quality) attribute, usability evaluation and design methods, usability-related process (usability engineering) and usability professionals.

It is largely agreed that User eXperience (UX) extends the usability concept, beyond its traditional dimensions (effectiveness, efficiency and satisfaction). The same ISO 9241 standard defines UX as "user's perceptions and responses that result from the use and/or anticipated use of a system, product or service" [1]. It also specifies that "users' perceptions and responses include the users' emotions, beliefs, preferences, perceptions, comfort, behaviors, and accomplishments that occur before, during and after use".

Proposed in the early '90s, heuristic evaluation is one of the most popular usability evaluation methods [2]. A heuristic evaluation is performed by a small group of experts (usually 3 to 5) based on a set of principles/rules/guidelines, called heuristics. Nielsen's ten usability heuristics [3] are well known, but are often considered too general, unable to detect domain-related usability problems. That is why many other sets of heuristics were proposed [4, 5]. Heuristic evaluation may be used to asses several UX aspects, not only usability [6].

Teaching the heuristic evaluation method and forming evaluators is challenging. We think the practice is the best way to understand the heuristic evaluation protocol and the usability heuristics nature [7, 8]. We performed a comparative study on the perception of novice evaluators over Nielsen's heuristics, involving Computer Science students from a Chilean and a Spanish university [9, 10]. This paper presents a follow-up study, including experimental results in two new case studies.

The paper is structured as follows. Section 2 introduce the "Evaluator eXperience" concept and describe the questionnaire that we developed and used for several years to assess the (novel) evaluators' perception. Section 3 presents the experiments that we made from 2016 to 2018 on three major online travel agencies websites, Atrapalo.com [11], TripAdvisor.com [12] and Expedia.com [13]. Section 4 discusses experimental results. Section 5 highlights conclusions and future work.

2 Evaluator EXperience

Heuristic evaluators are particular kind of "users" of particular "products" (artifacts): (1) the set of usability/UX heuristics and (2) the heuristic evaluation method. Both artifacts may be evaluated in terms of their "usability". We may think of Evaluator eXperience as a particular case of UX, which may also be assessed.

We conducted studies on the perception of evaluators over generic and specific usability heuristics for several years [14–17]. All participants are asked to perform a heuristic evaluation of the same case study. Then they are asked to participate in a post-experiment survey.

Heuristics quality is an important topic, as it highly influences the heuristic evaluation's results. At least one heuristic quality scale was proposed [18]. We developed our own scale, a questionnaire that assesses evaluators' perception over a set of usability heuristics, based on 4 dimensions and 3 questions:

- D1 – Utility: How useful the heuristic is.
- D2 – Clarity: How clear the heuristic is.
- D3 – Ease of use: How easy was to associate identified problems to the heuristic.
- D4 – Necessity of additional checklist: How necessary would be to complement the heuristic with a checklist.
- Q1 – Easiness: How easy was to perform the heuristic evaluation, based on the given set of heuristics?
- Q2 – Intention: Would you use the same set of heuristics when evaluating similar software product in the future?
- Q3 – Completeness: Do you think the set of heuristics covers all usability aspects for this kind of software product?

Each heuristic is rated individually, on the 4 dimensions (D1 – Utility, D2 – Clarity, D3 – Ease of use, D4 – Necessity of additional checklist). But the set of heuristics is also rated globally, through the 3 questions (Q1 – Easiness, Q2 – Intention, Q3 – Completeness). In all cases, we are using a 5 points Likert scale (from 1 – worst, to 5 – best).

Additionally, two open questions are asked, to collect qualitative aspects of evaluators' experience:

- OQ1: What did you perceive as most difficult to perform during the heuristic evaluation?
- OQ2: What domain-related aspects do you think the set of heuristics does not cover?

3 Experiments

We made several experiments on the perception of Nielsen's heuristics when evaluating online travel agencies, from 2016 to 2018. The experiments involved novice evaluators, Computer Science students from Chile and Spain:

- *Graduate and undergraduate students in Informatics Engineering at Pontificia Universidad Católica de Valparaíso, Valparaíso, Chile, and*
- *Undergraduate students of the Bachelor in Computer Engineering in Information Technologies at Universidad Miguel Hernandez de Elche, Elche, Spain.*

All students were enrolled in Usability/UX-oriented Human-Computer Interaction introductory courses. In all cases they were asked to perform a heuristic evaluation based on Nielsen's heuristics, following Nielsen's protocol. With few exceptions, it was the first time they performed a heuristic evaluation; it was also their first contact with

Nielsen's heuristics and his evaluation protocol. After performing the heuristic evaluation, the students were asked to answer the questionnaire described in Sect. 2. All students participated voluntarily in the survey, there was no sample selection.

Experiments involved 112 Chilean and 31 Spanish students, as follows:

- *Atrapalo.com was evaluated by 31 Spanish undergraduate students, 17 Chilean undergraduate students, and 33 Chilean graduate students;*
- *TripAdvisor.com was evaluated by 27 Chilean undergraduate students and 22 Chilean graduate students;*
- *Expedia.com was evaluated by 13 Chilean undergraduate students.*

Results obtained when evaluating Atrapalo.com were presented in detail in previous work [9, 10]. Section 4 synthetizes these results, describes the results obtain when evaluating TripAdvisor.com and Expedia.com, and compares them with the Atrapalo.com results.

Observations' scale is ordinal, and no assumption of normality could be made. Therefore the survey results were analyzed using nonparametric statistics tests (Kruskal-Wallis, Mann-Whitney U and Spearman ρ). In all tests p-value ≤ 0.05 was used as decision rule.

As three groups of students (with different background) evaluated the same set of heuristics (Nielsen's one), Kruskal-Wallis test was performed to check the hypothesis:

- H_0: there are no significant differences between the perceptions of the three groups of students,
- H_1: there are significant differences between the perceptions of the three groups of students.

Mann-Whitney U tests were performed to check the hypothesis:

- H_0: there are no significant differences between the perceptions of two groups of students,
- H_1: there are significant differences between the perceptions of two groups of students.

Spearman ρ tests were performed to check the hypothesis:

- H_0: $\rho = 0$, two dimensions/questions are independent,
- H_1: $\rho \neq 0$, two dimensions/questions are dependent.

4 Results and Discussion

The Atrapalo.com experiments where presented in two previous papers [9, 10]. In summary, the experimental results show significant differences between the perception of Spanish and Chilean students, in several dimensions and questions (as presented in Table 1).

Table 1. Mann-Whitney U test for Spanish and Chilean students. Case study: Atrapalo.

	D1 – Utility	D2 – Clarity	D3 – Ease of use	D4 – Necessity of additional checklist	Q1 – Easiness	Q2 – Intention	Q3 – Completeness
p-value	0.001	0.001	0.013	0.054	0.001	0.777	0.918

On the contrary as described in our previous papers [9, 10], there are no significant differences between the two groups of Spanish students (participants in the experiment in 2016 and 2017), in none of the dimensions and questions. The perception of Chilean undergraduate and graduate students is also similar; there are significant differences between the group of undergraduate and the group of graduate students only regarding question Q2 (intention of future use). It seems that the level of studies (graduate/undergraduate) does not influence students' opinion, at least in our experiment. So, there are significant differences between the groups of Spanish and Chilean students, but not really among the members of the same group.

We also noticed that Chilean students have a better opinion that their Spanish counterpart, on all dimensions and questions (Table 2). It is especially notable that even if the Chilean students have a better perception on heuristics' utility, clarity, and ease of use, they still fill the need for additional evaluation criteria (checklist).

Table 2. Average scores for dimensions and questions. Case Study: Atrapalo.

	D1 – Utility	D2 – Clarity	D3 – Ease of use	D4 – Necessity of additional checklist	Q1 – Easiness	Q2 – Intention	Q3 – Completeness
Spanish students	3.86	3.47	3.32	3.75	2.77	3.90	3.26
Chilean students	4.39	4.19	3.75	4.27	3.12	4.42	3.60

We did not have evidences to suspect that the differences between Spanish and Chilean students are due to their background or cultural-related aspects. Based on some of the Spanish students' comments, we identify as possible cause the methodology that was used when introducing Nielsen's heuristics. In the case of Chilean students each heuristic is first explained by examples, and then students have to identify usability problems related to each heuristic in several case studies. The problems they identify are debated in the classroom.

As we couldn't repeat the experiment in Spain using the same methodology as in Chile, we decided to repeat it in Chile in 2018, in three courses, using two others online travel agencies as case studies: TripAdvisor and Expedia. So we made new experiments with three groups of students:

- *A first group of 22 Chilean graduate students evaluated TripAdvisor.com;*
- *A second group of 27 Chilean undergraduate students also evaluated TripAdvisor. com;*
- *Finally, a third group of 13 Chilean undergraduate students evaluated Expedia. com.*

All three groups were using Nielsen's usability heuristics. The way we introduced Nielsen's heuristics and we perform the experiments were identical as in the experiments made in Chile using *Atrapalo.com* as case study.

Table 3. Kruskal-Wallis test for three groups of Chilean students, 2018.

	D1 – Utility	D2 – Clarity	D3 – Ease of use	D4 – Necessity of additional checklist	Q1 – Easiness	Q2 – Intention	Q3 – Completeness
p-value	0.528	0.463	0.056	0.996	0.014	0.021	0.014

The Kruskal-Wallis test indicates no significant differences between the three groups of students, concerning dimensions D1, D2, D3 and D4, even when their background (undergraduate/graduate level), and/or the case study are different (Table 3). Significant differences occurs only on the overall perception of the heuristic evaluation method (Q1), intention of future use (Q2) and Nielsen's set of heuristics completeness (Q3).

We then applied the Mann-Whitney U test for each pair of groups (Table 4). Results show very few significant differences:

- *One between undergraduate and graduate students that evaluated TripAdvisor, concerning the heuristic evaluation easiness (Q1);*
- *Two between undergraduate students that evaluated Expedia versus the ones that evaluated TripAdvisor, concerning Nielsen's heuristics ease of use (D3), and the intention of future use of Nielsen's heuristics when evaluating online travel agencies (Q2);*
- *Two between undergraduate students that evaluated Expedia versus graduate students that evaluated TripAdvisor, concerning Nielsen's heuristics ease of use (D3) and Nielsen's heuristics completeness (Q3).*

Table 4. Mann-Whitney U test for pairs of groups of Chilean students (p-values), 2018.

	D1 – Utility	D2 – Clarity	D3 – Ease of use	D4 – Necessity of additional checklist	Q1 – Easiness	Q2 – Intention	Q3 – Completeness
Undergraduate vs. graduate students (case study: TripAdvisor)	0.569	0.872	0.984	0.976	0.002	0.131	0.105
Expedia vs. TripAdvisor (undergraduate students)	0.705	0.284	0.038	0.930	0.169	0.012	0.061
Expedia (undergraduate students) **vs. TripAdvisor** (graduate students)	0.187	0.244	0.022	0.945	0.734	0.069	0.007

Table 5 presents the averages scores for dimensions and questions for the three groups of Chilean students that participated in the 2018 experiment. It also includes the results of the 2017 group of students. As the opinions of all groups of Chilean students are similar, it also shows the averages scores for all Chilean students and, for comparison purpose, the averages scores for Spanish students.

Table 5. Average scores for dimensions and questions.

	D1 – Utility	D2 – Clarity	D3 – Ease of use	D4 – Necessity of additional checklist	Q1 – Easiness	Q2 – Intention	Q3 – Completeness
Chilean graduate and undergraduate students (50, Atrapalo, 2017)	4.39	4.19	3.75	4.27	3.12	4.42	3.60
Chilean graduate students (22, TripAdvisor, 2018)	4.05	3.84	3.40	3.99	3.09	4.05	3.59
Chilean undergraduate students (27, TripAdvisor, 2018)	4.07	3.84	3.43	4.02	2.52	4.26	3.07
Chilean undergraduate students (13, Expedia, 2018)	4.14	4.07	3.90	3.93	2.92	3.31	2.31
All Chilean students (112)	**4.22**	**4.02**	**3.62**	**4.12**	**2.95**	**4.18**	**3.32**
All Spanish students (31)	**3.86**	**3.47**	**3.32**	**3.75**	**2.77**	**3.90**	**3.26**

The four groups of Chilean students have a better perception than their Spanish counterpart in all dimensions. They perceive Nielsen's heuristics more useful (D1), clear (D2) and easy to use (D3). But they also feel a higher necessity for additional evaluation criteria (checklist, D4). They perceive the heuristic evaluation as easier to perform, comparing to the Spanish students, excepting the group of undergraduate students that evaluated TripAdvisor. Chilean students also express a higher intention of future use of Nielsen's heuristics (with one exception, the undergraduate students that evaluated Expedia). Concerning Nielsen's heuristics completeness when evaluating online travel agencies, Chilean students have divided opinions; two groups have a better perception than Spanish students, but other two groups have a less favorable perception. However, when comparing the opinion of all 112 Chilean students with the opinion of the 31 Spanish students, Chilean students have a better perception in all dimensions and questions. So, new results are consistent with previous findings [9, 10].

Table 6 shows the correlations between dimensions/questions when considering the three groups of Chilean students that participated in the 2018 experiment.

Table 6. Spearman ρ test for all Chilean students (2018).

	D1 – Utility	D2 – Clarity	D3 – Ease of use	D4 – Necessity of additional checklist	Q1 – Easiness	Q2 – Intention	Q3 – Completeness
D1	1	0.344	0.293	Independent	Independent	Independent	Independent
D2		1	0.602	Independent	0.276	0.260	Independent
D3			1	Independent	Independent	Independent	Independent
D4				1	Independent	Independent	Independent
Q1					1	Independent	Independent
Q2						1	0.363
Q3							1

Few correlations occur when analyzing each group of Chilean students that participated in the 2018 experiments (Tables 7, 8, and 9).

Table 7. Spearman ρ test for graduate Chilean students. Case study: TripAdvisor.

	D1 – Utility	D2 – Clarity	D3 – Ease of use	D4 – Necessity of additional checklist	Q1 – Easiness	Q2 – Intention	Q3 – Completeness
D1	1	0.423	Independent	Independent	–0.549	Independent	Independent
D2		1	0.752	Independent	Independent	Independent	Independent
D3			1	Independent	Independent	Independent	Independent
D4				1	Independent	Independent	Independent
Q1					1	Independent	Independent
Q2						1	Independent
Q3							1

Table 8. Spearman ρ test for undergraduate Chilean students. Case study: TripAdvisor.

	D1 – Utility	D2 – Clarity	D3 – Ease of use	D4 – Necessity of additional checklist	Q1 – Easiness	Q2 – Intention	Q3 – Completeness
D1	1	Independent	Independent	Independent	Independent	Independent	Independent
D2		1	0.535	Independent	Independent	0.494	Independent
D3			1	Independent	Independent	Independent	Independent
D4				1	Independent	Independent	Independent
Q1					1	Independent	Independent
Q2						1	0.405
Q3							1

Table 9. Spearman ρ test for undergraduate Chilean students. Case study: Expedia

	D1 – Utility	D2 – Clarity	D3 – Ease of use	D4 – Necessity of additional checklist	Q1 – Easiness	Q2 – Intention	Q3 – Completeness
D1	1	Independent	0.611	Independent	Independent	Independent	Independent
D2		1	Independent	Independent	0.771	Independent	Independent
D3			1	Independent	Independent	Independent	Independent
D4				1	Independent	Independent	Independent
Q1					1	0.708	Independent
Q2						1	Independent
Q3							1

As in our previous studies, few correlations occur in relatively small groups of students. When considering altogether the three groups of students, more correlations occur, and most of them are also consistent with our previous studies. The D1 – D2 correlation is particularly frequent: when heuristics' specification is perceived as clear, heuristics are also perceived as useful.

Open questions OQ1 and OQ1 are evaluating some qualitative aspects of evaluators' perception. What the three groups of students pointed out is similar to what students of previous generations expressed [9].

According to what the students say in their comments, the use of Nielsen's heuristics seems to require positioning themselves in a new paradigm of thinking, to perceive and evaluate a website based on an evaluation perspective to which they are not accustomed to. In this way, the comprehension of each heuristic, its identification, adaptation and mode of application to different products, are aspects that the evaluators identify as difficult for their work.

Based on this, they highlight the importance of having elements that help familiarize themselves with both the artifacts they are using (Nielsen's heuristics), as well as the services offered by the evaluated products (TripAdvisor and Expedia websites in this case). In this sense, the evaluators emphasize the need to count with technical reports that would provide them examples of heuristic evaluations which have been previously carried out (either by them or by others). On the other hand, the evaluators highlight that the websites they have been evaluating should provide strategies to facilitate their understanding by the people who use them (for example through tutorials), a good organization, distribution and precision of the information that helps to a better understanding. They consider that novice users are also facing the adjustment of their way of thinking and operating to what offer and allow the websites they use.

On the other hand, it is interesting that the evaluators point out that although their work consist in evaluating products, they experience difficulties to take a critical look, especially to detect problems that are not major, evident, or common. It seems that the evaluators are guided mostly by functionality and effectiveness criteria (based on the achievement of final results); they think the problems would be detected while the ongoing actions are carried out. However, following that direction, aspects of the subjective and personal experience of the real users may thus be underestimated and unattended. In this sense, it seems that the evaluators have difficulties to identify problems until they constitute complications for themselves, according to their own way of using the product and according to their own experiences. The evaluators highlight in this way that they notice difficulties in putting themselves successfully in the place of other users, especially in the place of novices. Complications seem to also arise because each evaluator has to understand others evaluators' opinions. The evaluators emphasize that it is difficult for them to coordinate their opinions and perceptions regarding the carried out evaluations, in order to reach consent with the rest of the evaluation team.

5 Conclusions

Heuristic evaluation is probably the most popular usability inspection method, but forming evaluators is not an easy task. Heuristic evaluation results depend highly on both heuristics quality and evaluators experience. Evaluators are using specific artifacts, the set of usability/UX heuristics and the evaluation protocol. The protocol seems to be less challenging, but properly understanding and correctly applying heuristics in practice is much more demanding, especially for novel evaluators. Heuristics' "usability" may be assessed, based on heuristics quality scale. Evaluators experience may also be assessed.

We systematically conduct studies on the perception of (novice) evaluators over generic and specific usability heuristics, based on a questionnaire that we developed. The questionnaire allows evaluating each heuristic individually (Utility, Clarity, Ease of use, Necessity of additional checklist), but also the set of heuristics as a whole (Easiness, Intention, Completeness). The questionnaire also allows expressing evaluators' perception through comments.

In a comparative study that we have done before, we noticed significant differences between the perception of Chilean and Spanish Computer Science students when evaluating the same online travel agency (Atrapalo) based on Nielsen's heuristics. The perception of Chilean students with different background was similar. The perception of two generations of Spanish students was also similar.

As we did not have evidences to suspect cultural or background-related issues as possible cause, we think the reason could be the methodology of introducing Nielsen's heuristics, when teaching the heuristic evaluation method. We checked our assumption on two new case studies (TripAdvisor and Atrapalo), with three new groups of Chilean students. New results are consistent with our previous findings. Chilean students' perception was systematically better than Spanish students' perception.

As future work we would like to check (if possible) if the methodology that we are using with Chilean students would lead to similar results when applied to Spanish students.

Acknowledgments. We thank all the students involved in the experiment. They provided helpful opinions that allowed us to prepare this and (hopefully) further documents.

References

1. ISO 9241-11:2018: Ergonomics of human-system interaction—Part 11: Usability: Definitions and concepts. International Organization for Standardization, Geneva (2018)
2. Nielsen, J., Mack, R.L.: Usability Inspection Methods. Wiley, New York (1994)
3. Nielsen, J.: 10 Usability Heuristics for User Interface Design, January 1995. http://www.nngroup.com/articles/ten-usability-heuristics. Accessed 24 Jan 2019
4. Hermawati, S., Lawson, G.: Establishing usability heuristics for heuristics evaluation in a specific domain: is there a consensus? Appl. Ergon. **56**, 34–51 (2016)
5. Quiñones, D., Rusu, C.: How to develop usability heuristics: A systematic literature review. Comput. Stand. Interfaces **53**, 89–122 (2017)
6. Quiñones, D., Rusu, C., Rusu, V.: A methodology to develop usability/user experience heuristics. Comput. Stand. Interfaces **59**, 109–129 (2018)
7. Botella, F., Alarcon, E., Peñalver, A.: How to classify to experts in usability evaluation. In: Proceedings of the XV International Conference on Human Computer Interaction Interacción 2014. ACM (2014)
8. Rusu, C., Rusu, V., Roncagliolo, S.: Usability practice: the appealing way to HCI. In: The First International Conference on Advances in Computer-Human Interactions (ACHI 2008) Proceedings, pp. 265–270. IEEE Computer Society Press (2008)
9. Rusu, C., Botella, F., Rusu, V., Roncagliolo, S., Quiñones, D.: An online travel agency comparative study: heuristic evaluators perception. In: Meiselwitz, G. (ed.) SCSM 2018. LNCS, vol. 10913, pp. 112–120. Springer, Cham (2018). https://doi.org/10.1007/978-3-319-91521-0_9
10. Botella, F., Rusu, C., Rusu, V., Quiñones, D.: How novel evaluators perceive their first heuristic Evaluation. In: Proceedings of the XIX International Conference on Human Computer Interaction Interacción 2018. ACM (2018)
11. Atrapalo online travel agency website. http://www.atrapalo.com. Accessed 24 Jan 2019
12. TripAdvisor online travel agency website. http://www.tripadvisor.com. Accessed 24 Jan 2019
13. Expedia online travel agency website. http://www.expedia.com. Accessed 24 Jan 2019
14. Rusu, C., Rusu, V., Roncagliolo, S., Apablaza, J., Rusu, V.Z.: User experience evaluations: challenges for newcomers. In: Marcus, A. (ed.) DUXU 2015. LNCS, vol. 9186, pp. 237–246. Springer, Cham (2015). https://doi.org/10.1007/978-3-319-20886-2_23
15. Rusu, C., et al.: Usability heuristics: reinventing the wheel? In: Meiselwitz, G. (ed.) SCSM 2016. LNCS, vol. 9742, pp. 59–70. Springer, Cham (2016). https://doi.org/10.1007/978-3-319-39910-2_6

16. Rusu, V., Rusu, C., Quiñones, D., Roncagliolo, S., Collazos, César A.: What happens when evaluating social media's usability? In: Meiselwitz, G. (ed.) SCSM 2017. LNCS, vol. 10282, pp. 117–126. Springer, Cham (2017). https://doi.org/10.1007/978-3-319-58559-8_11
17. Rusu, C., Rusu, V., Quiñones, D., Roncagliolo, S., Rusu, V.Z.: Evaluating online travel agencies' usability: what heuristics should we use? In: Meiselwitz, G. (ed.) SCSM 2018. LNCS, vol. 10913, pp. 121–130. Springer, Cham (2018). https://doi.org/10.1007/978-3-319-91521-0_10
18. Anganes, A., Pfaff, M.S., Drury, J.L., O'Toole, C.M.: The heuristic quality scale. Interact. Comput. **28**(5), 584–597 (2016)

Purchase and Its Sign Analysis from Customer Behaviors Using Deep Convolutional Neural Networks

Shintaro Saito[1]($\boxtimes$), Kohei Otake[2], and Takashi Namatame[1]

[1] Department of Industrial and System Engineering, Chuo University,
1-13-27 Kasuga, Bunkyo-ku, Tokyo 112-8551, Japan
a14.s8tm@g.chuo-u.ac.jp, nama@indsys.chuo-u.ac.jp
[2] Department of Management Systems Engineering, Tokai University,
2-3-23, Takanawa, Minato-ku, Tokyo 108-0074, Japan
otake@tsc.u-tokai.ac.jp

Abstract. In this paper, we predict purchase from access log data and consider customer behavior about purchase sign on E-commerce site. In addition, applying Convolutional neural networks to this study, we discuss probability of purchase or not purchase and data preprocessing. By extracting hidden layer of model, we consider customer behaviors about purchase and not purchase. Furthermore, we discuss the way of transforming no image datasets to image-like data. We think about probability of using its networks for no images data through this study.

Keywords: Access log data · Purchase sign · Convolutional neural networks

1 Introduction

Recently, we become able to access detail customer data on electronic-commerce (EC) site and can analyze customer behavior more than before. In particular, using access log data, it extends the possibility of analyzing customer behavior and it become express customer information searching behavior. In this paper, mainly using web access log data, we predict purchasing and related behaviors in EC.

Nowadays, neural network or its extended method is applied to explain various business objectives. There are many types of research of applying deep learning to various tasks based on the improvement of computer performance. Especially, convolutional neural networks (CNN) which is often used in image recognition is applied to the churn analyzing [1]. AlphaZero might be the most famous among them [2]. For classification or predicting tasks, most of the deep learning models have a better performance than the conventional machine learning approaches (e.g. Support Vector Machine (SVM), logistic regression model), while there is a problem about incapable of explaining how the models decide for these tasks. In this study, we attempt to find features of time-series customer access log data by convolutional neural networks and consider purchasing sign from hidden layer state. Furthermore, we discuss transforming datasets of no images to image-like data.

© Springer Nature Switzerland AG 2019
G. Meiselwitz (Ed.): HCII 2019, LNCS 11579, pp. 464–474, 2019.
https://doi.org/10.1007/978-3-030-21905-5_36

2   Datasets

In this study, we use purchase record and web access log data on a golf EC site. Aggregating session log data by the users for days in a month, we make datasets of 30 rows and 11 columns for users. 11 columns are types of access pages which are new item pages, old item pages, news pages, and so on. Also, we label purchasing or not purchasing in the next month as supervised learning. We use various datasets, locate features in a certain order, in order of high correlation with purchasing or rearrangement placing features in some rules. These are enumerated in Tables 1 and 2 (Fig. 1).

Table 1. Locating features samples

Feature samples	Locate feature
1	In order of high correlation
2	High correlation form side to side

Table 2. Correlations of features about purchase

Feature name	Correlation with purchase
New item pages	0.023
Old item pages	0.027
Outlet pages	0.120
Sale pages	0.011
Lesson pages	0.019
News pages	0.120
Event pages	0.083
Gear pages	0.029
Reserve pages	0.067
Reserve cv pages	0.087
Purchase done pages	0.051

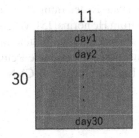

Fig. 1. The image of input data.

3   Methods

3.1   Convolutional Neural Networks

Convolutional neural networks (CNN), which is one of Deep Learning method have some convolutional and pooling layers. In convolutional layers, it is filtered small images with numbers to extract features, and it transform a certain area of images into a rough feature. In pooling layers, features which are mapped in convolutional layers are additionally summarized in maximum or average feature. After convolutional layers, we can grasp features through activation layers. Activation layers put them into a certain state. Then, we get output values from networks, then do back propagation which calculates errors of every unit in layers. These layers can make feature maps from images. This algorithm is as follows.

$$\begin{cases} u_{m,n,k}^{l+1} = \sum_{p,q,k} w_{p,q,k,k'}^{l+1}\, y_{m+p,n+q,k}^{l} + b_{k'}^{l+1} \\ z_{m,n,k'}^{l} = h\left(u_{m,n,k}^{l+1}\right) \end{cases} \tag{1}$$

$$where \begin{cases} k : chanel \\ k' : kernel \\ m, n : length\ of\ row\ and\ column \\ p, q : size\ of\ filta \\ p = \{1, 2, \ldots, P^{l+1}\} \\ q = \{1, 2, \ldots, Q^{l+1}\} \\ k = \{1, 2, \ldots, K^{l}\} \\ k' = \{1, 2, \ldots, K^{l+1}\} \end{cases}$$

$$\begin{cases} u_{m,n,k}^{l+1} : output\ of\ (m,n)\ pixel\ at\ (l+1)layer\ in\ k'\ chanel \\ w_{p,q,k,k'}^{l+1} : weight\ of\ (p,q)\ pixel\ at\ (l+1)layer\ and\ k\ chanel\ in\ k'\ kernel \\ z_{m,n,k'}^{l} : output\ of\ (m+p,n+q)\ pixel\ at\ l\ layer\ in\ k\ chanel \\ b_{k'}^{l+1} : bias\ every\ chanel \\ h(x) : activation\ function \end{cases}$$

Every filter of convolution layer is determined in some rules. In this study, we determined the weights of filters from He normal [5]. When n is the number of filter pixel, the weights are generated from normal distribution that mean is 0, and variance is $2/n$.

There are some activation functions, for example Relu, sigmoid, Leakly Relu. They are as shown below in Fig. 2. The architecture of CNN is shown like in Fig. 3.

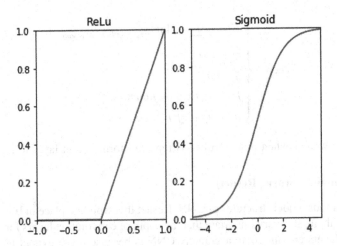

Fig. 2. ReLu and Sigmoid.

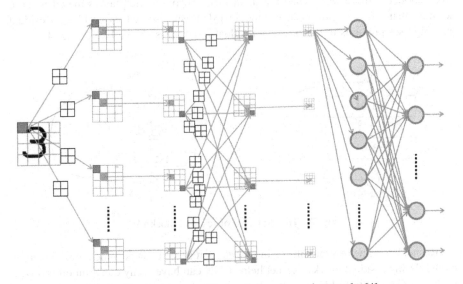

Fig. 3. The Architecture of convolutional neural networks [4].

The back propagation is as follows.

$$w_t = w_{t-1} - \eta \frac{dE}{dw} \tag{2}$$

$$\frac{dE}{dw} = \frac{dE}{dy} \frac{dy}{dt} \frac{dt}{dw} \tag{3}$$

$$
\text{Where} \begin{cases} E = -\sum_{n=1} \log(y^{[n]}_{correct\ label\ at\ n\ sanple}) \\ \frac{dy}{dt} = f'(t) \\ \frac{dt}{dw} = u \\ f(t) : activation\ function \\ u : output\ of\ hidden\ layer \end{cases}
$$

We get new weight when this calculate is repeated form output layer to input layer.

3.2   Residual Network (Resnet)

There are famous model structures of CNN, Resnet that won first place in ILSVRC 2015 [3] is one of them. It is very important that the depth of convolution layers for CNN. The more deep layers are, the more accurately CNN is because it can extract feature maps from convolution layers. However, it is said that the accuracy of many convolution layers model is more worse than not it. In fact, 20 convolution layers model is more accurate than 56 convolution layers model [3]. Resnet solved its problem. Residual learning uses previous input for every residual block. It is shown like in Fig. 4.

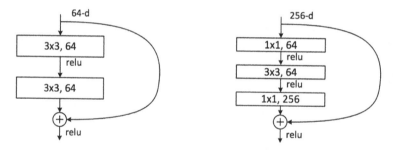

Fig. 4. The examples of residual block [3].

Resnet has some residual blocks in model, then Resnet can become more a accurate model. Using residual blocks, Resnet helps CNN can have many convolution layers, it is shown like in Fig. 5 [3].

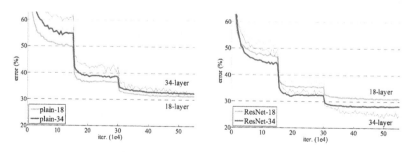

Fig. 5. The results of Resnet about ImageNet [3].

We use Resnet architecture in this study. This paper constructed a convolution layer in first convolution layer and final it, and 9 residual blocks like left on Fig. 3 every residual block have batch normalization layers after convolution layers. The filter size of every residual blocks is 3 × 3, channels are 64, training batch size is 64, and so on. To summarize, the CNN architecture is as follows Table 3.

Table 3. The architecture of CNN

The architecture	Contents
Filter size (first convolution layer)	5
Filter size (the others)	3
The number of filters	64
Optimization	Adam
Activate function	RRelu
Batch size	64

4 Data Preprocessing

Access log data is very sparse data, so in order to discriminate purchase data, we transform every pixel value into new it of subtracting it from 256. In addition, we produced impulse noise and median filter data from purchase and no purchase data to increase patterns of train data. In the end, we standardized all data. Lastly, we separate all data into train and test data, and make validation data from train data.

5 Modeling

We get the result from fitting the train and test data. These results are shown like in Table 4.

Table 4. Score of model

	Datasets 1	Datasets 2	Datasets 2′	Datasets 3
Accuracy	0.68	0.60	0.61	0.57
Precision	0.46	0.41	0.40	0.48
Recall	0.068	0.51	0.441	0.58
F-measure	**0.12**	**0.45**	**0.42**	**0.52**

- Datasets 1: not adding noise to train data in order of high correlation
- Datasets 2: adding impulse noise and median filter to train data in order of high correlation
- Datasets 2′: adding impulse noise and median filter to train data in order of high correlation from side to side
- Datasets 3: adding impulse noise to train data in order of high correlation

6 Discussion

First, we discuss the datasets. As you can see from datasets 2 and datasets 2′ of Table 4, the best way of locating feature is that every feature locates in high correlation. Furthermore, adding noise to train data is good way for modeling. It is based on datasets 1 of Table 4. Also, adding median filter is not so good preprocessing to increase the data patterns. However, impulse noise is good preprocessing for the image-like data of customer behaviors. We can say that it is good for the discrimination. In short, for the discrimination of image-like data of customer behaviors, impulse noise is should be added to the data which is sparse data.

Fig. 6. Feature maps of maximum probability purchasing from last convolutional layer. (Color figure online)

Next, we discuss purchase behaviors. From here on, the data sets are regarded as Data sets 3. We extracted feature mapping from hidden layers of maximum probability purchasing or not purchasing and minimum probability purchasing or not purchasing. They are shown like in Figs. 6, 7, 8 and 9.

Fig. 7. Feature maps of minimum probability purchasing from last convolutional layer. (Color figure online)

It shows how networks extract features from inputted customer behaviors log data. Using this figure, we can monitor the purchasing or not purchasing trend. We use CNN for mapping time-series customer behaviors in a month, and grasp purchase or not purchase sign. Each pixel expresses the value when the color is near blue, the active value is high and red is low. As you can see Figs. 6 and 7, customer behaviors of

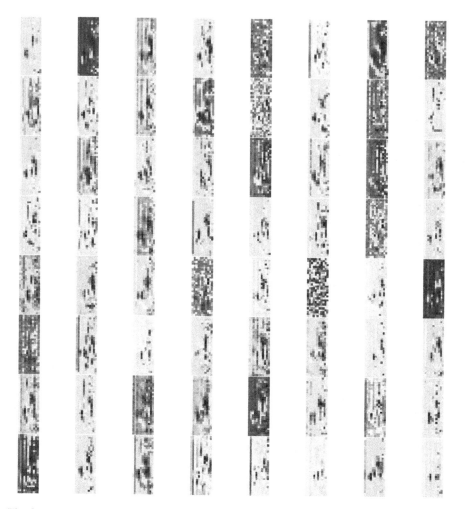

Fig. 8. Feature maps of maximum probability not purchasing from last convolutional layer. (Color figure online)

purchase class are time-series features in left edge. Namely, when time line customer behaviors are active about news pages outlet pages, gear pages, and old item pages, the possibility of purchase is high. On the other hands, there are active behaviors somewhere in a month, the possibility of purchase is low. Considering kinds of pages about max possibility of purchase, the time-series activity of customers about news pages or outlet pages is thought to be purchase sign. And, customers behaviors are active at the end of month, possibility of purchase is low. In terms of not purchasing class, when customer behaviors are active about such new item pages or sale pages, the possibility is low. They may use this E-commerce site for viewing products. Customers for minimum probability of not purchase are active about center of data. Thus, they are active users for reserving golf course and do not use this site not E-commerce site as reserving site.

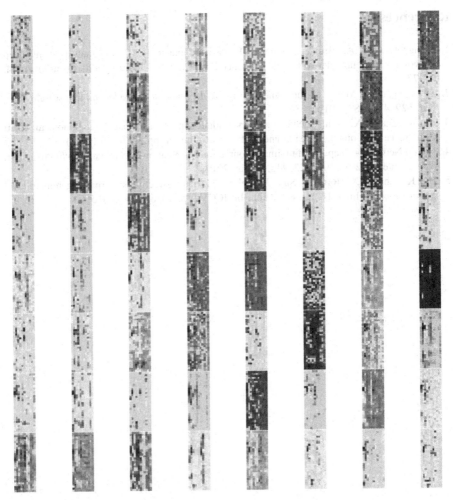

Fig. 9. Feature maps of minimum probability not purchasing from last convolutional layer. (Color figure online)

7   Conclusion

In this study, we proposed a CNN model to predict purchase and grasp its sign. Especially, to visualize hidden layers, we could grasp customer behavior from time-series its access log data by using CNN. So, this study expanded ability of applying CNN to no images discrimination. However, some studies are remaining, for example, more interpreting the characteristics of hidden layers or improving model accuracy. These are our future works.

References

1. Wangperawong, A., Brun, C., Laudy, O., Pavasuthipaisit, R.: Churn analysis using deep convolutional neural networks and autoencoders. Cornell University (2016). arXiv:1604.05377
2. Silver, D., et al.: Mastering the game of Go with deep neural networks and tree search. Proc. Nat. **529**, 484–489 (2016)
3. He, K., Zhang, X., Ren, S., Sun, J.: Deep residual learning for image recognition. In: IEEE Conference on Computer Vision and Pattern Recognition, pp. 770–778 (2016)
4. Neural Network - Deep Learning image source for presentation or seminar. http://nkdkccmbr.hateblo.jp/entry/2016/10/06/222245. 31 Jan 2019
5. He, K., Zhang, X., Ren, S., Sun, J.: Delving deep into rectifiers: surpassing human-level performance on ImageNet classification. In: ICCV, pp. 1026–1034 (2015)

Analysis of the Characteristic Behavior of Loyal Customers on a Golf EC Site

Yue Su[1(✉)], Kohei Otake[2], and Takashi Namatame[3]

[1] Graduate School of Science and Engineering, Chuo University,
1-13-27, Kasuga, Bunkyo-ku, Tokyo 112-8551, Japan
a15.xwsr@g.chuo-u.ac.jp
[2] School of Information and Telecommunication Engineering, Tokai University,
2-3-23, Takanawa, Minato-ku, Tokyo 108-8619, Japan
otake@tsc.u-tokai.ac.jp
[3] Faculty of Science and Engineering, Chuo University,
1-13-27, Kasuga, Bunkyo-ku, Tokyo 112-8551, Japan
nama@indsys.chuo-u.ac.jp

Abstract. In recent years, with expansion and growth of electronic commerce (EC) market, it is expected that the competition of getting customers will be fierce. The EC company is required to find new customers who have the potential of becoming loyal customers as soon as possible. In this study, we analyze customers' behavior using customer membership information data, purchase records data and web access logs data on a golf EC site. Firstly, we evaluate the loyalty of customers using RFM analysis to divide customers into the loyal and general ones. Next, we perform logistic regression to discriminate loyalty by using the first-time purchase and browsing behaviors. Through our analysis, we built a model to predict loyal customers and clarify the characteristic behaviors of high loyal customers.

Keywords: Customer behavior · RFM analysis · Logistic regression

1 Introduction

In recent years, electronic commerce (hereinafter called "EC") continues to evolve at a rapid pace [1]. With expansion and growth of the EC market, it is expected that the competition of getting customers will be fierce. Choosing appropriate target customers is very important for expanding sales and improving profitability.

Therefore, the EC company is required to find new customers who have the potential of becoming loyal customers as soon as possible. Here, the first purchase date can be considered a point. We look forward to the common behaviors of these customers in their initial purchases. Customers raise customer satisfaction, so that companies improve sales and profits. It is desirable to have such a relationship between both sides that can benefit from each other.

Figure 1 shows the framework of customers hierarchy. First, customers visit the website. Upper-level customer purchase frequently and high amount. Then, finding these loyal customers and developing new loyal customers are very important strategies for the retail company.

© Springer Nature Switzerland AG 2019
G. Meiselwitz (Ed.): HCII 2019, LNCS 11579, pp. 475–485, 2019.
https://doi.org/10.1007/978-3-030-21905-5_37

Fig. 1. Framework of customer hierarchy

In this study, we focused on new customers and the purpose is to clarify the characteristic behaviors of high loyal customers using customer's membership information data, purchase data and access historical data.

2 Datasets

We target on a general electronic commerce website (hereinafter called "EC site") relating to golf. The EC site provides some services such as EC of golf equipment, reservations for golf courses, manage golf score, etc. From among these services, we used the following data.

- Customer information data (age, sex, registration date, etc.)
- Purchase history data (category of purchase items, purchase date, whether purchased item is brand-new or secondhand, etc.)
- Access history data (log in date and time, URL of access page, URL of referrer page, etc.)

The category name of the product included in the purchase data is shown in Table 1.

Table 1. Category name of item

Category	Item
Men's wear	Tops for men, pants for men, etc.
Lady's wear	Tops for women, pants for women, etc.
Golf club	Putter, iron, etc.
Accessory	Golf ball, golf glove, etc.
Other	Calendar etc.

Target Customer

In this study, we analyzed 5,553 customers who purchased for the first time from May 1, 2015, to July 30, 2015, and purchased more than twice a year from the initial purchase date. We exclude the customer who has passed for more than one year from registration.

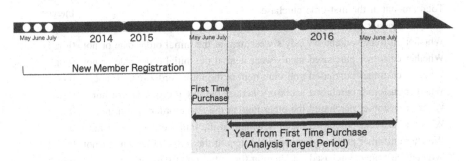

Fig. 2. Target period

In Fig. 2, we show the target period used in this research.

Explanatory Variables

We considered the impact factors to the first purchase using the above data. Based on the result, we created the explanatory variables such as customer's member information (5 variables), purchasing behavior at the time of initial purchase (11 variables) and web browsing behavior at the initial purchase date (13 variables) [4].

Details of the explanatory variables are shown in Tables 2, 3 and 4.

Table 2 presents demographic variables created by membership information data.

Table 2. Demographic variables used in the model construction.

Variable name	Data type
Gender (male = 1, female = 0)	0 or 1
Age	Integer
Whether customer lives in capital or not	0 or 1
Whether the member registration date matched the initial order date or not	0 or 1
Whether customer updated membership or not	0 or 1

Table 3 demonstrates purchasing behavior variables created by purchase data.

Table 3. Purchasing behavior used in the model construction.

Variable name	Data type
Total number of items purchased at the first-time purchase	Integer
Total amount at the first-time purchase	Integer
Average amount at the initial order date	Integer
Whether customer purchased lady's wear item at the initial order date or not	0 or 1
Whether customer purchased men's wear item at the initial order date or not	0 or 1
Whether customer purchased golf club item at the initial order date or not	0 or 1
Whether customer purchased accessory item at the initial order date or not	0 or 1
Whether customer purchased the other item at the initial order date or not	0 or 1
Whether customer purchased brand-new item at the initial order date or not	0 or 1
Whether customer purchased secondhand item at the initial order date or not	0 or 1
Whether customer purchased sale item at the initial order date or not	0 or 1

Table 4 shows Access History Variables created by web browsing data.

Table 4. Access history variables used in the model construction.

Variable name	Data type
Average login time of all session at the initial order date	Integer
Number of log in at the initial order date	Integer
Average number of page view at first purchase date	Integer
Whether browsing golf lesson page or not	0 or 1
Whether browsing golf course reservation page or not	0 or 1
Whether browsing golf movie page or not	0 or 1
Whether browsing golf news page or not	0 or 1
Whether browsing golf style page or not	0 or 1
Whether browsing golf second-hand goods shop page or not	0 or 1
Whether browsing golf gear page or not	0 or 1
Whether browsing golf new goods shop page or not	0 or 1
Whether browsing management golf score page or not	0 or 1
Whether browsing golf event page or not	0 or 1

3   Analysis of Loyal Customer

In this study, we analyze the behavior of the initial order date for customers who purchase more than once a year using customer membership information data, purchase records data and web access logs data on a golf EC site.

As an analysis, firstly we evaluated customer loyalty for new customers by RFM analysis. We determined customers' loyalties with three purchasing behavior indicators (Recency, Frequency, Monetary) and categorized them as loyal customers and general customers based on this.

Next, we created variables related to the initial purchase and exploratory behavior and constructed a discrimination model of customer loyalty by logistic regression analysis. Through these analyses, we worked to grasp the characteristics of customers with high loyalties at the initial order date.

3.1 RFM Analysis

RFM analysis is one of the most common approaches in database marketing. RFM analysis is a proven marketing model for behavior-based customer segmentation. It groups customers on recency, frequency, and monetary value can indicate customer.

RFM analysis segments customers on recency, frequency, and monetary value can indicate customer We evaluated the loyalty of customers using RFM analysis to divide customers into loyal and general ones [2]. Commonly, the F in RFM analysis is determined by the number of purchases. Here, we defined F by the total number of logins instead of the number of purchase, because frequent browsing behavior is also relates to customer's loyalty for the website.

RFM stands for the three dimensions:

- Recency: Period since last purchase
- Frequency: Total number of logins within the period
- Monetary: Amount of purchase within the period

The approach to RFM is to assign a score for each dimension on a scale from 1 to 5. The maximum score represents the preferred behavior.

Customers are divided into five scales equally for each of recency, frequency, monetary. The maximum score of RFM stands for the three dimensions:

- Recency: The maximum score (5) represents the shortest number of days that have passed since the customer last purchased within a year.
- Frequency: The maximum score (5) represents the longest number of logins within a year.
- Monetary: The maximum score (5) represents the highest value of all purchases within a year.

3.2 Binomial Logistic Regression

The purpose of this study is to predict the high loyal customers by using the initial purchase and browsing behaviors. When the objective variable to be predicted is binary, binomial logistic regression models are often used.

The Binomial logistic regression model is a type of classifier that performs class discrimination. By interpreting significant explanatory variables in the constructed model, it is possible to clarify the characteristics that affect the presence or absence of repurchase. In the binomial logistic regression analysis, the customer's repurchase probability p_i is expressed by the following equation [3].

$$p_i = \frac{\exp\left\{\sum_{j=0}^{m} \beta_j X_{ij}\right\}}{1 + \exp\left\{\sum_{j=0}^{m} \beta_j X_{ij}\right\}} \tag{1}$$

X_{ij} : Factors affecting repurchase ($X_{i0} = 1$)

β_j : Parameters for each explanatory variable (β_0 is intercept)

We prepared variables related to demographic variables, initial purchase behavior and exploratory behavior (Tables 2, 3 and 4) and constructed a discrimination model of customer loyalty by binomial logistic regression analysis. Here, we label the loyal customer as 1, and the general customer as 0.

In logistic regression analysis, when the explanatory variable is excessive, it may be difficult to interpret the regression equation, or the versatility of prediction of the objective variable may decrease. It may occur multicollinearity problem due to some variables have a high correlation. Therefore, in this study, to select true effective variables, we used stepwise method based on Akaike's Information Criterion (AIC).

In order to confirm the discrimination accuracy of the model, we divided the data used in the logistic regression analysis into two groups (Group A, Group B), and performed a 2-fold cross-validation method.

The cross-validation method is mainly used in settings where the purpose is a prediction, and one wants to estimate how accurately a predictive model will perform in practice.

In order to confirm the prediction accuracy of the constructed model, we performed hold-out validation by using the training data and test data. Specifically, we created a confusion matrix like Table 5 and we calculated prediction accuracy of the constructed model by using the following equations.

Table 5. Confusion matrix

		Predicted class	
		Positive	Negative
Actual class	True	True Positive (TP)	True Negative (TN)
	False	False Positive (FP)	False Negative (FN)

Accuracy (ACC): Percentage of the total number correctly predicted among the total number predicted.

$$ACC = \frac{TP + TN}{FP + FN + TP + TN} \tag{2}$$

Precision (PRE): Percentage of the total number that is a positive class actually among the total number predicted positive class.

$$PRE = \frac{TP}{TP + FP} \tag{3}$$

Recall (REC): Percentage of the total number predicted positive class among the total number that is a positive class actually

$$REC = \frac{TP}{FN + TP} \tag{4}$$

F-measure: harmonic mean of PRE and REC

$$F\text{-measure} = 2 \times \frac{PRE \times REC}{PRE + REC} \tag{5}$$

4 Results and Discussions

In this section, we show our analyzing results and discuss them.

4.1 RFM Analysis

Customers were divided into five equal scales equally for each of recency, frequency, monetary. Categories for each attribute of RFM are shown in Table 6.

Table 6. Categories for each attribute of RFM

Score	Recency (/days)			Frequency (/times)			Monetary (/yen)		
5		~	34	326	~		60950	~	
4	35	~	97	160	~	325	27667	~	60949
3	98	~	198	77	~	159	14001	~	27666
2	199	~	307	30	~	76	6801	~	14000
1	308	~			~	29		~	6800

Although the number of target customers in this research was 5,553, at the time of model construction, we randomly sampled the number of general customers by setting the number equal to the number of loyal customers.

The number of datasets (Group A, Group B) used in these model constructions are shown Table 7.

Table 7. Datasets used in prediction model

	Target customers	Analysis data		
		Group A	Group B	Total
Loyal customers	961	480	481	961
General customers	4592	480	481	961
Total	5553	960	962	1922

4.2 Binomial Logistic Regression

In each iteration, the model will be fit to one group of the data, and used to predict the other group.

We built two models that predicts loyal customer for the customers using binomial logistic regression analysis with AIC based the stepwise selection method.

The evaluation indicator for confirming the prediction accuracy are shown Table 8.

Table 8. Evaluation indicator of model for customers (%)

	Training data: Group. A	Training data: Group. B	Average
ACC	82.22%	82.40%	82.31%
PRE	84.60%	83.16%	83.88%
REC	78.79%	81.25%	80.02%
F-measure	81.59%	82.19%	81.89%

Table 9. Partial regression coefficients.

Explanatory variables	Partial regression coefficient	
(Intercept)	−5.460	***
Whether customer updated membership or not	0.798	**
Whether the member registration date matched the initial order date or not	0.754	***
Total number of items purchased at the initial order date	2.590	***
Average amount at the initial order date	0.736	***
Whether customer purchased lady's wear item at the initial order date or not	0.405	
Whether customer purchased men's wear item at the initial order date or not	0.744	**
Whether customer purchased golf club item at the initial order date or not	0.887	***
Whether customer purchased accessory item at the initial order date or not	0.709	*
Whether customer purchased sale item at the initial order date or not	0.724	*
Average login time of all session at the initial order date	0.179	.
Whether browsing golf gear page or not	0.449	

$***p < 0.001, **p < 0.01, *p < 0.05$

Both models are over accuracies. Since the conventional researches on the EC site had the accuracies about 60%, it can be said that this research gained sufficient prediction accuracy.

The accuracy is high when group A is used as training data. Table 9 shows the partial regression coefficients.

There are 11 variables selected from 29 candidate variables.

From Table 9, we can see that variables created from purchase data are selected much. In addition, the confusion matrix for the test data of this model is shown in Table 10.

Table 10. Confusion matrix of model for customers

		Predicted class	
		Positive	Negative
Actual class	Positive	390	90
	Negative	79	401

4.3   Discussions

We selected the explanatory variables which the coefficient of the significant probability of less than 0.05. There are 8 explanatory variables selected (Table 11).

Table 11. Estimated value of selected partial regression coefficient

Explanatory variables	Partial regression coefficient
Total number of items purchased at first purchase	2.590
Whether customer purchased golf club item at the first purchase or not	0.887
Whether customer updated membership or not	0.798
Whether the member registration date matched the initial order date or not	0.754
Whether customer purchased men's wear item at the initial order date or not	0.744
Average amount at first-time purchase	0.736
Whether customer purchased sale item at the initial order date or not	0.724
Whether customer purchased accessory item at the initial order date not	0.709

Overall, since all the partial regression coefficients are positive numbers, it was found that the higher the value of all the selected variables, the more likely to become loyal customers.

In all the variables, total number of items purchased at the initial order date is the highest partial regression coefficient. It seems that the loyalties will be improved by raising customer satisfaction such as giving coupons or gifts to customers with high purchase quantities at the initial order date.

Since partial regression coefficient of "Whether the member registration date matched the initial order date or not" is positive as well, we considered that customers who were interested for a long time and took a long time to purchase. From this result, it seems that recommendations of similar items promote purchase.

It seems that recommending the items of men's wear, golf club, accessory on sale items to the customers registered as a member and did not purchase leads to promotion of purchasing.

It is considered that it is necessary to improve the loyalty of customers by recommending goods to be compared without limiting prices at the initial purchase.

4.4   Verification

We verified with the data of the same period two years later using the prediction model built this time. The results are shown in Tables 12 and 13.

Table 12. Confusion matrix of model for customers

		Predicted class	
		Positive	Negative
Actual class	Positive	894	135
	Negative	946	3483

Table 13. Evaluation indicator of model for customers (%)

ACC	PRE	REC	F-measure
80.19%	48.59%	86.88%	62.32%

Here, although high prediction accuracy was obtained, the precision was low. It is considered that this model distinguishes loyal customers and general customers well, but it could not confirm loyal customers correctly.

5   Conclusion

In this study, we determined customers' loyalties by RFM analysis and constructed a discrimination model of customer loyalty by logistic regression analysis to find characteristic behavior of loyal customers on a golf EC site.

Through our analyses, we built a useful model to predict loyal customers using the web access logs and purchase records data at initial purchase on a golf EC site. As a result, we could clarify the initial purchase and browsing behavior of high loyal customers and tried to propose marketing measures. Even for the data after two years, the model we made this time got a high accuracy.

However, we are conducting a prediction from the data at one point in this study. It is important to check the prediction accuracy of loyal customers by analyzing the data at the transition time.

Acknowledgment. We thank Golf Digest Online Inc. for permission to use valuable datasets and for useful comments. This work was supported by JSPS KAKENHI Grant Number 16K03944 and 17K13809.

References

1. Ministry of Economy, Trade and Industry: Foundation for Data-Driven Society in Japan (Market Survey on Electronic Commerce) (2018). (in Japanese)
2. Nakamura, H. (ed.): Market Segmentation - Discovery of Sales Opportunities Using Purchase History Data, Hakuto Shobo (2008). (in Japanese)
3. Yamashita, H., Suzuki, H.: Analysis of purchasing behavior of customers focusing on sale items: logistic regression analysis with consideration of clustering of binary data. Commun. Oper. Res. Soc. Jpn. **60**(2), 81–88 (2015). (in Japanese)
4. Sato, Y., Namatame, T., Otake, K.: Analysis of the characteristics of repeat customer in a golf EC site. In: International Conference on Social Computing and Social Media, SCSM 2017: Social Computing and Social Media. Human Behavior, pp. 223–233 (2017)

Extraction of Product Features from Customer's Perspective Using User Review at the Golf EC Site

Ryota Takahashi[1(✉)], Takashi Namatame[2], and Kohei Otake[1]

[1] School of Information and Telecommunication Engineering, Tokai University,
2-3-23, Takanawa, Minato-ku, Tokyo 108-8619, Japan
6bjm2l18@mail.u-tokai.ac.jp, otake@tsc.u-tokai.ac.jp
[2] Faculty of Science and Engineering, Chuo University,
1-13-27, Kasuga, Bunkyo-ku, Tokyo 112-8551, Japan
nama@indsys.chuo-u.ac.jp

Abstract. Due to the spread of the electronic commerce site (EC site), it changed to an era where shopping can be done without going to a real store through the Internet. Under these circumstances, a review is one of the important information to consider purchasing at the EC site. In this study, we use the reviews posted on golf portal site and we analyze the characteristic of products using a text mining method. Moreover, we extracted characteristic words and we evaluated 6 products of golf.

Keywords: EC site · User review · Text mining

1 Introduction

Along with the spread of the EC (Electronic Commerce) market, it is easier to order some products and get some information about an item. Due to the above convenience of customers, the market size of the EC site is increasing [1].

Focusing on the service contents provided by the EC site, the user-contributed review service has been introduced at many EC sites. The review contains a lot of important information for customer impressions and customer experiences. Therefore, it is very helpful when the customer cannot decide to buy a product. The review has a strong influence on consumer's decision making. The review has positive content and negative content, which is also a factor for decision-making for consumers [2].

In this study, we use the reviews posted on a golf product for a golf portal site. Consumers want to find golf reviews that match their golf player level when considering purchasing products with reference to golf reviews. However, it is not easy to find a review that matches his or her golf level. In addition, we compare the characteristic words of the review by each golf player level and clarify noteworthy items that appear in the review.

© Springer Nature Switzerland AG 2019
G. Meiselwitz (Ed.): HCII 2019, LNCS 11579, pp. 486–494, 2019.
https://doi.org/10.1007/978-3-030-21905-5_38

2   Data Summary

In this study, we focus on the reviews posted by members of a golf portal site. In addition, we target reviews about golf products. Reviews include some texts that express the content, and evaluation score (5 stages, 1 is very bad, 5 is very good). Generally, after purchasing the target product, reviews are posted on the portal site. The total review number was 98,265. The review data includes the following items.

Table 1. Data of items

User attributes	Age of review
	Height
	Weight
	Golf type (athlete, semi athlete, enjoy)
	Round
Golf skill	Golf score
	Point
	Head speed(mph)
	Trajectory
	Shot
	Satisfaction level
	Distance
Review	Text

3   Dataset

First, we removed missing and outlier during the data. Next, we selected the target product. Specifically, we targeted products with more than 100 reviews in the data period. This is because it is difficult to identify the characteristics of the product from the review unless it was a product that had been reviewed to some extent. As a result, six golf product IDs were targeted. These six products were all included in the category "Ball". Table 2 shows the number of reviews posted for 6 products.

Table 2. Number of reviews posted for each product IDs

Product ID	Number of reviews
3534	165
3900	302
4071	102
4088	107
4089	183
4156	117

4 Analysis of Characteristics of Review

4.1 Summary Statistics

First, we compiled information on user who posted reviews for each product ID. The results are shown in Tables 3, 4, 5, 6 and 7.

Table 3. Percentage of average reviewers golf score for each golf product

Average score	3534	3900	4071	4088	4089	4156
~73	0%	0%	1%	0%	1%	0%
73~82	2%	5%	13%	10%	10%	4%
83~92	32%	47%	42%	54%	58%	38%
93~100	33%	36%	33%	30%	25%	38%
101~110	21%	10%	8%	5%	5%	16%
111~120	7%	2%	1%	1%	2%	3%
121~130	1%	0%	1%	0%	0%	0%
130~	3%	1%	1%	0%	0%	0%

Table 3 is construction ratio with respect to round score level. Generally, it is called that round score under 93 is an advance player, 93 to 110 is an intermediate player and over 111 is a beginner player.

Table 4. Cross tabulation golf level vs product

Golf level	3534	3900	4071	4088	4089	4156
Advance	35%	51%	56%	64%	68%	43%
Intermediate	54%	46%	41%	35%	30%	55%
Beginner	12%	3%	3%	1%	2%	3%

As a result, all the looks like for the intermediate player. Especially, the highest percentage among 3534 and 4156 is 93~100. It is mean that these products often used by the intermediate player. Besides, 3900, 4071, 4088 and 4089 highest percentage is about 83~92. These products are usually used for intermediate player and advance player.

Among the six product IDs, 3534 and 4156 are the high percentage of the intermediate user and also the high percentage of the advanced users.

- Product ID 4089 is the highest percentage of reviews among "advance" users.
- Product ID 4156 is the highest percentage of reviews among "intermediate" users.
- Product ID 3534 is the highest percentage of reviews among "beginner" users.
- When classifying the six products into groups, we defined "beginner to intermediate," "intermediate to advanced" and "advanced".

Next, we focus on the satisfaction of the review. Satisfaction shows that the user expresses what feelings to the product.

Table 5. Satisfaction level vs product

Satisfaction level	3534	3900	4071	4088	4089	4156
Good	90%	83%	86%	90%	89%	66%
Normal	10%	16%	13%	9%	11%	30%
Bad	0%	1%	1%	1%	0%	2%
Surprised	0%	0%	0%	0%	0%	2%
Anger	0%	0%	0%	0%	0%	1%

All Six products satisfaction level are mostly felt good. However, 4156 is not so satisfying compared with other product.

- Product IDs 3534 and 4088 is the highest proportion among "Good".
- Product ID 4156 is the highest proportion among "Normal".
- Product ID 4156 is the highest proportion among "Bad".
- 5 product IDs (3534, 3900, 4071, 4088 and 4089) percentage of "Good" is very high.
- However, ID number 4156 had not only ordinary and dissatisfied but also special icons such as anger and surprise.

Next, we focus on the evaluation score of the review. Evaluation score is how satisfactory the user is with the product by 5-step evaluation. Here, 5 is the highest score and 1 is the worth score.

Table 6. The result of tabulation on the evaluation score

Evaluation score	3534	3900	4071	4088	4089	4156
5	67%	56%	73%	75%	80%	33%
4	25%	37%	25%	18%	17%	50%
3	8%	7%	2%	7%	2%	13%
2	0%	0%	1%	0%	0%	2%
1	0%	0%	0%	1%	1%	2%

- Product ID 4089 is the highest proportion among "evaluation points 5."
- Product ID 4156 is the highest proportion among "evaluation points 4."
- Product ID 4156 is the highest proportion among "evaluation points 3."
- Most of the product IDs evaluation points are 5.

Next, we focus on the golfer type of the review. Golfer type represents the user's competitive motivation for golf. It is arbitrarily selected by the user from three options.

Table 7. The result of aggregation on golfer type

Golfer type	3534	3900	4071	4088	4089	4156
Athlete	3%	5%	12%	8%	9%	4%
Semi athlete	21%	27%	39%	48%	48%	28%
Enjoy	76%	68%	49%	44%	42%	68%

"Athlete" type has a highly competitive motivation. They can be inferred to be a type that practices regularly and tackles stoic. "Semi-athlete" type has middle competitive motivation. They can be inferred to be a type that enthusiastically engages in practice even though it is not as extensive as "Athlete." "Enjoy" type is not high in competitive motivation.

As a result, all the 6 product IDs usually reviewed by "Semi-athlete" and "Enjoy" type of player. Especially, 3534, 3900, 4071 and 4156 reviewed by "Enjoy" type of player. On the other hands, 4088 and 4089 reviewed by "Semi-athlete" and "Enjoy" type of player.

- Product ID 4071 is the highest proportion among "athletes."
- Product IDs 4088 and 4089 is the highest proportion among "semi athletes."
- Product IDs 3900 and 4156 is the highest proportion among "enjoy."
- When classifying the six products into groups, "Enjoy," "Semi athletes to Enjoy" and "Athletes to Enjoy."

4.2   Analysis of Features Included in the Review

We performed natural language processing analysis in order to clarify the characteristics of the reviews. Natural language processing is used for analysis of text data and many types of research are targeted on reviews on the EC site [3].

First, we compiled the reviews for each product into one document. Namely, we created six documents. Next, we performed Morphological analysis on each document. Here, we used MeCab [4] which is a Japanese dictionary for morphological analysis. In this study, we extracted nouns, verbs, adjectives, proper nouns, place names, organization names, and part-of-speech of proper nouns from review sentences.

Next, we try to identify words (characteristic words) that characteristically express each category. Specifically, we extract words that frequently appear in a specific category by the TF-IDF [5] method. TF-IDF method was adopted by the following Eqs. (1) to (3).

$$TF - IDF_{i,j} = tf_{i,j} \times idf_i \tag{1}$$

$$tf_{i,j} = \frac{n_{i,j}}{\sum_S n_{S,j}} \tag{2}$$

$$idf_i = \log \frac{|D|}{|\{d : d \in t_i\}|} \tag{3}$$

Here, $n_{i,j}$ is the number of appear frequency about word i in the sentence j. $\sum_s n_{s,j}$ is the number of appear frequency of all words in the sentence j, $|D|$ is the total number of all sentences. $|\{d : d \in t_i\}|$ is the number of sentences containing words i.

Table 8 shows the characteristic words with the high TF-IDF value for each product (Top 20).

Table 8. The top 20 words obtained by the TF-IDF method

Rank	3534	3900	4071	4088	4089	4156
1	cute	Bridgestone	tight	happy	distance	straight
2	woman	yellow	act	make	sense	name
3	glad	cost performance	match	change	wonderful	like
4	price	think	orange	glad	maker	cost performance
5	gift	distance	distance	coupon	number	attract
6	man	orange	model	excite	pro	product
7	look	down	compare	model	durability	turn
8	peace	Bridgestone	iron	stop	balance	distance
9	fun	try	feel	distance	sale	score
10	girl	tour	stretch	say	takes	ace
11	colorful	winter	driver	head	new	myself
12	can use	pat	ace	can buy	objection	peace
13	golf	level	green	feeling	complaint	find
14	product	cold	different	back	match	trajectory
15	me	fall	course	mild	me	iron
16	optimal	white	back	change	club	stop
17	repute	favorite	soft	try	know	match
18	a lot	great buy	turn	price	surmount	price
19	carriage	cost	patter	soft	feeling	green
20	conspicuous	sale	hard	patter	model	driver

5 Discussion

Based on the above results, we point out the characteristics of reviewer condition of each product IDs using Tables 3, 4, 5, 6 and 7.

As an overall trend, the average score shows that the ratio of "83 to 92" and "93 to 100" is high by looking at the six product IDs. For the golf level, the proportion of Advance and Intermediate is high, and the satisfaction degree accounts for the majority of good and normal. It turns out that most of the evaluation points occupy the ratio of 4 to 5. For golfers, the proportion of semi athlete and enjoy type is high.

Product ID 3534 has a high percentage of "intermediate" users with an average score of "93 to 100" and satisfaction is also high. The proportion of the evaluation points was high, and the type was found to be a lot of the "enjoying" type. We inferred that this product is for low motivation people from the "beginning" of golf to "advanced" people.

Product ID 3900 is the percentage of middle and "advanced" in the average score "83 to 92" of high, the satisfaction level is high, the percentage of "evaluation point 5" is the highest. There are also many golf player types. We inferred that this product is for users who can easily enjoy golf.

Product ID 4071 is a high percentage of medium and advanced in the average score "83 to 92". The satisfaction level is also very high, and the percentage of the "evaluation point 5" is also high. The percentage of "enjoying" types is high for golfers. We inferred that this product is for golf experienced and low motivation users.

Product ID 4088 is a high percentage of "advanced" users with the average score "83 to 92." The satisfaction level is also high, the percentage of the "evaluation point 5" is also high. It turned out that the proportion of "semi athlete" was high. We inferred that this product is for users who are experienced in golf and can be satisfied with high motivation or low motivation. Moreover, we inferred that this product is for users with confidence in golf and regular motivation.

Product ID 4089 has a high percentage of "advanced" users with the average score "83 to 92." The percentage of satisfaction and "evaluation point 5" is the highest. The proportion of golf player type semi-athlete is high. We inferred that this product is for users with a sense of golf and motivation is normal.

Product ID 4156 is a high average score of the for users of middle and advanced users of "83 to 92 and 93 to 100." Satisfaction degree is the highest but uses special satisfaction such as surprised and angry. As a result, the percentage of the "evaluation points 4" is the highest. We inferred that this product is intended for users who play golf and have low motivation.

Next, we discussed the characteristic words of each product using Table 8.

Product ID 3900 is used the word "Bridgestone." This is the name of a very famous golf company. Also, there is some word "yellow" and "orange." It means that this product has some color variation. The words "sale," "cost performance" and "great buy" which means this product is a bargain product with the standard product of the manufacturer.

Product ID 3534 is mostly used words like "cute," "woman" and "colorful." It means that golf product for girls due to the cute design of the product. It is understood that there are many people who purchase mainly for the purpose of using in the golf competition.

Product ID 4071 used the words "iron," "green," "driver" and "distance". We understood that it is evaluated about shot performance.

Product ID 4088 used the word "maker." That is mean this product developed by famous company. There were words "price" and "coupon" which means the price is affordable products. The word "happy" and "glad" means that this product can use for a gift.

Product ID 4089 used words "wonderful" and "feeling". This product is known excellent functionality such as sense and durability. Therefore, it can be inferred that such words appeared in the reviews.

Product ID 4156 shows that the performance of the ball is good which used the word "score" and "straight". It can be inferred that the performance of the ball was evaluated. Moreover, it can be inferred that the words "trajectory," "turn," "iron" and "driver" evaluated good flight distance in the first shot and approach scenes.

Finally, we evaluate each product IDs using the result of reviewer condition and characteristic words.

Product ID 3534 has a high percentage of "intermediate" users. Moreover, product ID 3534 is mostly used words like "cute," "woman" and "colorful". Additionally, satisfaction and evaluation points are nearly full. We evaluated this product is a commodity for gifts pleased even for women.

Product ID 3900 is a bargain product with goods of a famous manufacturer. We can see the characteristics that the performance is substantial. We evaluated this product is for the gift of competition.

Product ID 4071 is characterized by excellent performance. Exercises and scenes used in the course emerge. It is understood that it is perfect for users looking for products with particularly good performance. We evaluated this product is for using for practice golf and using at golf course.

Product ID 4088 is a product for gifts enough to please opponents. It is a pleasing tendency to send a gift to someone for famous manufacturers and for bargain reason. We evaluated this product is for a gift to make the person happy.

Product ID 4089 is a bargain product and has good characteristics. It seems that it is used for practice to understand the tendency to use as a premium for preparing as a good prize and to use it even in the course. We evaluated that this product is for gift of competition.

In product ID 4156, the performance part of the product is evaluated, and in addition, the cost performance is good. We evaluated this product is for golf playing.

6 Conclusion

In this study, we focus on the reviews posted by members of a golf portal site and targeted review about 6 golf product IDs. First of all, we compiled information on members who posted reviews for each product IDs. We targeted products with more than 100 reviews in the data period in this study. After that, we compared information on members who posted reviews for each product ID. Moreover, we performed natural language processing analysis in order to clarify the characteristics of the reviews. Finally, we evaluated each product IDs using the result of reviewer condition and characteristic words.

In the future, we need to increase the number of target data. It is possible to compare various golf products and to judge what kind of products are suitable for what users. Moreover, we judge whether the review sentence is positive or not and estimate what emotions the review wrote from the sentence.

Acknowledgment. We thank Golf Digest Online Inc. for permission to use valuable datasets and for useful comments. This work was supported by JSPS KAKENHI Grant Number 16K03944 and 17K13809.

References

1. Ministry of Economy, Trade, and Industry (Japan): Results of the E-Commerce Market Survey Compiled (2017). http://www.meti.go.jp/press/2017/04/20170424001/201704240012.pdf. Accessed 01 Feb 2019. (in Japanese)
2. Egawa, Y., Ichifuji, Y., Konno, M.: Effect of the user review of EC site on purchase behavior. In: Proceedings of the 73th National Convention of IPSJ, 2 M-6, pp. 591–592 (2011). (in Japanese)
3. Shiraishi, R., Otake, K., Namatame, T.: Proposal of the review recommendation system using the concurrent network. In: Proceedings of 2016 Future Technologies Conference (FTC) (2016)
4. KH Coder. http://khcoder.net/en/. Accessed 30 Jan 2019
5. Inui, T., Itaya, Y., Yamamoto, M., Shinzato, K., Hirate, Y., Yamada, K.: Structuring opinions by relative characteristics for user-opinion aggregation. J. Nat. Lang. Process. **20**(1), 3–25 (2013)

Searching for Community and Safety: Evaluating Common Information Shared in Online Ex-Vaxxer Communities

Alicia J. W. Takaoka[✉]

Communication and Information Sciences Program, University of Hawai'i at Mānoa, Honolulu, HI 96822, USA
ajwilson@hawaii.edu
https://www.hawaii.edu/cis/

Abstract. This study examines a collection of artifacts passed on from some closed Facebook groups of anti-vaxxers. The study conducted a thematic analysis to determine whether or not the group is a community of practice, evaluate and categorize the types of information shared in these groups, and determine the sources of over 1,100 links across two compiled documents to address a series of questions related to claims of ex-vaxxers when compared to anti-vaxxers and the types of data commonly referenced. Findings indicated that ex-vaxxers and anti-vaxxers have separate and distinct claims, abstracts are the most commonly shared scholarly document, and select information is most often taken out of context. This data set can be analyzed for valence and language use in future studies. The purpose of this study is to evaluate information shared in among anti- and ex-vaxxer parents. This study does not seek to validate a specific position or point of view, nor does the researcher want to explore or determine correctness of beliefs.

Keywords: Anti-vaxxer · Health information sharing · Community of practice · Support group

1 Introduction

Many parents want the best for their children. This includes their health and safety as well as emotional well-being. What happens when you believe in the power of science and vaccines, but you watch your child have a violent reaction or become "vaccine damaged" as a result of a vaccine injection (Anonymous, personal communication, July 21, 2018)? This is an uncommon occurrence for many parents, but it does happen [6]. While it is not an experience that may make parents become anti-vaxxers (those who do not believe in immunization or the current vaccination schedule), it is an experience that makes some question what is in vaccines, the vaccine schedule in their country, and barriers to

A. J. W Takaoka—Partial funding for presenting this publication was received from University of Hawaii at Manoa's Graduate Student Organization.

G. Meiselwitz (Ed.): HCII 2019, LNCS 11579, pp. 495–513, 2019.
https://doi.org/10.1007/978-3-030-21905-5_39

vaccination research. This community of parents is called ex-vaxxers, and the community is growing in number as they experience first-hand the reactions their children have to vaccines.

To date, no literature about a schism in the anti-vaxxer community in the United States exists, and scholarly research exploring anti-vaxxers and the information they share is a growing field. This study first seeks to identify the beliefs of the ex-vaxxer community and compare these with the beliefs of the anti-vaxxer community. Next, this study examines a small subset of compiled documents to determine the nature of information shared to conclude whether or not the information is scholarly research. Finally, this study identifies whether or not these closed Facebook groups are communities of practice.

Since many ex-vaxxers still believe in the concept of herd immunity, which is the need for a percentage of the population to be immunized against viruses and bacteria for the survival of the community ([13]), their desires and motivations appear to be different from anti-vaxxers. Next, this study explores whether or not the ex-vaxxer community is a community of practice with claims distinct from the anti-vaxxer community. Whereas anti-vaxxers spread conspiracy theories, disinformation, and misinformation about vaccines on social media ([40]), the demands of ex-vaxxers include the need to research safer adjuvants and other additives in vaccines that do not react with unique allergies [3]. Finally, a thematic analysis was performed on a data set passed on from a member of several ex-vaxxer Facebook anti-vax groups to determine if the data is peer reviewed or consists of unfounded claims.

The purpose of this study is to evaluate information shared in the anti-vaxxer community. This study does not seek to validate a specific position or point of view, nor does the researcher want to explore or determine correctness of beliefs.

2 Literature Review

It should be noted that a prevalence for conspiracy theories exist in the anti-vaxxer community. As Stein writes "Conspiratorial beliefs have become endemic among anti-vaccination groups" [40]. Stein lists several common conspiracies spread on social media today including the belief that airlines inoculate passengers through the ventilation system on planes. Opposition to vaccination is not new. This opposition dates back to the Victorian age and since the 18th century, fear and controversy accompanied the introduction of every new vaccine.

2.1 Language

Fear language is common in anti-vaxxer literature. When talking with new or young mothers, in "Recovering Trust," Boser explains that anti-vax beliefs are rooted in fear. In her conversations with mothers and analysis of literature to convert anti-vaxxer to pro-vaxxers, Boser writes, "The implied danger is mainstream medicine. Medical professionals were said to be 'authoritarian'... and medicine an 'impersonal monolith'...Mothers recount fear and a fundamental need to protect their children from the unnecessary poisons present in vaccines" [5]. A fear was also found when discussing the possible reporting of outbreaks on university campuses [35]. Also, fear and fear-based decision-making is the focus of Guillemard's paper on addressing concerns about vaccines in writing [15].

Other papers that have examined the claims of the anti-vax community include Kata's research about tropes and tactics of the movement as a whole [23], Murakami et als.' visualization of argument analysis in vaccination debates [31], Nichols' information credibility analysis [32], and the importance of patience when discussing vaccines with a member of the anti-vax community [10]. While these are interesting approaches to researching engagement with anti-vaxxers, none are cited by the community itself.

One study examining the language of anti-vaxxers in debate examines the use of science language in context in a Facebook post. This research about the comment thread accompanying an image posted by Mark Zuckerberg, Facebook CEO, is by Faasse, Chatman, and Martin (2016). Referenced often in anti-vax documents, this study superficially reinforces the narrative that anti-vaxxers are well-researched. The researchers, however, found that, "Although the anti-vaccination stance is not scientifically-based, comments showed evidence of greater analytical thinking, and more references to health and the body. In contrast, pro-vaccination comments demonstrated greater comparative anxiety, with a particular focus on family and social processes" [12]. It shows that anti-vaxxers can reference information but not necessarily that it is properly understood or interpreted. Additional research in health information sharing led to the development of the following question:

Are the claims of the anti-vaxxer community different from the claims of those who identify as ex-vaxxers?

It is worth examining social media and health information trends in order to situate the current landscape.

2.2 Health Information and Social Media

Sharing health concerns and health information on social media platforms is growing, and so is this area of research (e.g. [26]). Not only do people share their personal experiences with family, followers, and friends in social networking sites, they also reach out to try to create change in their communities, seek support and share information. Facebook groups are one such example. Ilhan [22] explores why users join fitness groups on Facebook from a uses and gratifications perspective. In addition, some niche platforms exist for solely for this purpose. Cancer care (cancercare.org) for example, is one such site where the goal is to get support from a community for cancer survivors, those in treatment, and caregivers of those living with or recovering from cancer. Research on cancer support groups is growing, as can be seen in [4] and [20]. Another group that seeks online support and knowledge sharing is the anti-vax community.

Some of the data shared in this community includes the Vaccine Adverse Event Reporting System (VAERS) (see [6,9,47] for more information), the economy of vaccines [28], and compiled documents with links to information about vaccines, vaccine injury, and vaccine research. Included in this list is also misinformation about vaccines. Research about health information sharing led to the development of the following question:

What types of information are shared in ex-vaxxer communities?
Information is shared in these groups to educate, so it is worth evaluating whether or not these groups can be considered communities of practice.

2.3   Communities of Practice

Communities of practice are peer to peer groups that focus on knowledge-sharing and problem solving and are driven by the participation of a willing membership [37]. Wenger-Trayner and Wenger-Trayner [43] define a community of practice as "...[a] group of people who share a concern or a passion for something they do and learn how to do it better as they interact regularly" (2). Some ways in which a community of practice might emerge are to exchange data or knowledge or accomplish a task. These groups engage in continuous communication in order to create a sense of belonging where it is safe to discuss or try to change a given "area of shared inquiry" (1). Communities of practice also provide a social aspect for their membership. This may include creating and sharing biographies or profiles or directories, facilitating online meetings, or nesting subgroups in online forums.

In many ways, Facebook is a wonderful platform for communities of practice. The Group feature allows like-minded people to gather together around ideas, causes, concepts, or events. Park, Kee, and Valenzuela examined uses and gratifications in a 2009 study of college students in Facebook groups. They found that gratifications varied based on engagement and relationships, but participants who were willing to get involved in an online community were satisfied overall [33].

In addition to evaluating Facebook groups for gratification, several studies have examined the effectiveness of Facebook groups as communities of practice (e.g. [44]). Duncan and Barczyk examined using a Facebook group in conjunction with a class in a university setting. Social learning and a sense of belonging were enhanced, but the community of practice was not statistically significant when compared with other classes that only met face to face [11]. Pi, Chou, and Liao evaluated knowledge sharing, an important aspect of a community of practice, in Facebook groups [34]. Research about communities of practice led to the development of the following question:
Can the anti- or ex-vaxxer community be considered a community of practice?

In the 2013 study, the group dynamics of information sharing were evaluated. Findings indicated that "...reputation would affect knowledge sharing attitude of Groups members and sense of self-worth would directly and indirectly (through subjective norm) affect the attitude" [34]. While Duncan and Barczyk showed that sharing information was enriched because of the connection afforded by Facebook groups, Pi, Chou, and Liao found that information is only as respected as the user sharing it. This may become problematic in groups where misinformation is frequently shared to maintain group norms (see [19] for information about knowledge management). Exploring these questions led to the development of this study, which employs a grounded approach to data collection and interpretation.

3   Methods

To evaluate the first research question, a grounded approach using open coding and thematic analysis of the data set passed on from an informant in several closed anti-vax Facebook groups was conducted. This analysis catalogued and counted the types of media passed on over a six-week period from July 19, 2018 to August 31, 2018. The informant volunteered to pass on information from these groups because it is understood that entry is difficult to obtain, and questions about group activity are closely monitored [1]. In addition, because the informant is an active participant in this community, certain information was selected to be passed on for its value in one or several of the communities. This data set, called the Original data set, consists of memes, scholarly articles, vaccine inserts, messages about interpretation or information and context to frame certain articles, videos, newspaper articles, and infographics.

This collection was sorted into a table to identify specific type and count information using thematic analysis. The information collected in this thematic analysis was the author name, type of content, year it was published, country of origin (where the research took place or the location of the first author), where the research was published, the title, whether the information was the full version or an abstract or abbreviated in some way, whether the information is open access or accessible without a paywall, if the source was peer reviewed, the subject or tags or keywords identified, and the conclusion of the argument. The data set was then examined further.

After the information was sorted, the scholarly articles were checked to determine whether or not the study was retracted or edited and whether or not the journal is peer reviewed. This information was then evaluated by descriptive statistics. Another subset of data, the compiled documents, were then evaluated for nominal variables. Content in tables were listed in the order in which they first appeared.

Several collections of data are shared in these groups. They are accessible as Google Docs, as a collection of links and quotes housed on an external resource server. Some are partially accessible with most hidden behind a paywall. These documents are shared among members of the Facebook groups and are generally deemed credible. These compiled documents were evaluated to determine the accuracy of source information. Links were coded by source type using a thematic analysis and open coding approach.

In addition, some links on one document, Vaccine File, had claims either preceding or following links. These claims were evaluated in the surrounding links to determine whether the information could be identified or if it was unfounded based on its presence or absence in the linked source. This was determined by copying and pasting a quote in Vaccine File and searching for the quote using the Find or Search feature in the abstract, article, or web page.

One researcher read for stated claims and beliefs held by anti-vaxxers in publicly accessible memes and posts in two prominent Facebook groups shared in the Original data set and the compiled documents using a close reading approach. These claims were then distilled into broad categories of claims using thematic analysis. These claims were compared and contrasted with claims stated from an informant in the ex-vaxxer community about what they (the self-proclaimed ex-vaxxer community) believe. In addition to this interview, artifacts from several closed ex-vaxxer groups were evaluated employing thematic analysis and open coding techniques in a grounded theory approach. Some interesting results and findings will now be explored and hypotheses posited.

4   Results

4.1   Claims Found

Claims from ex-vaxxers were gathered from an interview with an informant speaking on behalf of the self-proclaimed ex-vaxxer community while anti-vaxxer claims were gathered from open coding and close reading from links and memes generated the Facebook groups Dr. Tenpenny, Stop Mandatory Vaccination, and Revolution for Choice. Some claims are listed in the compiled document Vaccine File. Most anti-vax claims revolve around vaccines causing autism and other spectrum disorders. While these claims continue to be disproved in current scientific research, (e.g. [21, 30]) the claims of anti-vaxxers persist in their current iterations. The anti-vaxxer claims as found in memes created and disseminated by two Facebook groups are listed below:

1. Vaccines cause mental disorders.
2. Vaccines cause autism.
3. Childhood vaccinations contain mercury.
4. Mandating vaccines is government overreach.
5. The science behind vaccines is disputable.
6. Vaccines cause the diseases.
7. Doctors get paid by pharmaceutical companies to give vaccinations.
8. Society does not need vaccinations.
9. Measles is a harmless disease.
10. "Natural" immunity (i.e., immunity gained by infection with the disease) is better or lasts longer than immunity gained by a vaccine.

(see [27] for the Facebook groups from which the majority of anti-vax posts originate).

It appears as though ex-vaxxer claims can be distinguished from anti-vaxxer claims in content. These claims are primarily based on experience, but in cases where research backs up those claims, those articles have been referenced. The ex-vaxxer claims are:

1. Vaccines don't cause mental disorders, but parents have watched their children have seizures after receiving a vaccine [3, 46].
2. Recent studies of brains of patients with various spectrum diseases and disorders revealed an accumulation of aluminum in the brain [29]. Since not all bodies can process aluminum, alternatives to aluminum should be incorporated into vaccines.
3. Vaccines contain many things that need further study [2, 14].
4. The vaccine schedule should be amended so adverse reactions in children can be better monitored.
5. Because we acknowledge the reality of vaccine injury, less harmful adjuvants should be added to vaccines [3, 16, 17].
6. Vaccines cause adverse reactions [18, 36, 42]
7. We need to maintain herd immunity, but not at the cost of children [3].

It should be noted that a study published in February 2019 found that the majority of Facebook posts relating to anti-vaccination come from a relatively small number of people. Madrigal writes, "the top 50 Facebook pages ranked by the number of public posts they made about vaccines generated nearly half (46%) of the top 10,000 posts for or against vaccinations, as well as 38% of the total likes on those posts, from January 2016 to February of this year. The distribution is heavy on the top, particularly for the anti-vax position. Just seven anti-vax pages generated nearly 20% of the top 10,000 vaccination posts in this time period" [27]. Therefore, the use of the subset of memes and posts by these groups was sufficient to establish the claims listed. These memes can be seen in Vaccine File, a compiled document.

As seen in the above section, the claims made by ex-vaxxers can be argued for using current scientific research. One study is McLachlan et al. published a 2019 study on aluminum build up in neurodegenerative diseased brains post-mortem [29]. While this study did not find an overabundance of aluminum in brains with autism spectrum disorder, some neurodegenerative diseased brains did exhibit more aluminum. This study was conducted using a network of brain banks. Amaral et al. highlight the importance of a network of brain banks for post-mortem research on spectrum disorders, metal accumulation, and brain development [2]. Because of the contrasting claims and a reliance on current research, it can be hypothesized that

Anti-vaxxers and ex-vaxxers are separate and distinct groups with different goals for national vaccination.

4.2 Types of Information Shared

The initial data set shared from the Facebook groups in the original data set consisted of several types of media.

As seen in the table above, the number of articles shared from the informant totaled the same as the memes and comments. Each of these categories account for 16.7% of the shared content. While all of these types of data were interesting, and meaningful studies could be produced from this data set or newly

Table 1. Types of content shared in a six week period.

Type	Total	Peer reviewed	Open access
Article	9	4	8
Meme	9	0	2
Documentary	2	0	0
Book review	2	0	2
Book	1	2	0
Comment	9	0	3
Posts	1	0	0
Insert	1	0	1
Compiled doc	3	0	1
Blog	1	0	1
Court order	1	1	1
Facebook group	1	0	0
Anon analysis	3	0	0
op.ed post	1	0	0
Screenshots	2	0	0
Statistical report	1	0	1
Website	1	0	1
Donation request	1	0	0
Videos	5	0	4

constructed data sets based on these types of media, the next part of analysis in this study focused on the compiled documents.

The compiled documents only account for 5.5% of the shared information, but these files are stored online, publicly available, and are rich with links and claims for analysis. Some of the content in these documents were then analyzed.

Vaccine File. Vaccine File is a complicated document. When printed to PDF on 15 February 2019, it totaled 88 pages. This document was then copied and pasted to a spreadsheet where it totaled over 17,000 lines of text. It was cleaned to 483 links and 177 statements. The link types can be seen in the following table.

As can be seen in Table 2, 31.5% of the links were broken, 22.8% were redundant and appeared multiple times throughout the document, and 6.7% were Facebook posts. A total of 23.6% of links in this document led to scholarly databases. The majority of those were terminal abstracts with articles either only accessible behind a paywall or not accessible at all. Abstracts accounted for 15% of the total links but are 63.2% of the 114 scholarly links.

A unique aspect of this data set were the retracted articles and articles with commentary. It should be noted that 11 links to corrections and commentary

Table 2. Vaccine file links.

Source type	Total
Broken links (all)	152
Abstract	72
Article (OA)	23
Full text available	19
Compilations	8
News article	6
Second hand news article	2
WHO	3
CDC	6
Web page	7
Vaccine insert	2
Facebook post	32
Buy book	5
Vaccine documentary	4
Video	9
Untrusted site	6
Retracted article	2
Blog search	3
Redirected video	4
Database search	1
Facebook group	1
Institution of education statistics	1
Letter	1
Login required	1
Meme	1
Trailer for documentary	1
USFDA	1
Redundant (Total)	110
Total	483

were available on 4 abstracts. Only 2% of the articles were redacted, but commentary and amendments were available by link on approximately 7% of the abstracts. Again, this would be an interesting data set to explore in further research, especially since this document leads to eight additional unique compiled documents. This data set was reviewed for descriptive information about sets of links like, Doctors who explain clearly why vaccines aren't safe or effective. Those statements were removed from the document upon analysis. This file contained 177 meaningful statements. These consisted of claims, arguments, and quotes from articles. An example of this type of text is:

"Tylenol (Acetaminophen) depletes glutathione levels in the body, which are essential for detoxification. Vaccines have alum adjuvants and other ingredients (See attached link to see specific vaccine ingredients and adverse reactions associated). If you give your child Tylenol before or after vaccines, they can't process these toxins and they become even more susceptible to autism and other vaccine injury, as these peer reviewed scientific studies affirm [no citation]."

Another example in which a link is provided is, Wild animals don't have food allergies unless vaccinated. People in countries without modern medicine available to them do not have food allergies. (That is used as the reasoning behind the hygiene theory of food allergies. See www.medscape.com/viewarticle/842500). Unfortunately, this link is broken at the time of data analysis and writing. When a search for the statement is conducted using Bing and Google, no results are found. Again, these 177 claims analyzed did not include descriptive statements about the links, but such statements were in the document.

Of the claims made, like this one, approximately 75% are unfounded. This does not mean these claims are fabricated; rather, these claims cannot be found in the document either preceding or following the statement. This result could have been averted by properly citing documents. If this document was compiled like an annotated bibliography, finding sources and quotes again would be easier for future researchers. Five of the 177 claims relate to requesting a religious exemption. Finally, 11 claims have been omitted from this evaluation as they are, admittedly, conspiracy theories. One interesting subset of data was the redundant, or repeated, links.

Redundant posts made up 22.77% of the total links available, but 33.23% of active links in this data compilation. The redundant links were defined as a repetition of a link which connected to the same article, abstract, post, web page, or other source of information that was previously mentioned. A table of categories and total of each can be seen below (Table 3).

Table 3. Redundant and repeated source categories.

Redundant type	Total
Abstract	55
Article	24
Compiled documents	6
Facebook posts	4
Government news	5
Secondhand news	8
Webpage	8
Total	110

The other compiled document evaluated was the Vaccine Research Guide.

Vaccine Research Guide. Vaccine Research Guide is a file that houses links and descriptions of documents including vaccine schedules and inserts. The Vaccine Research Guide is the easiest document to navigate. It consists of clickable links that are easy to identify. As seen in the table below, only 4.6% of the links were unclickable, and 15% were broken. An overview of the types of material in that file can be seen in Table 4 below.

Table 4. Vaccine research guide links

Resources	Total
CDC	2
Book	2
For profit website	66
Database search results	5
Patent	3
Full peer reviewed article	4
Scientific information about compounds	18
NIH	1
Blog	1
Medline	2
Abstract	11
Uncontextualized data	2
Digital image	2
US news outlet	1
Video	1
Vatican analysis	1
Broken link	23
Unclickable	7
Total	152

Looking back to Table 1, it can be seen that the majority of information shared in this time frame was not scholarly, peer reviewed studies. While that is the case, it is all information that is needed for a good foundation in the reasons and beliefs of this community from the perspective of the informant.

Posts of solidarity seemed to be the most important type of information conveyed among users. This again reinforces the idea of a support group and to know that if your child or you experienced some adverse reaction to vaccines, a group of people also understand and share your pain.

Table 5. Comparison of data in originally shared artifacts and Vaccine File, and Vaccine Research.

Resources	V. Research	V. File	Original
Abstract	11	72	0
Anonymous analysis of information	0	0	3
Blog	1	0	1
Blog search	0	3	0
Book: about, buy, or review	2	5	3
Broken link	23	152	0
Centers for disease control	2	6	0
Compiled documents	0	8	3
Court order	0	0	1
Database search results	5	1	0
Digital image	2	0	0
Documentary	0	4	2
Donation request	0	0	1
Facebook group	0	1	1
Facebook post or comment	0	32	12
For profit website	66	7	1
Full text article, not peer reviewed	0	0	5
Full text available (open access)	0	19	0
Full text, peer reviewed article	4	23	4
Institution of education statistics	0	1	0
Letter	0	1	0
Login	0	1	0
Medline	2	0	0
Meme	0	1	9
National institute of health	1	0	0
Op ed post	0	0	1
Patent	3	0	0
Redirected video	0	4	0
Redundant (Total)	0	110	0
Retracted article	0	2	0
Scientific information about compounds	18	0	0
Second hand news article	0	2	0
Unclickable	7	0	0
Uncontextualized data	2	0	1
Untrusted site	0	6	0
USFDA	0	1	0
US news outlet	1	6	0
Vaccine insert	0	2	1
Vatican analysis	1	0	0
Video	1	9	5
Video trailer	0	1	0
World Health Organization	0	3	0
Total	152	483	54

A comparison of the types of data shared in the original data set shows that Facebook posts and comments were the most often shared (22.2%), followed by memes (16.7%) and then full texts of articles that were not peer reviewed and videos at 9.25% each. Compared to the types of data shared in the other compiled documents, visible in Table 5, personal interaction is most highly valued in the Facebook groups.

As Table 5 shows, the publicly housed data sets have broken and redundant links, but the originally shared artifacts did not have any broken links. Everything shared from the informant was accessible. Some things to consider are that, according to these data sets, scholarly articles appear 7.4% of the time in the Facebook group, 4.8% in Vaccine File, and 2.6% of the time in Vaccine Research. Converted to rations, a reader is likely to find an open access, peer reviewed article 7 out of 100 times in the original data set, 6 out of 125 times in Vaccine File, and 13 out of 500 times in Vaccine Guide. From these results, it can be hypothesized that

The amount of scholarly articles in compiled documents are not statistically significant when compared to broken links, for profit links, and other types of media shared in anti-vaxxer and ex-vaxxer groups.

After evaluating the types of information most commonly shared in these groups, it is now possible to evaluate whether or not these groups are a community of practice.

4.3 Community of Practice

Even though the members of these Facebook groups may feel as though information sharing and learning are priorities, these groups cannot be classified as a community of practice. Based on their information sharing habits and what was shared from the informant, it may be likely for these groups to function like support or self-help groups. Bender, Jimenez-Marroquin, and Jadad researched support groups on Facebook. They identified support groups as the most commonly created type of group relating to breast cancer is support for survivorship or support for caregivers of survivors [4]. It seems likely that Facebook groups for anti-vaxxers and ex-vaxxers may fall into this category, but more research must be examined.

First, Katz and Bender define support groups as "Voluntary, small group structures for mutual aid and the accomplishment of a special purpose. They are usually formed by peers who have come together for mutual assistance in satisfying a common need, overcoming a common handicap or life-disrupting problem or bringing about social and/or personal change" [24]. Huber distills this to mean that support groups have been used to improve individuals psychological, behavioral, physical, and interpersonal well-being [20]. The primary focus of a support group is not learning or developing a skill or accomplishing a task, as it is in a community of practice.

Instead, Zambelli and DeRosa (1992) define support groups as a modality that emphasizes peer support and can serve as an additional system. They further indicate that support groups typically do not aim to ameliorate interapsychic or interpersonal difficulties, even though this may occur as a result of participation in the group [45]. This seems to be one form of relief in sharing posts about experiences or seeking positive feedback from other members of anti-vax and ex-vax communities.

While there are several types of support groups, it must be examined whether or not ex-vax and anti-vax groups are self help groups. Some common characteristics of self-help groups that are associated with some cognitive behavior modification programs include their:

- "voluntary nature- they are run by and for group members, have regular meetings, and are open to new members (17);
- generally being formed in response to a particular issue, e.g. no access to education for children with disabilities, limited income-generating opportunities;
- clear goals, which originate from the needs of group members and are known and shared by all members (15);
- informal structure and basic rules, regulations and guidelines to show members how to work effectively together;
- participatory nature involving getting help, sharing knowledge and experience, giving help, and learning to help oneself (18);
- shared responsibility among group members each member has a clear role and contributes his/her share of resources to the group;
- democratic decision-making;
- governance by members, using an external facilitator only if necessary in the formation of the group (15);
- evolution over time to address a broader range of issues;
- possibility of joining together to form a federation of groups across a wider area." ([25], p. 3)

The agenda-setting, roles, rules, and democratic nature of self-help groups are not applicable to ex-vax and anti-vax groups. While members in these groups come together as a result of a particular event, the lack of governance, structure, and goals set self-help groups apart from the communities evaluated on Facebook.

One research question sought to examine whether or not anti-vax and ex-vax groups can be considered communities of practice. While the anti-vax and ex-vax communities are knowledgeable about some of the risks associated with vaccines and vaccine injury, communities of practice also have clearly defined goals and rules, regulations, and guidelines. Based on this information and the sharing practices exhibited by the original data set, it can be hypothesized that *Ex-vaxxer and anti-vaxxer communities in Facebook groups are support groups and not communities of practice.*

It is now possible to examine the shortcomings and future study possibilities for this area of study.

5   Discussion

Limitations for this study existed in several areas. First, this study only evaluated the data shared in communities by one member in a six week time span. Many factors of information retrieval may have impacted the data set. The member of the community may have excluded articles that did not favor a specific position or that may have come from unreliable sources. Additionally, the member might not have seen every piece of information shared in the community. It must be acknowledged that this study evaluates only a portion of information shared by ex-vaxxers.

Next, because data for this study was not collected directly from closed Facebook groups, random sampling could not be employed for further evaluation. The idea for this study was to evaluate scholarly articles to determine information accuracy, but there was no guarantee that all of the scholarly articles shared in the groups were passed on or that the data set constructed by the informant was comprised only of artifacts shared during the six week window. As a result, one future study on this topic is a participant observation, where researchers in the community observe and record events, artifacts, and conversations. Another area of future research is to evaluate compiled documents using content analysis with interrater reliability. Further, the subset of information shared within communities to what exists in the scope of scientific and scholarly journals only accessible behind paywalls can also be evaluated using thematic analysis and content analysis.

Linguistic and semantic studies on the originally shared content and compiled documents should be conducted. Some studies like [7, 8, 12, 31, 38, 39] have shown several approaches to evaluating language, rhetoric, and narratives in anti-vaxxer and vaccine debates. These approaches could be applied to any subset of the data collected from the original data set to evaluate language choices and the agendas set by these groups.

Another future study is to take each compiled document file and individually examine the statements, quotes, and claims for valence and use of emotional language. This type of study will provide insight to the agenda shared in each compiled file. In addition, teasing out the language and valence of each statement may help clarify true statements from created narratives. Like Faasse, Chatman, and Martin write, anti-vaxxers are better able to use scientific language in discussions about vaccines because they read excerpts from these studies [12]. While anti- and ex-vaxxers are not experts or even scientifically trained in these complex concepts, distilling the studies and concepts for mass dissemination will help communities as a whole better understand the issue and dispel some of the myths on both sides of the argument.

Another future study is examining the interpretations of information by members in the community. This study did not seek the opinions of community members, nor did the study solicit the interpretation of highlighted, non-annotated information that is publicly accessible. The study also did not ask members of the community to interpret any of the passages to ensure the continuity of meaning or continuity of conclusions reached in the published article.

To better understand the proliferation of scholarly articles in this community, examining the meaning, comprehension, and interpretation internalized from articles by community members is a crucial area of future research.

Perception studies about highlighted information in the Vaccine Guide should be conducted with members in the ex-vax and anti-vax community Facebook groups. This file includes a court case with only highlighted information on the first two pages of a 50+ page document highlighted [41]. A null hypothesis about information interpretation can be evaluated using a Mann-Whitney U-test and communication with other members of the closed Facebook groups. A follow up study on Vaccine Guide, the vaccine schedules, and Vaccine File should be the next phase in this line of research.

Finally, there was no way to evaluate the level of engagement in or between the groups in which this information was shared. Another avenue for future study is the evaluation of popular articles or most popular posts in groups as well as cross-group members and cross-group posting. The dynamics of community and information-sharing from a network perspective may possibly contribute to which articles get read, shared, or liked. This area should receive attention in the future.

6   Conclusion

What started off as a simple sharing of information turned into an evaluation of the presence of and access to information. The three compiled documents and the originally shared information became a complex data set of 1,105 links, claims, and highlighted information that were manually tested and coded by one researcher. This area of research should be continued in order to better understand the claims, experiences, and fears of those who have witnessed vaccine injury. In addition, research of the commonly shared documents in ex-vaxxer and anti-vaxxer communities can help to reach an understanding about where and how information gets misinterpreted. Finally, research in health information can further discourse about public health and safety. Future studies should be pursued by researchers interested in communication, health information, information sharing, and the interpretation of complex data.

References

1. Aaen, J., Dalsgaard, C.: Student Facebook groups as a third space: between social life and schoolwork. Learn. Media Technol. **41**(1), 160–186 (2016)
2. Amaral, D.G., et al.: Autism BrainNet: a network of postmortem brain banks established to facilitate autism research. In: Huitinga, I., Webster, M. (eds.) Handbook of Clinical Neurology: Brain Banking, vol. 150, pp. 31–39. Elsevier (2018). Chapter 3
3. Anonymous informant.: Correspondences via Facebook Messenger. https://www.messenger.com (2018). Accessed 01 Sept 2018
4. Bender, J., Jimenez-Marroquin, M.-C., Jadad, A.R.: J. Med. Internet Res. **13**(1), e16 (2011)

5. Boser, B.L.: Mothers anti-vax to pro-vax conversions. In: Lake, R.A. (ed.) Recovering Argument. Routledge, New York (2018)
6. Braun, M.: Vaccine adverse event reporting system (VAERS), usefulness and limitations. JH S Cont M (2017)
7. Brice-Saddler, M.: Teen Who Defied Anti-Vax Mom Says She Got False Information from One Source: Facebook. The Washington Post (2019)
8. Capurro, G., Greenberg, J., Dube, E., Driedger, M.: Measles, moral regulation and the social construction of risk: media narratives of "anti-vaxxers" and the 2015 Disneyland outbreak. Can. J. Sociol. **43**(1), 25–48 (2018)
9. Che, R.T., et al.: The vaccine adverse event reporting system (VAERS). Vaccine **12**(6), 542–550 (1994)
10. Coleman, M.C.: The role of patience in arguments about vaccine science. Western J. Comm. **82**(4), 513–528 (2018)
11. Duncan, D., Barczyk, C.C.: Facebook in the university classroom: do students perceive that it enhances community of practice and sense of community? Int. J. Bus. Soc. Sci. **4**(3), 1–14 (2013)
12. Faasse, K., Chatman, C.J., Martin, L.R.: A comparison of language use in pro-and anti-vaccination comments in response to a high profile Facebook post. Vaccine **34**(7), 5808–5814 (2016)
13. Fine, P., Eames, K., Heymann, D.L.: Herd immunity: a rough guide. Clin. Infect Dis. **52**(7), 911–916 (2011)
14. Fortner, K.B., et al.: Reactogenicity and immunogenicity of tetanus toxoid, reduced diphtheria toxoid, and acellular pertussis vaccine (Tdap) in pregnant and nonpregnant women. Vaccine **36**(42), 6354–6360 (2018)
15. Guillemard, M.: Addressing vaccine hesitancy in writing. Med. Writ. **27**, 39–42 (2018)
16. Guy, B.: The perfect mix: recent progress in adjuvant research. Nat. Rev. Microbiol. **5**(7), 505 (2007)
17. He, P., Zou, Y., Hu, Z.: Advances in aluminum hydroxide-based adjuvant research and its mechanism. Hum. Vacc. Immunother. **11**(2), 477–488 (2015)
18. Health, Resources and Services, Administration and others: National vaccine injury compensation program: revisions to the vaccine injury table. Final rule. Federal Register **82**(12), 6294 (2017)
19. Hoadley, C.: What is a community of practice, and how can we support it? In: Land, S., Jonassen, D. (eds.) Theoretical Foundations of Learning Environments, pp. 286–302. Routeledge, New York (2012)
20. Huber, F.N.: Communicating Social Support Behind Bars: Experiences with the Pennsylvania Lifers' Association. The Pennsylvania State University (2005)
21. Hviid, A., Hansen, J.V., Frisch, M., Melbye, M.: Measles, mumps, rubella vaccination and autism: a nationwide cohort study. Ann. Intern Med. **170**(8), 513–520 (2019)
22. Ilhan, A.: Motivations to join fitness communities on Facebook: which gratifications are sought and obtained? In: Meiselwitz, G. (ed.) SCSM 2018. LNCS, vol. 10914, pp. 50–67. Springer, Cham (2018). https://doi.org/10.1007/978-3-319-91485-5_4
23. Kata, A.: Anti-vaccine activists, web 2.0, and the postmodern paradigm-an overview of tactics and tropes used online by the anti-vaccination movement. Vaccine **30**(25), 3778–3789 (2012)
24. Katz, A.H., Bender, E.: Self-help groups in western society: history and prospects. J. Appl. Behav. Sci. **12**(3), 265–282 (1976)
25. Khasnabis, C., et al.: Community-Based Rehabilitation: CBR Guidelines. World Health Organization (2010)

26. Li, Y., Wang, X., Lin, X., Hajli, M.: Seeking and sharing health information on social media: a net valence model and cross-cultural comparison. Technol. Forecast. Soc. **128**, 28–40 (2018)
27. Madrigal, A.C.: The Small, Small World of Facebook's Anti-vaxxers. The Atlantic (2019)
28. Martin, G.: The economics of vaccine act cases. J. Legal. Econ. **17**(2), 87–98 (2011)
29. McLachlan, D.R.C., et al.: Aluminum in neurological and neurodegenerative disease. Mol. Neurobiol. **56**(2), 1–8 (2019)
30. Meyer, S.B., Violette, R., Aggarwal, R., Simeoni, M., MacDougall, H., Waite, N.: Vaccine hesitancy and web 2.0: exploring how attitudes and beliefs about influenza vaccination are exchanged in online threaded user comments. Vaccine **37**(13), 1769–1774 (2019)
31. Murakami, K., Nichols, E., Matsuyoshi, S., Sumida, A.: Statement map: assisting information credibility analysis by visualizing arguments. In: Proceedings of the 3rd Workshop on Information Credibility on the Web, pp. 43–50. ACM (2009)
32. Nichols, E., Murakami, K., Inui, K., Matsumoto, Y.: Constructing a scientific blog corpus for information credibility analysis. In: Proceedings of the Annual Meeting of ANLP (2009)
33. Park, N., Kee, K.F., Valenzuela, S.: Being immersed in social networking environment: Facebook groups, uses and gratifications, and social outcomes. Cyberpsychol. Behav. **12**(6), 729–733 (2009)
34. Pi, S.-M., Chou, C.-H., Liao, H.-L.: A study of Facebook groups members' knowledge sharing. Comput. Hum. Behav. **29**(5), 1971–1979 (2013)
35. Provenzano, S., Santangelo, O.E., Lanza, G.L.M., Raia, D.D., Alagna, E., Firenze, A.: Factors associated with reporting adverse reactions after immunization, study in a sample of university students. Ann. Ig. [Internet] **30**, 436–442 (2018)
36. Ridgeway, D.: No-fault vaccine insurance: lessons from the national vaccine injury compensation program. J. Health Polit. Polic. **24**(1), 59–90 (1999)
37. Serrat, O.: Building communities of practice. Knowledge Solutions, pp. 581–588. Springer, Singapore (2017). https://doi.org/10.1007/978-981-10-0983-9_61
38. Shelby, A., Ernst, K.: Story and science: how providers and parents can utilize storytelling to combat anti-vaccine misinformation. Hum. Vacc. Immunother. **9**(8), 1795–1801 (2013)
39. Smith, N., Graham, T.: Mapping the anti-vaccination movement on Facebook. Inform. Commun. Soc. 1–18 (2017)
40. Stein, R.A.: The golden age of anti-vaccine conspiracies. Germs **7**(4), 168 (2017)
41. Supreme Court of the United States (SCUS): Bruesewitz et al. v. Wyeth LLC, FKA Wyeth Inc, et al. Syllabus. Certiotari to the United States Court of Appeals for the Third Circuit, Washington (2011)
42. Weibel, R.E., Caserta, V., Benor, D.E., Evans, G.: Acute encephalopathy followed by permanent brain injury or death associated with further attenuated measles vaccines: a review of claims submitted to the national vaccine injury compensation program. Pediatrics **101**(3), 383–387 (1998)
43. Wenger-Trayner, E., Wenger-Trayner, B.: Introduction to Communities of Practice: A Brief Overview of the Concept and Its Uses. Grass Valley (2015)
44. Wong, K., Kwan, R., Leung, K.: An exploration of using Facebook to build a virtual community of practice. In: Kwan, R., Fong, J., Kwok, L., Lam, J. (eds.) ICHL 2011. LNCS, vol. 6837, pp. 316–324. Springer, Heidelberg (2011). https://doi.org/10.1007/978-3-642-22763-9_30

45. Zambelli, G.C., DeRosa, A.P.: Bereavement support groups for school-age children: theory, intervention, and case example. Am. J. Orthopsychiatry **62**(4), 484–493 (1992)
46. Zheteyeva, Y.A., et al.: Adverse event reports after tetanus toxoid, reduced diphtheria toxoid, and acellular pertussis vaccines in pregnant women. Am. J. Obstet. Gynecol. **207**(1), 59.e1–59.e7 (2012)
47. Zhou, W., et al.: Surveillance for Safety After Immunization: Vaccine Adverse Event Reporting System (VAERS), United States, 1991–2001. MMWR Surveill Summ. (2013)

Algorithms and Advertising in Consumption Mediations: A Semio-pragmatic Perspective

Eneus Trindade(⊠)

Universidade de São Paulo, Sao Paulo, Brazil
eneustrindade@usp.br

Abstract. This paper seeks to discuss the theoretical notion of algorithmic sign mediation in advertising and brand consumption, based on the theory of mediations [16], considering the sociocultural understanding of this new ontic status of the digital language of the market, based on the storage process, organization and interpretation of data for the establishment of interactions between brands and consumers. Thus, the reflection adds to the view of mediations a semio-pragmatic perspective, to understand the principles of algorithmic writing of advertising and its narrative and interactional dynamics in relations between brands and consumers.

Keywords: Digital advertising · Brands · Mediations · Algorithms · Consumption

1 Introduction

The ecosystem of brands, in algorithmic mediation, brings a new ontological status to the signic mediation of advertising. It is understood that signs give the communication mediations and that these mediations are founders of the sociocultural realities. Mediations, in this work, can be understood from a philosophical perspective, as a sort of materialist phenomenology [4, 16].

The materiality of digital signs, via algorithms, invites us to a new dimension of the writing of things in the digital humanities, which goes beyond the mediation of technicality, and spreads in the logic of production, industrial formats, institutions and cultural matrices, generating new sociabilities and new cognitions that are manifested in the mediations of the consumption of the brands with their appropriations and new rituals for consumers.

The communicative condition of the mediations of things in consumption was our object of the previous discussion in Perez and Trindade [18], which supported the propositions of the semiotics of Charles Sanders Peirce, sought to understand the aesthetic, ethical and logical dimensions of consumption signs, including in this kind of research, advertisings and every ecosystem of brands with their expressiveness.

At the same time, it also sought to observe the interfaces of these dimensions of consumption in the sociocultural realities in which such phenomena occur. In this theoretical complementation between cultural mediations and signic mediation, consumption is seen as a communicational mediation that would articulate regulatory or

G. Meiselwitz (Ed.): HCII 2019, LNCS 11579, pp. 514–526, 2019.
https://doi.org/10.1007/978-3-030-21905-5_40

intermediary instances of sociocultural dynamics, based on the Martín-Barbero model/map of mediations [16].

Such a model is discussed in its intermedialities implied to the interactional dynamics of goods, services, and brands with consumers for the constitution of signic sense links in cultural life, as outlined in the previous paragraph. It is perceived in this theoretical intersection that communication would function as pragmatics of social discursivization.

This theoretical effort enunciated in the previous lines now seeks its adaptation to the phenomena of digital advertising, manifested in the algorithms mediation. It is noteworthy that, in the opportunity of this text, although also consider the contribution of Charles Sanders Peirce, the reflection will be held on the same principle of this combination Semiotics and mediations, but now this theoretical crossroads is more oriented by the perspective of the French semiotic approach as proposed by Algirdas Julien Greimas.

Nevertheless, regardless of the semiotic approach used, this work continues to perceive signic mediation as a communicational condition in a philosophical-theoretical perspective phenomenological-materialist, as discussed by Couldry and Hepp [4], since the semiopragmatic in the Peirce or Greimas aspect is seen here in the material and symbolic condition that the signs of the algorithms assume in the processes of communication and consumption, in the media studies, whether these are defended in the concepts of communication mediations of the cultures or by the concept of mediatization.

It should be clarified that Martín-Barbero's theory of mediations [16] is not the same thing as the theories of mediatization. However, we work with the possibility of approximation that authors like Couldry and Hepp [5] present as currents of the studies of mediatization and in which they approach with Martín-Barbero on the concept of communicational mediations in cultures. With both concepts (mediations and mediatization) we seek to understand the processes that correspond to the media's modes of presence and performance in the transformations of cultures. This is the aspect worth emphasizing here since our interpretation of the questions of definitions about mediations and consumption mediation has already been discussed in other papers [21].

We are interested, specifically, at this moment of reflection, in the questions of the communication mediations in the consumptions, starting from the algorithms as mediating instances of daily life. The algorithms assume a relevance for the definition of new cultural patterns of interaction, being this a prominent aspect of the media studies in the contemporaneity.

It is not uncommon to find news in business journals or corporate websites dealing with investments and gains in competitiveness, from the use of applications (app). In the Brazilian case, in retail, Pão de Açúcar Supermarket Group invests in an application for the online food trade[1]. In the United States of America, Adidas brand declares an increase of more than 1000% in the average ticket in e-commerce sales, thanks to the

---

[1] Pão de Açúcar investe em apps para avançar no varejo online de comida. https://www.infomoney. com.br/negocios/grandes-empresas/noticia/7897626/grupo-investe-em-apps-para-avancar-no-varejo-online-de-comida Viewed in 30/01/2019.

use of the "Complete The Look"[2], an app, which offers combinations of other products, from the query of a single item, basing its combinations on consumer database.

The examples, many of them in retail, signal a transformation in the buying and selling actions, but that interfere in the logic of consumption of several segments of products and services. The calculations made by algorithms from databases shows a new social logic of consumption that puts the theme as a new challenge to be understood.

As Gillespie [9] said, in his studies, aspects of the relevance of the algorithms are identified, which can allow an understanding of the writing of this new ontic status of digital humanity. In this sense, it is possible to think of the application of these aspects of the mentioned author, from the perspective of a semio-pragmatic theory to the understanding of the algorithmic advertising signal processes of the brands in their interactions with the consumers, going beyond the technique, considering the conditions of interaction and of the production and circulation and consumption of its discursive forms.

The elements of Gillespie's [9], propositions are: algorithms promote patterns of data inclusion through the actors; the algorithms perform calculations of anticipation and predictability of occurrences; the algorithms promote the evaluation of the relevance of occurrences with non-visible criteria of calculations; the algorithms operate the supply of objectively calculated options; there is the idea of the impartiality of the offer on the part of the algorithms, although these offers are the result of subjective processes delegated by those who conceive the algorithms; the algorithm gains the condition of directing the life of the users by performing the mixture in the entanglement of calculations of occurrences, based on the practices of public uses, allowing the conception of a predictable public.

The results of semio-pragmatic applications on these aspects are related to contributions on the logic of production and appropriation potential of the dynamic way of algorithmic advertising actions, which in turn help to think the logical narrative and discourse of consumption cultures in digital mediation.

The theoretical and methodological proposal presented here is theoretically supported in works on the media brand [2], as well as applications of semiotics to advertising and marketing in the Brazilian context [20]. Thus, a pragmatic understanding of algorithmic advertising for the cultural dynamics of consumption in its new writing mode and specific contexts, such as the Brazilian for example, is constituted.

In this sense, it should be clarified that the text will be organized in three axes, namely: the production logics and powers of appropriation of algorithmic advertising in its writing; Algorithm and suggested narratives for consumption: a socio-cultural writing; and the manifestations of risky interactions [14], adapted to relations between brands and consumers in algorithmic advertising mediation, considering the tensions between programmed, accidental interactions, manipulation, and adjustment interactions regimes.

The four possibilities of meanings of the risky interactions allow to see modalities of communicative actions between brands and consumers in the mediation of the

---

2 Como Adidas mudou a receita do seu e-commerce usando inteligência Artificial https://portalnovarejo. com.br/2019/01/como-a-adidas-aumentou-a-receita-de-seu-e-commerce-usando-inteligencia-artific-ial/?fbclid=IwAR1IX8F2C98xpT8TLhWi8ptO5zSbnopo5NlUsKeIfACJyp2iIccaY8qlc78.

algorithms, namely: the programmed refers to the actions determined in the affordances of the platforms of interaction of the brands with consumers; the interaction in the adjustment works the calculations of occurrences in front of the most recurrent uses of the processes of interaction brands and consumers. The manipulation considers the selection manifestation of the algorithms in front of the calculations of relevant recurrences in the interaction of consumer brands and programming interests; finally, the accident configures the interaction regimes of the order of the less predicted elements of poetic/aesthetic tone, but possible to happen, that makes the process of sense of the interactions gain some degree of unpredictability, novelty.

This perspective seeks to offer, from the theoretical point of view, a communicational reading of advertising, toward the possibilities of algorithms adjustments in realities of consumptions, which explains our option for the theory of mediations as theoretical support that makes possible to understand the contexts on digital humanities in their socio-cultural heterogeneities and permanent negotiation processes.

2 The Logics of Algorithmic Advertising in Its Writing

Advertising and multiple expressions of brands live a transmutation against their classic definitions and formats. This can be seen in texts such as those of [2, 17, 22], that brands occupy a place of media-brand in a great variety of media, crossing by discursive genres and formats that initially shows a sense of depublicitarization of brand expression that, paradoxically, hyperpublicitizes the whole environment of consumers' lives, making the media-brand present and interacting in different ways with consumers.

Digital advertising, in this sense, reflects a new form of advertising, at the same time, revealing a new underlying expressiveness of suggestions and inductions to consumption, based on calculations of big data and Artificial Intelligence (AI), because there are, on the days present, a certain predisposition of the human to delegate to the algorithm its decisions. Thus, the question can be raised: what will the advertising industry become when the algorithms calculate all consumption possibilities and AI data systems can define the consumption patterns of humanity? What will be its ontic status? Is it in the same expressiveness that we know today of the speeches of advertising and brands? There is new writing in conformation. What remains? What changes? But none of this eliminates the senses of branded experiences. Algorithms can recognize, describe, indicate, induce, but they can not experience or feel.

The previous questions pose essential challenges to communication studies for the understanding of how this algorithmic logic works in communicational terms about market and consumption. How would be the processes of production, circulation, and consumption of brands and the interactions of brands with consumers in the logic of algorithms? What would be this algorithmic writing of advertising?

At this point that we recover the valuable contribution of Gillespie [9], on the six aspects of relevance of the algorithms, mentioned in the introduction, to find possible ways of answering the presented questions, crossing the informational/communicational aspects of the six relevant elements of the algorithm versus the dimensions of production, circulation/interaction and reception/consumption.

When thinking about the production of data in algorithms, we realize that the promotion of standards for data inclusion happens through the actors. Such actors are not necessarily human since AI has data capture machines. This finding favors the dialogue with the actor-network perspective of Latour [15], which studies the actors in connection in the digital networks and their flows of meanings. That is the narrative/discursive course of the networks, as a new domain of understanding of society and culture.

It should also be thought that this pattern of the form of data inclusion is previously thought by humans, but not all actors of this big data production are human. This process corresponds to the size of the production of the communication in algorithms to perform calculations that predict probabilities of occurrences, seeking to anticipate to consumers the offers of their most recurrent consumption practices. These calculation criteria are not visible and comprise the 'black box' of the algorithms. Besides, there are also groundbreaking discussions on the theme such as Beer [1], that deals with the studies of algorithms beyond the technical question and thinking about their power logic in cultural life, considering the productive intentionality, materialized in software and the uses in daily consumption of these products.

Recent international papers about the subject like Bucher [13], acknowledge that studies on production in algorithms and how they work are in greater quantity than studies on their circulations and their effects, perceptions, what could be interpreted, in the last case, such as studies about the imaginary of the reception of algorithms. This is a subject little discussed in international scientific journals. See also Filho [23], about this discussion, which emphasizes that most of the studies on algorithms are demarcated in the discussion of their functionalities and applicabilities or demarcated by the interest in data privacy and the surveillance issues of the actions of social subjects, considering the ethical implications of such processes. The effects of the algorithms and their processes of appropriation in the cultures are little studied.

At any rate, this strong aspect of the social production of an algorithmic sense reinforces what Gillespie [9], identified as an "algorithmic promise of objectivity," though idealized by the intentionality of production, but generalized in usage and consumption, since, these are based on a belief that such devices work in the perspective of an impartiality, in the sense of what they offer to consumer users as algorithmic truth. This aspect is false, because what is a selection of occurrences within commercial interests and what happens in greater probability, which also favors the commercial aspect of what is offered in the research of the data in its programmings.

The circulation/interaction and reception of the algorithm gain relevance from Gillespie's [9], perspective by the condition of directing (manipulating) users' lives by performing the mixture that induces, in the entanglement of occurrence calculations, from the practices of public, users-consumers, allowing the design of a predictable public. However, stays the question: what would be the level of adjustment and the accidental in the algorithmic interactions? If there is a probability of occurrence of a fact, however, small it is, this fact may occur. This aspect takes place in the third and fourth stages of this reflection, which consider the sociocultural contexts of the influence of algorithms as narratives and as forms of interactions that predict the most frequent as the central aspect of manipulation and that tends to be generalized, the merges of brand and user-consumer interactions by the cross-data that favor a revealing dynamic of the actual data flows and the accidental one that would demarcate the unusual occurrences and often out of commercial interests, but predicted as minimal or rare probabilities and also an instance of fruition or cathartic aesthetic experience.

3 Advertising Algorithm and Narratives: A Sociocultural Writing

Calculations of occurrences determined by algorithms in consumption are reflections of data interpretation. The induction or manipulation of determined occurrences happens in the interactions/circulations in the actions of users in the digital platforms toward the previous determinations of possibilities that a given platform offers to the anticipated conceptions of uses, denominated affordances. That is the concept that designates the potential of an object to be used as it was designed to be used. This understanding of the term, roughly, was offered by the psychologist Gibson [10], whose contribution stimulated reflections from design to man-machine interactions. But there are unanticipated uses and unusual occurrences that the algorithm calculus recognizes and can resize their offers and their predictability (adjustment) versus uses in realities.

This finding allows us to say that the algorithm does not act in the same way in all contexts and that the sociocultural and determinant aspect of adjustments to the cultural practices of consumption. Thus, as we study the issue of advertising and identity of Brazilian culture in 2012, realizing that the thematization and figurativization of Brazilian aspects in commercials created the identification and the link of pertinence and belongings to consumption [20], we can state that algorithm advertising also seeks the adjustments with the public which allows understanding in the perspective of Hall [11], that there are ideological processes that are specific to the contexts of interaction/communication, being a purpose of the research in the area the search for the nexus of the social production of meaning in their specific contexts, allowing us to think that through the relationship between communication and ideology there is a theoretical path to understand in practice the differences that the contexts of digital humanities can present. Moreover, the calculations in the discursive formulations, oriented to the consumers, will present thematizations and discursive figurativizations that reflect the context of identification with the culture that is inserted.

In addition to the discursive level, we perceive that, in terms of a francophone semiotics, it is as if the algorithms gave us an auxiliary narrative program that would be subordinated to a main narrative program of the big commercial brands that would be configured, in the perspective of looking for the conjunction with object of cognitive and pragmatic value of brands, profit, which in turn depends on the consumer's narrative auxiliary program with the brand in the conquest also of an object of value (cognitive and pragmatic offered by the brand) to consumers.

From the perspective of the semiotics in Peirce, applied to advertising [19], with a view to the study of the semiosis of the senses of brands and consumers, in the mediation of the algorithm, this semiosis would be framed in the perspective of the interpretation of the data, on a scale of dynamic interpretants that would go from the occurrences of the most recurrent to the rarest and unlikely.

The formulations above, which are said in this way, make it appear that everything would be programmed in the digital world and that the sociocultural world would be determined by algorithmic logic. In a sense, this can be understood as true, but it is only one way of a complex process in tow directions. The algorithm can determine reality, but reality can also determine the algorithm. Thus, we return to the question raised in the previous section of this discussion: but how is the question of the possibility of adjustment and the accidental in the algorithmic interactions? Have the algorithms for consumption served only retail? Or the offerings of brands would inhabit the minds of consumers also in actions of an affective, cognitive order related to brands?

4 The Interactions in the Algorithmic Relations of Brands and Consumers

Landowski [14], considers that the senses carry a risk, for although there is an order or regime of programming of living to the conjunction of every living actor toward death, for all actors of the great narrative of life, there is also in the narrative process of life, facts that leave the logic of regularities, which are tensioned by a randomness that, in turn, make the tensions between logics of an intentionality that contradict each other, by the logic of the sensible and allows the adjustment for this sensitive aspect, towards an accidental possibility (event), which can be good or bad.

The author emphasizes that the semiotics, in Greimas's proposition, was always occupied with the programmed and manipulative dimension of the senses and that it gave little space to the accidental, and the adjustment, which is the exact space of aesthetic experience, in terms of communication lived in the uses and media consumptions with cultural products, including brand messages and advertising.

Algorithms as a device of mankind do not escape this maxim. But their condition of writing is underlying as mathematical meta-language, constitutive of digital humanity, therefore, constitutive of the realities in their mediation condition, as Coudry and Hepp [4] treat, when considering data mediatization, or realities in datafication process.

The algorithm interaction considers the scheduling, manipulation, adjustment and accident regimes, the last two results of the circulation processes and the media uses and consumptions of the digital platforms and that by the AI conditions fit the possibilities of the identified data in the real dynamics of interactions.

At the same time, that such action in the uses of the algorithms, in theory, directs us hypothetically to the accidental, as Landowski [14] thinks, but in the case of commercial consumption it seems that the adjustment is always cooptated by the intentions of the intentionality of the commercial production, becoming the sequence in possibility manipulated of occurrence, when the accident interests. The mechanisms of AI seem to seek the agile overcoming of the adjustment and annulment of the accidental (not interesting), in the allotropic order of the permanent self-organization of the programming of the algorithm. This allows the occurrence of accidental as a record that tends to be incorporated or canceled.

It is important to say that in the risks of the senses, the accidental aspect can be good or bad for the brand and/or consumers. Accident as an event capable of altering the flow of narrative meaning of interactions is not necessarily a condition of digital interaction. There would be other factors that would influence the digital world out of adjustment and accidental processes.

This is why we consider Stuart Hall's [10] studies in which one, the author presents, in his discussions of communication and ideology, the idea of communication as an interdisciplinary theoretical regionality that seeks to understand the nexus on social production of meanings between events, cultural phenomena in the face of their specific contexts.

Although the quantitative digital aspect of the mathematical ontic state of the algorithm overlaps, its calculations are the result of an appropriation of big data interpretations for specific contexts. The datafication of the world should not be understood as homogeneous as it argues Couldry and Meijas [6]. This phenomenon happens appropriately to the contexts which the data refers. Although we know that there is a tentative standardization or colonization of the algorithmic programming of consumption in the world, which constitutes a globalized Babel trying to meet the commercial interests of large international corporations and the programmed logic given as certain and regular, profitable.

On the other hand, such interests are strained by the adjustments and accidents of the local contexts of interactions, with the random, irregulars and sensitives aspects that are constituted from the uses and consumptions of the specific contexts, sometimes escaping to that programmed by affordances and demanding adjustments of the algorithm for action in specific contexts.

Today the algorithm devices find great advances in the retail sector and create links between brands and consumers in the processes of buying and selling. Databases are being fed, but there is still a path to be improved in these relationships in the field of affectivity and cognition, which form stronger linkages between brands and consumers in AI mediation.

In this sense, the study of algorithmic advertising must develop an agenda for the investigation of social production of meaning in consumer cultures that must pass through the communication, production, circulation, reception/consumption contexts, combined with an understanding of morphology, semantics, syntax and the pragmatics of the algorithms in human interactions and with their social institutions for an understanding of their logic, always glimpsing the ethical dimension, since the dimension of commercial intentions is not the only defining elements of the social environment, which is also the environment of the economy of consumption. The algorithm needs to be humanized in its purposes.

The algorithms, as we expose at the beginning of this exposition, can describe, configure, induce, predict, but can not feel. The universe of the sensible can be calculated, stimulated, described, provoked, but can not, or can not yet, be felt by the non-human. The professionalization of the advertising area requires today digital knowledge that was not relevant for two decades. However, today they are.

The new modalities of interactions mediated by digital algorithms in the consumption and in the various dimensions of the digital humanity imply to know this new language of media circulation, that is, to open the 'black box' for the understanding of the morphological structures that make up the base of the algorithm code, its semantic assignment forms (which means understanding the modes assign meanings, functions, values/hierarchies). These dimensions would be in the horizon of the scheduling regime, observing the regularities (including statistics) and intentionalities, for the constitution of syntax, an ordering as a basis in the occurrences and possible functions predicted for the users-consumers, that is, the affordances.

On the other hand, the determination of affordances, from the circulation in the interaction with the consumer and their form of appropriation, make it possible in the AI dynamics to adjust the algorithm to the accidental real (positive or negative for the brands), this new semantization and syntax constitutes within a pragmatic of the digital language, 'mathematizing' the social life.

The proposition of a semio-pragmatic discussion justifies precisely because of the ontological aspect of the digital sign, algorithm, which in its writing and narrative seeks to determine in the interface with the human, the meanings that can be established in cultural life in detriments of other possibilities.

In addition to the discussion of commercial interests, the ethical, moral intentions that constitute human relations and AI are included. What do we want from this intelligence? What consumption society do we want? The high level of regularity of interactions in commercially programmed intentions understood in their contexts can lead to a society that values the meaning of the profitable for few in the logic of production in detriment of the interests of the majority of consumer society. What consumption society do we want? Sustainable? Selfish or selfless? How to think collectively in this logic?

The algorithms will be what we program to make them work. The semio-pragmatic and cultural mediation of algorithms signs for consumption emerges as a proposal that goes through the agenda of understanding its structuring signs (morphology and semantics), its rules of order (syntax) that in the interactions of the logic of functioning (pragmatic) given in the circulations, uses and consumptions for the appropriations of subjects and institutions of social life.

These aspects are fundamental for a deeper social critique of the conformation of the digital humanities and are the essential substratum for a good dialogue with a new political economy of digital humanities communication in spite in Fuchs' works [7, 8], about the data fetish and the consequent social criticism of media, which should be made for this positivist, administrative and often enthusiastic look at the practices of social class, economic dynamics and implications for the life of consumption that this digital presence brings, from a world given by the logic of the data, the algorithms.

This research agenda should also include, in addition to what has been commented on algorithmic language structures and processes, three approaches, namely: the first one refers to the understanding of how the ecosystem of brands is represented discursively in digital communications and in the suggestions that foresee for the uses of the algorithmic logic in the consumptions. This type of work shows in the action of the media agents of the brands a logic of the present time that confers the representative status of the digital sense to the imaginary of the social life in the lived moment. These studies can be synchronic and diachronic, allowing the comparison between the forms of representation of each temporal/spatial context and in their updates in time and space.

Hepp emphasizes the importance of synchronic and diachronic studies to understand the reality mediated by communication, by the mediatizing action of the media in time/space, that is, in the contexts in which they are circumscribed, since the synchrony reflects the actuality of the phenomenon and diachrony allows us to understand it in the confrontation with the different media configurations of previous contexts. The communicational configurations are specificities to be analyzed in their actuality and their historical senses, glimpsing possible communicational configurations in a future perspective [12].

The second aspect concerns research with users-consumers regarding the perceptions that they have about algorithms in consumption in their lives, to understand the types of the logic of appropriation of such references in daily life. This type of research is in line with Bucher's work [3] which, as previously mentioned, discusses the imaginary of perceptions about the algorithms and puts in the screen the discussion of the effects and reception that are presented, as an approach with great potential to be explored in the field of research on the subject.

Finally, the researches on digital interactions presuppose as a constitutive process the semio-pragmatic analysis the understanding of the processes of enunciation in digital networks that would support the understanding of their logic and narrative flows. Here, Bruno Latour's actor-network perspective is an articulating element of the narrative flows in digital networks [15]. At this way, we can observe the brands in their expressivities, not only as discourses, but as actants and actors of the process, perceiving in the semantic and syntax of these flows the narrative programs of the actants and their manifestations in discourses as actors, in the thematizations and figurativizations of discursive temporalities and spatialities manifested in the discursive updating of the platforms to interactions in networks. This process also requires understanding the enunciation as communication in productive processes, circulation and consumption and appropriation of speeches. The traditional protocol of narrative and discursive semiotics already exists and only needs adaptations to the reality of narratives and discourses of digital, algorithmic.

It should be emphasized that the field of circulation and consumption requires an anthropological competence of the culture to detect media uses and consumptions, requiring besides the socio-discursive understandings, an ethnographic and ethnological view for a full understanding of this communication mediation of the culture in digital humanity, via algorithms and individuals in their life contexts.

Only from this, it becomes possible to accumulate a set of information about the discursive formulations of algorithmic advertising and to analyze the regimes of interaction in their concrete manifestations.

5 Conclusions

On the other hand, this aspect of the volume of data creates a difficulty for the semio-pragmatic proposal, since it would not apply to the general data of a brand phenomenon, but to a reduction of consumer realities, from the selection of data better delimited, envisioning a deeper understanding of their social logics of meaning production.

This means that the semio-pragmatic perspective is limited to an understanding of medium-range phenomena, related to its contextual characteristics, which is aligned with the perspectives of studies of communication mediations as proposed by Martin-Barbero [16], because the algorithms in their communicational action would be in the centrality of the political-socio-cultural and economic life of the daily consumption realities. And the intermedialities as dimensions of cultural mediations, manifested by the logic of production and consumption and cultural matrices and industrial formats, in which these devices are embodied in cultural life, shows specific forms of the institutions of brands in their ways of generating sociabilities and cognitive processes of consumer practices, such as cultural practices, together with consumers witch, through the mediation of communication interactions, through algorithms and uses of digital platforms, presents rituals of uses and consumptions that are proper to the relational universes on the consumption of brands with their consumers in their appropriations of realities.

In this sense, we rescue the principle that advertising algorithms are constituents of consumption realities while being co-fabricated by the realities that are inserted. And the study of cultural mediations combined with the semio-pragmatic perspective of the relations brands and consumers are a privileged way to understand this phenomenology of the symbolic materiality that ideologically conforms the senses of the social, backed by a philosophical-theoretical axis in the media studies, that allows the most powerful configuration of the theoretical regionality of communication, aspect that when we start the text, was presented on the basis of Couldru and Hepp [4], which defend the philosophical-theoretical position that contemporary reality is mediated by the communication condition of the algorithm signs as a constituent element of this new conformation of realities by data.

In the view proposed here, Couldry and Heep [4], although referring to the concept of mediatization, which was not the subject of a deeper discussion of this work, may be equated with the idea of communicational mediations in cultures of Martín-Barbero [16], as we have already discussed, in Perez and Trindade [18], when we deal with the signic mediations of consumption and its philosophical-theoretical status.

The relevant aspect of this work is to demarcate a possible theoretical path of investigation in communication that seeks its space and voice, from a perspective, more adjusted to the accidental regimes that constitute the specificities of the communicational phenomena of consumption in the Brazilian context in Latin-American.

References

1. Beer, D.: Power through the algorithm? Participatory Web cultures and the technological unconscious. New Media Soc. 11(6), 985–1002 (2009)
2. Berthelot-Guiet, K., Montety, C., Patrin-Lecrère, V.: Sémiotique des métamorphoses Marques-Médias. In: Berthelot-Guiet, K., Boutaud, J.-J. (Orgs.) Sémiotique mode d'emploi, pp. 255–291. Collection Mondes Marchands. Le Bord L'Eau, Paris (2014)
3. Bucher, T.: The algorithmic imaginary: exploring the ordinary affects of Facebook algorithms. Inf. Commun. Soc. 20(1), 30–44 (2017). https://doi.org/10.1080/1369118X. 2016.1154086. Accessed Jan 2019

4. Couldry, N., Hepp, A.: Mediated Construction of Reality. Polity Press, Cambridge (2017)
5. Couldry, N., Hepp, A.: Conceptualizing mediatization: contexts, traditions, arguments. Commun. Theory. **23**(3), 191–202 (2013). http://onlinelibrary.wiley.com/doi/10.1111/comt. 12019/pdf. Accessed Jan 2019
6. Couldry, N., Mejias, U.A.: Data colonialism: rethinking big data's relation to the contemporary subject. Telev. New Media 1–14 (2018). https://journals.sagepub.com/doi/ pdf/10.1177/1527476418796632. Accessed Jan 2019
7. Fuchs, C.: From digital positivism and administrative big data analytics towards critical digital and social media research! Eur. J. Commun. **32**(1), 37–49 (2017)
8. Fuchs, C.: Social Media: A Critical Introduction, 2nd edn. Routledge, London (2017)
9. Gillespie, T.: The relevance of algorithms. In: Media Technologies: Essays on Communication, Materiality, and Society, Cambridge. (2014). http://governingalgorithms.org/wp-content/uploads/2013/05/1-paper-gillespie.pdf. Accessed Jan 2019
10. Gibson, J.J.: The theory of affordances. In: Shaw, R., Bransford, J. (eds.) Perceiving, Acting, and Knowing: Toward an Ecological Psychology, pp. 67–82. Lawrence Erlbaum, Hillsdale (1977)
11. Hall, S.: Ideologia e teoria da comunicação. MatriZes. Revista do Programa de Pós-graduação da USP. **10**(3), 33–46 (2016). http://www.revistas.usp.br/matrizes/article/view/ 124648/121876. Accessed Jan 2019
12. Hepp, A.: As configurações comunicativas de mundos midiatizados: pesquisa da midiatização na era da "mediação de tudo". MatriZes. Revista do Programa de Pós-graduação da USP. **8**(1), 45–64 (2014). http://www.revistas.usp.br/matrizes/issue/view/6358. Accessed Jan 2019
13. Hjarvard, S.: The Mediatization of Culture and Society. Routledge, London, New York (2013)
14. Landowski, E.: Interações arriscadas. Estação das Letras e Cores, São Paulo (2014)
15. Latour, B.: Reengendrando o social. Uma introdução à Teoria Ator-Rede. EDUFBA/ EDUSC, Salvador/Florianópolis (2012)
16. Martín-Barbero, J.: Dos meios às mediações. Comunicação, Cultura e Hegemonia, 2 edn. UFRJ, Rio de Janeiro (2001)
17. Perez, C.: Os signos da marca. Expressividade e sensorialidade, 2 edn. Cengage Learning, São Paulo (2016)
18. Perez, C., Trindade, E.: Três dimensões para compreender as mediações comunicacionais do consumo na contemporaneidade. In: Anais 27° Encontro Anual da Compós. COMPÓS/PUC-MG, 2018, Belo Horizonte. GT-Consumos e Processos em Comunicação (2018). http:// www.compos.org.br/data/arquivos_2018/trabalhos_arquivo_2IQ07E9AMLM2VTATOXZ-T_27_6520_26_02_2018_09_28_31.pdf. Accessed Jan 2019
19. Santaella, L.: Semiótica Aplicada. Cengage Learning, São Paulo (2002)
20. Trindade, E.: Propaganda, identidade e discurso. Brasilidades midiáticas. Sulina, Porto Alegre (2012)
21. Trindade, E.: Mediaciones y mediatización del consumo:una nueva perspectiva para los estudios sobre el fenómeno publicitario. In: Hellín Ortuño, P., Nicolàs Romera, C.S. (Org.) El discurso publicitário. Bases simbólicas, semióticas y mitoanalíticas.Salamanca: Comunicación Social Ediciones y Publicaciones by Pedro J. Crespo, Editor y Editorial, vol. 1, pp. 222–231 (2016)

22. Trindade, E.: Tendências sobre Publicidade e Consumo em Revistas Científicas da Comunicação Qualis A2 entre 2006 a 2017. Publicidade e Consumos Digitais em Foco. In: Anais 41° Congresso Brasileiro de Ciências da Comunicação. Univille/Intercom, Joinville (2018). GP2- Publicidade e Propaganda. http://portalintercom.org.br/anais/nacional2018/resumos/R13-1165-1.pdf. Accessed Jan 2019

23. Filho, C.T.: O Algoritmo nas Pesquisas em Comunicação: possibilidades para o estudo da publicidade e do consumo na contemporaneidade. In: Anais XXXXI Congresso Brasileiro de Ciências da Comunicação (INTERCOM). Univille/Intercom, Joinville (2018). GP2- Publicidade e Propaganda. http://portalintercom.org.br/anais/nacional2018/resumos/R13-0407-1.pdf. Accessed Jan 2019

Author Index